The Bumper Book of Common Sense

David Croucher

<David Croucher>
<2014>

Copyright © <2014> by <David Croucher >

All rights reserved. This book or any portion thereof may not be reproduced or used in any manner whatsoever without the express written permission of the publisher except for the use of brief quotations in a book review or scholarly journal.

ISBN 978-1-291-67129-2

First Printing Second Edition: <2014>

PREFACE

Common Sense is about how we think about the world and decide what it is reasonable to believe. Common Sense is about how we approach problems and how we make decisions. Common Sense is about how we view and interact with other people. Common Sense is about how we choose to live in the world.

The world is a complex and often confusing place, and the proper application of Common Sense enables us to interact far more effectively with the world than we would otherwise do. Many of the problems we have in our lives can be largely avoided or can be significantly reduced through the proper application of Common Sense. Common Sense will carry us through the perplexities of life.

You will find in this book most of the guidance and general guidelines you need for the proper application of Common Sense. Everything you do has in some specific or analogous way been done before and having access to how others have approached it is useful input to sit alongside your own thoughts, either as additional thoughts or as reinforcement to the thoughts you have already had. The specifics of your life and the situations you find yourself in however are yours alone, and it is up to you whether or not you follow the Common Senses given in this book given your unique circumstances.

Just one piece of Common Sense used when otherwise you wouldn't have done can change your life. There are over 4,500 statements of Common Sense in this book.

If you find some of the guidance in this book useful please visit www.aboutcommonsense.com which from late 2015 will provide learning and test material which will significant improve your day to day instinct for and ability to apply common sense.

CONTENTS

INTRODUCTION   1

OBSERVATIONS RELATING TO COMMON SENSE   3

THE CORE PRINCIPLES OF COMMON SENSE   6

COMMON SENSE THINKING   18

    TRUTH AND BELIEF   18

        Nothing is Certain   18
        Some Truths are More Reasonable than Others   18
        We Should Continually be Looking to Improve what we Believe to be Reality   21
        Faith and Belief   22
        Living without Absolute Truths   23

    SCIENTIFIC LAWS AND RULES   23

        The Origins, Limitations, and Usefulness of Scientific Laws and Rules   23
        Useful Scientific Laws, Rules, and Principles   25

    (LOGICAL) ARGUMENTS   26

        Valid and Reasonable Arguments   26
        The Form, Validity, and Use of Deductive Arguments   27
        Getting to the Bottom of Arguments   29

    USE OF LANGUAGE   30

        Assumptions and Definitions   31
        Inappropriate Use of Words or Expressions   32
        Use of Generalizations, Simplifications, Analogies, and Metaphors   34
        Fuzziness   36

    CLEAR THINKING   37

        Principles of Clear Thinking   37
        Cause and Effect   40
        Barriers to Clear Thinking   42
        Inappropriate Ways of Thinking   44
        Improving Your Clear Thinking Skills   45

    FALLACIES   46

        About Fallacies   46
        Examples of Fallacies   47

    BIASES   52

    UNCERTAINTY   57

        Certainty and Uncertainty   57
        Probability and Statistics   60
        Catastrophe and Chaos   64
        Predicting, Foresight and Hindsight   65

    SYSTEMS AND SYSTEMS THINKING   67

        Complex Systems   67
        Systems Thinking   69

COMMON SENSE INTERACTING WITH OTHERS 73

The Influence of Emotions 73
General Observations about Emotions 73
You and Your Emotions 74
Interacting with Others who are in a Heightened Emotional State 77

Groups 78
Belonging to Groups 78
Behavior and Behaving in Groups 79
Conflicts between Groups 80
Groupthink 80

People: The Way They Are And The Way They Think 81
How People See and Respond to the World and to Other People 82
People are Not Good at Seeing their Own Shortcomings 84
A Propensity for Passivity 87
Differences Between People 88
Prejudice and Stereotyping 89
What Motivates People 91
The Influence of Status 91
Self-Interest or Vested-Interest Behavior 92
Observations about People 93
How you Potentially Appear to Others 95
How We See the World and Others 95

How You Should Treat and Interact with Others 97
Treat Others as Equals 97
Recognize and Respect Differences 98
Be Positive Towards Others 100
Helping Others 102
Be Honest and Fair in Your Dealings with Others 103
Give People the Benefit of the Doubt, but Don't Let Them Take Advantage of You 104
Co-operation, Competition, and Conflict 105
Take an Interest in and Get to Know Others 109
Asking Others for Help and Advice 111
Don't be too Concerned about What Other People Think about You 112
Verbal Arguments and Debate 113
Responding to Negativity or Put Downs 115
Interacting with Difficult, Awkward, or Dishonest People 116
Ways of Seeing Others 118

Common Sense in Close Relationships 119
In General 119
Relationships between Husband and Wife or Equivalent Partners 121
Relationships between Parents and Children 126
Relationships with Teenagers 131
Relationships within Families in General 135
Relationships with Close Friends 136
Having and Looking After Pets 136

Influencing and Persuading 137
In General 137
Salesmen's Tactics 139
Use of Power 140
Psychological and Physiological Factors 141
Influencing Tendencies 144
Peer Influences 147

> *Responding to Authority* 148
> *Scarcity and Censorship* 149
>
> ## SMALL TALK AND CONVERSING 149
>
> *Why Small Talk?* 149
> *Meeting New People* 150
> *Topics to Raise or Not to Raise During Small Talk* 151
> *Interacting During Small Talk and Conversations* 152
> *Preparation for Small Talk* 153
> *Improving your Small Talk and Dealing with Small Talk Failures* 154
>
> ## MORALITY AND BEING A GOOD PERSON 154
>
> *What is Moral Behavior?* 155
> *We Choose our Own Morality* 155
> *How to Increase your Morality* 156
> *Benefits of Striving to be a Good Person* 157
> *Some General Observations Relating to Morals* 157

COMMON SENSE PLANNING AND DOING 159

GOALS AND OBJECTIVE SETTING 159

> *Why set Goals?* 159
> *Set Inspiring and Challenging Long Term Goals?* 159
> *Goals for Everyday Living* 161
> *Going from Long Term Goals to Short Term Goals* 162
> *General Characteristics of Good Goals (Long and Short Term)* 163
> *Regularly Monitor Progress Towards your Goals, and Adjust Accordingly* 163

PLANNING AND MONITORING 164

> *Why you Need Plans* 164
> *The Basics of Producing a Plan* 165
> *Estimating How Long* 167
> *Be Clear about Dependencies* 168
> *Confirm Feasibility* 168
> *Modify or Deviate from your Plans if Necessary* 169
> *Implementation and Monitoring* 169

TIME MANAGEMENT AND GETTING THINGS DONE 170

> *The Importance of Time Management* 170
> *Making Best Use of your Time* 171
> *Short Term vs Long Term* 173
> *Don't Waste Time* 174
> *Be Effective and Efficient in Doing Tasks* 176
> *Take Relaxation Time* 177
> *Get it all Down onto Lists* 178
> *Prioritizing and Doing what's Important* 181
> *Planning to Do Things* 183
> *What to Do Next* 184
> *Review Progress* 185
> *If you're Failing to Make Progress, do Something About it* 186
> *Focusing and Environment* 187
> *Be Positive and Persistent* 188
> *Multitasking* 190
> *Overcoming Procrastination* 190
> *Increasing your Ability to Control or React to Events* 194
> *Effective Management of your Time when Interacting with Others* 195
> *Getting On With It Aphorisms* 196

WORKING WITH OTHERS 197

Try to See Things from Other's Point of View	*197*
Deciding Whether to Work Alone or With Others	*198*
Gaining Other People's Support and Input	*199*
Providing Support to Others	*200*
Effective Working Within a Group	*200*
Negotiating	*201*

DECISION MAKING — 205

The Approach to Making Big Decisions	*205*
Personal Decisions	*207*
The Timing of Decisions	*209*
Judging Decisions	*210*
Overturning Decisions	*211*
General Considerations when Decision Making	*211*

PROBLEM SOLVING — 214

What to do When Initially Faced with a Possible Problem	*215*
Ensure you Understand the Problem	*217*
General Approaches to Problem Solving	*218*
Looking for Possible Solutions	*221*
Assessing Possible Solutions	*223*
Once we Have a Solution	*224*
Solving Logical and Lateral Thinking Puzzles	*225*

ANALYSIS — 226

Creating and Using Mental Models	*227*
Correlation	*228*
Lazy Thinking	*229*
Conducting Analysis Activities	*230*
Perception and Focus	*232*
Sorting Through Information	*233*
The Devil in the Detail	*235*
Outputs from Analysis Activities	*236*

MISTAKES, THEIR CAUSES, AND MITIGATING AGAINST THEM — 236

COMMON SENSE LIVING — 239

BEING ALIVE AND ATTITUDE OF MIND — 239

Live your Life in the Present	*239*
Today is the Day	*242*
Do the Right Thing Right Now	*244*
Be Positive, Happy, Optimistic, and Appreciative of what you have	*245*
Be Proactive	*249*
Do what you Believe is Right	*252*
Face up to Your Fears	*253*
Do the Best You Can in the Circumstances	*256*
Take Control of Your Own Mind and Thoughts	*257*
Don't just React, Think	*262*
Work Hard and Overcome Adversities	*263*
Life isn't Always Fair; Accept It and Move On	*266*
Accept and Embrace Change	*268*
Continual Self-Development and Improvement	*269*
Life is What you Make Of It	*271*
Live your Life with Purpose	*273*
Play to your Strengths	*276*
Sometimes Do Nothing	*276*
Daily Living	*277*

SELF-TALK   280

Why Self-Talk is Important?   *280*
What to Say to Yourself   *280*
The Importance of Positive Self-Talk   *281*

PERSONAL CHARACTERISTICS AND BEHAVIOR   282

We are able to Modify our Characteristics and Behavior   *283*
Always be Looking to Improve   *283*
Understand Yourself   *285*
Be Curious and Open Minded   *286*
Be Aware of your Surroundings and Circumstances   *287*
Be Positive and Confident and Appreciative of Being Alive   *288*
Relating to Others   *289*

SELF-MOTIVATION (AKA WILLPOWER)   291

What is Self-Motivation?   *291*
Why you should Look to Improve your Self-Motivation   *291*
Self-Motivation is Like a Muscle   *292*
Manage and Take Account of your Energy Levels   *293*
Have and use Inspiring Goals   *296*
Take Inspiration from Others   *297*
Self-Motivation is your own Responsibility   *298*
Get into the Right Mindset   *298*
The Use of Visualization   *301*
Learn to Take Control of your Now   *302*
Making Changes   *303*
Overcoming Temptation and Bad Habits   *304*
Understanding and Tackling Addiction   *310*
Implementing Good Habits   *311*
Keep Getting Back Up   *313*
General Self-Motivation Tips   *314*

DEALING WITH STRESS AND WORRIES   317

Dealing with Trauma or Despair   *317*
Recognizing and Managing Depression and Stress   *318*
Learn from Mistakes and Failures and Put Them Behind You   *322*
When Feeling a Bit Down   *323*
Take Responsibility for Dealing with your Unhappiness, Worries or Problems   *324*
Turning Problems and Worries Round   *328*

MEMORY   329

Memory Tends to be Meaning Focused   *329*
Make Associations and Patterns   *329*
Write it Down   *330*
Pay Attention   *331*
Memories can be False or Mislead   *332*
Impact of Health and Way of Life on Memory   *334*
Some Everyday Memory Tips   *334*
Some Observations Relating to Memory   *335*
Memory Training Tips   *336*

COMMUNICATION   337

Face to Face Communication and Listening   *337*
Body Language   *341*
Presentations and Public Speaking   *346*
Meetings – When you're Responsible for Them or Leading/Chairing Them   *349*
Meetings - As an Attendee   *351*
Meetings – Other General Points   *352*

Written Communication Including E-mail for Business	*353*
Use of Different Forms of Communication	*357*
General Effective Communication Tips	*358*
Potential for Miscommunication	*361*

Creativity   362

General Observations about Creativity	*362*
Sources of Creative Ideas	*363*
How to Boost your Creativity	*365*
Brainstorming	*368*
Ways of Encouraging or Discouraging Creative Thinking	*370*

Getting and Being Organized   372

Being Organized Sets you Free	*372*
How to Get and Stay Organized	*372*
Organize Your Workspace(s)	*374*
Make Extensive Use of Written Reminders	*375*
Always have Pen and Paper with you	*375*
Manage your Finances	*375*
Maintain your own Personal and Professional Portfolios	*377*

Learning and Teaching   378

Learning is Good for You	*378*
Never Stop Learning	*379*
Learning is your Own Responsibility	*380*
Most People can Learn Most Things	*381*
Learning Styles	*381*
What to Learn	*383*
Attitude of Mind Towards Learning	*385*
How to Learn Tips	*386*
Effective Reading	*390*
Obstacles to Effective Learning	*391*
Tips for Exams	*392*
Teaching	*393*

Fitness, Diet, Health, and some Notes about How your Brain Works   394

General Health	*394*
Diet and Eating	*397*
Exercise and Breathing	*401*
Sleep	*403*
Meditation and Relaxation Techniques	*405*
Body Posture	*406*
Your Voice	*408*
Dealing with Pain	*408*
How your Brain Works	*408*

Common Sense Working for a Living   410

Take Responsibility for Enjoying and Finding Meaning in your Work	*410*
Take Control over your Work and Responsibility for Getting the Right Things Done	*411*
Boosting your Employability	*412*
Be Professional in How you Behave	*414*
Work Life Balance	*414*

Common Sense Living on your Own   415

Common Sense Relating to Getting Older   416

Common Sense Survival Tips   418

DAILY LIVING ADAGES AND APHORISMS	424
GENERAL	428
Some Well-known Principles, Laws, and Razors	*428*
Relating to Experience	*429*
Taking Advice	*429*
HOW TO IMPROVE YOUR COMMON SENSE	431
COMMON SENSE ON A GLOBAL SCALE	432
FURTHER READING	**434**

INTRODUCTION

* There is something that can usefully be called Common Sense, which relates to how we should view and interact with the world if we don't want to be continually having difficulties and stresses that bother us.

* The dictionary definition of Common Sense talks about good sense and sound judgment in practical matters. And much of this is built upon the principles of good thinking, and avoiding the many errors and fallacies in thinking that are often the root cause of failure to say and do what is Common Sense. But, in this book at least, Common Sense is much wider in scope and also covers a range of rules of thumb and observations about how the world works, about how we work, and about behavior and attitudes of mind. Anything to give the reader a ready reference source of practical guidance and advice that will help him or her better interact with the world.

* Most of the difficulties we face in our lives have their root causes in our poor understanding of how the world works and our poor judgment in the decisions we make or avoid making. And even where our difficulties are not overtly of our own making, we could often have avoided them through different ways of behaving, and can better deal with them through having appropriate attitudes and ways of thinking.

* This book contains over 4,500 rules of thumb or useful observations relevant to pragmatic living in the real world. Use them to better understand what's going on and better deal with the complexities of life. The better you are able to apply Common Sense the better you will be at interacting with the world. You will solve more problems, make better decisions, plan more effectively, get more done. You will develop a more realistic view of life, find things going your way more often, and be less stressed. Following these principles and guidelines won't mean everything will go your way. But they will improve the odds. And like it or not, that is as much as we can ever ask.

* You may not agree with all of the principles and guidelines given in this book. And indeed some of the Common Sense guidelines seemingly conflict with others. This is because the application of Common Sense is context specific. What is appropriate in one circumstance, with its particular variations and nuances, is not necessarily appropriate in another.

* If you disagree with some of the statements or advice, good for you. Thinking for yourself is an essential element of what makes us what we are. If you find yourself disagreeing with a lot of what is here, I suggest you look more closely at yourself rather than simply be critical of this book.

* This book is largely for dipping into, or referring to when faced with particular circumstances in which you are looking for some guidance. You don't need to read it all at once. But at different points in your life different things will occur to you and some of the Common Sense given in this book will be particularly useful. And from time to time just dip in and see what you find.

* A particular way I would encourage you to use this book is as a basis for creating your own Personal Handbook of Common Sense. Simply identify those topics of most interest to you, or which strike a chord with you, and write down what you consider to be Common Sense guidance in your own words. Add your own topics and paragraphs. It is your Personal Handbook after all. See it as a continual work in progress. But return to this book again from time to time because as you progress through life you will doubtless find other parts of this guidance striking a cord when they didn't before.

* Use this book, and your own Personal Handbook of Common Sense, to help you get into an iterative loop of self-improvement and personal upgrade. Take some of this Common Sense guidance and look to apply it. If it doesn't seem to be working look at how you could improve it for your own application. Continue trying to improve and you will.

The Bumper Book of Common Sense

* There is some repetition in this book both in terms of saying some of the same things in different ways, as well as the same idea appearing under different topic headings. I make no apology for either. Saying the same thing in different ways both helps reinforce the idea, and also different people will more readily take to different ways of expressing an idea. A given idea might pass over someone's head if expressed in one way, but will strike a chord if expressed in another. And I have sought to make the topics stand-alone without overt cross-referencing. This has meant certain ideas do appear under multiple topic headings. However I have sought to avoid too much repetition, and the reader may find points he expected under a given heading appear under another related heading.

* I have not attributed specific rules of thumb or observations to particular authors or books. For the most part the items in this book are of a generic nature and whilst given authors may have talked about them in their books they will be ideas that have been around for a long time and talked about in many different books or websites. I have however included as Further Reading a number of books and websites that have struck a chord with myself and strongly encourage the reader to follow up on these. The route to improving your own Common Sense is to learn as much as you can from others but to adapt it to your own particular circumstances. Make the effort to improve your Common Sense and you will succeed, to the significant betterment of your life and the lives of those around you.

OBSERVATIONS RELATING TO COMMON SENSE

* Common Sense is not a set of absolute rules that you can simply apply without thought as the unquestioningly right thing to do in a given situation. Life is too complicated, full of subtleties and particular circumstances, for that. However there are ways of thinking and ways of behaving that are generally better than others and are more appropriate than others in particular circumstances.

* Common Sense is seeing things as they are, and doing things as they should be done. Common Sense is practical and helpful.

* Common Sense is sound and prudent judgment based on as objective a perception of the situation or facts as we can reasonably obtain.

* Common sense is largely the wisdom of the ages applicable in a modern context.

* The application of Common Sense enables us to extract useful meaning from a large volume of information, much of which is contradictory. It enables us to put things into context.

* Common Sense is, for the most part, broad rather than deep, general rather than specific. It is a set of general principles to be applied to particular circumstances rather than a rulebook to be followed.

* Common Sense is not all that common, although everyone thinks that they have it to a greater extent than others.

* Common Sense is not about knowledge and facts per se, though it would be difficult to exhibit much Common Sense if you had no or very little knowledge. Common Sense is a kind of meta-knowledge that helps us to apply our knowledge in an effective manner.

* Many older people believe Common Sense and Wisdom comes only from old age, and that because they are old they have it. Nonsense. Old age only brings Common Sense and Wisdom to those who have spent their time searching for it: to those who have reflected upon circumstances as they have passed by, who have learnt from their mistakes, who have sought out new experiences, and who have an interest in a wide range of subjects. Many people are as ignorant in their old age as they were in their youth. They are just better at hiding it behind their lack of energy.

* An argument sometimes heard is that Wisdom and Common Sense on a given issue can only be acquired by personal experience. Following this argument, presumably the only good doctor is a dead doctor. A doctor who learnt only from personal experience would be little better than the hacks of centuries past.

* Common Sense is not the same as common beliefs or notions. Common Sense is not simply what most people believe to be true or most appropriate. Conventional thinking can be, and often has been, mistaken. There are many examples of majorities believing or acting in ways that are clearly not Common Sense.

* Some aspects of Common Sense are culturally determined, and we should adapt the way we apply our Common Sense to the culture within which we live. However, much of Common Sense transcends culture and relates to a basic view of humanity that most people would like to be a part of.

* The application of Common Sense requires us to think for ourselves. This does not mean we need to invent for ourselves all the principles and guidance given in this book and elsewhere. It does

mean however that we need to think for ourselves how best to apply them in the particular circumstances we find ourselves, and adapt them as appropriate to our own needs. We should even disagree with them and adopt our own principles if we believe it is right to do so. But if you stray far from the guidelines and principles given in this book you are likely to find things won't turn out as you hope or expect.

* Just because everyone else is going off in a given direction, it does not mean they are right to do so. Decide for yourself what you think the best thing to do is. Whilst sometimes it might be prudent to go along with the majority, this doesn't mean you have to believe they are right.

* Common Sense is an explanation that fits the facts, without having to manipulate the information to fit preconceived notions, and which does not ignore or avoid conflicting evidence. Common Sense is the simplest explanation that meets these criteria.

* There are extreme situations where we cannot determine whether or not something is Common Sense; in the same way there are extreme cases where we cannot determine whether or not something is true or whether or not it is right. In these extreme cases the judgment becomes subjective. However in the vast majority of everyday situations we can identify things as being, for all practical purposes, true or false, right or wrong, and we can determine whether things are or are not Common Sense.

* Common Sense can be learned and improved through having guidelines about what is Common Sense and looking to apply them and adapt them to your everyday life. Anyone can improve their Common Sense if they make the effort to do so.

* We should encourage others to improve their Common Sense thinking. We are affected by the irrational thinking of others even if we do not take irrational actions ourselves.

* Common Sense is not intuitive, though as with any skill it will become more intuitive for those people who work at improving than for those who don't. The many people who think they have an intuition for Common Sense, but who don't make the effort to improve it, are kidding themselves.

* The application of Common Sense does sometimes require effort. Most people are too lazy to apply good Common Sense, which involves thinking through logical arguments, questioning their own prejudices, and admitting they might be wrong.

* The main principles of Common Sense derive from:
    o Clear thinking, with a focus on correctly structuring arguments and using words correctly and appropriately;
    o Avoidance of specific thinking traps and fallacies;
    o An understanding of Probability and Risk;
    o An understanding that the world as we perceive it is not a simple black and white of absolutes, but is in many cases grey and occasionally chaotic;
    o Understanding other people and how to interact with them;
    o Understanding ourselves and having some degree of self-control;
    o Recognizing practical limitations in the real world.

* Personal characteristics which aid the development and application of Common Sense include:
    o An ability to grasp situations and put things into context;
    o An ability to concentrate the mind;
    o A keenness of perception;
    o The ability to exercise reasoning power;
    o An ability to work and live with uncertainties and approximations;

- o   Calmness and self-control

* The main barrier to Common Sense arises from the belief that we have more Common Sense than other people and thus we don't need to make any particular effort to improve it. As a result most of us interact with the world far less effectively than we might otherwise do.

* You can usually get away with ignoring Common Sense in the short term, but in the medium to long term it will catch up with you.

* Common Sense is a collection of rules-of-thumb that provides guidance on how things should be done. But what is Common Sense in any particular circumstances is itself dependent upon the particulars of the circumstances. Whilst the guidance given in this book will tend to provide a good set of directions in most circumstances, it won't in all.

* The proper application of Common Sense does not guarantee things will always turn out for the best. There is a high degree of chance in how things turn out, and whilst we can make allowances for chance we can't predict outcomes with any certainty. Common Sense does however improve the likelihood things will turn out the way we are working for them to do so, and enables us to avoid the worst consequences should they not do so.

* What the Common Sense thing to do in a given circumstance is dependent upon the circumstance and dependent upon our goals and what is important to us. Whilst we may consider a given action on the part of someone else to be contrary to Common Sense it may be that the action makes perfect sense given that person's particular goals and given their perception of circumstances at that time.

* Some of the guidance identified as Common Sense is seemingly contradictory, at least in a purest logical interpretation of the wording. This is because Common Sense is intended to be applied in real life practical circumstances and the best Common Sense advice in a given circumstance will depend upon the specifics of the circumstances.

THE CORE PRINCIPLES OF COMMON SENSE

We cannot be certain about anything

* We can never be absolutely certain about anything in the real world. We can never prove, in an absolute sense, that something about the real world is true.

Reasonableness

* Notwithstanding our inability to be absolutely certain about anything in the real world, there is a consistency, a 'stickiness', about the real world which means for the most part that what we sense seems to be the same things other people sense. Facts are phenomena that we and others can observe and agree about. Truths derived from these facts can be considered reasonable if they are consistent with the known facts; are capable, at least in principle, of being proven false; and are the most general consistent with the previous points. Obscure explanations should be rejected in favor of simple explanations, unless of course they better fit the evidence.

* We should base our explanations, decisions, and actions on the reasonableness of truths, and not be put off by the fact that we cannot be certain.

* Sometimes we cannot get at truths and only have possibilities that we consider to be more or less likely to be the case. Generally we should act on the basis of what is most likely. However when the consequences of being wrong are severe it may be prudent to act in a way that would avoid severe consequences should it turn out the less likely is in fact the case.

* Whilst you should act with decisiveness on the basis of what you believe to be true, or most likely to be true, you should nevertheless remain open to the possibility of being wrong. Do not be closed minded about evidence that might point to the contrary. Whether or not you should change your actions as a result of contrary evidence depends upon the particular circumstances. Sometimes it is appropriate to continue on a course of action even though you know the original presumptions were wrong.

* The world is as it is, not as we would like it to be. Our mental models about the world are only ever the best we have so far, and we should always be on the lookout for better ones. We should see evidence that the world is different to the way we think it is as an opportunity to get closer to an understanding of how it really is. We should be curious about, rather than upset about, experiences or information that contradicts our existing beliefs.

* Most concepts and truths have a fuzziness about them. Their definition is good enough for most everyday purposes, but can become more subjective at the extremes of the definition. This difficulty at the extremes does not invalidate the definition for general everyday use.

* If you want to test a hypothesis do not seek out tests that confirm the hypothesis. You cannot prove a hypothesis no matter how many examples you find. Rather perform tests that would disprove the hypothesis. If the hypothesis is false you will probably quickly find out. If it survives these tests then it becomes a reasonable hypothesis to hold on to. Note however that this is the opposite of what most people do: they look for examples that confirm what they already believe to be true, which of course do no such thing.

Disagreements

* Left to their own devices, people usually act on the basis of prejudice rather than logic. For the most part, what people usually think of as being logical is in reality rationalization of something about which they have already made up their minds.

* When faced with a disagreement, focus on trying to understand the reason for the cause of the disagreement, rather than on trying to impose your own beliefs or views. In exploring the reason for the differences you will learn something new and you will be much more likely to come to an agreeable way forwards. By simply trying to impose your own views you are unlikely to make any progress.

* Just because someone holds different beliefs to yourself doesn't mean you should try to change their beliefs. You are better off exploring the reasons for the differences, and each be left to decide for yourselves whether or not the understanding arising affects your current beliefs.

Pragmatism

* Just because we are not certain about something does not mean we need to act in an uncertain manner. We cannot be certain about anything in the world, but we can recognize some things as being more likely than others, and act accordingly. Take decisive action on the basis of the best information you have.

* Pragmatism depends upon knowing what we can and cannot control. We can't necessarily control what happens to us, but we can control how we react to what happens to us, and we can control our decisions and actions.

Uncertainty

* Be cognizant of uncertainties, and recognize when your conclusions and decisions about action are dependent upon the uncertainties. If the outcome is dependent upon the uncertainty then it may be appropriate to focus on reducing the uncertainty before taking action.

* It is likely that unlikely things will happen. Something that has only 1 chance in 1,000 of occurring is likely to happen if there are enough occurrences. There are many thousands of things that may have only a 1 in 1,000 chance of occurring, so it is not miraculous or odd when one of them happens. It is just probability. Sometimes unlikely things will happen more often than average, just as sometimes they will happen less likely than average, though we probably wouldn't notice this.

* People readily see patterns in random events and assume some causal dependency, when there isn't one. Our brains are forever seeking out patterns in what we see around us; thus the shapes we see in clouds and elsewhere. Given the randomness in everything around us, things will often group in ways that we see as having some pattern. Mostly these are nothing more than our brain having picked out from the many millions of patterns it can conceive of some resemblance to what we are seeing. Occasionally the pattern may be real, and discoveries arise from the ability to see meaningful patterns where others have not, however the vast majority of the unexpected patterns we observe are simply the result of the way our brains work and are not real.

* People generally have a poor grasp of probabilities. It is common for example for people to overestimate probabilities based on the fact that they can bring particular examples to mind. Many people also misunderstand the rules of chance, and believe that chance events even themselves out, for example believing that after a sequence of heads during a coin toss, there is a greater chance of tails in the future in order to get back to the 50-50 ratio.

Systems thinking

* Entities are often part of or exist within multiple systems. By seeing an entity solely in terms of one system, and making changes accordingly, we can miss consequences arising from its existence within other systems. Our actions often have unintentional consequences as a result of our not paying attention to their impact on systems other than the one we were thinking about.

* What we do, or don't do, has consequences. And those consequences have consequences. We may not be able to fully appreciate the consequences of what we do or don't do, but we can usually avoid the worst of undesirable consequences by thinking things through first.

The Bumper Book of Common Sense

* In some circumstances small changes in one thing can lead to very large changes in something else.

* Highly optimized systems are often unstable. They work at the point of optimization, but as soon as there is some disturbance they can react in an unpredictable manner. It is usually best to build into complex systems some redundancy that can be brought to bear when the unexpected occurs. This same idea means that if in a given circumstance you have some surplus, then you can stay in control should there be some unexpected events; if however you have no surplus you are likely to find yourself a victim of circumstances.

Goals and objectives

* If you want to achieve things, you need to be very clear about what it is you want to achieve. Most people aren't. If you are not working towards your own long-term goals, then you are simply a pawn in the lives of those who are.

* Set goals that inspire you and excite you and help you get up in the morning. Don't be afraid to set big audacious inspiring goals. It is better to aim for great things and risk missing them, than to aim for not very much and achieve it.

* In setting your goals note that you cannot find meaning in simply being able to manipulate the world and satisfying your physical needs. Meaning is found in having a higher purpose. For many, this higher purpose is found through religious beliefs. For those without religious beliefs it can be found through a self-awareness of being part of the human race, through helping other people, and seeking to be an active part in its continuing survival and progression. We cannot and will not find meaning simply through selfish pursuit of our own ends.

* Choose goals where you can make a difference and that have meaning to you personally. Life is not about ticking off the achievement of goals; it is about doing things where you feel as though you have made a positive difference. Don't simply have the same goals as lots of other people, or goals based on other people's expectations of you. It is your life; do the things that matter to you.

* In setting goals don't lose sight of your relationships with others, particularly with your family. You need to work at your relationships and put time into them, and in addition to any personal achievement goals you might have you should also have goals relating to maintaining or improving your relationships with persons who are, or who should be, important to you. Achievement of personal goals is rarely of any long term satisfaction if you don't have anyone close to share them with.

Plan

* Without a plan it is difficult to know whether or not what you are doing is genuinely taking you towards your goals or is just doing something. And even if you are moving towards your goals are you getting there fast enough, and is it the most effective way of getting you there. It is easy to look and feel like you are doing something, to be busy, but not so easy to be sure you are doing the right something.

* Plan, do, monitor, review, (re-)plan, do, monitor, review, (re-)plan, ... If what you are doing is not getting you to where you want to get to, then you either need to change what you are doing or change where you are trying to get to.

* Planning is not just about what we need to do, it is about planning to timely obtain the facilities, and resources and tools and whatever inputs we need to enable us to do what we need to do. It is about recognizing what might go wrong and taking action to either reduce the likelihood of them going wrong or reducing the negative consequences should they do so.

Determine what is important

* It is important to find the right balance between the long term and the short term. Too much focus on the long term generally leads to things not getting done. Too much focus on the short term

results in simply going from crisis to crisis and never having the time to do the things that will prevent the next crisis.

* One of the primary applications of Common Sense is to be effective at sifting what is important from what is not. Generally what is important are: the things leading to your long term goals; the things that if not done now will lead to disruptions or lead to them having to be done later with more effort; and the things that are making you stressed because you haven't yet done them.

Appreciate, use, and manage your time

* It's up to you what you do with your life, the universe doesn't care.

* Learn to live most of your life in the present, rather than continually beating yourself up about things from the past or worrying about the future. The present moment is all we ever have. Now is the only time we have power to do anything or the time to appreciate being alive.

* If you don't like the moment you are in look to change it if you can, and if you can't change it then simply experience it. Like it or not, it is still the totality of your life.

* Manage your discretionary time. It will run away from you if you don't. Discretionary time is the time you can truly decide what to do with, as opposed to the time you spend doing paid employment or doing what other people want you to do or doing necessities such as eating and washing, etc. For most people their discretionary time just disappears to no good end. However you can choose to put it to a good use by using it to develop yourself and using it to follow up on your personal goals and on ideas that are important to you. If you want to make good use of your discretionary time you need to explicitly recognize it and plan how to use it in advance.

* You can't do everything at once, but you can do something at once. When feeling overwhelmed or uncertain about what to do, be wary of ending up doing nothing. Focus on doing something, and don't worry that you are not doing everything.

* You can only do one thing at a time. Decide what is the most important thing for you to be doing right now, and then get on with it to the best of your ability. Resist the temptation to multitask anything that requires intellectual effort: you don't really do such things in parallel; you do them one at a time whilst rapidly switching between them, to the detriment of both tasks.

* Look to understand the value adding opportunity costs with respect to anything you do. It is not just about whether you are doing something useful or value adding: it is about whether or not the useful or value adding thing you are doing is the best use of your time and resources that it can reasonably be.

* Determine what matters most, and will give your life most meaning. Eliminate the non-essential, both in terms of things and in terms of what you spend your time on. Organize to ensure you get on with what matters most. Get routine things that need doing done as effectively and efficiently as you can. Put your energies into the things that matter whilst looking after your body and mind such that you don't do yourself damage or burn yourself out.

* Don't obsess about the use of your time. Take time to relax. Take time to be with people who matter to you. Take time to sit and think.

Follow through

* It's important to have ideas, but it's also important to be able to turn ideas into action. Great ideas are nothing without the self-motivation and perseverance to follow them through to implementation, and through the early difficulties new ideas often face. Most good ideas go nowhere because not enough effort is put into developing and refining them, and following them through.

The Bumper Book of Common Sense

* New ideas will have resistance. Identify assistors and resistors. Use divergent thinking to identify both. List them out. Ask Who What When Where Why How? Select the most important and generate actions to leverage assistors and overcome resistors. Build up an action plan.

* In everything that you do, do the best you can. If you are in paid employment, do a little more than what you are paid for.

Be organized

* Be organized so that you can find things quickly. Clear up clutter and have some clear workspace. You will save a lot of time and feel more motivated to get on with things. In the medium to long term it takes much less time to get and stay organized than it does searching for things you can't readily lay your hands on. It also significantly reduces stress, and significantly increases your productivity as you make good use of information and tools you then have readily to hand.

* Have a time and a place for everything, and do and put everything in its time and place. You will accomplish much more, have more leisure time, and will feel much better about yourself. This includes having places for commonly used items such as keys and phones, which is where you put them when you are not carrying them around with you.

* Checklists are enormously powerful productivity tools. You make use of other people's experiences in addition to your own, and by keeping them live you can ensure they, and you, are continually improving. Their use ensures you don't forget things, particularly when in a rush or in a stressful environment. They also free up your consciousness to focus on other things.

Avoid common thinking biases

* Whether we believe it or not we are liable to a number of particular and common biases in our thinking. The following are some examples, but note there are many others:
  o The Attribution Bias, where we blame our own errors on external factors, but other people's errors on internal factors. Thus when we make mistakes it is because of circumstances or the fault of someone else, when others make mistakes it is because they were careless or had nefarious motives.
  o Availability Bias is when people give far more weight to examples they can bring to mind than more abstract but representative statistical information. Thus people who know someone who smoked till they were very old will be less inclined to believe smoking is very bad for your health.
  o Distinction Bias is the tendency to see two items as more dissimilar when evaluating them together than when evaluating them separately.
  o Endowment Bias is our tendency to place more value on something we own than on something we don't own.
  o False consensus bias is the tendency of a person to overestimate how much other people agree with them.
  o The Frequency illusion is where something that has recently come to our attention then appears to be everywhere, with far greater apparent frequently than previously.
  o Hindsight Bias is the tendency for people to believe they knew it all along after a given event has occurred. This can even lead to memory distortions as people often fool themselves about what they had really believed before the outcome became known.
  o Ingroup Bias is the tendency for people to give greater weight or preference to those who are members of groups of which they are themselves members.
  o Omission Bias is our tendency to see harmful actions as being worse than equally harmful inactions.
  o Optimism Bias is the tendency for some people to overestimate the likelihood of positive events and underestimating the likelihood of negative events.

- o The Overconfidence Bias is our tendency to be overconfident in our judgments. We all suffer from it to some extent, some more so than others. For example about 90% of drivers rate themselves as better than average. Most people are overconfident in their ability to accurately assess risks.

- o Pattern bias is our tendency to see patterns in random data. There are an infinite number of patterns we can envisage, and therefore finding one to match a set of random data after the event it not difficult. This makes many people susceptible to believing conspiracy theories.

- o Unconscious Bias is our tendency to make unconscious assumptions about another person based upon a single characteristic, such as their sex, gender, place of origin, etc.

* A poor understanding of cognitive biases, or a naïve view that we are somehow magically immune to them, leaves us open to the influencing and persuading of others, whether by salesmen, general advertising or through being targeted by scammers.

* It is very difficult to overcome our cognitive biases, but we can to a large extent. The greatest barrier to doing so is our belief that they don't apply to us. And thus the most important step towards overcoming them, or at least significantly lessening their hold and impact on us, is to accept without question that we too are susceptible to them, in the same way as we readily see that others are. Once we accept this we can better overcome our biases by: being clear about what is clearly facts and what is opinion or assumption, with far more being the later than we may otherwise have realized; actively listening to or seeking out alternative viewpoints and opinions; being aware that others are also susceptible to biases, including experts and friends; being aware that circumstances play a major part in what people do and decide, and that often you may not be aware of those circumstances; and ensuring you are not rushed into making up your mind or rushed into accepting what you feel is instinctively right.

Continually self-develop

* You can and should be continually developing yourself physically, mentally, and emotionally. There are hundreds and possibly thousands of opportunities each day when you can make decisions to be improving yourself: most in small ways, but they accumulate. Small decisions about what you do or don't eat. Opportunities for a bit of exercise. Opportunities about how you do or don't let your mind wander and about your self-talk. Opportunities about what you choose to do next, and about whether or not you choose to continue or to stop what you are doing. Opportunities to control your instinctive and emotional responses to what is happening around you. Every day hundreds and hundreds of opportunities, some big, most small, to get better and better, if you choose to do so.

* Try to know a little about a lot and a lot about a little. Don't try to know a lot about a lot because you will fail and dissipate your energies.

* Regular small improvements, even very small improvements, will add up to big improvements over time. Don't worry that you can't make big improvements all at once, focus on making small improvements. Improve just a little each day and you will take great strides.

* Our brains are far more flexible and malleable, far more capable of being upgraded, than most people think. When we do things we build up neural pathways in our brain. The stronger the neural pathways in our brain the easier and more natural we find doing the things they are associated with. Thus the more we practice something, the stronger we make the associated neural pathways, and the easier we are able to do it in the future. Our brain reconstructs itself, rewires itself, as a result of our learning experiences and what we practice doing. Even mental practice contributes to this rewiring of your brain, though not as strongly as with physical practice.

* It is not with others we should compare ourselves; it is with our past selves. Continual self-improvement makes life fulfilling.

The basics of succeeding

The Bumper Book of Common Sense

* Take 100% responsibility for your own life. Most people behave as though someone else is responsible for their lives, and thus they have an excuse for not achieving. Your life is down to you and you alone. Events may or may not go your way, but the outcome from events is dependent upon your response, which is down to you.

* Most people if things are going wrong tend first to blame others, then circumstances, and rarely then look at themselves. If you want to succeed first ask yourself what is it you are doing that is contributing to the problem and what can you do that is different. Then ask about circumstances. Finally ask about others, but in terms of what you can do different in your interaction with them.

* Be clear about what you want to achieve and have faith that you can. Make plans for getting there and be organized. Get on doing the things that will take you closer to where you are trying to get to. Work much harder than those around you, and spend time learning how to do things better. Do not let setbacks or failures put you off. Keep going for it with all your heart and energy. Have patience. Keep focused and opportunities will arise, often when you least expect them. You make your own luck by continually trying.

* If you want to achieve something worthwhile, expect there to be difficulties along the way. If you accept that there will be struggles and obstacles to overcome then you are less likely to get downhearted and demotivated when they occur. When you make a commitment to achieve a goal also make a commitment to tackle and overcome the difficulties. When times are tough remind yourself that it was never going to be easy but that the end is worth it. If you have a 'why' you can endure almost any 'how'.

* Take small steps. If a given step is too large just break it into the size of steps you can succeed at, one at a time.

* On balance your own competitive advantage in the world is better served by capitalizing on and improving on your strengths rather than on improving on things you are not so good at; though there may be some weaknesses that you do need to overcome in order to avoid squandering gains from your strengths. Being very good at one thing is generally of more value than being mediocre at lots of things.

* Seek to involve others in your endeavors. You can achieve great things in cooperation with others.

* Some of the reasons people fail to achieve what they are capable of:
    o Lack of purpose or goals;
    o Lack of ambition to rise above mediocrity;
    o Choosing goals they are not suited to;
    o Lack of knowledge or skills in their chosen area of endeavor;
    o Lack of self-discipline;
    o Lack of a plan to get them to where they want to go;
    o Lack of focus or ability to concentrate;
    o Lack of enthusiasm for what they are doing;
    o Frequent procrastination;
    o Tendency to avoid hard work;
    o Unwillingness to make the effort without an up-front guarantee of reward;
    o Overindulgence in pleasurable or lazy activity;
    o Lack of persistence;
    o Lack of energy brought about by poor diet and exercise habits;
    o Tendency to be negative;
    o Frequent indecisiveness;

- o   Over cautiousness, and a lack of willingness to take calculated risks;
- o   Poor interpersonal skills, or an inability to co-operate with others;
- o   Failure to recognize the need for continual self-development;

If any of these apply to you, do something about it.

The importance of self-control

* People who are able to exert self-control are generally happier, healthier, able to deal with life's downs, get on better with other people, do better in their careers, and live longer than those less able to. And we are all able to significantly increase our self-control and change our behavior if we choose to do so and make the effort. Our past failures and our current circumstances are no excuse. It is our conscious ability to choose to change that defines us as human beings.

How to increase your self-control

* The foundations of self-control are self-awareness and remembering what matters most. Frequently bring yourself into the present, and frequently remind yourself of your life's goals and the need to be working towards them in small ways whenever you can.

* Self-control is about doing the harder but more valuable thing, when you have the option of doing the lazy or easy thing. Self-control is like a muscle that we can strengthen through persistent effort to do so. And just as it takes time to build up a weak muscle, so will it take time to build up your levels of self-control. You would not expect a weak muscle to suddenly be strong simply because you started to exercise it, so don't get disheartened when your willpower doesn't either. But if you keep at it, if you persist, if you focus on small victories that you can build on, you will eventually succeed.

* By practicing to resist temptations you get better at resisting temptations. By practicing doing the right thing when it should be done, you are both improving your willpower for the particular task and you are also improving it in general. There are many hundreds of opportunities every day for seeking to do the right thing. Don't get despondent because you don't always succeed in doing so, just keep trying.

* Stress impairs willpower. It leads to short term focus, whereas willpower is about being able to focus on the long term. Don't allow yourself to be continually stressed. Understand what is stressing you and do something about it. Note in particular that most of our large problems arise from not facing up to and dealing with small problems when they arise, or from not doing the things that need doing when they ought to be done.

* If you plan and schedule something then you are far more likely to get on and do it than if you just have some vague idea that you ought to do it sometime. Ensure you have regular planned times for progressing your goals. And if there's something you know you need to do, decide specifically when you are going to do it and reserve the time in your calendar or organizer.

* Regularly read inspirational books and listen to motivational audio. Read about people who have overcome adversity or who have achieved great success having started out with nothing very much. The more you expose yourself to inspirational and motivational material the more it will seep into you, and the more you will come across ideas or tips that you can try out and occasionally find of real benefit. You will come to realize that those who have succeeded despite difficulties are for the most part people not unlike yourself.

* The outcome you expect is the outcome you will probably get. Believe you are going to have a great day, and you probably will. Believe you will have a horrid day, and you probably will. Be positive and things are much more likely to turn out positively, so long as you are not unrealistic and so long as you work at them.

The Bumper Book of Common Sense

* Don't kid yourself that there is some future best time to get on with the things you need to get on with. The best time to get on with whatever needs to be done is as soon as you can, irrespective of whether or not you feel like it. Don't wait until you feel motivated to get on with what is important to you.

* Employing will power to do something drains your energy. Use your self-control to develop good habits, which then become automatic and don't then continually require will power. Like a path through the undergrowth, the more times you follow the path the clearer the path becomes and the easier it is for you to go down the same path in the future. Persistence will lead to you succeeding in ingraining good habits.

Problem Solving and Decision Making

* Don't just solve problems. Understand and resolve the issues that gave rise to the problem in the first place.

* To make sense of disparate pieces of information you need to represent it in some structure. Whilst this helps you, it also constrains you. Putting the information into a different structure will reveal different insights about it.

* When confronted with a problem, look at the assumptions you are making about the situation as well as the situation itself. Think about the context within which the problem has arisen. Problems are often not what they appear at first sight to be, and the best solution to problems is often not where you might initially think it will be. In particular be wary of simply tackling the symptoms of what is in fact a deeper rooted problem.

* Frequently we need to home in on solutions, rather than attempt 'big bang' solutions. Homing in on solutions is about gradually eliminating certain options, looking at promising options in a little more detail then homing in again on the more promising ones, etc. At each stage the amount of effort is the minimum required to determine which direction to go in.

* When problem solving or decision making about issues that involve others, look to understand other people's views and beliefs; express your own; identify the common purpose; and work with others to achieve it. All too often we simply want to impose our own preferences. Whilst this may get us more quickly to a seeming solution, in the longer term it often leads to solutions not as good as they could have been. Sometimes of course a given solution or decision must be imposed, but this should only be after we have made the effort to involve and listen to others.

* A good decision is one that is the best you could have reasonably made at the time based on the information available or which you could have reasonably been expected to have gone out and uncovered. Ways of helping ensure you arrive at good decisions include: being open about your decision process and the rationale for your choices; ensuring the decision is documented or reasoned through in a clear and traceable manner; and not ignoring the viewpoint of others just because they don't align with your own. Actively seeking to understand the reason for conflicting viewpoints is usually a valuable source of useful considerations.

* Disagreement is an essential part of effective decision making. There is a greater risk of poor decisions being made when everyone comes to an agreement with little or no debate than if opposing views are expressed and defended, and the reasons for the opposing viewpoints actively explored. However it is important that the participants retain respect for others and their rights to have different views, otherwise egos can get in the way of the best options being selected.

* Don't agonize over unimportant decisions. They will wear you down. Don't go seeking out lots of choices. Get to a small number of options quickly, and come to a decision quickly, then move on. If you find you can't decide between 2 options, having thought through as best you can the costs and consequences and risks, then it doesn't matter which you choose. Go with the one that is the most interesting or is different to what you have done before.

* Don't worry about your decisions once they are made. If you believe a decision was wrong, you can either change it or not. If you can change it, and you believe it is the right thing to do, then do so. If you can't change it, then make the best of it that you can. But don't beat yourself up about it either way.

Be positive

* Don't worry. Be optimistic that life's problems can be solved. Get on with things: try to improve things when you can; try to change them if you have good reason to try; and accept the things you can't do anything about. Stay calm in the light of difficulties. Look to see the big picture and keep a sense of proportion. Do the best you can in the circumstances.

* Think not of the shortcomings of the past; think not of what others may think of you; do what you know to be right; fill your mind with noble principles; endure; be constantly in command of yourself; be ever looking to improve; be firm and persist and keep in mind your resolutions and commitments; act now; if and when you fall get back up and renter the fray with renewed vigor.

* Think of yourself as an essential cog in the universal consciousness, as important and as significant as any other cog. Our lives and everyone else's lives are governed mostly by chance, and it is chance that we happen to have been born in the environment we were and with the characteristics we were born with. It is thus not how successful you are that matters, since this is mostly the result of chance, it is how you make the best of whatever circumstances you find yourself in. You can be as significant as anyone else in the universe simply by making the most of the particular circumstances you find yourself in and by being aware of yourself and your environment as you do so.

Do the right thing

* Find work that you are suited to and love doing. Work is likely to be a big part of your life, and you will have a far more satisfying life in a job you enjoy, even if you earn less, than in a job you don't enjoy, assuming of course you don't earn so little you have to struggle to make ends meet.

* A good life is significantly aided through trying to do the right thing, respecting the rights of others to be different, having fortitude, and living modestly.

* People are often unreasonable and self-centered. Forgive them anyway. If you are kind, people may accuse you of ulterior motives. Be kind anyway. If you are honest, people may cheat you. Be honest anyway. If you find happiness, people may be jealous. Be happy anyway. The good you do today may be forgotten tomorrow. Do good anyway. Give the world the best you have, and it may never be enough. Give your best anyway. (Mother Teresa)

Other people and how to interact with them

* All men and women are born equal, even though they don't all have the same capabilities or opportunities. There is worth in everyone. You may or may not immediately jell with everyone you meet, but remember they are human beings with the same rights as you, and probably many of the same concerns and fears and hopes. Seek to instinctively like and respect everyone you meet and see any characteristics you find annoying as simply who they are, and not something to be judged.

* Welcome people with different views. Seeking out common ground with them will often give you different perspectives and lead to you developing and gaining a deeper understanding of your own views.

* Deal with people as you find them; don't be angry or frustrated just because they are not as you would wish them to be.

* People behave the way they do because of their particular background and beliefs, and because of their viewpoint in the particular circumstances. They don't behave the way they do because they are

The Bumper Book of Common Sense

stupid or evil people or because they are out to get you. Thus be tolerant of people behaving differently to the way you believe they should, and seek to understand their viewpoint.

* When others don't perform we tend to put it down to being a character flaw. When we don't perform we put it down to circumstances.

* Co-operation allows far more to be achieved than conflict, and is more likely to lead to long-term success. We achieve great things when working together in teams so long as we are all going in the same direction. If you want to achieve great success you need to involve others, and create a group of people who have an interest in helping you.

* When negotiating seek to find a win-win position where both parties feel good about the outcome. Understand what is important to you and what is important to the other person or group and see the negotiation as a joint problem solving activity of seeking out a position acceptable to you both. You want however to be negotiating with someone who is also seeking a win-win position. If you detect the other is not, then you need to be much more hardnosed about any trades you make or information you give away.

* Don't worry about what other people might be thinking about you. Other people are rarely thinking about you; they are mostly thinking about themselves, and probably worrying about what other people are thinking about them.

* You will not please everyone, and some people will be critical of you. Don't be put off by other people's negativity towards you. Do not let it play on your mind. Concentrate on doing the things you believe to be right. If you are working towards something you believe in, many people will be negative or discouraging because you are showing up their mediocrity.

* People are rarely out to upset you, so forgive them. Most negativity and put-downs come from people seeing things only from their own viewpoint and being what they think of as honest, albeit with a lack of sensitivity.

* We have a tendency to believe we are more reasonable than others and that we are more often right in our words and actions. Other people feel the same way about themselves. Whilst we readily see the shortfalls in others, we are largely blind to the shortfalls in ourselves

* Poor writing skills will be noticed by others and hold you back. Check your grammar and spelling. Be sure your tone and words and style is appropriate to your audience and means of communication. Be clear about what you want to say and get to the point quickly. Make sure each point in your message is clear and flows and is useful. Use headings and sub-headings and bullets to break up text. Proof read anything before you send it out.

Influencing and Persuading

* Factors used in persuasion include: reciprocation, our tendency to respond in kind; consistency, our tendency to want to appear consistent; social proof, our tendency to do the same as others; liking, our tendency to be more willing to believe people we like; authority, our tendency to do like what authority suggests or tells us to do; and scarcity, our tendency to think scarce things are more desirable and better. Those trying to sell us something will often be looking to exploit one or more of these tendencies.

* People buy on emotion and justify with fact. Arguments that appeal to people emotionally are often more persuasive in practice than arguments that are based simply on logic.

* If you want someone to take action, or to provide you with a response, make it as easy for them to do so as you can. Don't give them any excuse to put it aside to come back to later.

* Power itself is neither good nor bad. We need power to get things done. What is good or bad are our motivations for wielding the power we have, how we apply it, and the ends to which we put it.

* People faced with a large number of options are less likely to make a choice than people faced with a smaller number of options. People faced with too much choice often become paralyzed and avoid making a choice at all.

* People hate to lose things more than they like to gain them; people are generally loss averse. Thus whether or not a transaction is framed as a loss or as a gain can significantly influence behavior. For many types of products you are more likely to lose customers if you increase your prices than you are to gain customers by decreasing your prices.

Small Talk

* The world is full of people. And most of them are much like us, in their own way. Knowing how to be comfortable with other people through being able to engage in small talk is part of making the most of our lives. It opens up opportunities to making new friends and brings us closer to people we already know.

* Take the risk of meeting new people. Most people want to meet new people, but are hesitant about making the first move – so let it be you. The more you do it the better you will get at it. Be the first to chat to someone new to your area. Find out who they are and what makes them tick. If you make the effort when they are new they will be positively disposed towards you in the future. And don't be put off by the occasional person who does not respond. Be respectful and move on.

* Converse with everyone you come across: people you're in a queue with, neighbors, people on the bus, waiters. Use every interaction with others as an opportunity to practice and improve your small talk and intercommunication skills.

* Your opening when talking to someone you've not met before will generally relate to the immediate surroundings or circumstances. Assuming you get some response then you can follow up on any cues offered by the opening interchange or move on to introducing yourself or your reason for being there. In doing so you need to provide some hooks for the other person to follow up on, and also give the other person the opportunity to offer up similar information. Once you've got into conversation use the direction of the conversation to prompt further questions, revealing something of yourself as you do so. You are seeking out something to connect you to this other person. Thus be open about your interests and information about yourself. It gives other people an opportunity for identifying common ground with you. Note that you need to be prepared to answer any questions you ask others since it is likely you will get asked the same questions back.

* Keep a journal or notebook to write down conversation pieces. Unusual facts or news events. Funny or interesting stories. Quotes that appeal to you. Novel metaphors or analogies. Observations. Seek out a new one or two every week so you have something topical. Regularly review your notebook so the items are fresh in your mind.

COMMON SENSE THINKING

Truth and Belief

Nothing is Certain

* We can never be absolutely certain about anything in the real world.

* Sometimes certain beliefs have been accepted as true for such a long time that they are not questioned, and may indeed be seen to be 'Common Sense'. However there are no supposed truths about the real world that are unquestionably true, and there are many false beliefs that have been widely but mistakenly taken as true for long periods of time.

* Just because something is widely believed doesn't make it true.

* Some people are absolutely certain about certain truths. This says more about them than it does about the truth.

* Only the ignorant have no doubts.

* There is no, and there can be no, concrete and absolute test of what is true in the real world.

* Sometimes a group is strong enough to impose its beliefs or its will on others as the truth, and it is sometimes prudent for others to at least pretend to believe. This of course doesn't make these beliefs true.

* We do not see the world as it is, but as it appears to us to be. This is dependent not only upon the world as it is but upon our perceiving senses and upon our processing brains. Our attention, thoughts, and preconceptions affect what we believe we see.

Some Truths are More Reasonable than Others

* Some truths are more reasonable than others. We should base our explanations, decisions, and actions on the reasonableness of truths, not on some unachievable absoluteness of truth. The term 'truth', when applied in an everyday context, should thus be taken as reference to what it is reasonable to believe.

* Just because nothing in the real world can be absolutely proven, does not mean that all things have an equal right to be believed. We should look to get as close to what we can perceive to be the truth as we can, and not be put off by the fact that we cannot be certain.

* Notwithstanding our inability to be absolutely certain about anything in the real world, there is a consistency, a 'stickiness', about the real world which means for the most part that what we sense seems to be the same things other people sense. We can however be readily mistaken in what we sense if we are only given a few moments to sense it, or we are only able to partially sense it, or we are distracted by other things when we sense it.

* We should differentiate between what we sense, and what we assume or derive based upon what we sense. For example, we sense the sun rising above the horizon in the morning; we do not sense either the sun going around the world or the world going around the sun.

* Circumstantial evidence is where there are a number of probably true relationships that compound to give a likely true statement. The final statement is not absolutely proven, but is what is judged most likely to be the case. Generally we should act on the basis of what is most likely. However when the consequences of being wrong are severe it is often appropriate to demand a greater level of compounded probability through more circumstantial evidence. And we should keep in mind that that circumstantial evidence leads to probable, not certain, and thus remain open to potentially contrary evidence.

* The reasonableness of truths can be determined using guidelines that are useful and generally accepted. These guidelines are:

    (a) The 'truth' should be consistent with the known facts, both facts that indicate it is true and facts that might indicate it to be false.

    (b) The 'truth' must, at least in principle, be capable of being proven false. Ie. it must be possible to conceptualize examples which, if they occurred, would demonstrate that the truth was false. It is this that distinguishes many statements derived from science from statements of faith. Statements of faith are often not capable of being proven false.

    (c) The 'truth' should be the most general and most simple consistent with (a) and (b). Obscure explanations should be rejected in favor of simple explanations, unless of course they better fit the evidence.

* The most useful truths are usually those which are general, and can be widely applied, but which are easily capable of being proven false should they be so.

* If someone is not willing to accept the guidelines for determining the reasonableness of truth, then there is no point in arguing with them about what is and isn't true.

* The discovery of what it is reasonable to believe about the real world should be sought through direct measurement of the real world, and the deriving of rules based on patterns observed. These rules however are only ever the best we have to date, and can and should be modified when we gain further reliable observations that don't fit these patterns. Indeed the advancement of our scientific understanding of the world is based on actively looking to find examples of where our methods don't work or are wrong, and then modifying our understanding to account for the shortcomings.

* We do not need to see all the evidence for third party verification in order to believe something. After all the vast majority of what we believe is based on third party verification and we do not have time to verify it for ourselves. But we need to have some reasonable confidence that the third party verification exists and that we can go and look at it if we want to.

* There is an immense amount of third party information, and much of it is contradictory. The following are guidelines on what it is reasonable to believe:
    o Information which is widely accepted and we know has been widely tested;
    o Information which whilst it may not be widely accepted (yet) is practically testable, and if there is any doubt can thus be tested;
    o Information we know comes from a source that has a reputation for honesty and integrity;
    o Information we believe makes sense in that it fits in with the other things we believe, recognizing the risk that we may believe this because of rationalization.

* Circumstances when we should be wary of third party information include:
    o Information that cannot be readily verified;

The Bumper Book of Common Sense

- o Information generated by those with a strong vested interest;
- o Information that comes from a source we know to lack honesty and integrity.

However these guidelines are not absolute. For example, information generated by those with a vested interest is not necessarily biased, and often it is only those with a vested interest who make the effort to gather certain types of information.

* Sometimes it is necessary to distinguish clearly what we take to be the truth from the conclusions we draw from it. Truths are sometimes 'inconvenient'. Nevertheless we should not pretend they don't exist. What conclusions we choose to draw from truths are rarely an inevitable consequence of the truths themselves. Thus genetic differences between different peoples and races and genders are, at least statistically, real. Because some people then wrongly draw conclusions about superiority or inferiority does not mean the genetic differences don't statistically exist.

* People often believe something because they would like it to be true, or because it would be of benefit to them if it were true. Whilst this may be more comforting for them, it will usually lead to difficulties and ultimately more problems than would be the case if they accepted a more objective truth.

* Just because something is true does not mean it will be accepted as such or believed, or that it will be more accepted than something that is not true. Some of the things we now accept are true were once rejected by most people.

* Unless something is blatantly and obviously true, then we should accept that it might not be, even if for practical and everyday purposes we act as though it is true.

* Just because you can't prove something is true doesn't mean it is false. Just because you can't prove something is false doesn't mean it is true.

* In simplistic terms, a truth remains true as long as it is the best to be had; it becomes false as soon as it can be bettered.

* Most personal beliefs are largely driven by a hypothesis quickly arrived at based on past experience and prejudices, followed by looking for evidence to support the hypothesis. People do not naturally seek out evidence to refute their beliefs. They are more likely to read books and newspapers that confirm their current viewpoints rather than question them. Nevertheless it is by getting alternative viewpoints and being willing to modify our beliefs that our personal beliefs improve in terms of being more aligned with how the world really is rather than how we would like the world to be.

* People tend to view evidence that confirms their beliefs as reliable, and evidence that goes against them as questionable. Thus their current beliefs are relatively easily reinforced and strengthened.

* Information that is vivid, concrete and personal tends to have a strong impact on us, much more so than abstract or second hand information. Personal experiences have a greater impact than ones we read or hear about. However our personal experiences are often atypical; they are after all rare events, and it is likely to be hit or miss whether or not they are representative. Nevertheless people often give far more weight to events they personally experience than to statistical information. People sometimes base their whole value judgments and lives on generalizing from a single intense personal experience. Yet it is the statistical information that is the more representative and useful in terms of how the world really is.

* Whilst we can talk about something being 'subjective', in that it is a particular person's viewpoint, it is not possible to be sure that something is truly 'objective', ie. completely independent of any viewpoint. Like 'truth', how can we know? Nevertheless some things are more objective than others, and rather than considering subjective and objective as two sides of a coin, we are better off seeing them as two extremes, with our knowledge about things lying somewhere in between.

* The majority of people think there is something in astrology or the paranormal, despite the fact that they defy all the known laws of physics. No psychic or paranormal event has ever been proven under controlled conditions and there is long history of fraud.

We Should Continually be Looking to Improve what we Believe to be Reality

* Don't necessarily take facts at face value. If you have any reason to doubt them, check them if you reasonably can. There are many statements claimed to be facts that are not.

* Be curious about unexpected experiences or outcomes, and never ignore evidence or facts that contradict existing 'truths' or beliefs. By all means question the contradicting evidence or facts since they may be unreliable; however never ignore them simply because they are inconvenient. There are many examples of evidence that was initially ignored or covered up and later proved to be important and the basis of new understandings. We should always think of our current beliefs as simply being the best we have to date, and see any contradictory evidence as an opportunity to improve our understanding.

* Seek out the most persuasive arguments that challenge your existing opinions. It is not defending your opinions irrespective of whether they are right or wrong that is important, it is defending opinions you believe are right. You should thus always be willing to test whether or not they are right by listening to the strongest arguments you can find to the contrary.

* Much of the progress about how we view the world is through resolving the conflicts of opposing ideas. With respect to some given subject conflicting extreme views emerge. Eventually the resolution of the conflict is through some new viewpoint that includes aspects of both extremes, as a synthesis of the extremes.

* Just because there is evidence that contradicts what we currently believe, it doesn't mean we should simply abandon what we currently believe. We need to ensure our truths and beliefs account for both new evidence and old. Usually a modification of our previous truths and beliefs will allow us to account for both the new and old evidence. Only occasionally will we require a complete reversal and change in previous truths and beliefs.

* Be wary of believing information is reliable simply because it is quoted in many different places. Information that has been independently verified many times is likely to be reliable. However often information from a given source is simply re-quoted by others without any additional verification, and often hundreds or thousands of quotes for a given piece of information may all be reliant upon a single source, which may or may not be reliable.

* If you want to test a hypothesis do not seek out tests that confirm the hypothesis. With the exception of the trivial case where there is a limited number of items, you cannot prove a hypothesis no matter how many examples to support it that you find. Rather perform tests that would disprove the hypothesis. If the hypothesis is false you will probably quickly find out. If it survives these tests then it becomes a reasonable hypothesis to hold on to.

* There are some things we will never know, either personally, or as a species, though this shouldn't stop us trying to find out. After all, we don't know what it is we won't find out, and we might find out things we didn't think we would be able.

* It is better to know a little about things that are important than to know a lot about things that are unimportant.

* The world progresses through the evolution of ideas. And as with the evolution of species, each evolutionary step begins with a single individual.

The Bumper Book of Common Sense

* Personality gets in the way of truth. Pride and arrogance in particular stand in the way of many people seeing things as they really are.

* If you believe you already know it all then you will make no effort to learn anything new. Many people are severely limited by their own pigheadedness and suffer accordingly, at a loss to understand why the world doesn't just fall into place around them.

* From time to time, ask yourself about some particular belief you hold, what if this were not true, or maybe the opposite of it were true? You will find that it probably isn't such an inconceivable idea, and it will make you more open to considering evidence that contradicts your current beliefs which you might otherwise have simply rejected.

Faith and Belief

* Beliefs that rely on faith cannot be proved or disproved. For example: belief that we are an alien experiment with the aliens manipulating us, cannot be proved false. However nor is it a particularly useful belief in that it does not help us better interact with and control the real world.

* If someone declares something as certain, then they are exhibiting faith, not rationale thinking.

* Some people have absolute conviction in the truths they believe in. The strength of their conviction has no bearing whatsoever on the extent to which what they believe is a reasonable truth to hold.

* Most of our deep engrained beliefs arise implicitly as a result of the environment we are in, where we simply pick up the beliefs without thinking of those around us. By the time we are able to question these beliefs they are already inherent, and our natural tendency is to only pay attention to or to credit evidence that confirms our existing beliefs and to ignore, avoid, or discredit evidence that might contradict these beliefs.

* We often form initial judgments, the beginning of a belief, based on first impressions or scant evidence. However once we have formed this initial judgment, unless we actively and deliberately ensure we seek out objective evidence for and against, we will naturally start to look for evidence to confirm that initial judgment. And unless we counter them, biases will then dictate how we view potential evidence and we will get into a cycle of seeing confirmatory evidence whilst largely ignoring or failing to seek out evidence which would have contradicted it. And as a result weak initial evidence becomes the beginnings of strongly held convictions.

* Whether or not we believe something is not dependent solely upon an objective weighing up of the evidence. It is, at least in part, dependent upon what impact it might have on our lives. We have a strong tendency to believe things that are beneficial to us, and disbelieve those that are disadvantageous.

* If someone talks of having witnessed a miracle, ask yourself which is more likely: the occurrence of the miracle, or the person having been mistaken or exaggerating or lying.

* There are many people who will tenaciously hold onto strong beliefs despite there being no reasonable evidence, and even where there may be much evidence to the contrary. Convincing such people that their beliefs are wrong or inappropriate is more a question of psychology than it is the application of rational argument.

* People's political or religious beliefs are largely dictated by the environment they grew up in and by those around them.

* A person who is stubborn will tend to hold on to their existing beliefs no matter what further evidence comes to light. A person who is fickle will be continually changing their beliefs dependent

upon the most recent piece of evidence. Stubbornness ignores new evidence; fickleness ignores old evidence. A stubborn person will tend to ignore what the latest person has said, and a fickle person will tend to ignore what persons other than the latest person have said. We should strive to be neither stubborn nor fickle and take account of both old and new evidence.

* Just because someone holds different beliefs to yourself doesn't mean you should try to change their beliefs.

* Religion, or any heartfelt belief in some unseen order underpinning existence, provides many people with a route to a satisfying and fulfilling life.

* Sometimes friendship is worth more than being proven right.

* The most savage controversies are those where there is no clear evidence, and no clear way of differentiating between evidence, one way or the other.

* Having faith in a higher being is not a bad thing. Using faith as a reason to discriminate negatively against others is a bad thing. Forcing faith aggressively on others is a bad thing.

* We have an innate desire to know what our future holds for us, with many people believing that their future includes some form of life after death. Any belief system that includes life after death needs to have a clear view of what sort of life after death if it is to gain traction. And belief systems that do offer a clear view will be more attractive to people than those that leave it vague.

* During times of uncertainty, such as during economic upheavals that affect people's daily lives, the clear message provided by extremists are far more attractive to people than the vagueness provided by moderates, irrespective of the dangers following extremists invariably brings. A lesson is that moderates must also make their vision clear.

Living without Absolute Truths

* Whilst there are no absolute truths, we still need to act and behave as though there were. If we are to act effectively in life we need to do so without continually questioning everything. There are thus truths we should accept as being 'beyond reasonable doubt', albeit always being willing to question them should circumstances or more information throw some doubt on them.

* There is nothing hypocritical about acting firmly on the basis of something as though it were true, even though we know it might not be true. To get things done in this world we need to act decisively. However we should also keep an open mind about how things really are, and be willing to change our minds if there is convincing evidence that we should.

Scientific Laws and Rules

The Origins, Limitations, and Usefulness of Scientific Laws and Rules

* Whilst we can never be absolutely certain about anything we nevertheless appear to live in a world that behaves, for the most part, in a consistent manner. A particularly important set of 'truths' defining how the world appears to behave are those relating to scientific laws and rules. They enable us to manipulate the real world. They generally come about through:

The Bumper Book of Common Sense

- o The result of specific observations in which we find patterns which can be expressed mathematically, and which are then successfully used to explain other observations; or
- o A modification of some general truth or law we are already using, and for which some examples that don't follow the rule are found. Rather than simply abandoning the truth or law, we modify it in some way; or
- o We come up with a theoretical framework in some way unrelated to any specifics and then find that it applies to some specifics. There are many mathematical ideas which were worked out in detail as 'pure mathematics' and only later was it found that they were applicable to real world phenomenon.

* In deriving reasonable rules and theories we must ensure:
  - o They are consistent with known facts and other rules we accept, they are capable of being proven false, and they are the best of the alternatives;
  - o We understand the range and scope of their applicability, and ensure that the 'evidence' supports the full range and scope we claim;
  - o We are able to investigate the causal relationships that underpin the rule or theory, though just because we may have not yet identified the cause does not mean we should reject it.

* Scientific experiment is aimed at determining the causes of events through isolating the crucial variables, and identifying which factors if present lead to the effect, but which if not present, lead to the effect not occurring.

* Science is based on a willingness to accept and even seek out examples that prove current beliefs are false, or at least limited in scope, and that they are always in potential need of modification. Science accepts that the rules we currently take as true are at best approximations that seem to work, and should be seen as tentative until something better comes along. Evidence of a rule's shortcomings are to be welcomed and enable us to modify the rule or to search for a better rule. Pseudo-science on the other hand expects us to simply accept as fact the rules it holds. It lacks the desire to seek out its own limitations as a means for its further development.

* Science is forever self-correcting and changing. If something is put forward as an absolute truth – it is not science.

* Never ignore practical evidence that contradicts established rules. Some people consider that questioning long established rules is being unscientific. This is not the case. The identification of contradictory evidence should be seen as an exciting possibility rather than something to be embarrassed about or suppressed. If it is truly contradictory then it will ultimately lead to new insights and more general and better rules.

* When we find exceptions to a rule, this might not be a case of the rule having to be abandoned, but rather that there are additional aspects to it, or scope statements that must be included within it. Of course it may be an indication that we need a completely new way of thinking.

* Just because evidence contradicts an established rule, or a given rule doesn't explain all circumstances, this doesn't mean the rule should not be used. It may still be the best to be had, or still be useful. We should however use the rule in full recognition of its limitations, and take account of them in the way we use the rule and in any conclusions we draw from its use.

* It is the predictive nature of scientific rules that make them useful to us; simply being able to explain past phenomenon would be of little value. Being able to explain past phenomena using laws and rules that then enable us to predict future phenomenon is key to our being able to interact effectively with the world.

* Whilst given rules are not themselves Common Sense, ensuring we understand basic scientific laws, rules and principles which are applicable to our normal lives is Common Sense.

Useful Scientific Laws, Rules, and Principles

* First Law of Thermodynamics, also known as Conservation of Energy: the total amount of energy in a system remains constant over time: it is said to be *conserved* over time. A consequence of this law is that energy can neither be created nor be destroyed: it can only be transformed from one state to another.

* The second Law of Thermodynamics: Energy flows from places of higher concentration to places of adjacent lower concentration. Thus, for example, over time, differences in temperature and pressure tend to even out in a system that is isolated from the outside world, and so heat flows from hotter locations to colder. Scientists describe this in terms of the entropy of an isolated system tending to increase over time.

* Newton's Laws of Motion are not absolutely 'true' on very small and very large scales, but they work for all our everyday observations. These three laws state:
  o The velocity of a body remains constant unless acted upon by an external force;
  o The acceleration of a body is parallel to and directly proportional to the net force and inversely proportional to the mass;
  o The mutual forces of action and reaction between two bodies are equal, opposite and collinear (to every action there is an equal and opposite reaction).

* The universal Law of Gravitation: Two objects exert a gravitational force of attraction between them that is proportional to the product of their masses and inversely proportional to the square of the distance between them.

* Archimedes Principle: Any object, wholly or partially immersed in a fluid, is buoyed up by a force equal to the weight of the fluid displaced by the object.

* Boyle's law: For a fixed amount of an ideal gas kept at a fixed temperature, Pressure and Volume are inversely proportional. In fact Boyle's law is one consequence of a more general gas law which states that the the product of pressure and volume is proportional to the temperature of a system.

* Bernoulli's principle: Under ideal conditions the speed of a fluid increases with a decrease in pressure.

* Ohm's law: The electrical current through a conductor between two points is directly proportional to the potential difference across the two points, and inversely proportional to the resistance between them.

* Hooke's law: Up to a limit the extension of a spring is in direct proportion to the load applied to it.

* Refractions: When light passes through a transparent material, its velocity slows, causing the light to bend. The angle of bending varies dependent upon wavelength.

* The Doppler affect is the change in pitch you notice when a siren approaches and then moves away from you. When something is moving towards you, the sound waves bunch up closer together leading to an increase in pitch. When something is moving away from you the sound waves are more spread out leading to a decrease in pitch. The Doppler effect also occurs with electromagnetic waves.

* The principle of natural selection is that members of a species with characteristics best matched to surviving in their environment will more likely do so, and pass on those traits to their offspring. Natural selection does not in itself account for the origin of the different traits within the members of a species, which is a result of minor statistical variations or mutations. Note however that natural selection does not necessarily give rise to some optimum solution, since it only selects from the alternatives available. And if populations are small there may also be an element of luck involved.

The Bumper Book of Common Sense

* The Superposition Principle is the concept that when a number of influences are acting on a system, the total influence is the sum of the individual influences. Note that this is only true in what are termed Linear Systems.

(Logical) Arguments

Valid and Reasonable Arguments

* An Argument is about using one set of statements (premises) to derive another set of statements (conclusions). The analysis of Arguments is about determining the extent to which the conclusion definitely or reasonably follows from the premises. The form of an Argument could be a long sequence of premises and conclusions, whereby conclusions from one part of the Argument act as premises for a later part of the Argument.

* The term 'validity' with regards to Arguments, applies in the context of Deductive Arguments. An Argument is said to be valid when if the premises are true then the conclusion must definitely be true. An Argument is said to be invalid, when the truth of the conclusion does not necessarily and always follow from the truth of the premises. Note that an invalid argument does not mean the conclusion is necessarily false, just that it is not proven by the argument used.

* A valid deductive argument can tell us nothing new about the world. It merely tells us that if our premises are true then the conclusion must be true. The truth of a valid argument is thus dependent upon the truth of the premises.

* 'Induction' is the term used when we take a number of specific examples or instances and derive what we consider to be a general rule arising from some pattern we see in the specific examples. Learning by experience is an inductive process. In contrast to deduction, which tells us nothing new about the world other than what is already inherent in our starting assumptions, induction tells us something new. Unfortunately we can never 'prove' that what we have derived is in any absolute sense 'true'.

* We apply induction to derive general truths or beliefs, and then apply our criteria of 'beyond reasonable doubt' to determine whether or not it is a reasonable truth to believe in, in terms of our practical lives. Once we have some 'premises', derived by induction, that we can believe in we can then use deduction to realize things we hadn't realized before, and make predictions about what is likely to occur in the future.

* There is a certain irony in that we cannot be certain about anything that tells us something new about the world, and we can only be certain about arguments that tell us nothing new.

* A reasonable argument is an inductive argument about the real world where we judge that the conclusion can reasonably be assumed to follow from the premises. An unreasonable argument is an inductive argument that is presented as though it were reasonable, but has some flaw in it.

* There are a number of general conditions that must be adhered to for arguments; failure to comply with which is often a root cause of invalid or unreasonable arguments. These are:
    o Terms used must be used consistently through the course of the argument;
    o The terms used in an argument should mean what the people to whom the argument is made think they mean;
    o The conditions under which a general statement is made must be the same conditions under which more specific statements are made, and vice versa;

- o The 'external conditions', ie. everything else not forming part of the statements themselves, must be unchanged, in so far as they might impact on the statements used in the argument.

These conditions appear fairly obvious, however in practice there are many ways in which they might not be followed, some obvious, some very subtle. The Latin term 'ceteris paribus' means 'all other things being equal', and this is an implicit assumption underpinning valid or reasonable arguments.

* If an argument is a sequenced chain of deductive arguments each of which is intended to be valid, then one weak link is a weakness in the argument as a whole. If however there are a number of circumstantial arguments all contributing in parallel to a conclusion, as is frequent with some types of inductive argument, then one weakness does not necessarily invalidate the whole argument, though it might.

* An argument that is not falsifiable, ie. one for which there is no real or theoretical way to check the claim, cannot be considered valid or reasonable. It is an unsubstantiated opinion or statement of faith.

* A common form of argument is that 'If A is not B then it must be C'. Such statements must be considered very carefully, and unless they are blatantly obvious are usually incorrect. Common causes of error include mistaking things that are merely different for things that are mutually exclusive, and believing that only two states exist when in fact there is a continuous series of variations, for which the two states may be the extremes.

* The argument "A is better than B, and B is better than C, therefore A is better than C." is only true where A, B, and C relate to some one simple one-dimensional concept. However where 'better' involves combining a number of different measures then this is not necessarily the case. This might occur when A, B, and C are made up of a number of different characteristics which combine in some way to give rise to a single 'better than' measure.

* An argument that is true for one specific may not be true for many specifics. For example if there is a shortage of something, then getting there early may ensure you get one. However if everyone 'gets there early' then you can no longer be sure you will get one.

* It is quite possible to write a clear and persuasive argument in support of faulty ideas and beliefs. Charismatic dictators are exceedingly good at this. The fallacies in their arguments, of which there will be many, are hidden by the emotions they instill relating to some particular idea that appeals to the self-interests of their audience.

* Necessary conditions are not the same as sufficient conditions. Just because something is necessary doesn't mean it is enough on its own.

The Form, Validity, and Use of Deductive Arguments

* Deductive arguments usually take the form of a general rule, followed by a specific statement leading to another specific statement. Examples of a valid deductive argument:

    If A then B, and x is A, then x is B. "If it always rains on Mondays and tomorrow is Monday; then it will rain tomorrow."

    A valid consequence of this argument is If x is not B, then x is not A (If tomorrow it is not raining then tomorrow is not Monday.)

* For a deductive argument to be valid it must be absolutely true, not just might be true. Examples of an invalid deductive argument:

The Bumper Book of Common Sense

> If A then B, and x is B, then x is A. "If it always rains on Mondays, and today it is raining, then today it must be Monday".
>
> Or
>
> If A then B, and x is not A, then x is not B. "If it always rains on Mondays and today is not Monday, then today it is not raining."

* Once a deductive argument is reduced to a simple form, it is usually easy to spot the fallacies. However it can be much more difficult in real life, particularly when such arguments are spoken.

* Determining whether or not an Argument is valid is nothing to do with whether or not the premises or the conclusion are true. "If Brian is a Unicorn, and Unicorns have a horn, then Brian has a horn" is a Valid argument, subject to certain conditions such as we are talking about the same Brian and the same horn in the earlier part of the argument as we are in the latter part of the argument. The argument is valid irrespective of whether or not Unicorns exists or of whether or not Brian really is a Unicorn.

* Just because an argument is invalid, such that the conclusion is not proven to be unquestionably a result of the assumptions/premises, this does not mean that the conclusion itself is false or untrue. It is merely unproven by the particular argument.

* Once arguments are reduced to their basic structural form, their validity is fairly easy to spot. However arguments are rarely in such a simple convenient form, and one of the skills in thinking clearly is to recognize the form that a given argument is taking and thus being able to spot whether or not it is valid.

* One way of reducing arguments to their basic form is to replace the nouns by labels such as A and B.

* Another form of analyzing arguments is to represent them in Venn Diagram form. For example:

    > If A then B, can be represented as a small circle, which represents A, as sitting entirely within a larger circle, which represents B.
    >
    > x is A is then represented as an x within A, which can then be clearly seen to be also within B. Thus the argument "If A then B, and x is A, then x is B" is valid.
    >
    > x is B is represented as an x which could be anywhere within B. Whilst this x could also be within A, it could also be both inside B but outside A. Thus the argument "If A then B, and x is B, then x is A" is invalid, since it is possible for x to be B whilst not A.

* Deductive arguments are not concerned with the truth of the premises.

* Just because a deductive argument is invalid does not mean the conclusion is false. A deductive argument is invalid when the conclusion does not follow necessarily from the premises, which is what is being claimed when the argument is made.

* Even long complex deductive arguments can be reduced to a fairly simple sequence of premises and conclusions where the conclusion from one part of the argument is used as a premise for another part of the argument. The argument is then valid if and only if every sequence used in reaching the conclusion is valid.

* Almost the whole of mathematics can be proved deductively from some fairly simply definitions that are taken as premises. Whilst we can apply mathematics to the real world this does not mean we can use mathematics to prove anything about the real world. There are an infinite number of different 'mathematical models' that might be applied to the real world, and we cannot prove that one of these is correct. We can only make comparisons between what we observe in the real world and what our models predict, and use those models that best correlate with what is observed in the

real world. Our understanding of what models are best however is continually changing in minor ways and occasionally changes in major ways.

* Having determined that a given mathematical model provides a good representation of the real world we can use that model to determine other things that might also be true and go and look to see if there is reasonable evidence for them.

Getting to the Bottom of Arguments

* Sometimes it is necessary to put an argument into a standard form before it can be assessed either for logical validity or for reasonableness. Thus we need to clearly identify the conclusion, the premises, and the structure of the argument that takes us from the premises to the conclusion. This is often complicated by the fact that there is often a string of premises and conclusions, many of the premises or assumptions are not explicitly stated, and there is also often a lot of irrelevant information or claims. Care must be taken in putting the argument into a more easily understood form, to ensure that this process does not itself change the meaning of the argument

* If P then Q can be shown to be false only by showing an instance of P and not Q. Yet people focus on looking for examples of P then Q which, proves nothing, rather than seeking out an example of P and not Q (and failing to find any given a genuine attempt to do so gives some confidence in P then Q). Whilst the falsifiability rule is very useful it is not natural for most people.

* We need to learn to pick out arguments from written or verbal communication, which means identifying premises and conclusions, and the reasoning that links them. Sometimes arguments use wording such as 'therefore', 'thus', 'so', 'hence', and 'it follows that' which makes it easy to identify the conclusions. However sometimes it is far less obvious.

* In practice many arguments fail to be clear in what they are trying to conclude, and fail to make progress because in fact the two parties are actually arguing about something different. Take a simple example of whether or not there should be capital punishment. If two people have opposing views the arguments generally oscillate between being arguments about whether or not it is morally wrong and whether or not it acts as a deterrent. If the argument remained purely about whether or not capital punishment was morally wrong, or about whether or not it acted as a deterrent, the argument would quickly come to a conclusion: either that both parties had different premises about morality, or that they did not have enough information about the deterrent effect of capital punishment. But because the argument keeps shifting between the two possible conclusions, it usually ends up going round in circles continually covering the same ground.

* Some tips for when preparing for and engaging in an argument or debate with someone with both sides looking to convince the other of their point of view.
  - Ensure you keep calm. If you become emotional you are less likely to be able to keep your argument together, will fall into traps set by your opponent, and impartial bystanders will assume you are losing the argument.
  - Facts are hard to refute so gather together any facts that will support your argument. Note however that people's eyes often glaze over with statistics so it might be useful to have them supported by some anecdotal examples.
  - Prepare for and ask lots of questions. 'What evidence do you have for that?' 'What if everyone did that?' 'What exactly is it that you are objecting to?' Seek to turn questions asked of you back into questions on your opponent.
  - When you can, appeal to moral motives. 'Shouldn't we all be trying to …?'
  - Listen carefully to the argument being put forward by your opponent. You may well find weaknesses and flaws.
  - Try to make use of analogies. They are readily understandable by others and if accepted can put others in a very positive frame of mind towards your argument.

The Bumper Book of Common Sense

- o If others use analogies look for differences between the analogy and the issue at hand which makes the analogy invalid. The analogy may however still stick in people's head and if you can you should seek to counter with an analogy of your own.
- o Keep focused on strong elements of your argument. If you also use weak elements of your argument you leave them open to attack and if parts of your argument are refuted your whole argument appears weak.
- o Be wary of the other party looking to distract the argument away from the issue in hand. If they do so, acknowledge the different topic, but make it clear that it is something to be discussed another time.
- o Speak slowly and retain a strong sense of confidence in your own argument.
- o Be prepared to use silence if you have presented a strong argument that your opponent is having difficulty countering. Let your opponent flounder.

* See other people's arguments in the strongest possible light, even if you are not sure it is what they really meant. If you can defeat strong counter arguments against your own arguments, then you can certainly defeat weaker ones. Besides you want your arguments to be the best they can be, and change them if they are not. You should thus welcome strong counter arguments as a way of strengthening your own arguments or as identifying a need to change them.

* When your opponent in an argument commits a fallacy rather than simply pointing this out by naming the fallacy, it is better to pose questions back which indirectly use your understanding of the fallacy to show up the weakness in the other's argument. Thus, for example: "Can I just clarify. What you are saying is … . Is that what you are suggesting?"

* Sometimes an opponent in an argument will seek to derail you through introducing irrelevancies or trying to shift what the argument is about. It is important to keep focused on the original argument at least until it is adequately addressed or you mutually agree to move on from it. If necessary you can agree to discuss other issues raised, but insist on only doing so after you've addressed the initial issue in so far as you are going to.

* When you have two opposing theses, instead of trying to determine one or the other as true, you should seek out a solution that resolves the contradictions though identifying modified arguments which embraces parts from both theses. This is known as dialectic reasoning. Of course it may be that one of the theses is in fact correct and the other wrong, this however should emerge through the reasoning. This is related to the idea that many things are not black or white but are a shade of grey, albeit they may be a dark shade or a light shade. In some ways the dialectic method contrasts with the analytic method, in that it is looking to bring ideas together to form a synthesized result whereas the analytic method is focused on breaking a whole down into its constituent parts.

* People are generally reluctant to abandon long held beliefs in the face of logical argument, and rarely do. To be successful in changing someone's mind you will need to first of all show why their original beliefs were in fact logical given the circumstances, and then show them how new evidence leads to a change in circumstances and thus to a different concluding belief.

* It is important to differentiate unproven hypotheses from disproved hypotheses. For an unproven hypothesis ask yourself what sort of evidence would you expect to see, or to not see.

Use of Language

Assumptions and Definitions

* We categorize and label the world around us using words for different types of entities. This is essential to enable us to learn so quickly and learn so much, since we can then learn how to react to classes of entity in particular ways rather than having to treat every entity we come across as unique. However the way we categorize and label is not a reflection of the how the world really is, but rather a reflection of how the culture we are a part of has learned to interact with the world. As such, different cultures have different ways of viewing and categorizing entities. Neither our way nor their way is right or wrong. They are simply different ways that have arising through different environmental pressures.

* We characterize entities according to whether or not they have certain characteristics or groups of characteristics. This reduces the complexity of our environment and enables us to use language to communicate with others. It enables us to learn and to improve how we interact with the world. However there are many different ways we can characterize according to characteristics and the ones we use are those that are useful to us in some way in our environment. Given different environments different ways of characterizing and thus grouping up entities have different utilities.

* The very act of labelling something exaggerates its differences from other things.

* We make assumptions all the time without thinking about them and without even being conscious that they are assumptions. And by and large we couldn't do very much without making assumptions all the time about most things. Making assumptions is not a bad thing, it is a necessary thing. However in certain circumstances certain assumptions become important and can be mistaken and we need to be explicit about them to determine whether or not they are reasonable in the circumstances.

* Assumptions are difficult to detect as they are implied rather than explicit; we are usually not consciously aware of them. They stem from our personal and cultural experiences, and are things we take as givens without any real evidence.

* Prejudices are general assumptions people hold about a group. These are assumptions about the characteristics of people in that group and assumptions about how people in that group behave. For example, most people make implicit assumptions about genders and particular jobs: assuming that a surgeon is a man, or that a receptionist is a woman.

* Assumptions make many people feel comfortable in that they don't have to think about alternatives. However effective thinking means we should regularly look to explore alternative viewpoints on any given subject, and thus should be looking to uncover our own and other people's assumptions.

* Trying to identify the assumptions that underlie the ideas, beliefs, values, and actions that we and others take for granted is central to critical thinking and the effective application of Common Sense.

* A good way of becoming aware of our assumptions is to discuss a matter with someone who has very different views to our own. It should quickly become clear that assumptions we take for granted are not in fact held by everyone.

* Much of our language is ambiguous, but for everyday usages it is usually precise enough for the purpose in hand. However in specific contexts, including our use of deductive or inductive arguments, we often need to be more precise. Many a misunderstanding or disagreement has at its heart different definitions or nuances in the terms used. Many disagreements can be resolved by clarifying the terms as used in the particular context of the argument.

* In simplistic terms, we define a term by identifying what it is like, and then identifying how it is different from the things it is like. The key characteristics of a good definition are that:

The Bumper Book of Common Sense

- o It should state the essential characteristics of the term being defined. This is best done by stating the group to which the thing belongs and then giving the peculiar marks or qualities that distinguish it from other members of the same group;

- o It must not be circular or a tautology, ie. it should not contain the word to be defined or a direct synonym or derivative of it;

- o It should not be too broad or too narrow. Care must be taken to ensure it encompasses all the things denoted by the term and excludes things not covered by the term. This latter aspect is often forgotten about;

- o It should not be expressed in obscure, ambiguous, or figurative language. A definition defeats its own end if it is more difficult to understand than the item it is supposed to define;

- o It should not be negative where it can be positive. A definition is supposed to explain what a term means, not what it doesn't mean.

Inappropriate Use of Words or Expressions

* The words people choose can be and often are used to conceal the truth, mislead, confuse and deceive.

* Words can be misused accidentally, or deliberately.

* Many disagreements have as their root cause the fact that different people are using a given word in different ways, or have different emotional attachments to a given word.

* A category mistake occurs when we think and treat something as though it were an example of some given category when it isn't. Thus, for example, by thinking of The Mind as an object we get into a lot of philosophical difficulties, which go away if we think of it as a set of capabilities and temperaments.

* Anthropomorphism is the error of projecting uniquely human qualities onto something that isn't human. Usually this occurs with projecting human qualities onto animals, and then, for example, using this to explain the animal's behavior.

* Words are symbols used to represent things and ideas. The connection between words and what they represent is no more and no less than what we choose it to be. The connection that we make may or may not be the same as the connection someone else makes. Whilst dictionaries give some level of consistency, without which words would be of little use to us, they are not precise and they do not include our personal experiences relating to given words.

* Words can change their meanings over time, and the way a word is used by older people may be different to the way it is used by younger people. The terms gay and wicked are examples.

* Dictionaries, at least in the English language, record current usage rather than try to dictate how given terms should be used. Thus dictionaries are living documents that require regular updating.

* Many words have different meanings, and their use in a particular situation can be ambiguous. If you are not sure of the meaning of a given word then you are in danger of being misled.

* Words can sometimes be used in so vague a manner as to make them meaningless or make them open to interpretations that can be deliberately exploited to mislead.

* A word can have different connotations for different people. These connotative meanings play an important role in arguments. Speakers and writers whose goal it is to persuade will exploit such connotations to elicit particular emotions.

* Some words can have an emotional association for some people, and that association will be different for different people as a result of their different experiences. For example the word 'collaboration' is largely neutral for many people, but for some people it can be very negative because of its association with wartime collaboration in occupied countries. People's names can have certain associations - we may have known people with a given name as being a bit thick, flirty, or untrustworthy, and when we come across someone else with that name unjustly make the same association. We may associate certain characteristics with certain products, such as reliability or unreliability, based upon our own personal experiences that may or may not be the same as other people's experiences.

* For many ideas there are a number of words we could choose which, whilst expressing the same underlying idea, also carry very different emotive connotations, which can be used to convince people of certain ideas, for good or bad. Thus for example a crowd might be described as a mob, or administration might be described as bureaucracy, or a person may be described as a terrorist by someone who disagrees with their actions and a freedom fighter by someone who agrees with their actions.

* The emotive use of words is far more common and effective in speech than it is when written down.

* There are many adverbs or adjectives which are similar in meaning but have either a positive or a negative spin on them. For example: someone's actions can be described as either bold or reckless, as cautious or cowardly; an idea as either innovative or hare-brained; someone could be thrifty or miserly, determined or obstinate, masterful or domineering, loyal or servile.

* A person may be mistaken in their use of a given word, confusing it with another word, or simply be mistaken about its meaning. This is particularly the case with obscure words that we use only occasionally.

* Some words are open in terms of their scope, with different people having different views as to whether certain extremes are within the scope of the use of the word or not.

* Some words have multiple meanings, and whilst one person may be using it with one meaning, another involved in the same argument or circumstance may be using it with another meaning. Some examples include: a specialist using a word in the narrow sense applicable to their specialization; different nations using a word differently, such as use of billion in the UK and the US; use of words which have both literal and metaphorical meanings. This can also occur with the word 'or' where "a or b" could either include or exclude the case of "a and b", and with the word 'if' which may or may not be used to mean 'if and only if'.

* Words used in translations from one language to another may not reflect the original intent. This generally occurs when words are translated individually rather than when they are translated in the context of the sentence in which they are used.

* A given word may exist in two different languages with subtly different meanings. A word like' democracy' means a very different thing to the West than it does to countries like China and other far Eastern countries. Both countries in the West and those in the East consider themselves to be democratic.

* Use of technical terms outside of the technical environment within which they have well defined usage is inappropriate. When it is done, it is often done to make the speaker or writer seem more authorative or knowledgeable than they genuinely are.

* A particular misuse of words is to define the scope of a word such that the argument is then true by definition. For example: 'Any true Englishman would do XYZ.' The way someone would use this expression would be such that they would judge whether or not someone was a true Englishman by whether or not they did XYZ.

The Bumper Book of Common Sense

* It is not practical or useful to state precisely what we mean by the terms we use every time we use them. We implicitly assume that the other person means the same thing as we do. Generally this implicit mutual understanding is close enough. But we must always be aware that if we find ourselves in disagreement, it is the word meanings that may be the root cause, rather than any fundamental difference of opinion. If you suspect this may be the case, explore with the other person precisely what they mean by given terms.

* Ultimately we may need to explicitly define a given term for the purpose of the argument or discussion in hand. Words should thus be viewed as useful or confusing, convenient or misleading, rather than right or wrong, real or mistaken.

* We need to be consistent in our use of words within a given argument or circumstance. An example of subtle changes in the use of words is where in an early part of an argument the speaker uses a phrase that would be true if the word 'some' appeared in front of it, and later in the argument using it as though the word 'all' appeared in front of it. For example: money being spent on X is being wasted therefore we should stop spending money on X. In this argument there will often have been a subtle change in the use of the word 'money', with the early part of the argument referring to some money, and the later part referring to all money.

* Examples of subtle changes in the use of words abound in politics and is often used to drive one's opponents into making more extreme statements than intended.

Use of Generalizations, Simplifications, Analogies, and Metaphors

* Simplifications and generalizations are often useful. The fact that there are specific cases where the simplification or generalization does not work does not invalid the use of the simplification or generalization for many purposes. We must however always be aware of the scope or limits of the simplification or generalization and not use it beyond or outside of them.

* The laws of nature, science, and engineering are invariably generalizations and simplifications. As are the rules of thumb we use consciously and sub-consciously in our daily lives. We must be wary of not mistaking these generalizations or rules of thumb for the reality of how things are.

* With respect to generalizations we must recognize the circumstances under which the generalization is valid. Whilst something may be true in general, it may not be true in particular circumstance or with regards a particular instance.

* Finding a specific exception to a generalization does not in itself undermine the generalization. A generalization is just that, not an absolute. Of course a lot of specific exceptions could undermine the generalization.

* Some people make generalizations based on a single instance. Eg. 'Jim smoked all his life and lived to be 85': therefore the inappropriate generalization that smoking is not really bad for you. 'Ray never got any qualifications and look how well he did': therefore the generalization that it doesn't really matter whether or not you try to get good qualifications. Single instances of this type are not a reasonable basis for generalization. They do however counter absolute statements such as 'smoking will lead to an early death', or 'you need qualifications in order to succeed'.

* Our ability to generalize from past experience is an important skill and saves us huge amounts of time and energy with regards learning about the world. We don't need to go around questioning everything because we can assume most of what we see is similar to what we've seen and had experience of in the past. However this can also be misleading because we can end up generalizing in circumstances when we shouldn't. For example when we stereotype certain nationalities or groups of people based upon one encounter with someone from that nationality or group.

* One of the ways we make sense of the world is through categorizing people, objects, and events. In so doing we take some particular characteristic, and group together the entities which have that

characteristic. This is a natural and useful process. However in so doing we often implicitly assume that those entities then share other characteristics. Sometimes this is useful, however at other times it can be harmful and ill-judged.

* Whilst generalizations are very useful and a necessary part of daily life, don't treat them as perfect. In particular be wary of the strong tendency to want our generalizations to be valid, because it makes our life easier, and thus tending to see things through a filter which notices when things are consistent with the generalization and turns a blind eye to things that are not.

* Simple statements are often used which, whilst they have a ring of truth to them, are in fact over simplifications. Such statements are often used in arguments and used to draw conclusions which are invalid because they rely upon the simplification being always true which it may not be in particular circumstances.

* An analogy is where we compare two things and find one or more similarities then assume further similarities. We draw analogies between people, places, things and situations. A metaphor is an analogy that is used implicitly without drawing attention to itself, such as when we say someone is as gentle as a lamb. Some metaphors have been used for a long time and many people do not even realize when they are using them.

* We are both enlightened and restricted by analogies and metaphors. If we see ourselves as ships on the water we can think in terms of being able to make adjustments and improvements to ourselves as we progress through life but will limit our thoughts about being able to completely rebuild ourselves. Analogies and metaphors provide new insights about the world but we mustn't confuse them with reality.

* Use of analogies provides us with a very powerful problem-solving tool. When making an analogy we are noting a similarity or relationship between two things or situations, and then assuming that some other similarity or relationship may also exist. The solution to one problem may therefore suggest a solution to another 'analogous' problem.

* Analogies are useful in suggesting that there might be some commonality between entities or circumstances that can then be investigated by some other means.

* Inappropriate analogies can mislead and lead us to an incorrect or inappropriate solution or conclusion.

* There is often a tendency to compare a complex problem with a simple problem, and then arguing that the solution to the simple problem will also apply to the complex problem. This often has an appeal that can be difficult to combat, and sometimes it might even be appropriate. All too often however this is an oversimplification that will lead us to taking actions that give the illusion of progress but that don't actually solve the complex problem.

* We cannot prove anything by analogy. Just because something has one thing in common with another does not mean it must therefore have other things in common. Where someone uses an analogy as though it were a proof they are in practice merely using it to help defend some position that they already hold. It is a form of rationalization whereby we consider analogies to be correct when we agree with their outcome, and incorrect when we disagree.

* Analogies and metaphors allow us to use what we already know so we can conceptualize things we don't know. They are a valuable aid to learning and to thinking in general.

* There are some common analogies that many people take as though they are actual representations of reality. For example, likening an atom to a planetary system has been a useful analogy. But for many people this is exactly how they think atoms are. Similarly likening gas to a cloud of little balls is one that lingers in the minds of many people.

The Bumper Book of Common Sense

* Much of UK law is about analogies, where lawyers try to demonstrate that current circumstances are analogous to some previous circumstances and thus the same judgment should be arrived at; whilst other lawyers try to show that the circumstances are not analogous.

* To attack or weaken an analogy you need to see and focus on differences. To argue against given analogies and metaphors you must find examples that follow the same logic but which are clearly incorrect or inappropriate.

* In general terms, whether or not someone believes that a given analogy or metaphor is appropriate will usually depend upon whether or not they accept the consequences of its use. If they believe the consequences they will consider the analogy or metaphor a good one; if they don't, they won't.

* People who believe analogies to be real will sometimes reach conclusions that are false. In practice for people in their everyday lives this is not usually a problem, though it may mislead them into believing that life is simpler than it really is, and thus surprised when things don't unfold as they had expected.

* Believing in the reality of analogies can prohibit and limit our ways of thinking, since we tend to limit our thoughts to areas of commonality and find it difficult to think about or even notice areas where the analogy or metaphor does not work.

* Metaphors and analogies are commonly used in literature and can help evoke emotional responses. This is a legitimate use. For this very reason however they should not be used in purposeful arguments and discussions, except where being used to help illustrate something. They should never be used as an attempt to prove something or to draw any conclusions.

* A euphemism is where some less offensive word or expression is used in order to weaken the impact of something that might otherwise have aroused much stronger feelings or disapproval. Thus we talk about someone having 'passed on' rather than 'died', or about 'collateral damage' when people are hurt or killed unintentionally. Whilst euphemisms can be used positively to avoid hurting someone, they are often used deliberately to deceive and excuse what would otherwise be questionable behavior.

Fuzziness

* Many words have a fuzziness associated with them. For example when is a table not a table: take bits of it away and keep asking yourself if it's a table.

* Logic generally relies on the concept that things are either A or are not-A; for example something is red or it is not red. This leads to a very black and white view of the world. A type of logic, fuzzy logic, recognizes that many things are in fact grey, and on a scale with no clear dividing line as to when we might consider it falling into a simple A/not-A category. When precisely does red become orange?

* Fuzzy logic, expresses the greyness between things being Black or White, A or not-A, by saying that things are at the same time partially A and partially not-A. Thus a given shade of Grey is partially Black and partially not-Black, ie. White. It may be more Black than not-Black, or it may be more not-Black than Black. In the extremes it is Black or it is not-Black.

* Fuzzy logic reflects the way we often think in the real world. When we use words we use an interpretation of words that ultimately might be very personal and unique to ourselves. There are many words that are shaded by our personal experiences that leads us to mean subtly different things by them.

* The fuzzy logic way of thinking provides us with a realization that different persons may mean subtly different things with regards given words. Whilst for many arguments our conclusion may

not be sensitive to the subtle differences, in some arguments it may. Where we suspect this is the case we need to be explicit about precisely what each person means by given words, and often we will find our disagreements come down to the differences in meaning. We will often then find that both sides of the argument are correct or understandable given the particular meanings they are putting on the words.

* Fuzzy logic helps us overcome some of the seeming contradictions that occur when we use a more conventional way of thinking. For example, when does red become orange? With fuzzy logic this is not a problem to be solved. We simply have different degrees of red and not-red. The color can move in the direction from red towards not-red without there needing to be a particular point at which it becomes fully not-red except at the extreme point we may call orange; just as we can move along a line between two points. Similarly, when is a man bald? We have an extreme of bold which is having no hair at all, but various degrees of not-bald which move towards an extreme of having what we would consider a full head of hair, ie. fully not-bald.

* Just because words are fuzzy, this does not in any way make them any less useful. Just because there are no sharp delineations between different colors does not mean we cannot usefully use terms such as red, purple, orange, etc. What it means is that there are certain circumstances where we cannot be specific. If these circumstances are important to us then we must decide what to do about them in those particular circumstances.

* With an appreciation of fuzzy logic we can consider that we believe in things to a greater or lesser extent, rather than simply believe or not believe. As time goes by the extent to which we hold particular views can change, and there may come a point where we consider ourselves to be more a non-believer than a believer.

* Taking a simple black and white view is often a simplification that is useful in helping us get things done. What we gain in simplification however we lose in accuracy, and we may find the 'greyness' we have ignored becomes a dominating factor affecting what we are trying to do.

* In order to be able to communicate with each other we need some core common views on what particular words mean. The recognition of fuzzy logic does not take this need away since we need to be able to label the extremes simply so we can refer to the fact that we are somewhere between them. We can, should, and will, continue to use words much as we do already. And we can continue to argue about the meaning of words. However rather than arguing about what a word really means in some absolute sense, we are arguing about what we should best choose the word to mean to be useful in our particular circumstances.

* There are many directions in which something might move towards being 'not-red'. Thus the color red might move in the direction of becoming orange or in the direction of becoming pink. Whilst we can talk generally about 'not-red', if we are using it in particular circumstance we must be clear about its particular use.

Clear Thinking

Principles of Clear Thinking

* A summary of guidelines for clear thinking:
    o Get to the root of the question you are trying to answer, and the specific purpose of your thinking;
    o Suspend judgment;

- Stick to the point;
- Seek structure, though be aware of the constraints a given structure may impose;
- Separate what is relevant from what is not;
- Be clear about premises and assumptions;
- Consider the reasonableness of premises and assumptions;
- Seek out any missing information that may be important;
- Seek out options and possibilities;
- Seek out alternative viewpoints;
- Summarize complex ideas;
- Consider facts dispassionately;
- Judge on merits;
- Keep calm and cool;
- Listen patiently and tolerantly to other people's opinions;
- Avoid getting defensive;
- Be willing to reconsider in the light of new evidence or argument;
- Be persistent in trying to get to the bottom of the issue or issues;
- Explain the rationale behind decisions or conclusions reached.

* Be sure that your thinking has a purpose. Many of the thoughts we have are more of the nature of idle dreaming rather than being purposeful. Thus if you're thinking about something in order to come to some form of conclusion, ensure that you are asking yourself specific questions, and not vague, indeterminate ones.

* Keep focused on the matter in hand. Failure to think clearly about an issue is very often a result of irrelevancies becoming part of the consideration, for example when one or more person involved: throws in pet topics; or seeks to take advantage of who is there to discuss something else that is important to them; or focuses on some secondary issue without the primary issue having been properly considered; or focuses on the people themselves rather than the matter under consideration. It is important, when irrelevancies begin to surface, to quickly bring the subject back to the matter in hand. This need to keep focused applies as much when we are thinking to ourselves as when we are interacting with others.

* An important aspect of clear thinking is distinguishing relevant from irrelevant facts. There are often many pieces of information around, some of which might be very interesting or provoke an emotional response. However it may not all be relevant to the particular issue under consideration. Being able to differentiate what is and isn't relevant will help us go a long way towards thinking clearly about an issue.

* Seek clarity in your thinking and in your understanding of concepts and terms. Lack of clarity leads to miscommunication and to misconceptions. Thus look out for ambiguities, vagueness, and ideas or terms you don't understand. Seek clarification of others and of yourself. Look to present ideas as clearly as you can, possibly using illustrations and specific examples.

* Be honest about what you do and don't understand, at least to yourself, and be wary of allowing yourself to be impressed with and accept on faith something you don't understand. Fear of being seen to be ignorant leaves us exposed to accepting invalid arguments. Thus, if you don't understand something that is important to you, make the effort to do so.

* Look for hard data wherever possible, rather than assumptions or opinions. Ensure the data is itself reliable, preferably coming from multiple but unrelated sources.

* Be clear about what you know and what is conjecture based upon what you know. If there is an increase in reports about something, it doesn't mean that the something is on the increase; only that there are more reports, which may, for example, have come about through changes in the way it is reported.

* Being able to ask useful questions is an important part of clear thinking. In asking useful questions you need to be clear about what you are trying to find out and avoid ambiguity or vagueness.

* Sometimes there is simply not enough data to allow any particular conclusions to be drawn. Don't pretend that there is, if there isn't. If you are accepting a matter on faith then be honest about it. An example is the existence of aliens: there is not being enough data to prove or disprove the existence of aliens, and those that categorically believe or disbelieve in aliens do so for reasons other than through rationale argument or proof.

* Sometimes there is too much data and information and it is difficult to determine what is and isn't relevant. In order to sort through information we need to identify ways of categorizing or grouping it. There is no one correct way of categorizing information but there are ways that are more useful than others. We need to categorize it and group it up in a way that is relevant to the particular issue at hand. Be aware however that in categorizing you are also constraining the way you think; you can't help this, it is the price you pay for being able to make sense of the information: nevertheless be willing to adopt or consider other categorizations if they are also useful.

* How much detail you need about something, or how accurately you need to know something, should be determined by the matter under consideration. It is counterproductive trying to obtain details or accuracies that are beyond what you need to come to a conclusion about the matter in hand. You should not go seeking further detail or accuracy just because you can.

* If the information used in arriving at a conclusion changes, then you may need to re-examine the conclusion.

* An important aspect of clear thinking is recognizing assumptions, whether stated or un-stated. Once the assumptions are clearly recognized we can then decide whether or not we accept them. Many arguments are dependent upon assumptions that we don't even recognize, but if we did, would not accept.

* When making comparisons ensure you are comparing apples with apples. If is not uncommon for comparisons to be made inappropriately, for example by using only one particular characteristic for the purpose of comparison when in fact multiple characteristics should be taken into account.

* Ensure you understand the meaning of terms used as part of any thinking you are doing, and if others are involved ensure you have the same meaning as they do with regards any terms that are important or are differentiators in terms of alternative viewpoints.

* It is important to understand what terms mean in the particular context in which they are being used. Terms have many subtleties and potential associations that can differ dependent upon context.

* An essential element of effective thinking is not simply being able to think clearly about what is in front of you, but to think clearly about what might have been omitted, or what isn't there and maybe should have been.

* No manner or amount of logic will make up for ignorance. Clear thinking requires good knowledge to ensure that the premises on which arguments are being built are reasonable and appropriate to the matter in hand. Good logic cannot compensate for poor or inappropriate premises.

* Have a healthy level of skepticism. Knowledge is difficult to obtain and we should be skeptical of people telling us of some easy knowledge that we should simply accept. Generally we should consider new ideas and knowledge as being false or at least unproven until we have either seen good evidence or we understand and agree with the logic behind it. This is particularly true of

The Bumper Book of Common Sense

miraculous claims that do not match our own experiences of the world. Note however that being skeptical does not mean we have to be cynical.

* If you never change your mind, you are not thinking clearly. We do not know everything, and thus we will come across things we didn't know before. If we are open minded then new information should at least refine and occasionally completely overturn our previously held opinions and beliefs.

* Clear thinking requires both humility and confidence. You must always be prepared to humbly admit when you are wrong, and sometimes you will be. On the other hand you must be confident in your ability to think things through for yourself and stand by those beliefs you have arrived at through logic albeit always being willing to listen to arguments to the contrary and accept them if they are stronger than your own arguments.

* Express things as simply as you can. If you have difficulty understanding something then it is more likely than not because it is poorly expressed or described.

* It is a general truth that anything should be expressed as simply as possible. The more complex something is the more effort that is required to understand it and the more likely it will be that there will be misunderstandings and misinterpretations. If you have produced something always spend a little time looking to see if you can simplify it. Discard or disregard anything that is unnecessary or irrelevant.

* Simplification should not lead to the loss of what is being expressed. It is easy to simplify if one is willing to lose part of what is expressed. If that part was important then the simplification is counter-productive.

* The simpler something is the more likely it is people will believe it and act on the basis of it.

* In hypothesis testing we are looking to be able to accept something that is true and reject something that is false. However we could reject something that is true, which is known as making a Type I error, or accept something that is false, a Type II error. These errors are inherent in any hypothesis testing. How tolerant we are to one or other of these errors should be dictated by circumstances.

* Our clear thinking can be significantly affected by our mental and physical state. We should avoid making important decisions when tired or stressed or emotionally aroused or under the influence of drugs.

Cause and Effect

* A good understanding of cause and effect relationships is important because it underlies the rules we use to help us understand what has happened in the past, what is happening in the present, and what is likely to happen in the future, or what might happen, if we do or don't do certain things. Many problems are largely about identifying the cause of a given effect.

* Just because B has occurred shortly after A does not mean that A has caused B. It could be just a co-incidence that B has occurred after A. Or it could be that there is something else that has caused both A and B without there being any direct causal link between A and B themselves.

* Generally before we have high confidence in a cause and effect relationship we should seek to have some understanding of the underlying phenomenon giving rise to the relationship. However, just because we don't have an explanation that doesn't mean the relationship doesn't exist.

* For A to be the cause of B, then the occurrence of B should always indicate that A has occurred, and the absence of B should mean that A did not occur. Failure to take this into account is a

common cause of poor thinking. Adverts on TV frequently fall foul of this. Some super fit person is shown eating some particular breakfast cereal. However it is almost certainly the case that the person is super fit irrespective of whether or not they eat that particular cereal, and there will be many cases of people who eat the cereal who are not super fit. It is blatantly not true that the breakfast cereal has led to the super fitness.

* Many arguments that claim a later event is a consequence of an earlier event show only that the earlier event was a contributory cause of the later event. However they often fall short of showing that the earlier event was both a necessary and sufficient cause of the later event.

* It is very common that there are many potential contributory 'causes' to a given effect. For example, if a house collapses in a storm, is the cause the storm, poor design of the house, some particular weakness of a given material? In circumstances such as these we should look for what was out of the ordinary. Was the storm more severe than the house could reasonably be expected to have been designed for - what happened to other similar houses round about; was there a flaw in the design we would not have expected to have been there - and was not present in other 'similar' designs; was there some material used which was outside of the usual specifications for such a material?

* When looking for an explanation for something, the cause of an effect, ask 'why' did the effect happen. And if you identify a cause, then ask why again; is it itself an effect of some other cause. You should continue to ask yourself why and seek out root causes that are often missed by simply accepting some superficial explanation. Of course you need to stop somewhere, but it will usually become obvious when you have got to a root cause about which you can take effective action.

* Any given happenance is dependent upon an infinite number of specific happenances in the past. If past happenances had been different, today's happenances would be different. This does not mean the past happenances caused today's happenance. True we could pick any one of a vast multitude of past happenances and say if it were different today's happenance would be different. But why pick out any one in particular. There are a multitude of others we could say the same of, and a multitude of even earlier happenances upon which any given one we chose itself depends. If we keep asking why something happened there is usually a whole chain of 'causes', ultimately reaching right back to the beginning of the universe.

* When looking for cause and effect relationships recognize that there may be other changes also having an effect. For example there may be changes that would naturally happen irrespective of whether or not the given 'cause' occurred. It can often be difficult to differentiate between such naturally occurring changes and changes that may have been brought about by the 'cause'.

* A common fallacy in thinking is identifying a possible cause and effect relationship and then assuming that this is the only one possible.

* In considering hypotheses to explain an event or circumstances, think about absence of evidence, not just the evidence itself. If the hypothesis were true, what should you be seeing that you might not be?

* The mistaking of correlated events for causal relationships is a frequent one, both in everyday life and in the scientific community. There have been numerous cases of causal effects being declared based on evidence of correlation only for it later to be found that there was some other cause that gave rise to both or that the correlations were just normal statistical variations with researchers simply having picked on some of the more extreme sampling results.

* Once we have identified a plausible cause and effect relationship based on particular evidence, we tend to continue to believe in the relationship even if the evidence that led us to it in the first place is found to have been faulty.

* The link between cause and effect is often of a probabilistic nature. Smoking causes lung cancer, but not everyone who smokes will get lung cancer. It is arguably better in many circumstances to talk in terms of influencing factors.

The Bumper Book of Common Sense

* When there are lots of people doing something for which there is a significant element of randomness, then things will go well for some and bad for others as a result of chance. Those for whom luck is on their side will usually believe that they have succeeded because of their own skill.

* The gambler who has a string of good luck will believe he is more skillful than others, or he is fated in some way. When his luck changes he will continue to believe in his own skill, but find excuses for his then losses.

* With regards people who play the stock market and traders for large financial organizations. In a given year luck plays a significant part of their success, and those that are successful get huge bonuses. And of course in the years they make losses they do not have to repay the huge bonuses they received in earlier years.

* We have a tendency for believing that causes and effects resemble each other. Thus we expect big noises to be caused by big things, and a major event to have a major cause. However it is not uncommon for a little thing or what in normal circumstances would be a minor incident to have a major impact – such as in Chaos or Catastrophe Theory. People generally however tend to dismiss this and seek what to them are more 'obvious' explanations.

* Superstitions are often a false belief in cause and effect relationships. Thus people believe in lucky charms because they remember incidents where they were lucky in the presence of the lucky charm, but forget incidents when they were not lucky despite being in the presence of the lucky charm.

* Reverse causation is where what appears to be X causing Y is in fact Y causing X. Thus is an author famous because he sells a lot of books or does he sell lots of books because he is famous. It can be difficult to distinguish. Are we good at the things we like or like the things we are good at? Is violent crime the result of high levels of gun ownership, or are the high levels of gun ownership due to the high levels of crime, as people seek to protect themselves? Which came first, the chicken or the egg? There is, in such instances, often a reinforcing loop relationship between X and Y so they are both the cause and the effect of each other. In some sense either X or Y may have been the initiating cause of the other, but once there is a reinforcing loop relationship it no longer makes sense to insist on one being the cause and the other the effect.

Barriers to Clear Thinking

* Some common clear thinking errors:
    o Over simplifying, including black and white thinking;
    o Over generalizing on the basis of small samples;
    o Comparing apples with oranges;
    o Ignoring relevant evidence;
    o Attributing effects to a single cause when there are multiple contributory factors;
    o Confusing cause and effect;
    o Hindsight bias;
    o A tendency to put other people's behavior down to their personality but our own behavior down to circumstances;
    o Having negative expectations, or being overly optimistic;
    o Rationalization;
    o Failing to think through consequences.

* The basic principles of Clear Thinking are often not applied, partially as a result of ignorance of what they are, but more so for psychological reasons. Thinking is hard and threatens our ego.

* We are limited by the predisposition of our own thoughts.

* It is easy to fall into a drone mentality, where we go through life without thinking, and without paying too much attention to what is going on.

* Arrogance and intolerance severely limit many people's ability to think clearly.

* We are conditioned by our social background and upbringing. Most people fail to recognize or appreciate this and their thinking is seriously constrained and biased as a result. However if we acknowledge and apply the basic principles of Clear Thinking and Common Sense, we can overcome our social conditioning. In particular we should readily recognize that there is nothing inherently superior in our own culture, and that all cultures are simply different, though some may be more successful than others, and some may be more open and attuned to accepting the principles of Clear Thinking.

* We are conditioned by our particular experiences. Just as with our social conditioning, we need to acknowledge that our personal experiences are not necessarily typical, and we must keep true to the principles of Clear Thinking and Common Sense.

* Egocentric thinking is viewing everything in relation to oneself. It impedes critical thinking because egocentric people are closed minded to the thoughts and ideas of others. Many egocentric people are not aware that they are significantly more self-centered than others. You should always be on the lookout for ideas from others, and you will find your own ideas are often significantly improved through modifications as a result of ideas coming from others.

* Making good decisions sometimes takes time. If we are pressured into making important decisions quickly then we are at significant risk of making mistakes and making poor decisions that then cause significant problems later. It is a common saying in large organizations that there is never enough time to do it right first time, but always enough time to do it again.

* Rationalization in terms of Common Sense thinking relates to someone finding justifications for what they already believe, rather than seeking out an objective explanation. It is a very common barrier to clear thinking, problem solving, and the application of Common Sense in general.

* People do not like being seen to be wrong. As a result they go out of their way to justify their existing beliefs, and this seriously clouds their judgment and prevents clear thinking.

* Much of what people think of as reasoning is looking for arguments that justify what they already believe.

* People often evaluate the validity of an argument based on whether or not the conclusion is true or at least what they believe or would like to be true, rather than on whether or not the argument itself stands up in terms of premises and argument structure leading to the conclusion. It is easier for them to make a judgement about the conclusion than it is to follow and assess the validity of the argument.

* People often use justifications that cannot be proven to explain away facts that refute what they want to be true. For example, clairvoyants will find all sorts of reasons why a given prediction didn't turn out as they said; assuming of course they have predicted something specific, rather than something so vague it could fit almost any potential future.

* People are most likely to listen to and accept logical arguments when the subject matter is seemingly complex and they have not firmly made up their minds. Once they have made up their minds their focus then shifts to defending their viewpoint through rationalization.

Inappropriate Ways of Thinking

* Seeing a fault as something to be fixed rather than a problem to be overcome limits us. If you think of a fault as a problem to be overcome you may find you don't need to fix the fault at all, but can find a more effective way of overcoming the problem. Thought of in this way faults sometimes become opportunities in that you find better ways of doing things than you might otherwise have done.

* People often simply stick to approaches that they are familiar with rather than think about what might be best in the particular circumstances.

* People all too often develop a theory based on just a few facts and then proceed to rationalize further facts against the presumption that the theory is correct.

* Why waste time listening to alternative viewpoints when the first argument sounds so convincing? Why look for further alternatives when the first solution we come across seemingly solves the problem?

* Incorrect ways of thinking are often acquired because of an engaging narrative which has some complexity to it, which can appeal to those of moderate or even high intelligence. Example include conspiracy theories, tax evasion schemes, get rich quick schemes, ways of beating the stock market, ways of winning the lottery. The fact that they have some complexity to them is an important part of their appeal to intelligent people, with the implication that those less intelligent wouldn't understand them and thus not be able to take advantage of them.

* We often believe and assume that deep down other people think the way we do. We are often mistaken.

* Being able to explain the origin of a type of behavior does not justify it. Just because someone had a hard up bringing does not justify their becoming a murderer or a thief. There are many people who have had a hard up bringing who have not become a murderer or a thief.

* What is perceived to be 'normal' in our society or culture is usually specific to our society or culture, and in no sense is it some objective measure of normality. Many of the people that are seen as deviants are simply people who don't conform to our society or cultural norms. Whether or not society in general, or we as individuals, should try to prohibit or punish behavior that is away from the norm should be dependent upon the damage it could physically do. Insisting everyone behaves in some absolute 'normal' manner is not healthy for a society and is a characteristic of authoritarian and totalitarian societies that irrespective of their initial well-meaning invariably become oppressive. On the other hand 'anything goes' can also be damaging. Generally we should err on the side of tolerance and freedom of thought and action where it doesn't harm others in a physical sense or in a severe psychological sense.

* Future success is often inhibited by our making procedures to formalize what generated a previous success. Circumstances are continually changing and what is necessary for future success is likely to be different to what was necessary for past successes. By all means understand and document what went well and what went badly in the past, but the more you proceduralize it the less flexible it will be. Success often breeds failure.

* Don't believe everything you read. Be particularly wary of information gleaned from the internet. It is not all factually correct. Even if information appears in many different places on the internet, it is possible it is merely the same information from a faulty source which has simply been repeatedly copied.

* We all have vivid imaginations, and we tend to get lost in our fantasies. Life is a series of ordinary events that follow the laws of logic and probability. Ordinary events are indifferent to our fantasies.

* Just because something can't be proven to be false this does not mean it is reasonable to believe it is true. However many people justify their belief in absurd ideas on the fact that they cannot be

proven to be false. You can't prove that there are no pixies but this doesn't mean it is reasonable to believe there are.

* Many people use particular personal experiences, or recalled stories, as short cuts to thinking. The very fact of being able to bring to mind a particular memory leads people to overestimate the likelihood of it or similar other events occurring. People often justify their decisions through use of particular examples even though they may be highly unrepresentative.

* Our gut reactions can be useful, however they can also mislead. A gut reaction can be our subconscious weighing factors up in a way our conscious mind is unable to do so. However our gut reactions can also be our prejudices overriding our rationale judgments.

* Some characteristics of arguments where there is a lack of application of clear thinking principles:
    o A lack of any structure to addressing the issue, with a scatter gun approach to addressing the different aspects of the issue;
    o Over simplifications;
    o Questionable premises being used without justification;
    o Unsaid assumptions which are critical;
    o Use of specific rare examples with the implication they are commonplace;
    o Inclusion of information or considerations which are irrelevant.

Improving Your Clear Thinking Skills

* Most people think they have good thinking skills. They don't. But whether your thinking skills are good or bad you should be forever trying to improve them.

* Becoming an effective thinker requires the continual questioning of your own thinking and ideas as well as questioning the thinking and ideas of others. This will separate you from the crowd.

* Write down your thoughts and arguments. What might seem to make sense in your mind may not do so once written down.

* Errors of judgment are often systematic rather than random. They are more often the result of biases which can be avoided than they are resulting from any inability to take account of the factors in front of you. If you learn about common fallacies and biases, and watch out for them in your own thinking, you will be apply to apply good judgment - as best you can given the circumstances and information available to you – most of the time.

* When faced with an argument leading to a conclusion, in order for you to understand the argument it is important you are able to think it through based on the information given rather than based on what you thought before you were given the information, ie. be able to separate structure from content.

* Seek out conflicting and alternative views. Talk to people about your ideas and encourage them to pick out weaknesses. Try to get someone to act as a devil's advocate, or try to do so yourself. If you disagree with a view be sure you can clearly articulate why. Hidden away in conflicting or alternative views are usually ideas that can improve your own ideas and views, either to modify them or to enable you to articulate more clearly their strengths.

* Look to understand principles that arise from cultures different to your own. We are at best only vaguely aware of how strongly we are conditioned by our culture. By looking to understand other cultures, and accepting that they are as valid as our own, we learn to be more open-minded.

The Bumper Book of Common Sense

* Improve your vocabulary. Good thinking requires a rich language with plenty of subtlety. The more extensive your vocabulary the greater the potential for your thoughts.

* Inconsistency is a sign that something doesn't line up. It is usually a sign that some of your current assumptions about how things are need refining; and it may be appropriate to do this, or it may be easier just to live with the inconsistency. It's up to you in the circumstances. But be wary of simply dismissing inconsistency by pretending it doesn't exist. Thus if someone you thought of in simplistic black and white terms (he's a bad person) does something that is 'out of character' (something kind), it is more likely to be a sign that your assessment of them is too simplistic (like everyone else, they have good and bad points) rather than some hidden motive that really fits in with your existing assessment (their kindness was really an act of deviousness).

* Life is rarely clear-cut or black and white. Don't expect it to be.

* If you want to be right as much as possible, then you have to stop caring about being right in any particular circumstance. It is only by accepting that you might be wrong, and thus listening objectively to arguments for and against, that you will be more likely to be right in the future.

* Avoid making judgments whilst listening or gathering information or receiving sensory inputs. There is a time for understanding facts and a time for analyzing the facts to draw conclusions. Don't mix the two. The longer you can delay judgment the more informed your conclusions will be.

* In the face of finding yourself rationalizing about something, ways to keep yourself objective include: not getting personally attached to your beliefs and rather than seeing them as your beliefs see them as just beliefs which could be gone in the future; don't see disagreements as win or lose, see them as an opportunity to develop a new idea drawing upon both sides of the argument; recognize that admitting you are wrong from time to time strengthens your case when you stand by your beliefs since people can't accuse you of always being obstinate; feel good about changing your mind since it makes your beliefs stronger, since presumably your new belief is based upon stronger arguments than your old beliefs.

* Remember there are multiple viewpoints with respect to most situations. Don't assume yours is somehow correct. Different people will often have different viewpoints, and other people's viewpoints will often be just as valid as yours.

* When someone has a different viewpoint to yourself, try to understand why. If you understand the rationale for them having the opinions they have, you will gain an understanding that may help you to improve your own viewpoint.

* Personal experience rarely becomes wisdom unless also enlightened by the wisdom of others.

* Approaching issues with clear thinking is no guarantee you will find satisfactory solutions, but it significantly increases the chances of coming up with the best solutions that are available in the circumstances.

Fallacies

About Fallacies

* Although we may not be conscious of it, most of our purposeful thinking involves the use of logical arguments. A fallacy is an argument that is intended or claimed to be correct but which contains an error. Note that the fallacy relates to whether or not the argument itself is valid or

reasonable, in that the premises can reasonably be considered to lead to the conclusion. It does not relate to whether or not the conclusion itself is true or false. Just because there is a fallacy in an argument this does not necessarily mean the conclusion itself is false.

* Fallacies have been understood for a long time, and they have names and definitions. Many have a Latin name as well as being known using standard English terms. Learning the names of particular fallacies helps us more readily spot them, and helps us be more precise with others when trying to point out a given fallacy.

* Fallacies are commonplace, but can be difficult to spot. They are particularly difficult to spot when spoken. If someone's logic in support of an argument appears to be flawed, then it probably is. If it is important to you that you understand whether or not a given argument is valid, then get it written down, simplify it as much as you can to reduce it to its essential form, and then check it for fallacies.

Examples of Fallacies

* The Fallacy of Accident is the applying of a general rule inappropriately to a particular case that is outside the scope of the general rule. Thus the claim that everyone has the right to free speech is taken as the right to make racist statements. Or someone may believe that penguins can fly because they are birds and birds can fly.

* The Fallacy of Amphiboly refers to sentences or phrases which are grammatically ambiguous and can be interpreted in more than one way. Widely used by Groucho Marx, such as in the classic: "One morning I shot an elephant in my pajamas. How he got into my pajamas I'll never know." Can be used to deliberately deceive, such as in "We oppose taxes which slow economic growth." Do they oppose all taxes or only those that slow economic growth.

* The Fallacy of Argument By Selective Observation is where we count the hits and forget the misses. For example when someone talks about what a bad state the world is in, as a result of them paying attention to all the bad news but ignoring the good news. Casinos encourage the selective observation tendency. There are bells and whistles to announce slot machine jackpots, but losing happens silently. This makes it much easier to think that the odds of winning are good. Some specific examples of this fallacy include the Fallacy of Suppressed Evidence, where some particular evidence is ignored, and the Fallacy of Confirmation Bias, where only evidence that supports an argument is sought.

* The Fallacy "Ad Hominem", Argument To The Man, is where it is the person who is making the argument that is attacked rather than the argument itself. Thus it might be stated we cannot believe an argument because the person making it is a cheat, or an ex-convict, or foreign, or just plain stupid. Such statements are usually irrelevant to the argument. Only if the person's credibility is itself part of the argument - where for example they ask us to believe something because they are an expert - is it valid to then question whether they are truly an expert in the matter under consideration.

* Much of our knowledge comes from listening to authorities or experts and we can make an Appeal to Authority as a legitimate part of an argument. However, an Appeal to Authority is a fallacy under circumstances such as the following: when the authority appealed to is not really an authority in this particular subject, or the particular aspect of the subject under consideration; when the authority cannot be trusted to tell the truth such as there being vested interests which may be distorting the authority, or where the authority might be under pressure or have other distractions; when there is significant disagreement between authorities, or a poor record of being right for the particular authority being quoted; or when the authority is misquoted.

* An Appeal to Consequence, is arguing that something is true or false based on whether or not we find the consequences acceptable. Thus you might believe someone to be innocent because they are a close friend and it is inconceivable that a close friend would do such a thing. When we engage in Wishful Thinking we are exhibiting this fallacy.

The Bumper Book of Common Sense

* The Fallacy of Appeal to Emotions is when someone appeals to you to accept their claim merely because of the feelings and emotions aroused, such as fear, love, outrage, guilt, pity, pride, sympathy, etc. This is commonly used in advertising and in politics. For example, when people who have suffered some tragedy are treated as though they are experts on related topics. Use of this fallacy as an influencing technique can be very effective in practice, as emotion often holds more sway than logic. Of course, use of emotions to persuade people to take action is not necessarily a bad thing, and is a part of how we motivate others for good. However as a basis for belief in what is true or false it is a fallacy.

* The Fallacy of Appeal to Human Nature is the claim that some general behavioral trait is built in to us as a result of our evolutionary past. Where such is claimed however it is almost always some prejudicial statement for which there is no objective evidence. Opinions vary widely as to what are true general behavioral traits resulting from our evolutionary past, and at best such statements are applicable to some but not all people.

* The Fallacy of Ad ignorantiam, an Appeal to Ignorance, is an argument that basically states that a specific belief is true because we don't know that it isn't true. It is often used to unreasonably shift the burden of proof. There are many things that can't be proven not to be true, ranging from the eminently possible to what most of us would consider the absolutely ridiculous. However just because something can't be proven doesn't mean it is a reasonable thing to believe.

* An Appeal to Money is the fallacy of supposing that because something costs a great deal of money, then it must be better, or to suppose that if something is cheap it must be inferior.

* A Fallacy of Appeal to the People, Ad Populum, is to suggest that something is true because it is what most other people also believe. There have however been plenty of examples of popular opinions being wrong.

* An Appeal to Ridicule or Mockery is dismissing a claim as ridiculous without actually offering up any evidence for why.

* The Fallacy of an Appeal to Silence, is where because someone doesn't say they disagree then we take it as agreement.

* The Fallacy of Appeal to Vanity is a claim that by believing the same as some famous person or elite group, then we are in some way similar to that famous person or we are part of that elite group.

* The Fallacy of Assuming the Antecedent is where expressions are used which implicitly assume the correctness of the conclusion without actually offering any supporting evidence. Thus, for example, 'As everyone knows …', or 'Obviously …'.

* The Fallacy of Avoiding the Issue is where an argument goes off at a tangent rather than staying focused on the supposed issue. Also referred to as missing the point, straying off the subject, digressing, and not sticking to the issue. When this is done deliberately to distract attention away from the argument then it is often said that someone has introduced a Red Herring.

* A Fallacy of Changing the Goalpost, or raising the bar, occurs when evidence is provided to support a claim, but it is then insisted that further evidence is required for a further more extreme claim. This is usually done in a way to distract attention from the face that the initial claim has been demonstrated to be valid.

* Circular reasoning occurs when an argument simply brings you back to where you started. For example a dictionary definition that refers you to another term, with the definition of the other term referring you to the original term. A particular form of circular reasoning is Begging the Question, in which a conclusion is derived from premises that presuppose the conclusion. For example, the argument "women shouldn't fight bulls because a bullfighter is and should be a man," is nothing more than saying women shouldn't fight bulls because women shouldn't fight bulls. Or 'X was mad.' 'How do you know?' 'He must have been; no sane person would have done that.'

* Cum Hoc Ergo Propter Hoc translates to "with this therefore because of this" and is the name of the fallacy whereby correlation is taken to imply causation. For example blaming foreigners, or gypsies, or people with funny accents for all sorts of things simply because they are there.

* Fallacies of Composition and Division: What is true of the whole or a group is not necessarily true of the parts or individuals taken separately; and what is true of the separate parts, even of all of them taken separately, is not necessarily true of the whole. It is common in arguments to find people accidentally or purposefully using part of an argument to refer to individuals but their conclusion concerns the group, or vice versa. Thus a politician might argue that because a few people are abusing some particular system that the whole system should be scrapped.

* The Fallacy of Confusing an Explanation with an Excuse. Just because we can explain something this does not mean we should excuse it. For example, trying to explain why someone committed a crime is taken by some people to be an attempt to excuse the crime. To them, because the crime is inexcusable there should be no attempt to explain it. Another example is where we find a supposed explanation for someone's bad behavior in their distant past – their parents divorced when they were young – and offer it up as a reason for why they shouldn't be punished. There are many people whose parents divorced when they were young who did not then go on to exhibit the bad behavior.

* Fallacy of the Continuum is the belief that small incremental differences can be ignored because they are inconsequential on a larger scale.

* The Fallacy of Distortion is where someone's view is twisted to something other than what they intended in order to make it easier to attack. An example is the Straw Man Fallacy, also known as the Fallacy of Extension, whereby an exaggerated or caricatured version of the intended argument is attacked. For example, the fallacious response to someone questioning something that is written might be that you can't question everything that is written.

* The Domino Fallacy is where it is assumed that one small event will lead to another and that in its turn to another, and thus the small event will inevitably lead to some greater event.

* The Fallacy of the Dope Pushers Defense is the argument that if I don't do it, someone else will. It is an approach that leads to the lowest possible standards becoming the norm. We can and should consider those using such an argument for their own selfish ends as being morally corrupt and untrustworthy, not just with regards a particular topic but as regards any other dealings we might have with them as well. We should have as little to do with them as we can.

* The Fallacy of Double Standards occurs when we ought to judge two things by the same standard, but don't. This is very common, and foreigners and strangers will often be judged to a different standard than friends. Indeed we often judge ourselves to different standards than we judge others. We readily find excuses for our own behavior or that of persons close to home, whilst we would consider analogous behavior in others as inexcusable.

* A Fallacy of Emphasis or Accent, is the deliberate use of ambiguity arising from shifting the emphasis on certain words within an argument. Thus the statement "A thinks B" as a spoken statement could be a simple statement of belief about A thinking B, or if a strong emphasis is put on the word "thinks" it could be intended to mean that A is mistaken in thinking B.

* The Fallacy of Equivocation is the use a word or phrase to mean one thing in an earlier part of an argument, and then later in the argument use it to mean something different.

* The Fallacy of the Excluded Middle is one of assuming there are only two alternatives when in fact there are more. For example, assuming Atheism is the only alternative to Fundamentalism, or being a traitor is the only alternative to being a loud patriot, or that reckless spending is the only alternative to austerity. This fallacy is also sometimes called a False Dichotomy or False Dilemma.

* The Fallacy of False Analogy is where we identify something in common between two things and then assume other things will also be common, without any particular evidence to justify it.

The Bumper Book of Common Sense

* The Fallacy of False Balance is the view that because there are different viewpoints on an issue that therefore all viewpoints are equally valid. For example, some people will argue that because all experts do not agree about all the details of evolution that therefore evolution is no better a theory than any other. However just because experts don't agree about the detailed mechanisms of evolution this does not change the fact that the vast majority of experts do believe in the general principles of evolution.

* The Fallacy of False Continuum is the idea that because there is no definitive demarcation line between two extremes, that the distinction between the extremes is not real or meaningful. Thus someone might argue that there is a fuzzy line between cults and religion, therefore they are really the same thing. However there is no clear point when red becomes purple, but we still use the terms.

* A Fallacy of False Precision is when information is treated as being more accurate than it really is. For example if a measurement estimate for item A is x and that for item B is x+1, then item B may be assumed to have a measurement value greater than item A. However if the accuracy of the measurements is only +/- 5, then there is a significant possibility that this is not true. Or an instruments measurement might be given to an accuracy of millimeters, whilst the actually measurement may only be accurate to within meters: e.g. A GPS device.

* The Fallacy Argumentum ad Logicam, also known as the Fallacist's Fallacy, occurs when because we find a fallacy in an argument we assume that the conclusion is therefore false. This however is clearly not the case. The conclusion has simply not been proven by that particular argument.

* The Gambler's Fallacy is the belief that future chance events are influenced by the outcomes of previous events. Thus a run of heads when a coin is flipped is viewed as meaning it is more likely there will be a tail next time in order to 'even out the odds'. Of course it is not unreasonable to judge that future events are more or less likely as a result of past events. However only because we are seeking out some possibly hidden causal explanation. If events are truly random then there is no law of nature that overrides this. In practice, if you get a long run of heads, it may be that there is an unintended bias in the coin tossing, and you might be better off guessing heads next time. Or it may be that the coin tossing is being deliberately manipulated, in which case you need to think through how and why. Or of course it may be just chance.

* A Fallacy of Group Identity is the appeal to a belief on the basis of it being what gives the group its identity. A common use of this fallacy is in nationalism where people are expected to believe things that put their nation in a good light and disbelieve those that don't.

* The Fallacy of Guilt by Association is where we reject an argument because it was held or supported by someone widely accepted as having been wrong about other things. The fallacy of course is that whilst someone may have been wrong about other things it doesn't mean every view they held was wrong.

* A Hasty Generalization is the fallacy of taking a few instances, often personal experiences, as the basis for a general rule. In any hasty generalization the strength of an argument that is based on small sample sized is overestimated. A specific example is the Fallacy of Anecdotal Evidence where people give far greater weight to anecdotes than they do to statistical evidence.

* The Hindsight Fallacy, or Historian's Fallacy, is judging past circumstances based upon information only known afterwards. Thus we might attribute past decisions to deliberate conspiracy because the consequences of those decisions are so obvious. However they are often only obvious in hindsight.

* The Fallacy of Hypostatization is the error of inappropriately treating an abstract term as if it were a concrete one. For example when we talk about 'nature' deciding who lives and who dies in the wild: nature can't make decisions.

* The Loaded Question Fallacy is where the question contains an unjustified assumption. For example: 'When did you stop beating your wife?'

* The Fallacy of Moderation, or Fallacy of the Middle Ground, is when it is assumed that the middle position between two extremes must be right. Whilst it may well be, there is no logical reason why it must be, and people sometimes deliberately take more extreme than reasonable positions simply to seek a middle ground that is in their favor.

* The Fallacy of Poisoning the Well refers to deliberately using terms to create an atmosphere that is prejudicial against a particular argument or against the person who is making an argument.

* The Fallacy of Positive Ad Hominem is where we accept an argument because we are positively disposed towards the person making the argument, rather than on the strength of the argument itself. We tend to more readily accept arguments made by people we like.

* Post Hoc ergo Propter Hoc translates to "after this, therefore because of this". Often referred to as the Post Hoc Fallacy, it relates to the frequent line of argument that 'A occurred then B occurred, therefore A caused B'. People often fall into this fallacy when it is a regular occurrence, or when it suits what they want to believe. However there are other reasons why B may always follow or appear to follow A. Both events may themselves be the result of some other cause. Or it may be selective attention and we fail to notice that B often occurs even though A doesn't, or A sometimes occurs when B doesn't.

* The Prosecutor's Fallacy is the mistake of over-emphasizing the strength of a piece of evidence due to a lack of attention to the context. For example a test for a rare disease might be described as 99.9% accurate. Many people who test positive for the disease are likely to then believe they have the disease. However a 99.9% accuracy means that the disease will misdiagnose 1 time out of every 1,000. If, say, on average 1 in a million people have the disease, then for every 1 million people tested 1,000 will test positive even though, on average, only 1 of them will have the disease. Thus being tested positive still only means there is 1 in a 1,000 change of having the disease.

* The Fallacy of Rationalization is very common, whereby someone takes a possible explanation as though it is the only explanation; usually because it is of benefit to them.

* The Sharpshooter Fallacy gets its name from the case of someone shooting a rifle at the side of the barn and then going over and drawing a target and bulls eye concentrically around the bullet hole. Someone who makes many predictions is likely to get some of them right. If when they get one right they loudly use it as proof that they can predict the future, and quietly ignore all the times they got it wrong, then they are guilty of this fallacy.

* The Fallacy of Single Cause is where it is assumed there must be a particular cause to a given outcome rather than accepting there may be a combination of multiple causes, no one on its own which would have brought about the outcome.

* The form of a Slippery Slope Fallacy looks like this: A leads to B; B leads to C; C leads to D ... Z leads to Hell. You don't want to go to Hell. So, don't take that first step A. In practice even relatively high percentages of each step leading to the next will lead to a relatively low percentage of A leading to Z and thus Hell.

* The Spotlight Fallacy is the implicit assumption that all members of a group exhibit the same characteristics as a few prominent members.

* The Fallacy of Style Over Substance occurs when the style with which an argument is presented is taken as adding to the substance or strength of the argument. Thus an argument presented by a person dressed smartly might be taken as having more substance than one presented by someone dressed scruffily.

* If you say or imply that a practice must be OK simply because it has been seemingly wise practice in the past, you commit the Fallacy of Traditional Wisdom. This is not, of course, to say you shouldn't accept or use past practices, however they must be judged on the merits of the current circumstances and options, which may be different to what they were in the past. Similarly a practice is not OK simply because it is new or modern, the Fallacy of Appeal to Novelty.

The Bumper Book of Common Sense

* The Fallacy of Tu Quoque is committed when we reject an argument because the arguer does not, or did not at some point in the past, practice what they preach. Whether they did or not is usually irrelevant to the validity or reasonableness of the argument itself.

* The Fallacy of the Unexplained is the presumption that because something is unexplained then it is inexplicable. However just because we do not currently have an adequate explanation for a phenomenon does not mean that it therefore defies the laws of nature or requires a paranormal explanation.

* The Victim Fallacy is someone believing they are being discriminated because they are the member of a group that is sometimes prejudiced against. There are people who, if not performing well, will shift the blame from their own poor performance to a claim that they are being victimized because they happen to belong to a particular group. Of course, prejudice is also sometimes real.

Biases

* Cognitive Biases are instinctive ways we think and behave which are actually inappropriate in particular circumstances. They largely arise as a result of our brain seeking to maintain a positive self-image so we feel good about ourselves, and our tendency to be lazy and want to do things, including thinking, with the minimum of effort.

* Actor-Observer Bias: when it comes to explaining other people's behavior, people overemphasize the influence of personality and underemphasize the influence of circumstances, but do the opposite when it comes to explaining their own behavior. People thus see themselves as flexible and responsive to circumstances but see others as fixed in their ways. This is also sometimes referred to as a Trait Ascription Bias.

* Ambiguity Bias: people tend to select options for which they can estimate the probability of the outcome over those for which they are unable to make any such estimate. People tend to avoid options for which they don't have adequate information.

* Anchoring or Focusing Bias: people tend to rely heavily on one particular piece of information when making decisions, often a piece of information they obtained early on. For example people often make big purchase decisions, such as for a house or car, on some relatively minor feature. This is often deliberately used by those who wish to manipulate us as they seek to plant some particular idea in our head that favors their position.

* The anchoring and adjustment process is where we begin by anchoring on the most easily retrievable relevant number and then adjust up and down based on information available. However our adjustments tend to be 'sticky' and stay relatively close to our anchor, thus if the initial anchoring number is not appropriate then we will not get to a reasonable outcome. This is often exploited by salesmen. Where a negotiation starts can well be the primary influence on where it ends up.

* Attention Bias: we notice far less of what is going on around us than we realize, and we tend to only really notice that which we are explicitly paying attention to. For much of the rest of what we believe we are seeing, the background, our brains is often filling out the detail based on past experiences rather than based on what is really there. The more you are paying attention to something in particular the less likely you are to notice something unusual in the background.

* The Attribution Bias: if I make a mistake or do something wrong there is a good reason, and I am innocent; if others make the same mistake or do wrong they are guilty and should accept the consequences.

* Availability Bias: people overestimate probabilities based on the fact that they can bring particular examples to mind, and tend to be much more influenced by information that is readily to hand. This includes a tendency to be more persuaded by information presented in a visual form rather than that provided as a relatively long piece of text, and also to be more influenced by information that produces strong emotions or is otherwise dramatic.

* Bandwagon Effect Bias: as more people come to believe in something, others jump on the bandwagon without thinking too much about it, either because they want to conform, or because they are lazy in their thinking and take the view that something popular must be right, particularly if it is advantageous to themselves in some way.

* The Barnum Effect Bias: individuals will readily accept as highly accurate, descriptions of their personality that are supposedly tailored specifically for them, even though the descriptions are in fact vague and general enough to apply to a wide range of people.

* Base Rate Bias: Say a detection system has a 1% failure rate, whereby it fails to go off when it should 1% of the time, but also goes off when it shouldn't 1% of the time. Most people in finding the detection system has gone off will assume it is correct 99% of the time. This however is likely to be wrong, and could be badly wrong. Take the case of whatever it is being detected only occurring 1 time in a million. If all 1 million things, whatever they are, were tested, the system would not only detect the 1 occurrence in the million, but would also claim another 10,000 detections due to the 1% failure rate. Thus even if the system claims a detection, the likelihood of it being a correct detection is actually only 0.01%.

* Belief Bias: people's evaluation of the strength of an argument is strongly influenced by whether they are already prejudiced towards or against the conclusion. If they don't agree with the conclusion they are more likely to reject what is actually a good argument, and similarly accept poor arguments if they agree with the conclusion.

* Benefit Bias: people generally view something that would be of benefit to them as less risky than they would do if it had been neutral or disadvantageous to them.

* Blind Spot Bias: people see themselves as generally 'better than average' when it comes to having positive traits and 'less than average' for negative traits. This includes believing themselves to be less prone to biases than most other people.

* Even-Chance Bias: many people believe that chance events even themselves out such that if, for example, a sequence of 13 heads occurred on a coin toss, they will believe that for a while afterwards it is more likely that tails will occur, so as to even out the run of heads. This is not the case.

* Choice Supportive Bias: our memories are not absolutely true and become distorted. The distortion is strongly biased towards seeing ourselves in a positive ego enhancing light, and we often believe that we were right in our past beliefs and decisions. For example we believe we knew things would turn out the way they did before they did. In reality we didn't have any more idea than anyone else, but once things have happened we remember any thought we might have had towards the way things turned out and forget the thoughts we had about alternatives. It is not particularly unusual to have completely false memories, or to remember as our own beliefs things we might have read or been told by others.

* Clustering Bias: people underestimate the likelihood of patterns in random events and see them as having significance. It's because they underestimate how many different patterns there can be.

* Conservativism Bias: people tend to cling to their existing views at the expense of acknowledging new information. This is also where people tend to underestimate high values and high probabilities and overestimate low ones.

* Confirmation or Preconception Bias: people give greater weight to information that confirms their beliefs or is otherwise advantageous to them. They tend to interpret ambiguous evidence, and

The Bumper Book of Common Sense

evidence on its own is often ambiguous, in their own favor, and ignore or undervalue evidence that goes against their beliefs. In a particularly suspicious atmosphere, confirmation bias can even lead to the absence of information being seen as a confirmation.

* Congruence Bias: people place greater reliance on direct testing of a hypothesis than on indirect testing (ie. a test which eliminates alternatives leaving only the one hypothesis remaining). This can lead to bias when there are a number of hypothesis some of which can be directly tested whilst other cannot. Better to focus on tests that would differentiate between the hypotheses. Note that Sherlock Holmes clearly did not suffer from this bias with the famous quote: "when you have eliminated the impossible, whatever remains, however improbable, must be the truth".

* Consistency Bias is the tendency to believe we were always the way we are now. When our attitudes or beliefs change we tend to alter our memories to be consistent with our changed attitudes or beliefs.

* Contrast Bias is when we perceive something as more extreme than it is as a result of having just been exposed to something else with the same characteristic but a different value. Thus the same water may seem to us hot or cold depending on whether we had just been exposed to more extreme cold or more extreme hot water. Or if we are interviewing candidates and we interview a particularly good (or bad) candidate, the next candidate is likely to be perceived as worse (or better) than they really are. Contrast Bias can be a particular issue with regards decision-making because the idea or option that arrives right after a bad idea or option will tend to be rated much better than it would have been rated if presented at a different time.

* Control Bias is where people underestimate risks if they believe they can control them.

* Distinction Bias is the tendency to see two items as more dissimilar when evaluating them together than when evaluating them separately. Our mind exaggerates the differences as a means of distinguishing the items. Thus if viewing the quality of two TV screens next to each other one may appear significantly worse, whilst if we'd seen them at separate times we might not have noticed the difference. Or if we get a good suggestion for a solution after a bad suggestion, we tend to rate the good solution as much better than it might actually be. This is used as an influencing technique when we are pushed towards one option in particular because of the way it is presented together or alongside other options.

* Early Evidence Bias: information that appears earlier is weighted more strongly than information that appears later. Note however there is also the Recency bias where recent information is also more heavily weighted. Between them the Early Evidence bias, sometimes referred to as the Primacy bias, and the Recency bias, lead to bias against information in the middle.

* Early Reward Bias is when given two similar rewards, people show a preference for the one expected to arrive sooner rather than the one expected to arrive later. We are said to 'discount' the value of the later reward; the more so the longer the delay.

* Egocentric bias is when people see their role in things as more prominent than they actually were. For example claiming a greater role for themselves in joint action or in meetings, or remembering past events in a far more favorable light with regards themselves than was actually the case.

* Endowment Bias is our tendency to place more value on something we own than on something we don't own. As a result people will demand more to give up something they own than they would be willing to pay to acquire it.

* Extreme Aversion Bias is the tendency to avoid extremes and to choose something in between.

* Observer Expectancy Bias occurs when someone subtly and unintentionally communicates their expectations of an outcome, which then causes biased behavior in another person. The wording of a question for example can subtly suggest an expected or preferred response. With regards undertaking experiments or tests involving people, this unconscious influencing of participants by the experimenter is termed The Experimenter Expectancy Bias.

* Expectation Bias is where we see what we expect to see even when it is not there.

* False consensus bias is the tendency of a person to overestimate how much other people agree with them.

* Familiarity Bias is where we notice and are more positively disposed to things we recognize or are familiar with. We give more weight to the correctness of something we are familiar with, and tend to reject or disbelieve things we are unfamiliar with.

* The Framing Bias is when we look at a situation from a particular viewpoint and fail to recognize there are other viewpoints which might enable us to think differently about it.

* The Frequency illusion is where something that has recently come to our attention then appears to be everywhere, with far greater apparent frequently than previously.

* The Halo Effect Bias is a tendency to view a person or thing favorably, or unfavorably, based on a single incident or trait.

* Hindsight Bias is the tendency for people to believe they knew it all along after a given event has occurred. This can even lead to memory distortions as people often fool themselves about what they really believed at the time before the outcome became what it became. Given any event, after it has occurred most people seemed to have 'known it all along,' even though few of them seem to have been so definitive prior to the event occurring.

* An Illusion of Control Bias is the tendency for people to overestimate their ability to control events which are in fact largely determined by chance. They thus praise or criticize themselves for outcomes over which in reality they had little or no say. Many gamblers suffer badly from this bias.

* Implicit Assumption Bias is where an opinion is implicitly taken as though it were fact. This is often expressed through use of certain adjectives such as 'he justifiably …', or 'it is obviously the case that …'.

* Information Bias is the belief that the more information that can be acquired in support of making a decision the better, even though often the more information is irrelevant to the decision.

* Ingroup Bias is the tendency for people to give greater weight or preference to those who are members of groups of which they are themselves members.

* A Just World Bias is where people believe that the world is essentially fair, and as a result those who are poor or are suffering or are victims, have, in some way, only themselves to blame. This can readily lead to prejudices and discrimination.

* A Negativity Bias is the tendency for people to pay more attention or give more weight to negative information or experiences than to positive. Thus a piece of negative information about someone or something will outweigh an equivalent piece of positive information. A good and a bad experience of similar weight occurring together will leave one feeling down rather than up or neutral. People tend to notice risks or threats more readily than they notice opportunities.

* The Normalcy Bias is where people who are experiencing extreme circumstances significantly underplay the seriousness of the situation, seizing on any ambiguities as signs that things aren't as serious as they in fact are.

* Omission Bias is our tendency to see harmful actions as being worse than equally harmful inactions.

* Optimism Bias is the tendency for some people to overestimate the likelihood of positive events and underestimating the likelihood of negative events. It is, for example, a continual problem when planning projects based on subjective estimates of how long things take.

The Bumper Book of Common Sense

* Outcome Bias, strongly linked to hindsight bias, is when a decision is judged based upon how it turned out rather than what could reasonably have been known at the time the decision was made.

* The Overconfidence Bias is our tendency to be overconfident in our judgments. We all suffer from it to some extent, some more so than others. For example over 90% of drivers rate themselves as better than average. People who were 100% confident in their spelling of certain words were in fact only right 80% of the time. Most people are overconfident in their ability to accurately assess risks.

* Partsum Bias is the tendency to estimate the probabilities of parts of a whole as summing up to more than estimates of the probability of the whole itself.

* Pattern Bias is our tendency to see patterns even where they don't exist. Thus we readily see images of faces or animals in clouds. Or we interpret vague statements such as given in astrological predications as specific to us because we focus on aspects that match and ignore those that don't or fail to realize that statements are so general anyone could find a match.

* Personal Validation Bias is where a person is more likely to consider information to be correct if it has some personal meaning or significance to them. People will often give far more weight to personal experiences and anecdotes than they will to objectively measured probabilities.

* Pessimism Bias is the tendency of some people to overestimate the likelihood of negative things happening.

* Recall Bias is where we estimate as more probable things we find interesting or memorable. When we can recall specific examples of an event, we generally believe it is more common than it really is. Similarly if we cannot think of examples of an event we judge its probability to be lower than it really is. Thus chance or coincidental events that are memorable are often judged to be far more common than they really are.

* Recency Bias is where more recent information will tend to push out older information, and thus we are more likely to be influenced by it. Albeit noting the Early Evidence bias where early information is also more readily remembered. To keep an appropriate balance we need to ensure we keep good notes and review them regularly, so that newer or more readily remembered information doesn't inappropriately bias our decisions.

* Restraint Bias is the tendency for people to overestimate their self-control, and thus they are more likely to put themselves in the way of temptation.

* Risk Framing Bias is the fact that people tend to be more risk adverse when faced with positive options, but more likely to take risks when faced with negative options. Thus people are less likely to take chances when looking to gain something than when faced with losing something.

* Secrecy Bias is when people give greater weighting to information that they believe is restricted and not openly available in some way.

* Selective Outcome Bias occurs when we only use the results that favor our viewpoint and suppress those that don't. If you run 10 sampling tests then you will get a spread of results. If you then only present the results from one test at the extreme you will get a biased viewpoint.

* Social Comparison Bias is claiming an argument on the basis of some social comparison, such as a parent claiming they are right because they are the parent and the other the child.

* Unconscious Bias is the tendency to make unconscious assumptions about another person based upon a single characteristic, such as their sex, gender, place of origin, etc. It is a natural process and the fact that we are subject to it does not make us prejudiced, because we are all subject to it to a greater or lesser degree. However we should be aware of it, and actively seek to compensate for it, and when we don't then we are being prejudiced. Thus whenever we find ourselves having reservations about someone that we don't have personal experiences of interacting with, then there is likely to be unconscious bias at work.

* The Zeigarnik Effect is a bias towards wanting to complete unfinished tasks, and the fact that we haven't can keep intruding on our consciousness when trying to do other things. It can be more extreme in some people and lead to them going out of their way to get something finished even when there are more important things to be done.

* Biases can be deliberate, though often they are not. We more readily see biases in other people than we do in ourselves, and even when we are intellectually aware of the possibility of bias in ourselves it can still be difficult to counter.

Uncertainty

Certainty and Uncertainty

* If you're absolutely certain about something whilst other people are not, ask yourself why are you certain. Might there be other alternatives, or are they for some reason impossible. Why are they impossible?

* If you're absolutely certain, but other people aren't, ask yourself what if you are wrong. You don't need to believe you are wrong, but ask yourself the question anyway. If the consequences are particularly undesirable you might want to double-check your certainty or at least have contingency plans.

* Uncertainty derives partially from our lack of information about something and partially from the inherent randomness that exists in the world. A given uncertainty may be biased towards one or other of these, or may be entirely the result of one or other of these.

* Subjective uncertainty is due to our viewpoint and lack of information. Someone with a different viewpoint, or more relevant information, could well have a different perception of the uncertainty, or may not have any uncertainty at all. I may be uncertain when the next train is due, but someone with a timetable won't be.

* Objective uncertainty is the uncertainty that derives from the randomness inherent in the world, and is, for practical purposes, genuinely indeterminate, such as the fair toss of coin.

* Whilst we cannot predict the specific value a given objective uncertainty may take on a given occasion, we can know about the percentage of times it will take a given value following a large number of occasions, and thus the likelihood of it taking a specific value on a given occasion. This distribution of the percentages is what is termed a Frequency Distribution.

* Many uncertainties in the real world are a mixture of subjective and objective uncertainties. With more information or a different viewpoint we can reduce many uncertainties, but not necessarily eliminate them altogether.

* Uncertainty can be considered to be of one of two types. Statistical uncertainty which follows distribution patterns, typically the normal distribution, and rare event uncertainty, which when it occurs it comes out of the blue. The rare event uncertainty may itself be either something we know will happen at some point, we just have no way of being able to predict any pattern in its occurrence (ie. known unknowns), or it may be something that happens which we hadn't thought of (ie. unknown unknowns).

* Gambling relies upon people believing that many events are more subjective than they really are, and thus that their special knowledge or ability can predict the outcome better than others.

The Bumper Book of Common Sense

* Casinos don't generally need to cheat. They understand the true odds, and they play games that have a small advantage in their favor. This leads to their gains as a result of the large number of games played.

* Many uncertainties can be reduced through gaining more information. With regards subjective uncertainties this might be through getting a better viewpoint. For objective uncertainties it is through improving our ability to know the underlying frequency distribution.

* When faced with uncertainty, and having done what we reasonably can to reduce it, we should then prepare an approach that is generally flexible or robust in the light of however the uncertainty might turn out. However it can be costly or unrealistic to prepare for severe outcomes and we often have to take a 'realistic worse case' viewpoint. Or if none of the outcomes are particularly severe we could simply ignore the uncertainty and just deal with the outcome as it occurs.

* The stock market relies upon a certain unpredictability in future shares. Without it people would not be interested in 'risking' their money. But 'insider' knowledge can significantly reduce this unpredictability for particular firms. Part of the reason insider trading is illegal is it that it puts the whole stock market system on which western economies are critically dependent at risk. Who would be willing to risk their money if they know others have an unfair advantage.

* The insurance market relies upon not having definitive information about individuals. Take for example Life Insurance. The market depends upon uncertainty about when given individuals might die. If we had detailed profiles of individuals and were able to predict to within a few years when they were likely to die, baring accidents, then only those who had a likelihood of dying in the near future would want to take out life insurance.

* It is not true that because all things are possible, that all things are therefore equally probable. Most things are possible. There are an infinite number of things which are possible, most of which are highly unlikely. There are only a few things that are probable.

* Most people are very poor at calculating the chance of a co-incidence, and whilst they focus on con-incidences that do occur don't notice the ones that could have occurred but didn't.

* Uncertainty is not something we should be afraid of and avoid, but is something that we should see as an opportunity for development and learning. The uncertainty exists irrespective of whether or not we choose to ignore it. Just as we seek to learn facts about the world to better understand and interact with it, so should we seek to understand uncertainties and related frequency distributions. The more the uncertainty the more we can usefully learn about it.

* Information is structure brought out of what previously was perceived to be random. New information is new structures we had not previously been aware of. The 'richest' information is that where there was previously the greatest uncertainty.

* Be wary of mistaking luck for skill. Note that doing better than others may be partially or completely due to luck. Some people will be luckier than others, just as others will be less lucky. A few people will be much luckier or unluckier than others, though the longer the period the less likely they will remain lucky or unlucky. If they are consistently lucky or unlucky it is probable that other factors are at play, such as good or poor application of Common Sense.

* Having been lucky in the past does not mean you are more or less likely to be lucky in the future, albeit noting that some people adopt behaviors that make them appear to others to be lucky or unlucky.

* If you are doing better than others due to skill rather than luck then you should be able to explain why, you should be able to do it consistently, and you should be able to help others do better.

* You can make your own 'luck'. It is possible to be apparently more lucky than others by:
    o Recognizing situations as ones that can be taken advantage of;

- Being prepared to take advantage of certain situations when they arise;
- Trying lots of times such that although the probability associated with any single try might be low, the combination with lots of tries gives a greater chance of some success.

An example is where someone gets an idea 'out of the blue'. The 'clever' idea that certain people have is often not due to luck in terms that anyone might be lucky, but due to the individuals having lots of ideas and continually searching for more. Most of the ideas go nowhere, but occasionally there is one that really works out. Someone who expects a good idea to just occur to them one day, without actively searching for it, is unlikely ever to have it; or if they do, they won't recognize it or be able to act on it.

* Some people are 'unlucky' because of their behaviors. For example they may jump into doing things without thinking first. Whilst sometimes they will get away with it, and may even gain advantage, there are times when things will go badly.

* Whilst in many cases you cannot ensure something will happen or not happen, you can often increase the likelihood of something happening, or not happening.

* People generally don't like randomness of events and seek a reason for why things happen. Thus if they perceive a pattern in the randomness they hook onto it. However randomness can and often does give rise to sequences of events that we can readily fit into patterns after the events have occurred: after all there are an infinite number of potential patterns to pick from. Given any sequence of truly random numbers one can always find an equation that links them, and if one is looking for an equation that only approximates the numbers it is much easier. And if one is then also willing to make excuses for why certain of the random numbers can be excluded, it gets easier still. Thus given a number of random events people readily see some causal relationships to fit some pet theory they come up with, and find excuses for why the more blatant examples that disprove their theory should be discounted.

* When something very unlikely happens, it may simply be the normal consequence of probabilities. However if something occurs significantly more often than expected it may be a sign that there is something else going on. It is not necessarily a sign, but it may be worthy of investigation. And if unlikely things keep happening there is probably something else going on.

* A general belief that things happen in threes is a result of perception. Things happen once or twice all the time and we pay no attention to them. But once something happens three times it often then sticks in our mind. In terms of things occurring, there is nothing magical about three times.

* Following a string of unlikely things happening, some people will assume they will continue to happen, such as when they consider themselves to be on a winning or a losing streak. However occasional strings of unlikely things will happen from time to time. Of course, in the real world, it may be that there is some underlying reason for the unlikely occurrences, which might be worth investigating.

* Low probability events stand out more than higher probability events. We tend to remember them and may find ourselves remembering a number of low probability events whereas we do not remember the probabilistic equivalent of a large number of higher probability events. This can mislead some people into refusing to believe the low probability events are due to chance alone.

* Some seemingly unlikely events are in fact more likely than many people realize. An example: with 23 people in a room there is a greater than 50% probability that two or more will share the same birthday.

* Whilst a given low probability event is unlikely to happen, there may be many possible low probability events and thus the likelihood of one of them happening may be relatively high.

* People often value the complete elimination of a risk, even if the risk is very small, such as going from 1% to 0, more than the much greater reduction, but not elimination, of a larger risk, say going from 30% to 20%. In part this is because people think in terms of proportions where the reduction

from 1% to 0 is a 100% removal of the risk whilst going from 30% to 20% is only a reduction in a risk.

* If something is important you need defense in depth or contingency plans to take account of the unexpected or of things not going as you would like them to.

* Playing the percentages is about optimizing your longer-term strategy in the light of uncertainties. A basic rule for playing the percentages is to choose the options which give you the greatest rate of return, except avoid circumstances with unacceptable consequences, and if the cost is low you can afford to take bigger gambles. Ideally the rate of return should be greater than 1, so that you get more out than you put in, though sometimes all you can do is choose the best of those available and thus limit your losses.

* A factor we need to consider in playing the percentages is the opportunity cost of any outlays, in terms of whether better opportunities exist or may arise in the future. We should be wary of so committing ourselves that we cannot take advantage of significantly better opportunities should they arise. Albeit if we hold back because we believe we may be able to get better returns in the future, then we are losing the returns we could already be getting if we had already committed. What we should do in particular circumstances depends on what we perceive to be the various percentages, and likelihood of gains now and in the future.

* Seek out small advantages. For example, given a seemingly 50-50 bet, rather than betting for something, bet that it won't be the opposite. Taking the example of tossing a coin, rather than bet it will be heads, bet that it won't be tails. In the unlikely event that a third option might then arise, such as the coin landing on its side, you win.

* In the real world, if you were betting on the tosses of a coin, and 7 heads had come up in a row, it would be prudent to bet on heads again. If there are no biases you have lost nothing. However if it comes up heads 7 times in a row it is possible there is a bias, and the bias is more likely to be towards heads. Of course if after it comes up heads 7 times someone asks you to place money on the next toss, it may be that they are trying to manipulate you into choosing heads. So pay careful attention to context.

Probability and Statistics

* Some things are random, leading to outcomes that are just chance. Uncertainty is all around us. We cannot ignore it. We need to work with this uncertainty and we need to communicate with others who work with it. Probability and Statistics are the mathematical language of uncertainty.

* The better we understand the true probabilities associated with possibilities the better the judgments we can make. You should in general choose the option with the highest expected value, with the expected value being the possible gain multiplied by its probability of occurring and subtracting the possible loss multiplied by its probability.

* Terms such as 'almost certainly', 'probably', 'unlikely', 'little chance', etc. are interpreted in quantitative terms very differently by different people, leading to their drawing very different conclusions from statements which use these terms.

* 'The Frequency Distribution' represents the likelihood that a parameter we are interested in will take a particular value. There are two types of commonly used frequency distributions: the flat distribution curve, where the value is simply known to fall between two extremes, with any given value between these extremes being equally likely, and the normal distribution curve which takes a bell shape. Although the normal distribution curve may appear odd, many distributions occurring in the real world approximate to this distribution. If you understand the frequency distribution of an uncertainty you will be able to more accurately predict what is likely to occur.

* Frequency distribution curves may themselves be approximations of what is being represented. There may be uncertainties in our understanding of a given uncertainty.

* Most people have a very poor understanding of probability. Given a large sample then unlikely events will happen. Coincidences are highly likely when you don't predetermine which particular coincidence. The likelihood of some coincidence is likely given there are a lot of coincidences that could happen.

* People often have a misleading view of the rarity of rare events because their very rarity makes them newsworthy when they occur, and the publicity makes them appear more common than they are.

* Small samples are likely to give atypical results.

* It is likely that unlikely things will happen. When there are thousands of things that may have only a 1 in 1,000 chance of occurring, it is not miraculous or odd when one of them happens. Sometimes unlikely things will happen more often than average, just as sometimes they will happen less likely than average, though we probably wouldn't notice this.

* If something is likely, its' none occurrence does not prove it wasn't.

* People have a very poor instinctive feel for real world probabilities. There are many biases in our thinking that leaves us believing certain rare events are much more likely than they are, and that common place events are less likely than they are. The way the news is reported is a significant contributor to this when we are bombarded by rare events but hear nothing of common place events.

* Many people mistakenly believe probabilities even themselves out in some causal way. That if they have had a sequence of 6 heads in a coin toss, that a tail is then more likely so as to even out the probability to the known 50%. This is mistaken. The next coin toss remains a 50% likelihood.

* Many people are bad at estimating the probability of a sequence of events even when the individual events are known. They often stick with estimates close to the individual events rather than multiplying them together which will give a far smaller value.

* The world around us may not be truly reflecting the probabilities we believe it to be. Thus we may believe a give coin toss is truly 50% and when we see a pattern that is biased towards heads or tails believe this is just an example of the randomness that is inherent in probability. However in the real world it may also be due to a biased coin. Thus whilst randomness does allow and indeed expect temporary deviations from the probabilistic norms, we should also be aware of the possibility of underlying causes that mean the true probabilities are not as we assume them to be.

* People generally fail to understand how a base rate impacts a probability. Take the example of a diagnosis for a disease that is described as 99% accurate, in that only 1 in 100 diagnoses will be incorrect. Most people if then diagnosed as having the disease will consider it highly likely that they have it. However if the 'base rate' is that only 1 person in 1 million has the disease, this means that if everyone was tested for the disease 10,000 people who didn't have the disease would be diagnosed as having it. Thus although someone is diagnosed as having the disease, there is in fact still only a 1 in 10,000 chance that they actually have it.

* In testing the effectiveness of medicines or other 'measures' it is essential to have and to understand the results from a control group. Take for example the case of:
    o 200 people given the treatment and improved.
    o 75 people given the treatment and didn't improve.
    o 50 people not given the treatment and improved.
    o 15 people not given the treatment and didn't improve.

The Bumper Book of Common Sense

Many people will see the treatment as effective, since 200 out of 275 seems high. However the improvement amongst those not given the treatment 50 out of 65 is even higher and thus the treatment is completely ineffective.

* Where a value is presented as an average be aware that there are different types of average, the most common being the 'mean' (add the items and divide by the number of items), the 'mode' (the most common item) and the 'median' (the one in the middle when the items are put in order). Where the type of average is not stated it is usually intended to be the mean, but sometimes it might be one that is being deliberately used to give a misleading impression. Taking a different average might lead to a totally different conclusion.

* Averages can be misleading. They can easily be skewed by a few extremes.

* Statistics is about inferring information about a large population by examining characteristics of a randomly chosen small sample.

* It is not true that you can prove anything with statistics. At least not to someone who has a basic understanding of statistics. If you understand the basic principles of statistics then you are much less likely to be misled, and you will be able to distinguish valid statistics from invalid statistics.

* Core questions to ask yourself when faced with statistics include:
  o Is there a sufficient sample? Where relatively small samples are taken, or the population is itself small, it is unlikely that any significant conclusions can be drawn;
  o Is the sample unbiased? If the sample is not chosen in a random way from the entire population that is relevant then it is biased;
  o Where the statistic relates to a comparison, is like being compared with like?
  o Is all the evidence gathered being presented, or only the evidence that favors a particular viewpoint? If not all the evidence gathered is used then the statistics will be highly biased;
  o Are the scales being used to present the statistic appropriate to what is being presented?

* Be sure that where comparisons are made the same 'units' are used throughout the comparison. A particularly frustrating and unfortunately common tendency in the media is to use an absolute value for part of a comparison and a ratio or percentage for a different part, such that the complete comparison cannot be understood. For example: this year 1 in 10 of the fish have died from pollution, whilst last year only 3000 did so.

* Don't be fooled by false accuracy. It is not uncommon to see numbers given to a decimal place accuracy when the numbers on which they were based are only accurate to the nearest 1,000 or so.

* Where statistics, and trends in general, are presented in a graphical or visual form be sure you look carefully at the axis origins and intervals on the graph. Different use of origins and scales can create very different impressions. Try drawing the results using different origins and scales and see if the same impression is given.

* Be wary of extrapolation of data beyond the limits within which the data was gathered.

* Statistics are often used to show causation by showing that there is a relationship between two variables. However simply because there is a relationship does not imply one has caused the other. Correlation does not imply causation. They may both be caused by some other factor. Correlation however does suggest there is some relationship albeit possibly indirect which should be explored.

* Note that where statistics are intended to show a trend over a period of time, other conditions may have changed which could account for part or all of the difference. For example a seeming increase in unreliability may not be due to increased unreliability but be due to more comprehensive gathering of information. There is also in certain areas a tendency to change the rules associated with what information is included in or excluded from a given statistic.

* Where statistics are used to lead to a conclusion be sure that there were not 'side-effects' which would impact upon the decision but which were not presented. For example, a drug could be presented as significantly reducing cancer, whilst not mentioning that it increases some other major medical condition.

* Be wary of arguments where statistics are presented as the proof that a given course of action is right or appropriate, particularly when presented by persons or groups with a vested interest. Whilst given statistics might support a given course of action, they cannot 'prove' it is right. There are often many factors to consider when judging a course of action, and the statistics themselves will only be one of them.

* A common use of statistics is in taking polls of people's opinions, for example relating to a given product, or to try to predict an election, or to determine tastes. When taking polls we must consider:
    o Are people telling the truth? Often people will say what they think they should say or what they think the pollster wants to hear, rather than give their genuine opinion;
    o Are the questions clear or are they open to misinterpretation or different interpretations by different people?
    o Are the choices sufficient to allow people to express what they believe?
    o Are the people who respond to the poll a representative sample?

* Bias can creep into the responses to polls: through the experimenter or pollster; through the sampling technique; or through the respondent. For example, a common problem with telephone polls is that they are biased towards people who have accessible telephone numbers, who are in when the pollster calls, and who are willing to take part in the poll. Or polls which rely on a response being sent in are biased towards those who are motivated to respond, which is unlikely to be a random sample.

* Just because we have a large sample, this does not make its results valid; there may be significant bias. Asking 1 million Christians whether or not God exists and getting a 99% positive response - don't ask about the other 1% - does not mean most people believe God exists.

* The experimenter or pollster may have a vested interest in the outcome of the experiment. This may accidentally or deliberately affect their approach, for example:
    o they may give the benefit of the doubt to results that support their position, and not for those which contradict it.
    o they may bias their experiments towards those more likely to produce positive results.
    o they may exclude negative results for a variety of reasons they rationalize away to themselves.
    o they may deliberately falsify the results.

* It is difficult to get sampling right. A particular problem is getting access to the full population such that a genuine random sampling can be applied. A significant problem is where there is individual choice on the part of the respondent as to whether or not to take part. Often only those with a vested interest will be willing to take part.

* Responses to questionnaires suffer from the respondent's tendency to respond with what feel they should do or think rather than what they do do or think. Or respondents may not really understand the question but not wish to say so and therefore respond regardless. Questions may be truly ambiguous leading to different respondents responding to different interpretations.

The Bumper Book of Common Sense

Catastrophe and Chaos

* There are very real dangers of things changing dramatically and catastrophically, even though there has been no major 'cause' of such a dramatic change.

* Small changes can have big impacts. Whilst the difference between two things may be very small in some absolute measure, the consequences of the difference can, in certain circumstances, be huge.

* Catastrophe and Chaos are two concepts that have their roots in mathematics but which manifest themselves in science and which affect the psychology of how we view the world. They are both concerned with the concept that things can change suddenly, dramatically, and in ways we cannot predict.

* What is termed catastrophe theory, is concerned with things that are in a given state, and the fact that under certain circumstances, some small change, rather than leading to some small change in the thing's state, leads to some very major change. Chaos theory is concerned with things that are changing all the time, and the fact that under some circumstances, rather than there being gradual predictable changes there may be changes which simply cannot be predicted. To the non-mathematician the differences are not important, and so we shall consider catastrophe and chaos theory as being the same concept.

* An often-stated illustration of chaos theory is that a butterfly flapping its wings in Japan could lead to a storm somewhere across the Pacific. And this is true in the sense that if the butterfly had not flapped its wings the storm would not have occurred. This of course does not mean that all storms over the Pacific are caused by butterflies in Japan.

* There is a tendency for complex systems to gradually change and evolve for most of their time, but to have occasional bursts of dramatic change. There is evidence that this occurs in living creatures, and it is also a tendency for man-made systems. Gradual change and evolution occurs as opportunity arises for small improvements. The occasional dramatic change occurs as a result of large numbers of small changes leading to stresses and strains whereby the system either suddenly snaps or a radical overhaul is required during which advantage can be taken of more significant improvements that could not be introduced as minor changes.

* Catastrophe or chaos theory tells us that there will be things we will never be able to predict. As a consequence we should look to predict as best we can when we can, in areas where such predictions are of significant use to us; look to understand the limitations in our ability to predict, so we don't waste effort trying to predict what can't be predicted; and where we cannot predict, look to see if we can take mitigating action in the light of the possibility of the unpredictable occurring.

* Global disasters are very real possibilities. Just because we have not had global disasters in recent history does not mean they cannot occur. Just because people have predicted global disasters in the past and they have not occurred does not mean they won't occur. But then just because they might occur does not mean they will occur. However our actions do make such disasters more or less likely to occur, and the polluting and environmentally damaging impact we are having on the world is making disasters much more likely to occur.

* Although under certain circumstances our ability to predict is limited, we are still able to significantly improve our ability to predict. Models of the weather do get more and more accurate and useful as time goes by. The fact that they can never be perfect is not a reason for not continuing to improve them.

Predicting, Foresight and Hindsight

* Be wary when predicting what might be possible in the future based upon what is possible now, particularly where technology is concerned. Much of what we take for granted today would have been unthinkable a hundred years ago, and would have been seen as magical a couple of hundred years ago. Who knows what might be possible in the future. For example, just because we have not yet created true artificial intelligence does not mean we never will – it is highly likely it will eventually happen.

* The future is a very uncertain place, and the further we look into the future the less certain it is.

* We suffer from an 'illusion of control' that fools us into thinking that the future is more predictable and less uncertain than it really is. We believe tragic events only happen to others, never to us. As a result many people fail to make contingency plans when they ought.

* Our ability to predict certain types of change will always be limited.

* The best way to predict the future is to create it.

* The predictions of several people or models usually results in more accurate forecasts than if we relied on a single person or method. This is because the data we observe consists of a combination of underlying patterns plus noise, and when we undertake averaging we are cancelling out the noise. Whereas some noise distorts the pattern in one direction other noise distorts it in other directions. In the process of averaging the distortions cancel each other out and reveal the underlying patterns.

* Simple averages of people's judgments provide surprisingly accurate estimates. Thus when people are asked to estimate something, such as sweets in a jar, or the weight of a cake, then the average estimate is nearly always more accurate than the single guess that wins the prize. It is however important that the estimates are independent.

* Just like human beings, statistically sophisticated methods for analyzing data find illusory patterns or relations that don't exist. The more sophisticated the statistical method, the better the fit to past data. However, unless what is being measured is a physical phenomenon, there is often no correlation between how well methods explain the past and how accurately they predict the future.

* Even if we have the means of predicting accurately based on past data, there is no guarantee that circumstances in the future won't be different such that our extrapolations are no long valid.

* Even though there are sometimes limits to what we can predict, we can improve our ability to predict most things and this can be of value. How much effort we spend trying to predict should be traded off against the likely success and benefits.

* Everyone can and should make the effort to understand and estimate their chances of success and failure in all that they do. Such insights would reduce bad surprises and disappoints as well as help prepare for certain common failure.

* When something happens, it arises as a result of circumstances that existed before it happened. Whether or not a happening can be predicted based on circumstances is dependent upon: how much we know about the initiating circumstances; how well we understand or know the laws of nature and other 'predictive' models; how good our predictive models are; and what other influencing factors may be relevant and how well we can account for them.

* Clouds gather before a storm. Frequently, before problems engulf us there are early warning signs that if we are sensitive to enable us to take action before the issues become a crisis. Thus with regards safety a number of 'near misses' is usually a sign that something serious is likely to occur unless we do something about it.

The Bumper Book of Common Sense

* We should understand the limitations in our ability to predict, and not waste effort trying to predict what can't be predicted. Sometimes, rather than trying to predict the likely outcome we would be better off trying to ensure our preferred outcome comes about, or making plans about what to do in the light of the different possible outcomes.

* We can't predict most of what happens to us, let alone control it. But there are things we can do to minimize the negative consequences of our inability to predict.

* Where we cannot influence or predict, we should look to see if we can take mitigating action in the light of possible undesirable events occurring. We could avoid being somewhere that might be prone to certain undesirable events. We could build in redundancy, such that we have spare capacity in the event of the unexpected occurring. We could put in place the means of recognizing undesirable events occurring and the means to compensate for them, such that their full consequences can be limited.

* When something occurs that we didn't predict and didn't make any allowances for, we should cope with it as best we can, and look to learn from it. Do not waste effort bemoaning the fact that it occurred.

* When trying to predict the future, rather than work forward from where you are now, you could instead work backwards from various hypothetical futures. When working forwards our thinking is often prejudiced and we would see certain events as unlikely. If however, instead, we imagine an unlikely event occurring and then work backwards to see how it might have come about, we may find to our own surprise there are perfectly rationale and feasible explanations.

* Use 'hindsight' to imagine realistic possibilities for the future. Imagine a future state and then rationalize how it might have come about. You will find yourself able to think up alternatives you might not have otherwise done, or to rationalize what you might otherwise think of as highly unlikely events.

* People over estimate the accuracy of their past predictions. They tend to remember the ones they got right and forget about the ones they got wrong. They thus remember themselves as being right far more often than they were.

* Knowing how things turn out profoundly influences the way we perceive and remember past events. People 'remember' themselves having been correct to a far greater degree than they actually were.

* When we get hindsight information about a situation our brains unconsciously re-evaluates information and knowledge we already have, and changes the weighting associated with different factors. Factors we had previously considered of little relevance may be seen to be important, and others may diminish. And unless we had previously explicitly articulated our earlier thinking, or written it down, we 'forget' our previous thought process. We will have overwritten in our minds the previous weightings and genuinely believe that the new weightings were in fact the ones we held before. Thus we overestimate our own abilities. Even when we know about these psychological biases we have limited success in overcoming them.

* Analysis after the fact will usually conclude that events were far more readily foreseeable than in fact they were, since those doing the post event analysis will subconsciously give greater weight to factors they know only in hindsight were important.

* When reconstructing the past there is a strong tendency towards believing that what occurred was inevitable given the circumstances, and therefore should have been predictable. Those who didn't 'predict' are then unfairly castigated.

* If someone makes a large number of predictions they will probably occasionally get some of them right. If someone frames their predictions in vague language then they can fit many possible outcomes into them. If lots of people are making predictions about the future some of them will be right by chance.

* We can usually find a line of reasoning that both leads to observed outcomes and is compatible with what we already believe. Most belief systems, such as religions, have features that allow this to be done. It is for example impossible to prove something was not fate or was not due to some given influence. Those who believe in fate or in some given influence can thus always attribute to this fate or influence what has happened.

* If predictions are vague there will be some truth that can be assigned to them which a believer can then home in on as 'proof' of the truth of the prediction. Vague predictions can be readily twisted or interpreted after the event to align with the actual outcome.

* A person's ability to predict things should not be judged on their ability to explain why what happened in the past was inevitable. Most of us can do this to a greater or lesser extent. A person's ability should be judged on their record relating to what they said before the event happened; and not just what they claim to have said.

* There is a great asymmetry between how readily we can explain the past on the one hand and predict the future on the other. Anyone can find a rational for why past events were the way they were. But no-one can explain or predict the future in advance.

* Horoscopes and astrological predictions are of a very general and vague nature, and rely upon a greater commonality between people than most of us are aware of. For example, most people would consider the following as being specifically relevant and insightful descriptions of their own personalities:
    o Sometimes you are extroverted and sociable, whilst at other times you are introverted and reserved;
    o You pride yourself on being an independent thinker;
    o Whilst you may appear disciplined and confident on the outside, you often worry and are less secure inside;
    o You believe you are capable of much more than you have in fact achieved;
    o You have a tendency to be critical of yourself;
    o You have a desire to be liked and admired by others.

* Remember that if those who claim to know the future genuinely knew the future they wouldn't be doing whatever it is they are doing

Systems and Systems Thinking

Complex Systems

* A system is something that is made up of a number of parts working together but for which the behavior of the system is fundamentally different to the behavior of the parts. A system has 'emergent' properties that do not exist as regards its parts. Systems can be man-made or naturally occurring.

* Simple high level features and characteristics can sometimes emerge from complex interactions of the lower level features and characteristics of many parts. Take a car: the detailed workings of a car are complex, yet the high level workings of a car are relatively simple, at least when it is working correctly.

The Bumper Book of Common Sense

* A feature of a system is that the parts only have a purpose in the context of the system. You cannot understand how the system works simply by understanding how each of the parts works in isolation from the other parts.

* A system's complexity is not determined by the number of parts, but by the number of different ways the parts can interact with and influence each other whilst the system is operating within its environment. A system with a small number of parts interacting in complex ways is generally far more complex than a system with a large number of parts that interact in simple ways.

* In complex systems, whether naturally occurring or man-made, one thing is linked to another. All things exist in a web. All strands in the web have a role. In taking away or altering any strand we are changing some aspect of the whole web, for good or bad.

* Loosely coupled systems are ones where each of the subsystems performs a significant role within the context of the system as a whole but without many complex interactions between them. Tightly coupled systems are ones where the subsystems only perform their role through extensive interactions with the other subsystems. Tightly coupled systems tend to require less subsystems and parts than loosely coupled systems and are, in theory at least, more efficient and, if man-made, cheaper to produce. However as tightly coupled systems age there is an ever greater likelihood of something unexpected going wrong. Whilst loosely coupled systems may not have as high performance as tightly coupled systems, they are likely to be more reliable and easier to upgrade.

* Adding more complexity to a complex system as a means of providing additional safeguards is likely to be counterproductive. The more complex a system the greater the likelihood of there being things that can go wrong in specific circumstances. Adding complexity to deal with a particular mode of operation that we can foresee is just as likely to add additional modes of operation that we can't foresee.

* Automation enables a lot of work to be done with little human input. However it also means an error or fault can be very costly requiring highly skilled human input to spot it and correct it.

* A characteristic of systems is their stability. Some systems can be highly tolerant of change in one part and readily readjust. Other systems can be highly unstable, with a small change in a particular part leading to major changes in the system or leading to its complete failure.

* A system under pressure can seemingly resist the pressure for a long time, but slowly be becoming less stable such that a time arises when a small change has a major impact: 'the straw that breaks the camel's back'.

* In designing systems we need to design them not just for 'normal operation' but also for use under abnormal circumstances or circumstances where part of the system might have failed in some way. It may be that under these circumstances we still want the system to continue performing in a safe manner, albeit we may accept some degradation. In designing for such eventualities, considerations we need to give include:
    o The likelihood of extreme circumstances arising – bearing in mind that over the life of the system or over the life of a number of instances of the system, the likelihood may become relatively high;
    o The consequences of various types of failure of the system. Clearly the more catastrophic, the less acceptable even low probabilities of occurrence might be;
    o The costs associated with making provision for rare circumstances – a concept of ensuring safety risks are ALARP, As Low As Reasonably Practical, is often applied whereby the designers must justify that they have taken all reasonable measures in the circumstances;
    o The extent to which the system can be designed to fail or degrade in a safe manner;
    o The extent to which mitigation actions can be put in place, such as procedures for use or warnings – albeit recognizing the 'human factor' issues associated with whether or not individuals will follow the procedures or warnings as intended.

* In complex systems, parts are bound to fail. Complex systems thus need redundancy to ensure failure of parts is not catastrophic to the system as a whole. Note the following with respect to redundancy:
    o Redundancy might be: by having identical parts which continue or start to operate when another or others fail; by having other parts which whilst different can undertake the same or similar functionality; by being able to achieve the purpose of the part in a different way when it fails; by being able to do something completely different which still satisfies the underlying purpose;
    o Building in redundancy is building in additional complexity, which might bring other problems;
    o Ensure that the redundant systems are not at risk from the same failures that might strike the normal use system;
    o There must be controls and checks for ensuring that the redundant elements operate as and when required, recognizing that they may have been dormant for a long period of time and then expected to suddenly start working.

    The amount of redundancy to build in is a trade-off between the costs and consequences of not building it in vis-à-vis those of building it in.

* Ironically highly reliable systems can be prone to catastrophic failure because no one spots the problems. Having monitoring systems and checks to spot emergent problems is essential.

* In a complex system, identifying and assessing 'near misses' can give us insights into modes of operation that might in other circumstances be catastrophic.

* During development and testing, subject systems to stress tests, ie. simulations of extreme conditions the system could be subject to. This will give you the chance to modify and improve it before it actually becomes subject to such conditions for real.

* In developing a system we need to ensure we understand the environment within which we expect or want it to operate. In doing so we need to understand not just the current normal environment, but also understand potential extremes that may occur in the environment, and also ways in which the environment may change. A system optimized for a particular environment may perform poorly or not at all should the environment be, or become, different to that assumed. It is often prudent to recognize that we may not fully understand extreme or future environments and thus build in capability margins to cope with extremes, and build in flexibility to make it easy to upgrade the system. This however usually comes at a cost and therefore must be explicitly recognized as an essential requirement for the system otherwise cost optimization will focus purely on being cost-effective in meeting the requirement that is stated.

Systems Thinking

* Much of the world around us can be viewed as a hierarchy of systems, and focusing on parts without understanding the systems of which they are part will frequently lead us to inappropriate conclusions about them and inappropriate courses of action.

* Systems Thinking is about seeking to understand the full environment and context within which something exists, and reacting accordingly.

* Systems Thinking provides an approach to problem solving where instead of trying to break a problem down into its component parts and solving the component parts, we instead focus on the wider context of the problem as a whole, and see the problem as arising from issues of how the parts interact with each other and with the wider environment within which the problem exists.

The Bumper Book of Common Sense

* You gain knowledge through analysis, breaking a problem into parts. You gain understanding through synthesis, through Systems Thinking, through thinking about parts in the context of the whole. You need both though one or the other is often most appropriate for a given problem.

* Interactions between parts within an environment often lead to interdependencies and feedback loops that give rise to complex behavior, beyond what can readily be understood or predicted by studying the parts in isolation. These relationships can be drawn in diagrammatic terms using what are sometimes labeled Causal Loop Diagrams, and the subject that makes use of them in a structured manner is what is termed System Dynamics.

* When representing problems or processes in terms of Causal Loop Diagrams it is usually best to start with as simple a representation as we can, showing the basic elements that might be increasing or decreasing and the dependencies giving rise to these increases or decreases. You can then add complexity as necessary to get a better representation of what is going on.

* Feedback loops arise where a change in one part of a system leads to a change in another part of the system which itself, either directly or indirectly, leads back to changes in the original part of the system. Reinforcing feedback, often marked as a '+' on Causal Loop Diagrams, leads to amplification of the changes, whilst Balancing feedback, often marked as a '-', leads to a dampening down of the changes.

* Reinforcing feedback can be of benefit, or it can lead to a spiraling out of control. Eventually something stops a reinforcing feedback loop, such as the system breaking, or other factors coming into play to dampen it down.

* The application of Systems Thinking can help you analyze a system and thereby recognize sensitivities between the behavior of the parts and behavior of the system as a whole. Small changes in the behavior or characteristics of some parts can have a large impact on the behavior or characteristics of the system as a whole; whilst large changes in other parts could have little or no impact on the whole. Systems Thinking can help you find the key 'leverage points' where you should focus your efforts.

* The application of Systems Thinking should help us recognize the potential for unintended consequences of our actions. Our actions often have an impact on multiple systems, not just the particular system that is superficially of interest to us. By explicitly looking to seek out and understand what systems could be impacted by our actions we are more likely to recognize the potential for impacts beyond what we intend. By explicitly mapping out an assessment of potential consequences arising from given actions or decisions, and inviting input from others, we can leave behind a record of our thinking which can help protect us from those who would apply hindsight to argue certain consequences should have been obvious.

* For want of a stud, a shoe was lost. For want of a shoe, a horse was lost. For want of a horse a battle was lost. For want of a battle a kingdom was lost. Small things can have big consequences.

* Systems Thinking includes the realization that things are interconnected, and that changes are always likely to have consequences other than those we plan for. We can reduce the unexpected consequences of change if we search them out systematically and with an open mind in advance.

* By viewing a problem or process in terms of its elements and feedback loops we can think about what might be done to change the overall system behavior. Thus the system we may be investigating might be some business problem, a relationship issue, a health issue. Changing interactions between elements, or adding new elements, or changing how an element behaves, or changing how we use the system, are all means of adjusting the overall behavior of the system under consideration.

* Measurement systems are used to determine the difference between what is desired and the present state, and thus provide information to determine what action to take. Too sensitive a measurement system can lead to damaging continual micro adjustments, and too insensitive a measurement

system can lead to no action when action is required. And of course measurement systems can also sometimes give incorrect results.

* What you measure in a system, and how you measure it, will limit what you see and therefore what you can do. Just because you are not measuring something does not mean it is not more important than what you are measuring in terms of impact on your end goals. Often people only measure what is easy, rather than what is important but difficult.

* If you find yourself seemingly solving a problem, but then find the problem or similar problems keep coming back, then is likely you need to apply a more structured systems thinking approach. In particular you need to think about what other systems your problem is a part of.

* Systems Thinking is not just about solving problems. It's about identifying and resolving issues that give rise to the problems in the first place.

* A common Systems problem is where all parties act in a way that is reasonable from their own viewpoint, but which because everyone is acting in the same way is damaging to the wider 'common good'. A quiet holiday spot for example might be completely ruined by large crowds all attracted to a quiet holiday spot. Or with regards fishing in the oceans whereby each nation acting in its own short term national interests would lead to overfishing and long term collapse of the fishing industry. This is sometimes referred to as 'the tragedy of the commons'. Solutions to this problem usually require some form of regulation whereby usage is shared or controlled in some way.

* When thinking in terms of a system solution to a problem we can often recognize that there is no one 'cause' but a set of interdependent circumstances which need to be restructured to mitigate against the continuing problem.

* The relationship of inputs to outputs for a system is often complex and rarely linear. Some common characteristics include:
    o Sometimes a threshold needs to be reached before there is any output at all;
    o There is often an optimal working range for a system, outside of which strange behaviors may result;
    o Systems can have different states, with different behavior in the different states;
    o Once a system has gone into a different state it may not be able to return to a previous state;

* A system works as well as its weakest link. If you want to improve a system, focus on its weakest link. Note however that continuing to improve what had originally been the weakest link may stop being of value once the weakest link then becomes some place else.

* Optimizing a part without considering the whole could lead to no improvements in the whole or could even lead to actually making the whole worse – for example through putting increased strains on other parts.

* By optimizing a system you can make it super-efficient in its particular environment, but actually less able to respond to or adapt to change. And change will come. Sometimes it is best to have some slack, and thus non-optimization, that is then available when the situation changes.

* Systems of tight control that minimize waste are not very responsive to change, and can behave in unpredictable and undesirable ways when change or disturbances occur, as they will. Just In Time, for example, works very well when it works well, but if there is a disruption and it's late, who knows what the consequences might be. Beware of putting everything on the critical path.

* When we make changes in order to bring about some effect, we need to be careful about 'assuming' all other things will remain unchanged. Our change might bring about other effects, and of course other things might also happen at the same time. Systems Thinking is in part about acknowledging that change in one area can have knock on consequences in areas other than those

intended. Thus building bigger roads in order to ease traffic often results in changes in behavior about how the roads are used, which can make things worse.

* Systems Thinking includes our recognizing that we are part of the problems and issues being thought about – either physically or as a result of how we mentally think about the problems.

* Outputs are dependent upon inputs, upon the environment, and upon the transformations made to the inputs. All three factors have a part to play. Thus, just because an institution gets good results this does not mean it is a good quality institution. If input is high quality and the environment is favorable then high quality output can be obtained without significant transformational quality. Rewarding those responsible for transformational quality solely on the basis of output is thus shortsighted. If input is poor quality or the environment is unfavorable, but good quality output is still achieved, then it is likely there is significant transformational quality which should be rewarded.

COMMON SENSE INTERACTING WITH OTHERS

The Influence of Emotions

General Observations about Emotions

* Emotions arise as a natural result of our being human. They are not necessarily good or bad, they are simply a fact of life. If is generally unrealistic to try to deny our emotions. We can however usually intervene between our emotions and our actions in order to hold ourselves back from behaving inappropriately: just because we feel angry doesn't mean we need to act out our anger.

* When in a highly emotional state you will be unable to keep a measured response towards arguments or situations, and there will be a general suppression of Common Sense. You will tend to see the world in a distorted and prejudiced way. Do not try to kid yourself you are being rationale or level headed when you are feeling strongly emotional, and don't expect others to be so.

* When we are rationale we look at the evidence before drawing our conclusions. When we are emotional we draw our conclusions then look for the evidence to support it.

* When we feel threatened it is our emotional selves that respond first, and will continue to respond all the time we feel threatened.

* Jealousy and envy make us prejudiced, and prone to many of the failings of clear thinking. In particular jealousy and envy will lead to the rationalizing of other people's motivations and actions in a negative manner, which is often partially or completely unjustified.

* It is relatively easy to appeal to people's prejudices when they are emotionally aroused and they will often readily accept arguments which are nonsense and false.

* We all have particular emotional triggers that cause irrational and relatively extreme emotional response. It is worthwhile learning what these are and developing tactics for deadening their impact on us. Similarly if we are aware of the triggers for those close to us we can make a significant effort to avoid them.

* If we are tired and not getting enough sleep then we will be far more emotional than we would be if we had plenty of rest and sleep. This applies to us and it applies to others.

* Our emotional brain responds much quicker than our rationale brain. However we can quickly become aware of our negative emotional responses and then redirect our thinking and emotions.

* Pride can have an extreme effect on behavior, though more so with some people than others. In extremes individuals have committed suicide rather than be forced to admit they might have been wrong.

* Increasing happiness increases the likelihood of insights, whilst increasing anxiety decreases them.

* People are more likely to make a gut response to something when they are in a happy mood, and more likely to weigh up the pros and cons when they are in a sad mood.

The Bumper Book of Common Sense

* It is easy to get upset by small injustices when tired. This accounts for many bad feelings. For example after a hard day at work minor issues at home may explode out of all proportion.

* Exclusion and rejection is physiologically very painful.

* Emotions in themselves are not bad. They are an important part of what makes us human. Emotions motivate and inspire. If we can align our goals and our thinking in a positive way with what motivates and inspires us then we are more likely to see them through to a useful end.

* Moods and emotional states are highly infectious.

* Emotions aren't bad and we shouldn't try to suppress them. We do however need to control extreme behavior that can result from our emotions. Some believe that venting their anger is a healthy release of that anger: that violent video games for example is releasing natural pent up violence that might otherwise be released through other means. This is not however generally the case. Better to learn relaxation techniques. Aggressive behavior generally leads to further aggressive behavior.

* Emotions serve important and useful functions. Fear for example can protect us from excesses, and hope is an important motivating force.

* Sad events are inevitable. You should accept and feel the emotions that result, and in time the pain that results from sad events will lessen.

* Use of the passive voice when describing events keeps people detached from them, and helps dampen down emotional responses. If talking to someone about a third person with whom they are angry or upset, use the passive voice to talk about the third person.

You and Your Emotions

* Don't fake or hide or suppress your feelings, and don't apologize to yourself or others for having emotions. They are real and you have a right to feel emotions. However nor should you let your emotions result in your behaving inappropriately. If you do, apologize for that.

* We overestimate how obvious our emotions are to other people. We often feel our own emotions intensely and assume they are therefore obvious to others, but often they are not. People are far more focused on themselves and their own emotions, just as you are on yours. Even when people are paying attention to your emotions, or you to theirs, they and you overestimate the accuracy with which they are interpreted.

* When we are concerned about something we assume it is obvious to others: usually it is not.

* It is when we are emotional that we are prone to getting into arguments, using the everyday sense of the word. However such arguments rarely have a clear purpose and rarely come to any reasonable conclusion.

* If someone proves or demonstrates that you are wrong, rather than be upset you should be pleased. It is better to have an illusion corrected than to continue to believe it. Many people think they lose credibility if they are seen to be wrong. However a willingness to continually learn and improve generally carries far more credibility than demonstrating an unwillingness to do so.

* Sometimes people will unjustly criticize you. Don't get upset. Listen to what they have to say, and look to see if you can take anything positive from it. If you can, do so. If you can't, put it behind you. This is of course easier said than done, particularly when you feel the criticism is unjustified. However remember that the more you respond emotionally to criticism, the more people will see it as potentially justified.

* Accept insults and slights from others without getting angry or tense or upset. They either didn't know what they were doing, or they are not worth bothering about.

* Holding on to anger or regret or an inability to forgive others, physically harms us, and makes us more prone to illness.

* Seeking vengeance or revenge is almost always harmful to yourself. When you become revengeful you are letting someone else dictate your behavior. If someone does something to which you need to respond, do so for a clear reason that is to your benefit, rather than simply to get back at them.

* When emotions are aroused it is not uncommon to make more extreme statements than intended. Try to avoid getting drawn into arguments when you are feeling emotional since others will often take advantage of you, drawing you into extreme statements that can't then be defended.

* Sometimes our emotions get the better of us and we say or do something we regret. When you hurt someone else then apologize afterwards, and mean it. Don't let your pride stand in your way of apologizing.

* Our emotions are influenced to some extent by our environment. Colors and sounds can tip our emotions in given directions. Thus you can use colors and sounds to influence your emotions. For example common associations with colors include: red – high energy, love, willpower; orange – creativity, courage, enthusiasm; yellow – cheerfulness, vitality, communicative; green – harmony, healing, luck; blue – calm, truth, hope; indigo – intuition, change, flexibility; violet – spirituality, self-improvement. Similarly some sounds and music relax us, some irritate us. Pay attention to color schemes in your house and workplace.

* It is not situations that cause our changes in state of mind, but our reaction to them.

* Don't try to control everything; loosen up.

* Keep a look out for when your emotions are dictating your thoughts and words. If you have been hurt your immediate response will probably be emotional and destructive rather than creative. Try to be slow to respond and slow to react when you are feeling emotionally charged.

* Be wary of anything you write when you are feeling emotional which you intend to send to someone else. Always put it aside and have another look later. Do not fire off e-mails when you are in a heightened emotional state.

* Be aware of your own emotional state, in particular of when you are getting frustrated or annoyed. Your effectiveness is likely to start dropping and it may be appropriate to take a break.

* It is not circumstances that make us angry, it is the thoughts we have about the circumstances. Anger is how we let ourselves react to circumstances, and is often a defense against a loss of self-esteem.

* Our negative responses to things are generally stronger, faster, and longer lasting than our positive response to things: a natural consequence of survival instincts that developed when there were real life threats all around us. If we find negative emotions kicking in then we need to divert our attention to other stimuli and thoughts as soon as possible before negativity takes a strong grip of us.

* Our negative emotions frequently derive from situations where the world is unfolding differently to the way we believe it should be. If we can be less judgmental about the way the world is we will find ourselves reacting less negatively towards it.

* Observe without judgment and you will avoid being a slave to your reactions.

The Bumper Book of Common Sense

* Understanding your own and other people's emotions is a useful skill to have. You can practice and get better at it. If you can be aware of your own or other people's emotion you can adapt your behavior to avoid negative consequences.

* We are constantly reacting to our experiences, feeling positive, negative, or possibly indifferent to them. Be more aware of your reactions and feelings. Don't fight them, just be more aware; this gives you a greater ability to control your follow up reactions in a positive way rather than just react automatically and often negatively.

* What we most dislike in others is often the things we see but hate in ourselves.

* Don't rise to sarcastic comments. They are often not deliberate and more often than not the result of the other person being tired or just having a bad day.

* We don't need to ignore or deny our emotions and bad feelings: we should accept and manage them. Our mind has power over our emotions, even very strong emotions. We can learn to control our emotions. We do not need to be a slave to them; it is our choice whether or not to be so.

* Our first and instinctive reaction to situations is emotional. This is not a bad thing, it is simply part of who we are as human beings. However we can learn to quickly take control of our emotions and think rationally about how to physically and mentally respond to our initial emotions and the ongoing circumstances.

* Each of us has the power to direct our thoughts. Through directing our thoughts we can control our emotions, enabling us to neutralize any harmful effects resulting from our strong inner urges such as instincts and passions that we have inherited or acquired and which seem to push us into doing things we later regret.

* Your emotions follow your thoughts. To change your emotional state you need to change how you are thinking about the problem or situation at hand, possibly through looking to distract yourself.

* You are not your emotions. Your emotions are something you experience and you can change them almost instantly by simply choosing to let them go. When in an emotional state ask yourself, 'Can I let this go?' Answer Yes or No out loud, whilst exhaling. Be honest to yourself. If you say No, repeat the question a little later. After a few times you'll most likely find yourself saying and meaning Yes.

* The more you are in a given mood the more you'll tend to be in that mood in the future. Some people stay in a bad mood for days, weeks, even years. To change a negative mood you need to give yourself a jolt.

* We can increase our control over our own emotions through practicing to do so, and we should practice doing so. Letting our emotions control us leaves us less able to achieve our goals and less effective in our interactions with others. We should be able to use our emotions to help motivate us when we wish to do so, and to help us in effectively communicating with others.

* Analyze the circumstances where your emotions have gotten the better of you and look to understand the triggers that gave rise to any loss of control. Plan for what you might do in similar circumstances in the future.

* By acting as though you are in a good mood you can put yourself into a good mood. Smiling will help you feel happier.

* Being in a good mood is infectious. And being in a bad mood is infectious. Be the one in a good mood: smile a lot and be enthusiastic about what you are doing, and be interested in and enthusiastic about what other people are doing. Be strong willed such that your good mood defeats other people's bad moods every time.

* Learn to shift your emotional states. By being aware of your emotional state you can practice rising above and out of negative states, possibly by a bit of self-talk and reminding yourself of bigger issues. If your partner has annoyed you, remind yourself of some positive moments and that you do love them. If you are frustrated with a task remind yourself of the longer term goals of which it is part.

* If your emotional arousal feelings are high, take some time to calm down. In particular avoid ruminating about whatever it is that has given rise to your strong emotions. If you do it is likely to prevent you from calming down.

* If you are feeling angry, go for a walk or do some exercise. Take yourself away from anywhere you risk venting your anger on other people. Drinking a glass of water can help alleviate anger.

* One way of dampening down our emotional feelings is to think about and label our emotions.

* You tend not to be in both a positive and a negative emotional state at the same time. If you find yourself in a negative frame of mind – such as fearful, jealous, hateful, vengeful, greedy, angry – try to replace it with a positive frame of mind – such as enthusiastic, hopeful, loving.

* People, including you, are poor judges of the causes of their own moods and emotions. For example the day of the week is often a far greater factor than whether or not they have had a good nights sleep.

Interacting with Others who are in a Heightened Emotional State

* Other people have emotions too, and sometimes their emotions get the better of them. Just like you, when your emotions get the better of you, this is not necessarily who they are. Thus be understanding and forgiving and tolerant. This doesn't mean you ignore or continually let them get away with unacceptable behavior. But give them the benefit of the doubt from time to time, and don't let a single incident sour your life relationship with them.

* Do not let others use emotions, real or pretend, to push you to where you do not want to go: if you avoid responding to their emotions in an emotional way you should have little difficulty. If you let yourself become emotional you can easily be manipulated by others.

* Do not try to argue with someone who is in a highly emotional state, whether negatively or positively. They will not be able to think clearly, irrespective of whether or not they are aware of this themselves. Walk away or humor them or try to calm them down, which ever appears most appropriate.

* Reasoned arguments and Common Sense will not hold sway with someone in a heightened emotional state or with someone who is depressed.

* People do not like to be proven wrong, and will often defend inappropriate positions to avoid what they see as the embarrassment of being proven wrong, particularly if any potential 'public exposure' is involved. Rather than simply attacking a person's position, it is better to give them room for maneuver, for example by focusing on assumptions they may have made which can be demonstrated to have been inappropriate, or on how circumstances may have changed or not have been as they imagined them to be.

* The barriers of 'pride' and 'face', will lead to people holding onto inappropriate views long after they should in all reasonableness have given them up. Certain people, highly intelligent in other ways, can be particularly prone to what could be called pigheadedness. Don't underestimate the strength of feeling that pride can give rise to. You must help them find a way of changing their view without wounding their pride.

Groups

Belonging to Groups

* We have a very strong instinct for belonging to and feeling loyalty towards groups, a sort of 'tribal' instinct. In belonging to a given group we distinguish ourselves from others who are not part of that group and feel a much greater sense of loyalty to those within the group than to those outside.

* An important hierarchy of groups to which people belong is: our immediate family; our extended family; our neighborhood; our village, town, or city; our county or region; our country; our continent or some affiliation of countries. We can feel some sense of belonging to each of these groups, though the degree of the sense of belonging can be different to different levels within this hierarchy. Some people, for example, feel a stronger sense of loyalty to their region or country than they do to their own family.

* Some people derive a strong sense of belonging to groups of persons they share some affiliation with, such as persons who share the same religious beliefs, or who work for the same organization, or who support the same football or other sports club, or who share a craze for a given pop star or pop group, or who went to the same school. For some people their allegiance to persons within these groups can be stronger than their allegiance to their family, at least for a while.

* People generally feel their strongest allegiance to whichever group or groups most recognize them as an individual, and gives them a strong degree of respect. Whilst for most people in normal circumstances this will be their own family, it is not always so and individuals can become or feel estranged from their own family and their sense of belonging can then be strongest elsewhere. People with low self-esteem, or a poor self-image, will be particularly prone to attaching themselves to any group that seemingly welcomes them and, for a while at least, boosts their self-esteem and self-image.

* We are far more positively disposed towards those within the groups we belong to than to those outside the groups. This extends to the belief in the superiority of the groups we belong to, believing them, for example, to be more tolerant than other groups and better informed.

* People within a group think of the members within their own group as being more diverse than members within other groups.

* People within a group tend to view people in other groups in a very stereotypical manner. They will tend to view negative behaviors within other groups as being typical whilst negative behaviors within their own group as being a justifiable response to particular circumstances.

* The stronger someone feels a part of a given group the stronger will be their feelings of superiority and animosity towards other groups. People can be and are pushed towards extremism simply through strengthening their ties to a given group. Many people simply looking for something to be a part of can be and are deliberately and cynically exploited in this way.

* People can and do have allegiance to many different groups at the same time. Sometimes these allegiances can come into conflict, leading to unpredictable behaviors as they consciously or subconsciously seek to resolve the conflict.

Behavior and Behaving in Groups

* We should, to some extent, conform to the customs and practices of the people we live amongst and the groups we find ourselves part of. Not to the degree of losing one's own identity and individuality, but enough to avoid regular conflict. We should think of ourselves as guests who have been offered a home by others; and we should respect this.

* Groups, particularly smaller groups, often have some distinguishing mark or feature which visibly differentiates them from other similar groups.

* If you want to stir strong feelings of loyalty, then talk about how well some rival group is temporarily doing. We want our group to be better than others and having this threatened binds us more strongly together, so long as we see the rival group's success as a short-term issue that our superiority can overcome.

* The harsher the initiation ceremonies to a group, the greater the resulting group solidarity.

* The more distinctive the dress or visible differentiation a group has the more likely the members will behave in an extreme or irrational manner.

* We have 'tribal instincts' which lead to us being influenced by the groups we feel part of. If everyone else within the group behaves in a certain way then we will tend to ourselves, unless we deliberately set out to do differently.

* Faulty ideas can spread like an epidemic through a crowd or group. Pyramid schemes are an example of this as were lynch mobs.

* To be successful in the long term, groups, including society itself, need to tolerate non-conformity and differences. Without these, a group will not be able to effectively evolve and adapt and react in the light of changing or unexpected circumstances.

* Individuals will sometimes exhibit selfish behavior that puts the whole group at risk. As such, it is sometimes necessary for groups to curtail some freedoms. It is then for individuals to decide whether or not they wish to remain within the group given its rules for membership.

* Within a group, ensure you look after your own interests. This does not have to be at the expense of others, and it may involve compromising.

* People's perceptions of their role and contribution to a group is usually far greater than it actually is.

* When a group of people are working together to achieve a common goal individuals have a tendency to work less hard than if they were working on their own, so long as their own individual contribution is not being measured. If however their individual contribution is being measured and is visible to the group as a whole, they will tend to work harder than they would if they were on their own.

* If you want to break away from the normal behavior within a group, you usually need to break away from the group as a whole. If you want to adopt a certain behavior, join a group for which the given behavior is a norm.

* We become like the people we spend time with, and there are enormous social pressures to conform to the groups we are part of.

* If you are looking for action or help from a group of people you are far more likely to get it if you target individuals within the group rather than make a general appeal to the group as a whole. In a group everyone will leave it to someone else.

The Bumper Book of Common Sense

Conflicts between Groups

* The way to break down hostility or conflict between groups, as between individuals, is to give them some common cause or goal they can work together on. However it is important the group succeeds or at least largely succeeds in the common task otherwise they are likely to blame each other for the failure.

* When strengthening the co-operation and respect within a group by giving them a common goal, be careful to ensure that this is not at the expense of creating or increasing feelings of dislike and discrimination against other groups. It is not uncommon for one set of conflicts to be overcome but at the expense of increasing conflicts elsewhere.

* A way of attacking and creating conflicts within groups is to force them to be more aware of the differences that exist within the group.

* Rivalry can be very readily created by simply separating people into two groups and then putting them into competition with each other.

* Where conflicts and antagonism arise between groups they are often most intense between groups close by and similar rather than between groups which are further away or are clearly different.

Groupthink

* Groupthink is what most other people within the group think. More than this, it is what everyone in the group is expected to think.

* Some characteristics of groupthink:
    o Members develop an illusion of invulnerability and extreme optimism;
    o Inconvenient facts are ignored;
    o There becomes strong support to 'means to an end' thinking at the expense of moral thinking;
    o Other groups or viewpoints are stereotyped;
    o Dissent and doubt and views not in line with the preferred group thinking are suppressed and there is an illusion of unanimity.

* Groupthink occurs when members of a group believe it is more important to support each other than it is either to get at the truth or to behave with complete integrity. Groupthink is usually a recipe for poor group performance because any ideas that are different to those publicly held by the majority are discouraged or actively suppressed.

* Groupthink constrains and prohibits effective thinking. As the saying goes: "When everyone thinks alike, no one thinks very much."

* Group decisions tend to be more extreme than decisions people would make on their own; either riskier or more conservative, dependent upon the particular group. Group decisions also tend to be more dogmatic and more moralistic. Irrational decisions are more likely to emerge from groups then they do from individuals. Moreover the members of the group will be more confident about the correctness of the group's decision and more likely to attempt to justify extreme positions than they would be about their own decisions.

* Groupthink occurs when one or more of the following are present:

- - A group leader or small group of strong-minded persons have already made up their mind and sell it to the others;
  - A group that sees reaching a consensus as more important than reaching a rational and honest decision;
  - A strong sense of uncertainty with an underlying strong message that they are all expected to agree a given course of action;
  - External pressures leading the group to behave in a highly defensive manner against a common enemy.

- Groupthink tends to evolve through the following stages:
  - High level of uncertainty;
  - A small group arrives at (or already has) a preferred solution early;
  - A preferred solution is pushed onto the other members as ' the obvious way to go';
  - Aggressive suppression of dissent;
  - Increasing social pressure on any further holdouts;
  - Rationalization of the chosen course of action.

- A group leader will tend to listen to those who most closely agree with his or her own views, and these people will often look to please the leader by expressing not only views that agree with the leader's views but are often a more extreme form of those views, which in turn encourages the leader to move towards a more extreme form of his or her own views.

- To avoid groupthink, alternative viewpoints need to be sought and encouraged. For example: have someone act as a deliberate devil's advocate, but choose someone who will be good at this; give voice to those who go against the grain; bring people together from different parts of the business; ask people who are not experts on the matter in hand, recognizing that naïve viewpoints will often open up different ways of thinking; using outside consultants, though be wary of their adopting an approach which is simply to tell you what they think you want to hear as a strategy for staying in business with you.

- Some counters for groupthink:
  - Involve people from a wide range of backgrounds;
  - Involve some independents, people who are outside experts or otherwise not involved;
  - Have the group leader or most senior person present avoid stating their view before others have clearly expressed theirs, or even avoid them giving their view at all;
  - Avoid trying to come to a consensus too quickly;
  - Feel comfortable with disagreements, but keep them focused on views about the task, not about the people;
  - Look to come up with multiple options to be decided between;
  - Focus on evidence rather than opinions.

People: The Way They Are And The Way They Think

The Bumper Book of Common Sense

How People See and Respond to the World and to Other People

* People respond to the world not as it is, but as they perceive it. Given the way they perceive it, their behavior is entirely rational. If their behavior appears irrational to you it is because they are seeing the world differently to the way you are seeing it.

* Underlying most behavior is positive intent, albeit biased towards their own interests. People rarely go out to deliberately harm or upset others, except where it is a choice between others and themselves. But their behavior and actions derive from their viewpoint, not yours.

* Many people interact with the world as they would like it to be rather than as it is. They get upset when the world does not behave as they think it should.

* Most people do not like anything that threatens their established way of living, or which tries to force them out of their comfort zone.

* People have a strong tendency to simplify. They will ignore or forget inconvenient details that don't fit in with their simplified models or views of the world.

* When times are hard many people will resort to wishful thinking and allow themselves to believe the unrealistic promises of extremists.

* There is much uncertainty around us, and should the uncertainty become threatening people often back away from considering the consequences and instead adopt unrealistically optimistic attitudes.

* We see what we expect to see, as our expectations strongly influence our perceptions. Thus people given a placebo but told by someone they believe that it will significantly reduce pain, do indeed experience significantly reduced pain. Someone given a non-alcoholic drink and told it is alcoholic will experience and exhibit symptoms of someone who has drunk alcohol. We will experience expensive wine as tasting better than cheap wine even though if given a blind taste test we would not be able to tell which was better.

* We all have different upbringings, different experiences, different learning, leading to different knowledge and information and beliefs. As a result we all see the world in slightly different ways. We mean and understand different, albeit sometimes only subtly different, things when we use or hear given words.

* Many people have a tendency to reject new information when it contradicts their established beliefs.

* If new information is consistent with our existing beliefs then we find the new information well founded and useful. If it is contrary we consider it biased or mistaken. When people are forced to consider evidence that contravenes what they believe they will find ways to criticize it or otherwise dismiss its validity.

* People become totally convinced in the absolute truths of their beliefs and their own world view because they only subject themselves to information that is consistent with those beliefs and ignore or avoid any information that might be contrary or point to alternatives.

* It is not easy trying to see things from someone else's point of view, so most people don't try.

* People have a tendency not to change from established behavior unless there is a strong incentive to change.

* Where people stand generally depends upon where they sit. The morality of 'have-nots' is likely to be an appeal to laws other than man made laws, such as ideals of equality. The morality of 'haves' is likely to be an appeal to man-made laws such as law and order and property rights. 'Have-nots' generally want change and 'haves' want stability.

* People much more readily listen to things they agree with than things they don't agree with.

* The way we see the world is to a large extent conditioned by the age and culture we live in, and the language we have available to us. In today's world we largely see the world in scientific terms, and more specifically often in computer analogy terms. In the past the world has been seen in scientific mechanical terms, religious terms, and even in animalistic terms. Doubtless future generations will see the world differently to the way we see it now.

* People act to align themselves with how they believe other people perceive them. Thus if we believe people see us as charitable, we are more likely to act charitably.

* People feel more comfortable and at ease with people who are similar to themselves, and will react more favorably towards those with whom they have something in common.

* People are more likely to support and agree with people who appear to be like them. Any type of likeness can have an effect: dress, speech, age, background, religion, politics, food preference, first names, body language, ….

* People feel closer to each other when they agree about common dislikes to a greater extent than they do when they agree about common likes.

* What people see in others is often a reflection of what is in themselves.

* People think highly of themselves, it is part of the way our brains work, a self-protection mechanism. We are aware of our positive traits and downplay the negative. We believe we are special, albeit having been held back by circumstances, whilst everyone else is just part of the crowd.

* Most people are very reluctant to accept responsibility for their actions should they turn out to be wrong or harmful. When confronted with evidence that what they did was wrong in some way they will tend to look to defend or justify their action or shift the blame to others. 'They started it.'

* People generally perceive their successes to be the result of their own skill and actions, but their failures to be due to circumstances outside of their control or due to lack of support from others. Thus most people take credit for success but deny responsibility for failure.

* Many people look to maintain their self-esteem through refusing to accept any responsibility for things that don't go right. Any failure must be the result of some external factor, some circumstance outside of their own control. They become very defensive at any hint that something they did might not have been the right thing to do.

* People who yield to cheating justify themselves by saying it's something everyone would do if they had the chance, or that the means justify the ends with regards their future career. Those who resist the temptation to cheat will become more extreme in their condemnation of cheats. Those who almost give in to temptations but resist, become most intolerant in their condemnation of those who do yield.

* We tend to consider other people's behavior as being largely determined by their internal personalities rather than by the particular circumstances, but see our own behavior as highly responsive to external circumstances. Thus if someone trips over something we will tend to see them as clumsy, whilst if we did the same thing we would blame the circumstances, such as poor light, or being distracted, or the object we tripped over being in a stupid place.

* The more dramatic an outcome resulting from an event the more likely we are to attribute the outcome to a person involved rather than to the circumstances. For example, if we are injured we will generally believe someone is to blame, whereas if someone we don't know is injured we will often believe it was just bad luck given the circumstances.

The Bumper Book of Common Sense

* People believe they themselves are flexible in terms of their behavior and moods and that their responses are dependent upon the particular circumstances, whilst they believe other people are much more fixed, with their responses being largely determined by their personalities.

* We know that we ourselves are complex beings. Whilst we often try to do the right thing we know that sometimes we don't always succeed due to particular circumstances or due to momentary weakness or due to our having been distracted. Our occasional lapses do not define who we are. Yet when we see such in others we often do take it as who they truly are. We rarely notice their everyday behavior but immediately notice any transgression on their part and often define them by it.

* We judge our own actions by our intentions: generally we mean to do good, but if it goes wrong, due to circumstances or other people's reactions, we know that at least we meant well. However we don't have ready access to other's intentions, only their actions and the consequences of those actions. If they come out wrong we then attribute it to deliberate intent on their part, or to their stupidity or incompetence.

* Everyone believes that their own load is the heaviest, and are generally blind to the privileges that have been handed them.

* People generally think in relative terms rather than absolute terms. A rich man in a poor neighborhood will generally be happier than a poor man in a rich neighborhood, irrespective of their actual worth. People in modern society are often depressed and feel hard done by yet their lives in absolute terms are many times better than the lives of the vast majority of people for most of history.

* People with strong beliefs often see persons who are neutral on the subject they feel strongly about as being biased against them.

* People overestimate how well they understand others, and often believe they know others better than those others know themselves. However they would never accept that others may know them better than they do themselves.

* Some people assume that because they know what they themselves are thinking and feeling, that others do too; that it is obvious. Unfortunately the external manifestation of how they are feeling is usually ambiguous from the viewpoint of an external observer.

* People who find certain tasks relatively easy tend to assume others do as well. They often underestimate how much they know and have learnt. This is often a problem with those producing learning material or instructions, who assume certain information or steps because it is obvious; however it is only obvious to those who already know it.

* People's behavior is often dependent upon whether or not they believe others are watching. People tend to be motivated to avoid shame, and shame arises when we believe others are aware of actions we believe they would disapprove of or would see as weakness. Those who believe in an all-seeing god thus have a greater motivation against shameful acts than those without such beliefs.

* Some people believe that life is about being happy all the time; that life is meant to be easy. They then get depressed when it isn't, or justify to themselves criminal or unethical activities aimed at getting them a 'fairer share' of life.

People are Not Good at Seeing their Own Shortcomings

* People often subconsciously project their own negative thoughts or emotions onto others. An example is where someone who is having thoughts about infidelity believes their partner is having

these thoughts and thus it is ok for them to have an affair because their partner would do so if they had the opportunity.

* Most people don't know that they are just like most people when it comes to general behaviors and capabilities.

* Self-deceit exists on a massive scale.

* Even the most evil and hateful person thinks they are a good guy.

* Intuition is that instinct that tells us we are right, whether we are or not. Whilst our intuition may be useful when looking to quickly make relatively unimportant decisions, it is rarely a replacement for hard thinking and systematic analysis of pros and cons and weighting of different factors for important decisions. People's intuition is based upon a subconscious focusing on certain facets which in truth results as much from biases and prejudices than from some magical ability to ascertain underlying truths.

* Most people believe they do not suffer from the shortcomings of most people. Most people thing they are objective whilst others are biased. When others don't agree with them it is because the others are biased.

* People generally believe they are far less biased than they actually are. If someone has a vested interest they will probably be biased, either consciously or sub-consciously.

* People accept that most people are unrealistic about how unbiased they are, however they don't believe it applies to them.

* People see prejudices in everyone but themselves. Prejudices are irrational or mean-spirited, and no-one sees themselves as being that way – therefore any negative feelings or dislikes they have about others must be justified.

* People frequently fail to see their own hypocrisy. They criticize others for some given type of behavior, but fail to see analogous or similar behavior in themselves.

* People justify their own actions as being due to the way they are, and see it as a virtue. But they criticize other's actions as being the result of the way they are, and see it as a fault.

* When faced with evidence that their existing beliefs may be wrong, many people react by rejecting or ignoring the evidence, or finding reasons why it isn't valid. As a result many people fail to learn and improve.

* People are very reluctant to admit their mistakes and will either deny that a mistake has been made, or if the evidence is undeniable will make all sorts of excuses for why it was not their fault.

* Rather than admit they may have made a wrong decision or done something wrong people will often pursue highly destructive courses of action. They may continue to follow inappropriate and possibly dangerous processes, they may treat people even more harshly because they deserve it, they may want silence or harass people who have different views or who might expose them.

* People who are always looking to 'control' situations may think of themselves as leaders or as assertive, others may well see them as control freaks, or aggressive.

* People often overestimate their ability to control a situation. They make plans for how they will make things happen but don't recognize that other people will not act the way they want them to just because they want them to. Those who play a lot of video games for example can get a distorted view of how the world will react to their real world actions.

* Overconfidence, and an inadequate appreciation of the vagaries of chance, can lead to highly irrational behavior, particularly if pride or greed is involved.

* People generally overestimate how much other people agree with them. They tend to assume their opinions and values are normal and commonplace. Even people who accept that their views are minority views will strongly overestimate the number of others who share their views.

* Other people frequently notice when we contradict ourselves. We rarely notice our own contradictions.

* People tend to hear what they want to hear, see what they want to see, and remember what they want to remember, all aimed at seeing things in a way that puts themselves in a positive light.

* For the most part people only accept evidence that agrees with the views they already hold.

* Those holding pseudo-scientific beliefs display confirmation bias, fail to consider alternative hypotheses, ignore chance as an explanation for an outcome, do not critique their beliefs, and fall for fallacies of probabilistic thinking.

* People will often come to believe their own lies. When they exaggerate or distort the truth for effect they will frequently come to believe the exaggerations or distortions to be fact.

* People consistently over estimate their own capabilities, with 50% of people often putting themselves in the top 10% whilst very few consider themselves below average.

* People generally overestimate their abilities relative to others, and this is most pronounced amongst those with the least skill. With respect to IQ however, whilst those with lower IQs tend to overestimate their IQ, those with higher IQs often underestimate their own IQ.

* People with a high IQ often believe they are more intelligent than others and thus less prone to making thinking errors of believing wrong things than others. However IQ only measures a very narrow range of thinking ability, to do with analysis of given information, and those with a high IQ are just as prone to many thinking errors prevalent in the real world as are those with a lower IQ.

* People who are incompetent at what they do tend to overestimate their own level of skill and fail to recognize high levels of skill in others.

* A lack of understanding of probability is widespread and is the source of much irrational thought and action. Many people who are deemed highly intelligent fail to understand or put to effective use probabilistic judgments.

* Many people have a tendency not to face up to shortcomings in themselves, but to make excuses for their behavior: 'I was in a rush'; 'My parents divorced when I was eight'. In practice, having been 'caught out' the person simply identifies something out of the ordinary in their past as the cause, when in fact it has no causal relevance. There are people who go through their whole lives rationalizing their behavior in this way, as a result of which they never take any true responsibility for it, and thus make no attempt to change it. In the long term it is to their own detriment.

* Everyone believes they are free thinking open minded individuals. Most people are wrong.

* Most people believe they are open-minded. However being open-minded means being rational, non-judgmental, without prejudices, and willing to listen to any views irrespective of whether you agree or disagree with them. It means accepting that your own views may be wrong or in need of modification and being open to new information. In practice most people tend to be opinionated, judgmental, defensive, and believe there are justified reasons for their prejudices. They consider themselves to be open-minded but that they will not need to change their minds because they know they are right

* Most people believe they are far less susceptible to being influenced or persuaded by advertising and the media, and that they are far less gullible, than most other people.

* Most people are too self-satisfied and too self-absorbed to recognize the shortcomings in their own thinking, much of which is over simplistic and prejudiced.

* Most people are held back from effective thinking through laziness and pride. They take the easy route of accepting what they are told, particularly when it fits in with their own self-interests. And they don't like to think that what they know might be wrong.

* People who are desperate don't look very hard at the evidence and readily give in to wishful thinking. Thus the reason many people get readily taken in by scams, and the popularity of extremists when times are hard.

* People are often very certain about things they know little about.

* People are generally overconfident about what they believe they know to be true. Much of what they know is at best only a matter of opinion, and some of what they know to be true is in fact false. Moreover their overconfidence holds them back from seeking new and better information, and they fail to look for evidence that would reduce their faith in their current beliefs.

* Most people believe they are good at understanding other people, and are confident in their assessment of why other people behave the way they do; which they mostly put down to what they see as that other person's inherent personality and behavioral traits. Even when people behave in ways that are contrary to their expectations, there is a ready rationale for why it is still really consistent. Most people are wrong about their understanding since most behavior has a strong situational context.

* People who hurt others through words or deeds often barely notice it, whilst those on the receiving end may feel the pain or resentment for years.

* People who criticize or look down on others for being judgmental are often judgmental themselves, albeit about different things.

A Propensity for Passivity

* People have a tendency to be lazy in their thinking. Thinking requires effort and it is much easier simply to accept common notions or opinions, or accept those of the people around you.

* To some extent we must all be lazy in our thinking sometimes, for the same reason as we need to sometimes physically rest: it is simply not possible to think about everything in depth any more than it is possible to be continually physically active. However many people are often lazy in their thinking about important things when they don't need to be. They are simply taking the easy way out. And some people are lazy in almost all their thinking. They have never gotten into the habit of genuinely thinking for themselves.

* Many people want a 'quiet life', and dislike anything that threatens or disturbs that. Hence a general prejudice against change or innovation. This, along with a desire for self-survival, leads to a willingness to accept great wrongs by the state or culture as a whole, and a willingness to go along with the crowd.

* Many people don't do what is most important; they do what is easiest.

* People feel more responsible for their actions than they do for their inactions, even when the outcomes are the same.

The Bumper Book of Common Sense

* People have a strong aversion to reading instructions. Long or complicated instructions or warnings are highly unlikely to be read.

* People often follow the path of least resistance, irrespective of whether it is right or wrong.

* In some circumstances when there is more than one person witnessing an event it can be less likely they will intervene or report it than if there is only one person, because they will each think it is someone else's responsibility to intervene or report it. This is sometimes known as the Bystander Effect.

Differences Between People

* People have different abilities and capabilities, partly as a result of their genetic make-up, and partly as a result of their life circumstances.

* There are different types of 'intelligence' that people have to differing degrees. There are different 'models' of how to name and define these different types of intelligence, with the following being a particular way of defining them:
    o Abstract Intelligence: the ability to reason in logical or mathematical terms;
    o Social Intelligence: the ability to interact effectively with other people;
    o Emotional Intelligence: our ability to be aware of and to manage our own emotions, and to be able to accurately sense the emotions of others;
    o Kinesthetic Intelligence: our ability to effectively manipulate our own body;
    o Aesthetic Intelligence: our ability to appreciate aesthetics such as music, art, and literature;
    o Practical Intelligence: our ability to see the world as it really is and cope with the challenges and opportunities of life.

* Intelligence as measured by IQ tests is a fairly narrow measure of thinking ability, and deals with only certain types of analytical thinking. IQ tests do not measure how well we can adapt to the environment or circumstances, our ability to make rationale real-life decisions, or general common sense and creativity. People with a high IQ are not necessarily any better at dealing with practical issues in the real world than people of lower IQ. People of high IQ are just as capable of believing absurd ideas, being dogmatic, failing to think through all options, or falling for scams as those of lower IQ. Many pseudo sciences were invented by and believed by people of high IQ intelligence. There are 20 times more astrologers in the United States than there are astronomers.

* People of higher IQ however do tend to be better at applying strategies, including good thinking strategies, once they have been shown how to apply them.

* People have different propensities with regards how they think with regards to:
    o The extent to which they collect information before making up their mind.
    o The extent to which they seek out various points of view before coming to a conclusion.
    o The extent to which they explicitly weigh up pluses and minuses before coming to a decision.
    o The extent to which they think extensively about a problem before responding.
    o The extent to which they think about whether or not their opinion is consistent with the available evidence.
    o The extent to which they think about possible consequences before taking action.

* People have different styles of thinking. There are different ways of grouping up people's thinking styles, and the following is just one example:

- o Clarifier: Are we solving the right problem? Methodical. Asks lots of questions. Gathers information. Looks at details. Can over analyze.
- o Ideator: Looks at the big picture. Produces ideas. Toys with different ideas. Intuitive. Conceptualist. May overlook details.
- o Developer: Tinkers and improves ideas. Generates workable solutions. Gets lost in a single idea. Perfectionist tendencies.
- o Implementor. Quick to action. Brings ideas to fruition. Decisive and determined. Can leap into action too quickly.
- o Integrators. Focus on collaboration.

* People have different personality types. There are various models for personality types. For example the Myers-Briggs types which measures people on scales of Extraversion – Introversion; Sensing – Intuition; Thinking – Feeling; Judging – Perceiving. Or those deriving from Transactional Analysis that identifies people's behavioral states and tendencies in terms of Parent, Adult, or Child. These can be very useful in helping us understand an individual's behavior and understand how best to interact with them, but the measures are at best gross simplifications and are not in any sense an absolute truth about a person. Moreover people can behave differently in different circumstances, and can change over time, particularly if they consciously set out to do so.

* People have different thresholds that control when they decide to act and seek to change something in their environment. To one person a room may be unacceptably untidy, whilst to another it is perfectly ok. This can be a source of considerable conflict in relationships where one person finds they are always doing the tidying because their threshold is significantly different to that of another person.

* Recognize that people are different. Some are open, honest, and simply trying to do the best they can. Some are deceitful and only interested in themselves. Most are somewhere in-between. It is important to recognize the differences in people, and to be able to judge which people are which to what extent in what circumstances.

Prejudice and Stereotyping

* Prejudices are assumptions about how people in a particular group or with particular characteristics behave, and it is the assumption that they all behave in the same way. Prejudices are almost always unfounded and negative. They are often deliberately encouraged by those with a vested interest in isolating those they are prejudiced against, but many others often go along with it, sometimes without realizing it.

* Some people form long term and deep rooted prejudices based upon brief impressions. For example, a particular experience with someone of a given nationality can give someone a deep rooted prejudice against anyone of that nationality.

* Prejudices readily form when times are difficult or when people feel they are being disadvantaged. The prejudices provide us with a potential route to improving our position by discriminating against those we are prejudiced against.

* Prejudice mixed with generalizations is a particularly unpleasant mix and underlies racial, sexual, and many other types of discrimination.

* People act out their prejudice in ways that vary from verbally expressing negative attitudes, through discrimination, to physical violence, through to extremes, which have been common in the past, of extermination and genocide. As prejudice takes hold it often starts to increase in intensity unless prevented in some way from doing so.

The Bumper Book of Common Sense

* Stereotyping, which leads to prejudice, enables us not to feel guilty about how we treat others. People who are prejudiced against a particular other group are sometimes capable of extreme cruelty without having any feelings of remorse.

* Prejudice is self-reinforcing. A prejudiced person selects facts that fit their preconceived opinions. Facts that contradict their prejudiced opinions are ignored. They thus accumulate lots of arguments and examples in favor of their prejudices, which are reinforced in a self-delusional manner.

* Prejudice means people concentrate their attention in a particular direction and ignore other directions that are, from a logical viewpoint, equally or more valid. This often makes the person blind to the application of logic and Common Sense. If the same prejudicial arguments where presented for something they felt neutral about they would readily see the illogicality in the argument.

* Prejudices are invariably based on ignorance. People are prejudiced against other groups of people because they see them as different. The more you get to know others the more you realize we are all largely the same, just conditioned by a different environment.

* Prejudice is often broken down when people have to work together with particular individuals to achieve a common goal. Everyone has good and bad points, strengths and weaknesses. Prejudice means we only see the bad and weak points. When we work with someone on something of mutual interest we come to also see their good and strong points and build up levels of mutual respect.

* We are more prejudiced than we realize. We may believe ourselves not to be prejudiced at all in a given way, and yet tests would quite likely show we have biases. This does not make us bad people. But we should try to keep an eye on potential biases and try to compensate for them through keeping focused on facts and reasoning and context and remembering that people are individuals.

* Instinct can be very prone to prejudice.

* What we see is dependent on who we are. We are more tuned in to seeing details of those similar to ourselves than those who are different. All foreigners looking alike is not prejudice, it is how our brains work. Thinking that all foreigners are alike is prejudice.

* We don't have the time to get to know everyone we come across. Stereotyping, based on some characteristic we can use to group people, provides us with a quick and often useful way of interacting with a large number of people. However it is also often misleading particularly when we need to interact more closely with particular individuals.

* A well-known psychological tendency is the halo effect where we take one characteristic of a person as a strong indicator of other characteristics. A common manifestation of this is that a person who is physically attractive is generally seen to be a good, happy, intelligent, and successful person, whilst someone who is unattractive is generally seen to be a bad or less competent person. Attractive people thus get the benefit of the doubt more often, and get more breaks in life than do unattractive people.

* People who are different from the majority stand out and we notice bad behavior on their part more than we notice on the part of the majority. Thus even when in general those in a minority group may be better behaved than those in the majority group they will still be perceived by many of those in the majority group as being worst behaved. This leads to or strengthens prejudices against minorities.

* Some common stereotyping that most of us are prone to:
    o Women wearing glasses are more intelligent than those that don't;
    o Men in suits and ties are more important than those without them;
    o People wearing bright clothes are friendly;
    o Taller people are more intelligent than shorter people;

- o People who talk slowly are less intelligent.

* Most fundamentalists are fundamentalists first and extreme believers in whatever their fundamentalism is about second. If they had been born in the place where opposing fundamentalists had been born they would have been believers in the other fundamentalism. Of course, the nature of their fundamentalism is such that they would never accept such an argument, despite the fact that it is blatantly so.

* Extremists see moderates as extremists.

What Motivates People

* People want to be noticed. They want to be appreciated. They want to feel that they matter to and are important to other people.

* People are far more motivated by the thought of losing something than they are by the thought of gaining something.

* Most people value fairness as a primary need. They are happier receiving less so long as it is a fair share, than more if they feel as though they didn't get their fair share.

* People's general state of happiness is influenced more by their state relative to their peers and those around them than is by their absolute state. Most people would be happier being poorer, if they were better off than most of those around them, than they would be being better off but worse off than those around them.

* All people are motivated to some extent by self-interest, some more so than others. However there is a big difference between those whose self-interests leads to them being willing to lie, deceive, and worse in order to get what they want, and those who look after their own interests but try to balance this with other people's interests when they can.

* The use of rewards to motivate can be counterproductive. Use of rewards can change someone's perception of the task being rewarded. If you reward someone for doing a task that they might have been self-motivated to do they will often lose the self-interest in the task and do it solely because of the reward, and if the reward is withdrawn lose interest in doing the task. Thus rewards can appear to work in the short term but be counterproductive in the long term.

* People are for most everyday activities best motivated through the simple pride of doing a good job, rather than through being rewarded or punished for how well they do the job.

The Influence of Status

* People will go to great lengths to protect or increase their status, and a sense of decreasing status can make people feel like their life is in danger. The desire to increase status or avoid reduction in status can drive people to incredible feats of endurance.

* Many of the arguments and conflicts at work and in life have status issues at their core.

* An increase in status is one of the world's greatest feelings; a decrease in status is one of life's worst.

* You can increase a person's feeling of status simply by noticing them and thanking them for what they have done.

The Bumper Book of Common Sense

* A feeling of high status helps people process more information, including more subtle ideas, with less effort, than a feeling of low status.

* People sometimes get into a mode in which their being 'right' is more important than almost anything else.

* When someone is trying to solve a problem, simply giving them your solution will often not be well received. They will often see it as a status threat, a potential acknowledgement that you are smarter than they are because you came up with a solution when they couldn't.

* People who think of themselves as superior or better than others tend not to adopt Common Sense approaches but merely look to impose their will. Clever people are particularly prone to jumping to conclusions very quickly; and whilst they may often be right, they won't always be.

* Powerful people are more likely to follow through on their thoughts, whether good or bad, than less powerful people. Most of us have bad thoughts as well as good, but rarely follow through on our bad thoughts. It is not so much that power corrupts, but that power leads to our bad thoughts being more likely to see the light of day.

* Power without accountability is a recipe for abuse.

* Politicians usually set out with good intent, and believe they are incorruptible. However once they experience power, or see the opportunity for power, as a means for getting things done, they justify small compromises in their morals as the means for achieving ends, and rapidly find themselves on a slippery slope.

Self-Interest or Vested-Interest Behavior

* People are hundreds of times more interested in themselves than they are in you.

* Common Sense is not the same as integrity. Self-preservation is sometimes best served by saying you agree with or doing something you disagree with. You might do this because you believe it is the best way to achieve what you believe is right in the long term, such as through working from within the system rather than trying to change it from without, or simply because you have more to lose than you are willing to risk.

* There are people who will take advantage. There are people who will deliberately lie and cheat and deceive. A very few people will do it frequently and at any opportunity. More will do it occasionally dependent upon particular circumstances and possibly dependent upon the mood they are in at the time.

* It is hard to be dispassionate when we have a vested interest.

* If you are looking for objective feedback on an important piece of work avoid friends and avoid people with a vested interest.

* Just because someone has a vested interest it doesn't mean they are necessarily distrustful, though they might be. The extent to which a person allows vested interests to affect their behavior and decisions is largely determined by the person rather than by the circumstances. If looking to determine whether a given person is allowing vested interests to affect them look to understand whether or not the person has a track record of being trustworthy and behaving with integrity.

* People often make decisions on behalf of others, such as an employing organization or a club. Some people will make such decisions on the basis of their own interests rather than in the interests of those they supposedly represent. The degree to which someone will do this will vary from person to person and from circumstance to circumstance.

* People are psychologically predisposed towards egocentric thinking and behavior. It is not necessarily conscious or deliberate.

* That people have a tendency to look after their self-interests is not in itself a bad thing. It is normal and healthy. However it is when those self-interests mean harming or taking advantage of others, when there are reasonable alternatives, that it becomes a bad thing.

Observations about People

* A person who is intelligent and wise in one area of life is not necessarily intelligent and wise in another.

* People have an innate desire to improve, to do quality work, to be curious, and to accomplish. What holds many people back is an expectation that others are responsible for creating the environment that would enable them to flourish.

* People always want more. Once we have achieved one thing we move on to wanting something else.

* Many people confuse their wants with their just dues. They want to be paid more, but don't ask themselves if the work they are doing and the effort they are putting in justifies them getting more. They thus work less when they feel they are not being paid as well as they think they should be, and thus justify why they are not being paid more; rather than working harder to justify why they should be paid more.

* Many people seem to believe they have rights without duties. The world however doesn't give something for nothing, and those that get something for nothing are reliant upon others who give more than they get.

* People tend to see themselves as more deserving of beneficial circumstances than others when those circumstances are in their favor, and more hard done by than others when circumstances are against them.

* People tend to see themselves as having played a greater part in joint decisions or actions than an impartial observer would have judged them to have played.

* People often think about what it is easy to think about rather than what needs or ought to be thought about. Which is why meetings with lots of people or without a pre-agenda keep going off at a tangent; different topics are easy for different people.

* People aren't perfect. They say the wrong things, they make mistakes, they forget things. Don't get upset about it. It is the way they are. You are like it as well.

* For the most part people are less extreme than they seem, whether they seem good or bad.

* People are resentful when unfairness goes unpunished.

* Those we term 'crazy' or 'insane' are people whose mental models differ very significantly from those of the rest of us. Not that the rest of us all have the same mental models. We don't; we all have our own unique models. However there is usually sufficient overlap for us to communicate and work together. This is not the case for those we consider 'crazy' or 'insane'.

* When people behave in ways we consider to be contrary to Common Sense, there may be specific physiological reasons, for example children's and teenager's brains go through developmental stages.

The Bumper Book of Common Sense

* People don't only pick up particular bad habits from others; they also pick up behaving badly in general. However it also works in reverse and we can pick up good behavior and good self-control from those we see as role models. Bringing them to mind helps us be a little more like them.

* The best predictor of what a person will do is what that person believes others are doing or will do.

* Once someone has made up their mind about something it is very difficult to get them to change it, because they will see any suggestion of potential change as an attack on their ego, and as an accusation that they have made a bad choice. For the same reason, once someone has started to use a given brand they will become very defensive towards that brand.

* People are capable of extreme cruelty if unfettered by law or the belief they are likely to get found out and punished.

* Most people tend to pay more attention to the negative than the positive. An insult or criticism plays more on their mind than a complement or praise.

* When someone criticizes another it usually says more about the person doing the criticizing than it does about the person being criticized.

* Most people, regardless of how they might appear, are as filled with self-doubt as are you; particularly just before the dawn.

* The number one fear of most people is rejection, and the number one need is acceptance.

* Most people feel threatened by feedback; see it as criticism. Most feedback conversations revolve around people defending themselves rather than looking for ways to improve.

* People like people who are similar to themselves, and will tend to spend more time with them.

* People who are abusive, arrogant or act in a demeaning manner towards others lack self-esteem. They put others down because it makes them feel better about themselves.

* Much of people's behavior can be traced to them looking to protect their ego. People, for the most part, want to feel good about themselves, and for various reasons are often unable to do so in the circumstances they find themselves. They thus subconsciously adopt tactics which either dulls the pain of not feeling good about themselves or provides a way that makes excuses for them not feeling good: they take drugs or alcohol; or they take out their frustrations on other people, particularly those physical weaker than themselves.

* People can change their moods very suddenly: in particular when they 'lose their temper'. Frequently the thing that makes them lose their temper is in itself some minor incident, however it will have built upon a number of other incidents such that some threshold is passed.

* People who are under significant stress are more likely to act and think in impulsive and instinctive ways, even though their impulses and instincts will be more prejudiced and short term focused than if they were not so highly stressed.

* Just because man is a rationale creature this does not mean men always, or even usually, act in a rationale manner.

* Just because someone doesn't say they disagree with something this doesn't mean they don't. Just because people don't complain doesn't mean they don't have just cause for complaint.

* Just because someone is assertive or aggressive it doesn't mean they are right. Assertiveness or aggressiveness is often mistaken for strength of knowledge or the voice of authority; and modesty and tolerance attributed to weakness or ignorance. People can and often do express strong feelings

about something they know little about, or are simply wrong about. Thus the adage: 'it's the empty can that makes the most noise'.

* People are not right just because they say they are, or just because they believe strongly that they are. Do not be intimidated by people with strong beliefs, or who are insistent that they are right.

* People who lack self-awareness lack the ability to program themselves and are therefore relatively easily programmed by others. This in part is why authoritarian regimes come down so hard on intellectuals, because it is intellectuals who are most self-aware and most aware of the nefarious programming of the regime, and thus the greatest challenge through infecting others with this realization.

How you Potentially Appear to Others

* Be aware that you may not appear to others the way you think you appear, and others may not actually be the way they appear to you. For example: you consider yourself logical, others may see you as unfeeling; you see yourself as decisive, others may see you as obstinate, inflexible, or over hasty; you see yourself as caring, others may see you as a busybody or intrusive; you see yourself as organized, others may see you as bureaucratic; you see yourself as flexible, others may see you as indecisive; you see yourself as cooperative, others may see you as conspiring.

* People judge others based on appearances because it is all they have to go on. Accept this as a fact and thus dress in a way appropriate to whatever impression you wish to make. When people know you better then your appearance will matter much less, but until then.

* People will react to our looks and demeanor, particularly when they first meet us or don't know us very well.

* People assume we have the same personality traits as our friends.

* We have a natural instinct to treat strangers as foes until such time as we have had reason to treat them as friends. Thus the importance of icebreakers at workshops and establishing a rapport when meeting new people.

* Be aware of your own behavior and its potential effect on others. Do you have a tendency to be negative or to put others down, without meaning to? Do you find yourself frequently in conflict with certain people? Do you find certain things trigger a strong emotional reaction in you? If people react to you in a negative manner then try to be more aware of your own behavioral traits, and seek to modify them.

* If you are unreasonable, then don't be surprised if others lie to you, or mislead you. Examples of being unreasonable include: not listening to people's genuine concerns; asking people to do things which are unreasonable or not realistically feasible; punishing or criticizing people for things which were out of their control and which they could not reasonably have done anything about; being inconsistent, and wanting one thing at one time and another thing at another; not giving credit where credit is due.

How We See the World and Others

* We believe others are far more aware of us than they are. When we make a mistake we think everyone notices, but usually they don't, or if they do they quickly forget about it. In truth most people spend the vast majority of their time thinking about themselves, and the tiny fraction of the time they spend thinking about us is shared with all the other people they come into contact with.

The Bumper Book of Common Sense

* The way we see others is often dependent upon our own emotions at the time. When we are feeling down we will see people as being very different to how we see them when we are in a good mood.

* We are selective about what we notice. We cannot deal with the vast amount of sensory input in terms of paying attention to it all, so our brain filters it dependent upon what is of interest to us or what represents a potential threat.

* By being selective about what evidence we focus on or ignore, we can convince ourselves of the truth of almost any hypothesis.

* The way we see the world is largely a self-fulfilling prophecy. Once we start to see the world in a particular way we find many examples that seem to confirm that particular way of thinking.

* We tend to see people not as they are, but as we are. A thief thinks everyone steals, or at least would do if they had the chance. Freudians see everything in terms of sex and phallic symbols. An accountant may see everything in terms of finance and money. Revolutionaries may see everything in terms of a struggle with government and with accepted ways of doing things. Someone who is disabled will see a very different world to that of those who are not disabled.

* Do not assume everyone's actions derive from rational decisions based on clear goals.

* Because we see the world in a particular way does not mean this is some underlying truth about the way the world is.

* People have a tendency to believe that the way they do things is best. Very often they are mistaken, but it is only by coming up against people who do things differently that they get the chance to question and possibly improve – assuming of course they are sufficiently open minded. Whilst we may feel comfortable with people similar to ourselves, we improve and grow when we mix with people who are different to us.

* If you want to understand someone you need to see things from their perspective, you need to become them, at least for a while.

* Be wary of assuming others think as you do, and thus that they would behave the way you would in similar circumstances.

* We typically project our own viewpoint into the minds of others and presume they can see the same things that are obvious to us. A simple illustration of this is tapping out a popular tune with your fingers. Most people in doing this will believe that it will be obvious to others what is being tapped out, whereas it rarely is to the listener.

* Be wary of believing you know what other people are thinking. Sometimes you might be right, but often you will be wrong.

* The way people describe others often tells us more about them than the people about whom they are talking. Someone who sees everyone else as out for what they can get is somebody who is out for what they can get.

* We have a tendency to see people who are the victims of misfortune or adversity as having done something to deserve it. This is a result of us wanting to believe that such things won't happen to us; which we can if we can think in terms of our not doing things that would put us into such circumstances. This can lead to us blaming the victim of a crime – 'they were asking for it' – rather than focusing all our blame on the perpetrator, and can lead on to discrimination and bullying. Don't allow yourself to be drawn into this way of thinking.

* People will appear to you the way you believe them to be.

* There is a natural tendency to dislike someone who brings us bad news, even though we know that person was not to blame. On the other hand we are positively disposed to those who bring us good news.

* Be wary of making judgments about what other people think. If necessary ask them and seek clarifications.

* Be wary when looking for explanations for an individual's behavior. There is a frequent tendency to identify some particular event from someone's past and say it is to blame. However this is usually rationalization. There are probably many others who had similar events in their past but who did not then go on to exhibit that behavior.

* Cognitive dissonance is the uncomfortable psychological state or feeling of anxiety that occurs when we experience two incompatible beliefs or thoughts. We then have a very strong tendency to resolve the conflict by rationalizing or altering our view of one or both of the beliefs. Thus we might seek to attribute motives to people to 'explain' why they might have done what they did. For example we might judge someone who rejected one of our ideas as having some ulterior motive for doing so, thus protecting in our minds the belief that our idea was really very good. Or if someone we know and like did something despicable then it must have been someone else's fault. Or that our cheating in an exam is really the fault of the teacher for not having prevented us from doing so, since everyone else would have done the same if they had had the chance.

* If you have bad thoughts about someone and then something bad happens to that person, don't blame yourself. You cannot bring about changes in the physical world through thought alone. It is not your fault.

How You Should Treat and Interact with Others

Treat Others as Equals

* Treat people well. Treat them the way you yourself would like to be treated. Do this even if they don't treat you well.

* All men and women are born equal, even though they don't all have the same capabilities or opportunities. Other people have as much right as you do to exist, and have a right to respect.

* Avoid arrogance or thinking that you are better or more deserving than other people. Just because you are more highly skilled or an expert in certain topics this does not make you better than people with less skill or expertise. And always remember all others have some skills and abilities that you don't, and that even in your own areas of expertise you are not all knowing.

* Try to see things from other people's perspective.

* Show respect for other people's opinions. Never tell them they are wrong. You can tell them you disagree with them, and why you disagree, but avoid the arrogance of telling they are wrong.

* Seek out other people's experiences. You learn much from experience, and you can learn much from other people's experiences if you listen to them. Of course you don't need to take everything at face value, and you can be skeptical of more extreme claims or claims you might have reason to doubt. But for the most part other people are open and honest about their experiences and you can empathize with them and add them to the wealth of your own experiences, albeit recognizing the potential for some bias as they see things through the filter of their own viewpoint.

The Bumper Book of Common Sense

* Be mindful of wanting or expecting others to do things your way, and getting upset when they don't. It shows a basic lack of respect for others. They have their views just as you have yours. You need to respect that and come to some agreement with them, not get upset because you are not getting your way.

* Treating people as equals means being open and honest with them, unless you have a particular reason for not being so, such as a reasonable belief they will seek to take advantage of you. It should be rare however for you not to be open and honest with others.

* Treating others as equals means you keep your commitments to them, or if you can't you apologize and let them know in advance. This includes arriving on time for meetings with them.

* Treating others as equals means remembering their name once you have been introduced to them.

* When you are talking with someone else then show them some respect by paying attention to them, and being responsive to them. Don't spend the time you are with someone else wishing you weren't there or thinking about other things.

* Respect other people's personal space, and local social etiquette. Otherwise you are likely to find other people getting on your nerves and you are certainly very likely to be getting on other people's nerves.

* Treating others as equals means respecting the cultural norms of those around you. By all means push the boundaries a little, but go out of your way to try and avoid offending others, unless you have a very clear moral point you wish to make and are willing to accept the consequences.

* Be wary of ethnocentricity, the belief that our culture is superior to others. When we think this way we also think we are superior to those from other cultures, and see this as justification for any discriminatory action we may take.

* In most societies, though not all, there is such a thing as freedom of speech. However if you insist on loudly exercising it in a way, right or wrong, that offends others, don't expect them to like you and don't be surprised if they react. You are not 'in the right'. You are merely being insensitive. In most circumstances you can stand up for what you believe in without openly offending others.

* Don't play one-upmanship. Avoid trying to better someone's story to you, though by all means relate similar incidents.

* The law is society's way at seeking a balance between the needs of the many and the needs of the few. When we deliberately flout the law we are putting our own interests before the needs of the many, and saying we should have more rights than others. Whilst we doubtless find ways of justifying this to ourselves, it is nevertheless a selfish act. If we believe the law is wrong we should seek to get it changed, not simply flout it.

Recognize and Respect Differences

* There is worth in everyone you meet. You may or may not immediately jell with everyone you meet, but remember they are human beings with the same rights as you, and probably many of the same concerns and fears and hopes. Seek to instinctively like and respect everyone you meet and see any characteristics you find annoying as simply who they are, and not something to be judged.

* We should be wary of assuming others should think and act like we do. The way people think and act is to a great extent conditioned by their particular circumstances both in general cultural terms and in particular individual terms. We are conditioned by our culture and particular circumstances, and others are conditioned by theirs. If we had been brought up in their circumstances we would likely think and act more like they do than like we do.

* We should be sensitive to the possibility of others seeing the world differently to the way we do, and recognize that our differences with them may be due to this different way of interpreting the world.

* Most interpersonal relationship problems arise from one person having expectations of the other. Usually we apply our own standards and expect others to behave to them. However whilst clearly there are reasonable expectations at the extreme, we should be tolerant of others having different standards to our own. After all we would think it unreasonable for other people to expect us to confirm to their standards.

* Be tolerant of differences, and have respect for honest alternative viewpoints. People, within reason, are as entitled to their opinions as we are to ours.

* Welcome people with different views. Seeking out common ground with them will often give you different perspectives and lead to you developing and gaining a deeper understanding of your own views.

* Some people have behaviors they can't help. People with autism, and there are milder forms of autism that might not be readily obvious, behave as they do because of how their brain is wired. Rather than be upset, you can usually find an effective way of interaction with them if you make the effort.

* The fact that others are different to us, including the fact that they are better than us at certain things, is to be embraced not begrudged. You have more to gain by working with someone who is better than you in some way relevant to the given task, than you do by working with people who are worse than you.

* When you are in conflict with someone, or have a difference of opinion, you have the opportunity to improve your own views. We learn far more from listening to those whose opinions differ to our own than we do from those who simply agree with us.

* Deal with people as you find them; don't be angry or frustrated that they are not as you would like them to be.

* Other people will usually perceive their own interests differently to the way you perceive them. They may also perceive your interests different to the way you perceive them.

* Be wary of stereotyping, based on some particular characteristic someone has, or the way they dress. Whilst it provides a quick way of deciding how to react to someone, stereotyping is a sloppy and ineffective way of reacting to individuals, and is usually based on prejudices. There is far greater variation in individuals within a group than there is commonality. Failing to recognize this will lead to poor interactions with others.

* Be wary of your perception when judging people. For example, one man's disorder is another man's order. A cluttered desk may seem disordered to a casual observer but the user of the desk may know exactly where everything is, and may be more effective at finding things than someone else with everything neatly tucked away in cabinets. Of course, a cluttered desk could be a cluttered mind, and the person may be hopeless at finding anything. The point is, it is not the appearance of the cluttered desk that necessarily tells you the way the person is.

* Don't begrudge differences between yourself and certain others. If someone is better than you in certain ways, accept it, and work with it, but don't be jealous. We all have different abilities and capabilities. If you believe you can be as good as or better than the someone else then embark on a program of self-development.

* Look to understand the background of others and how it might be a factor in the way they are and the viewpoints and attitudes they have. This includes your own family, relations, and friends.

The Bumper Book of Common Sense

* People behave the way they do because of their particular circumstances and background and beliefs. They don't behave the way they do because they are evil people or because they are out to get you. Remember this and you are more likely to be tolerant of people behaving differently to the way you believe they should.

* There is a point of reasonableness with respect to respecting other people's point of view and rights to free speech and action. Whilst we should err on the side of tolerance, it is right that law should prevent the preaching of hate and violence and discrimination. Whilst there are sometimes excessively authoritarian and oppressive regimes, where there is some justification for unlawful activities, the vast majority of societies are democratic countries in which the rule of law should be respected, even though we may not agree with all of it. In such societies, those who believe it is right to kill in the name of their own particular beliefs should be prevented from either doing so or from encouraging others to do so.

Be Positive Towards Others

* Be friendly towards others, those you know, and strangers. Say thank you regularly. Hold open doors for people. Pick things up for them. Smile when you catch someone's eye. Be friendly at any excuse.

* Show gratitude for what others are doing or trying to do for you, even if it is not perfect. Thank people, and praise people, whenever you have a genuine opportunity to do so. Thank anyone who helps you.

* You are not perfect, and other people are not perfect. Forgive yourself and forgive others for mistakes, though look to see how you can lessen the likelihood of them being made again.

* We get better results in dealing with people and situations if we approach them with a positive co-operative spirit rather than with an antagonistic spirit. However we often let a fear of someone taking advantage of us override our openness and keep us on our guard.

* Have and show respect for anyone and everyone. When you are with them give them your full attention.

* Praise people whenever you have an opportunity to do so. Acknowledge good work, and acknowledge people making an effort.

* Enhance other people's self-esteem. One way of doing this is to respond positively every time they use the word 'I'; respond either verbally ('well done'), or non-verbally through a smile or nod of the head.

* Life is short. There is too little time to hold bitter thoughts in your heart and your mind.

* Our life, or those of people we know, could end at almost any moment. Be thoughtful about how you speak or act with others because you may not get the chance to correct that which you regret.

* People are often unreasonable and self-centered. Forgive them anyway. If you are kind, people may accuse you of ulterior motives. Be kind anyway. If you are honest, people may cheat you. Be honest anyway. If you find happiness, people may be jealous. Be happy anyway. The good you do today may be forgotten tomorrow. Do good anyway. Give the world the best you have, and it may never be enough. Give your best anyway. (Mother Teresa)

* Think kindly of others and you will feel much better than you would otherwise have done.

* Overcome hate by love, anger by calm, greed by generosity. Be positive in response to negativity.

* Forgiveness is strongly linked with happiness. Those that can forgive others are generally much happier than those who hold on to their resentment.

* Forgive people and accept them as they are. Let go of any resentment or anger towards them. You will feel much better.

* Don't wait for an apology before you forgive someone. The only person you are hurting when you allow yourself to get upset by someone else's behavior, actions or words is yourself. People rarely realize how upset they have made you feel, and they didn't really mean it. So forgive them unconditionally. You'll feel much better for it.

* If you bear a grudge against someone the only person you are harming is yourself. Let grudges go.

* Be kind and courteous, though not gullible, irrespective of whether or not your kindness and courtesy is returned.

* Good manners and civility cost nothing. Say please and thank you. Hold open doors. Don't go barging into people as you pass them. Let people speak without interruption.

* Show appreciation for those in whose company you are. A kind word can make someone's day.

* When you talk or gossip about other people, the listeners transfer the characteristics you use to describe other people onto you. If you talk about how incompetent someone is, the listener applies that incompetence to you. Thus it is much better to talk about others in a positive manner.

* If others beat you in a competition or game do not feel bad about it. Congratulate them and feel genuinely happy for them. Be happy that there are other people with the same interests as you, and who possibly feel as passionately about those interests as you do. If they are better than you then you get better as a result of playing or competing against them, and so you should be grateful to them.

* Value the people you meet, and they will be positively disposed towards you, and all sorts of opportunities and interesting experiences will result.

* You will be happier if you think positively about others, are willing to help without reward, and feel good about being in their presence.

* Your expectation of how someone is, often becomes a self-fulfilling prophecy as you behave towards them in accordance with your expectation and they respond in kind.

* Criticizing or shaming people as a result of their lack of self-control will sometimes just further weaken their self-control. Better to focus on anything positive and encourage them.

* The way we think about others is a choice we make, not something that is imposed on us. We can see people as largely self-interested and selfish if we choose to do so, or we can see them as human beings just trying to make their way in the world if we choose to do so.

* The way we see others is more a reflection of how we are than of how they are.

* See the best in others at every opportunity.

* Look to treat people not as they are but as they are striving to be; most people are striving to be a better person. People act as they are expected to act, and they become what you treat them as being. As such they are capable of far worse or far better than we might suppose.

* Don't get annoyed at other people for doing what it is they are doing, such as taking a long time in the queue in front of you. Feel a connection to them as fellow members of the human race.

The Bumper Book of Common Sense

* Be careful what negative or cruel things you say to people. You will not be able to unsay them. If negative thoughts pop into your head, keep them to yourself and don't dwell on them.

* Given that people in general focus more on the negative than the positive, you need to be seeking to have a lot more positive interactions with people than negative ones. Thus, ensure you give far more praise than you do criticism.

* Many interactions can be viewed as a bid by one person seeking a response from the other. The response could be a turning towards the other person, which acknowledges the bid and offers a response that takes the interaction forward in a positive way, or the response could be a turning away in a hostile way which is leading towards conflict or disengagement. Seek to ensure your responses to others are positive rather than negative.

* Respond enthusiastically to any good news that someone shares with you.

* Help others to look good in front of others.

* Build bridges, not walls.

* Be good to other people and your life will be worthwhile.

Helping Others

* Be ever friendly and ready to help others. Any excuse to help someone should be taken. Always be looking for ways to help others.

* Take any opportunity you can to do good; you may not get another.

* Do not begrudge your own generosity. There is a lot of truth with regards one's own piece of mind and feeling of self-worth in the adage 'It is better to give than to receive.'

* Favors have their strongest effect when they occur between people who don't know each other very well and when they are small but thoughtful.

* If you give something to someone, you must give them the opportunity to repay you if they try to do so.

* Do some things out of pure altruism. Do something for someone else without any expectation of reward or return of favor or even of recognition. Preferably do it without them even knowing. You will feel better. But be careful you are not giving charity to someone who will actually feel hurt or embarrassed by it or who will become resentful.

* Try to do something altruistic every day, something that helps someone else. Indulge in acts of kindness without any thought for reward.

* You will do more for someone by helping them improve with regards some everyday activity than by doing them some great service just once.

* Help other people get what they want. Help other people to be self-motivated. Point out their strengths and help them exploit them.

* There is good in everyone. Help them to find it.

* To help people solve problems hold back from simply giving them your solution, no matter how good or obvious you think it is. Help them think about the problem for themselves by asking them

leading questions, possibly offering up alternatives, in a way that enables them to come to their own conclusion.

* For many people, what you see as positive statements or actions can be taken as put-downs. For example, you try to help someone and they see it as you thinking they can't cope. You suggest a solution to a problem and they see it as you thinking them too stupid to find their own. In most circumstances rather than impose yourself or your ideas, better to explore whether that is what they actually want. Try to get to a position where they ask for your help.

* Life can always be made meaningful through finding a way to help others; altruism is one of the best ways to boost your happiness. You can help others in terms of the moment, or help others longer term. Helping others to achieve their goals can be particularly satisfying.

* If someone is in trouble in a public place it is not uncommon for no-one to help. This is not due to the low morale standards of people today, but due to the psychology of the situation whereby everyone fears embarrassment should the help not really be needed, and everyone is waiting for someone else to step in and show them that the help really is needed. In such circumstances you should be the first to step in to help. Once you do, others will readily also step in. Better to risk a momentary embarrassment than a life time of regret at having not helped.

Be Honest and Fair in Your Dealings with Others

* When interacting with others, respond to the specifics of the circumstances rather than to your attitude towards the person.

* Better to say No to doing something, and then change your mind, than say Yes and then change your mind. If you are unsure, say No. Don't leave people thinking you will or you might if you won't.

* There is a time and a place for frankness. Being frank when someone is not in the mindset to listen will create bad feeling regardless of the truth of the matter.

* Don't spare a person's feelings only for them to be devastated later. It is often unnecessary to be brutally honest, but within reason it is usually best to be honest.

* Encouraging high self-esteem in others gives them confidence to do things they might not otherwise have done, and also means they will feel good about themselves. However it does not increase their ability. Indeed undeserved self-esteem often has a negative effect through encouraging arrogance, conceit, a belief in personal superiority, and an expectation for reward without making much effort.

* Do unto others, as you would have them do unto you. Would you be happy if other people did to you the thing you want to do or are doing to them? Would you be embarrassed if the way you are treating someone else was common knowledge?

* Most people know someone else they 'trust' with a secret, including the person you pass a secret on to. If you want to be trusted with secrets, don't pass them on to anyone.

* Be wary when passing on a secret that has been told you. You become beholden to the person to whom you have passed on the secret.

* Don't steal other people's successes. Give credit where it is due. If you build upon someone else's work then openly acknowledge it. By giving praise to those who have helped you, whether they did so deliberately or not, you will find people are more likely to help you in the future and you will also gain general respect.

The Bumper Book of Common Sense

Give People the Benefit of the Doubt, but Don't Let Them Take Advantage of You

* Think positively of others, and give them the benefit of the doubt unless you have a reason to do otherwise. Assume that they are acting in what is to them a rationale manner, that they are moral, and that they are well meaning.

* If you don't understand why someone is behaving the way they are, don't be too quick to attribute it to some negative personality trait. It may well be due to some particular information or circumstance you are not aware of. If you were aware of it, you may well see their behavior as perfectly normal.

* If you see error in others, the error may be in your own misconception.

* When others don't perform we tend to put it down to being a character flaw. When we don't perform we put it down to circumstances. If people don't perform be sure you give them the opportunity to explain why not.

* When we see someone consistently being what we perceive to be incompetent, and assuming our perception is reasonable, then keep in mind that it is not because that person is incompetent as a person; it is merely that they are doing something to which they are not best suited. That same person is likely to be very good at doing something else.

* Never attribute to malice that which can be explained by ignorance or incompetence.

* People often attribute malicious behavior where it is not due and see conspiracies where there are none. Incompetence or chance happenings, accidents, mistakes, misunderstandings, or con-incidents are usually a far more likely explanation of events than is conspiracy.

* Be wary of pigeon-holing people based on some particular incident. We may have one particular experience with them and then see them as being the same as someone else we know, and immediately judge them and treat them as such. People are invariably more complex than that, and just because they seemingly share some characteristic or behavior trait with someone else does not mean they share others.

* Do not be too quick to judge others. We may not know the specific circumstances that underlies their particular behavior or actions.

* Don't be jealous of others or the things they have. You don't know what burdens they are also carrying. Don't begrudge another's good fortune. You do not know what misfortune they have had to bear.

* Speak well of others, even if you do not think well of them. Dwell on people's good points rather than on their faults. Speak of the little good you see in others rather than of the abundant bad.

* It is unfair to judge someone who has done an evil without being sure that they had a realistic alternative that was less evil.

* Be quick to forgive others; though don't let them take willful advantage of your willingness to forgive. If you are able to forgive someone you will release a lot of negative feelings that will be eating away at you, and you will feel healthier and stronger.

* It can be a fine line between being gullible and being distrustful. Always be on the lookout for being one or the other with respect to a given issue. On balance it is usually best to err on the side of being trustful, and thus risk being gullible.

* Steer a course between gullibility and cynicism. Don't accept everything at face value, and don't look for diabolical motives in everything.

* Some ways of helping to determine whether people are basically looking to be fair or looking to take personal advantage include:
    o Your past dealings with them;
    o Other peoples view, particular the views of those you respect;
    o More generally their reputation, assuming they have one;
    o The way they talk about other people and situations. Do they talk in competitive terms, of winning and losing? If they do they are likely to be competitive themselves and concerned with winning;
    o Your own instincts, probably based on body language. Though remember that these can mislead.

* If someone's behavior is irritating you, think about the good things in your life, to put yourself in a generous frame of mind. Then tell yourself there may be something going on in the other person's world that might warrant their behavior: they might be having a lot of worries, or had some bad news, or generally just be having a bad day.

* Accept that people's behavior and attitudes can change. Do not assume that because someone was once a particular way that they necessarily still are. In particular a lot of people are pro-active in improving themselves, which includes their behavior, and many are successful at doing so.

* People often judge an accused criminal on the severity of the crime rather than on the strength of the evidence. But you can't apologize to a dead man and many an innocent man has been hanged. Err on the side of letting the guilty walk free rather than the innocent be condemned, but this should not be too hard over.

Co-operation, Competition, and Conflict

* Cooperation is generally more useful to us as individuals than competition. We achieve great things when working together in teams so long as we are all going in the same direction. That this has been so through our evolutionary past is exhibited through our strong tribal and group instincts.

* Most people believe in fairness and do not like being taken advantage of. Whilst people might in certain circumstances behave in a highly co-operative and fair manner, if one or more people start to exploit the situation and take advantage, many others will often also start to do so just to avoid being taken advantage of. Greed can thus become contagious not because people are inherently greedy but because people believe in fairness. It is appropriate that those who take advantage of others are exposed and castigated for doing so, otherwise such behavior will gradually become widespread to the disadvantage of the majority.

* Competitive games between unequal players merely cause frustration and is of little positive gain to either player. Better to turn them into co-operative games where you are trying to succeed together. Eg: rather than playing against each other in badminton or table tennis, try to go for long rallies.

* Co-operation allows far more to be achieved than conflict, and is more likely to lead to long term survival. A lot can be achieved through sustained cooperation.

* To achieve great success you need to involve others, and create a group of people who will help you.

* We are, whether we like it or not, dependent upon others. If we truly tried to go it alone we would live a miserable existence.

The Bumper Book of Common Sense

* Game Theory is a branch of mathematics that relates to working out optimal strategies in circumstances where people could either betray each other or co-operate in order to 'win'. Whilst in one off situations there are benefits in betraying, in circumstances where there are repeated plays the optimal tactical is generally one of tit for tat. This is a strategy that is basically one of initially acting in cooperation, and subsequently responding in like to the last action of your opponent. This results in an approach close to maximum benefit whereby we gain the advantage of long-term cooperation with those who are willing to cooperate whilst not allowing ourselves to be significantly exploited by those looking to take advantage.

* Whilst there may appear to be benefit in taking advantage of the people we are only likely to meet once, in practice it is rarely so simple. We may, for example, unexpectedly come across someone we have taken advantage of, and they may remember. Or we may get a reputation for being untrustworthy, such that people become very wary of working with us. Or we may make an enemy who goes out of their way to get revenge. Or we may meet people like ourselves and hurt each other significantly. Or we may find ourselves behaving in an instinctive selfish manner even when with people we interact with regularly. Being someone who is continually trying to take advantage of others can be very stressful, and people like that often have more health problems and often die younger.

* A cooperative car driver is someone who is willing to let others out and pass where it appears sensible, and a non-cooperative car driver is someone looking to take advantage of every opportunity without giving way himself or herself. The non-cooperative driver will succeed frequently in getting past cooperative drivers, saving themselves a few seconds or possibly minutes on their journey. However every now and again such a driver will come across someone similar to themselves, and the two of them will engage in some quite aggressive and dangerous maneuvers which are far more likely to lead to an accident. Are those few moments really worth it?

* The statement 'one person can't make a difference' is frequently heard as an excuse for not behaving responsibly. But all the time each individual believes this then things will continue to get steadily worse. Our apathy or selfishness at the individual level leads to what can only be described as insanity at the group level, where the combined actions of individual behaviors leads to slow death at the group level. Thus the need for governments to enforce certain behavior or curtail certain freedoms, and also the sometimes need for social pressure on individuals. With respect to the later however we must be wary of the potential fine line between those who do not do their fair share and those who simply do not conform.

* Some degree of competition does potentially spur innovation. During the post war period, for example, the capitalist West was far more innovative than the centralized East. There is also significant evidence that the Greek heyday, and also the rapid developments in the Western world in the 17th, 18th and 19th centuries, were significantly facilitated by the fact that there was significant competition between the Greek City States and between the different countries and states in Europe. Though one wonders whether true cooperation between those involved might not have led to even greater things.

* Do not fear or avoid competition. Competition pushes us not only to do our best, but also to keep improving. Without it we often lack the stimulus to keep getting better.

* Cutthroat competition can sometimes be bad for all parties concerned. Ways out of cut throat competition where both parties can only see themselves winning through the other side losing, include seeking to increase the overall size of the market so both sides can win relative to their starting positions; or increasing specialization and differentiation so both sides can win but in slightly different markets.

* A situation where cooperation can be of significant benefit is where organizations work with suppliers to get overall costs down in a mutually beneficial manner rather than trying to get as much from each other as possible. There is also a lot of evidence that children develop best not in a competitive environment but in a secure and stimulating environment where they can experiment through play. Human evolution may itself have advanced quickest when the environment was relatively safe allowing for safe experimentation. The commonly held view of nature being 'red in tooth and claw', and being a highly competitive environment in which only the strong survive, is far

too simplistic, and is certainly misleading when it comes to humans with their high degree of self-awareness.

* In general terms we should look to avoid conflict. However in doing so we can sometimes make matters worse, if underlying tensions are allowed to fester, or if one party sees the desire on the part of the other party to avoid conflict as being a sign of weakness. By seeking to understand the root causes of the conflict, rather than simply trying to ignore it, we may well arrive at not only a mutually agreeable position, but also a position that may be of greater benefit than had the conflict not arisen in the first place.

* When faced with conflict we can adopt one of the following styles:
    o Avoidance (lose-lose): behaving as though the conflict doesn't exist. Eg. Doing nothing, changing the subject, avoiding the person, saying you'll do something but not getting around to it. The problem doesn't get solved. We can lose our credibility. There are occasions however when we may need to use it, such as when the other party has more power and will impose on us an unwanted resolution, or the risks involved are too great, or no resolution is possible, or you genuinely believe it will blow over.
    o Competition (win-lose).
    o Compromise (no win – no lose), such as splitting the difference. Sometimes compromise is necessary but it is used more often than it should or needs to be. It is better to seek win-win rather that no lose – no lose. Holds us back from getting the best deal. It may however be appropriate if we've tried for a win-win but been unable to achieve it.
    o Accommodation (lose – win)
    o Collaboration (win-win)

    Different styles may be appropriate in different circumstances, and if one style fails we can fall back on another.

* Conflict can give rise to opportunities. In understanding the root cause of a conflict, or in looking how to resolve it, we often find better ways of doing things, which we may well never have identified had the conflict not occurred. And people who have worked together to successfully resolve a conflict will often come out of it with more mutual respect that can be drawn upon to benefit in the future.

* Where circumstances can be seen to be giving rise to conflict then it is sometimes best to get this out in the open and tackle it. In doing so either the conflict might be resolved or at least become less severe than if might have if left ignored.

* In most conflicts you should be looking to resolve them with a win-win, rather than merely looking for some compromise, or seeking a win-lose outcome. 4 principles for win-win are:
    o Separate people from the problem.
    o Focus on interests not positions. Ie. the reason behind the positions being taken. Seek to understand why are we and they taking a given position, rather than just defending and bargaining with our positions.
    o Generate options for mutual gain. Look for lots of options, not just one or two. Work together to generate them using brainstorming techniques.
    o Base choices on objective criteria, that are agreed in advance and reflect both sides interests.

* In seeking a win-win, look to identify shared goals, and treat the conflict as a shared problem or challenge you can work on together to find solutions. In doing so note that the conflict arises not necessarily because of differences, but rather because of the perception of differences. When you dig a bit deeper into the reasons for the perceived differences you usually find a lot of commonality that can be built upon.

* Different viewpoints can be seen as analogous to looking at an entity from different angles and from different distances away. The entity can look very different from different viewpoints, just as

a conflict can look very different from the different viewpoints of the different parties. It is not that one viewpoint is right and the other wrong: they are just different. And if you can both see from the viewpoint of the other you can work together to mutual benefit.

* Much conflict arises from what is termed the fundamental attribution error: what I do is dictated by circumstances, what you do is determined by who you are. Thus we tripped because some fool had left an obstacle in the way, you tripped because you are clumsy.

* In violent conflicts each side sees itself as being the injured party, and thus entitled to retaliate. And of course both sides are the injured party, just as both sides are the cause of injury. However the pain inflicted on us is far more intense than any pain we may inflict on another, and thus we see ourselves as justified in whatever response we make, even when it is a significant escalation.

* When setting up a meeting with someone in order try to resolve a conflict ensure you contact them face to face or over the phone. Refer to the conflict as a problem to be addressed, and the desire to find a solution in both parties' interests. Ask them when would be best. Ensure you come prepared to the meeting, ready to explain your point of view and ready to listen to the other parties' views, feelings, and suggestions. Thank them for being there. State the purpose and what the issue is. Ask how they would like to proceed. If the other party tries to hijack the agenda, agree to talk about their issues after you've discussed why you are here – or meet some other time. Be wary of cycling round issues. Keep focused on where you are trying to get to and moving towards that. Steer the conversation towards something you can agree on.

* When looking to resolve a conflict recognize that there are multiple aspects of what each party wants, their goals, which need to be taken into account. There is what might be termed the topic goal, whatever it is the conflict is most obviously about. In addition however there are relational goals, relating to how the parties want to be treated, and there is what is termed the identify goal, which is how the parties wish to be perceived by each other. Failure to take account of relational and identify goals can prohibit coming to satisfactory resolution of the topic goal.

* Explicitly articulate to yourself what your goals are regarding the topic and relationships. If they are in conflict, which is most important? How do you want to be treated? How do you want the other person to perceive you? What are you identify goals and how do they conflict with the other goals? The clearer you can be about your goals the better armed you are for managing the conflict. It makes it easier to identify where you can give way in letting the other person better achieve their goals.

* What do you know about the other party's goals – topic, relational, identity?

* The more equal the conflicting parties are in power, the better are the chances of working out a good resolution. The greater the disparity, the less likely a satisfactory resolution will be arrived at. Thus seek to equalize power. If you have more power seek to give some of it up by acknowledging the benefits of interdependencies.

* When trying to resolve a conflict:
    o Treat others with respect. If people have alternative views it is for a reason, not because they are stupid or out to take advantage;
    o Keep people separate from the issues. Don't get personal about the issue or turn it into a general 'you always …';
    o See it as a mutual problem to be resolved rather than about trying to determine who was at fault;
    o Be clear about where each person or party is coming from. Try to ensure both parties understand each other's point of view;
    o Come to an agreement about what the issue is that is to be resolved;
    o Get into a brainstorming mood with regards looking for solutions;
    o Negotiate a solution.

* There may be circumstances where potential conflict should be kept hidden or unspoken about if in so doing it is genuinely believed that things will get better. It is often a subjective judgment as to whether or not it is better to tackle or to leave it. All that can reasonably be asked is that this judgment is an honest one; based upon the best interests of all those likely to be affected rather than the desire of an individual or individuals to avoid of create personal conflicts.

* When faced with complex negotiations, try to build from the things you can agree on. Focus on identifying what you can agree on rather than focusing on what you disagree about.

* People are much more positive and co-operative if they have choices. Much of teenage rebellion is a seeking of choices when they feel they are not being given any.

* If you are going into battle, metaphorically or literally, try to choose your battleground such that it is favorable to your own way of fighting. Never enter a battle without knowing what the surroundings are.

* When two dogs fight for a bone they risk a third running off with it.

* Be conscious of escalating conflicts where both sides see themselves as the good guys reacting to unreasonable provocation from the other. To break out of this cycle either one side needs to have the courage not to react to the latest response of the other, or both parties need to raise their vision and identify some higher-level common position that overrides their simple tit for tat reactions to each other.

* When someone has wronged you, retaliation may well be justified. However in retaliating you are then harming the other and giving them a justification for retaliation of their own. This often leads to a cycle of revenge harm which ultimately does far more damage to both parties than either party would have suffered if the original wrong had not been responded to. Of course sometimes you need to show that you will not allow yourself to be taken advantage of. However this is often relatively rare circumstances. Revenge action is a form of self-harm. If you think of the harm you have already suffered as 'sunk harm' then your revenge actions are simply going to risk further harm to yourself.

* There are different types of professional help that can be called in to help resolve conflicts. At the extreme is the courts. Less extreme is arbitration which is still a win-lose negotiation but avoids courts. An arbitrator is someone independent of both parties but who both parties accept as someone they can put their cases to and by whose decision they will both abide. A better option is mediation, where a trained mediator is brought in to work with both parties to word towards an agreeable solution. Other options include use of an ombudsman or people recognized as counsellors in a given topic such as marriage.

Take an Interest in and Get to Know Others

* To make someone feel important, take an interest in them. Give them your undivided attention. Listen intently. Ask questions. Everyone has a need to feel important. The more they feel you are listening to them, the more important you make them feel, and the more they will value their relationship with you.

* People have a very strong desire to be appreciated. Make people feel valued and special albeit without being dishonest. Be sincere by noticing their good points.

* Take an interest in other people and they will find you more likeable. Learn to be genuinely interested in and to like everyone. Seek out the beauty and the history that is in everyone, and revel in their uniqueness rather than expect them or want them to be different.

The Bumper Book of Common Sense

* When trying to get to know someone better, look for connections such as common interests or places or people you both know. Don't fake your interests however: it is usually very obvious and you will quickly lose any credibility you may have had.

* If you encourage people to talk about themselves you will make much more progress in getting to know them and getting them to like you, than you will by telling them about yourself.

* Ensure you listen to what other people have to say, and understand what is important to them. By making the effort to understand others and show that you understand you significantly increase the likelihood that they will make the effort to understand you.

* The better you understand other people's motivations they better you are able to predict how they will behave in given situations or circumstances. Even if you don't like someone it is still worth trying to understand how they think and what is important to them.

* Remember people's names and other small details about them like their partner's name, or what their children are doing, or where they go on holiday. Unless you have a particularly good memory it is best to write such information down somewhere private.

* Make the effort to learn a little about the people you come into regular or occasional contact with. Seek out common ground and find out what interests them. And remember it – keep your own written notes if your memory is not particularly good. Having common ground or knowing someone's interests provides you with a ready opener when you meet them and can then lead on to other topics.

* Mistrust is generally borne of ignorance. When we don't know someone else, or some other group, we tend to think the worse in terms of them potentially wanting to do us harm. Once we know them better we usually come to realize they are driven by the same concerns as we are. It is hard to hate someone when you know their life story.

* Try to understand things from other people's point of view. Other people are just as logical or illogical in their thinking as you are, and thus behave the way they do and do the things they do, not because they are incompetent or bad people, but because of the way they see things. Try to understand how it is that they see things.

* In broad terms we can better understand and empathize with others if we have been through similar or analogous experiences. However some people are so self-centered that they fail to empathize with others despite having had similar experiences, and there are those who are able to genuinely understand and empathize without having been through the same experiences.

* One way of better understanding the mood or feelings of another person is to imitate their postures, gestures and facial expressions. Do not, however, do this openly.

* Network. Networking isn't about trying to hang out with important people. Networking is about building mutually respectful relationships at all levels inside and outside of your work environment. A good way to network is to join associations and to attend conferences.

* Build a network of like-minded people.

* Look out for the people who know lots of people and be friendly with them. They will provide you with the opportunity to meet many others.

* You don't need to get to know well everyone you meet, and most people can stay in the category of acquaintances rather than friends. However you should look to have sufficient knowledge about them to know when they might know things that are of interest to you.

* Make friends. Be willing to talk to people. Be willing to make the effort. Be positive and smile a lot.

* People more openly talk when eating. If you share a table with someone when they are having a meal you significantly increase the likelihood that they will engage in some level of conversation, and thus have the opportunity for building or strengthening a relationship with them. Assuming of course you are not unreasonably intruding upon them.

* To feel the warmth of others you must be willing to share and to give of yourself.

* One of the most important ways our lives are given purpose is through our being meaningful to others; and being loved by them and loving them in return.

* Our happiness is strongly dependent upon the quantity and quality of our social connections. Having friends helps you think better and see things from novel perspectives. Loneliness significantly increases the risk of death from stroke and heart disease.

* Having met someone new with whom you wish to follow up and get to know better, ensure your initial follow up is within 24 hours of first meeting them. Use of e-mail is good, or find an excuse to talk to them on the phone. You should ensure you do a further follow up within about a month. Of course you need to ensure that following your first meeting you have the means of following up, such as e-mail address or phone number, and preferably you leave them with a reason for a follow up, such as 'I'll find out about … and let you know.' or 'I'll send you some further information on …'

Asking Others for Help and Advice

* Don't be too proud to ask for, and take if you believe it is appropriate, the advice of others.

* Consider the advice from others alongside your own thoughts when deciding on the best way forward. Others may not know the full circumstances, which may tend against their advice if it conflicts with your own; on the other hand others may have more experience about the matter in hand, which may tend towards their advice. Where the balance lies is for you to determine given the specific circumstances.

* Do not feel duty bound to follow the advice of others. But do take it into consideration.

* Sometimes the best person to clearly see the most appropriate way forward is someone who is detached from the situation.

* When asking for advice from others be careful not to ask leading questions. If you ask your questions in a certain way it could strongly influence their response, away from being truly objective. Make questions as neutral as you can: 'What do you think I should do about xxx?', rather than 'Do you think I should do yyy?'

* When receiving advice from others that it is contrary to what you believe, then it might be worth exploring why it is different. You are not in competition with others for the best advice, you are trying to get at the best way forward. When faced with any conflicting information, the resolution of the conflict is often through digging a bit deeper, with the resolution often emerging from an understanding of the underlying reason for the different viewpoints. Circumstances will dictate however whether or not it is reasonable to attempt to question the other person about why they have offered the advice they have, noting the need to be careful not to make it seem like you are attacking or criticizing them for the advice they have given.

* If you ask someone for their advice, and you don't like it, don't then criticize them. By all means ask follow up questions to better understand why they have offered the advice they have; maybe they haven't fully understood the particular circumstances, maybe their advice is based on some specific incident from their own past. However it is not their responsibility to try to double guess

The Bumper Book of Common Sense

what you want to hear. It is their responsibility to provide an independent viewpoint, which you can then decide whether or not to take into account.

* If you take someone's advice, and it doesn't work out, it is not their fault. The responsibility for whether or not you take someone's advice, is yours, not theirs. Only you know the full and specific circumstances.

* If you want someone to help you then ask them. People are often quite willing to help, but can only do so if they know you would like some help. If they say no to your request for help, then don't push them.

* If you want something from someone don't be afraid to ask. Often we don't ask because we assume the answer will be no. But this is not necessarily going to be the case. There are more things in this world that are negotiable than many people give credit for. Simple things like hotel prices or expensive items are often, though not always, negotiable. After all, you usually have nothing to lose; you can always accept or reject what is on offer. "Nothing ventured, nothing gained."

* If you don't tell people what you want, don't be surprised if they don't know. What you want may be obvious to you, but it rarely is to other people.

Don't be too Concerned about What Other People Think about You

* Don't worry about what other people think of you. Some will think positively some will think negatively. It doesn't matter. If you think positively about yourself, without being arrogant, more people will think positively of you more of the time. You can't please everyone all the time. So don't try. Just be yourself, and think positively about yourself.

* Don't worry about what other people might be thinking about you. Other people are rarely thinking about you, they are mostly thinking about themselves, and probably worrying about what other people are thinking about them.

* Too often we hold ourselves back through worrying about what other people might think of us; like embarrassed teenagers. But why should we let our actions be dictated by thoughts that may or may not be in someone else's head, and most likely are not?

* Do not be concerned by others not appreciating you; be concerned about you not appreciating others.

* Don't worry about what other people think. They don't know who you really are.

* No-one can make you feel bad about yourself without your consent.

* Don't be obsessed or even concerned with whether or not people think they are better than you. If you believe people are looking down on you, and trying to make you feel inferior, then recognize that it is their problem, not yours.

* If you want to understand how others see you, it is vital you do it uncritically. Don't focus on whether they are right or wrong to have the views that they have, just seek to understand what views they do have. Then with regards any negative viewpoints, don't seek to deny it, but ask yourself why it is that you might come across to others that way. Once you understand this, you can decide whether or not you want to make any changes.

* Most other people want you to be average, to be just like them. If you strike out on your own to do the things you want to do, you will often get others criticizing and disapproving. Don't let this dissuade you. Have faith and belief in yourself. Be self-reliant.

* Let your own feelings guide you; do not be distracted by others. Doing things to suit others, if they don't also suit you, will only consume your energy and time and won't make much difference to how they think of you anyway.

* Don't be afraid of criticism. Take it as feedback which is either useful to you or it isn't. Once you've made use of it, forget it.

* Be different to other people. Have something unique about your look or what you wear that means people will remember you after they have met you. Don't do this in an offensive manner or a manner that might offend.

* Beware of sinking into mediocrity because you don't want to upset others. You can seek out your own goals with a certain selfishness without being completely heartless.

* Don't take too personally somebody's comments or behavior towards you. It is unlikely they are deliberately getting at you; more likely they are like that with everyone. Or there was something else on their mind and they were not aware of the seeming slight they gave you. Or it was a spur of the moment thing, and for them it is already out of mind.

* You are not in this world to live up to other people's expectations of you, any more than others are in this world to live up to your expectations of them.

Verbal Arguments and Debate

* When engaged in a verbal argument, ensure you clearly understand what is being argued about, and that it is something you want to argue about.

* When engaging in an argument or debate ask yourself what it is you want to achieve. Some possible reasons for engaging in an argument include:
    o We are trying to show off how knowledgeable or clever we are in the belief it will increase our standing with the person we are arguing with or others who might be listening in;
    o We are looking to defend our self against what we see as an attack on our beliefs or our integrity or our competence;
    o We are looking to maintain or improve our social connection with the other person by engaging in some hopefully friendly banter;
    o We are looking to persuade the other person of an idea or to take some action, or find ourselves responding to someone who is trying to persuade us;
    o We are looking to learn something or better understand something than we did before.

   Of course few arguments achieve any of these things. They usually turn into some form of sporting dual, possibly friendly, possibly not. Try to be aware of when an argument is not serving any useful end and look to get out of it, either by changing the topic or politely backing away, possibly with the offer to discuss another day.

* Just getting louder when arguing with someone will not make your case more persuasive.

* If you find yourself in an argument, be sure you understand the other person's point of view. Even if you don't agree with it, you can still learn from it.

* To understand someone's current position, listen to their reasons for rejecting your arguments.

* When faced with a disagreement ask yourself: What is the disagreement about and are both parties arguing about the same thing? Do you have the same views about the facts? Are you using terms in the same way? Does the disagreement matter, or is it best just to agree to disagree?

The Bumper Book of Common Sense

* Avoid arguments with someone who is obviously not interested in listening to your point of view.

* When people claim they are not lying, this does not mean that they are telling the truth, the whole truth, and nothing but the truth. People can easily mislead without lying. And of course they could be lying about not lying, or be lying but not know it.

* People do not always say what they believe. Not necessarily because they are being dishonest, but because of particular reasons relating to the moment which might be stronger than the desire to say what they truly believe. People often get swept up in the moment when arguing, and may take up positions simply in order to take up an opposing view to that of the other person.

* A common trick used in verbal debates is to drive one's opponent towards making statements more extreme than they intended.

* A common misuse of spoken arguments is to include within the argument many statements of a seemingly relevant nature that can be easily agreed with and then concluding that the final statement therefore follows, without actually have demonstrated any logically valid link. Keeping tabs on the logic and the specific relevance of the earlier statements can be difficult, and the arguer relies upon your having agreed to a lot of seemingly relevant statements to lead you into almost then automatically accepting the concluding statement.

* If a verbal argument is complex it can't be relied upon to prove anything. There are many ways for fallacious verbal arguments to sound convincing. In practice a complex verbal argument will be believed more on the basis of how it is said rather than on the basis of what is said.

* Daily argument and debate isn't about logical correctness. Fallacies are common. Only if they are central to the argument should you disrupt the argument flow to point them out. Verbal arguments are mostly about persuasion, which is more a question of psychology than it is of logic.

* Complex spoken arguments are almost impossible to assess. If they sound convincing this may be more to do with how it is said rather than what is said. From an influencing viewpoint the way a verbal argument is presented is usually far more powerful and persuasive than the logic of the argument itself. Some of the particular problems with spoken arguments include: emotional reactions; being able to remember precisely how terms have been used, and whether or not their meaning has subtly changed; simply not having time to follow the structure of the argument; and being able to clearly identify which of the statements made are relevant.

* If an argument is important it should always be written down, and if the person making it is reluctant to write it down, then this is itself a sign that they recognize there are some hidden flaws.

* Our own thoughts can be seen as verbal arguments with ourselves. Anything complex should be written down. People who consider that their thoughts are 'too deep to be put into words' are kidding themselves, and kidding us. Thoughts that cannot be expressed in written language are of no practical use.

* If you spend all your time expressing your own opinions all you'll hear is the sound of your own voice. You learn more by listening than by speaking: as the Chinese proverb goes – 'From listening comes wisdom and from speaking comes repentance'. However you should speak from time to time to expose your own beliefs to the hard reality of other people's opinions and to direct discussions to topics of interest to you.

* Rather than declaring generalizations or your own opinions as absolute truths, get into the habit of self-reference, 'It seems to me ...' or 'So far as I am aware ...'.

* Be very wary of making someone out to be a fool in a verbal argument involving others. You can very easily make an enemy for life.

* Let your opponent score some points, so long as they don't seriously damage your case.

* Your audience will find you agreeable if you meet their expectations. If you want to influence others then behave the way they expect you to behave.

* When in verbal arguments, most people are mostly concerned about winning the argument, or at least not losing it, especially if there are 3rd party onlookers. If they find they are losing they will generally resort to defensive tactics such as attacking the other person, or getting louder, or feigning anger. However a far more constructive and useful approach is to embrace the fact that you have learned something. The real winner in a verbal argument is the person who comes out of it knowing more, or better able to construct future arguments.

* Most arguments break down into being about blame, values, or choice. Blame is about the past and is argued using the past tense, values are about the present and argued in the present tense, and choice is about the future and argued in the future tense. Arguments often shift between these and as a result often fail to come to any acceptable conclusion. Try to keep your argument in the right tense for the issue at hand.

* Avoid arguments in the past tense with family and friends. They tend to focus on blame. Shift the argument to the future tense.

* If your argument is about choice, keep it in the future tense. If you don't you will find yourself quickly getting off topic.

* Many arguments are about moral viewpoints. There is no 'winning argument' when it comes to arguing morality. You can however give people food for thought by expressing your arguments in a clear manner, and using novel analogies that mean something to them. Don't however expect them to agree on the spot. The best you can usually hope for is that what you say strikes a chord with them and they continue to think about it later.

* The best response to anger is silence.

* When engaging in verbal arguments try to avoid it becoming a win-lose encounter.

* A discussion is an exchange of knowledge; an argument is an exchange of ignorance.

* Look to understand your style when in a conflict argument. Common styles include: avoidance of conflict and hoping it will go away; giving in, even though you haven't been convinced; or getting mad, which stops you thinking constructively. Better to try to stay calm and seek out innovative solutions that benefit both parties. You can of course also seek out compromises, but these often leave both sides feeling they have to some extent lost, though sometimes this may be the only reasonable outcome.

* In seeking compromises try to avoid simply stating your preferred solution. You need to try to get the other party to feel some ownership of the solution. For example suggest a number of potential solutions that suit you and give the other person room to assess them from their viewpoint.

Responding to Negativity or Put Downs

* Don't be put off by other people's negativity towards you. If you are working towards something you believe in, many people will be negative or discouraging because you are showing up their mediocrity.

* If someone puts you down, don't go out seeking revenge, or trying to get even; go out to improve and get better. Even if you think they are wrong, the best riposte is to just keep getting better and better.

The Bumper Book of Common Sense

* You will not please everyone, and some people will be critical of you. Do not let it play on your mind. Concentrate on doing the things you believe to be right.

* Sometimes it is best simply to put up with unjust criticism or complaint. For example, the criticism or complaint might be by someone stronger than you and you judge that pointing out the unfairness will simply make things worse. Or when someone is in an emotionally charged state, it may be better to accept their criticism or complaint at that time, and possibly look to have a more rational discussion with them later.

* You will often come across negative people, people who see problems in everything, people who always believe things will turn out badly, people who are cynical about others and are often complaining. Such people can be very draining, and an obvious way of dealing with them is to avoid them and keep away from them. This however is often not possible or practical. Some tips for dealing with such people include:
    o Don't get drawn into their negativity. Be at best non-committal in response. Do however respond positively to anything they say which is of a positive nature;
    o When engaging with negative people try to do so in a group. People tend to be less negative in the presence of a group than when talking to an individual;
    o Don't take negative comments personally, even when they come across this way. People don't usually mean it personally, but they tend not to be sensitive enough to recognize that it is coming across that way;
    o Try to find topics about which the person feels more positive. What subjects do they enjoy?
    o Do positive things for people who are negative, try to put positive thoughts into their head;
    o Limit the time you spend with people who are being negative. Why put yourself in a negative frame of mind by spending a lot of time with them.

* A way of disarming someone who is being critical of you is to agree with the criticism. You are not perfect, and the person being critical might have a point. Agree that they have a point and then explore a bit more, in particular ask them what should positively be done as a result. You could well learn something, and you will often find the other person then becomes more positively disposed towards you and will help you in any follow up action.

* When you get upset by someone else's actions or behavior you get stressed. Nobody else cares. So don't you either.

* People are rarely out to upset you, so forgive them. Most negatively and put-downs come from people seeing things only from their own viewpoint and being what they think of as honest, albeit with a lack of sensitivity. You do it yourself to others. You don't notice when you do it to them, and they don't notice when they do it to you.

* If someone is out to upset you, which though it may not feel like it is actually very rare, then don't give them the pleasure of succeeding.

Interacting with Difficult, Awkward, or Dishonest People

* Avoid toxic behavior: people who make others feel devalued, inadequate, angry, frustrated, or guilty. Prefer nourishing behavior, people who make others feel valued, capable, loved, respected, and appreciated.

* When you have a toxic relationship you can either: try to change it; accept it and adjust as best you can; or leave it and end it. However if you choose to accept it you must bear some responsibility for the continuation of the relationship.

* Some people are highly critical and talking to them can be a real downer. They rarely, if ever, offer a compliment. They seem to always be focusing on the negative and the problems. When meeting such people:
    o Don't take their comments or views personally. They are not aimed at you, since such people are the same way with everyone;
    o Note that such people often don't realize the way they are. They think they are just being open, honest, and helpful, and don't realize how socially tactless they are. Try to see behind their method and understand what they are trying to say. There will often be something useful in what they are trying to say, and it will invariably be an honest viewpoint;
    o If you feel uncomfortable with their comments ask yourself why. There is probably something about what they are saying that is striking some inner chord with you. Understanding what it is and doing something about what it, is likely to be a useful learning and self-improvement exercise;
    o You do not need to accept the negativity emanating from them. We are responsible for how we allow ourselves to react to other people;
    o Don't react angrily or try to enter into an emotional exchange with them;
    o People who are critical are often those most in need of some kindness themselves. Be generous to them, and pay them complements. It will help them learn to be more generous themselves;
    o Remember you have a choice. You can disengage from them.

* When you come across a person who is consistently mean, ungrateful, or dishonest, don't get angry at them for being what they are, just avoid them and work your way around them.

* In dealing with people with delusions, rather than confronting them directly, which is very likely to fail, accept their delusion, enter into it, and then gently lead them in another direction.

* Do not simply ignore or put down awkward or difficult people. They often have a lot to offer in terms of ideas even if they don't put them across very well. Be as patient and tactful as you can be, and you may well get something positive out of them.

* When dealing with difficult people try to see if there is a way of adapting your approach into a way that works more effectively with them. People are rarely if ever deliberately difficult, they just lack flexibility in how to deal with others. If you can be flexible you can often find a way of working with them.

* When dealing with difficult people, actually when dealing with anyone, focus on their positive qualities and traits. You might find they become less difficult if you regularly complement them.

* When dealing with difficult people take responsibility for your contribution to the difficulties, and seek to be flexible and willing to compromise. Ensure you keep focused on real issues and keep away from getting personal. Dealing with difficult people provides us with an opportunity to seek to improve our own interpersonal skills and to better understand ourselves.

* Do not be angry with others for their narrowness and pettiness. It is the way they are. Respond in an open and generous manner, albeit without letting yourself be taken advantage of, and maybe they will become a little less narrow and petty.

* We learn more about ourselves from the people who make us angry.

* Tactics for dealing with certain types of difficult people, or people who are being difficult in particular circumstances:
    o People who complain: be careful not to agree with the complaints or to apologize – at least not until you are sure it is the right thing to do; don't become defensive or confrontational; ask for clarification and details; seek out a solution in terms of what they expect to happen to resolve the issue.

The Bumper Book of Common Sense

- o People who make promises they are unlikely to be able to keep: you need to encourage them to be more realistic and frank, but without confronting them.

- o Know it alls: don't attack their ideas directly, but suggest alternatives. Seek out more details. If it's clear they don't know as much as they think they do, ensure you don't show them up in public.

- o The pessimist: don't argue with them. Focus on making and responding with positive and optimistic statements. Suggest a range of alternatives relating to the subject they are being pessimistic about, and let them contribute.

* There is little point in playing a game unless all sides accept the rules. Avoid playing games with persons you consider might break the rules to take advantage. This holds true not just for games but for any endeavor whereby you are working with others.

* There are people who will take advantage if they have the opportunity. This doesn't mean you need to mistrust everyone you meet. Nevertheless you should be sensitive to the possibility, and under certain circumstances back away from being in a position in which you can be taken advantage of.

* There are some people who will commit violence under relatively normal circumstances. Fortunately they are few. Nevertheless they exist. Avoid being around someone that has a reputation for violence, or places that have a reputation for violence, and if faced with physical violence it may be better to give in to those threatening you rather than risk extreme violence or death.

Ways of Seeing Others

* How people see the world is to a significant extent revealed through what they do and don't talk about, and the language they use.

* See everyone as individuals just trying to make their way in the world as best they can. There is something to admire and like in everyone. There is something to be learned from everyone.

* You can understand anyone if you can see the world as they see it.

* You can be readily influenced through expectations. If you are told that someone you don't know has some particular personality or behavioral traits, then when you meet them you are likely to interpret their behavior in a way that reinforces those preconceived expectations.

* People are often not the way you assume they are, and people often do things for very different reasons to the ones you assume. Talk to people and ask them, rather than assume.

* Be wary of judging people against standards you create for them. If someone doesn't do something you expected them to do, think before you judge them too harshly. Were your expectations unreasonable? How would the expectations have looked from their viewpoint? Would they even have been aware of your expectations?

* Be wary of looking for explanations for someone's behavior in some incident in their past life. Almost any current behavior can be rationalized against almost any past incident, just as hindsight can be used to explain why almost any current event was inevitable.

* We have a tendency to believe we are more reasonable than others and that we are more often right in our words and actions. However remember that other people feel the same way about themselves. Whilst we readily see the shortfalls in others, we are largely blind to the shortfalls in ourselves.

* You have very limited control over other people's behavior. However you have, if you choose to exercise it, significant control over how you interpret and respond to other people's behavior.

* If you are lonely, be aware that there are many others just like yourself. If you are willing to open up to others for companionship, and make the first move, then others will open up to you.

* You can feel at one with humankind and the world as a whole. You don't have to feel lonely. You can be aware of many many others just like you and feel an affinity with them, even if you don't know them.

Common Sense in Close Relationships

In General

* Whatever relationship problems you may be having you will not be the first to have experienced them. There will be lots of advice and help readily available on the internet or through advice centers or elsewhere. The first essential step is to recognize there is a problem and then deciding not to let it lead to an irreconcilable breakdown of the relationship. Having done this look up and use the plenty of good practical well proven advice.

* Regular interactions with close friends and family is the number one source of happiness in most people's lives. And when we are happy we are less stressed and think clearer.

* Having and maintaining good relationships has significant health benefits and increases the quality and quantity of your life.

* Nothing gives more pleasure than a return of affection, and the mutual interchange of kind feelings.

* Be appreciative of your contacts and relationships with family and friends, they don't last forever. We are all mortal and death could strike down anyone at almost any time.

* Treat people knowing you may never see them again. Ensure your encounter with them is not one you would regret if you never saw them again.

* Relationships thrive and survive on mutual support and agreement. Hints of criticism have very negative effects. It is important to add lots of positive into any negative, or what might be perceived as negative, statements.

* You can be close to someone without having to believe that everything they do is right. If a friend makes a mistake, the friend remains a friend and the mistake remains a mistake. It is not being disloyal to friends or family to disagree with them if you believe what they are doing is wrong or inappropriate.

* If you want someone to love you more find out what makes them happy and do more of it. Find out what makes them unhappy and do less of it. Always greet them with a smile. Always be positive and encouraging. Tell them you appreciate them. Respect their space.

* Show gratitude whenever you can: say thank you, write thank you messages, send thank you cards.

* Be generous, though genuine, with compliments.

The Bumper Book of Common Sense

* Good relationships are maintained through small gestures and acts of kindness.

* Maintaining good relationships requires give and take, by both parties. People need love and respect most when they don't deserve it.

* If you want to stay or be close to someone you need to respect them for how they are, and accept that they are not how you would like them to be.

* If you say or do something hurtful or which you regret, say you are sorry. Never let your pride get in the way of saying you are sorry. Being too proud to apologize is never worth it and means good relationships will deteriorate.

* Be wary of taking close friends or family for granted. It can happen over time without you really noticing it. You may become less considerate, and show less interest. Be sure to listen to anyone you are close to and to show them appreciation.

* Always consult before making decisions that affect the other person in a close relationship.

* It may be appropriate in close relationships to set up a regular time, once a week, once a fortnight, when you can discuss issues that are bothering you in a safe manner.

* Don't force yourself on others. Give relationships time to develop. Trying to get people to like you is likely to backfire. Be friendly and respectful and a good listener, and your relationships will gradually develop and improve.

* Successful relationships require some work. Don't take them for granted. Maintain open communication and be honest, at least in the things that really matter.

* You get out of relationships what you put in. If you want to be loved, you need to give love. If you want friends you need to be friendly. If you want to be understood, you need to be understanding.

* We change, and the people we have relationships with change. Your relationships may need to adapt to these changes. Don't hold yourself back from change just because of your relationships, and respect the right of others to change. However if you want to maintain relationships through changes you will need to work at it and in particular need to be tolerant of other's behaviors and attitudes to a greater extent than you may have been before.

* If a relationship that is important to you isn't working, don't go looking to blame the other person. Look to yourself. You are far more likely to improve a relationship that is having difficulties through adjusting your own behavior than you are by trying to adjust the other person's behavior, despite the fact that you probably feel it is the other person that ought to.

* If others have hurt you, forgive them. In most cases they will not even know they have hurt you, and will not have done it deliberately. Don't therefore hold it against them, though if it is a regular occurrence let them know so it is less likely to happen again. If someone has deliberately hurt you, again forgive them in terms of putting aside the resentment, but you need to decide whether or not the relationship is one you wish to continue with. If they continue to deliberately hurt you, then you need to get out of your relationship with them.

* If someone close to you has upset you or done something you consider to be wrong, tell them. But don't go on about it, don't lecture them.

* Many members of families or previously close friends fall out over relatively minor matters and once good relationships can be lost for life over trivialities. Where you find this happening to yourself put the matter into context: is it something life threatening? Normally it is a matter of pride on both sides. Be the one willing to let it go. Is it really worth the loss of the friendship? Better to be flexible and bite your lip from time to time in order to maintain harmonious relationships.

* Sometimes close friends or family can be a bit grumpy and be a bit short or disrespectful to you. Try not to react. Try to be yourself. A touch of sympathy if appropriate but not too much. Get them on to neutral topics or get on with activities. For most people, most of the time, grumpiness will pass soon enough. If however you react through getting upset with them it will turn into much more and can spoil your whole day.

* You will come into conflict from time to time even with close friends and family. We are all individuals and want different things. It is normal. The trick is either to mutually seek out some equitable resolution of differences, or to limit the damage by not letting the conflict spill over or to create longer-term antagonisms. Be quick to offer an olive branch after any conflict and be quick to accept any olive branch that is offered to you.

* Beware of self-righteousness over some relatively minor action or words on the part of a friend or relative that has upset or hurt you. If only they would apologize you would be more than willing to forgive. But they are in the wrong and they must make the first step. Many a good relationship has gone sour over minor incidents where both sides felt it was the other side that should make the first move, and neither does. Or where one side has imagined a slight which the other didn't notice or mean and the resulting changed behavior has led to a permanent deterioration of the relationship. Brush off occasional upsets caused by friends or relatives.

* Understand common causes of friction in your family or your relationships and find ways of dealing with them or reducing the likelihood of them occurring.

* Do not get into heated arguments with people, there's rarely if ever anything to be gained.

* Big relationship problems do not come out of nowhere. There are plenty of signs and small problems. It is important to tackle small problems as they arise.

* When you have relationship problems to solve, do so with your head, not your emotions.

* Avoid generalizations and absolutes in describing someone else's behavior to them. Thus avoid 'You always ...' or 'You never ...'.

* When someone you know well comes to you complaining about something, recognize that they may or may not be asking you to help them solve it. Listen and work out whether they are simply looking for a bit of sympathy, a bit of support, or indeed help to find a solution. Often the best thing you can do for them is to be there for them and to help them feel good about themselves in general so as to reduce any stress they may be feeling.

* Be very reticent in solving other people's problems for them, even those you love. For one thing it means they don't get the opportunity to learn and grow. It can also sour rather than help your relationship with them, particularly if issues arise with your solution. If someone directly asks for your help about doing something specific, and you are better placed than they are to do it, then by all means do it. However when it comes to advice about what they should do, avoid telling them directly such as through 'you should ...', and stick with 'have you thought about ...', or 'maybe you could try ...'. Give them options and ensure they decide what to do because they believe it is the best thing to do, not because they believe you believe it is the best thing to do.

Relationships between Husband and Wife or Equivalent Partners

* Life is better if you share it with a partner.

* Of what value are personal experiences without someone to appreciate them with?

* Have plans and dreams that you share with your partner. Something you are working towards together.

The Bumper Book of Common Sense

* Couples who take part in joint, relatively unpredictable, exciting and active activities will maintain a greater sense of the excitement of when they first got together, and are more likely to stay together.

* Make the effort to make your partner's birthday special and memorable. This could be through any combination of:
    o A special thoughtful gift;
    o Taking them out somewhere you've never been to before;
    o Make efforts you wouldn't normally do, do the cooking maybe if you don't usually do it, or do all the clearing up and cleaning afterwards.

* Don't forget your wedding anniversaries. Celebrate them in some way.

* Ask yourself from time to time: 'What have I done recently to make my partner feel loved and appreciated?' You might be surprised to realize that the answer may be nothing, and not for a long time. If you love someone you should be showing it in some way every day. It is easy to fall into routine and habits which become almost business like and with little real affection attached. Thus the need to stop and ask yourself the question from time to time.

* Build up knowledge about your partner. Know their clothes, shoe, and ring sizes; their favorite foods; their favorite color; particular likes and dislikes, etc. If your memory is not all that good, write it down. Keep this knowledge up to date.

* Keep a diary of the special times you have had with your partner, possibly alongside a joint photo album. It is easy to forget the good times. If you have a record of them you can remember them when times get a bit fraught, and they will help you feel good towards each other.

* Anyone can fall in love. The trick is to stay in love once the automated infatuation has passed, which it will. It is a natural process. It is then that a decision to stay in love and make the effort to continue to develop your relationship, rather than move on to the next infatuation, will bring you lifelong companionship.

* For a relationship of mutual respect to last after the early infatuation, which will pass, then the participants must retain their own identity. They must have their own interests outside of the relationship, and they must respect and be comfortable with the fact that they each have other friends. However the relationship itself should be and remain the most important one in their lives and they must feel they are stronger in the relationship than they would be out of it.

* Over time good relationships can get stale, and partners can come to regularly see each other in a negative rather than a positive light. They can get frequently annoyed at each other's habits and behavior. This is normal. The key to a relationship is whether this continues in a downward spiral leading eventually to irreconcilable differences or whether you work to counter it. Whilst expecting or trying to recreate a continual 'first love' environment is unrealistic, you can create an environment of continual love and mutual respect by:
    o Doing things together, which you both enjoy;
    o Giving each other both time when you listen to each other but also time apart;
    o Seeing the positive in each other rather than the negative;
    o Both be willing to make the first move;
    o Responding positively to moves by the other. Never dismiss them as not enough;
    o Cuddling up to each other. Don't treat all close contact as sexual. Hold hands.

* Taking your relationship with your partner for granted will slowly kill it. Ensure you have a period of a couple of hours at least once a week where you get a chance to talk together without either of you doing something else and without distractions or disruptions. Maybe go out somewhere, for a walk holding hands or to a restaurant. Just the two of you.

* Tell your partner from time to time how important they are to you, and how happy you are to have them in your life.

* Treat your partner like you would a friend who has come over to visit. How would you behave as a good host? Isn't your partner important enough to deserve such treatment?

* Find out what your partner needs to feel loved: what they think they need, not what you think they should need. Is it praise, compliments, physical closeness, to be listened to? Ask them if they feel loved, and follow up with the question of why or why not. Make sure they regularly get what they need to feel loved.

* Be regularly intimate with your partner, and be comfortable with intimacy that doesn't involve or lead to sex. Just being close together with arms around each other, or a slow dance together in the living room, or even just sitting opposite each other at a table holding hands.

* Surprise your partner every now and then. Buy them an unexpected present. Do something for them that you wouldn't normally do.

* Don't get upset when your partner doesn't do something you had wanted or expected them to do. Remember that your partner doesn't know what you are thinking, no matter how obvious it is to yourself.

* Focus on the small positive things about your partner rather than the flaws. Don't praise only actions, praise personality and appearance.

* Dwell on your partner's positive traits, not their faults. See actions that irritate you as being caused by temporary factors such as them having had a long day, and see their positive actions as being the result of the type of person they are.

* Give at least 80% positive feedback to your partner. Don't assume they know. Give them positive feedback on a regular basis. They will then be more open to occasional negative feedback.

* Small things matter enormously in close relationships. Such as looking pleased to see the other person, inquiring about the other's day, paying attention when the other is talking, keeping arrangements. These little things matter much more than grand gestures such as expensive presents or trips.

* The perfect relationship doesn't exist, and don't judge your relationship against it. Your partner has negative traits and so do you. Don't focus on them or expect your partner to change them. Accept them as a very small price to pay for the positives in your relationship.

* Don't try to change the person you are in a relationship with. Be supportive of them. And be an example to them. But don't try to change their behavior. If it's a major problem to you, talk to them about it. But only they can change their behavior and only because they choose to do so.

* Remember that your partner does not think the same way as you do. You need to respect the differences and learn what does and doesn't matter to them. You need to listen to them and not judge them by your own standards.

* Forgive your partners slip-ups as being due to circumstances, but give them credit for the good things they do. Always give them the benefit of the doubt.

* Recognize that when your partner is complaining, they may not be complaining about you, and they may not be looking for you to do something about it. They may be simply looking to let off a bit of steam, or looking for a bit of sympathy.

* Women tend to respond emotionally and are seeking emotional responses back. Men tend to give informational rational responses and try to avoid emotional responses. Neither is right or wrong,

The Bumper Book of Common Sense

they are just different expectations and both partners should recognize the differences and seek to meet the others needs and expectations as best they can.

* A common cause of angst between a man and a woman in a close relationship is when she talks about a problem and he, trying to be helpful, offers a solution. However she just gets madder because it is not a solution she is looking for, it is empathy, someone to listen to her as she talks about her feelings. She also sees him as assuming he can handle her problems better than she can. He of course doesn't understand why she is getting madder, after all he is only trying to help.

* Don't psychoanalyze everything your partner does, or even very much that your partner does. Lighten up.

* If you have a need to forgive your partner for something, and you decide to do so, once you have made the commitment to forgive them, and told them, never bring it up again.

* Husbands and wives, or partners, need to take joint responsibility for the upbringing of their children. Husbands who blame their wives, or visa-a-versa, for the bad behavior of their children are being irresponsible.

* Don't expect to agree about everything. Respect different opinions and look to come to compromises when action is required. If you respect each other's views rather than judge them, then the compromises you come to can be better than either of you would have come to alone. Compromises however shouldn't be simply middle ground. If you respect each other you are looking for the best of the combined views, which will often be largely based on the views of one or other partner, but then improved by the perspective of the other.

* If you have differences of opinion from your partner on political or non-family related issues, don't get into negative debate. Either respect each other's views or keep off these topics.

* If you have disagreements with your partner keep them private. Never argue with your partner in public.

* When you are in an argument with, or feeling negative towards, a loved one, try to see things from their point of view. Look to understand why they are behaving the way they are. Then imagine trying to surround them with an imaginary hug.

* When you have a disagreement with your partner, try to see things from their point of view. Literally try to explain things as though you were a lawyer speaking on their behalf.

* If you have fallen out with your partner and are waiting for them to make the first move of reconciliation, don't wait. Get on and make the first move yourself. And if they don't respond make the second move and then the third.

* Take responsibility for making a relationship work, through: focusing and emphasizing the positive; being willing to give in most of the time; seeking out the other's point of view; not letting negative emotions well up within you; overlooking any seeming insult; and listening even when you don't like what is being said.

* Close relationships can suffer a major disruption: serious illness or injury; being made unemployed; etc. It is vital in such circumstances to talk things through regularly and get taboo topics on the table. You need to get to a new normal in your relationship which will be different to what it was before. It may be necessary to get professional help.

* Relationships are about give and take in an environment of mutual respect and trust. Don't let your relationship become a competition between you, with each trying 'to be right'. Solutions to issues should emerge through working together not through one trying to impose their will on the other.

* Listen to your partner's criticisms and concerns without getting defensive. Overlook small irritations and solve any major problems that arise.

* Do not make excuses for everything. If you messed up, say so. Your relationship will be stronger for it. If you've always got an excuse for everything that goes wrong, or always finding a way to blame the other person, your relationship will get weaker.

* You will sometimes get angry at your partner. It is not a sign of a permanent breakdown in your relationship. There is a big difference between anger and rage. If there is rage you need counseling as a couple, or to get out of the relationship.

* If you feel yourself getting resentful or angry towards your partner, tell them. Don't let it build up until it explodes. Talking about your feelings will often help keep them under control.

* Don't take every argument as a threat to your relationship. Calm down and say sorry.

* Don't feel a need to share everything about your respective pasts. It's past. By all means do so if you are comfortable about it, but a loving relationship doesn't require it.

* Don't bring up old wounds if you get into an argument with your partner, and certainly don't keep score. If you carry around resentments then you need to let them go, or talk with your partner about them. Otherwise your relationship is at serious risk.

* Relationships with your partner start well. Many relationships however eventually end in divorce. The following should be treated as warning signs that a relationship is deteriorating: less respect; greater disappointment in the other; more negative criticism; arguments where one or the other feels angry; doing less together; less intimacy and touch; feelings of rejection; less joint decision making; less sharing of thoughts or feelings; less helping each other. Don't let these gradually become the norm, because if they do your marriage is in difficulty.

* If you believe there is something not right in your relationship then you are probably right. Talk to your partner about it and try to work it out between you, but keep it to yourselves. If you both agree, see a professional counselor. But keep family and friends out of it.

* It is not uncommon for partners to find themselves in a loop of recriminations, where one sees themselves simply reacting in a normal way to the provocation of the other. Whilst both see the other as being to blame, in fact it is neither, and they have simply got themselves into a loop of action and reaction where their behaviors feed off each other in a negative fashion. If you find yourself in this situation, and many couples do at some point in their relationship, then to break out of it you need to jointly analyze and understand how it is that your respective behaviors are triggering negative responses in each other. This is not about who is right, but a joint understanding of the facts of how you are reacting to each other and the destructive impact it is having on your relationship. If one or other of you starts to use the analysis to justify why you are right or the other wrong, stop the analysis and try again later. Assuming you can get through the analysis and gain an understanding of how you are negatively influencing each other, you should be able to identify ways of breaking the loop through agreeing different ways to respond to trigger events. Clearly this analysis should not, and cannot, be done whilst in the loop of destructive behavior itself. You must both be in a good receptive mood and willing to listen to each other. If you find you are no longer ever in such a receptive mood then best you go and get some counseling.

* Couples who drift apart often do so slowly over a long period of time, with a slowing increasing pattern of blame and recrimination. Each sees the other as doing wrong, whilst seeing their own ways of doing things as justified. There is a growing intransigence on both sides and a gradual taking up of opposing positions each with a strong feeling of self-righteousness and self-justification. Each party's self-justification leads to them seeing their own behavior and attitudes as completely reasonable or at least understandable, but getting angrier and angrier at the unreasonable behavior and attitudes of the other.

* Once a relationship reduces to contempt, sarcasm, mockery, name calling, and blame it is on its last legs.

The Bumper Book of Common Sense

* A tip for dealing with a deteriorating situation between you and your partner is to whisper rather than shout. If you can agree to and get in the habit of doing this you will find anger dissipating quickly.

* Don't judge your partner for things they did before you met them. Do not go through their private possessions from before you met them. They may well have had strong feelings for others before they met you, and still have positive feelings for others. However unless this is interfering with your relationship let them have their past privacy. Trying to 'dig up the past' is far more likely to damage your relationship than strengthen it, unless your relationship is already badly damaged and it is a necessary part of trying to repair it.

* The grass is rarely greener on the other side. Other people are not all living in perfect or even good relationships: the large number of divorces makes that obvious, and they are just the extremes. Moving on to another person will make you feel good for a while, just as the start of your existing relationship will have made you feel good. But you will eventually experience the same issues as your present relationship. Best to put your energy into fixing your existing relationship.

* Financial problems are a common cause of marriage breakup. If you have financial problems it is essential you sit down together and figure out how you will jointly address them. If necessary go to a reputable credit counseling service.

* There are some people you shouldn't be in a relationship with. If you are being mistreated, or not treated with respect, or being led in directions you don't want to go in, get out of the relationship. It might be difficult for a while, but in the long term it will be better.

* If you are at the receiving end of any form of abuse from your partner either get professional help or get out. If abuse is tolerated it will become the norm.

Relationships between Parents and Children

* Don't fixate on being a perfect parent. There is no way to be a perfect parent, but lots of ways to be a good one. Just do the best you can, enjoy as much of it as you can, and try to let your children become what they want to be. The rest will follow.

* Children are shaped by a mixture of genetics and environment. You can't do anything about genetics, at least not once you have a child, but you can do an awful lot about the environment. And the biggest environmental factor in your child's life is you, assuming you are responsible for caring for him or her.

* Babies and young infants need love. Whether or not they get it can significantly influence how they will cope with stress and difficulties in later life.

* Young children who are neglected when crying cry more often than children whose mother comes to them whenever they start to cry.

* Like parents like children. Children don't do what their parents say; they do what their parents do. You can't just talk about ideals; you need to live them.

* Children learn mostly from our example, not from what we actively try to teach them.

* Children have more need of example than criticism. You must keep to the same standards you expect from your children, including with respect to swearing, putting things away, showing respect for others, and basic manners.

* You don't absolve yourself of responsibility for your children's behavior and attitudes simply because you told them to behave. Parents need to be patient in helping their children adopt

appropriate behaviors and attitudes, and ultimately accept responsibility for how their children turn out. It will often be difficult, however any parent is capable of accepting responsibility and seeking to do the best they can.

* Don't just tell your child, or shout at your child, to clear up their room. Go in there and do it with them, and help them and show them how to do it in terms of where to put things. Help them to ensure they have a place for everything, and to put things back there when they are not using them. Help them to ensure they have somewhere to put rubbish and the habit of clearing away their rubbish on a regular basis. Ensure clothes are not left lying around, but are put away if still to be worn or put in laundry baskets if not. Ensure plates, glasses or other crockery is taken out of the room not long after being finished with. You may have to do this quite a few times, but so long as you do it with them rather than do it for them, they will eventually get it, even if only to stop you from continually coming into their room.

* Help your children develop good habits with regards getting ready for school and doing schoolwork. Ensure they take responsibility for their school clothes being washed and ready for the new week. Ensure they hand over any letters from school as soon as they are home. Ensure they keep schoolbooks in a set place so they know where to find them when they need them. And try to teach them the habit of doing homework as soon as they can rather than as late as they can: this will significantly reduce stress for them and for you.

* Be careful what labels you put on your children, such as 'clever' or 'sporty', even if just in jest. It tends to instil a fixed mindset in them, that that is how they are, and they are likely to live up to it, and be less inclined to explore for themselves what they are good at or what they enjoy. Such labeling often happens without you noticing it, often as a result of contrasting one child with another.

* Be very wary of praising children, including teenagers, for being smart. For many this will hold them back since they will often be less likely to try in future, fearing that if they do it might show them up as not as smart as they think others believe they are. Much better to praise children for working hard, for getting on and doing things, and for persisting in the face of difficulties.

* Hard work is of far more long-term benefit than any supposed natural talent. Having a child believe they are talented can be a significant drawback since they are then less inclined to believe that they need to work hard, and will tend to become demotivated when the going gets tough. Those that do work hard will sooner or later, usually sooner, overtake those that don't, no matter how talented, and leave them far behind. Focus your praise and rewards on attitude and effort rather than on ability and achievements.

* Parents shouldn't rely on school to teach their children everything they need to know. Some particular areas parents should seek to supplement or emphasis schooling are with regards to:
    o Developing good language skills;
    o Learning to love reading;
    o Learning to play a musical instrument;
    o Thinking in terms of options and possibilities;
    o Developing a tolerance for ambiguity and complexity;
    o Articulating problems, coming up with options, and working their way through solutions;
    o Making decisions for themselves;
    o General creativity and being able to think up original ideas;
    o Sharing their ideas with others;
    o Being able to get on with others and tolerate differences.

* You should seek to ensure your children learn analytical, practical, and creative thinking skills. An ability to deploy all three will help them in later life. Analytical skills include the ability to critique and evaluate and to compare and contrast options. Practical skills include the ability to make use of

The Bumper Book of Common Sense

what is readily available, and to recognize what is likely to work and what isn't. Creative skills are about being able to imagine things in new ways and to be open to and be able to adapt ideas which are not their own.

* Teach your children to express feelings in terms of 'I' messages, to listen to other people without judging, to consider the other parties point of view, to take responsibility for their part in a conflict and apologize if appropriate, to seek win-win solutions and invite the other party to do so also, to learn how to calm down their own emotions, to not hold grudges, and to practice their conflict skills with you.

* Try to encourage your children to read. When they are very young read stories to them. Let them see you reading. Try to ensure they have access to reading material they will find interesting. It doesn't matter too much what they read, so long as they get into the habit of reading.

* Talk to your children about past events, and encourage them to talk about them. This helps improve their long-term memory of those events and also helps improve their conversational abilities.

* Children learn better by listening and doing, rather than just by listening.

* A child's brain goes through various stages of development. You can't get a child to do certain things until his or her brain has reached the relevant stage of development. For example, before about 7, though it varies from child to child, children are very egocentric, and it is not until they are about 11 or 12 that they can start to think in abstract terms. And it is not until late teens or even adulthood that the parts of the brain that relate to self-control and being able to make balanced judgments are fully functional.

* Given the way our brain develops whilst children, with those parts relating to self-control not being fully developed until late teens or early twenties, simply appealing to their willpower is sometimes unrealistic. You often need to adopt strategies with children such as using incentives or coming to agreements with them.

* Notwithstanding the fact that their brains are still developing, it is still appropriate to help your children exercise self-control, and help them learn tactics for avoiding putting themselves in the way of temptation.

* It is a natural instinct to want to protect our children, however if we protect them too much they never learn how to protect themselves. Clearly you need to protect them from circumstances which might lead to real harm, but you also need to teach them how to deal with such circumstances, gain confidence in their ability to do so, and then let them deal with such circumstances on their own. You won't always be there when they cross the road.

* Give your children room to make mistakes and to learn from them. If you do everything for them they'll get little practice in how to deal with the real world once they've left home.

* Do not let your children overextend themselves in terms of clubs and activities. Some activities are good for them. Too many leave them stressed and with no time for family activities or homework.

* Avoid having unhealthy snacks and soft drinks in the house; have healthy snacks and teach your children to get in the habit of mostly drinking water when they are thirsty.

* A major cause of, or at least significant contributory factor to, disruptive children is them not getting enough sleep. Lack of sleep impairs willpower. Pay attention to how much sleep your child is getting and look to ensure they get enough. It is in your and their interests.

* If you don't treat your children with respect, they will not treat you with respect. Treating them with respect means recognizing that they have rights of their own and that they are valuable members of the family. You thus talk to them about issues that affect them, and listen to and take account of their views.

* If your child wants your attention give it to them. Never be annoyed by their wanting attention, particularly if it is not something they are continually demanding. They will be gone soon enough so make the most of the time they want to spend with you. If they are continually demanding your attention then there is an issue you need to learn about and deal with.

* Children believe in fairness. Rather than telling them to stop something, say it is your turn.

* When wanting a child to do something, rather than say "I want you to …", instead say "Would you be willing to …"

* Be as consistent as you can with your children, and try to be consistent with your different children, albeit respecting differences particularly ages. Thus younger children shouldn't have all the same rights as older children. And both parents need to be reasonably consistent with each other.

* Siblings bicker. A little bit of bickering is normal and healthy. However if it is allowed to get out of hand, or it starts to become their primary means of communicating with each other, then you should try to overcome it. If not they will have little to do with each other once they've left home, and quite possibly little to do with you either. Some tactics relating to dealing with bickering include:
    o Bickering in the evening is often due to tiredness. Try to create a relaxing evening, - eg. watching a film together. Avoid situations where they are competing with each other;
    o Have them set rules with each other about sharing possessions – such as always asking rather than taking them, or maybe having tokens that they exchange for borrowed possessions. Set the rules when they are getting along with each other;
    o Set rules about not invading each other's space such as going in each other's room without permission, or in each other's area if they share a room;
    o Don't allow children to put each other down;
    o Try to give children some relatively easy tasks they can accomplish together.

* Remember that the worse influence on children is other children: their peers. You need to give your children the skills and ability to say no to their friends. However telling them who they can and can't be friends with will almost certainly backfire.

* If certain other children are being a particularly bad influence on your child then you can't just turn a blind eye, unless you have good reason to believe it is just a short term fad. Many a child who would otherwise have grown up to be a decent and happy member of society gets pulled towards disruptive and eventually self-harming and criminal behavior through the influence of certain friends or groups of friends. Whilst it is not easy to try to distance your child from certain friends, sometimes it is necessary to try. Don't criticize such friends directly since this is more likely to lead to them binding themselves closer to those friends rather than to distancing themselves. However you do need to make it clear to your child what is and isn't acceptable behavior, and whilst you shouldn't be too dictatorial about it, there are limits. You should also ensure that you do notice and reward good behavior, that you ensure you spend some quality time with your child and that you regularly give them a chance to talk to you and that you listen to them without judging them. It is very important to be someone they feel comfortable being around you, which they won't be if you are always criticizing them or their friends.

* Once your child starts regularly going out with their friends, get a telephone list of their friend's home numbers and mobiles. From time to time your child will have their phone powered down or switched off. Knowing how to get hold of their friends can save a lot of hassle and heartache. Also knowing that you may try to contact them through their friends will make them more likely to ensure you can get in touch directly.

* When your children or teenagers go out with friends, set ground rules about knowing where they are and contacting you if their plans change. Also set an agreed time by which they must be back, or letting you know if they are going to be late. If they persist in being late, or don't let you know, then you need to admonish or lightly punish them in some way.

The Bumper Book of Common Sense

* Bullying should not be tolerated, whether of children or adults. Schools take bullying very seriously so involve them if necessary. If your child is being bullied look up and teach them strategies for dealing with it. Also try to spot if your child might be one of those doing the bullying and help them to stop.

* Don't seek out psychological root causes for current behavioral issues with your children. Not only will they be at best tenuous, but they will not help you solve current behavioral issues. And they will often leave you thinking you can't deal with the issues, which is not true. Behavioral problems can be solved, particularly if you accept that your own behaviors will be a significant contributory factor.

* Be wary of inadvertently conditioning your child to be annoying. If you give your child a biscuit to stop him crying you are teaching him to cry when he wants a biscuit. If you frequently stand up to your child for a while but eventually give in, you are conditioning your child to keep at you even when you say no. They are learning that by going on and on they will eventually get their way. If you do make a stand against your child it is important you stand by it, or at least if you do give way do so in a 'conditional' way, whereby you expect something in return, so that they do not see you as simply giving way, and thus having their continual nagging rewarded.

* Children need clear boundaries defined through rules and discipline if they are to function effectively in later and adult life. Enforce rules in a consistent manner. Punish them, albeit without hitting them, for doing bad things. They will turn out to be more able, well adjusted, and happier. Giving in to a child's every whim is not respecting them, it is putting your desire for a quiet life above your responsibilities as a parent.

* Children who are under mild threat for misbehaving are less likely to misbehave when the threat is removed than children who are threatened with severe punishment.

* As they get older some of the boundaries you impose on your children can and should change. However you should explicitly discuss this with them rather than have them see them as arbitrary changes.

* In teaching children boundaries it is likely parents will need to punish their children in some way. Different parents will have different views on what constitutes acceptable punishment; the golden rule however is to have the child's best interests at heart, not your own. All too often the punishments are aimed at making the parents life easier.

* Punishing children has 3 facets: consistency, speed, and severity, with their importance being in that order. Being consistent is most important, followed by doing it soon enough after the event for it to be clearly associated as feedback from the event. Severity is least important, and being too severe will usually be counterproductive. Unfortunately many parents do the reverse. They let their children get away with many misdemeanors and then 'lose it', leading to some severe punishment which seems grossly unfair to the child, and indeed is with regards the particular event, and leads to resentment, rebellion, and secretive underhand behavior. Inconsistent or severe punishing of children leads to them becoming more concerned with not getting caught than with adopting improved behavior.

* Telling children not to do something often makes them obsess about doing it. Much better to tell and talk to them about positives and what they should do rather than about negatives and what they shouldn't do.

* Threats against children might work in the short term, but are usually counterproductive in the long term. Children are often attracted to whatever it is they are being threatened about. Better to simply state you don't want them to do something, and if they want reasons encourage them to try to think through and play back to you what some of those reasons might be.

* The carrot and stick approach does not work very well as children get older. There is a greater need to negotiate with them. This is not a bad thing, as some parents believe. It demonstrates to them that you are treating them as an independent human being with wants of their own. And they are

more likely to keep to their end of a negotiated agreement. It is also teaching them a valuable life skill, though try to not to turn every interaction with them into a negotiation. You shouldn't need to 'negotiate' everyday good or respectful behavior.

* As children get older, good types of 'rewards' are an increased sense of autonomy, giving them more chances to make their own decisions, and more opportunities to interact with friends.

* Be sensitive to the fact that your children don't stay kids for very long and eventually you need to start treating them more like adults and negotiating with them if you are to remain friends with them when they grow up.

* If you unjustly shout at your children, apologize unreservedly. If you shout at them albeit with what you consider to be justification, still apologize but explain their part in it.

* If you criticize other members of your family in your child's presence – for example criticizing your own parents – then your child will see this as normal. They will not only be learning to be critical of your parents, they will also be learning to be critical of you.

* Criticism of your partner in the open hurts your child.

* Children pick up on the moods and stresses of their parents. Better to admit you're stressed but trying to deal with it, rather than just being stressed around them but trying to hide it. Your stress will result in short temper and lack of attention, which they will react badly to and assume is to do with them unless you are open and honest with them.

Relationships with Teenagers

* It is easy to drift apart from your teenagers, and if you do so they are likely to drift apart from you when they become adults. You need to find some things you can do with your teenagers, some common interests, that you and they feel comfortable doing together: cooking, going out to events, even watching common interest TV so long as it prompts conversation.

* You can't expect to have serious one to one conversations with your teenager if you don't regularly converse in a no pressure environment about nothing in particular. You need to spend time simply being in each other's company – eating, watching films, doing odd jobs, walking, etc. Buying off your teenager as a guilt driven replacement for not spending time with them is not the basis for a decent relationship; now or in the future. Moreover small intense periods of what you might term 'quality time' does not make up for simply lots of time. Your children need your presence more than they need your presents.

* Spend some dedicated time with your children even when they get older. Ensure you are comfortable around them and they are comfortable around you. If not, you won't see much of them after they have left home.

* Appreciate your teenagers whilst they are home. They'll be gone soon enough. If they ask for help with schoolwork, or anything else, try to give it to them, though do so in a way that they learn, rather than simply doing it for them.

* Your teenager will develop their own interests and abilities. Encourage them in anything, within reason, that they feel passionate or strongly about, even if you can't understand why on earth they would want to do that. Don't try to push them in a direction they clearly don't want to go. It won't work and they'll become alienated from you.

* Parents who criticize their children's choices, particularly once they become teenagers, end up strengthening the desirability of those choices. Criticizing a daughter or son's choice of friends makes those friends more desirable and is thus counterproductive.

The Bumper Book of Common Sense

* When your teenager has friends round don't hang about. If you do they are likely to stop bringing them round, then you'll lose track of the people they hang out with.

* Ensure your home is somewhere your teenager can be comfortable and feel safe. Ensure they know you love them, and that they can talk to you about anything that worries them and can come to you for advice. Though don't tell them what to do; only what they could do.

* Do not belittle your teenagers concerns. What to you with your many years of experience might be minor matters, to them can fill their very being. Teenagers do get depressed and some even try or succeed to commit suicide over things that 10 years later wouldn't bother them at all.

* Teenagers can and do get stressed. Try and teach them strategies for coping. Exams in particular can be very stressful. Ensure they start their revision a long time in advance and help them understand the basics of the topics they are learning.

* Teenagers feel insecure in society. Their constant texting, for example, is a form of mutual grooming. Don't be critical of it.

* Expect some defiance and rowing with your teenager. It is a part of them growing up and becoming independent. It is part of the shift towards them becoming your equals, which you need to accept, and ought to support and encourage, or you will become alienated from them.

* Teenagers often say hurtful things. Don't demand an apology, which will just inflame things. When things have calmed down point out that what they said was unkind or hurtful. But leave it to them whether or not they apologize. And they usually will. Demanding they do will not help matters.

* Being dictatorial with your teenager will back fire. They will rebel, and you will end up with an estranged relationship. Much better to negotiate with them. You can and should have rules, but be willing to come to compromise agreements respecting their views and needs. Do however be tough when agreements are broken without good reason.

* Just because your teenager has done something you consider to be wrong you do not need to necessarily punish them. Often just making clear to them that it was wrong is enough, though you may need to discuss it with them since they may have a different view of right and wrong than you have. However don't let them take advantage of you through deliberately defying you, knowing they will always get away with it.

* Should you need to punish your teenager, ensure that the punishment is one relating to whatever you are punishing them for. Punishments should be focused on teaching your teenager that some actions are wrong and have consequences for others.

* Do not get into a habit of continually nagging your teenager. Come to agreements with them about what needs to be done, by when, and the consequences if they are not.

* When you find yourself in the middle of an escalating row with your teenager:
    o Take a few deep breaths – but don't make it seem as though you are sighing;
    o Keep to the topic of the argument;
    o Avoid overstating ('you always ...', 'you never ...');
    o Focus on behavior, and the consequence of the behavior on others, not the person;
    o If you feel you are going to lose your temper, back away.

* Teenagers value independence. Rather than tell them to do something give them a choice of what to do. For example, don't tell them they must do X now, but ask them if they want to do it now or at some specific time later.

* Praise your teenager for good behavior or actions without qualifying it with a but. Be genuine however, teenagers can readily spot phony praise.

* Be an active listener when your teenager is talking to you. Don't do other things, or jump in with your pearls of wisdom.

* Because of the way teenagers' brains develop they have heightened emotions before they have developed the rational means to control them. This leads to irrational outbursts and risk taking. No point in your getting upset about it. Develop strategies to cope, such as spending regular no conflict time with them. Also talk about what can happen as a result of risky behavior, but in a matter of fact tone that doesn't seem like it is directed explicitly at them.

* Remember that teenagers largely think themselves invulnerable, and that bad things happen to other people. It is often best to appeal to their vanity when talking about any bad habits they may be developing such as excessive drinking or smoking.

* Many teenagers die every year as a result of car accidents, most of them resulting from their own actions or the actions of other teenagers they are with. Once your teenager has learnt to drive go with them a few times to identify any particularly bad habits, and also go with them when they first drive in bad weather or at night. Ensure they understand that loud music, phones, eating, or other distractions whilst driving are potentially lethal. Instill a habit of being a courteous driver by being one yourself whenever you are driving and they are with you. And insist on rules such as no driving if they have had anything alcoholic at all to drink, or if they are tired.

* Discuss 'what if' scenarios with your teenager. What if they were with friends who were drinking and then going to drive? What if they felt someone was following them? Discuss this with them when they are in a good mood and relaxed.

* Have only a few important rules you stick to with regards your teenager, not lots of them. Set your rules with them, and explain the reasons behind them. Be willing to negotiate. Some potential reasonable rules include:
  o Safety: Keep in touch; be home at a reasonable time; don't take drinks or substances or lifts from strangers;
  o Everyone has rights to live in a comfortable home. They should put their stuff away when left in common areas, and should not force their loud music on others;
  o Everyone should help with certain chores, such as washing up and tidying up after meals, and doing their own laundry;
  o Everyone has a right to their own space, but no crockery or left over food left lying around or rotting in bedrooms.

* Some basic safety rules you need to teach your children once they start going out without you:
  o No lifts from strangers;
  o No lifts from friends who have been drinking;
  o When walking alone at night keep aware, no listening to music;
  o When walking alone stick to busy roads, avoid deserted alleyways or paths;
  o Keep valuables out of sight;
  o Keep away from dangerous situations or ones that make them feel uncomfortable;
  o Drink sensibly;
  o Be forceful if being threatened sexually.

* Pass on your tips for getting organized. Encourage them to be organized though don't try to force them.

The Bumper Book of Common Sense

* Teach them how to manage money effectively – give them a weekly or monthly allowance but be clear about what it is and is not for, and don't top it up simply because they've spent it. As they get older you can increase the allowance but have it cover more of the things you might otherwise have bought for them and thus give them choices about what to spend their money on.

* Before your children leave home ensure they have learned about basic financial management. And don't leave it till just before they leave. Aspects of financial management to instill in them include:
    o How to protect financial and personal information, including the need not to keep pin numbers or other personal information written down where they could be stolen along with their credit card;
    o In terms of daily expenses to spend less than they earn. Exceptions include things like mortgages and particular big expenses like cars. However even with these they need to ensure they can afford the payments, and not just the interest payments but regularly pay back some of the capital owed;
    o How to budget, and do basic budget calculations;
    o How to manage a bank account and sensibly use credit cards so they are not paying interest on them;
    o What investments are all about and how to go about investing;
    o How to shop for bargains, and to ensure that what they are buying are things they really want rather than getting taken in by advertising to buy things they will discard within days;
    o The importance of starting to save for their retirement as soon as they start a regular paying job.

* Try to teach your teenager some basic critical thinking skills. Teach them that there are often two sides to most arguments, and that they should make their judgments after understanding what they are rather than leaping to conclusions. A way to do this is to discuss with them topical news items and ask them what they think, and put alternative viewpoints to them. Keep it as matter of fact as you can and try not to get into emotional arguments with them about such topics.

* Try to ensure your teenager develops a positive outlook on life. That even if things look bad, they will get better. Teach them that rather than complaining about things they should take responsible for trying to make things better, or if things are truly outside their control to accept them and get on with doing what they can.

* Teach your teenager how to deal with the demands of homework and revising in plenty of time rather than as a last minute rush. They will be prone to procrastination just the same as adults, and you need to provide them with examples of how to overcome this. Best to get them to do weekend homework at the beginning of the weekend rather than at the end. Teach them to plan for the work that needs doing.

* Help your teenager develop listening and conversation skills. Teach them the basics of small talk. When they finish with school or college, whether they continue higher education or start work, they will regularly be meeting new people. Help them feel comfortable doing so, rather than awkward. An essential element of this is ensuring they develop good listening skills.

* Ensure your teenager gets the opportunity to learn practical skills. Basic cooking skills, how to change a light bulb and a plug, how to use tools safety, how to read electricity and gas meters, how to do laundry, how to clean around the house, how to do basic repairs, how to top up the oil and water in a car and change the bulbs. In fact anything that you do in terms of keeping your house, garden, or possessions in a good state of repair are things you should show your teenagers.

* Teach your teenager how to appreciate being in the present rather than continually being traumatized by the past or worried about the future. Teach them to appreciate the moment.

* Children and teenagers are not born with an inherent ability to be responsible. They need to learn it. They need to learn that their actions and behavior have consequences. You need to give them

room to suffer and learn from their own mistakes, albeit without putting them into any serious danger. It is better they learn the consequences of irresponsible behavior whilst still under your roof, rather than only learn after they've left home and when the consequences could be catastrophic.

Relationships within Families in General

* Family life has the potential, for most of us, to be the greatest happiness in our lives. But don't take it for granted. Be willing to work at it, and that means making compromises.

* The best of times are days out with the family.

* If you are in a family ensure there is family planner or calendar that includes everyone's events. If there are conflicts in each other's schedules you want to see this well in advance and resolve them before they become the cause of considerable friction.

* Families need some joint events to give them memories of being a family. This might be joint holidays or joint days out, or joint attendance of particular events.

* It's important to have some traditions in families, around Christmas for example, to give your children something to remember and to nostalgically look back on when they've left home. However it's also important to let traditions go when their time has passed. If maintaining certain traditions becomes a stress, let them go.

* If you have children, then your family life will be subject to change. Your children won't stay the same forever, and will gradually change from being totally dependent upon you to being fully independent people deciding for themselves. Don't fight against this change; it is going to happen. Appreciate the time you have with them, and help them to become independent of you.

* If your children are disrespectful to your relatives, then it's because you are disrespectful to your relatives.

* Small talk in families is important. Ask open questions. Rather than 'Did you have a good day?', 'Tell me about what you've been doing today.'

* Fix the little problems around the home. A little at a time, but regularly. You will feel much more comfortable and have less family arguments if you do.

* Look for little improvements you can make to your home. Brighten it up a little. Make it a little more comfortable. This will help facilitate more harmonious family relationships.

* Don't begrudge the good you do. Many people find themselves helping others in their family, either parents as they get old, or others with disabilities. They can come to see this as a major constraint on their lives, something holding them back. It is easy to get into a mindset whereby they don't do anything for themselves, but nor do they take pleasure in the good they are doing for others. Two points:
   o Firstly, helping others is one of the most worthwhile purposes you can have. Most of what makes our lives worthwhile and purposeful is our relationships with others. If others need help and you give it to them, take pride and pleasure and meaning from doing so. If you don't this will almost certainly reflect onto your relationship, and both you and the other person will be poorer for it.
   o Secondly, you can and should also pursue your own interests and goals alongside helping others. There is always a way of doing this, and those who use their helping of others as an excuse for not doing so are invariably the people who even if they had all the time to themselves would still find nothing purposeful to do.

The Bumper Book of Common Sense

* Children, whether young or teenagers, can be severely traumatized by parents going through a divorce. They will frequently see the troubles between their parents as being at least in part their, the child's, fault. It is important that parents remain close and loving to the children and avoid acrimony between themselves when any of their children are in proximity. They must also avoid badmouthing the other to their children or trying to get children to take sides. A parent who tries to get their child or children to take sides is being very very selfish, since the children should be allowed to retain good long-term relationships with both their parents.

* Forgive your parents for not being perfect. When you have children of your own you'll realize that for the most part you are simply trying to do your best in an environment where it is far from obvious what is really best. It was the same for your own parents.

* Remember, how you treat your parents is how your children are likely to turn out treating you. If you are continually making excuses for not visiting or not getting in touch with your parents, or continually complaining or being negative about them, then your children will be learning that as normal behavior. Once your children have left home you will no longer be the most important people in their lives. If you treat your own parents with respect and warmth and remain friends with them, then it is far more likely your own children will do so with you.

Relationships with Close Friends

* Friendship is borne out of proximity and shared interests. Find somewhere you can be in close proximity with people who have similar interests to yourself and you are likely to come across people you can be friends with.

* Join a group. People who are members of a group tend to experience greater happiness.

* A few close friends will help you get through life: a few people you can be close to and with whom you can talk to about more or less anything.

* You'll never be lonely if you have a true friend, but you'll never have a true friend unless you pay attention to them. Treat them well and they'll treat you well. If you want friends to be there for you then you need to be there for them.

* Be willing to help others and others will be willing to help you.

* If someone does you a good turn send them a thank-you card.

* Just as with family, close friendships can come under considerable strain. You need to be careful not to take close friendships for granted, and be quick to forgive. You may also need to adapt your friendships to changing life circumstances, your own and your friends. There is no reason close friendships can't survive changed life circumstances, but they will probably need to adapt. Regular nights out with friends when you are both single is likely to be less acceptable or feasible when you or they are in a relationship, and particularly if one of you has children and the other doesn't. But if you and they are willing to be flexible and adapt in a way that works for you both then close friendships can well survive.

Having and Looking After Pets

* Only have a pet if you are willing to put in the time to look after it. Recognize that children are very fickle when it comes to having pets. If you buy them a pet ensure you are willing to take full responsibility for looking after it should your child lose interest, which is a common occurrence.

* Ensure you are willing to spend money on setting up appropriate living conditions for your pet or pets, feeding them, having them looked after when you go on holiday assuming you can't take them with you, and, for many types of pet, vet bills.

* Don't blame your child for maltreatment of a pet. You are the adult; you take responsibility. If your child maltreats a pet it is because you gave them the opportunity to do so, and you did not teach them not to. Note that children can be cruel and it is your responsible to ensure they are not given the opportunity to be so. Cruelty or failure to care for a pet is a crime.

* Learn about any pets you have. How do they need to be cared for? Don't assume you know, unless you do know because of past experience. Find information, particular to your type of pet, covering diet, living conditions, extent to which they should or shouldn't be kept with others - either of the same species or different, the amount of exercise they should be given if appropriate, and how to look out for and deal with illnesses.

* Ensure your pets are looked after. Ensure they are fed regularly, given fresh water regularly, and their toilet areas are cleaned out regularly. If they need taking for exercise ensure it is done. Ensure you don't simply abandon them. Regularly talk to them and stroke them if they are the type of pet that can be stroked. Ensure they are not left in places that are too hot or too cold or otherwise dangerous for them. If you leave pets in cages in the garden, ensure they are secure from foxes or other wild animals. If they are injured or ill take them to see a vet. Even if the pets have been bought for your children, ultimately they remain your responsibility.

* With certain types of pets you need not to leave them alone in the presence of young children, or possibly even older children. There are, for example, certain breeds of dog that can be dangerous, and whilst you may be convinced your particular pet is completely house-trained, there are circumstances where even the most placid animal can become a danger.

Influencing and Persuading

In General

* If you want to influence others:
    o Be clear about what you want;
    o Plan your approach;
    o Keep your message simple and short;
    o Use open friendly body language;
    o Understand the other person's point of view;
    o Look for commonalities with the person or people you are trying to influence – people like people like themselves or who have similar backgrounds.
    o Respect the other people – think of them as equals;
    o Interact at a time when it is convenient to them;
    o Seek give and take;
    o Be confident;
    o Appeal to their self-interest and the benefits to them;
    o Ensure your ideas are practical or useful to them;

- o Surprise people, find an unusual way of presenting your message;
- o Start at one end of your position, though ensure it is reasonable, and slowly move towards a compromise position;
- o Ask them to come on board with your ideas.
- o Be clear about your agreements as they are made. Preferably get them written down.

* Factors used in persuasion include: reciprocation, our tendency to respond in kind; consistency, our tendency to want to appear consistent; social proof, our tendency to do the same as others; liking, our tendency to be more willing to believe people we like; authority, our tendency to do like what authority suggests or tells us to do; and scarcity, our tendency to think scarce things are more desirable and better.

* In a complex environment people will tend to accept or stick with the default options offered to them.

* Don't give advice; suggest options.

* If you want to persuade someone of something you need to pick your time. Pick the wrong time and you will fail. Timing is important. There is a time to reap and a time to sow. A time to keep silent and a time to speak.

* People buy on emotion and justify with fact. Arguments that appeal to people emotionally are almost always more persuasive in practice than arguments that are based simply on logic. Often the most persuasive arguments, by politicians, or salesmen, or even fanatics, intentionally lack logical argument.

* Style will often triumph over substance when it comes to influencing what people believe. The emotion and immediacy of witnessing something will have a far stronger impression than abstract arguments or statistics to the contrary.

* It is hard to persuade people with abstract ideas and statistics. You need concrete examples which people can relate to to support the ideas you are trying to get across.

* Words can be used to deliberately arouse feelings, or bias someone positively or negatively, often though the use of adjectives. It is important to look out for the emotional content of language, and keep focused on the meaning of the words in their particular context.

* People are more likely to listen to you and do what you ask if you talk less and spend more time listening to them.

* Not all that glitters is gold. Don't be fooled by appearances. If something seems too good to be true, then be very wary, and do lots of checks.

* When looking to reach agreement with someone avoid being judgmental. State the facts and tell them what your point of view is. Invite them to give their point of view and then talk around the various possibilities and options until you find a course of action that suits both parties.

* If you want someone to take action, make it as easy for them to do so as you can.

* If you need to criticize someone, in order to try to improve their future behavior, ensure it is a specific aspect of their behavior or their output that you are criticizing rather than being critical of them or their behavior in general. In many cases you don't even need to actually criticize their behavior but merely point it and its consequences out, and leave them to judge themselves.

* People will not listen to you if you are simply critical. You need to be positive if you expect people to listen to what you have to say.

* If someone is trying to persuade you of something, whose interests are they serving, yours or theirs?

Salesmen's Tactics

* A common sales technique is to bump and drop. Put the price up and then offer a discount, or a 'special offer' or a sale price.

* People will pay more for an item when in an environment in which other things are expensive. It is a common sales technique to initially show you something expensive so as to make what they really expect to sell to you appear cheap or at least good value. Related, is the idea of selling you accessories after you have purchased an expensive item. The accessories may be at a price you wouldn't buy them at if they were all you were going to buy. But relative to the something much more expensive you have just bought they don't seem so expensive and you can easily get drawn into buying them, especially when they are offered up to you one at a time.

* A salesman ploy is to make a good offer, gain a strong commitment from the prospective customer that they want the product, and then find a reason why the original offer cannot be upheld. Often the commitment is by then so strong that the customer accepts the increased price, particularly if there is a good plausible reason for why the original offer had to be withdrawn. In such circumstances, ask yourself if you would have wanted the product at the new price if it is what had been on the table initially. If not, walk away. You may of course find that the original offer comes back onto the table.

* Moral licensing is where someone makes you feel virtuous or good about yourself, and then leads you into temptation, as a reward. Thus TV advertising such as 'because you're worth it'.

* A sales ploy is to claim something is scarce – buy now as later it will not be available. A variation on this is when information is presented as though it were a secret or restricted. Thus many books will claim to offer 'The Secret of ….'.

* People will feel more comfortable about a decision if they believe it is one that many others have or would make. This is an effect advertisers try to exploit, when they set up testimonies from people like us – which of course are usually carefully scripted.

* Salesmen and TV advertising will often appeal to our vanity, and our desire to be part of a special elite group. Thus the association of famous people with given products, and the implication that by buying that product we are entering an elite group that includes those particular famous people.

* People will often go out of their way to be consistent with earlier actions or decisions. Even if their actions or decisions become irrational in the new circumstances. Thus a sales ploy is to start as though doing a survey, 'how would you respond if …', asking the question in a way that leads you to giving a reply that makes yourself look good. They then put you in that position, leaving you with the choice of either doing what you said you would in the survey or being seen to having been a liar. Most people will do what they said they would, even though a direct approach to them would not have led to such an outcome.

* We have a deep human desire to reciprocate. If someone does us a favor, we have a natural instinct to want to return it, even if we don't particularly like the person that has done us the favor. Most of us feel uncomfortable with a sense of indebtedness and will do a lot to release ourselves from it. We also have an instinct to receive a favor: it seems impolite to refuse a favor. Our inherent instinct to receive and want to return favors is exploited by some salesmen or persons who want to influence us, as they create a small sense of indebtedness, for example through giving us a free sample, or a small gift, or even a try before you buy. They will then try to draw us into a situation where we 'return the favor'. Of course the favor we are being drawn into returning will be substantially greater than the relatively minor one they will have done us. This is often done so subtly we don't even notice it going on. To respond to this we need to see it for what it is, a sales technique, and thus counter any instincts to respond. We can always turn down 'gifts' or if they are

forced upon us in a way we cannot refuse simply take them and walk away. We do not need to feel guilty about not being manipulated by others – and indeed can see our keeping a gift in these circumstances as our simply responding to a manipulative ploy with a reciprocated manipulative ploy. If we are interested in the product being offered, then we should turn down the gift before we talk to them about it, and indeed refuse to discuss the product with them unless the gift is withdrawn. If you like the product and buy it, you can always then take the gift, they will not begrudge you it if they have made the sale.

* When being sold something by a salesman who we find ourselves liking it is important to distance ourselves from them. We have been manipulated into liking them. We need to think objectively about what is on offer. Would we have been interested in the product if we had heard about it from a leaflet that came through our door?

* People manipulate us to do things we don't really want to do by getting us to focus on one or a limited number of features rather than seeing things in the round and in their wider context.

* We rely on partial information to make decisions when we are rushed, stressed, uncertain, distracted, or tired. People who want us to make decisions in their favor will often manipulate us into one or more of these states.

* Smells trigger wants in our brains and retailers such as supermarkets and fast food establishments exploit this. The smells themselves are rarely the result of the food or products themselves, but are specially manufactured smells being deliberately pumped into the atmosphere. Baked bread smell is a particular favorite, and it generally instils a feeling of comfort and nostalgia in most of us.

* Supposed psychics and mind readers influence people through techniques whereby they use general but vague terms which many people can pick up on because of some loose connection to themselves, and then the supposed psychic adapts to the way people respond to home in on more specific truths. There is nothing magical in it. They are often skilled readers of body language and picking up other clues, and also generally focus on people who have a tendency or willingness to believe in the first place. They also play on people's tendency to believe in statements of authority and statements that show them in a positive light.

Use of Power

* Power is the ability to get others to do the things we want them to do. There are broadly two forms of power - influence and compulsion. We should try to influence people rather than force them. Relying on compulsion often has undesirable side effects.

* We can gain power to influence through being knowledgeable and skilled. We can thus increase our influencing power through increasing our knowledge and skills.

* The best power to accumulate is that which comes from a respect for your capabilities and ability to get things done.

* Power itself is neither good nor bad. We need power to get things done. What is good or bad are our motivations for wielding the power we have, how we apply it, and the ends to which we put it.

* We should not see the accumulation of power as a bad thing, and avoid it. We simply need to stay honest in our use of power.

* By not using power to achieve your ends you are ceding to others the use of power to achieve their ends.

* We do not need more power than others in order to be able to influence them. We simply need enough power through interdependence to make it in the other person's interests to have us on board with a solution.

* If you use power to push people too hard, they will tell you what you want to hear rather than what you want to know. When the Spanish in the 16th century were looking for El Dorado in America they used to torture the natives so that they would tell them. So of course the natives told them. 'It is hidden in the jungles to the East', or 'It is high in the mountains far to the West', or whatever. And there are of course many many examples of analogous situations, including everyday 'management' situations where managers want their staff to give them good news, not bad; so they do.

* The threat of punishment is used more often than the potential for reward as a means to supposedly motivate people: adults and children. However it leads to inappropriate learned behavior, including procrastination, fear of failure, and the feeling that nothing you do is good enough.

* Power has a habit of corrupting. People are far from perfect beings, and to some extent are held in check by constraints. However the more power we have the more we can overcome the constraints or come to believe the constraints don't apply to us. Be wary of seeking too much power.

* 'Might is right'. This is true only because Might says it is. It is a tautology, rather than a statement of truth. When Might says something that we believe to be wrong or unjust it is often Common Sense to hold back from saying so; since in certain circumstances our pointing out the error will merely bring the wrath of the Might upon us, rather than leading to Might objectively listening to and responding to what we have to say. Fortunately in today's democratic societies the greatest Might lies with the state, and whilst there is still opportunity for abuse of power it is far less prevalent than in other societies or than it has been in the past.

Psychological and Physiological Factors

* Someone who is experiencing intense emotions is more receptive to ideas and is thus in a relatively suggestible state.

* To change someone's mood, tell them a story. The more vivid you make it the more you affect their mood. It also works well with an audience.

* If you are deliberately trying to manipulate someone emotionally, keep your language simple.

* Don't expect someone who is in pain, or otherwise suffering, or who is generally in a bad mood, to be receptive to your new ideas. There is a time and a place to get someone's attention to new ideas.

* Note that people will be more conservative in their decision making when their glucose levels are low: which is generally later in the day, or after having made lots of other decisions.

* When our willpower is low we are more likely to put off making decisions or take decisions that keep our future options open. We are more likely to procrastinate over making decision.

* When our willpower and energy levels are low we tend to go for the easiest option. We are less able to make trade-offs and will adopt a simple approach such as going for the cheapest option, or the one that is being pushed most aggressively at us. A sales technique is thus to get us to make lots of minor decisions and then lead us down a path of least resistance comprising the default options they wish to sell to us. This, at least in part, is why impulsive buys are positioned near the checkouts in supermarkets.

The Bumper Book of Common Sense

* People faced with a large number of options are less likely to make a choice than people faced with a smaller number of options. People faced with too much choice often become paralyzed and avoid making a choice at all.

* People's behavior is strongly dictated by default circumstances. People in general do not 'opt out' of defaults. This can be exploited for good or bad. For example, countries where the organ donor option is opt-in have far fewer donors than those where the option is opt-out.

* People will be more positively disposed towards you if you reflect back some of their attitude and opinions, and even adopt, albeit not too obviously, some of their physical mannerisms.

* To persuade others, you need them to believe you share their values. One way to do this is to claim you once held your opponent's view but overwhelming evidence led you to change your mind.

* You are more likely to persuade someone to do something they probably would rather not, by first getting them to see themselves as the sort of person who does. Ask them if they are the sort of person who does X. Once and if they say they are, then ask them to do X. They are more likely to do so than if you had just asked them to.

* A one to one persuasion technique it to make a point by starting softly and looking down, then when you get to the key point stare intensely as you make the point. It gives an impression of strong sincerity.

* Don't try to change other people. Change yourself and be an example to other people. Children are influenced far more by the way their parents behave than they are by how their parents tell them to behave.

* Rules of Thumb and Stereotyped Behavior are an essential support to our dealing with the complexities of life. We simply don't have the time to work out from scratch how best to deal with most of the situations we come across. So we learn short cuts, rely on these for most of things we do, and conserve our energy and time to deal with things that don't fall into common patterns. Some people will exploit this. For example, a rule of thumb sometimes exploited is "Expensive = Good Quality". More often than not this is true, and the reason something is expensive is because much more effort went into its creation. However unscrupulous persons can take advantage of circumstances where it is difficult for us to readily confirm the quality, or circumstances where we cannot go back and complain later. They put a high price on simply to make us believe it is of high quality. Other examples of rules of thumb which can be exploited include "Higher demand = better value for money" and "What others are doing = what we should do."

* People will be influenced positively towards your proposals if they are presented with positive associations, even though it may be obvious that you are doing this deliberately and even if the associations are weak.

* People's experiences are strongly influenced by their expectations relating to those experiences. How something is presented and the environment in which it is set, can have a huge influence on what we actually experience. The same food presented one way in an expensive restaurant and another way in a cheap restaurant can taste very different.

* People's feelings about someone or something are influenced by physical circumstances. People holding a warm cup of coffee will be more positively disposed towards a stranger they are talking to than someone holding a cold drink. People sitting in hard seats are more likely to be argumentative than those sat in cushioned seats.

* We automatically assign to good-looking people favorable traits such as talent, kindness, honesty and intelligence, though subconsciously we don't notice ourselves doing it. We are more likely to give good-looking people the benefit of the doubt. Good-looking people have a significant social advantage.

* Men in the presence of attractive women, or having just been looking at pictures of attractive women, are more likely to make impulsive decisions; decisions aimed at the short term rather than the long term.

* People's natural tendency to associate things in close proximity to each other underlies most product advertising. Thus beautiful women are used in car ads, and statistically they do increase the sales to men, even though men will deny, and believe their own denial, that they have been so influenced. And of course celebrities are extensively used in advertising.

* Things that are important, or that we know to be of higher status, literally appear bigger to us. And things that are larger tend to be perceived as being of higher status. Taller people thus have a natural advantage over shorter people.

* People who go through a great deal of trouble or pain to attain something, or have paid a lot for it, will tend to value it more highly than someone attaining it with little effort. Conversely they will value something less if they have been unable to get: 'sour grapes'. If you are thinking of paying a lot of money for something, don't ask someone who has already done so since they will be highly biased towards it as a justification of their own outlay.

* If something is hard to get, it often becomes more desirable.

* People look to maintain consistency in how they appear to others, even if this pushes them towards making exaggerated or even less than truthful claims in order to be consistent with something they said earlier.

* People hate to lose things more than they like to gain them. People are loss averse and more prone to take risks to save losses than to make gains. Thus whether or not a transaction is framed as a loss or as a gain can significantly influence behavior. For many types of products you are more likely to lose customers if you increase your prices than you are to gain customers by decreasing your prices.

* Advertising slogans are repeated over and over because advertisers know that by such repetition the slogans become familiar to us and we have a greater tendency to believe things we are familiar with. Repetition and its resultant familiarity can be a more important factor in our beliefs than analysis or evidence.

* We often comply with requests that surprise us. Our state of uncertainty makes us more prone to agree with something we would have been less likely to agree to had we had more time to think about it.

* A common media technique is to propose 'What if ...' scenarios. By phrasing something as 'If ... then wouldn't it be terrible', they are not making an actual accusation, but they are creating an impression of wrong doing in the mind of the listener or reader. There are many media programs which base themselves entirely on this technique: 'What if aliens really existed and the government was covering it up'; 'What if there really was a conspiracy to ...'. This technique is also used in politics where should some wrong doing be associated with a person for reasons other than strong evidence, others can exploit the association by talking about how bad the wrong doing is, and phrases such as 'What a terrible thing it is. I'm not saying X did it, but if he had then ...'. There is no accusation here, but the association is being strengthened in the mind of the listener.

* If you are looking to influence powerful people then you need to get them into a situation where they don't feel so powerful, make your point, and then make them feel powerful again. If you try to influence them when they are feeling powerful they are likely to be confident and fixed in their existing opinions, and not open to your ideas; whereas when feeling less powerful they will be more open to different ideas. Ways of making them feel less powerful include ensuring they are in an environment where they are not surrounded by their power, away from their office for example, or just telling them something they didn't know and which for a short while shakes their confidence in their own omnipotence. Once you have made your case, then assuming it is a strong and logical

case, they will evaluate it. By then making them feel powerful again they will feel confident in their evaluation.

* Maintain good eye contact and people will be more positively disposed towards you, though be wary of strong eye contact which can be easily misconstrued or leave you seeming a little fanatical.

* Trying to change other people's thinking is very difficult to do. People only really change when they see or find out things they hadn't seen or known before. The best way to change someone is indirectly through helping them to have new insights.

* If you disagree with someone's views, simply telling them so is unlikely to influence them. Far better to ask questions about it. Seek a better understanding and guide them towards seeing the contradictions in their view. Openly disagreeing will generally destroy your influence. Questioning is far more powerful than argumentative confrontation.

* You can plant an idea in someone's head by denying it.

* People who are involved in the making of an agreement are more likely to live up to the terms of that agreement. People who, at the subtle request of the salesman, have written out the key parts of the sales agreement are less likely to cancel it during the cooling off period.

* When looking to get a largish group of people with divergent views to agree with you, you need to be as vague and general as you can get away with, a skill that is particularly important for politicians. The listener then interprets what you are saying in a way that suits them personally and they assume this is what you mean. The vagueness and generality also makes them feel more in control and they feel you are giving them more control.

* To sell or get agreement to something unpalatable, paint a worse scenario first, and then the unpalatable doesn't seem so bad.

Influencing Tendencies

* People are more often swayed by individual cases and anecdotes than by statistics even though the individual cases may be atypical. Stories that appeal on an emotional level, particularly those using fear, empathy, or pride, will beat statistics almost every time. However whilst strong testimonials can be very persuasive, they rarely provided the basis of good objective evidence.

* People are more likely to agree with you if they have already responded to you in a positive manner. Thus the tactic of getting people to respond positively to minor points before moving on to what you really want them to agree to. For example, if someone responds positively to your having politely asking them how they are, they are then more likely to comply with a subsequent request than if you had simply make the request direct.

* People are more likely to agree to a big request if they have already responded to a small one. Thus an influencing technique is to get you to make some small commitment that then triggers you being asked to make larger commitments.

* An influencing technique is to initially make a big request, and then when it is refused make a smaller request. Having initially turned down a big request people feel more obligated to respond positively to a smaller request.

* People are more likely to like you if they have done you a smallish favor. They are also more likely to do you a further favor. Note however that asking for or having people do you big favors can have a negative effect.

* Once someone has done you a small favor, they are likely to do so again.

* We like people who help us, and we help people we like. You scratch my back and I'll scratch yours.

* If you want someone to do something for you, give them something first. People have an implicit desire to reciprocate. Note however that people tend to be influenced more by small gifts than large gifts since they don't evoke ethical concerns.

* People are more likely to buy from people they have bought from in the past. The foot in the door technique is effective, in that once people have made even a very small purchase they are far more likely to make larger purchases in the future than are people who have not made any purchase at all.

* People are more likely to buy something at price A with something thrown in for free than buy it and the something at a price of A.

* People are more likely to respond positively to 'offers' that are expressed in an unusual way.

* If people are initially faced with a big unacceptable or extreme demand they are then more likely to respond positively to a more modest demand, than if they had been simply initially faced with the modest demand. Thus people will sometimes agree to crazy ideas because they are not seen as being crazy relative to the more outlandish ideas that were originally presented.

* You can make your own ideas seem more attractive by making alternative ideas seem extreme.

* If you are trying to influence others to take up a particular preferred option from a list that you have, then put your preferred option in the middle and put more extreme options at the beginning and end. However try to make sure your choice stands out and doesn't get lost amongst a long list of options, for example using very slightly larger font, a little more space before and after.

* When trying to persuade someone, throw in a bit of light humor, as it puts the recipient into a good mood; and people in a good mood are more giving.

* If you want someone to believe something, get them to write it down. Product companies run competitions where people write about how much they like the product. In writing positively about the product they are conditioning themselves to actually be more positively disposed towards the product.

* If people think you like them they will be more persuaded by you. We are all suckers for flattery, even when it is not particularly well deserved. If you flatter people in a way that is not too obvious then they will be more positively disposed towards you. If you are too obvious however it comes across as sycophantic and it can put people in a negative frame of mind towards you.

* We can significantly increase the likelihood of people liking us by appearing similar to them in the way that we dress, in what we say we like or dislike, and in our body language and posture.

* People are more positively disposed to others and to ideas whilst eating. It is easier to sell someone something whilst they are eating, assuming the eating experience is pleasant.

* People spend more money when they are hungry, and not just on food.

* We are more influenced by people we know and like than we are by strangers. We instinctively respond to cold callers by seeing them as a threat. Which is why salesmen try hard to make some connection to us before launching into their sales pitch. It is also why they try hard to get names of others from us so that when they go to see them they can refer to us and appear like a 'friend' who knows their friends.

The Bumper Book of Common Sense

* Availability shapes demand. If something is readily available people are more likely to buy it than if it is more difficult to find or get hold of. Thus people are more likely to buy items in a shop that are in prominent positions.

* We are strongly influenced by information that is readily to hand, or easy to locate. We have a tendency to be lazy and to simply accept easily obtained information. If some information has been provided for us, ask whether the person who has provided it has a vested interest. If so, we should seek out further information. In particular, we need to be careful about simply accepting information we readily come across on the Internet.

* We are more influenced by information that is easy to understand than by information that is difficult to grasp. It is thus worth trying to present information in as clear and simple a manner as you can, with analogies that help with difficult concepts. Better to get someone to have a simplistic view of something that is complex and roughly correct than no view at all. You can always tell them the view is simplistic and invite them to gain a better understanding. Expecting them to immediately grasp difficult concepts however is likely to lead them to making no effort at all to understand.

* We are more readily influenced by concrete information than abstract information. Charities in seeking out donations from the public now largely focus on individual cases we can visualize rather than simply provide us with abstract statistics. A picture of a single starving child influences us more than being told 15% of children in a country are starving.

* Base your arguments on what is good for your audience, not on what is good for you. How would they benefit?

* In a debate, the last speaker has the persuasive advantage. Not just because earlier speakers will be likely to be forgotten, unless they kept their message simple and repetitive, but because earlier speakers will have left uncertainty in the minds of the audience which a later speaker can exploit. An uncertain audience is more vulnerable to persuasion. Thus as a last speaker start your speech by reiterating the alternative views thus emphasizing the uncertainty. If you find yourself as an earlier speaker, keep your message simple and repetitive, also with some novel way of getting it across if at all possible, so that it sticks in the audience's mind.

* If you want to persuade someone to move to your position you need to start with where they are and the beliefs they hold as self-evident. You need to understand their current position and what is important to them and what arguments might move them from it. Don't tell them their current views are wrong, because they won't believe you. Confirm that their current views are right, but give them a path towards changing them to something better.

* In putting together a persuasive argument be clear about what you want to achieve, decide what you want to say and in what order, determine the style that best suits your audience, get it down in an appropriate format, and deliver it.

* Three main stages in an argument intended to persuade. Identify with those you are trying to persuade, and show you are just like them and understand their point of view. Then present your logical argument as simply as you can, including responding to opposing views. Then finish with some emotions. Show you care about your argument.

* You can influence people by emphasizing certain points whilst de-emphasizing others. Some of this is just a natural and normal part of communication. If it leads to blatant misrepresentation or falsehoods however it becomes unethical.

* Use of language that implies superiority but is too imprecise to be meaningful is commonly used as part of advertisements. For example saying something will last 20% longer but not being specific about longer than what.

* People are more likely to do what you want them to do if they know the reason why, assuming of course the reason is honorable.

* You are more likely to get someone to commit to doing something in the future than you are to get them to commit to doing it now.

* We tend to over estimate the extent to which we can successfully influence the behavior of others. This is because whilst we are familiar with our own efforts to influence another, we are much less informed about what other factors and influences might also affect their behavior.

* Whether or not someone will listen to a reasoned argument is often dependent upon whether or not they are already pre-disposed to the conclusion you are trying to reach. Thus an individual may be open to reasoned arguments on some topics, but not others.

* People won't hear the full sentences you utter, but they will often hold on to certain words. Be wary of repeating words that have a negative connotation. You can tell a child that there are no monsters under the bed, but what sticks in the child's mind is 'monsters under the bed'. Better just to be reassuring about how comfortable and safe the bed is and that you are there to protect them.

Peer Influences

* People are far more reluctant to change their opinions once they have been made public.

* People are more comfortable and confident doing things others are also doing. Most of us feel comfortable buying a product we haven't bought before if there are lots of good testimonials from others.

* We have a tendency to assume the actions undertaken by many others are correct. This can be exploited when certain behaviors are made to appear to be the norm. Of course if many others are also influenced because they believe it is the norm, it then becomes the norm.

* Social 'proof' can lead to people following the lead of a few, leading to a snowballing effect as many others then join in. This is particularly potent in the light of uncertainty about what to do.

* Just because everyone else is doing something, does not mean it is right. Just think of lemmings and cliffs.

* When there is significant uncertainty, we are more likely to look to and accept the actions of others as being correct. This can be inappropriate. For example when you see someone staggering around in a public place is it because they are drunk or are they having a heart attack. If others are ignoring them then it is likely you will too.

* If you find yourself in trouble in a public place, and those around you are ignoring you, pick out an individual, make it clear you are in trouble, and ask for their specific help. It makes it difficult for them to ignore you. Once one person starts to help, others will as well.

* Most people will be more strongly influenced by the example of others than by rationale arguments. Telling people of the dangers to health and wealth resulting from drinking too much will be far less effective than showing them that they are part of a despised group, and that they have smelly breath.

* People are socially influenced to a far greater extent by people who are similar to themselves than they are by those who are different. Highly publicized news stories will often lead to copycat behavior amongst those similar to those in the stories.

The Bumper Book of Common Sense

Responding to Authority

* Most people have a tendency to obey authority figures, even if they think the instructions are wrong.

* Obedience to authority is instilled in us from birth, and when there are also explicit or implicit punishments for none obedience, as there are often are, then unthinking obedience is common for most people. Moreover following instructions given by an authority figure means many people then no longer feel responsible for their own actions and can be induced to do great harm without feelings of guilt.

* Our instinct for obeying authority even when it is telling us to do things we disagree with or which don't make sense can be fatal. In medical circumstances there can be a tendency towards blind obedience of higher authorities such as doctors or surgeons. This can and often has had fatal consequences, where someone more junior has been aware there is clearly or very likely an error but either held back because of an authoritarian culture or were not listened to having tried to point the error out. And of course this is not limited to the medical field.

* If we have no respect at all for authority, and question everything we disagree with, then organizations will be unable to function, to the detriment of us all. If we choose to be within a given organization, then the authority within that organization has a right to be obeyed so long as it is behaving in an ethical and appropriate manner given the acceptable cultural norms. However those in authority do sometimes make mistakes, and if we have good reason for believing they are making a mistake we should reasonably expect a right to be able to say so, and a right to be listened to without being penalized or criticized. Not all organizations or individuals within organizations respect this right, but it is not an unreasonable expectation.

* Our instinct to obey authority is exploited in adverts where actors dress as doctors or scientists or other figures of authority.

* Conmen exploit our deference to authority by pretending to have authority they don't have either through the way they dress and behave, through associations they claim to have, or through titles and qualifications they claim to have.

* An authority in one area of endeavor is not necessarily an authority in another, yet our deference to them tends to attach to them as a person rather than to them as a person in a particular role.

* People underestimate their own deference to authority. When asked how they believe they would respond if asked to do things they disagreed with by persons in authority, they underestimate their degree of compliance compared with how they actually do respond in tests or in actuality. People are thus not as forearmed to being inappropriately manipulated by seeming or actual authority as they should be.

* Be aware of your natural tendency to automatically respond to authority, and ensure you question instructions or requests that appear odd or which you have good reason to be concerned about. Be conscious of the possibility of the authority being mistaken in the particular context, or of the authority trying to con you. In particular ask yourself:
    o Could the authority be mistaken in this instance? Authorities are not perfect and they can make mistakes;
    o Does the authority have a vested interest that might be consciously or unconsciously prejudicing it in the particular context;
    o Is this really an authority on the matter in hand? Could it be a conman, or someone whose authority is not relevant to the particular matter in hand, such as when celebrities endorse products.

* The masses can easily be manipulated by their leaders into acts of aggression simply by being told they are being attacked, and being told that anyone who says otherwise is unpatriotic and is

exposing them all to danger. The enemy of extremists are people who think for themselves and see through the lies and manipulation of the extremists.

Scarcity and Censorship

* People can be significantly influenced by information they believe is scarce and known only to a few. The persuasiveness of a piece of information is often increased if it is itself seen to be scarce: 'Keep it a secret, but …'

* Our desire to have something is greater the scarcer it is. Something we might normally have no interest in can become desirable simply because we learn it is scarce or is about to become scarce. Closely related is the idea of limited time offers. Recognition of this underlies many of the sales and advertising techniques where we are put under pressure to make a decision quickly, before the opportunity is lost: 'hurry buy now, limited stock'. This is also exploited through sales events, where a number of limited very good deals leads to large crowds of people who then get caught up in buying lots of other things where the deal is significantly less good.

* We have a tendency to believe that something that is rare is also better.

* Two jars of identical items; one full, one nearly empty. All things being equal, people will generally find the items that are in the jar that is nearly empty as both more desirable and better than the items that are in the jar that is nearly full.

* Rivalry and scarcity can be a potent mix, and exploited by those trying to sell to us. When people are competing for a rare or scarce item they can become far more focused on owning the item than on ensuring the item is of value in the context of what they want it for.

* When finding ourselves beset by scarcity pressures we should think carefully about why we want the item. We then need to see the price relative to what we want the item for, and be sure we don't get pressurized by circumstances, often deliberately construed, into paying more than what it is worth to us.

* The act of censoring something often makes it more desirable, and raises people's estimation of it or desire to get hold of a copy of it. Attempts at censorship often fail, because the very fact that something has been censored makes it something people have a greater desire to get hold of. Thus ironically, by banning extremist views we are, for some people, increasing the attractiveness of those views. And when a judge rules something as 'inadmissible' in court and to be disregarded by the jury, he is often increasing the value of that information and giving it greater prominence – as of course lawyers are aware and sometimes seek to take advantage of.

Small Talk and Conversing

Why Small Talk?

* The world is full of people. And most of them are much like us, in their own way. Knowing how to be comfortable with other people through being able to engage in small talk is part of making the most of our lives. It opens up opportunities to making new friends and brings us closer to people we already know. It also helps us pass certain times of our lives more pleasantly and memorably than might otherwise have been the case.

The Bumper Book of Common Sense

* People like to talk about themselves. By using small talk to encourage them to do so, you will build stronger relationships with them.

* People like people who let them talk about themselves. Listen to people and ask who, how, why questions.

* If you avoid opportunities for small talk or conversation people will likely see you in a negative way – as stuck up probably, or as being interested in no one but yourself.

* Small talk is not just about talking with people we don't know. It is about being able to be with and talk comfortably with people we already know, through having a ready supply of conversation pieces to maintain good and comfortable relations with people, even family and close friends.

* The more you can identify in common with someone else the more likely you are to get on with them. Small talk enables us to seek out points of common background and interests and of common likes and dislikes.

Meeting New People

* Take the risk of meeting new people. Most people want to meet new people, but are hesitant about making the first move – so let it be you. The more you do it the better you'll get at it. And don't be put off by the occasional person who does not respond. Be respectful and move on.

* Always be open to meeting new people. Be the first to chat to someone new to your area. Find out who they are and what makes them tick. If you make the effort when they are new they will be positively disposed towards you in the future.

* Everyone you meet is interesting and worth talking to. Be curious about them and ask questions to enable you to find out things about them. Try to find out what most interests or motivates them. Is there anything they are passionate about or have a special interest in? You can do this with almost anyone you meet unless there is a particular good reason not to.

* At social functions, smile, and be willing to go up to strangers: "I don't know many people here, do you mind if I just talk to you for a moment." Smile and keep smiling. Think of occasions for meeting people as opportunities, not nightmares.

* You will interact much more effectively with strangers if you first get a few minutes to know them a little. Try to find something in common even if it is just the traffic you have just been through.

* When you greet another person, smile. Show enthusiasm and warmth, albeit without going over the top. Be expressive. A tip is not to smile immediately you meet them but hold back a couple of seconds, then smile. It is then clearer that you are smiling at them rather than just smiling at everyone.

* Look for any excuse to compliment someone. If you are at an event they have been involved in setting up say some good things about it. If they are wearing something unusual you can complement them if you feel comfortable doing so in the circumstances. If they mention some success they have had congratulate them. Any excuse to make someone feel good about themselves should be taken.

* Practice. Converse with everyone you come across: people you're in a queue with, neighbors, people on the bus, waiters. Use every interaction with others as an opportunity to practice and improve your small talk and intercommunication skills.

* If you are meeting someone you've met only once or twice before then don't assume they remember your name. Generally you should look for the opportunity to repeat your name when you talk to them again. Thus you might introduce yourself again to them as 'Hi, David Croucher,

we met …', or if they are with others be sure you introduce yourself to the others and thus avoid the potential embarrassment should they not remember your name.

Topics to Raise or Not to Raise During Small Talk

* Questions to ask of people you haven't met before are about the surroundings and present circumstances, about mutual acquaintances, about recent news items, sports events, the weather, about how they have traveled, about family or job (usually after you've broken the ice a bit), about where they were brought up, about favorite music or books or magazines or films, or recently read books or seen films, or current TV programs, about whether they are members of clubs or gyms, about whether they do sport, whether they have pets, about where they go on holidays, about where they would most like to visit, about their hobbies and what they do outside work.

* Your opening to talking to someone you've not met before is dictated by the circumstance that has brought you together, but will generally relate to the immediate surroundings or circumstances. Assuming you get some response then you can follow up on any cues offered by the opening interchange or move on to introducing yourself or your reason for being there. In doing so you need to provide some hooks for the other person to follow up on, and also give the other person the opportunity to offer up similar information.

* Once you've got into conversation use the direction of the conversation to prompt further questions, revealing something of yourself as you do so. You are seeking out something to connect you to this other person. Thus be open about your interests and information about yourself. It gives other people an opportunity for identifying common ground with you. Note that you need to be prepared to answer any questions you ask others since it is likely you will get asked the same questions back.

* Once you are engaged in small talk, continuing the conversation will involve a mix of comments and questions. You need to strike a balance: too many questions can make the interaction feel like an interrogation, too many comments and you are not giving the other person much opportunity to talk. You will be looking to move from simple questions that might have only a few words as an answer to more open questions that gives the other person the opportunity to open up.

* Ways of introducing topics include "What do you think of...?" Have you heard...?" What is your take on...?"

* Stay away from negative or controversial topics, unless you know someone well, and refrain from long-winded stories or giving a lot of detail in casual conversation. Also avoid talking about finances or significant illnesses, and keep any discussion on politics relatively light in tone. Remember you don't know a lot about the other person or their views or their personal circumstances.

* Be careful about use of jokes amongst people you don't know very well. Many jokes are discriminatory, and you don't know the personal circumstances of whoever you might be talking to.

* You'll have something in common with almost anyone. You just have to find it. Asking and following up on questions should help you find it. If the person is completely unresponsive then politely move on. But keep positive.

* Be genuinely interested in other people. Ask questions. People are interesting. Find out more about them, find something in common, find out things they know that you don't, find out what they are interested in and the topics they like to talk about. Ask them about where they grew up, or where they've lived. Ask about whether they have any particular ambitions.

* Raising minor issues that annoy you can open up the opportunity for the other person to do the same. But be wary of getting into a spiral of negativity.

The Bumper Book of Common Sense

* If you struggle finding questions to ask, run through in your mind the interrogative pronouns: Who? When? Where? Which? What? How? Why? It should prompt thoughts.

* If you can get someone talking about something they know more about than you, take the opportunity to learn more about it by asking questions. Most people will be only too happy to talk about something they know a lot about.

* People often like questions about themselves, and also a bit of flattery. If you have an excuse to complement them, for example on an unusual or particularly attractive piece of clothing or accessory, then do so.

* Small talk with an acquaintance is a little different to that with someone you don't already know. If you can remember a little about them, and you should make the effort to do so, you can follow up on that. Questions about holidays, or children, or some hobby. Other more general questions are such as 'How was your weekend?', or 'How have you been?', or 'You having a good day?' You risk one or two word responses, which if you are just passing by each other may be enough, or you will need to follow up by seeking a bit more detail. If you still get a short response you probably need to leave it, or maybe start talking about something you yourself have recently seen or been doing or something about someone else you both know.

Interacting During Small Talk and Conversations

* To keep the flow of conversation going you need to be a good listener and pick up cues from what the other person says. Being a good listener means maintaining good eye contact, not finishing off other people's sentences for them, and not talking to yourself whilst they are talking. Never glance around the room while they are talking to you. Do not fold your arms in front of you whilst you or they are talking.

* When someone tilts their head when you're talking it means they are listening to you attentively. Arms crossed in front is a sign that someone is not listening to you. If you find someone is not listening to you, try to get them to do more of the talking.

* Add description - color, smells, sounds, etc. - when you are talking to other people; if describing a place for example.

* If someone pays you a compliment, do not be dismissive; accept it, and show you are pleased to receive it. Be liberal in your praise of others.

* When introducing people to each other try to get some snippet of information into your introduction, something they have in common, which will enable them to start talking together.

* When responding to questions asked of you, avoid answering with simply yes's or no's. Look to throw in a mention of something else that can be picked up on as topic of continuing conversation. Thus throw in mentions of hobbies or holidays or particular likes or dislikes, so long as it relates to what is being talked about in some way.

* Avoid doing all the talking, avoid lecturing or being lecturing to, unless of course it is a lecture, avoid gossip, avoid talking about major health or finance problems or bad relationships, and avoid getting into arguments with people you don't know very well.

* Be wary of assuming knowledge or understanding on the part of the other person. Try not to use abbreviations or specialist terms with anyone other than people you know are completely versed in the topic you are talking about.

* Speak clearly. If you have an accent then slow down your speech when talking to anyone not with the same accent. If you are talking to people who are not very good native speakers of your

language then try to limit your vocabulary. Not only do you need to be more careful with your words but also be aware of homonyms whereby given words sound the same but mean different things: this is unlikely to be much of a problem with native speakers but can be a problem with those who are not very good speakers of the language.

* Don't tell people they are wrong. By all means say you don't agree, but don't tell them they are wrong.

* Don't try or feel like you need to impress. Any attempt to impress is usually obvious to the other person and comes across as arrogant or insincere.

* End the conversation in an upbeat manner. Try to leave the conversation before you run out of things to say. Best to cut the conversation whilst there is still a flow of topics rather than wait till you've run out, though don't be seen to be breaking off the conversation prematurely. Ensure you end with a smile, and preferably a shake of hands and some compliment about being pleased to have met them. If you wish to meet them again, make this clear, and ensure you have contact details as appropriate. Try to keep farewells relatively short.

Preparation for Small Talk

* Remember people's names. Write them down, though not in front of them. Use their name whenever you meet them. Remember things about people, write them down. Have questions you can ask people should you meet them.

* Keep a journal or notebook to write down conversation pieces. Unusual facts or news events. Funny stories. Quotes that appeal to you. Observations. Seek out a new one or two every week so you have something topical. Regularly review your notebook so the items are fresh in your mind.

* Develop a niche interest, something that once people know you have the interest they will be able to ask you about and will remember your interest in it.

* Look to see how good communicators talk to each other. Pick up tips.

* Before going to a function, social or business, brief yourself on some topics of conversation and interesting things to talk about. Either something relevant to the particular function, or general newsworthy items.

* Conferences and seminars are particularly good places for meeting people and networking in general. It is likely that the primary benefit you will get out of a conference or seminar is new contacts rather than the information delivered itself. You should go out of your way at such events to seek out potential new like-minded contacts or people with shared interests. Identify particular individuals to seek out.

* If you're going to an event try to get a list of names beforehand, and take it with you. If you can find out something about the people you will meet then do so. Remind yourself of anything about people you have met before. Look to see if there are people going who some of your friends or colleagues may know and to whom you could introduce yourself as their friend or colleague.

* Think about what you want to happen at an event or function and verbalize it to yourself. Say it with conviction and enthusiasm. Work on your inner voice to make it positive and enthusiastic about what you are going to achieve.

The Bumper Book of Common Sense

Improving your Small Talk and Dealing with Small Talk Failures

* The only way to get better at small talk is to regularly practice. There are usually many opportunities every day, and in truth they are very low risk. Whilst you may feel embarrassed if someone does not respond to your attempts at small talk, the truth is they barely notice, and will certainly quickly forget, unless you keep trying to push them after they've clearly indicated they don't want to talk. So be ever ready to comment on your surroundings or to ask questions of almost anyone you find yourself with for a few moments: maybe observations about the weather or the surroundings, or ask questions such as 'You having a good day?'

* Most people prefer to talk about themselves rather than listen to you talking about yourself. So be ever ready to ask them questions, and to follow up on those questions. Ensure however that you pay full attention to them as you do so and as you listen to them. Asking questions but then seeming distracted will come over as very insincere.

* Small talk experiences, good or bad, will help you improve your skills. Take any opportunity, and certainly don't avoid situations because of a reluctance to engage in small talk.

* Learn from how others engage in small talk. Pick up tips from people who try to engage you in small talk, or who you overhear in queues or elsewhere. Some people are able to engage effortlessly in small talk. Look to learn from them and you'll find yourself developing the same skills.

* Not all your attempts to engage in small talk are going to be an outstanding success. Sometimes nothing will come to mind. Sometimes you won't get a response from someone you try to talk to. Sometimes you might even get a negative response. Don't let failures put you off. Just continue to learn and to better prepare.

* If you try to make conversation with someone and they don't respond, or you get a negative response, don't get upset. Move on. Maybe they are not interested in talking to you or indeed anyone at this time for reasons that are nothing to do with you.

* Don't be disheartened if you have difficulties communicating with certain people. It happens. You won't instantly get on with everyone.

* If you get regular rejections when trying to engage in small talk, try to see if there is something you are not doing right. Maybe you are not yet applying the basic principles of small talk. Maybe you have bad body odor or bad breathe: if so, do something about it. Maybe you are being too pushy? Maybe your body language is aggressive or closed? Your failures are the best feedback you will get and will enable you to learn and adapt and do better in the future. Don't see them in a negative light. See them as opportunities and use them.

* Some common failings in small talk are not being able to get beyond the initial interchanges relating to circumstances, and getting stuck on a favorite topic. If you find yourself regularly suffering from these failings, then the shortcomings result from either not picking up and responding to the cues given by the other person, or not being open yourself to giving cues which would allow the other person to hook on to. If you recognize these shortcomings in yourself you can work at overcoming them.

Morality and Being a Good Person

What is Moral Behavior?

* Behavior generally considered moral includes: avoidance of deliberate harm to others; a respect for other people's privacy and acceptance of their right to make their own decisions; a keeping of your promises and agreements; avoiding the deliberate misleading or defrauding of others; and a belief that others have a right to a minimum standard of living. Of course there are sometimes conflicts between these in particular circumstances, and also constraints brought about as a result of living in society, but that doesn't negate these being general guiding principles to live by in most societies.

* Morality is largely about recognizing and acting upon the fact that other people have needs and rights that, in so far as is reasonable, we should put on a par with our own. As such we should behave towards others in a manner that is honest, fair, and compassionate. This means all others, not just those who are close to us or those we personally know.

* There are some basic moral principles that are generally found in most religions in some form or other, though we don't need to be religious to accept them. Ultimately they underpin enabling large numbers of people to live in relative harmony together. Some of the underlying principles that make up such a morality are:
    o Treat others as you yourself would like to be treated;
    o Do the best you can in the circumstances;
    o Be honest and keep your promises;
    o Do not harm others except where they are a tangible threat to you;
    o Have a leaning towards charity;
    o Respect the rights and privacy of others and don't steal;
    o Seek to put back into your community what you take out;
    o Look after the environment: future generations are dependent upon you.

* Our morality should be based on the desire to create and live in a sustainable and fair world. Sustainable means that future generations matter, and fair means we should all have opportunities and a minimum standard of living and be free from physical coercion.

* Do your bit for the world you live in. Make personal sacrifices in times of shortage, for example by keeping to official guidelines during water shortages. Give to charities if you can afford it, or even get involved in charity work. Help to reduce pollution by being more environmentally aware and acting in an environmentally responsible way. Don't be wasteful when you have an option.

* We all have influence. It may be only over a few people, or it may be over many. But our influence then extends out from them. Look to ensure your influences are positive with the intent of making the world a better place.

* The fact that you can't help everyone is not an excuse for not helping anyone. The fact that you can't personally save the planet from pollution is not an excuse for polluting when you can reasonably avoid it. The fact that there are some others who selfishly don't care about others is not an excuse for you selfishly not caring about others. The fact that you cannot do the right thing all the time is not a reason for not doing the right thing when you can.

We Choose our Own Morality

* Life is without objective meaning. The meaning of your life is whatever you choose it to be or accept it as being. Life is what you make of it.

* You must take responsibility for your values and beliefs, and your moral code, and accept the consequences. Why not believe in a god or whatever religion attracts you. It is our choice. If that

The Bumper Book of Common Sense

helps you in your life it is as valid a choice as believing nothing and feeling empty and lonely your whole life.

* Having faith in some religion is choosing to be a member of a club. You are free to join the club of your choosing, but you should then expect to have to abide by its rules.

* One can choose to have faith, just as one can choose to reject all faith. Faith brings with it a way of life which for many is a better way of life than they would have through choosing not to have faith. Do not belittle those with faith, or those without faith, or those with a faith different to your own. Faith is a choice about how we want to live our lives.

* No amount of rational argument will bring the world into alignment with how we wish it to be. Our rationale however may help us to interact with the world in a useful way which either works for us or it doesn't. Choose whichever rationale works best, not because it is right, but because it works.

* We are all able to choose for ourselves high inviolable moral standards below which we will not go.

* When we avoid doing what we know to be the right thing, we are doing the wrong thing. Not to act when we should is as unjust as to act when we shouldn't.

* You can dodge your responsibility, but you can't dodge the consequences of dodging your responsibility.

* The Universe is what it is, but if we limit ourselves to its lowest sides – to biological needs, to creature comforts, to accidental encounters – we will lead a miserable life. If you recognize nothing but the 'struggle for survival', and the 'will to power' fortified by cunning, then your world will be limited.

* We cannot find meaning in simply being able to manipulate the world and satisfying our physical needs. Meaning is found in having a higher purpose. For many, this higher purpose is found through religious beliefs. For those without religious beliefs it can be found through our self-awareness of being part of the human race and seeking to be an active part in its continuing survival and progression, or simply through helping other people. We cannot and will not find meaning simply through selfish pursuit of our own ends and personal development aimed only at our own personal ends. There are many different religions and many different ways of finding meaning in life and they all have a right to exist so long as they don't violently try to impose themselves on others.

* There is no 'right way' to finding meaning, and we should all be on a journey of personal self-discovery. However the direction of travel is in looking outside of ourselves and see ourselves as part of the collection of self-aware beings rather than as selfish lonely beings. So long as you recognize this, and you are genuine about appreciating the right of all others to exist, then don't let anyone tell you you are on the wrong track.

How to Increase your Morality

* Test the morality of your decisions or actions by imagining them appearing on the front page of a major newspaper and your parents or family seeing it – would they be proud or ashamed of you?

* You don't have to commit fully to every good cause you come across. You can do a little bit as opportunity allows without feeling guilty that you don't do more. But there should be one or two good causes for which you do do more.

* Strive to be the best person you can be. Be clear about your core values and keep trying to live your life in accordance with them. Don't give up because sometimes you fail to live up to your own

standards. It is a good thing that you have standards, and it is good thing that you keep coming back to trying to live up to them every time you fail.

* Self-awareness is the route to self-development and self-realization. In the absence of a strong sense of self-awareness we act on the basis of mechanical self-interest, and lack the self-control or the direction to overcome our tendency to take the easy path rather than the path of long term gain.

* Meaning in our lives comes about through a genuine altruism, through helping others without thought of getting anything back in return.

* Make the effort to appreciate art. Art helps us feel a part of something bigger than ourselves. It helps us open up to a feeling of there being something that transcends our daily existence.

Benefits of Striving to be a Good Person

* Having a meaning in life will help us overcome most hardships. If we have a 'why', we can bear almost any 'how'. If our lives are without meaning we will tend to give up much quicker.

* Finding a meaning in your life, whether it is through religion or not, will increase your chances of living longer and having a healthier life. This is because you are less likely to engage in harmful bad habits, and you will have a more positive disposition that will cope better with misfortunes.

* In the long term, the good guys win more often than is appreciated.

* People who use dishonesty or overly selfish behavior as a way of making short or medium term gains are sometimes perceived as getting away with it. However these people are often stressed unhappy individuals, forever worried about getting caught out or of others taking advantage of them. And frequently, particularly over the longer term, they do get caught out and they find that others generally see them for what they are. Such individuals often find themselves very lonely in their later years.

* People who are inherently selfish find it difficult or impossible to have a long term loving relationships with a partner. And it is long-term loving relationships that bring us the most satisfaction in our lives.

* Giving to others creates a greater reward response in our brain than receiving gifts of similar value.

Some General Observations Relating to Morals

* We cannot use logic to determine our moral beliefs. However our moral beliefs should be consistent with logic, in that they should be coherent and consistent both in themselves and with regards our other beliefs.

* In all the history of mankind it has not been possible to demonstrate in any absolute manner that a given moral argument is true, nor even that it is true beyond reasonable doubt. So be wary of getting drawn into moral arguments that are claiming to be able to prove that a given belief is true.

* Different societies tend to accept different morals as the norm at different times. Morals can be seen as cultural influences on behavior. Frequently when a society judges certain behavior to be immoral this is due to practical factors whereby certain behavior is causing damage to the society generally.

The Bumper Book of Common Sense

* Whether we recognize it or not, it is likely that our morality is largely derived from and dependent upon the society within which we live.

* Common Sense cannot answer specific questions about morality. For example, if by killing one person we could save thousands, should we do it? What if the one person were a criminal? Or an innocent child? What if we could save millions? What if we could save 2 others? Don't expect Common Sense to give you the answer. Common Sense can however help you understand there are consequences of certain decisions, and can help ensure that you don't come to a decision through the application of faulty logic or beliefs.

* People's values can be dependent upon context. Different values could be applied to different aspects of a person's life.

* Being able to manipulate the world and others gives us power but it doesn't make our lives meaningful or worthwhile.

* Our moral choices are rarely between what is obviously good and what is obviously bad. Our moral choices are often between two choices both of which are, or appear to be good, or both bad. Sometimes we reject something not because it is wrong, but because we make another choice.

* All paths lead nowhere, but some journeys are better than others.

* The ends do not always justify the means. Sometimes the means have secondary effects for which the medium or long-term consequences are worse than the achievement of the ends.

* Circumstances are capable of turning most of us into bad or evil people. At a large group level the following are steps that have in the past led what would otherwise have been ordinary caring people into being bad people:
    o Some ideology which justifies discrimination;
    o An authority which legitimizes the ideology;
    o Giving people an important and meaningful role which is 'recognized' by the authority;
    o Avoiding use of direct terminology for killing or hurting those discriminated against;
    o Blaming those being discriminated against;
    o Legitimizing ever more extreme acts against those discriminated against;
    o Involve people in acts of discrimination, at first in relatively minor way, slowly increasing in intensity;
    o Allow those involved in acts of discrimination to avoid personal responsibility;
    o Do not allow any challenge or debate to the acts of discrimination.

Once the first two of these are in place, it is very common for the rest to follow. Be wary of supporting any ideology based on discrimination. And remember that those who direct such ideologies eventually move on to other areas of discrimination, and many of those who support the initial discrimination eventually find themselves in their turn being discriminated against.

COMMON SENSE PLANNING AND DOING

Goals and Objective Setting

Why set Goals?

* Those with long term goals, broken down into more immediate goals that they are working towards, are happier and more successful than those who just drift through life.

* Very few people control themselves and their affairs with a guiding purpose that they have chosen for themselves. Most are merely swept along, like flotsam on a river, at best spectators of life. Define for yourself what you want to be and achieve in life, define your own purpose, and keep reminding yourself of it.

* Hitting a target is much easier when it is clearly defined and visible.

* If you want to get somewhere and if you want to achieve things, you need to be clear about where it is you want to get to and what it is you want to achieve. Many people have a vague feeling they want to achieve something, without ever thinking about precisely what it is. They think they are moving but never check that they are moving in a particular direction.

* If you want to know which road to take you need to know where you are going to.

* You don't get to the top of Everest by simply wandering about.

* If you are not working towards your own long-term goals, then you are simply a pawn in the lives of those who are.

Set Inspiring and Challenging Long Term Goals?

* What would you like to be your legacy? Set goals that will set you off doing the things you want to be remembered for.

* Set goals that inspire you and excite you and help you get up in the morning.

* Don't be afraid to set big audacious inspiring goals. Don't be too willing to compromise on your goals. Set them and go for them.

* Choose goals where you can make a difference. Life is not just about ticking off the achievement of goals; it is about doing things where you can feel as though you have made a positive difference. Understand your strengths and your weaknesses and then look to succeed in areas that play to your strengths - or what could be your strengths if you developed them.

* Set goals in areas that have meaning to you personally. Don't simply have the same goals as lots of other people. Don't simply have goals that are ones you think other people expect you to have. It is your life; do the things that matter to you.

* Your long term goals should be either life time goals or goals a good number of years into the future. You shouldn't be looking for a large number of detailed long-term goals, and if you do they

are probably best seen as sub-goals to some other higher-level goal. Generally you should try to avoid having more than about 5 or 6 goals, and just one goal can be enough for some people.

* Set long-term goals that cover your working or professional life, your home or family life, and your own personal 'what I would really like to do' life. You should have goals that cover all of these though the same goal may cover more than one of them.

* Ensure you write your goals down. Those who do so are far more likely to achieve them than those who don't.

* It is important to differentiate dreams (wishful goals) from goals (actionable goals). Goals should be realistic and achievable and should derive from action you can take and have control over.

* Goals should be set on the basis of what you want to achieve rather than on the basis of what you want to avoid or escape. Goals about where you want to be are usually more motivating and interesting than goals about where you are trying not to be.

* Focus your goals on self-improvement and mastering skills rather than on winning. People who focus on their own skills will work their way through obstacles and feel good. People who focus on winning will often give up should it look like they might not win, and even if they are winning will often be anxious less they start to lose.

* For the most part it is harder, and more worthwhile, to create than to destroy. Have goals that create, not goals that destroy.

* Don't take your initial thoughts about what your long-term goals are at face value; examine the root cause of why you want to achieve them by asking why. And keep asking why until you get at what you feel is the real underlying reason. You might find that your real goals or desires are not what they at first appear to be, and thus the sub-goals and route to achievement may not be what you might otherwise have set out to do.

* Spend time getting your goals right. If you spend your time chasing the wrong goals you will not only waste much of your time but you will lose the opportunity of what you could have achieved had you spent the time doing something else. The right goals are ones which:
    o Are consistent with what you see as your purpose in life, and are ones you really want to achieve. They should be your goals, not goals you believe you ought to have.
    o Are more important to you than other possible goals. You can't do everything so choose the goals that matter most to you.

* If a long-term goal seems right, then set it and go for it. If it turns out it is too easy, get on with achieving it whilst setting a further goal for which your current goal can be seen as a stepping-stone. If you are falling a long way short either set your goal to be more realistic, change your plans for how you are trying to achieve it, or try harder.

* If you are unsure whether your goals are realistic or not, set out with them but set some clear early sub-goals that are focused on improving the attitudes and abilities you will need if you are to achieve your goals. Your progress in working towards these sub-goals will give you a better idea of what you are capable of, and then you can adapt your goals - they are after all your goals.

* Having identified a potential goal, before you settle on it, ask yourself the following questions:
    o What is the benefit of achieving the goal, what is the reason you want to achieve it? Is it worthwhile? Will you feel really good when you have achieved it?
    o Is the goal possible, recognizing you can learn new skills?
    o In striving for the goal will you be able to maintain your values?
    o Are you willing to make sacrifices in order to achieve the goal?
    o Can you objectively measure progress towards the achievement of the goal?

- How will you know when you have achieved the goal?
- What sub-goals either need to be achieved along the way, or are a useful measure that you are heading towards the achievement of the goal?
- What should you be achieving by when to ensure you are heading towards the achievement of the goal within a reasonable time?

As a result of answering these questions you may want to re-frame the initial statement of your goal, in which case do so, and you will then have an outline set of measures to keep you focused and to help monitor progress.

* Having given it some thought, don't use the excuse that you might not have got your long-term goals quite right as an excuse for not getting started. You can improve and adapt them as you go along. It is usually far easier to change direction once you are in motion than it is to get started in the first place.

* There is a huge difference between a long-term goal you are setting out to achieve and a someday/maybe goal that you may one day set out to achieve. A long-term goal is one that has a next action that you can get on with now. The latter is of no use to you.

* No matter how long term your goal, there is always a next action you can get on with right now.

* Once you've achieved your long-term goals, set some more. Though I suspect if they were challenging in the first place you will probably already have a very clear view of what you wish to do next because you'll now be that sort of person.

Goals for Everyday Living

* In addition to your long-term goals, you should set general daily living improvement goals. For example you may just want to lose a bit of weight, or get a little fitter, or watch a bit less TV, or earn a little extra money, or complete some pet project you just never seem to be able to get round to. As with long-term goals, you need to be as specific as you can about the goal, try to set it in terms of where you want to get to rather than what you are trying to get away from, be able to track progress towards its achievement, and have a clear understanding of by when you would like to have achieved it.

* Set a goal or goals relating to improving your relationship with those who matter to you.

* Don't set too many daily living goals at a time. It is usually better to have one daily living goal that you achieve at a time, over a period of a month or two, and then move onto another, than to have ten goals that you don't achieve. If you try to achieve too many goals at the same time there is a high likelihood you will fail in them all as you continually flip between them without much progress. If you tackle one at a time, or tackle the achievement of some tangible measured progress of one at a time, then you will find yourself making steady progress in terms of personal improvement.

* Be sure that any daily living goal you set out to achieve is one you truly want to achieve. If you don't, you are unlikely to make much progress; better to focus your time and effort on something else more important to you. To think through whether your goal is one you really want to achieve you need to understand your underlying motivation for wanting to achieve it: you may find that there is some other more appropriate way of seeking out to satisfy a given underlying motivation.

The Bumper Book of Common Sense

Going from Long Term Goals to Short Term Goals

* When we create a goal we create a tension with where we are now. To resolve this tension we need to move on from where we are now (or give up on our goal). Our short term goals are the steps we take to enable short term relaxation of the tension.

* Your short term goals should relate to action that is within your control. Of all the actions it is within your gift to take, which will best take you closer to your long term goal or goals.

* To achieve your long-term goals you need to understand what medium term goals you will need to achieve along the way, and then what shorter-term goals, and then the specific actions that you can be getting on with now. There is nothing to stop you achieving your long-term goals if you have a viable plan and you follow it. For every one of your long-term goals there should be something to be done in the short term.

* Work back from your life or long-term goals. Where do you want to be in 10 years? Where do you want to be in five years? In a year? In three months? In a month? By the end of next week? Our shorter term "to be"s should relate to steps towards achievements of our longer term "to be"s, and they should be things we know we can achieve, if we put in a bit of effort.

* To get from long-term goals to short term goals, start with the long-term goal in mind and develop a strategy for achieving it. What do you need to have achieved along the way? By when? What do you need to have accomplished? These then become the basis of medium term sub-goals. Having got medium-term goals then you need to develop the strategy for achieving each one of them. And work your way back towards short-term goals for which you can identify the specific action or actions you can be progressing with now.

* Ask yourself how do you get to a given objective? Take the response and then ask how again. And then again, iteratively, until you get to a set of steps that are easily understood and followed.

* A technique for teasing out intermediate goals is the use of storyboarding. Draw up empty boxes or more. In the last box draw up the final state you are looking for. In the first box draw up the current reality. In the intermediate boxes draw up the intermediate states that will get you from the first box to the last.

* Ensure that your medium-term and short-term goals are expressed in terms of some end point or specific outcome rather than just in terms of doing things. It is vitally important that you can measure progress towards the achievement of your goals and can readily see whether or not you are getting there fast enough. Just because you are moving it doesn't mean you are moving in the right direction or that you are moving fast enough to get to your destination before the barriers come down.

* Learning new skills, or improving existing skills, or gaining new knowledge, or improving your attitudes and behaviors is a common area of short or medium term goals on the way to longer term goals. However it is important that you identify some tangible outcome to achieve in a specific period of time. Otherwise you will just keep going on without explicitly moving on to the next sub-goals for which the skills or knowledge are an enabler. Of course, you can continue to further improve your skills or increase your knowledge after achieving the specific target that was your sub-goal, however you need to know when to move on to the next sub-goals. This self-discipline is vital, otherwise you will find yourself continually working towards your goal but not making the progress that will actually get you there.

* For any goal there is always either a next action that can be done right now, or a specific action to be taken once some input, which you have already taken action to ensure is on its way, arrives.

General Characteristics of Good Goals (Long and Short Term)

* Where possible, ensure your goals are SMART: Specific, Measurable, Attainable, Realistic and Time Bounded. The more specific your goals the easier it is to develop strategies to achieve them. You should also ensure your goals are Worthwhile and Challenging, and you should ensure you write them down.

* In setting your goals, ensure they are stated in the positive; about what you want to do, not about what you want to avoid.

* Ensure your goals are within your control; that you understand the resources needed, including knowledge and skills; that they are ethical and consistent with your personal values; and that it is clear what steps need to be taken, at least in the short term.

* Always assess and have confidence in feasibility before committing.

* By the time you have identified your Short Term Goals they need to be Positive, Immediate, Concrete, and Specific.

* Short term goals need to be action focused, be measurable, be achievable, and be important to you. Goals that don't stand up to these criteria are unlikely to be met, which is why most New Year resolutions fail.

* Most people tend to set goals which are unrealistic in terms of outcome and in terms of timescale. Learn to improve the realism about the goals you set.

* To aim for results which cannot be achieved is not being ambitious, it is being foolish.

Regularly Monitor Progress Towards your Goals, and Adjust Accordingly

* If you don't regularly provide yourself with objective feedback on whether or not you are making tangible progress towards your goals it is likely you will stop making real progress. It is all too easy to be doing things that give the illusion of progress but in fact are not taking you any nearer to your goals.

* If you do not continually remind yourself of your goals, and of the short term progress you are seeking to make, it is likely you will find days, weeks, months, even years will pass by without significant progress towards them. On the other hand if you keep them in the forefront of your mind you will find ideas keep popping into your head about how to keep making progress.

* Schedule a time with yourself each week to review what you have done that week and whether or not you have made progress towards your medium and long-term goals. Modify your short-term goals if necessary, and be clear about what you want to achieve in the coming week. Every month you should be able to explicitly identify something in particular that you have achieved as a step towards your long-term goals.

* Be wary of continually finding excuses for why you are not making progress towards your goals. If the route you are taking is not getting you noticeably and measurably closer then you need to find another route. And keep looking for better routes to ensure you make progress.

* If you are not regularly making good progress towards your goals it is likely some aspects of your behavior or way of doing things is holding you back. Adjusting your behavior, finding new ways of doing things and thinking about things, will probably be essential if you want to make progress.

* If you are struggling to make significant progress towards achieving a goal ask yourself what is stopping you achieving this goal? List out everything that comes to mind. Then ask of each point,

The Bumper Book of Common Sense

'how is this a problem,' and 'what do I need to do for this not to be a problem?' Then tackle the points that come up, identifying them as further sub-goals towards the achievement of your longer-term goal if appropriate. Ensure however that you don't simply deal with the easy things. If there are difficult things stopping you from making progress, then get on and work out how you are going to overcome them.

* If despite every effort you still find yourself not making progress towards a given goal, then you need to change your goal. There will be significant goals you can achieve, so don't spend your life chasing goals you can't.

* Look to maintain a goal diary where you write down your long-term goals, and the medium and short-term goals along the way, and you monitor your progress. Write down the things that get in your way and what you can do, and do do, about them. Don't expect your diary to be a record of continual success. It will be for the most part a record of your struggles. There will be many failures along the way. But if you keep up with it you will over time make progress; ensure you write down your successes along the way. If you want to keep honest with yourself however it is probably best to keep your goal diary private, as you would a personal diary.

Planning and Monitoring

Why you Need Plans

* It is one thing to have a clear understanding of where you want to get to, but if you don't have a plan then you are very unlikely to get there.

* Planning is necessary to ensure that what you do is what needs to be done, in the order it needs to be done in, rather than simply doing what can be done because it is easy.

* Without a plan it is difficult to know whether or not what you are doing is genuinely taking you towards your goals. And even if it is genuinely taking you towards your goals is it getting you there fast enough, and is it the most effective way of getting you there. It is easy to look and feel like you are doing something, but not so easy to be sure you are doing the right something at the right time.

* To get something done you will often need input from others. With a plan you can recognize this early and take timely action to engage with them so you get what you need from them when you need it, rather than come across the need and then have to wait.

* You can with a plan.

* The more prepared you are the more confident you become.

* As attributed to Eisenhower – 'No battle was ever won according to plan, but no battle was every won without one.' The act of planning enables dependencies and actions to be identified. Plans help ensure you are doing the right things. Plans help you mobilize large numbers of people to work together towards the same end.

The Basics of Producing a Plan

* Planning is about understanding what needs to be done, by when, based upon a realistic view of who, where, and how:
    o What sub-tasks need to be undertaken to achieve the task as a whole?
    o In what order do the sub-tasks need to be undertaken, noting that the outputs from some sub-tasks will be the inputs to others.
    o When do the sub-tasks need to have been completed by in order to achieve the overall task within an acceptable time?
    o Who needs to do what sub-tasks? Tasks get done by people, and you need to be satisfied you can organize the right numbers and types of people to get the tasks done.
    o Where will the sub-tasks be done? This is about ensuring you have the physical resources, in addition to people, to get the tasks done.
    o How will the sub-tasks be done? You must be satisfied that there is a feasible way of doing the sub-tasks in terms of processes and ways of working.
    o What are the inputs and dependencies required for each sub-task. Is it clear where these will come from, that they are likely to be available when needed, and it is clear who is responsible for providing them?

* One way of getting to an initial outline plan is to start with the end goal in mind, ie. the overall task, in terms of both what and when, and identify what the sub-tasks are that need to done by when to get to the end goal. Then you break up these sub-tasks into further sub-sub-tasks. You continue to break down the various levels of sub-tasks until you get to sub-tasks that you are confident you can achieve in terms of organization, resources, processes, and dependencies.

* For significant tasks you will often not have the resources and tools in place to get all the tasks done. Obtaining the resources and tools, and setting them to work, should thus become a part of the plan itself and thus be identified as some of the earlier tasks that need to be achieved before later tasks can be undertaken.

* In addition to simply obtaining resources and tools, you need to ensure they are in good working order for the purpose to which you intend to put them and that you know how you are going to use them. Good tools, appropriately trained people, and effective processes can significantly reduce the amount of time it takes to do a job. Poor tools, people inadequately trained, and ineffective processes, mean it will take longer and you are more likely to have mistakes leading to rework or even rejection of the end product. Include in your plan, sub-tasks relating to ensuring tools are appropriately set to work for the purpose in hand, people are appropriately trained, and processes have been developed and proven.

* When deciding in what order to do things recognize the following guidelines:
    o Do early the things upon which other things are dependent, and in particular the things that then allow the most other people to make progress.
    o If there is uncertainty affecting some of the things, do early the things that you know will need to be done anyway despite any uncertainty, ie. those things not sensitive to the uncertainty.
    o Do early the things that reduce uncertainty, but not at a cost that outweighs the benefits of the reduced uncertainty.
    o Do not do early anything for which there is any significant chance that it might become irrelevant as a result of other activities or possible changes in circumstances.
    o Match the order you plan to do things to the likely availability of resource.

These are not absolute guidelines and can be broken dependent upon particular circumstances such as the potential need to undertake certain high visibility or critical tasks early even where there are significant uncertainty risks. However in general you are seeking the route that will lead to the

The Bumper Book of Common Sense

required outcome whilst making most effective use of time and resources bearing in mind the uncertainties.

* Plans are based upon estimates of how long things will take and are based upon assumptions about inputs and circumstances. Many things can, and often do, go wrong to upset a plan: our initial estimates may be wrong; inputs may be delayed or not of the required quality; circumstances may change. If there are significant uncertainties then build in resilience at the expense of optimization. By doing so you are more likely to survive and stay in control when things don't go quite the way you would like. One way of building in resilience is to have some resources available but either not fully allocating them to tasks or engaging them on low priority tasks such that they are available for use when the unexpected occurs. Another is to have arrangements enabling additional resources to be quickly made available should they be needed. A further way of building in resilience is to ensure risky activities are kept away from the critical path. In these cases the overall cost or timescale of the project will be greater than a theoretical optimum dependent upon everything going perfectly. However given that things rarely go perfectly, with the resilience built in you are more likely to stay in control and bound cost and timescale overruns than you would when an optimized plan starts to go wrong.

* Leave some time in your plan for the unexpected, including the need to do additional tasks you hadn't thought about, or some tasks taking longer than expected, or the need to do rework if the outputs of a given task are not up to the required quality.

* Given the greater level of uncertainty associated with activities further in the future, it is often appropriate to adopt a 'rolling wave' approach to planning, whereby we have more detail on activities intended in the near future, and less detail on activities further into the future. General guidelines to support such rolling wave planning include:

    o The near term detail should be sufficient to support activities underway or which need to be gotten underway in the near future;

    o Longer term activities should be in sufficient detail that we understand what 'enabling' activities are necessary to be ready to undertake them when the time comes;

    o There is little point in adding detail to a plan in an area where the uncertainty is such that it is likely to significantly change;

    o It is often better to err on the side of having slightly more detail in the plan and recognizing a need to change it, than having too little detail such that the need to timely prepare for future activities is missed;

    o There needs to be regular review of the rolling wave plan to ensure that the next level of detail is added in a timely manner to support the continuing smooth operation of the plan as a whole.

* When you are undertaking complex tasks which have significant consequences for the future, make the effort to do them right first time. Be wary of skimping or trying to 'save costs' on the front-end activities of a complex project. The significant cost overruns of complex projects are often due to having to correct errors made early on, or not having adequately taken account of issues early enough. Put the effort in at the front.

* There are knowns, there are known unknowns, and there are unknown unknowns. With a bit of thought, research and effort we can turn many unknown unknowns into known unknowns or even into knowns.

* When you have long or complex tasks ensure you identify some clear milestones that represent significant progress along the way. These will enable you to track progress, and also give you a sense of accomplishment which will help keep you motivated.

* In putting together a plan you are looking at what you need to do to make the achievement of the plan close to being a certainty rather than a precarious affair. You need to think about how you need to arrange and leverage your environment. You need to understand what resources you need. And you need to understand what obstacles you might encounter and either mitigate against them getting in your way or how you will get around them should they do so..

* If you are putting together plans for others to undertake, ensure you involve them in the planning, and look to ensure they take ownership. People work harder to achieve if it is their own plan.

Estimating How Long

* People generally underestimate how long it will take to do something that they are or will be responsible for. More accurate estimates derive from understanding how long similar tasks have taken in the past, and from breaking a task into steps and then estimating the time for each step. Even then people tend to underestimate. If estimating for a complex task it is generally prudent to double any times that might be pure guesswork and add up to 50% to those you have some past data for.

* Be wary of wishful thinking, where you estimate how long based on what you would like to be the case rather than what some attempt at an objective measure gives you. Sometimes people will give you the estimates they believe you want, not their best objective estimates.

* Major projects significantly underestimate true costs and timescales because if they didn't they risk not being accepted in the first place. This is rarely deliberate dishonesty, just self-delusion, often on a vast scale.

* Be wary of idealistic planning, where you assume everything will go perfectly. A given task might, for example, only take a given amount of time, but only if you, or whoever is responsible for it, could devote all your time without interruption to it. In real life there may also be other tasks that need your attention at the same time.

* Planning is guesswork. The more complex and novel a task the more we are likely to underestimate how long it will take. In practice we should put in significant slack and contingency, although there will usually be pressures not to do this.

* Optimism bias is a very common problem on complex projects. Generally the view is that the chances of any given thing going wrong is small, and they are thus not taken into account. However there are many things that could go wrong and the chances that one or more of them will occur is actually very large.

* When estimating the time for a given task be sure to include time to do more detailed planning once the task is underway, time to get resources on board and working effectively, the time to do the task or sub-tasks themselves, and the time to finish off and get the outputs accepted, including possible rework following review of outputs.

* Parkinson's Law states that *'Work expands so as to fill the time available for its completion.'* Thus, if a project is given six months for completion, it will generally require six months to finish. If the same project is given two years for completion, it will require two years to finish. This is in part because when a deadline is far off, people work more slowly toward it, and put tasks for that project further down their priority lists. They will also do things which whilst relevant may not be the most important things necessary to get the project completed. As the deadline gets closer they become more focused on doing what is essential. Of course, because much of the work is left until nearer the deadline, it is often not until late on that many of the problems become apparent, leading to many projects then becoming delayed or even cancelled. This is why it is so important to have intermediate milestones and deadlines to ensure that there is continual momentum towards the completion of the project.

* It can be tempting to those responsible for a project to give it a short timescale in order to 'motivate' the people working on it. However unrealistic deadlines can be just as bad as no deadlines since people will know the deadline can't be met and therefore not accept responsibility for attempting to achieve it.

* You can improve your estimating for how long tasks take by regularly estimating and then measuring how good your estimate was. If you regularly do this, you can significantly improve your estimating, and thus improve your plans and improve your ability to stick to your plans.

Be Clear about Dependencies

* Not everything in your plan will be dependent upon your own effort. Include in your plan any dependencies on others and ensure others are clearly aware of what they need to do by when. In addition to simply showing the milestones for inputs from others, it is useful to include additional earlier milestone which if not met would give you advance notice of problems with the dependency.

* Where you have dependencies on others ensure they are clearly defined, understood and agreed by those on whom you have the dependency. Don't be vague about what you need or when you need it by or about your quality expectations. Ensure you have a way of objectively verifying when the dependency has been satisfied, including for example quality checks on any inputs provided.

* If you have dependencies on others, ensure you understand the risks associated with them delivering what is required, to the quality that is required, for when it is required. If the risks are significant build flexibility in your plan to keep the dependency off the critical path.

* Keep in regular and open contact with those on whom you have dependencies. Be wary of creating an environment where they hide their problems from you such that the first time you hear about delays is just before they occur and after you will have had time to make adjustments in your own plan.

* Remove or plan out as many dependencies as you can, so that your success is more within your own control.

Confirm Feasibility

* If someone says something can be done in principle, confirm that it can be done within acceptable timescales, with resources that can reasonably be made available given other tasks that also need to be done, and without some other consequences which are likely to be unacceptable.

* If someone says something can be done in principle, ensure you understand what they mean by 'in principle'. Often it is code for their belief that it can't be done in practice. There is no point in being able to do something in principle if it can't be done in practice.

* If someone claims something is feasible, they should be able to elaborate on why they believe it is feasible, through reference back to, for example, earlier analogous activities. If they are unable to give some degree of rationale for why they believe it is feasible, then be wary.

* If you ask for something that is feasible, people will generally try to give you what you want. If you ask for something that is infeasible, they will give you what is in their own best interests. Unfortunately many people ask for something they know to be infeasible because they think that people will put in extra effort in order to do the best they can. It doesn't work that way. If you ask for something that is infeasible people feel no sense of responsibility for it, and there is no telling what you'll get.

Modify or Deviate from your Plans if Necessary

* Plans are a means to an end. If you have a plan you should stick to it, but only because you believe it is the best means to achieve your end. If it is not, change it.

* You should always seek to have the best estimates and understanding of circumstances that you reasonably can. However once you have started to implement a plan, just because you have better information does not mean you should necessarily change the plan. Changes to plans once underway can be highly disruptive.

* Factors to take into account when deciding whether or not to change a plan as a result of better information include: benefits that might arise through changing the plan; the cost of making the change in terms of disruption, loss of momentum, and possible loss of motivation; the possibility of not getting the expected benefits; the likelihood of different possible consequences arising from not making the change.

* Estimating the costs and impacts of change can be very difficult. We need to be both as objective as we can in estimating costs and, subject to confidentiality issues, as open as we can. The costs of change can easily be underestimated or overestimated by persons with a vested interest in the outcome. The best guard against this is to ensure costs and assumptions are made explicit and open such they can be readily challenged.

* Even if you decide to stick with an original plan despite having better information, that in principle you would have used had it been available earlier, you should still acknowledge this better information. Don't pretend it doesn't exist just because it is inconvenient. It may still be useful and may help you analyze and deal with certain problems should they arise.

* If you are part of a team working in accordance with a joint plan, and you believe the plan is wrong, seek to get it put right rather than simply going off and doing your own thing. If a plan is being worked to by a large number of people, then whilst doing something different may be best for your part of the plan, if it then leads to a lack of integration with what everyone else is doing then it is likely to cause more problems than it solves.

* Change your plans if they are not working, in acknowledgement of the well-worn phrase: 'If you do what you always do, you will get what you always get.' However do recognize that sometimes the best way forward is persistence. You need to steer a middle course between the need for flexibility as a plan unfolds and a certain tenacity in sticking to the agreed plan.

Implementation and Monitoring

* Reasons our plans don't come to fruition include:
  - They are incomplete and we underestimate what needs to be done and then find we don't have enough time or resources.
  - Lack of motivation or perseverance, ie. we don't try hard enough.
  - Lack of skills.
  - Unanticipated difficulties.

  We need to pay attention to the completeness of our plans and their feasibility, we need to be committed to them, we need to ensure we have the skills to undertake them, and we need to anticipate as best we can the difficulties we are likely to encounter and take them into account.

* Just because something can be done, doesn't mean it will. You need both viable plans and a will to follow through.

The Bumper Book of Common Sense

- A poor plan well executed is sometimes better than a good plan poorly executed.

- You may know where you are trying to get to, but if you don't know where you are now how can you be sure you are going in the right direction?

- If you want to improve something, you usually need to measure it so that you know where you are vis-à-vis where you want to be, and can determine the extent to which your actions are taking you closer to or further away from where you want to be.

- Measure the wrong things and you'll get the wrong result. For example, measuring software development productivity by numbers of lines of code produced per day will lead to lots of poorly written and difficult to maintain code being written.

- What gets measured gets valued. Yet all too often what is measured is what it is easy to measure, rather than what it is important to measure. It is better to measure the right thing imperfectly than the wrong thing perfectly.

- Not everything that can be counted counts, and not everything that counts can be counted.

- You won't improve if your chief concern vis-à-vis metrics data is to manipulate the data to make yourself look good. Unfortunately that is often the primary concern behind the way most metrics data is used. They are initially introduced in circumstances where there are high hopes that targets can be met, but when performance starts to fall short the focus often shifts towards managing the metrics themselves rather than the issues being reported through the metrics.

Time Management and Getting Things Done

The Importance of Time Management

- Time is a limited resource. If you're not using it, you're wasting it. Don't however get paranoid about using every moment of your time. Use of time for recreational or relaxation purposes is not a waste of time, so long as it is part of a balanced use of your time.

- Deliberately and carefully manage your time. It is a vital limited resource, and when it's gone, it's gone. Final.

- If you want to live a reasonably fulfilling life, and avoid continual stress and crisis, effective management of your time is essential.

- Be aware of your use of time. Time will run away from you if you do not make a conscious effort to use it purposefully, and the hours will run into days, the days into weeks and months, the months into years. Get into the habit of being aware of the present moment and asking yourself whether you are making best use of your time, right now. Don't however become a slave to time. You do not need to fill every moment with activities, you should leave plenty time for relaxation and contemplation and just appreciating being alive.

- Problems do not go away just because they are suppressed or ignored. They will usually resurface, with consequences far greater than would have been the case if they had been dealt with at the time. Thus being able to get on with addressing an issue at an appropriate time is an important way of avoiding problems in our lives.

* Nothing is so tiring as having a task continually unfinished. Having things left undone after you'd intended to do them saps your energy, even if they are relatively unimportant. Moreover we usually focus at the end of the day on what we didn't get done rather than what we did get done. If you can manage your time to get things done you will have more energy and you will feel good about yourself.

* We have both much less and much more time than we realize. Every day is a finite step towards our eventual deaths. Whilst time appears to be here for ever, it is not. It is passing and the days that have gone are gone forever. For some people their deaths will come about much much sooner than they realize. But for all of us each day contributes to the weeks and months and years that relentlessly lead only in one direction. On the other hand we waste huge amounts of time every day and every week without realizing it. Through Time Management we can put large amounts of otherwise wasted time to good use and effectively live our days and weeks rather than have them just pass by.

Making Best Use of your Time

* Time is, in normal circumstances, the most precious commodity we have. We are either using our time to good effect or we are not. Regularly ask yourself which it is. And note that it is not simply doing things with your time that is important; it is doing the best thing you could reasonably be doing with your time that is important.

* Time management is not simply about getting more and more done. You will never get done everything that you could and ought to get done. Time management includes thinking about what is worthwhile and ensuring you do the things that are important to you. Be ready to say no to doing tasks that you don't want to get done and you don't have an obligation to get done.

* Stop trying to be busy. Put first things first and don't worry about the rest.

* Regularly ask yourself 'Is this the best use I can make of my time, right now?' If yes, get on with it. If no, stop what you are doing, and do what you believe is.

* Remember there is an opportunity cost in your use of time. If you are doing something of little value, then you are not using your time to do something of value. Be sure the projects you are spending your time on are those that are of value to you. Time you are spending on less important projects is time you could be spending on more important projects.

* You don't have to be perfect about everything. There is a 'good enough' which is good enough for most things. It is better to do something imperfectly than it is to do nothing perfectly.

* Completed imperfect work on time is usually of more value than more perfect work produced too late.

* Replace concerns about whether something is going to be just right with focusing on whether or not it is good enough for the purpose in hand.

* If you're doing something, do it as best you can in the time you're willing to allocate it.

* There's nothing wrong with paying people to do some of the housework drudgery that you hate, assuming you can afford it. There are plenty of people who will be glad of the paid work. And it may even free you up to earn more money, which is likely to be at a higher wage per hour than you are paying. Don't however outsource looking after your kids, except maybe occasionally.

* Get up early, between 5 and 6am. You will get more done and feel more alive during the day.

The Bumper Book of Common Sense

* Getting up early generally engenders an attitude of proactively and a can do now attitude. Getting up late generally engenders an attitude of can do later. People who get up late often find themselves working late to get things done, and whilst they often do, they will rush the tasks, not do them as well as they could have done, and generally feel hassled at the end of the day. The next morning they are then tardy getting up and facing the day, feeling they deserve a bit of a lie in, and gear themselves up for repeating the cycle. Over a period of time people who get up late and work late tend to achieve far less than those who get up early, get on with tasks early, and go to bed earlier.

* Getting up early and going into work early means you can avoid the pains of commuting at the same time as everyone else. This saves you time, means you get more done earlier in the day before the business of the day takes over, and can then commute home earlier, either each day or on some days, again saving you more commute time.

* If you get up early, say 5 am, and can get 2 or 3 hours uninterrupted work done, then you can get as much done in this time as most people get done in a day. Most people who get up early will identify it as being the most productive part of their day. It is time you can work on the projects and tasks that are important to you rather than just reacting to other people's demands. It also generally means you are more relaxed in the evening and have more time to spend and enjoy with family or friends.

* Getting up early provides you with the opportunity to see the dawn and possibly even the sunrise. It can be very peaceful and highly inspiring, engendering an appreciation of life and thoughts of wanting to make the most of the new day.

* If you want to start getting up early then you should adjust gradually. Start getting up about 15mins earlier for a while, for a few days or a week, then a further 15mins for a while. You will also need to start going to bed earlier. Once you are getting up earlier it is important you get out of the bedroom as soon as you are up and start doing things. Take benefit of the time so that you feel good about having got up.

* Understand your personal peaks and troughs through the day. Know when you feel full of energy and are able to concentrate, and when you feel tired. Then ensure you take advantage of the good times to get more complex tasks done and do easy tasks when you are feeling less energetic. For most people this means tackling the more complex or difficult tasks as early as you can in the morning.

* Think of your attention levels as an energy to be conserved and used effectively. Don't fritter it away. Do your attention high tasks when you have a fresh and alert mind – often early in the day. Put aside distractions like e-mails or the phone whilst you do so. However don't use the downs as an excuse to do nothing, but find something that is easier but still useful.

* You cannot be fully alert and effective all the time. It will burn you out. Allow yourself to take it slow from time to time. If you are feeling drowsy, a 15 minute nap can make a huge difference to how alert you feel.

* Do what works for you in terms of getting on doing things. When faced with a number of tasks some people prefer to tackle a difficult task first, some prefer to tackle a few easy tasks first. Do what works for you in terms of getting what is important done.

* Look to have lots of small goals through the day. Keep yourself motivated and focused rather than just wandering through the day achieving nothing in particular. For example, towards the end of the day you can set a specific task or goal to achieve before you finish up. Look to ensure you are in charge of your day rather than having your time dictated by a myriad of other people.

* We spend a lot of time in transition from one place or task to another. This may be a long period of travel, or it may be just a few moments or minutes. Within safety considerations, you should make use of this time, for example in thinking through whatever it is you are looking to get out of your next task. Clearly however if you are driving or are otherwise in what might be a potentially

dangerous situation, be aware of the dangers of distractions and give priority to your own, and potentially others, safety.

* Make use of the little blocks of time you have during the day whilst waiting for something. Even 5 minutes is enough to read or listen to something, to jot down a note, to learn something, to give someone a ring, or do a little bit of work on something. Always have something productive to do close to hand should you find yourself with some time to spare.

* The 80/20 Pareto Principle is the idea that most of our results come from a small portion of our actual work, and conversely, that we spend most of our time and effort doing things that aren't all that important. Figure out which part of your work is likely to have the greatest results and focus as much of your energy as you can on that part.

* For relatively minor tasks set short timescales for getting them done. Don't make a meeting an hour long if you can reasonably get through the business of the meeting in 30mins. If you give yourself longer it will just take longer.

* Don't try to do too little in a day. If you have only a little to do, you will only do a little. If you have many things to do, you should look to see how you can rise to the challenge of getting them all, or a substantial amount of them, done.

* If you are doing tasks try to ensure you do them properly so that you don't have to do them again or don't have them come back to place further demands on your time.

* Circumstances are rarely ideal for doing the things you want or ought to do. You can usually find some excuse to put off doing what you know you should do. You might be feeling a little tired and you will be more alert in the morning. Maybe there's something on TV you'd quite like to watch. There are many excuses you can doubtless find; and one of them may well be a good reason for putting something off. However circumstances are never ideal and the question is not one of whether circumstances are ideal but of whether or not you could, with a little bit of effort, make some worthwhile progress.

* Do enough, and only enough, unless there is a specific reason for doing more. And then move on to something else you could be usefully doing with your time.

* Make decisions about what you deliberately decide not to work on alongside decisions about what you will work on. Nagging thoughts in your mind that you could be doing something else can significantly impair you effectiveness in doing what you are trying to do.

* If you have the opportunity to have others doing some of the things that you might otherwise have to do yourself then you have the opportunity to save yourself a lot of time. It may be that others are more than willing to do certain tasks either for their own reasons or because they want to, or feel an obligation, to help you. Look out for such opportunities and look to take advantage of them if you are able. Note however that you want to do this in a way that does not leave the other person or persons feeling they have been inappropriately taken advantage of. In looking for opportunities to have others do things on your behalf, be conscious of what topics to pass to them, taking cognizance of both your own and their relative strengths and weaknesses.

Short Term vs Long Term

* Don't confuse motion with progress. Sometimes people are doing things that are of no value with respect to end objectives, or could even be disruptive with respect to achieving end objectives. Rushing to do something without first thinking about it will often lead to doing the wrong things.

* Many people and many organizations or projects see their being driven by short-term needs as a 'pragmatic' approach. In truth the need to be driven by short term needs is invariably a self-fulfilling prophesy in that if no time is spent considering longer term needs then everything will

The Bumper Book of Common Sense

    need to be addressed in the short term. And this invariably leads to missed opportunities and much time spent doing the wrong things.

* If you focus only on what has become a crisis you will always be focusing on a crisis. Most crises arise because you didn't deal with something you should have done before it became a crisis.

* As a very rough rule of thumb, which should be adapted to circumstances, you should spend between 5 and 10% of the effort associated with a problem looking at the longer term issues and consequences, such as how it arose in the first place, and whether or not there is a more fundamental problem to be solved. If you can afford to spend more, you should.

* In general you should seek to spend about 50% of your working day on tasks that are tangibly contributing to your long-term life goals, noting that some of your life goals should relate to what you want to achieve at or through your work, and also that work should give you extensive opportunity for self-improvement which will also be contributing to achievement of your life goals.

* There will invariably be times when genuine short term needs take total precedence over everything else. But this itself should never be more than 5-10% of the time.

* Ensure that short term solutions are properly written up, because they have a tendency to become long term solutions.

* It is easy to make the short term look good, if you take your eye off or are willing to sacrifice the long term. Focusing on the short term can look good for a while until you hit a brick wall, which is often catastrophic. Rewarding people for short-term behavior without greater rewards for the long term is asking for trouble.

* Think about the long term but act now.

Don't Waste Time

* Be conscious of the time you are spending doing nothing of any useful purpose. It is a lot. Imagine what you could achieve if you put it to good use.

* TV and the internet will steal a big chunk of your life away, arguably your most important time, your discretionary time, time you can choose what to do with. They take away your attention to very little useful end, and after you are often left unsatisfied. Rather than be relaxed you end up more anxious. There are good things on the TV and internet, however you need to limit your time and be very deliberate about what you watch or seek out.

* If you get rid of your TV you will free up a lot of time for doing productive stuff. For many people this could easily be 20 hrs or more a week. If you make productive use of your time whilst others are watching TV you will soon pull way ahead of them.

* If you can't give up your TV altogether, then watch it less. Depending upon your habits you should probably watch much less. TV is for many people the single greatest waste of their time. There are some informative programs, and sometimes a bit of TV for relaxation is not a bad thing. However watching TV for just 2-3 minutes induces a trance like state that is a form of hypnosis, and you can easily get into a channel hoping state where after hours you can barely remember what you have been watching. An effective way of watching less TV is to decide in advance what you want to watch, and only watch that – have the TV off at all other times. Another trick is to record everything you might want to watch and then watch it from the playback. You can then fast forward bits that are not of interest, which is often quite a lot.

* Rather than genuinely relax you, most TV actually saps your energy. After most TV programs people generally feel groggy, tired, and often grumpy. Whilst we may think of TV as a justified

relaxation, at the end of the day it does little to increase our happiness or well-being. People who watch a lot of TV are generally less satisfied with their lives than those who don't. Not only are they frittering away some of their most valuable personal time, but they are bombarded by unrealistic views of life.

* Spending hours aimlessly browsing the Internet can be as much of a waste of time and as pointless as aimlessly watching TV. Limit your use of the internet to when you have a particular purpose, and then quit once you've achieved that purpose.

* You need to schedule activities for the times you habitually watch TV otherwise you'll instinctively simply put the TV on. There are of course many things to do with the time you free up: Go out for dinner with friends, or invite them to you; learn a musical instrument, language or skill; take a course; go do some exercise down the gym or elsewhere; etc. etc. Don't however replace one bad habit by another, such as then spending lots more time down the pub.

* Don't obsess about the news. You can't do much about what is going on in the world, and it has little direct bearing on your life, so don't worry about it. Don't be ignorant about what is going on, but a couple of minutes a day will keep you abreast of the vast majority of what you need to know about since most of news is the same news repeated over and over. A quick glance at the headlines once a day is quite sufficient, and you can then follow up on anything that may be of particular interest.

* Spend less time reading newspapers or magazines. Don't read articles just because they are in front of you. Be selective about what you read, and use skimming techniques to home in on the bits that are of real interest to you; it may well be only one or two percent of the newspaper or magazine. Similarly if you are reading a book for a particular purpose adapt your method to your purpose. You can get the key ideas out of a book in a fraction of the time it takes to read every word.

* Don't become a slave to modern technology. Modern technology often requires a significant learning curve and sometimes a lot of maintenance time. Don't get drawn into spending a lot of time playing around with such technology to no useful end.

* Converting 2 hours a day of time otherwise wasted into productive learning or focused effort is the equivalent of freeing up over 700 hours a year, which is the equivalent to 100 7hr days. Think about what you can achieve with that amount of productive time focused on something of real interest to you.

* Be aware of where your time is going. For a week keep a record of what you are spending your time doing and how long you spend doing particular things. You might be surprised how much time you are allowing to simply fritter away.

* Feel free to procrastinate over less important tasks since by doing so you may find they get overtaken by events and don't need doing at all.

* If something doesn't need doing, and there is no good reason for doing it, decide not to do it. There are plenty of things that do need doing or which you ought to do.

* We waste a lot of time because of indecisiveness in deciding what to do with something. For example we might look at an e-mail several times before we decide what to do about it. We might look over junk mail multiple times in case there is something of interest to us. We prepare for but put off telephone calls or replies to letters. For most things you should make a decision on what to do with it, and do it, when you first take a look at it.

* Don't get sucked into time-consuming tasks that are not worth the amount of time you spend on them. For example, are you continually fixing or maintaining things; if so, are they things you really need, do they really need fixing, and would it be better to get someone else to do it?

* Nothing steals our time like laziness. Don't do for a reason, not because you just can't be bothered. Laziness and idleness make you unhappy. Resolve to be active and to do things. If you avoid being

The Bumper Book of Common Sense

idle you will always have enough time. It is those who most waste their time that most complain about not having enough time.

* If you have a tendency towards laziness, then look to keep busy. You will not be lazy all the time, but probably find that once you stop doing things you find yourself not getting started again for a long time. Rather than take breaks between activities try to get into the habit of going from one to the next. You can take a break later in the evening.

* Keep moving. Be willing to change direction, if necessary, if things are not going so well, but keep moving.

* Try to avoid driving when the roads are busy or going shopping when the shops are busy. You'll waste a lot of time. Whilst we don't always have a choice about when we travel or shop, we often do. And when you do, choose times when you will not be in queues.

* Just because you are busy that doesn't mean you are not wasting your time. There are many things we do out of habit which are of no or very limited value.

Be Effective and Efficient in Doing Tasks

* Try to be efficient in all the things that you do. Efficiency means doing things with the minimum of effort and resources. Of course it is also important to be doing the right things. But assuming you believe you are, also try to do them as efficiently as you can. There will always be plenty of other useful things you can do with the spare time or resources freed up.

* Don't just do; think about the best way to do. What is the best way of getting done what it is you want to get done? Be creative.

* Find standard efficient ways of dealing with common problems or recurring tasks. Each small amount of time saved on something that you do regularly adds up. Regularly look to see how others approach them and adopt the best practices you can find.

* The more often you need to repeat given tasks or activities, the more it is worth putting effort into being effective and efficient, and turning your approach into habits which require little mental effort.

* Every now and again think about whether your common ways of dealing with recurring tasks are still the most efficient. We have a tendency to keep doing what has worked for us in the past even though better ways of doing it may become available. Stay sensitive to the possibility of better ways of doing things.

* If you are learning to do a task you know you are likely to need to do again in the future, note down the steps so you can readily have them to hand when you need to do the task again.

* If appropriate create checklists and templates to support things you do regularly in order to minimize the amount of effort you need to put into them and to help reduce the likelihood of you missing something or making mistakes.

* Invest in the best productivity tools you can afford. Small improvements in your productivity can lead to big improvements in your outputs.

* Learn shortcuts with respect to using computers or other pieces of technology you frequently use. Not only does it save time, which can quickly add up, but it also helps keep your thoughts flowing through being less distracted by having to stop and think. If there are computer programs you use regularly ensure you know the basics well so that you don't have to keep looking up how to do things. Learn to use keyboard shortcuts for things you do regularly. If you understand how internet

search engines work in terms of how they combine words for search you will find what you want much quicker and more reliably.

* Learn speed-reading and how to touch type. If you don't know your times tables well, learn them.

* Shifting between different types of tasks requires effort and is an inefficient way of using your time. Better to batch up similar tasks and do them in a single session. For example, don't deal with e-mails sporadically throughout the day: do them in chunks 2 or 3 times during the day – and turn off any continuous notifications of new e-mails coming in. Do the same with voice mail, phone calls you need to make, responding to letters, filing, and so on. Any routine, repetitive tasks.

* If you can combine a number of tasks into a single task, do so, but don't make tasks too complicated. Simple tasks are far more likely to get done than complex tasks.

* If you have a lot of relatively minor quick tasks on your To Do List, put them all together and blitz through them in an hour or two.

* Make phone calls that you don't want to go on too long just before lunch or towards the normal end of the day. If the other person doesn't make the excuse to stop, you can.

* Don't let trivial tasks eat up your time. If tasks are trivial either decide not to do them, or get them done quickly.

* Something poorly done quickly is rarely as effective long term as something done properly albeit with more time. If you have only limited time decide whether poorly done is adequate or is it better to wait until you have enough time to do it well.

Take Relaxation Time

* Active relaxation, when we use parts of our brains that we don't normally use, is better for us than passive relaxation. Thus prefer painting, playing music, singing, playing computer games, sports, etc, to TV, drinking, reading pulp fiction, etc.

* A change is as good as a rest. The only recuperation time you need is sleeping. If you are feeling tired or stagnant whilst doing a particular activity do a completely different one.

* When you have completed a difficult task, relax and switch off for a while. Don't be in a continual state of stimulation. This will be damaging for your long-term health. However try to avoid TV, smoking, alcohol, or high sugar foods as part of your reward and relaxation.

* Don't be overly obsessive about managing your time. If you are having to manage every moment of your time in an optimal manner, then you are doing too much. You need to cut down on the amount of things you are doing. You need to manage your life.

* Schedule and keep reserved your leisure time. The time you spend doing things you enjoy will help you be more motivated and focused during your working periods, and less prone to procrastination.

* Look to have relaxation periods during the day and week. 5 minutes or so each hour, just a walk around or making yourself a cup of coffee: but be wary of getting drawn into long discussions around the tea urn or drinking too much caffeine during the day. Have at least a 15-30 minute period during the day when you listen to some music or do some yoga or meditation: but don't use TV as relaxation, it doesn't work. Have a more substantial period of a few hours or more once or twice a week when you are doing what you want to do, and not what other people want you to do. Note that listening to music with your eyes closed significantly intensifies the experience.

The Bumper Book of Common Sense

* If you have a planned pleasurable activity or event, try to schedule in 30 mins of quality work before you go. Knowing you've got the pleasurable activity coming up should make it easy to just get 30 mins in. It might also give your subconscious a chance to think creatively about your work during the course of the pleasurable activity – ideas often pop into your head under such circumstances – so ensure you have a pen and paper to jot them down.

* Try to have at least one day a week when you don't do any of your paid work activities, and focus on your own activities including home chores, being with family, working on personal projects. Treat this day off as sacrosanct.

* Occasionally find some time to be on your own, without any distractions, just thinking. No TV, no music, no reading, no eating comfort foods, with as little noise as you can get away with. Get rid of distractions such as phones. Paint, or draw, or write, or cook, or take a long soak in the bath. And listen to your thoughts.

Get it all Down onto Lists

* For your mind to be really effective you need to clear it of worries and distractions and the need to remember things that pop into your head. Get it all down on paper or in some form of electronic organizer. Understand what is most important. By freeing up your mind from having to keep track of things to do you are freeing it up to think creatively and to focus. You will find you have far more energy and you will be more aware of opportunities. Lists if used wisely bring order to your mind and your life in general.

* There are a myriad of things bouncing around in our heads that are continually distracting us, worrying us, stressing us, and causing us anxiety, and ironically actually preventing us getting on with things. You need to either do straight away something that is gnawing away at you, or if you can't, then get it written down. As a rule of thumb put it down onto a post-it note when it starts to keep coming into your head. It can stay on the post-it note for the rest of the day if you are intending to deal with it that day. If you don't however then get it onto one of your To Do Lists. Don't let post-it notes lie around for days on end.

* All the time you have your To Do List in your head you'll always be struggling to get the important things done. Urgent, easy, short-term stuff will win every time. To get important stuff done you need to get everything down onto lists and then ensure your short-term lists and calendar include items that are contributing to your long-term goals rather than simply include the urgent stuff that is in front of you. If you then prioritize what is on your list you can simply progress with tasks in priority order.

* Only when you have and maintain a complete list or lists of what you need to do will you make effective decisions about how to use your time. Note however it will usually be appropriate to manage lists relating to your work life separate from lists relating to your personal and home life.

* Have a complete list of all your projects in one place, and review it once a week without fail to ensure it is complete and current, and that you have planned in the next action. It is also important to manage a calendar into which you put specific things you intend to do at specific times.

* Be wary of having lots of To Do Lists. You need to identify what works for you, but a suggestion is:
  o A 'To Do Next List': This is a list of things you could get on and do straight away without having to wait for inputs from others. These items should typically be ones you are looking to get done within the next week. For important things on this list, you should be able to decide when you are going to do it. Once it is in your calendar you can strike it off your To Do List. Of course if you don't then do it, it may need to go back on. At the end of each day look to see if any calendar entries have not been done and either put them into a future calendar entry or back onto your To Do Next List.

- A 'Delegations/Interest List', which is areas of work you are responsible for, or have a strong interest in, but which is being undertaken by other people. If there are specific actions you need to take then they should go on your 'To Do Next List'.
- A 'Projects/Objectives List', which is areas of work you are responsible for but which require multiple actions to get them done, possibly over an extended period of time. Every project should have a Next Action sitting on your 'To Do Next List', or possibly be waiting for a particular trigger from someone else which will then make it actionable. If there is no 'Next Action' then you are not committed to the project and it should go on your Someday/Maybe List.
- A Repeat Activities List, which are activities you need to do on a regular basis, such as weekly or monthly reports, or timesheet approvals, etc. If the activities are relatively quick, then they may just go as calendar entries.
- A Someday/Maybe List. These are activities you would like to do if you have the time, but other priorities currently prevent you getting on with them. Having this list helps reduce the clutter of your other To Do Lists, and helps make them more effective working tools.

* In deriving your To Do Lists relating to your work life then consider the following:
  - What are your current tasks – typically a couple of hundred.
  - What are your current projects – typically 50 or so.
  - What are your areas of responsibility – typically 10 – 15.
  - What are your objectives over the next 3-6 months.
  - What is your vision for the next couple of years.
  - What are your career goals and expectations.

* In deriving your To Do Lists relating to your personal or home life then consider the following:
  - Do you have any personal projects, or topics you would like to learn about, or skills you would like to develop, or community activities you would like to be part of.
  - You should seek to have some goals relating to ever improving your relationships with family members, both close family and possibly extended family. You may also wish to do so with certain friends.
  - If you have children you should have some goals relating to helping them develop.
  - There may be various activities or goals relating to maintenance or improvement of your home, possessions, and garden if you have one.
  - You may have certain personal goals relating to your habits and general desire to be healthier both physically and mentally.

* Make the items on your To Do Next List as specific as possible. For example, Contact X, should be Phone X, or E-mail X. This reduces the decision-making effort and reduces the likelihood of procrastination. Some other characteristics of a good To Do Next action include:
  - It is a physical action, something you can readily visualize doing
  - It can be accomplished at a single sitting
  - It is something you can do now or at the next opportunity
  - It supports progress toward a recognized goal and it is worth doing (what would happen if you didn't do it?)
  - It is something for which you are the most appropriate person for the job.

Thus for example if you have a report to produce be specific about what you can do in a period of 15-30 minutes or so: produce initial contents list; or draft introduction; etc. Have a clear target for what you are looking to do within a relatively short period of time.

The Bumper Book of Common Sense

* Things on your general To Do Next Lists are either attracting you or repulsing you. What attracts you are the things you can get straight on with. What repulses you are the things you are not sure what to do about. Items and actions on your To Do Next List should be attracting you.

* If you've delegated tasks to others, then your 'To Do Next Action' relates to when you next contact whoever you have delegated to for an update of how they are getting along, assuming they haven't contacted you in the meantime. If you are waiting for something then your To Do Next Action is when, assuming you don't get it, you will take some action to chase it up.

* If there are things on your To Do Next List which you keep put off doing, then it is likely you haven't broken them down to a simple 'next action' readily do-able format. People often put items on To Do Next Lists that are really projects rather than 'next actions'. It is important to recognize projects for what they are, and then be clear about the specific 'next action' that will move you forward.

* Be wary of tasks that stay on your To Do Next List long after they should have been done by. From time to time, list these out, ask yourself why you keep putting them off, and identify some action that might help you get them unstuck, or at least make some progress. If you keep putting them off it may be that they don't need doing at all.

* Tasks on your To Do list can be Done, Deleted, Delegated, or Deferred. Get as much Deleted or Delegated as you can.

* Keep your To Do Lists up to date. Every day add on new items that come up and delete items that have been done. Once you have completed a 'To Do Next Action' it may give rise to another, particularly if it relates to a project or longer-term task. Every week go over the lists and ensure the items are still ones that need doing. In particular check over your Projects/Objectives List at least once a week and ensure every item has a corresponding item on your To Do Next List. Weed out anything that is either done or you have no intention of doing. Transfer items between different lists if appropriate.

* You don't need to put everything you could do down on a To Do List. If tasks can be dealt with at once, do so. And many tasks can. Got on the phone, skim through the report, reply to the e-mail. Similarly if you have something in your calendar you don't need to also include it on your To Do Next List, though any Projects or Tasks that have multiple activities associated with them ought to be on your Projects/Objectives List.

* Ensure you always have a means with you to note down any further To Dos that come up or occur to you. Then get them on to your managed To Do Lists at the next opportunity or the next review you've set up for yourself.

* Create Daily To Do Lists of the things you intend to do today. Don't try to pile more stuff on it than you can do: people often have a Monday To Do List which is more than they would be able to do in the whole week. Split your Daily To Do List into those things you Must Do and those you will Possibly Do, as opportunity allows.

* Think of your Daily To Do List as a finite sized container, and your To Dos as items to go into the container. You can only fit so many in, particularly Must Dos. If you have more tasks to add which will overfill your box you will need to take some of your existing tasks out, or don't put some of the additional tasks in. Of course if you can do tasks quickly and efficiently they will take up less space and you can fit more of them in.

* Make commitments to do the Must Do things on your Daily To Do List. If you have too many things on your Daily To Do List to make such commitments, take some of them off the list, and either park them away for later, pass them to someone else, or decide you are not going to do them. Don't treat your Must Do Daily To Do List as a dumping ground for everything that you should maybe do. It is a list of the things you are going to do.

* Persist in setting up effective To Do Lists that work for you. Don't expect these to work first time you try. Persist to get them set up and working as an effective tool. Their use could transform your life for the better.

Prioritizing and Doing what's Important

* The key to effectiveness is spending your time on doing the right things. You may be very busy, but are you actually progressing the things that are important to you. Are you moving towards your goals? Are you creating rather than just reacting?

* Say no to things you habitually do but which are of limited or of no benefit.

* You can, within reason, achieve almost anything, but you can't do everything. A small number of things to do are likely to get done, a large number of things are not. In simple terms the more you try to do the less likely you are to do any given thing. Heed the Russian proverb: If you chase two rabbits you will not catch either one.

* Don't try to do everything. There is far too much in the world for us to experience everything, for us to know everything, for us to do everything. Don't even try. You don't need to do the "100 things everyone must do before they die", or visit the "100 places everyone must visit before they die." Don't let yourself be dictated by other people's fantasies. Be dictated by your own. Think about the relatively few things you would really like to do, and do them. By all means try new things. But don't get obsessed about trying everything new, because you won't succeed.

* Be clear about your priorities and act on them. Most people get caught up in doing things that are not important but which are easy. Do the things that are right for the longer term. Don't feel bad about leaving unimportant things undone so long as what you are doing is important.

* In order to set priorities you need to be clear about what is important. Ensure you are clear about your long-term goals and you are clear about what you need to be doing in the short term to help you achieve them. Your high priority tasks should mostly be those that are of most benefit in the long term, though sometimes there are things you need to get out of the way because if you don't they will cause you problems.

* Be wary of simply being in reaction mode all day, where you are simply responding to the urgent things that are demanding your time and attention rather than doing the important things. You can easily find your day passing by with you having been busy all day long but having achieved nothing of long-term importance. If you find your day running away from you stop and take stock. Put all distractions aside for 5 minutes and think about, or remind yourself about, what you would like to accomplish today. What can you do to put yourself back on track?

* It's very easy to work hard and be busy all day long but not get anything of importance done. If you don't plan to get what is important done, your day is likely to fill up with what you'll recognize at the end of the day as not having been important. Your problem is not a lack of effort, it is a lack of focus.

* Identify tasks as High or Low Urgency, and High or Low Importance. As much as possible try to work on tasks that are High Importance but Low Urgency. If you find yourself having to spend a lot of time on tasks which are both High Urgency and High Importance then it is likely you are doing a lot of firefighting and going from crisis to crisis, probably brought about by not spending enough time on what were earlier High Importance but Low Urgency tasks. If you are spending a lot of time doing High Urgency Low Importance tasks then you are probably allowing yourself to be dictated by other people's priorities rather than your own. Tasks which are Low Urgency and Low Importance don't need to be done, though you may occasionally do so for relaxation purposes: generally however you should delete them from your To Do Lists.

The Bumper Book of Common Sense

* Sometimes low priority tasks are high priority tasks in waiting. Sometimes you should progress low priority tasks to avoid them becoming urgent problems in the future. Many lower priority tasks will never become significant problems if some effort is expended on them early. However if you ignore all lower priority tasks until they become high priority or a crisis you will never get control over your tasks.

* Sometimes you should progress low priority tasks because they are easier and sometimes you should do easy things to relax or avoid getting over stressed.

* A way of grouping tasks is as: Quick Wins, Major Projects, Thankless Tasks, Fillers. There will then be different best times to tackle different groupings:
   o Major Projects should be planned for your most productive time and timetabled as such.
   o Thankless Tasks should be timetabled for times when you know you are not at your best but will nevertheless get on with things.
   o Quick Wins will be done possibly as a break whilst engaged in your Thankless Tasks.
   o Fillers you should have with you and take advantage of small amounts of time that become available as they become available.

* When faced with a number of problems to be solved then think in terms of which will give the greatest return for the least relative input. Focus on those first.

* Every day we are faced with decisions about whether to take a difficult route or take an easy route. The difficult route is usually the one that takes us forward towards our goals; most people most of the time take the easy route. You don't have to be most people.

* Having too many priorities is the same as having no priorities at all. Be as clear about the things that are not priorities as you are about the things that are. And having identified some stuff as low priority, decide that some of it you are not going to do at all. By cutting back on stuff that doesn't need doing you free up more time for doing the things that do need to be done. Thus, in order to get what is important done, learn to leave much of what is not important or even much of what is important but less important, undone. Ensure this is through deliberate decision, and take what doesn't need to be done off your To Do List.

* Don't spend all your time thinking about how to solve other people's problems and working to other people's agendas. Be wary of forever being busy on tasks that only help others achieve their goals. Say No to things that are not your responsibility unless you have a good reason for doing them. Note however that one of your priorities should include keeping on good terms with others, so sometimes doing something for others should be important. Also, as part of an organization, your priorities include ensuring the success of the organization, so sometimes, although something may not be explicitly your responsibility, it is still the right thing to do from an organizational viewpoint.

* The inconveniences and obstacles thrown at you by daily life are not getting in the way of you living your life; they are your life. Don't put off doing what you want to do until you've got the other stuff out of the way, because you'll never get the other stuff out of the way. You need to do what is important to you alongside the other stuff.

* Set aside particular times during the week for working towards your long term goals. An average of just 1 hour a day on a long-term goal will help you make good progress over a few months or a year. If you find you are not able to dedicate this time, do something about it. There is plenty of time you can free up to work on your goals if they are important enough to you.

* Spend 10mins or so each evening being clear about what you want to achieve the next day. People achieve more the next day when they do this than when they don't.

* First thing in the morning identify the 2 or 3 most important things you need to do that day, list them out separately from your general To Do List, and go all out to get them done, as early in the

day as you can. You will feel as though you have achieved, and you will be inspired to make the most of the rest of your day.

* Don't be a slave to your To Do List and calendar. They are meant to free you not enslave you. If opportunity or strong desire to do something else of greater importance shows up, take it. However this should be relatively rare.

Planning to Do Things

* Thought precedes action. If our thoughts are muddled, vague, wandering, is it any wonder our actions lack focus and purpose, and we never seem to get to where we have some vague idea that we may want to get to.

* The desire to escape from doing hard and meaningful work is ever present. If you don't have a clear idea about what you want to do with your time, it will run away from you. You will be responding to other people's demands, or simply filling time with whatever is easy and in front of you. Plan out your day. Plan particular priority activities for particular timeslots, but don't fill up your day in this way. Have some unplanned time during which you can respond to things that come up during the day or deal with overruns on your priority tasks. Also have a list of relatively quick tasks you can get on with during the times you have not allocated. You don't have to then be a slave to your plan, and you can adjust to circumstances. However you will get far more done if you have a plan and adapt it than if you have no plan at all.

* Once you have set yourself a task be clear about when you intend to get it done by, and what steps you need to take by when to get it done. Be clear about when you are going to do the next action on it. If you have no deadline or plan of action then it is likely the task will just drift.

* If you are struggling to achieve certain goals, such as losing weight, then you need to get disciplined about achieving it. Be clear about precisely what your goal is. Devise a strategy for achieving it. Identify the specific elements of a plan to achieve the elements of your strategy. Get on with the planned elements, assess and track your progress, and adapt your plan as necessary based on what is working and what is not working. If there are barriers, work out how to overcome them. This works for businesses, it will work for you to.

* If you have a complex or long task, break it up into smaller specific tasks that can be completed in a single sitting.

* Prepare. We know about many events in plenty of time – Christmas for example is always sometime in late December, every year. There is no excuse for forgetting to send cards, or running out of time to buy presents. For any event decide when you should start preparing, and set yourself a reminder. Make sure it is plenty of time in advance because the first thing will be to make a checklist of everything that needs to be done and by when. Then put the things that need to be done into your diary, calendar, or organizer, with time to spare in case something should delay you or some unexpected problem arise. Then do things as set out in your diary, calendar or organizer; and if you miss an item do it as soon as you can. For regular events you might want to develop and keep a general checklist that you can reuse, and improve any time it is shown to have a shortcoming.

* For all the things you need to do, understand the next action. Then organize these next actions into groups around when and in what circumstances you can do them efficiently. Then plan to do them and do them when planned. If you don't do them when planned, get them back into your future plan.

* Be wary of spending too much time planning and not actually getting started. Be sure that your planning is not an excuse to avoid taking action. A good plan will help ensure you do the right things and don't waste time doing the wrong things. However planning is not doing, and at some point you need to get on with doing. If you have done enough planning to have confidence in what

The Bumper Book of Common Sense

the right things to be doing are, then generally it is best to get on with doing, even if in parallel you continue to do further planning. Most plans in any case will need adjusting as you go along, so don't plan in detail in areas where changes might be required.

* Have a Plan B when there are significant risks and uncertainties in your life, such as engaging in a highly risky venture, or the possibility that you might lose your job. When engaging in risky ventures, a Plan B can help you avoid catastrophic circumstances should events not turn out the way you would like. Explicitly work through the scenario where things don't go the way you would like, and ensure you have a viable route that does not lead to disaster. Where you have uncertainties in your life, again work up a Plan B. You don't need to spend lots of time on your Plan B - unless it is actually something you would prefer to do – but it should at least be realistic and be something you have some enthusiasm for. Thus, for example, if you did lose your job, what positives might come out of it, and what other opportunities might it open up.

* You don't necessarily have to plan everything. If you know what is important to you and you are able to just get on with it, then go for it. Planning and managing your time are a means to an end. If you are able to focus and make progress towards your own ends without planning, then good for you. Most of us unfortunately can't due to either the many other commitments we have to be continually balancing, or because we are not naturally as focused.

What to Do Next

* Do what is important. It is often tempting to do easy tasks first in order to get them out of the way before you get on with more important things. However this is a form of procrastination. Occasionally it is ok to do easy things but you should get in the habit of mostly getting on with what is most important first.

* Do the things that are worrying you. Deal with the things that are on your mind. Get them out of the way, or at least decide specifically when you are going to deal with them. If you don't, they'll stay on your mind interfering with everything else you are trying to do. Worrying, without deciding on and undertaking action, saps your energy.

* If it pains you not to be getting on with something you know you should be doing, just get on with it?

* If a problem is not going to get easier in the future you should tackle it as soon as possible. Otherwise it might get worse, and you will inevitably spend time worrying about the fact that you are not doing it.

* Unfinished tasks keep disturbing our conscious mind, nagging us, and interrupting other things we are trying to do. This is known as the Zeigarnik Effect. We can eliminate this effect by having a specific plan about what we are going to do to finish the task that is nagging us, with a clear understanding of the Next Action. However ensure that a Next Action is simple to do. If it isn't it is likely you haven't identified the immediate Next Action. Don't leave Next Actions as complex multi-step actions.

* If you are vague about what to do about something you will worry about it and you will put off doing anything about it. If you are specific about what you are going to do next, then you will generally be looking for the opportunity to get it done.

* To get things done effectively and efficiently, be clear about what needs to be done next. Do this for your goals and for everything and anything you want or need to get done. You can then take control of your life.

* Instead of focusing on all that needs doing, you need to simply focus on the next thing that needs doing. Instead of focusing on when you can finish something, focus on when you can next do a

part of it, when you can next spend a minimum of 30 mins quality time on it. If you keep starting, the finishing will look after itself.

* When you have some personal project you want or need to get done, you don't need to have everything planned out. Sometimes all you need to know is what is the next thing that needs doing. If you get on with the next thing that needs doing, what needs doing after that will become obvious.

* Any task that is worthwhile can appear daunting. But if you understand the direction you need to go, and you are taking steps in the right direction, you will get there. All you need to do is focus on the next step and occasionally raise your head to ensure you are still going in the right direction, adjusting your course if necessary.

* Replace feelings about a task being too big or important with focusing on taking one step at a time. If you can take one step at a time and then repeat it, you can go a long way.

* Sometimes, whilst you might not know precisely where you want to get to, it is better to start heading off in what you believe to be the right direction, and look to refine your course once you are on your way. You don't need to have all the answers in advance, just so long as you are confident you are heading in at least roughly the right direction. If is often easier to change course once you are moving than it is to get moving in the first place.

* Of all the things you could be doing now, decide which one you are going to do. Having decided, forget the other things you could be doing and concentrate upon the task at hand, and do it until you have completed it or made some tangible progress. Don't try to multitask; give your total and undivided attention to one task at a time. Whilst you are focusing on a given task blot out all thoughts of anything else and get on with it. If you find thoughts about other things keep distracting you, find somewhere to write them down so you can come back to them later – once written down they should stop distracting you. If that doesn't work, then you may need to stop what you are doing, put it away, and get on with whatever it is your mind is telling you is more important.

* If you're in two minds about whether or not you should be doing something then you'll not be effective in what you are doing. Decide when it's time to decide and then act on your decision. Don't worry that you could have chosen to do something else. If the thought that you should be doing something else keeps nagging away at you, stop what you are doing, decide what to do, and do what you decide.

Review Progress

* Regularly review how you are getting on with your active tasks: are you on target, and what is going well and what is going not so well. By constantly reviewing you can keep improving the chance of successfully completing what you have set out to do, or potentially change direction so you don't waste your time and energies on something that isn't working.

* Circumstances may change whilst you are embarked upon a given course of action, and necessitate a review of the approach you are taking to ensure it is still the most appropriate, or change it if it is no longer appropriate.

* If you are meeting or exceeding your targets then congratulate and possibly reward yourself. It is a great motivator to know you are succeeding.

* If you are failing to meet your targets then you need to understand why you are failing and take action. If your targets were unrealistic then reset them, and think about ensuring you make better estimates in the future. A common issue is with a given target being realistic but only if it was the only thing you were doing. In real life we have lots of things that need doing, and so we must be realistic about what effort we can realistically apply to any given task.

The Bumper Book of Common Sense

* After you have completed a task or a goal, or abandoned it, think about what went well and what went badly as part of a learning experience to improve your future performance. Try to pick out particular things you could and should have done differently and think about how you would do so in similar or analogous circumstances in the future.

* Keeping a time log can be a great motivator for using your time more effectively, since it makes you more aware of how you are using, or more often misusing, your time. Making a brief note of what you've been doing each hour takes only a few moments but both helps you become more aware of using your time more meaningfully, and also makes a great diary to look back on from a future time when your past will have mostly faded from memory.

If you're Failing to Make Progress, do Something About it

* If you are struggling to get something done, ask yourself why. What are the blockers to getting on with it? Are there particular limiting factors or barriers? List them out. What can you do to overcome those blockers? Not all seeming barriers are real, and they may be based on misconceptions about what can and can't be done.

* When it starts to get too much for you, or you keep pushing but aren't getting anywhere, relax. Let it alone for a while; let it simmer in your subconscious whilst you go and do something else.

* If despite everything you are unable to get on with the something you had specifically wanted to do, then stop trying. Free yourself from the guilt of not doing it and decide to do something else instead. Do something else that whilst it is not what you had wanted to do, is nevertheless something useful. Don't get drawn into a no-man's land of not doing anything useful because you feel guilty about not doing something in particular.

* Commit to making a little regular progress on tasks you struggle. Just 15mins a day and only continue if you feel like it. But always do the 15mins.

* It is better to make a beginning at something that may lead somewhere than to struggle endlessly with something that is leading nowhere.

* Too little stress is as much an inhibitor to effective working as too much stress. One way of increasing your stress levels, assuming you are feeling too un-stressed, is to imagine things going wrong. Imagine the embarrassment of being late for example, or of having your work criticized. Don't let this then dominate your thinking and take your stress levels too far the other way; just enough to avoid complacency.

* If at the end of the day you feel you have failed to get done the important things you set out to do, then review what it was that prevented you or distracted you or demotivated you. Seek to learn from such experiences to improve your future behavior and practices so as to increase your chances of progressing future activities. Look out in particular for the common issue of not having been specific enough about what you had intended to do as your next action.

* If you find your weeks and months are passing by unsatisfactorily, then track what you are doing with your time, in hour chunks. Keep a notebook with you and record in it every waking hour: time spent eating, time spent doing chores such as laundry or cleaning, time spent working, time spent watching TV, time spent going out, time spent being proactive with family, time spent on your own projects. Then analyze it by making up a daily or weekly chart in which you color code different types of activities. You should quickly become aware of patterns and can then plan where you want to make changes, and free up dedicated time for meaningful goals. It also makes you aware of how much time you really have in the week and helps you more realistically plan your time.

Focusing and Environment

* People perform better at a task when they set themselves a specific challenging goal, rather than simply 'doing their best'.

* When you start doing a task, have a clear idea of what your target is for the given session and do your best to ensure you achieve it, or at least have make some tangible progress. If you are having difficulty making progress try to at least identify some small step that leaves you feeling you've done something of value. Avoid giving up on a task earlier than you had intended simply because you are struggling to make progress.

* Having decided what you are going to spend your time on, look to make the best use of that time by totally focusing on it. Don't spend your time whilst doing a task thinking about other things that you could be doing, or by doing other things at the same time.

* Focus on what you are trying to achieve, not on what might go wrong. By all means look to understand what might go wrong and have plans for dealing with certain circumstances should they arise. But once you've done this and you're ready to get on with doing with whatever it is you want to do, focus on doing it. Most people who can easily walk across a wide plank a few inches off the floor would be unable to walk across it if it was high in the air. Because close to the ground they focus on walking the plank. High in the air their focus is on the possibility of falling off.

* The environment you are in can significantly impact your ability to focus on a task. A good environment for keeping you focused tends to be one with the following characteristics:
    o A cool temperature, though not cold - warm conditions are likely to make you feel drowsy;
    o Bright light;
    o Quiet, though the use of low volume instrumental or classical music can help concentration;
    o Comfortable, though not overly comfortable, seating;
    o No clutter or piles of things that keep drawing your eyes away from what you are doing;
    o Everything you need to do the task is at hand and you don't need to go looking for things;
    o No interruptions such as e-mail or phone alerts;
    o No other distractions such as drinking, eating, or smoking.

* Low lighting levels will make you feel lethargic and a bit down. If you want to get on with things try to ensure there is plenty of bright light about.

* Listening to music can help drown out potentially distracting background noise, however the music should be soothing and familiar to you so that it does not itself become a distraction. Note however that listening to music whilst you work will not disturb logical serial processing types of tasks, but it will inhibit creative thinking tasks since music is processed in the part of the brain that deals with holistic thinking.

* When working on anything important it is usually worthwhile switching off anything that might interrupt you, and going somewhere you won't be disturbed. If you are concerned about missing something important arrange for someone to come and disturb you with it if necessary. It will lead to significantly improved performance. Distractions are time consuming, tiring, and likely to lead to mistakes. Children who say they work better with the TV or music on, are deluding themselves. They would work even better without it, assuming you can get them to do so. However children are better able to work with distraction than older people, since the older we get the less effective we are at multitasking and switching rapidly between tasks.

* Ensure you prepare for a task by having everything you need to do it close to hand, in so far as is reasonable given the particular task. Once you start to focus on a task, having to get up to find or get things can disrupt your concentration and flow.

The Bumper Book of Common Sense

* If you get distracting or disruptive thoughts whilst trying to focus on a task it is important to get them written down. Always have a piece of paper with you where you can write down intermittent thoughts about things you want to remember for later. If you get them written down they will generally stop interrupting you, if you don't get them written down, they will keep coming back to mind.

* Keep a 'worry box'. One of the things that stops us getting on with things is our worrying about something else. It is important you get your worries written down. Either have a notebook in which you can list your worries, or have a box in which you can keep bits of paper with your worries written down on. If a worry occurs to you, get it written down and move on. Once you've done whatever it is you wanted to get on with, you can come back to your worry list and set aside particular time for working out what to do about items that are on it.

* Sometimes you have difficulty getting on with or focusing on a task because of lots of other thoughts cluttering up your brain. A way of clearing your mind which works for many people is to just dump your thoughts out onto a piece of paper or by typing into a word processor. Literally just write or type up anything that comes into your head for 10 minutes. Don't assess or think about what you are writing; just write it. Anything. Even your meta thoughts about not being sure what to write or type next. After about 10 or 15 minutes, sometimes earlier sometimes later, you should find your mind becoming clearer and you may well find yourself feeling more alert. You should then find yourself able to focus on whatever task it is you wanted to focus on. As for the scribbling you've written down just throw it away or put it away: you might want to have a look at it later to see if any useful or creative thoughts have happened to occur to you.

* If you are unable to focus on a task because of a given worry, and writing it down doesn't help, then think clearly about what is the best use you can make of your time right now. If it is doing something about whatever it is that is worrying you, then do so. If there is nothing you can do about your worry right now, be specific with yourself about when you will look to do something about it, say that clearly to yourself, and look to return to your given task.

* Watch out for using progress as an excuse for slowing down before you had planned to do so. Having made progress our conscious brains become less focused on our long-term goals and we become more prone to giving in to lapses through temptations. Rather than focusing on how much progress you have made, focus on your commitment to keep going and why you are looking to achieve the particular goal.

* Be wary of daydreaming whilst you are trying to get on with activities that require your concentration. If you find yourself daydreaming, or you mind continually wandering off, either get yourself refocused fully on the task or take a break from it. To help you refocus simply saying to yourself something like: 'Stop it, focus back on this now', can help. If you take a break but are keen to carry on, ensure it is just a short break, possibly a short walk or going to make a coffee.

Be Positive and Persistent

* Optimists tend to live longer than pessimists.

* Optimists are more likely to succeed in getting things done than pessimists. If you believe you can do something you probably can. If you believe you can't, you can't. The more positive you are, the more you will get done.

* Being positive is not about being unrealistically optimistic. Out and out optimists are at a disadvantage because they don't plan for how to overcome setbacks and adverse circumstances, and they tend to be less resilient than pessimists. By recognizing there are difficulties we can prepare and plan for overcoming specific difficulties and circumstances. Pessimists however generally get no further than recognizing there will be difficulties; they don't move on to working out how to overcome them.

* Pessimists look at a big task and say it is too difficult to get it done in one go and put it off for another day: they stop thinking about how best to do it. Optimists see the same task and look to see how much of it they can get done today, and get on and do it: they keep thinking about how best to do it. Pessimists are quitters, optimists get things done. Pessimists see difficulty in every opportunity. Optimists see opportunity in every difficulty.

* Pessimists think of themselves as realists. And to some extent they may see situations more accurately than optimists. However most things that are worthwhile have difficulties, but people who are creative and determined will overcome them. It is not realistic to believe you can't, it's just being pessimistic.

* Take pleasure from how much you have accomplished rather than continually beating yourself up about how much you still have to do.

* Small steps and victories are good. If you do little things well, you can do bigger things well. Get little goals done; you'll get big goals done. Step by step you can go a very long way.

* Persistence will enable you to get most things done. Persistence is a state of mind that can be cultivated, that can become a habit. However to be most useful it also requires a clear sense of purpose, a desire, and a belief that you can. It also requires the intelligence to ensure you persist in the right things: persistently beating your head against a brick wall is not necessarily the best way to get over to the other side.

* The man who will win is the one who keeps going when the going gets difficult and there is every excuse to stop.

* We limit ourselves by what we believe is possible. If you find other people can and are doing things you thought not possible then you are more likely to succeed in doing them yourself. Shortly after Roger Banister ran the 4-minute mile many others did it, whereas prior to this many considered it not possible. If you want to succeed in doing something that you are not sure is possible find others to take your inspiration from and reset your own expectations based on what others have already shown to be possible.

* Regularly tell yourself that one of the things that differentiates you from most other people is that you get on with things. You make more use of your time than they do. And you are going to succeed because when they are doing nothing in particular you are doing things for a reason, you are proactive, you are moving forwards.

* Whilst others are planning, over thinking, and generally going round in circles, be productive and proactive and you will soon be way ahead of them.

* Faced with something difficult that you need to do, don't focus on the worry of whether or not you will be able to do it, but focus on working out how best to approach it. And then get on with it.

* When someone says 'No' to you, sometimes you can treat it as a challenge to be more creative in getting them onto your side or to change their minds. If seeking a Yes is important to you, then a rejection should be a call to be more creative in finding a way to change the rejection around.

* If you are working on a task but not making much progress don't despair or lose concentration. Many activities, including learning new skills or doing creative writing, progress at an uneven pace, sometimes slowly and sometimes rapidly, and being persistent is a necessary part of succeeding. Do however ensure that what you are trying to do is worth the effort and also that you are not being overly perfectionist.

* If you are failing to make adequate progress or failing to overcome hurdles or barriers then analyze why, identify new strategies, and keep trying. What can you do differently in order to make progress?

The Bumper Book of Common Sense

* You'll never get something done if you don't try.

Multitasking

* We don't really multitask anything that requires any focused mental effort. We simply switch between tasks. Some people are better at switching between tasks and giving the illusion of multitasking, but the brain simply doesn't work that way. Tasks are more effectively done, with greater accuracy and performance, one at a time, assuming you can maintain the motivation and interest in doing so.

* Multitasking less attention intensive tasks can keep up your motivation for doing them longer. Doing some simple administrative tasks whilst watching TV can help you get them done with having hardly noticed you were doing them.

* You can multitask with activities which you've learnt to automate, and which thus don't need your focused conscious attention. This is why touch typing is such a useful skill to have, because you can learn to automate your typing such that your brain focuses on what you want to say, not on the typing itself. People who have to also focus on their typing are continually having their thoughts interrupted.

* Our ability to undertake different tasks at the same time is better if the tasks are very different. If the tasks are similar, such as listening to music with words whilst reading, the interference and decline in effectiveness is very significant. If you feel as though you need music to listen to whilst studying, ensure it is classical or instrumental music and that it remains background music rather than continually grabbing your attention.

* If you multitask whilst doing complex tasks you will be far less effective and much more likely to make mistakes.

* The illusion of multitasking can be, and frequently has been, fatal. Whilst many people think they can do complex things with phones or in-car gadgets whilst driving they are reliant upon nothing out of the ordinary happening. As soon as it does their reactions are slower than they would have been had they been giving full attention to driving, with possible fatal consequences for themselves or others.

* Decide on one thing to do, and how long you are going to do it for, and get on with it. If you have several tasks to get done, you will usually get them done quicker one at a time than you will by trying to do them all at the same time.

Overcoming Procrastination

* Procrastination is when we put off things we should be doing now and instead do something less important but more enjoyable or easier, or worst still do nothing purposeful at all. It is when we fail to do what we intended to do. Signs of a procrastination habit include filling our days with low priority tasks or distractions, having something important left undone for weeks or months on end, frequently reading e-mail several times but not taking any action as a result, sitting down to do a task and immediately getting up to make a coffee, waiting till you are in the right mood before getting on with something.

* Procrastination is a habit, and you won't break it overnight. But like any bad habit it can be broken if you work at it.

* We often sleepwalk into procrastination. It's easy and pleasant to watch a bit of TV or browse away on the internet or go down the pub. We know we should be doing something else but don't give it

much thought. However we should consciously give it some thought. We should force ourselves to be explicitly aware of when we are procrastinating. We should think about the consequences of what we are doing and the specific problems we are storing up for ourselves. We should assume that not doing it now means it won't get done later either, so what are the consequences of not doing it at all? Maybe we ought to do at least a bit of it after all.

* The three things that are at the bottom of most procrastination problems are: feeling like a victim; being overwhelmed; and fear of failure. The better you are able to recognize which of these is behind a given procrastination, the better you will find a way to overcome it.

* If you find you are procrastinating because of worry about whether you'll be able to do the task itself, then put yourself firmly in the present and think positively about what you are doing. Think in terms of it being a unique experience that at worse is a challenge that you can learn from.

* If you are procrastinating because you find the task overwhelming, then break it down into smaller steps, and then if necessary still smaller steps. You only need get on with one of the small steps at once, you don't need to get it all done at once.

* If you are putting off a task because you think it will be difficult, then recognize that once you get started most tasks turn out to be easier than feared.

* A common type of procrastination is putting off making decisions. However if you learn good decision making skills you will be less likely to do so. In particular if you can't decide between options then toss a coin. And then either go with which ever option comes up heads, or if that fills you with foreboding, go with the other one.

* Acknowledge that you are just as responsible for the decisions you don't make, but could have done, as you are for those that you do make. By delaying or not making a decision so that it gets made for you, you haven't avoided responsibility. You are just as responsible for the consequences that arise as a result of your not having made the decision.

* Procrastinators typically avoid one task by doing another. Rarely do they sit there doing nothing at all. Thus doing nothing is a tactic against procrastination. If you know you must do something then either do it or do nothing. Sit around looking out of the window or just walk around the house, but don't do anything else: no tidying, no reading, no listening to music or radio, no watching TV, no internet browsing.

* You can make procrastination work for you. Procrastinators often don't sit around doing nothing. Rather than let yourself waste your time watching TV or browsing the Internet, find something else worthwhile that needs doing.

* If procrastination is the result of lack of interest, then look to increase arousal by doing things differently. Even relatively mundane tasks can be made more exciting by setting challenges for yourself in terms of getting them done in record time, or doing them with some handicap.

* When faced with overwhelming worries, anxieties, and stress we often fail to act. Rather than move into a heightened state of action we often shut down altogether and distract ourselves with irrelevancies, doing things that are easy and familiar. Thus faced with some looming deadline that is not yet upon us we might watch some TV. To overcome your procrastination you need to understand and then focus on the immediate steps you can be getting on with now. It doesn't matter that you can't do it all; all that matters is that you can do some of it. Once you've done some of it, you will often find the rest is not as overwhelming as it had at first appeared.

* We overestimate the ability of our future selves to do things we don't want to do now. We put them off in the mistaken belief that our future self won't suffer from the procrastination habit of our present self. Yet time and time again we find our future self is really our current self with exactly the same procrastination habit. The best chance our future self has of overcoming procrastination is in our current self overcoming procrastination.

The Bumper Book of Common Sense

* Procrastinators often see themselves as always working and not having time to themselves. Though they put things off, they feel guilty about it and are left in a limbo between not doing their work but also not making the most of and enjoying the time they have to themselves. One way of breaking out of this is to schedule specific time for yourself. Knowing you have such time, to do the things you really want to do, will help you feel more motivated at other times. Knowing your work is not depriving you of your own time means you don't need to feel resentful towards it, since you know you are not ruining your life.

* Procrastination is often more tiring than simply getting on and doing whatever it is you are procrastinating about. Most people spend significant amounts of energy and time avoiding what they should be doing, or looking for excuses for why they didn't get something done. If that energy and time was spent getting on with what they are avoiding they would get it done.

* Nothing is more tiring than a task or goal you can't seem to get finished. Let go of any tasks or goals you are not committed to, or which you are not willing to give your all to get done. If necessary put them on a list of things to consider in the future, but get them off the list of things you are trying to do now.

* We often procrastinate for long periods of time on tasks that if we got on with would only take 30 minutes or so.

* Try to get into the habit of doing your most unpleasant task for the day as early in the day as you can. It puts you on a high and in the mood for a productive day.

* If you are dreading making a phone call, do it as soon as possible. If not, it will drain your energy until you do.

* If you have a particular unpleasant task that you just cannot make any progress on, then commit to doing just 10mins, and then tell yourself you can get on with something else. If after doing 10mins you are sufficiently motivated to carry on, then do so. If not, then put it aside and do something else. The next day, again, 10mins.

* Set yourself in motion and be content with what you get done, no matter how small. If you are having trouble getting started on something, then try starting it in slow motion, or with a very laid back attitude. Deliberately take your time. It is easier to get started on something if you don't feel under any pressure and are in no rush. Once you've started you'll find yourself picking up pace with no real effort.

* Don't focus on what needs to be done to finish a task, focus on committing to do 30 mins or so on it. Even 30 mins of quality work is usually enough to make noticeable progress, and infinitely more progress than results from doing nothing at all. When the 30 minutes is up then either go and do something else, or carry on with the task, whichever you feel like doing. Often having started on the task you will want to carry on. Ensure however that your first 30 mins is focused, without interruptions such as getting up to make a cup of coffee or checking your e-mails.

* Be wary of rewarding yourself for procrastination. If rather than getting on with something important you go off and do something enjoyable, you have rewarded yourself for procrastination. Much better to agree with yourself a certain minimum time, say 30 mins, of doing what is important, and then going off and doing something enjoyable. You'll both be conditioning yourself to get on with things, and also find your enjoyable activities more enjoyable because you will feel less guilty about doing them.

* Keep making the effort to at least get started on what you know you should be doing when you should be doing it. If you keep making the effort to do so, it will get easier.

* A technique for overcoming procrastination. List 5 or 6 tasks you want to get done in a morning or an afternoon. Write against them 10, 20, 30. Then start on task 1 for 10 minutes with a timer. When the timer goes off after 10 minutes stop working on that task, strike out the 10 against the task, and set the timer for another 10 minutes whilst you get on with the second task. Repeat until

you have done 10 minutes on each task and then continue doing 20 minutes on each task then 30 minutes. Clearly if you get a given task done you can simply strike it through and carry on with the other tasks. This technique can be highly effective in getting on with tasks because you are working to a deadline on each task, which tends to concentrate the mind. Also having started the tasks you get an urge to want to continue with them when the time comes round again.

* Being organized will help you overcome procrastination. If you know what the most important tasks are that need doing, and you know what the next steps are, and you have everything you need to hand to get on with them, then you are far more likely to at least make a start.

* If there is something you can get done straight away, do so, before you have a chance to procrastinate. For example once you have made a decision or set a goal, immediately take some action to progress it.

* You can build up a mental toughness and a feeling of being someone who gets things done by getting into the habit of being aware of yourself as someone who gets things done. Every night decide on one thing you will get done the next day. Not something difficult which you might not actually get done, but something you can and would like to get done. Then ensure you do get it done, and be aware at the end of the day that you have. Repeat the next day, and for a week. Then move onto things that whilst relatively small, are the sort of things you generally procrastinate about. Make a list of 7 of them and each night pick one that you will get done the next day. And do it. Then move on to bigger things. Things that are worrying you. Break them down into smaller tasks that you can easily get done during the day. List them and then tackle one a day. In doing this you will slowly build up a mental toughness and also tackle some of the underlying stresses that are likely to be eating away at you.

* If you are struggling with getting on with something, ask yourself whether or not it really needs to be done. Look for reasons not to do it, not to do it at all that is, not excuses for putting it off. If you can decide you really don't need to do it then you can get on with other things and stop procrastinating about the given task. If on the other hand you decide you really do need to do it, you should be clearer about why, and a little more motivated to get on and do it.

* If you are struggling with getting on with something, ask yourself if there is a different approach to take. Maybe it is the way you have decided to approach it that is repelling you, rather than the task itself. If you approach it in a different way you might find it easy to get on with.

* If you are stalling, and not getting tasks you had set out to get done today done, ask yourself if your life depended on you getting it done, or the life of your child, or if you were offered a million pounds to get it done today, could you. If the answer is yet, then clearly it is possible to get it done, it's your own mind that is holding you back, and you are in control of your own mind. So do you want to get it done or don't you?

* If you are struggling to progress a seemingly daunting task, then maybe it would be better to get it done quickly and not worry that it might not be as good as it could have been. Maybe you can get it done quickly and then look to improve it afterwards. Or maybe you should set yourself a short timescale to do it in and get as much of it done in that time as you can.

* If you have trouble starting something because you are concerned it might not be very good, or will fall short of your own high standards, then accept that it will be bad and get on and do it. Give yourself permission to produce a poor first draft. You can and will improve it later. Almost all published works did not get initially written that way, but got improved through reviewing and editing, often to a point where the words themselves are largely unrecognizable from the first draft.

* If you are putting off a task because it is unpleasant, then you need to try to get it over with as soon as possible, so it isn't weighing on your mind and you can then get on with something more pleasant. You might think of some reward for yourself once you've done it.

* Once you get started on a task it usually goes better than you feared it would.

The Bumper Book of Common Sense

* We don't usually procrastinate about everything. Procrastination is often in the light of particular tasks and circumstances. By being more conscious of what these are we are more likely to find ways to overcome them.

* Be aware of specific procrastination behaviors. Are there particular environmental or thought habits present at the onset of procrastination? You can adapt your environment to remove some of the prompts and temptations for procrastination. Switch off your computer or TV, for example, maybe even take the plug out for a while. Think about what makes it easy to procrastinate, and then make it harder.

* We are more likely to procrastinate when no one is looking over our shoulder. If you make visible to others what you are trying to do such that they can see when you are procrastinating, then you are less likely to procrastinate: peer pressure and pride are powerful motivators.

* Procrastinators who do work at the last moment often believe they produce better quality work under deadline pressure, but it is not true. Their work is lower quality than it would have been had they took more time over it.

* See instances of procrastination as an opportunity to better understand the root causes of your procrastination and practice techniques to overcome it. Don't get disheartened if they don't work; you've learned something, and can try other techniques.

* Try never to end a bit of work on a down. If you're stuck try at least to get to a point where you have a way forward. You should seek to stop a piece of work with some momentum that will help you get started again next time.

* Deciding not to do unimportant tasks, and doing other things instead, is not procrastination. Also, putting off a task for a good reason, such as you are feeling really tired, or there genuinely is a better time to do it, is not procrastination so long as you do then get on with it when you are no longer tired or the better time comes around.

* What you do makes a difference; what you put off doing, doesn't.

* Be ruthlessly honest with yourself about the reasons you are procrastinating. Write them down. Analyze them. Work out tactics for overcoming them, and get on and do so.

Increasing your Ability to Control or React to Events

* If you have a surplus you can control circumstances. However if you have no surplus you will be controlled by circumstances. This is true on many levels. For example with regards materials and resources for doing a job. For management of your time. Even for your own energy levels.

* Say No to tasks other people try to give you which are not in your own interests or which are not part of your area of responsibility or which you do not wish to take on for reasons of improving your relations with others.

* To succeed in circumstances you are not familiar with or which are unpredictable you need to be flexible, adaptable, and generally light on your feet. To a significant extent intelligence is about being able to respond to any situation, especially novel situations, by adapting one's own behavior.

* Have a plan for doing the important things that need doing. Keep updating the plan as necessary to make it or keep it realistic both in terms of ensuring the things in your plan are the right things to do in the right sequence, and in terms of having achievable timescales. Keep your plan up to date. If something doesn't get done when planned, either decide it no longer needs doing or readjust your plan to put it back in to the future. For the most part follow your plan, though not slavishly if due to circumstances it is not the right thing to do. You will find yourself much more in control if

you have the best plan you can put together, follow it, but be willing to deviate and adapt to emerging circumstances where necessary.

* Look to take benefit of other people's willingness to help you with your tasks. If someone else can do adequately well something you would otherwise have done yourself then you have freed up some of your time for doing other things. However to get a return from other people you need to have first invested to ensure they clearly understand what needs to be done, by when, and that you are confident they can and will do the job as well as is necessary. You may also need to monitor what they are doing just to check they have fully understood and to ensure they are making adequate progress.

* You will never have enough time. Beware of trying to solve your problems by simply working harder. You need to make smarter choices. Ensure what you do has value, and will count in the long term. Ensure you do what will have the greatest pay-off, not simply what is easy. Do non-urgent things that could become problems before they become problems. Push back on interruptions or tasks that are of low importance. Seek to align others such that they are helping you achieve your goals. Sometimes however you should be willing to work harder, but only sometimes.

Effective Management of your Time when Interacting with Others

* Don't let your time be filled up by other people's demands, and be willing to say no to their demands on your time. However your relationships with others are important, so sometimes you need to do things to keep those relationships in good working order.

* If you think of what you do as either creative or reactive, be conscious of the need to be creative much of the time. It is all too easy to end up spending most or all of our time reacting to other people rather than having them react to us.

* When someone comes to you asking for you to do something to help them, and you would like to do so, then ask yourself: Am I the right person? Is this the right time? Do I have enough information to be able to do what they want? Just because you can help someone doesn't mean you should. Just because you want to help someone doesn't mean you can. It may be that someone else is in a better position to help them, or that there is a more appropriate time for helping them, or that you need more information before doing so. On the other hand it may well be appropriate to help them.

* When interacting with others on a particular topic there is sometimes a right time and sometimes a wrong time to do so. Trying to push things before people are ready to accept your position can be hard work or doomed to failure, whereas waiting for the right moment can make it easier. Not that you always know when the right time is, but if you are sensitive to circumstances it is often obvious when the wrong time is.

* Be disciplined about dealing with e-mails. Only check your e-mails a couple of times a day, otherwise they will be continually interrupting you. When you do deal with them, respond to those that can be dealt with right away and delete those that are of no interest. Have a disciplined way of dealing with the rest. For example file those that contain information you wish to keep but don't require action, or possibly copy the information elsewhere and delete the e-mail. Have a To Do folder for those that require action but you do not intend to deal with just yet – add the action to your To Do Lists. Do not leave e-mails hanging about in your In-Box.

* If you have appointments, confirm them if there is any doubt. There is no excuse for turning up to meetings that have been cancelled or turning up at the wrong place or time for appointments.

* Turn up for meetings with others on time or early. If there is the potential for delays, recognize them and make allowances so you still turn up on time. Try to avoid back-to-back meetings, but if

they are unavoidable then recognize travel time between the meetings and ensure those responsible know you will need to leave a little early or arrive a little late.

* Many meetings lack focus and you can waste a lot of your time in them. Where you fear this may be the case either don't attend, or ensure there is a clear written agenda. Try to avoid going to lots of meetings that are not core to what you do; they take up a lot of time, and your contribution and what you gain will usually be limited.

* Be confident and assertive in your dealings with others and they will more likely respect you and support you in your endeavors. However this means you also need to respect other people's assertiveness, listen to their concerns and issues, and ensure you reach mutually agreeable way forwards with them, rather than simply try to impose your will upon them.

Getting On With It Aphorisms

* You can't do everything. But you can do something.

* You can't do everything that needs doing at once. But you can do something at once.

* The wise get on and do what the fool puts off for another day.

* One who sleeps doesn't catch fish.

* Never put off till tomorrow what can be done today.

* When it turns up, not when it blows up.

* Great books are written one word at a time; great journeys are undertaken one step at a time.

* All beginnings are small.

* Begin at the beginning and keep going until you get to the end.

* You will be remembered for what you do, not for what you think.

* All success comes from daring to begin.

* If you wait until everything is absolutely ready, you will never begin.

* If the wind won't serve, take to the oars.

* Who seizes the moment is the right person for the moment.

* Sometimes it is best to act; sometimes it is best to be still. Sometimes it is best to speak; sometimes it is best to be silent.

* If there is nothing else to hand, then why not clutch at straws?

* Do it right first time and you won't have to do it again.

* Look before you leap.

* Don't pour water into a bowl with holes.

* It's the little things that make the big things possible. By paying attention to the little things we are paying attention to the big things.

* If you don't know what you are doing, you won't know when to stop.

* Be a visionary when deciding what the right thing to do is; be a doer when you need to get it done: not the other way around.

Working with Others

Try to See Things from Other's Point of View

* You need to try to see things from other people's point of view, if you are to avoid conflict with them and be able to work effectively with them. To do this you need to learn good listening skills, and to suspend your own judgment and continual self-talk.

* If you understand where someone else is coming from you should be able to interact with them in a more effective manner. You can be more flexible in areas that are less important to you but which you know are important to them.

* Sometimes it is better to get conflict out in the open and deal with it rather than avoid it in a way that will make it worse later. On the other hand sometimes it is better to play down conflicts in the interests of working together and giving yourselves time to develop the sort of mutual respect that would in time allow you to openly discuss and resolve your differences.

* Seeing things from another person's point of view does not mean you need to agree with their point of view, though it may lead to you modifying your own point of view.

* From their own point of view, people are not acting illogically any more than you are from your own point of view. There is a reason they are acting the way they are which is logical from their point of view. Maybe they are seeing things differently to you as a result of having different goals and priorities. Or they have different information and understanding, which may be more or less than you have. Or they are being influenced by particular experiences that they may have had. Or they are being pressurized by others. Of course it is also possible they are applying faulty logic, but it's highly unlikely that the faulty logic itself is the root cause of the reason they are not fully aligned with your way of thinking.

* People don't do things that appear stupid because they are stupid. They do them because:
    o They don't know some key piece of information that you know;
    o They know some key piece of information that you don't;
    o They have different objectives than you do;
    o They have different objectives than you think that they have, possibly a hidden objective;
    o They balance different objectives in a different way than you do;
    o They have a different view than you do of what might or might not be feasible.

    If it is important to you, you should try to find out which one of these it is.

Deciding Whether to Work Alone or With Others

* Metaphorically speaking, and literally, a single architect will usually produce a better outline design for a building than a number of architects working in committee. On the other hand a single architect is unlikely to know all the details about everything required to produce and erect a building. You need to think carefully about when it is best to work alone and when it is best to work with others. And even when working alone, what you are doing will generally be part of some bigger plan, and you should work with others to ensure that what you are working alone on fits appropriately into the bigger plan.

* Even when working alone it is usually a good idea to invite input and comment from others at appropriate times. Writing a book is an activity that is usually best done by someone working on their own. However once the shape and initial draft of the book has been produced there is usually huge benefit in getting comments and suggestions from other people, so long as the author retains control over what is and isn't changed.

* For some things, many hands make light work. Particularly if they are hands that can do things and it is clear what needs to be done. However too many cooks can spoil the broth when they all want to do things their own way or they become a distraction to those that are doing things.

* We all have different capabilities and skills and different things we'd rather do and not do. When working with others there is the opportunity for each of us to work on what we are good at and avoid working on what we are not so good at. However this is dependent upon the mix of tasks to be done and the range of capabilities of those available. Sometimes we need to compromise and need to work on things we'd rather not.

* When working alone you have less distractions and can, in principle at least, get more done and be more focused. However it can also be very difficult to motivate oneself for an extended period of time. Whilst there are distractions when working with others there is also the pressure of having others able to see what you are doing. Most people find it harder to motivate themselves to doing a full 8 or 9 hour day working alone at home than they do in a working environment with others. A partial short-term compromise could be working alone but in a public place away from an interactive working environment, such as doing your work in a library or moving away from your usual desk at work and working somewhere else visible to others but not those likely to disturb you.

* For many jobs there will be periods of working with others and periods of working alone. Most work is a collaborative effort, but we have our own specific responsibilities as part of the overall effort. Ensuring everyone is going in the same direction is vitally important, as is ensuring that the efforts of each individual is part of a wider plan of complete and coherent set of activities that will deliver the end goal. This means we need to be in frequent contact with others. However there will also be some particular pieces of work that are ours and ours alone. Some time on our own will be necessary to progress them, though we may well need input from others and need to get others to review what we are doing or have done.

* In a typical working day we spend some of the time working alone, sat alone at our desk maybe, some of the time working with others, in a meeting or discussion for example. Depending upon the nature of our work we need to get the balance right since too much of one or the other will lead to less effective outputs.

* If we are working alone on something that is intended to contribute to some collaborative effort we need to ensure we regularly get input from others to ensure we do not going too far off in the wrong direction. When working alone we can feel as though we are making a lot of progress simply because we are producing a lot of output. However we can also be deluding ourselves about the value or relevance of what we are producing.

* Working and interacting with others exposes us to ideas that we would never have had if working on our own.

* Be willing to ask others for help. We are not experts in everything, or even in truth very much. Getting input from someone who knows more than us about something can save us a lot of time in trying to find out for ourselves and makes us less prone to getting it wrong. However respect other's time and don't be continually going to others when you should be capable of finding out and learning for yourself.

* Many people are looking for something to bring meaning into their lives. Working with others on some meaningful goal, is one of the most meaningful experiences to be had.

Gaining Other People's Support and Input

* Ask advice from people who can help you. If you want help from someone, ask them; don't wait for them to offer, because no matter how obvious it may be to you, they probably don't know you want their help.

* If people offer to help you, say yes, unless you very specifically don't want their help.

* The best way to get a task done is to have someone else do it for you, assuming you can be confident that it is the right thing, that it will get done on time, and that it will be done to the necessary quality. This might be through your delegating to someone who works for you or who is otherwise willing to do it for you. Or it might be through working with others who have similar interests and are willing to take on the particular task.

* If you tell people why you want something done they are more likely to do the right thing than if you simply tell them what you want done.

* Consult with people about what you want them to do, and gain their understanding and buy-in. Adapt the detail of what you ask them to do in response to what they say and want. Whilst it can take much longer to get started than simply telling them to do it, in the longer term you will need to spend much less time giving further instructions and there is a much greater likelihood the task will get done effectively without creating more problems.

* When people are simple told what to do, and are not consulted about what needs doing or how best to do it, they take no ownership or responsibility for the task, and generally make much less effort than they might otherwise have done. If what is being done is unrealistic or not feasible, they may or may not try to tell you so. Potential opportunities for doing things better will generally be lost.

* Involve others in decisions about the things that affect them.

* If you are looking to gain people's support to an idea, then you need to identify the stakeholders. Who is affected? Who has an interest? Who can affect the outcome? Who is likely to express discontent? Who can influence others? Who have clear roles in the plan? What is the current position of each of the stakeholders? Do they approve or disapprove, and if so how strongly? Where do you need them to be? How do we get them from where they are to where they need to be?

* It is usually better to get people's willing agreement to something rather than imposing on them. Negotiate with people as equals rather than make demands of them.

* If you have power you can often force people to do things for you, but you won't get as much out of them as you would if they worked for you voluntarily.

* If you want people to help you, you need to be ready to help them. Thus you need to be ready to do people favors, albeit without letting yourself be taken advantage of.

The Bumper Book of Common Sense

* People are more likely to help you if they like you. To help with this smile a lot, use the other person's name, show you are listening, talk about their interests, and make them feel important.

Providing Support to Others

* Don't always assume that what you think you are being asked to do is necessarily what is needed. Often instructions are poorly stated or are misinterpreted or incorrect assumptions are made. If you think the wrong thing is being asked for, then seek clarification. It is better to seek clarification than risk doing what turns out to be the wrong thing.

* Under promise rather than over promise.

* Help people to think better by helping them solve their own problems or come to their own conclusions. Rather than give them an answer, help them to think through the issue and options.

* If you don't point out errors in what other people are doing you are not giving them the opportunity to improve. However there are some ways of giving people feedback that are more likely to be listened to in a positive manner than are other ways. Simply criticizing someone is unlikely to get a positive response from them. Most people are immediately defensive in the light of criticism. You need to catch people in a positive mood. You need to include positive statements amongst any statements that will be perceived as negative, irrespective of how you mean them. You need to be specific rather than general when suggesting how someone might improve. And never provide negative feedback in public.

Effective Working Within a Group

* If you are to work effectively within a group you need to be at least tolerant of, and best be appreciative of, the fact that people are different. People have different views to you, different approaches, different strengths and weaknesses. This shouldn't upset you, and get you annoyed: it should excite you and make you feel upbeat about the fact that together you have a far wider range of skills, abilities, and approaches than you would have if you were all similar.

* When a group of people who haven't worked together come together for some particular purpose it is often appropriate to spend a little bit of time early on ensuring they get to know each other a little bit and to get everyone into the same open contributing mindset. Some ways of doing this include:
    o Have people introduce themselves together with providing some little known fact about themselves;
    o Have people tell everyone else what it is they are looking to get out of the group working session or period;
    o Have people interview each other in pairs and then introduce the other person to the wider group;
    o There are many short games or ways of passing from one person to the next that can get people interacting. These however are often most appropriate when the group is made up of relatively young people, up to about their mid-twenties. Older people will often find this quite condescending and even embarrassing.

* Try to avoid working with people who are continually critical and negative about what you are trying to do. Constructive criticism is to be welcomed; destructive criticism however is of no use. People who are continually criticizing, and not looking for solutions to the areas they are being critical about, are of little use to you and the people you are working with. They can seriously undermine the motivation of any group that are a part of.

* Be wary of simply working with yes men. They will tend to lack ideas.

* Effective working in a group requires a common goal and the understanding amongst all members of the group that they all win or lose together.

* People adopt particular roles within groups. Look to understand what role you are playing, and ensure it is playing to your strengths.

* Be tolerant of the fact that people have different ways of thinking, different capabilities and skills, different personalities and behavior traits. People being different is a benefit to group working, not a difficulty, so long as those in the group recognize this.

* Encourage the group to be clear about what it is trying to achieve, and to have clarity of who is responsible for what and who is doing what and by when.

* If a group needs to decide between a number of options then simply give each member of the group a number of votes which they can distribute amongst the options. Simply take the choice with the most number of options. Keep the voting between options secret to avoid groupthink. And just keep it simple. Don't try to complicate it by 1st preference, 2nd preference etc. A number of equal weight votes distributed amongst the options.

* One particular problem when people are together for some purpose, such as in meetings, is that different members of the group will often be in different mindsets, and this often leads to conflicts. A technique to help members in a group to get into a similar mindset at the same time is that created by Edward de Bono and known as the six thinking hats. Using this technique everyone agrees to think in a way that is consistent with the particular hat they have agreed to imagine themselves wearing at a given time. The six hats are:
    o White Hat: The information hat - people adopt a data gathering mindset, simply seeking out facts and information, without judging it or using it to draw any conclusions;
    o Red Hat: The emotion or feeling hat – people say how they feel about whatever is being discussed.
    o Yellow Hat: The optimism hat – people look on the positive side of whatever is under considerations.
    o Black Hat: The pessimism hat – people look at the negative or down side.
    o Green Hat: The possibilities hat – people look at what opportunities or creative ideas arise from the subject matter.
    o Blue Hat: The process hat – people consider how they should or are going about approaching the issue under consideration.

    Details of applying this technique can be found in the books by Edward de Bono. Alternatively, just being aware of the difficulties that arise when different people are thinking in different ways, such as some people looking to generate options and ideas whilst others are looking to evaluate and judge ideas, can help those involved in a group meeting or activity identify the root cause of certain conflicts and steer the group towards more overtly getting people in the same frame of mind as they attempt to address the issues under consideration.

Negotiating

* Decide whether or not negotiation is your best option. How interdependent is the other party on you? Consider context, is this the right time?

* Think win-win in all your relationships with others. Look to always be building a better relationship with others at every opportunity.

The Bumper Book of Common Sense

* Effective negotiation lies in finding win-win positions. A key basis for this is identifying factors that have different values to either side. Some of the parameters that may be of differing values to the different parties, and thus can form the basis of a position that is advantageous to both parties, include:
    * Up front costs vs longer term costs;
    * Delivery timing or schedule;
    * Time to reach agreement and sign contracts;
    * Support to setting to work;
    * Additional 'support' including possible repair/replacement arrangements;
    * Length of time over which support is provided;
    * Trade-in or buy-back options;
    * Agreements on loaning items rather than outright purchase;
    * Agreements relating to Intellectual Property Rights;
    * Agreements on warranties and guarantees;
    * Agreements on financing arrangements;
    * Training provision options;
    * Exclusivity options;
    * Agreements relating to other topics or collaborations not explicitly related to the matter under negotiation.

* Negotiation requires seeking out common ground. The more open both sides are the higher the likelihood of finding common ground and finding a deal that is beneficial or at least acceptable to both parties. However openness on the part of one party needs to be reciprocated by the other.

* Try to engender a feeling of being allies seeking a mutually agreeable solution rather than adversaries trying to get the best for yourself.

* When negotiating with others look to understand what their position is and what's in it for them. Concentrate on areas you know to be important to the others rather than waste time on areas that are not. Note that you often find these things out by asking them and by listening to what they say. If you ask more questions than they do you are likely to get more information and be at an advantage in seeking out a solution which best fits your needs.

* Ensure that your and the other sides starting positions are themselves reasonable. Negotiating will involve both sides changing their positions. Someone stating an unrealistic starting position means that they will be seeking concessions from you whilst not genuinely making any for themselves. This is not open and honest negotiation and you should not accept it as a start point. You should seek some reasonable justification for the other parties starting position, just as you should also be willing to justify your starting position.

* Prepare for negotiations. Have as much relevant information to hand as you can find. If you are looking to negotiate the price of something, it is useful to know the going rate but also how much it is likely to have cost the person you are buying it from. They are unlikely to be willing to make a loss on it, but they might be willing to significantly reduce their profit margin in order to make the sale. Also, if you know when their sales periods it might be possible to time your negotiation for when an extra sale is worth more to them than at other times.

* In negotiating, the more acceptable your alternatives, the easier it is for you to walk away, and the stronger your position. Always try to be clear about your best alternative to a negotiated agreement, abbreviated to BATNA. Also the better you understand the other party's alternatives the better you can emphasis certain features of what you are offering.

* When negotiating, know your bottom line, which is in terms of the alternatives available to you. Be prepared to walk away from a deal rather than make a deal that you know you will regret later.

* In preparing for negotiations ask yourself:
    o Who is involved?
    o What do they want?
    o What do you want?
    o Are there any time constraints, and if so what and why?
    o Is there past history to be aware of?
    o What is the environment?
    o How important is the deal to either party?
    o What are the primary benefits of the deal to the other party?
    o How do you respond to certain potential objections they may have?
    o What other factors may be relevant?
    o What are yours and theirs next best alternatives?
    o What tradeoffs can you offer?
    o Are their negative perceptions by you or them of the other that might prejudice the negotiations? How do you eliminate or reduce them?

* Negotiate with decision makers, or at least those likely to be able to influence decision makers.

* If you are looking to negotiate with persons from a different culture then get expert advice. Culture matters when it comes to negotiating.

* If you are part of a team then ensure the team remains joined up and consistent in terms of messages. A common tactic sometimes employed when negotiating is that of divide and conquer. Don't let that happen to you. The team members therefore need clear roles in the negotiations and regular get-togethers to discuss progress and priorities and common messages.

* Whenever the other party is speaking, or wishes to speak, let them do so. Every time they speak you are learning more and you are strengthening your knowledge position. Encourage them to speak and to explain their position or reasons for rejecting something.

* Avoid negativity. If you think negotiations will fail, they probably will.

* Separate people from the problem to be solved. If someone is reacting in a negative manner emotionally than try to understand why. There's probably something you've done or said unintentionally which has sparked an emotional response. If you can understand what it is you can probably correct it and get back to a more objective search for a commonly acceptable position.

* Don't go to extremes or issue ultimatums.

* Be aware of various tactics used by some people when negotiating, some more unscrupulous than others:
    o Saying a better offer is available from others, which may or may not be true;
    o Just saying 'you'll have to do better than that …' or otherwise belittling your offers;
    o Prematurely walking away from the negotiation or adopting a take it or leave it attitude;
    o Changing negotiators who then go back on certain previous agreements or understandings;
    o Introducing new key issues or requirements part way or most of the way through the negotiations;

The Bumper Book of Common Sense

- Asking for some down payment before the whole deal has been agreed;
- Seeking separate agreements on different parts of the deal;
- Creating artificial deadlines during which agreement must be reached;
- Making short term best or final offers;
- Saying they can only afford a certain low figure;
- Putting onus on unimportant or low priority aspects and then 'conceding them' and expecting concessions on important aspects in return;
- Having got to an agreement then say some other 'higher' authority has to agree, which then leads to further concessions being sought;
- Claiming other factors are relevant, but which can't be discussed because of confidentiality;
- Claiming expertise and knowledge which you don't have;
- Painting an overly black picture about what will happen if the agreement is not reached;
- Leaking certain aspects of the partial agreements to third parties who then put additional pressure on;
- Seeking to divide and conquer those in your team;
- Using delaying tactics if time is on their side;
- Bad guy/good guy tactics where one person is hard nosed with you whilst another pretends to be on your side getting you to agree a position other than which you would have otherwise agreed;
- Taking an extreme starting position then seeking to meet half way or part way;
- Attempting to offer some personal inducements to you or someone else on your team;
- Claiming that if you agree to this deal they will give you preferential treatment when it comes to future deals;
- Asking for further concessions after agreement seemingly reached and just before final sign off;
- Using flattery and appealing to your self-esteem in making the deal;
- Threatening bad publicity or other extreme threats if agreement is not reached;
- Trying to break the negotiation up into lots of small agreements;
- Introducing external (to you) standards that they say they must follow and thus affects what they agree to;
- Use of supposed facts which cannot be verified;
- Claiming some things are not negotiable without being clear about why;
- Continually demanding additional information;
- Refusal to continue until a concession has been granted;
- Offering only a limited set of options;
- Bringing in factors outside of either parties control.

* Albeit without being too idealistic, be prepared to confront those adopting unethical or unscrupulous negotiating tactics head on, and discuss what you consider to be appropriate rules for the negotiating process itself. If they don't respond, walk away.

* Some general guidelines if you are involved in tough negotiations:
    - Be prepared to ask for what you want;
    - Get as much relevant information as you can. Be prepared with the facts;
    - Try to learn about their negotiating style possibly by trying out negotiating on something not very important, or possibly observing when others negotiate with them.;

- Try to understand what is really important to the other party;
- Give yourself room to maneuver by not moving towards your 'bottom line' too early;
- When giving up something look to ensure the other party is also doing so, such that you get something in return. Seek to give up things that are less important to you, albeit try not to let the other party know they are not important to you;
- Be prepared to use body language to express not being happy with the proposed concessions from the other party, frown from time to time, and be ready to say nothing and let the silence linger;
- Be prepared to walk away from a deal that is not good for you;
- Don't go below your bottom line;
- Help the other person to feel good about a deal that is acceptable to you.

* Should the other party raise objections, rather than simply getting defensive, take it as an opportunity to ask them questions and better understand their position. Ask them to clarify why they are objecting, but be careful not to do this in an accusing manner. Do it in a manner that indicates you really want to understand the nature of their objection so ensure your body language and tone remains relaxed.

* Counters to the objection that your price is too high, is to focus on the value to them. Counters to the objection that it won't work for them, are testimonials of others similar to them. Counters to 'not now' are educating them about the benefits to them and the potential lost opportunity.

* If negotiations start to stall, find some less critical aspect of the negotiations that you can work to seek agreement on that might kick start a positive attitude.

* If negotiations are not going well then both sides have a tendency to overestimate the level of conflict and what they will see as the unreasonableness of the other side. It is often useful to bring in someone independent and trusted by both sides to look at the position and identify positions that will bring the sides back close together.

* If full agreement is unlikely to be reached, are there partial agreements that can be reached? Maybe there is some joint working that can be done that may help facilitate future negotiations.

* Negotiations that don't lead to an agreement are not necessarily a failure. It is better to realize there is no good deal available than to enter into a bad deal.

* If you get to a satisfactory negotiated position, get it written down and signed up to whilst you are still together. Leaving it till later is leaving open the very real possibility of differing memories of what has been agreed and changed minds.

Decision Making

The Approach to Making Big Decisions

* A simplified stepwise approach to decision making:
    - Define the problem;
    - Identify the decision criteria, ie. what factors of interest might be impacted as outcomes from the decision made;

The Bumper Book of Common Sense

- o Understand or weight or the relative importance of the decision criteria;
- o Generate options or alternatives;
- o Rate each option or alternative against each criteria;
- o Compute the optimal option.

* The outcomes of importance that result from a decision can be broken down into separate independent attributes. Each of these attributes can then be given a weight depending upon what its value, its utility, is. For each option score it against each attribute, and sum the scores times weights to give an overall score for each option.

* In approaching a decision:
  - o Clearly articulate what the decision is about, and how you will determine or know when you have the right answer;
  - o Be open minded in identifying options and alternatives and seek input from others. Be wary of dismissing options too early since good options are sometimes variations of a theme;
  - o Understand the pros and cons of each alternative, and the differentiators between them;
  - o Draw tentative conclusions in terms of the extent to which pros cancel out and outweigh cons;
  - o Analyze how critical your conclusions are to uncertainties in assumptions and evidence;
  - o Home in on the best solution having taken into account differentiators and uncertainties. Note that the chosen solution may not be the theoretical best, but one that is most robust in the light of uncertainties. It may also contain elements of the different options;
  - o Make your analysis and conclusions open and available for questioning by others, assuming circumstances allow;
  - o Be sure of effective follow up. Many important decisions are well handled as decisions to be made, but then lose many of the benefits through lack of clarity about who is responsible for what to ensure effective follow through.

* General strategies for making decisions include:
  - o Seek an optimum solution through identifying a wide range of options and following a structured process for deciding between them;
  - o Seeking a satisfactory solution, and going with it, not worrying whether it is optimal or not;
  - o Seeking the option with the biggest potential benefit, and going with it, without looking to trade risks. An 'all or nothing' type approach;
  - o Looking for the least worst solution. The option with the least number of downsides;
  - o Seeking a consensus option, one that everyone will agree to.

* The value of outcomes is dependent upon the use we can make of those outcomes, their utility, which can be different to different people, and can be different at different times. If we have only a little of something having a little more can be of great value. If however we already have a lot of something, having a little more is of much less value.

* With some types of decisions, weighting the different criteria against which the options will be assessed is important. Simply asking for what is important is of limited value because in an ideal world people want everything. Thus a way to get at what's important is to ask a series of question about which is the more important between any two criteria. Mathematical techniques such as pair wise comparison, or pair ranking, provides a means for using a sequence of simple pair wise decisions to derive an estimate of overall weighting of the different criteria.

* A technique for using a group of experts to try to come to a common consensus is the Delphi Method. The experts are independently asked for their viewpoints, often in the form of questions, and asked for the reasoning behind their answers. The answers and reasoning is then made

available by a facilitator to all the experts. The experts themselves are kept anonymous from each other to ensure they focus on the arguments and rationale. Having received the results from the group as a whole the experts are then asked to revise their views, again with reasons. The expectation is they will generally converge, possibly after a number of iterations, onto a common view.

* The person responsible for making a given decision does not necessarily have the necessary skill and knowledge to make the decision. They thus need to ensure they identify and involve those that do. And they need to do this in as an objective a manner as they are able since the quality of the decision will be critically dependent upon them doing so.

* Big decisions have big consequences. Think through all the options and think through all the consequences of the options.

* Confrontation and disagreement are an essential part of effective decision making. There is a greater risk of poor decisions being made when everyone comes to an agreement with little or no debate than if opposing views are expressed and argued. However it is important that the participants retain respect for others and their rights to have different views, otherwise egos can get in the way of the best options being selected.

* In the absence of objective evidence and well-reasoned arguments, decisions are made by the person the most senior, and based on personal interests and prejudices.

Personal Decisions

* Many decisions can be arrived at by simply listing pros and cons. Get the pros and cons written down and compare them. Strike out those that cancel each other out and then see what you have left. Leave it for a while to see if anything else occurs to you, then make a decision.

* For a given option write down the possible outcomes, the probability each will occur and the desirability of each outcome. You can compare options by comparing the sum of the probabilities multiplied by desirabilities.

* Don't agonize over unimportant decisions. They will wear you down. And don't go seeking out lots of choices. Get to a small number of options quickly, and come to a decision quickly, then move on. If it doesn't turn out as well as you would like, live with it, or decide to do something else.

* When evaluation options to arrive at a decision, keep firmly in mind what your objectives are.

* Not resolving a decision can lead to a bottleneck in our mind, where other decisions and actions get held up because our mind keeps returning to the unresolved decision. This can be very tiring. If a decision does not have significant consequences, or you have all the information you are likely to get, then get on and make it.

* Many decisions can be made quickly, particularly if the consequences of getting the decision wrong or non-optimal are not too serious. However if the decision is one that could have significant impact on yourself or others then ensure you spend more time on it, and approach it in a structured way.

* For the smaller decisions in your life get in the habit of making the decision quickly, within 60 seconds. Adopt a 'do it now' mantra. Being able to reach decisions quickly, albeit with having thought through the consequences, is an important characteristic of people who get things done.

* Decide what you're going to do with every input in your life as soon as you encounter it, learn to make bold decisions even when you're not really sure. Keep moving forward.

The Bumper Book of Common Sense

* Trying to continually optimize our decisions takes a lot of time and effort and leads to higher expectations and generally lower satisfaction because we are continually concerned we may have missed something. Making a decision that is good enough (satisficing) on the other hand and moving on makes us feel good with much less time and effort. Be wary however of then rationalizing that decision as being the best decision. It may or may not be. That doesn't matter. If it is good enough, it is good enough. Move on.

* Many decisions are made on the basis of simplified heuristics. We don't have the time or energy to agonize or try to optimize every potential decision that comes our way. Thus for many decisions we choose quickly based upon general rules we have learned. We make choices based upon our personal subjective experience of how good something is rather than objective evidence. For most everyday decisions this is fine. When we apply this to important decisions however, ones with significant consequences, then we can get ourselves into serious trouble or miss significant opportunities.

* Relying on simply heuristics or rules as a basis for personal decision making often works in a benign environment. But doing so leaves you exposed to being exploited, particularly where there are those who are seeking to do so such as salesmen, or scammers or through the bombardment of advertising we see when we switch on the TV, use the internet, or even go walking or driving about.

* One off decisions require thinking about. Particularly ones where you need to identify options for yourself rather than simply choosing between a number of constrained options in front of you. And often, even when you are presented with a number of options you may find you have the opportunity to identify others. Look to be innovative in your generation of options using creativity techniques, and look to generate many options from which you can then choose or maybe combine in different ways to best meet whatever it is you are trying to achieve.

* Be aware that decisions made quickly are likely to be very conservative and likely to miss opportunities. If you think there are opportunities that could arise from a given decisions then spend a bit longer thinking about it, though also be conscious that taking too long can itself lead to loss of opportunity.

* You can often get a lot of benefit through talking through a decision with someone else. Not only might the other person have different viewpoints which might be useful, but the very act of talking it through often helps you realize things for yourself or things that you might have otherwise missed. It is often best to have thought it through for yourself first, and then test your rationale and conclusions with someone else.

* Ask yourself whether or not you have the right information to make your decision. If there is other information you need and can reasonably go and get, then actively go and get it before you decide, assuming of course you can wait. If there are time constraints on the decision then these need to be respected and you may need to simply go with the best information you can make available in the time that you have.

* When making a decision as to whether to do or not to do, ask yourself:
    o What will happen if I do?
    o What will happen if I don't do?
    o What won't happen if I do?
    o What won't happen if I don't do?

* When our intuition points us in a particular direction with regards a decision, it is usually best to go with it. Our intuition is often our subconscious weighing up options below the level of our consciousness. However intuition is far from infallible and will often be strongly influenced by our prejudices. If a decision is important don't rely on intuition alone. Nevertheless err on the side of going with your intuition, particularly if after deciding to go with it you feel good about it.

* We are continually making decisions whether we notice it or not. We are 'deciding' whenever we continue with things as they are rather than looking to potentially change them. Thus a person who doesn't make a decision when there is a decision to be made, has made a decision, whether he or she realizes it or not. There are consequences that result from us not making a decision just as there are consequences resulting from us doing so.

* If you can't decide between 2 options then it doesn't matter which you choose. Go with the one that is the more interesting or is different to what you have done before. You should of course have already assessed any risks associated with this option.

* If you have doubts and don't know what to do, think carefully about pros and cons and come to a decision. If you can't come to a decision then either option is as good as the other. Toss a coin. Go with the result, unless you instinctively feel it is the wrong choice, in which case go with the other. Ignore any further doubt and move on.

* Too much choice often stifles decision-making. Large numbers of options lead to confusion, are time consuming, require more effort, and often lead to procrastination. People are more likely to make choices and follow them through if there are a relatively limited number of options to choose from than they are when faced with a large number of options.

* If you have a long list of options out of which you are looking for a small number of preferred options, then pass through the list once doing an initial identification of those you think best. Then go through this reduced list doing it again. Then again. You'll often find yourself getting down to a preferred small list fairly quickly.

* Every decision has consequences. Think them through and play them out in your head.

* If you have a lot of options to assess it can be useful to cluster the ideas and home in on and refine the most promising group of ideas.

* Sometimes the only choices you have are bad ones. But there is still the best choice to be made in the circumstances.

* Don't worry about your decisions once they are made. If you believe a decision was wrong, you can either change it or not. If you can change it, and you believe it is the right thing to do, then do so. If you can't change it, then make the best of it that you can. But either way don't beat yourself up about it.

The Timing of Decisions

* There is usually a best time to make a decision or to take action. Some people make decisions or take action as soon as opportunity allows, some leave it as late possible, or just do it when they have some spare time. They may be lucky and the quality of the decision or action may not be dependent upon timing. However often it is, and decisions are better, and actions are more effective, if taken at the appropriate time.

* Taking a decision too early occurs when not enough time is spent getting all the relevant facts or information, or when there is some future potential event that could have a significant impact on our decision. There may be uncertainties which could be reduced or resolve themselves if the decision is left till later.

* Taking a decision too late might mean there is not enough time to take effective action resulting from the decision. It also significantly increases the likelihood that someone else will end up taking the decision for you, in a way that is contrary to your own best interests.

The Bumper Book of Common Sense

* Make decisions too early means you are more likely to undertake inappropriate actions, too late means the actions you do take or try to take will not have the impact you would have liked.

* On balance you should look to make decisions early rather than late, so that you can get on with taking action. This is particularly the case if there is the opportunity, once you've started to take action, of adjusting your approach in the light of how things are turning out. However do ask yourself if there is good reason to believe that delaying the decision would lead to reduced uncertainty and a better decision being made, without any significant consequences arising from the delay.

* If a decision does not need to be made any time soon then sometimes it is best not to make it. Circumstances may change which either means the need to make the decision goes away, or significantly effects the decision itself. Sometimes making a decision before it needs to be made unnecessarily constrains you.

* You often have more time to make a decision than it might at first appear. Whilst relatively unimportant decisions can be made quickly, important ones usually need time. You need the time to think them through thoroughly, seeing them from many different viewpoints, ensuring you understand all the relevant factors and potential consequences. If you feel you are being pushed to making a decision before you are ready, think through the consequences of delaying the decision to give yourself more time to think it through properly.

* Decisions don't always need to be made. Sometimes things just sort themselves out.

Judging Decisions

* A decision maker should not be criticized based purely upon the consequences, but on whether or not the end result of the decision could have been reasonably predicted and whether or not better options were clearly available. Bad decisions are often only obviously so in hindsight.

* We often judge a decision to have been bad when the consequences turn out worse than we believe would have been the case if a different decision had been taken. However just because a decision turns out bad, this does not mean the decision maker made a bad decision. The decision maker should only be considered to have made a bad decision if they could reasonably have been expected to have made a better decision based on information available at the time and given circumstances extant at the time. The decision maker did not have the benefit of hindsight, so in judging them we need to consider what they knew at the time, or could reasonably have known if they had gone looking.

* When in the light of a poor decision the decision maker claims they didn't know certain things at the time, this may or may not be a reasonable excuse. We need to ask whether or not they could have reasonably obtained relevant information had they gone looking for it, and ask whether or not in the circumstances it should have been reasonable for them to have gone looking. Bear in mind that it is only in hindsight they we know a given aspect was important. If at the time it was only one of many potentially important aspects, or even not considered important, then it is unfair to criticize them for not having investigated that particular aspect more so than others.

* Whilst the outcome of a decision may have been bad, it may actually have been the least worst of the options that were reasonably available.

* If you are in an environment where you could be severely criticized for a given decision, then ensure you write down your decision making process at the time. Identify the factors you consider important and the weighting you give them, and why. Write down how you score your options and the basis for the decision you come to. Preferably invite others to review this as you do it. This will then help protect you if the decision turns out bad, and people with hindsight come in to assess it. You can demonstrate that your decision was reasonable given the understanding that was available at the time it was made.

* Only worry about whether or not you should have done something different from the viewpoints of whether or not you can learn something to help you make better decisions in the future, and whether or not you can do something about it.

* Look for feedback on your decisions. When you make significant decisions write down the basis for them at the time, then look back on them when the consequences have become apparent. Learn from outcomes you hadn't expected. Note that if you don't write these things down at the time it is likely your memory will be through rosy colored spectacles. We all to a greater or a less extent, and usually to a greater, adjust what we thought we thought based on hindsight. We 'knew that would happen' only after it happened.

* People don't set out to make bad decisions. Decisions are made based upon circumstances at the time, but those judging decisions often don't fully understand or appreciate what those circumstances really were.

Overturning Decisions

* It can be difficult overturning a decision or changing direction when a lot has been 'invested in it', and most are reluctant to do so. This can apply to individuals, groups, or corporations. Many individuals, groups, or corporations will continue to throw good money after bad in the hope things will improve. However it is very important to recognize that decisions need to be based on current circumstances – always ask yourself: "If you came to the particular situation anew, without personal investment, what would you decide to do?" Often it is obvious that you would make the changes you are reluctant to make because of your own past involvement.

* Be prepared to admit decisions previously made where wrong if they clearly were, and change them assuming it is appropriate to do so. However just because a decision was wrong in the past does not mean you should necessarily overturn it. Decisions need to be made based on where you are now, and circumstances now may not be the same as they were when the original decision was made. Also the options based on where you are now may not be the same as they were when the original decision was made, and thus it may not be simply a case of 'choosing the other option'.

* Sometimes you need to persist with a decision even if things aren't going as smoothly as you'd planned or hoped. The difficulty is judging when to persist, and when to change direction. There are no general rules other than being honest about where you are trying to get to and what you believe is the best way to get there.

* There is no contradiction in making decisions and acting firmly on the basis of them, whilst retaining an open mind as to whether or not they are right. As new facts come to light they may confirm us in what we are doing, lead us to modify what we are doing, or lead us to abandon what we are doing. Unfortunately many people have difficulty with the concept of acting decisively whilst retaining an open mind.

General Considerations when Decision Making

* Making a decision is not difficult. What is difficult is making a good and appropriate decision, and one that is capable of being effectively implemented.

* Sound decision making requires the decision maker to feel and accept responsibility for the decision outcome.

* When evaluation an idea: list out criteria, check criteria are independent but complete, check all positively expressed, identify a way of scoring options against criteria, evaluate each option against each criteria, look at what the scoring is telling you. However don't just choose a preferred option,

The Bumper Book of Common Sense

look at how you can improve the most promising or best idea by taking positive aspects from other ideas.

* For some types of repetitive decisions you can adopt some simple rules which experience shows work in the majority of cases, and then rather than agonize over every instance of the decision, simply follow the simple rules and accept the consequences of occasionally getting it wrong. You need to be satisfied that the occasional wrong decisions are not going to be a major problem. Whilst this may occasionally seem unfair, note that even when we agonize over each individual decision we will sometimes get it wrong, because of mistakes, or misleading information.

* If we apply simple decision rules, note that they may need to be modified or changed if the environment changes. Whilst simple rules may be highly accurate in the precise circumstances they were defined for, circumstances have a habit of changing.

* Some criteria to give consideration to when decision making include:
    o General cost-effectiveness of different outcomes;
    o The context and how well different options fit in with wider goals and interests;
    o What future opportunities are opened up or closed down as a result of different options;
    o How sensitive are different outcomes to specific assumptions noting potential uncertainties in those assumptions;
    o How flexible are different outcomes to future changing circumstances;
    o How easy are different outcomes to implement, recognizing potential difficulties or resistance with regards certain options.

* Some decisions can be reduced purely to monetary terms. The outcomes can be considered in terms of money, gains or loses, and the likelihood of different options occurring can be multiplied by the estimated monetary gains or losses.

* Many approaches to decision making include a balancing of pros and cons. However not all pros and cons are equal, and it is rarely a case of simply totting up the number of pros versus the number of cons. It may be appropriate to score each pro and con, say from one to five, and thus sum up the pro and con scoring. You may also need to take into account the likelihood of different pros and cons occurring and multiplying this by your scores to get a value for each pro and con.

* Seeking the best score of different options is not necessarily the only consideration when choosing between options. A given option may be unacceptable in some way or may have risks that are judged too great. Indeed a tradeoff between seeking optimum gains or benefits against how much risk to take is a frequent consideration when making many decisions.

* Inflation and interest rates means the value of money changes over time. Making decisions involving money over an extended period of time requires financial techniques to enable the worth of future monies to be compared to current day monies.

* Sunk costs are those you've already made. The term is usually used in a context where a project or activity has not proceeded as planned and decisions need to be made about whether or not to continue. Calling costs made to date 'sunk costs' is emphasizing the fact that they have already been spent and your decision to proceed should depend solely on where you are now. Of course in most circumstances having spent money you should have made progress and the logic to continue will be stronger than when you started. However new facts may have come to light that show your original estimates to no longer be valid, or other difficulties may have arisen. Your decision about proceeding should ignore what you've spent and simply decide on the best option given where you are now. This can be psychologically very difficult, particularly where doing so is an admission that we made an error in our earlier decision. However always keep in mind that no matter how bad things may appear, they can usually get much worse.

* In making decisions remember the past is past. You can't change it. What matters is the options open to you based upon where you are now.

* The value of something is its value now, and the value it might have had in the past is no longer relevant.

* In making decisions be conscious of opportunity costs, ie. the possibility that you could use the resources required to implement the solution on something completely different.

* Sometimes not all the information is available to make a clear decision about what to do. Sometimes you simply have to use the best that is available and accept the uncertainties.

* When making decisions we take into account both the likelihood of certain outcomes arising and the consequences should they arise. However be aware that our perception of likelihood can be influenced by what we perceive to be the consequences, and we will overestimate the likelihood of positive consequences and underestimate the likelihood of negative consequences. We are biased towards seeing things as we would like them to be rather than as they truly are.

* You never have 100% certainty to underpin your decisions. Get the best information you can and seek out more information only if you believe it could clearly make a difference. Think about what information might make a difference. If it is not clear that additional information would help, accept the uncertainty and decide based upon the best information you have.

* Truth matters. We should always seek to base our decisions on as true a version of reality as we can determine. Even when the truth is inconvenient it is still important that we understand it so that we can make the best decisions we can in the circumstances.

* If there is an ethical or morally right or wrong element to a decision then you should give it additional consideration. Ask yourself what your conscience is telling you to do. Explicitly ask yourself who might be hurt by the decision, and how you would feel if it was done to you. Ask yourself about how you will feel about it later, and what you think other people might think about you if, and when, they find out. Remember you will have to live with your decisions long after the particular urgency of the circumstances have passed.

* Sometimes you have to choose the lesser of two evils.

* Some common biases when decision making:
    o More weight is often given to information that is readily available or more easily remembered or understood, irrespective of its importance;
    o More weight is given to information provided at the beginning or end, and thus if a sequence of options are presented the ones at the beginning and end will be better remembered and there will be bias against the ones in the middle;
    o More weight is given to information that has personal relevance, or which is favorable to ourselves, or which is supportive of what we already believe;
    o People are overconfident in their own judgments, even when they don't know anything about the topic they are making the judgment in;
    o How a problem is framed affects decisions. People tend to be risk adverse, and more focused on avoiding losses than achieving gains. People can be manipulated into making different decisions against the same circumstances simply as a result of how the decision is framed;
    o There is often a strong desire to come to a decision that more senior persons will be happy with, rather than coming to a decision based on an objective assessment of the facts.

* For decisions that are important it is essential that the potential for biases is recognized and compensated for. Decisions can be strongly influenced by how options are presented, the order in which they are presented, the personal preferences of individuals involved, and many other factors that are not a part of arriving at a balanced judgment. An openly visible means of weighing and scoring options, and the involvement of independent third parties, is usually necessary to prevent either deliberate or unconscious biases distorting the path to a good decision.

The Bumper Book of Common Sense

* Some people will make decisions on the basis of their own interests rather than on the basis of the 'authority' asking them to make the decision.

* The decision someone arrives at is dependent upon how they see the world, and what they see as important. Someone who sees the world in largely financial terms could well come to a very different decision than someone who thinks in terms of human consequences.

* Most experts believe they know more than they in fact do, and believe their judgments are better than they in fact are. Experts tend to quickly form hypotheses and judgments based on key information, more quickly than they realize. More information rarely impacts on their judgments though it may impact on how confident they are in their judgments.

* We often seek the advice of experts when we have important decisions to make. However remember that experts have no magic crystal ball about the future. There are limits to what they can predict, and like everyone else they will assume the future will be like the past, which it may or may not be.

* An expert will tell you about his past successes, but is unlikely to tell you about his past failures.

* It's often not what you don't know that is a problem when making decisions, it's what you know you know but which is in fact not so.

* There are such things as good decisions and poor decisions. Whilst sometimes it becomes necessary to make a decision in order to get on with something, it is still appropriate to attempt to make a good decision. However this should not be an excuse for prevaricating. There often comes a time when it is necessary to make the best decision you can at the time. Ways of ensuring good decisions are made include:
    o Being open about your decision process and the rationale for your choices;
    o Ensuring the decision is documented or reasoned through in a clear and traceable manner, such that it can be challenged by others;
    o Don't ignore the viewpoint of others just because they don't align with your own. If you ignore someone's viewpoint be sure you have a clear explainable reason for doing so. Seeking to understand the reason for conflicting viewpoints is often a valuable source of useful considerations.

* If a decision is important you should look at it from different viewpoints. For example, what does the decision look like from a purely dispassionate numbers viewpoint? What does your instinct about the decision say? If you were to assume the worst about circumstances after the decision has been made, how might things turn out? If you were to assume the best about circumstances, how might they turn out? What does a pessimist have to say? What does an optimist have to say? If you were to bring in an independent consultant with no stake in the outcome what would they say?

* Be conscious of the fact that the environment or circumstances or available information may change during the course of a decision making process. Keep track of assumptions and whether or not they are constant or subject to change. If they change or new information becomes available you may need to rework aspects of your decision process.

* Turn decisions into actions as soon as possible. A decision without action is for the most part hypothetical thinking.

Problem Solving

What to do When Initially Faced with a Possible Problem

* When faced with a problem which you or someone else believes needs to be solved ask yourself:
    o Do you really need to solve it?
    o Do you want to solve it?
    o Is it worth the effort of trying to solve it?
    o Can you at least potentially solve it?
    o Is it really someone else's responsibility to solve?
    o Is someone else better placed or better able to solve it?
    o Is trying to solve this problem the best use of your time?
    o Does the problem need to be solved now?
    o Is there an optimum time for trying to solve the problem?
    o Has the problem been solved before?
    o Are you sure you understand precisely what the problem is?
    o What form do you expect the solution to take? Would you recognize the solution if you saw it?
    o Are there facts you should gather before attempting to find the solution?
    o Are there particular people you need to involve from early on?
    o What is the best approach to the problem. Directly trying to find an answer, or gradually homing in on a most appropriate solution.
    o Is there only one solution? If there is more than one solution how will you recognize if a given solution is the best or is at least good enough?
    o If the solution involves people, have you taken account of how people really are rather than how you might like them to be or believe they should ideally be?
    o Are there uncertainties that need to be taken account of?

* Some problems are just not worth the time and effort in solving them. You have more important things to do.

* If you have a number of problems that need or could be solved, then you need to think about which ones to solve. Evaluate the importance of different problems, high, medium, low, and the probability of likely success, high, medium and low:
    o Low prob of success – High Importance: Creative Challenge.
    o Low prob of success – Medium importance: Difficult endeavor.
    o Low prob of success – Low importance: Don't even think about it.
    o Medium prob of success – High Importance: Stretch goal.
    o Medium prob of success – Medium importance: Grey area.
    o Medium prob of success – Low importance: Why bother?
    o High prob of success – high importance: Just do it.
    o High prob of success – medium importance: Low hanging fruit.
    o High prob of success – low importance: A distraction.

* Not every seeming problem needs solving, or at least doesn't need solving straight away. Sometimes it is best to just let situations run and they will either resolve themselves in a perfectly satisfactory manner or a better time for taking action will emerge. The skill of course is knowing when it is best to leave alone and when you need to take action to stop something getting worse or turning into a crisis.

The Bumper Book of Common Sense

* If there is a problem to be solved caused by something not having been done right, get on and fix it, rather than spend your time trying to find out who was at fault. If the problem was caused by yourself be willing to own up to it if appropriate. It will give you more time to get on and fix it before it gets even worse. Whilst it may also be appropriate to understand how and why the problem arose in the first place, this is primarily so that you can seek to prevent such a problem happening in the future. Avoid seeking blame. Keep focused on solving the problem and learning lessons from it.

* Depersonalize problems. Let people know that the problem isn't with them but with how things have turned out. If you make it clear you are looking to fix the problem and avoid similar situations in the future, without blame attached, you may find they are open about what gave rise to the difficulty, and find that you fix more than the problem itself but also some underlying issues you hadn't been aware of.

* If you have a problem to solve ensure it is clearly stated before you start trying to solve it. Try stating it in different ways or seeing it from different viewpoints. Many problems can be solved simply through being expressed or thought about in the right way.

* How we frame a problem determines how we go about solving it. For example if a problem relates to someone having done something 'wrong' we can frame the problem in terms of that person's behavior, or we can frame it in terms of the circumstances that gave rise that that person's behavior.

* Problems as initially stated are not necessarily the real problem. Given a number of symptoms of a problem many people leap to assumptions about what the problem is. However there may be other explanations for the symptoms. Or there may be a hierarchy of explanations for the problem having arisen which can be teased through asking 'Why' a number of times – 'It was because of X.' 'Why did X come about?' 'Because of Y.' 'Why did Y come about?' …

* Sometimes you have to spend time clearing away irrelevancies in a situation before you can clearly see the problem or the route towards finding a solution.

* Ask yourself whether or not there are alternative perspectives or viewpoints that might frame the problem in a different way to that in which it has been presented to you. Sometimes a problem only exists because of the particular viewpoint someone has taken. Taking a different viewpoint can lead to it being seen in a very different way or even as not being a problem at all. For particularly complex problems it is often worth trying to see the problem from many different viewpoints rather than just one or even two.

* Look for analogies to the problem. To identify potentially relevant analogies describe the problem in abstract terms, focusing on the nature of the relationships between entities rather than on the entities themselves. If you can view the problem in terms of some analogous situation you may find you have an adequate ready-made solution. However before you implement a solution arising from analogy ensure you also understand differences between the problem you are trying to solve and the analogous one; sometimes these differences will be significant enough to invalidate the analogous solution.

* Check the accuracy of your perceptions and assumptions relating to a problem. If your perceptions are distorted or assumptions are wrong then your understanding of the problem or of where to go looking for solutions may be inappropriate.

* Whilst the general rule is that solutions must be precise and specific, there are circumstances where they should not be. An example is the situation where two parties are looking to come to some agreement in an environment in which there has typically been a lot of mistrust. In these circumstances looking for precise agreements too early will lead nowhere. It is sometimes necessary to progress on the basis of vague agreements that give time for common purposes and trust to develop.

* Do not try to solve a problem if you are on an emotional high or low. Strong emotions limit our ability to think clearly about a problem, and limit our ability to see problems from the different viewpoints that might be relevant.

Ensure you Understand the Problem

* When faced with a problem that seemingly needs solving, spend time ensuring you understand what the problem is. Spend time gathering up what information you can on the problem and the context within which it has occurred. Look for the who, what, where, when, how, and whys related to the problem. Look to be able to express it in specific terms and in a way that would enable you to understand what a solution would look like. It is worth spending this little bit of time ensuring you understand the problem so as to avoid the potential for wasting a lot of time solving the wrong problem, or trying to solve a problem that doesn't need solving.

* To find correct solutions, we must first ask the right questions. A problem properly stated is already half solved.

* If someone is passing you a problem to solve, ensure you get from them everything they know about the problem, including precisely what the problem is and why it needs to be solved.

* Being able to analyze and understand the problem is the most important part of solving a problem. Not only is the solution often hidden away in the problem itself, but if you are solving the wrong problem, as many people do, it doesn't matter how good your follow on skills are.

* There is significant correlation between time spent examining and clarifying a problem and the eventual efficacy of solutions and outcomes implemented.

* The solution to many problems lies in the circumstances of the problem itself. It is not uncommon to find that in seeking to understand the circumstances of the problem, and better understanding what it is about, that the solution becomes self-evident, or that there was no problem at all - simply misunderstandings.

* There may be many different viewpoints on a problem. Seek to gather them up. You will learn a lot about the problem through exploring inconsistencies and differences in the viewpoints.

* If you are looking to solve a problem where there many instances occurring, don't just focus on the occurrences, look also at where the problem didn't occur, but might have been expected to.

* Pay particular attention to ensuring that you are solving the problem and not just symptoms of the problem. It can be difficult to differentiate particularly with complex or difficult problems, so think clearly about it. Keep asking why with regards to the occurrence of the problem.

* By spending time exploring a problem with other stakeholders you are more likely to ensure everyone gains a common understanding of the underlying issues and work together towards arriving at a solution rather than working at cross purposes.

* Sometimes it is not just the immediate problem that needs solving, but the circumstances that have given rise to the problem. A given problem may itself be a symptom of a bigger problem.

* When problem-solving keep focused on what you are trying to achieve, the outcome you are looking for, rather than simply focusing on the details of the problem itself. Focusing on the details of the problem locks you into thinking about what you have done in the past; focusing on what you are trying to achieve helps you be more creative in looking at possibilities.

* One of the common traps of problem solving is getting dragged into solving an interesting problem, or one you know how to solve, rather than the real problem that needs solving.

* A reason why solutions to certain types of problem fail is because the potential impact of the solution itself is not adequately taken into account. For example, a new road is built to alleviate a particular traffic problem but then simply leads to further traffic problems. Inadequate attention is paid to the fact that people will behave differently as a result of the implementation of the changes intended as the solution.

* Try to express problems in simple terms. Even oversimplify if necessary just so you can get some new ways of thinking about the problem.

* Fix situations not people. Situations, more than individuals, are what produce difficulties, even though it usually looks as if it is individuals who are fouling up. Change reporting relationships, enlarge or reduce the expectations of the job, set up flextime arrangements, and so on. Circumstances are powerful determinants of behavior.

* Be wary of continually solving problems for someone who should be solving the problems for themselves. If you are too ready to solve someone else's problems for them they become dependent upon you. Rather than simply taking on someone else's problem, look to help them solve the problem for themselves. Don't suggest a given solution, but suggest how and where they could go looking for a solution, or suggest they list down a range of possible solutions, some of which you may indirectly give them, but only alongside other solutions that you encourage them to come up with for themselves. Try to avoid taking any credit for them coming up with a solution. If they take credit for themselves they are more likely to try to solve their own problems again in the future.

* Although it is often appropriate and necessary to consult others about problems you have or are responsible for, think the problem through for yourself first. You are likely to get more from other people if you have already explored the problem for yourself, tried to understand the relevance of information and data, and have formed some hypotheses. Other people will not have the same commitment as you and will start pulling you in different directions based on their own prejudices and misunderstandings. If you already understand the problem you can make use of their experience and knowledge to help you come to a better solution rather than simply be confused by alternative viewpoints. However ensure you then use your interaction with others to improve your viewpoint rather than simply trying to justify your viewpoint.

General Approaches to Problem Solving

* In problem solving there are 5 related states of mind or stages which we can and should switch between:
    o Data gathering mode: focused on gathering information, opinions and hypotheses – could include experimentation to generate new information and could be information about the problem or about potential solutions;
    o Opinion generation mode: focused on identifying potential options and solutions;
    o Judgment mode: critically evaluating the validity of options;
    o Assessment mode: putting together information, options, and judgments to identify preferred solutions;
    o Close out mode: once we have a preferred solution coming to the final acceptance of it and then determining the consequential actions that result.

* When problem solving it is very important to know or decide which stage you are in. Failure to do this lies at the heart of many shortcomings when problem solving. For example, leaping to conclusions about solutions before we have fully understood the problem or have tried to identify a range of options. When a number of people are involved in the problem solving it is common for different persons to be at different stages, with some still trying to identify what the problem is really about whilst others are into assessing particular solutions or even trying to gain acceptance of their preferred solution. Committee type meetings frequently suffer from this as they find

themselves going round in circles as different people keep leaping about between different stages of the problem solving. It is important in these circumstances that someone guides the meeting through the different stages and keeps everyone focused on one stage at a time.

* There's a time to consider far out ideas, and a time to come to a preferred solution; a time to gather information, and a time to put information to use; a time to refrain from judgment, and a time to judge.

* When faced with personal issues to be resolved it is useful to think of there being only one of 4 possible solutions, and thus choosing between them:
    o Solve the Problem: use problem solving techniques to seek out a particular solution; decide on the best, or least worse solution; and implement your preferred solution;
    o Change your perception, for example see difficulties as opportunities; or be grateful for what you have rather than be miserable about what you don't have;
    o Accept the situation: ie. just acknowledge it is what it is and stop thinking of it as an issue;
    o Continue, as you are, probably miserable. Whilst this is rarely a deliberate decision it is often the default decision, and thus why it is useful to think in terms of these 4 solutions.

* Some ideas to help solve personal problems include:
    o Write down a description of the problem;
    o If the problem can be stated mathematically or graphically, do so;
    o Ask others for advice;
    o Think about how others might solve the problem;
    o Look up suggestions on the Internet or in Self Help books;
    o Think about how this or analogous problems have been solved in the past.

* Some questions to ask when trying to solve ordinary life problems:
    o What am I trying to accomplish?
    o Have I done this sort of thing before? What was the outcome? What can be learnt from previous similar circumstances?
    o Could I do this some way other than the obvious, maybe in an opposite manner?
    o How did or would other people tackle this?
    o What kind of person or persons am I dealing with?
    o How can this situation be changed to fit me?
    o How can I adapt myself to this situation?
    o How about using more? Less? All of it? Only a portion? One only? Etc.
    o How about using something else? Something older? Something newer? Something more expensive? Something cheaper?
    o Could I do this in combination? With whom? With what?
    o What would happen if I did nothing?

* Detach yourself from the problem you are trying to solve. You are more likely to arrive at effective solutions if you approach a problem objectively rather than subjectively. This of course doesn't mean you should ignore your own interests. Your interests need to be looked after: but not obsessively or in an overwhelmingly selfish manner.

* Approach problems on the basis that they will be solved once hurdles have been overcome rather than that they can't be solved because there are seemingly insurmountable hurdles. Work on overcoming or getting round the hurdles rather than bemoaning how difficult the problem is because the hurdles exist.

The Bumper Book of Common Sense

* Gradual evolutionary change often goes unnoticed, and when we have been working on something for a long while we may miss changes that have gone on around us; assumptions that had been valid at one time may no longer be so. Having someone come new to a problem can often lead to new insights and they may notice things that those more intensely immersed in it had missed. Past experience is both an aid and a hindrance. Thus if you have been working on a problem for a long while, ensure new people are brought into your problem solving activities.

* When you have a problem to solve ensure you have had a look to see if it or similar problems have been identified and addressed in the past. You may find that there are already satisfactory solutions to the problem one of which suits your needs.

* Ensure you understand the quality of the information you are relying on either to define or to solve the problem. How reliable or accurate is it? Depending upon the importance of the decision and how much is dependent upon particular information, you may need to go and improve the quality of the information.

* Check over any assumptions that are relevant to your problems. Assumptions are often overly simplistic. It is often the case that a change in assumptions makes a problem much easier to solve.

* For complex problems we should look to apply both theoretical and practical thinking. Theoretical thinking on its own may fail to take account of some of the practical issues. Practical thinking on its own tends to be short-sighted and simplistic and rooted in past solutions. Theoretical thinking ensures we know what the right thing to do is; practical thinking ensures it can feasibly be done.

* We should seek to be skilled in both divergent and convergent thinking, and in when to apply which. Divergent thinking is opening out. Convergent thinking is narrowing down. Divergent thinking is when we are trying to open up different ways to get to the end, and indeed exploring the end itself and whether or not it is really what we should be aiming at. Convergent thinking is about bringing information together and focusing it on a particular end. Divergent thinking is best when we are initially faced with a problem; it helps ensure we approach it the right way and confirm it is the right problem to focus on. Once we have explored this and convinced ourselves it is, and we have identified a range of options, then convergent thinking enables us to assess them and come to a preferred solution or conclusion.

* For every complex problem there is a simple and obvious solution – and it is often wrong.

* In practice, people rarely choose the most logical solution, but usually choose solutions or explanations which:
    o Are agreeable and comfortable, avoiding what they dislike or dread;
    o Are novel, simply because they are novel;
    o Are risk adverse, simply because they are risk adverse;
    o Are similar to other solutions and explanations, because they are familiar with them and they understand them;
    o Confirm what they already suspect to be the case;
    o Are popular;
    o Support particular pet theories that they have.

* When your mind reaches an impasse in trying to solve a problem or come up with an idea, break away from your current thoughts. Take a break and do some mundane tasks to relax your mind and give your subconscious time to mull it over. However do something active rather than something passive. Do something different for a short while; get into a relaxed, calm, and happy state, and listen to subtle thoughts in your head. Write them down and brainstorm around them.

Looking for Possible Solutions

* Think about how best to go about trying to find a solution, rather than simply launching into finding potential solutions. Sources of ideas for solutions include: brainstorming either alone or with others; using checklists; talking to other people; undertaking research to derive more information; doing searches on the internet; looking through literature such as books or magazines; seeking out an understanding of what solutions have been tried on similar problems in the past.

* When faced with a problem, strategies that have worked in the past can get us to a solution quickly, assuming there is a genuine similarity. If not however, and we are mistaken in our belief in similarity, then past strategies can get in the way of coming up with new solutions.

* We must of necessity rely upon our past experiences and prejudices to allow us to quickly arrive at workable solutions for most of the daily problems we are faced with. We simply do not have the time to think through in detail every problem we come across. And for the most part the solutions serve us well. However for more complex problems, ones with significant consequences if we apply inappropriate solutions, then we should take more time and adopt a structured approach to identifying potential solutions.

* Think of a problem in terms of the end objective in solving it. This might help put the problem in a broader light where different types of solution may suggest themselves.

* Be open-minded. Think about what alternative solutions might theoretically be possible. You don't have to believe in them. Just recognize that they are possible. Then you can dismiss them, assuming you've got something genuinely better; or use them as triggers for other ideas.

* Arguably the most common shortfall in everyday problem solving is finding a solution, and then taking it as though it were the only solution. This is particularly prevalent when a situation is seemingly similar to one we have previously encountered and we assume the same solution is therefore appropriate. In fact the situation may not be as similar to the previous one as we think, or the solution to the previous situation may not itself have been optimal. Of course the solution may be entirely appropriate; however we should be able to reason why it is, rather than simply jump to conclusions.

* A common shortcoming in complex problem solving is stopping to look for solutions once you have a few to choose from. You need to try to search for solutions in a structured way such that you obtain an understanding of all potential solutions, even if you then quickly dismiss many of them once you start to undertake your assessment of them.

* There are many situations where finding a solution is not a case of choosing between a small number of readily identified alternatives, but is one of having to identify potential areas for looking for solutions, possibly without any clear criteria for determining what is a best or acceptable solution. This is often the case with major projects and large amounts of effort and resources may be required, which we can ill afford to waste. We must therefore ensure that the effort and resource we do apply is used effectively as part of 'homing in on the solution'. The primary considerations in these circumstances are: to be able to eliminate poor areas of solution quickly and without too much effort; ensuring that good areas of solution are not prematurely discounted; and to ensure any detailed work on the solutions themselves are focused on those most likely to be ultimately adopted.

* Some types of complex problems are best solved by breaking them down into simpler sub-problems, and then if necessary still simpler sub-sub-problems. However we must be sure that the sub-problems, once solved, will lead to the solution of the original problem. We must also think about whether the given set of sub-problems are the best way of breaking the problem down, at least in so far as we can practically determine. There may be different ways of breaking the problem down, and some of these may more readily lead to solutions than others.

* Many problems relate to looking for the cause of an effect, which you do through asking and investigating 'why' did the effect happen. And if you identify a cause, then ask why again; is it itself

an effect of some other cause. You should continue to ask yourself why and seek out root causes that are often missed by simply accepting some superficial explanation. Of course you need to stop somewhere, but it will usually become obvious when you have got to a root cause around which you can take effective action.

* Detective work, whether criminal investigations, scientific investigations, or just in everyday life, frequently involves applying deductive logic, whereby given some conclusion or outcome we try to determine the truth or falsehood of some possible premises through constructing a plausible chain of events. A common shortcoming of this in practice is that the chain of events offered as an explanation may only be one of a number of possible chains of events. Another common shortcoming is being wrong about some premise that we implicitly assumed to be true.

* Ensure you critically question any assumption that is making a problem difficult to solve or is preventing you accepting the validity of what might otherwise be a good solution.

* If you have an open ended problem that is proving difficult to solve then try using creative thinking techniques to generate and explore ideas you wouldn't otherwise have thought of. Initial ideas may not hold out much promise but if you keep exploring you may find a novel way to think of and approach the problem.

* A way of generating possible options is to work back from some future possible state and think through different alternatives for how it might have come about.

* You sometimes need to approach problems from a different direction or perspective. For example the best form of defense may be attack. Things intended for one purpose may be useful for some completely different purpose. Something intended to keep things in might also be used to keep things out.

* Some problems we would describe as a vicious circle, or a catch 22 situation, where the obvious solution merely leads to a chain of events that causes the problem to reoccur. For example a business is struggling so it cuts costs but the result of the cost cutting merely reinforces the difficulties the business is having. To break out of a vicious circle you need to see the problem in a different way, often from a higher level and wider context perspective.

* A way of generating alternative solutions is to look at different ways of expressing the problem or characterizing it.

* Thinking 'outside of the box' requires that you focus on the essentials and put all other assumptions and implications aside.

* To get your subconscious mind to help with identifying possible solutions to a problem:
    o Think about the problem, preferably giving it a name. Think about the different aspects and in particular those that are making the problem hard to solve;
    o Deliberately put the problem aside and do something completely different. You need to get the problem out of your conscious mind;
    o Keep pen and paper close and jot down emerging thoughts when they come to you.

* Ask other people their thoughts about problems that you have, preferably a group of people. They may well have ideas that have not occurred to you.

* It is often useful to talk through a problem with someone completely uninvolved. Even if they say little of value, you will be using a different part of your brain to think about the problem which can prompt new insights.

* Sometimes an issue is too knotty to unravel. You need to simply cut through it, as did Alexander the Great with the Gordian knot.

* Extreme problems may require extreme solutions.

* If you cannot find the solution to a problem then either you've misinterpreted the problem or you're looking in the wrong place for the solution.

* If you are undertaking a number of tests to identify a fault then think not only about what is most likely to be the fault based upon past experiences or available information, but also about how long it takes to undertake the test. The most effective strategy is one that optimizes the probability of it being the fault within a given period of time. Thus if it takes 30 mins to do a test which has a 50% probability of being the fault, but only 5 mins to do a test which has a 10% probability of being the fault, then assuming no particular constraints or other factors then doing the 5 min test first is the optimum strategy.

Assessing Possible Solutions

* Solutions are rarely about trying to weigh up all possible factors, but are about identifying and weighing up the most critical or important factors in order to arrive at a preferred solution and then checking to ensure that it has no unacceptable aspects with regards other relevant factors.

* When looking for information to help determine the best of a number of hypotheses we need to seek out information that helps us differentiate between the hypotheses.

* Not all problem solving needs to identify an optimal solution. If time is limited or the problem just needs a solution then options include: just selecting the first solution that appears good enough; selecting the solution likely to gain the greatest consensus; using analogy with a solution that has been used before and worked. In these circumstances however we shouldn't claim we have the best solution, simply that we have an acceptable solution.

* Sometimes you can't find a clear solution or explanation. There may be a number of solutions or explanations, without any clear evidence as to which is best, even after applying Occam's Razor. Or there may be none. Sometimes we must simply make a subjective judgment about what to do, based on instinct if we feel it, and accept the uncertainty and accept the fact that we may be wrong.

* For some problems we must pay a lot of attention to identifying appropriate assessment criteria. Often the solution is dependent upon the specifics of the assessment criteria and the weight we give them. We must ensure these are themselves objective and fair. Outputs can be, and sometimes are, manipulated through having assessment criteria that favor one option over another.

* Just because something is a solution doesn't mean it is the right solution, the only solution, or the best solution.

* It is better to have a solution that is roughly right than one that is precisely wrong.

* One of the major shortfalls in problem solving is the tendency to stop thinking once you have a solution. If you keep thinking you may find a much better solution.

* Coming up with a solution to a problem is not always difficult. What is difficult is coming up with the best solution that is reasonably available, and coming up with solutions that don't, in their implementation, give rise to new unexpected and unforeseen problems.

* A solution that was appropriate at one time is not necessarily appropriate at another time. Circumstances change. Thus just because a given solution was right last time, doesn't mean it is this time.

* People have a habit of making judgments about a solution quickly, and then being reluctant to change when more information becomes available. Rather than dispassionately considering the new

The Bumper Book of Common Sense

evidence they get into a frame of mind where they focus their efforts on justifying why their original judgment is still correct.

* When evaluating potential solutions to problems think about how they might go wrong or fail. The best solution is often one that is not the most optimal in terms of potential gain, but the one that is most robust and resilient to future changing circumstances.

* When evaluating ideas be wary of rejecting novel ideas too early. You may feel uncomfortable with new ideas because they are different, but be very wary of rejecting them. Make the conscious effort to keep novel ideas alive.

* 'Optimum' solutions are often unstable solutions, in that any slight variation has highly undesirable consequences. This is because in seeking an optimal solution any slack or margins that are rarely required are removed. However under certain 'abnormal' or unexpected circumstances there is then no slack or margin, and behavior can then be unpredictable and possibly even chaotic. Sub-optimal solutions can be far more robust in the face of the unexpected or when circumstances change.

* Don't just evaluate options, look at how you might adapt options to take them closer to your ideal solution. What is pushing an option away from the ideal? What is pulling it towards it?

* The best solution is often not simply one of a number of proposed options, but results from taking bits from the different options.

* Ensure your potential solutions are capable of being implemented. Understand what specific action would need to be undertaken, and be sure it is capable of being undertaken given realistic resources and tools and in the light of obstacles that may arise.

* A frequently heard argument is that something might be fine in theory but won't work in practice. This doesn't make a lot of sense. If a theory doesn't work in practice then it is not a very good theory since feasibility should always be an important consideration, even in theory.

* Ask others about what they think of your potential solutions to a problem. They are more likely to spot shortcomings than you are.

Once we Have a Solution

* Many problems can be seemingly solved in the short term but continue to exist or even get worse in the long term. Papering over cracks makes the room look good again for a while, but the cracks are still there, and if we cannot see them they may be getting dangerously worse.

* Be suspicious of continually finding yourself with similar problems despite continually solving them. It is an indication that you are solving symptoms, and that there is a deeper underlying problem that needs solving.

* Unless you understand the underlying causes of problems, and fix them, then fixing the seemingly immediate causes won't bring you any long term peace. If problems keep returning despite your fixes then you can be sure there is an underlying structural problem that is not being fixed.

* The solution we choose is sometimes a compromise, or is otherwise constrained by some particular practical factor. It is important that when we do this we don't then rationalize and pretend that what we have is the optimal solution. We need to keep our minds open to the possibility that the opportunity may arise for us to improve our solution should circumstances change.

* A common failure when solving problems is poor or no follow through of the solution. Often the implementation of a solution requires a number of actions to be undertaken. All too often the identification of these actions leads to the presumption that the problem has been solved, but then

no clear responsibilities are placed for ensuring adequate follow through. As a result the problem doesn't actually get solved. Thus once you have a solution to a problem which needs follow up action:

- o Be clear about what actions are required to implement the follow up;
- o Be clear about responsibilities for undertaking the actions and related timescales;
- o Ensure resources are made available to implement follow up actions;
- o Put in place a clear means for, and responsibility for, monitoring progress towards implementing the follow up actions.

Solving Logical and Lateral Thinking Puzzles

* Many logical puzzles are in essence questions of reducing the problem to a set of statements that take the form of a string of deductive arguments, and then applying the rules for validity of deductive arguments. If the argument is not obvious then look to reduce the argument to a form where nouns are replaced by labels such as A and B and then teasing out simple statements which you organize into the form of standard deductive argument, such as If A then B, and x is A, then x is B. Alternatively deductive arguments can be analyzed in Venn Diagram form where circles are used to represent entities and the relationship between entities is shown in terms of the extent to which the circles overlap, or are contained within each other. Much of the skill in applying such techniques is in being able to separate useful and relevant information from that which is not.

* There are some types of logical puzzles that can only be solved through the use of a little bit of mathematics. These puzzles are ones often encountered in puzzle books and riddles, but rarely in real life. The mathematics used however is usually very simple, and the only two things you need to be able to do to solve these types of problem is:

   a) Be able to turn the format of the problem into mathematical equations, which involves replacing words by letters and symbols such as A, B, +, =, etc. Note that it does not matter what letter symbols we use to represent things so long as having deciding on a symbol for something we always use that symbol for that thing.

   b) Be able to solve simple equations. This is usually a simple question of finding one of the equations which shows one of the symbols as being = to an expression involving some of the other symbols and numbers, and then replacing this symbol in all the equations. Eventually you get to an equation where the numerical value of the symbols left can be calculated as numbers. You can then use this to calculate the values of all the other symbols.

   Example: A man purchased two ties which together cost £12. One tie cost £8 more than the other. What where the individual prices of the ties.

   A + B = 12

   A = B + 8

   Therefore: B + 8 + B = 12

   ie.   2*B + 8 = 12

   ie.   2*B = 12 - 8 = 4

   ie.   B = 2

   Therefore A = 10

There are many seemingly complicated 'problems' that can readily be solved in this way.

The Bumper Book of Common Sense

* The basic approach to solving some common types of logic puzzles is to be able to represent the complete set of options in some tabular, grid, or other way that enables you to show the data in a structured way. You are looking to represent your options in a way that you can then mark up those relationships which are positive and those that are negative, possibly with a simple tick or cross. You then systematically go through the information you have, putting in ticks and crosses. You may need to go through the information many times since it is only once you have made use of later information that certain earlier information becomes useful. You will then find, assuming the problem has a unique solution, that the answer starts to emerge as you find for example a row of information which has crosses in all the options except one, leaving the one unmarked option as the tick and thus where the relationship you are looking for lies.

* Just working your way methodically though the options will get you to the solution of many logical puzzles. For certain types of logical puzzles you might find it useful to use some props like coins or matchsticks to represent the puzzle on the table in front of you.

* Lateral thinking puzzles generally require you to think creatively. As a result writing down the problem as you try to solve it can be counterproductive since this tends to activate the left hand side of your brain which is better at logical and verbal skills. Of course writing it down helps with logical problems. Being able to recognize what sort of problem it is will help you decide how to approach solving it and thus increase your chances of solving it.

* Do lots of lateral thinking puzzles and you will find the same ones keep coming up time and time again. When you find yourself impressed at someone solving a lateral thinking puzzle there is a good chance it is because they have come across it before.

* The following are some common uses of preconceptions or other tricks used in lateral thinking puzzles to try to fool or distract the reader:
    o Assuming the gender of someone based upon the type of job.
    o Assuming a given noun is what it usually is, but in fact it is being used as a name for someone or something (eg. A horse named Monday).
    o Use of words which have multiple meanings (eg. Shot could be with a gun or could be with a camera.).
    o Assuming you are approaching or viewing something from one direction, but in fact you could approach or view it from another (eg. Looking through the cellar door could be looking out of the cellar rather than into it.).
    o Assuming the person or object involved is 'normal', but in fact the person or object could be unusual – eg. A very small person, or a window in a spaceship.
    o When told half or part of something is X, assuming the other half or part is not X. However if half is X, the remainder could be as well.
    o Using terms in a more literal sense than they would be usually.
    o Use of the International Date Line to separate a few seconds elapsed time by a day. May also combine with use of leap years to separate a few seconds by a couple of days.
    o Use of ice or snow or other materials that can change its composition.

Analysis

Creating and Using Mental Models

* Our brains have evolved in such a way that they are continuously engaged in a search for patterns. Whilst essential to our everyday lives, it also means we are instinctively finding patterns where in fact there are simply chance events.

* Our brains create mental models, also referred to as frames of reference or mindsets, about how the world works. We then seek to fit new information into our mental models. However we must bear in mind that the models we create are just that, models, they are not reality. Creating such models is an essential part of thinking and how we can interact effectively with the world. They help us make sense of new information and enable us to predict what might happen as a result of different actions we may take. However they can also mislead us. Be open to seeing the world differently in circumstances where you recognize that your models, your preconceived notions, could possibly lead you astray.

* Analysis of complex situations or problems involves creating mental models, though we may not recognize them as such, which set out our understanding and expectations about cause and effect relationships. Newly acquired information is both interpreted in terms of the models we have created, and is also used to help validate or change the models. The models are used to help us predict things about the future, or understand why certain things may have happened.

* Analogies structure how we think about a situation and influence our predictions about future outcomes. Good analogies provide useful insights, poor analogies constrain our ability to think effectively about the matter in hand.

* How a situation is framed affects how we go about thinking about it. Since most situations can be framed in different ways there are many different ways we can think about or analyze a situation. If one way of thinking is not getting us to an answer or satisfactory resolution, then we should try to think about it in a different way. See it from a different viewpoint or find some other way of thinking about it.

* Analysis is about identifying the relationships and dependencies between entities. By categorizing whatever we are trying to analyze in terms of particular entities, and in choosing to represent and define the relationships and dependencies in a particular way, we are creating a mental model, which we can of course then write down and describe, and use to refine our own thoughts and use in discussions with others.

* Our ways of seeing the world are personal and unique to us as individuals, though many of us share some similar ways of seeing the world. Many people see the world largely in ways consistent with their particular religion. Others see the world in scientific terms, with mechanical analogies having been common for a long time, and with computer type analogies being common more recently. Our ways of seeing the world are not necessarily entirely based upon one model and we often adopt more than one, switching between them to describe different aspects of our lives. Some people have very specific personal models that can lead to them being considered mentally unbalanced.

* In seeking an explanation for events we are looking for one that fits in with some mental model that we already have. Thus a mystery is solved when it can be shown to be similar to something else, or an example of something we already know about or understand.

* Context is vitally important in our understanding and memory of something. Something that seemingly makes no sense on its own becomes blindingly obvious with a bit of context. On the other hand if we choose a context that is wrong, we may completely misinterpret what is going on.

* The very act of structuring data is imposing a given way of thinking about it. Given large amounts of disparate data we need to structure it to enable us to understand and make use of it. However the structure we use will itself constrain the way we think about the data, and we may miss important relationships that would have been obvious had we structured the data in a different way.

The Bumper Book of Common Sense

* We should not bemoan the fact that our minds create models, it is the way our brains work, and for the most part is immensely successful. However in complex situations we can be misled. The models are all about trying to make sense of what we perceive and know through seeking out patterns and simplifying. In more complex circumstances our models may be misleading or have limitations. We need to be conscious of this and as best we can make allowances. Sometimes we may need to shift over to use of a completely different model, something that is often termed a paradigm shift.

* It is often not difficult to conceptualize possible theoretical models for how or why things work. What is difficult is finding ways to reliably test the theoretical models to identify which one works or is best.

* If you are surprised by something, even something relatively minor, it is an indication that your current mental models might need some adjustment.

* Just because we don't understand how something works, doesn't mean it doesn't. Once we do understand something we previously hadn't we may find that our existing understandings and mental models need some modifications.

* A common cause of faulty analysis is when we simply reject new information because it doesn't fit into our existing mental models, rather than use the new information to modify or change our models. It is usually information that doesn't fit in with what we had expected that is most revealing and useful to us.

* Finding examples that are consistent with our mental models is rarely difficult. However it does little to prove our models are good representations of reality. If we want confidence that our mental models are good representations of reality we need to actively look for examples that would show they weren't. If we honestly seek out such examples in the best way we can, and then fail to find them, we can have confidence in our mental models. And if we do find shortcomings in our mental models we can use this information to improve them.

* We are more likely to interact effectively with the real world if we have the best mental modes we can derive, which we will only have if we actively seek shortcomings in the ones we currently have and use.

Correlation

* Correlation is not necessarily an absolute dependence between the occurrence of two or more events. Correlation is often a statistical term where there is a tendency for there to be a dependence. Thus finding instances where two events do not occur together does not mean there is no correlation, any more than finding instances where they do occur together prove there is correlation.

* People generally have a very poor intuition for correlation. People usually overestimate the existence of correlation through focusing exclusively on instances where the existence of A is then accompanied by the existence of B. However to get the full picture of the strength of a correlation we also need to understand:
    o instances where A occurs but B does not occur;
    o instances where B occurs but A hasn't;
    o instances where neither A nor B has occurred.

    People tend not to notice or have information on all these cases, and thus their judgments are usually based on incomplete and biased information.

* People generally notice the correlations that support their existing beliefs but ignore or don't notice those that don't. They thus get a highly biased view in support of their hypothesis.

* Just because A and B are correlated this does not mean A is the cause of B or B is the cause of A. There may be some other factor which is the cause of both A and B.

* A given seeming correlation could be a co-incidence. We can usually find a pattern in data if we seek it after the event, particularly if we place no constraints on what sort of pattern we are looking for.

* Two things A and B are independent, ie. are not correlated, if the probability of A occurring is not dependent upon the probability of whether or not B occurs, written mathematically as $P(A|B) = P(A)$, and $P(A|\text{not } B) = P(A)$: ie. the probability of A given B is the same as the probability of A, and the probability of A given that B does not occur is the same as the probability of A.

    A and B are positively correlated if: $P(A|B) > P(A)$, ie. the probability of A given B is bigger than the probability of A. Which also means $P(A|B) > P(A|\text{not } B)$.

    A and B are negatively correlated if $P(A|B) < P(A)$, ie. the probability of A given B is smaller than the probability of A. Which also means $P(A|B) < P(A|\text{not } B)$.

Lazy Thinking

* We are naturally lazy thinkers in the sense that we have a strong bias towards low effort thinking. Not only do we often default to such thinking, but we also don't even recognize we are doing so, and thus don't question it. For most everyday problems, particularly ones we frequently encounter, this works well enough, but for some problems, particular new or unique ones, it can lead us seriously astray.

* Lazy thinking is primarily a result of our brains seeking to find solutions based on what is from a cognitive viewpoint low effort automated thinking rather than high effort awareness thinking. Parts of our brain are essentially at war with each other, with our natural and often lazy instincts and tendencies being in conflict with the conscious awareness that we ought to do other things. This is a battle we are frequently aware of as we sometimes succeed and sometimes fail in the application of our willpower, as we attempt to override short term gratifications in order to better satisfy longer term interests.

* When trying to make judgments about a complex subject, people zero in on factors that are easily observed or assessed, or which are already familiar to them, and give them far too much attention.

* Our minds struggle with complex problems that involve ambiguous information, multiple players and viewpoints, and changeable circumstances. When faced with things we don't understand, rather than think it through, many people simply go with their instincts and prejudices. Whilst this is easy it often leads us astray. Better to learn strategies for approaching complex problems in a structured manner.

* People often judge probabilities based upon how readily they can imagine relevant instances or readily recall specific instances. Thus more recent events are usually given a higher weighting, as are more vividly remembered events. Whilst this is a quick and easy way of estimating probabilities it often leads to incorrect conclusions. A smoker who has known someone who has died from lung cancer will usually believe there is a greater risk from smoking than someone who hasn't. Much illogical thinking can be traced back to incorrect estimates of probabilities arising from over reliance, or total reliance, on a few vividly remembered instances.

* Lazy thinkers are allowing their attention and thus their lives to be manipulated by others.

* Be sure that the reason you believe something is true is because the evidence suggests it is, rather than because you would like it to be.

The Bumper Book of Common Sense

* Just because you have said something, by speech or by writing, this does not mean that what you intended has been understood. Just because you know what you meant to say, this does not mean the other person has understood what you meant. It is lazy thinking to believe your responsibility stops at the point of transmission. If you are trying to get a message across your responsibility only stops once you are sure the other person has got and understood your message.

Conducting Analysis Activities

* When making judgments and drawing conclusions we must think both about the issue itself, but also about how we are arriving at our conclusion.

* We don't need to know everything about a given situation, just enough to be able to draw the conclusions or make the decisions we need. If we understand where we are trying to get to, we can focus on what we need to know to enable us to get there.

* When undertaking an analysis or problem solving activity in the real world, as opposed to solving theoretical or mathematical problems, don't rely only on the information that is provided to you. Frequently you need to go out searching for additional information.

* Just because there may be aspects of a problem which are indeterminate, this doesn't mean the solution is necessarily indeterminate. Sometimes, if you run through all the options for the aspect of the problem which is indeterminate, you find that the solution still becomes apparent, either because all the options lead to the same solution, or otherwise there is a clear best solution despite there being a number of possible outcomes.

* Seek out an understanding of all possible states when considering options or solutions to a problem, and when seeking out alternative hypotheses. This is not difficult to do and is just a habit to get into. Simply ask yourself what alternatives might there be, or if there is something indeterminate ask yourself what the different states or options might be.

* Sometimes it is not what is there that is important, it is what is not there but should be.

* People when problem solving are often lazy in their thinking and stop if they come across information that is indeterminate. However if you think through all options you may be able to come to a conclusion even though you may not have all the information.

* Attribute substitution is when we substitute one problem which is hard for another problem, which we believe to be an equivalent problem, which is easier. This is often done subconsciously. For many problems this is useful and valid, however it can on occasion lead us astray.

* People base their judgments on the information they have and give inadequate attention to the fact that they may not have all the information that is relevant. Out of sight, out of mind. However either the missing information itself, or the fact that it is missing, may be the key to the judgment required.

* Just because something is low probability this doesn't mean it is not significant. If it has high impact, or there are many entities or events to which the low probability applies, it could be very important.

* A particular type of analysis activity is using past data to predict future data. We find some sort of mathematical fit to the past data which can then be used to extrapolate into the future. We should be wary of trying to be too sophisticated in our modelling. The past data will consist of a combination of the underlying trend we are looking for, the signal, plus noise, which results in the variability of the resulting data. Sophisticated modelling tends to find trends in the noise, which whilst accounting for past results, are not real and thus have no validity with regards predictions for future data. Often it is best to keep mathematical fits simple, unless there is some good reason to believe the underlying trend follows some particular type of pattern.

* Beware of focusing your information gathering on confirming your preferred hypothesis or option. Focus information seeking on what will be useful to help you differentiate between options. Just because information supports your preferred hypothesis or option this does not mean the hypothesis is correct. The same information may also support alternative hypotheses. Information that disproves hypotheses is usually more useful than information that supports hypotheses. The best hypothesis is generally the one with the least evidence against it, having honestly gone looking for it, rather than the one with the most evidence for it.

* A good analysis technique is to ask 'what evidence would make you change your mind, or make you favor one alternative over another?'

* We must be open about our assumptions and reasoning, making them explicit, and allowing them to be openly challenged by others. If there are better assumptions or lines of reasoning we should be willing to hear them and adopt them if appropriate.

* We bring a large amount of subjectivity to an analysis through our personal experiences and prejudices. However in trying to suppress these we are likely to also suppress much of the personal strengths we bring to the analysis. Rather than attempt to eliminate the application of our personal experiences and prejudices, it is better to make them explicit and enable them to be examined and challenged.

* When we look at situations from different viewpoints we can come to different conclusions. It is important we don't let ourselves be inappropriately pushed towards a given viewpoint and thus given conclusion. We should seek to see situations from different viewpoints and thus come to a more balanced conclusion. Note that a useful technique is to look at the discrepancies that arise from seeing different viewpoints and then seek to resolve those discrepancies. Unfortunately much of the reporting we are subjected to with regards conflict situations tends to be from only one viewpoint, and with others then having or being subjected only to a different viewpoint it is little wonder people become polarized.

* It is important to explore uncertainties and doubts, and if we don't know something be willing to admit it, at least to ourselves. This is not as an excuse to avoid action, but as a way of understanding what the best course of action is. This also helps in avoiding 'jumping to conclusions' since understanding the gaps in our understanding helps keep our minds open.

* When we come to a conclusion that is critically dependent upon some assumptions or premises, we should think about how confident we are in the assumptions or premises. If there is some doubt then we need to think about whether or nor our conclusion is sensitive to that uncertainty. If it is, then we need to focus on finding out more about the assumption or premise in order to reduce the uncertainty to a level below that to which our conclusion is sensitive.

* Questions to ask yourself when analyzing an argument:
    o Is there ambiguity, obscurity, or lack of information which in hindering a full understanding of the argument?
    o Is the argument an appeal to emotion, or is it intended to be a structured logical argument?
    o Is the argument clear in terms of basic premises, rationale, and conclusions?
    o Can you differentiate what is relevant from what is not relevant?
    o Are any premises or assumptions, whether explicit or implicit, reasonable?
    o Does the argument contain fallacies or biases?

* When trying to understand something, ask yourself and possibly others lots of questions:
    o What is the reason for …?
    o What possible explanations might there be for …?
    o What possible causes might there be of …?
    o What are the pros and cons of …?

The Bumper Book of Common Sense

- o What other explanations might there be?
- o How does it all fit together?
- o For a given conclusion to be true, what premises or assumptions must have been true?

* Dealing with new concepts is harder and more tiring than dealing with concepts we already know well. Thus we tend to believe whatever is most familiar and tend to reject, to disbelieve, what is unfamiliar. Try to avoid reviewing or considering new or unfamiliar ideas when you are mentally tired, otherwise you are likely to be biased against them.

* How effectively we undertake an analysis activity can be strongly influenced by our state of mind at the particular time. If we are tired, or under pressure, or our brains are sluggish, our analysis activities will be less effective. In such circumstances we are more likely to adopt short cuts based on stereotyping or focusing only on certain easily assimilated information. We are much more likely to miss more subtle but vital pieces of information.

Perception and Focus

* The world is not necessarily how you perceive it to be.

* Much of our so-called facts of observation consist of partial sense impressions completed by rapid interpretation or inferences supplied from imagination, memory, and previous experience.

* Perception is an active not a passive process. What we see, hear, smell, taste, feel, has already been through extensive processing in our brains, and much of what we perceive is what we expect to perceive. As a result it takes more focused deliberate awareness on our parts, to recognize phenomenon that are slightly or subtly different from the norm.

* What we believe we see and hear depends as much upon what we are thinking as upon what we are actually seeing and hearing as sensory inputs. If we are preoccupied then there is a significantly increased likelihood that what we thought we saw or heard was not in fact the case.

* We see with our eyes and our minds. When we see some words our eyes are seeing much as an animal might see but it is our minds that make sense of them as words. The 'facts' never speak for themselves because our knowledge and experience and mental models will always shape them.

* To a man who has only a hammer everything begins to look like a nail.

* The particular terminology and concepts we use to think about the world derive from our models of reality. For example an accountant may see everything in terms of money, and revolutionaries may see everything in terms of a struggle with whoever or whatever they are revolting against. Someone who is disabled will see a very different world to those without the disability.

* We often give people motivations that are more a reflection of our own motivations than are ones that we have any genuine evidence for giving them. For example: someone who is mean or always taking advantage sees everyone else as mean or taking advantage, and explains away seeming generosity in other people as hidden motives. As the saying goes: If you fish with a plankton net, you catch plankton.

* The way we see the world is largely a self-fulfilling prophecy. Once we start to see the world in a particular way we find many examples that seem to confirm that particular way of thinking. Anything new will be affected by the way we have seen things in the past. Whilst this helps us react quickly to things, it also constrains us and occasionally leads us astray.

* Our brain is capable of, and there are many optical illusion examples of, constructing images of what is not there, or distorting what is there. And even when we know something is an illusion, this does not necessarily enable us to correct for it.

* Our perception of what we see can be distorted. When we see a magician doing a magic trick, if he is good, we see things we know to be impossible. Yet we have nevertheless perceived them. There are many ways in which what we see can be a distorted or incorrect representation of what is actually going on.

* If something looks like magic, it's because you are following the wrong line of thinking. This wrong line of thinking is one that under normal circumstances would be the most probable explanation, but in the particular instance it is not.

* Our current concerns significantly filter and focus our perceptions. When you buy a particular make of car you suddenly see them everywhere. This selective perception affects a person's view of reality. They see what they expect to see and what they want to see. They seek out and give weight to information that supports the views they already have. They ignore or reject information that conflicts with what they already believe. The facts do not speak for themselves because they are only aware of a selected subset of the facts, or they interpret the facts in a particular way. Most information is ambiguous enough to allow more than one interpretation to be put on it, and they put on it the interpretation that meets with their expectations and with the way they think things ought to be.

* The emphasis we put on something is dependent upon our motivations and experiences. We pick out information that is of interest to us in some way. Ie. we are subjective in our listening to information, not objective.

* Perceptual consistency is a tendency to assume certain attributes go together, so that when we see one attribute, we assume certain others are also present. It derives from the brain's continual desire to make the world fit into the mental models we already have. It is not something we can and should try to resist, because it helps us function in an incredibly complex world. However we should be cognizant that it can lead us astray, and be on the look out for when it might be doing so.

* People perceive the time taken along routes they know well as taking less time than routes they do not know well. This is because people are more attentive when taking less familiar routes and thus more conscious of the time passing. People taking familiar routes can often go into an automatic mode and barely notice they've taken the route at all.

* By priming yourself to look out for certain things you are far more likely to notice them. People who are 'lucky' are often so because they are more tuned in to looking out for and responding to opportunities.

* People are far more likely to notice when something doesn't belong than they are to notice that something is missing.

* People underestimate how much they rely upon other people and third hand information when making judgments and coming to conclusions.

* You can improve your perception and focusing skills by practicing doing so. Take an everyday object and spend time examining it in detail. Examine its shape in detail, its color and blemishes in detail, feel it in your hand, its weight, its texture. Get in the habit of doing this regularly, at least once a week, with different objects. You might move on to trying to draw a part of the object, paying attention to detail that with your usual casual glances you would have missed.

Sorting Through Information

* Every day we're flooded with information from all sorts of sources, much of which is contradictory, ambiguous, incomplete and often quickly out of date. Moreover, there are people out there who try to persuade us of false ideas in order to further their own interests. Being able to

The Bumper Book of Common Sense

sort through this information, determine reliable information from bad, determine relevant information from distractions, is an important skill.

* When analyzing information keep firmly in mind your purpose in doing so.

* When looking to make sense of information think in terms of entities, events, and causal relationships. This will help you make sense of the information and help you uncover missing information or contradictions. It also helps if you try to represent information and relationships between it in some diagrammatic format, using for example causal loop diagrams, mind-maps, flow-charts, trees, tables, etc.

* Look at organizing your information into structures. How can different bits of information be related to each other into groups and how can the groups be related to each other. You need to do this to make sense of lots of disparate bits of information. However the way you group the information will itself then limit the way you analyze it. If this gives you the output you are looking for then all well and good. If it doesn't you should look at alternative ways of grouping up the information. It may be useful to have other people independently look at ways they might group up the information.

* Information must be both relevant and useful. If it is not, discard it, at least for the purpose in hand. Though in discarding it, put it somewhere you can get at it again should you wish to do so. Sometimes you may discard information but later, as a result of further information or understanding, recognize that stuff you had previously discarded may be relevant.

* If you are dealing with a lot of information, all of which may be relevant, then it may be necessary to prioritize it. You may not have the time or the ability to make use of it all, and therefore you need to cut down the amount of information you are dealing with to a more manageable subset. Thus pick out the information which is of most relevance or importance with regards the matter in hand, and put the other information aside. Once you have had a pass at making use of the information you consider most relevant you might then glance at the information you put aside just to check there is nothing that in hindsight you believe might have a significant bearing on any conclusions or decisions you may have come to.

* Matrices are useful analysis tools in a range of circumstances when two variables can be sorted into 4 outcomes. For example, sorting tasks into Important/Unimportant against Urgent/Not Urgent. Set up matrices so that all options fall into 1 of the 4 possible outcomes though feel free to break your own rules if it is useful.

* Group up information into a smallish 3 or 4 number of meaningful 'chunks', rather than see it as lots of bits of independent data. The brain can only deal with a small number of concepts at a time, so it will be doing this anyway, and the number it can deal with is not the ubiquitous 7 +/-2 often quoted: it is about 3 or 4. Best to be conscious of it. This also then relates to when you structure headings for a report or an agenda for example: You can have a longer list of headings if they are simply different facets of a single concept, but each set of headings and sub-headings should only deal with about 3 or 4 independent concepts.

* Recognize that information may be incorrect or wrong. If the use to which you are putting the information is particularly critical then you may need to pay more attention to the potential reliability of the information. Many a person has been legally sentenced to death only later to have been found innocent – a posthumous pardon doesn't really cut it.

* Questions to ask yourself about information include:
    o Is the information relevant in the context of the give issue?
    o What or who is the information source, and is it reliable?
    o Is the information presented in a professional manner or at least in a manner consistent with its purpose?
    o Is the information well argued as regards any conclusions it is being used to support?

- Are there implicit assumptions not stated or without supporting evidence which is essential to the conclusions drawn?
  - Are there any obvious biases in the information?
  - Is the information complete with regards its intended coverage, or is there some information conspicuous by its absence.
  - Is the information up to date, or at least not outdated or superseded?

* It is important to distinguish facts from opinions and assumptions.

* How we perceive and process information is strongly influences by our past experiences, education, cultural values, roles we fulfill, organization norms, and the specifics of the information received. This leads to filters being applied which limits us in terms of the information we pay attention to or seek out.

* Our current concerns tend to strongly influence our perception and interpretation of information. If our mind is pre-occupied with something in particular we will often ignore or fail to appreciate important information relating to other topics.

* If we have a particular belief, we will interpret ambiguous data as support for that belief. Given that most information is ambiguous we generally interpret it in a way that fits with our expectations. We also tend to ignore or not notice information that might conflict with what we believe or expect.

* We generally give a greater weight to information that is consistent. However just because we can find many 'sources' for a given piece of information this does not mean they are necessarily independent. It is not uncommon for a single piece of information to be re-quoted many times without independent verification and often without acknowledgement of the source.

* Always try to keep things as simple as possible. But beware of oversimplifying.

The Devil in the Detail

* The term 'the devil is in the detail' is used in circumstances where something can readily be agreed in general terms, but the difficulties will arise when needing to consider the detail. It may be that, if these details were known, it could have impacted on the high level agreement. Nevertheless it is usually appropriate to make agreements in principle, and then return to them once the details have been investigated.

* Whilst we are addressing something at a high level we generally cannot and should not address the detail at the same time. However we should be sure that we understand the detailed consequences enough to have confidence in what we are doing at the high level. This may involve looking at certain key aspects of the detail. Sometimes there is a fine balance to be struck between:
  - The need to assess feasibility;
  - The effort involved in addressing feasibility and other issues in detail;
  - Taking account of the uncertainties involved;
  - The need for the agreement to be comprehensive, which does not necessarily mean detailed;
  - The need to avoid addressing difficult issues before they need to be or before a common purpose and sense of trust has been developed.

* The devil may be in the detail, but if you delve straight into the detail the devil will win. You defeat the devil in the detail by ensuring you have a clear vision of the context in which to see and resolve the detail.

The Bumper Book of Common Sense

* It is often appropriate to first agree guiding principles which can then be applied to addressing issues arising from looking at the detail rather than delving straight into the detail and trying to address many small conflicts without commonly agreed principles in place.

Outputs from Analysis Activities

* Ensure you present the outputs of your analysis in a clear format relevant to the audience. Executives in organizations for example are unlikely to have the time to read through a detailed report. Ensure you provide a clear up front summary with the conclusions and primary basis for those conclusions, with pointers to where they can get the detail and supporting rationale should they wish to do so. Ensuring you have a well-structured report well suited to the audience can be as important as the analysis activities themselves. A poorly structured report can lead to an otherwise valid analysis being rejected or ignored.

* When presenting the output from an analysis activity don't pretend to be more certain than you are. Be explicit about the degree of uncertainty and what additional information or milestones would reduce or remove the uncertainty.

* Circumstances are rarely static. Be wary that they may change even whilst you are undertaking assessments. Thus once you have an output or conclusion, satisfy yourself there have not been changes since you started out which might make it no longer appropriate or optimal.

* If you want to get better at making judgments, you need objective feedback on the outcomes of the judgments you make. Thus look to follow up on your outcomes to see how they turned out, and if they didn't turn out as you expected, look to understand why not. It may not have been your analysis that was at fault, though approach your assessment with an open mind as a learning activity not as an ego protection activity.

* Just because something worked out or was successful doesn't mean it was the best option. Other things could have worked even better or been more successful, or achieved the same more efficiently or effectively, or achieved the same with fewer undesirable side effects.

* There will often be multiple hypotheses that fit the evidence. Just because there is evidence that fits the hypothesis does not mean that it is right. Conspiracy theories are difficult to counter because they are generally self-consistent. The hypothesis most people favor is the one that fits their own prejudices and past experiences rather than the one that best fits the evidence. Thus if we have come to a conclusion from an analysis activity do we simply have an output or do we have what can reasonably be considered the best or most appropriate output with a clear rationale for why.

Mistakes, their Causes, and Mitigating Against Them

* Crisis management can become self-perpetuating and create a sense of security that is misplaced. Fixing a crisis generally distracts from taking action to ensure crises don't happen in the first place. An organization can get into a cycle of crisis management where because it is continually attending to a crisis it is allowing the next crisis to simmer because no adequate action is being taken to ensure it does not occur. Moreover the sorts of people who are often good at sorting out a crisis are often not so good at preventing them in the first place, sometimes they are even the people who precipitate crises in the first place. But the kudos they get from fixing a crisis, possibly even substantial reward, leaves them insisting that the focus needs to be retained on managing the current crisis. An organization can go on for a long time being effective at managing crises. Eventually however there is usually one crisis too many, or a crisis too severe, and the business is severely or fatally damaged.

* Authority is not necessarily right. Experts are not infallible. If we believe authority or an expert is making a mistake we should say so, though our willingness to do so will depend strongly on the environment we are in. By mistake however we are referring to something we think the authority or expert would realize if they were conscious of it, not merely our having a different opinion.

* Positions of authority don't automatically bring the wisdom and capabilities that is expected to go with them.

* Organizations which do not encourage more junior staff to question the actions of their superiors when it comes to matters of safety are asking for trouble. Senior people make mistakes.

* Overconfidence is a major flaw in much decision-making and action, and thus a common cause of mistakes. Just because someone is very confident, doesn't mean they are right.

* Short-term fixes that then become long-term fixes are often a root cause of major problems. Sometimes a particular problem arises and a short-term fix is implemented. Unfortunately such a fix can be too successful since it then takes off any pressure to find and implement a more appropriate long-term fix. Eventually the short-term fix gives way leading to further significant and possibly disastrous consequences.

* Sometimes people having uncovered an error or a mistake simply replace it with another one. They are particular prone to this if trying to hide or keep secret the initial error or mistake.

* Poor human factors design will lead to human errors. If sometimes you turn dials to the right to do something, and other times you turn them left, then sometimes people will turn a dial the wrong way, particularly if they are under stress. Likewise objects of similar appearance will get confused with each other; which can be lethal if, for example, different medical drugs are kept in similar looking bottles.

* When designing operator interfaces, simplify where you can and build in constraints to block errors.

* A lack of sleep causes errors. People who have not slept enough do not think their lack of sleep will be the cause of more mistakes or errors, but statistically it will.

* We make mistakes when we are tired. We forget things, become lazy, and more prone to simply going along with the crowd. We are also more prone to making and accepting poor thinking. Avoid doing important things when tired. Don't be pressured into making hasty decisions when tired.

* Mistakes are not just what we do that we shouldn't have done, but also what we don't do that we should have. However whilst the former are generally obvious, the latter are often not.

* We see what we expect to see, and don't see what we don't expect to see. We will often miss things that are 'out of place' unless they come into our narrow clear area of high resolution – which is an angle of only about 2 degrees; beyond that everything gets blurry. Our brains instinctively avoid spending time looking for things that probably aren't there.

* Hindsight bias often leads to unfair blame being attached to a problem or failure. Thus someone might be blamed for not having paid sufficient attention to X, the physical cause of the problem or failure. However before the event X may have been just one of a multitude of factors that could have gone wrong. Whilst with hindsight bias it is obvious that more attention should have been paid to X, it may or may not be reasonable to have expected this before the event. It may be simply chance that X occurred as opposed to one of the multitude of other things that could potentially have gone wrong. A consequence of attaching blame to the person in this way is that the 'solution' to the problem is to punish the person, rather than see what could be done about the fact that X or a range of other factors could go wrong and have the consequences they did.

* Don't hold someone responsible for an action without first considering what others would have done in the same circumstances.

The Bumper Book of Common Sense

* Accept and admit your mistakes. Don't look for excuses or transfer of blame. We all make mistakes. What differentiates us is how we react to making mistakes. Some people refuse to accept it was a mistake, or refuse to accept their part in it. Such people learn nothing from their mistakes and are likely to make the same or similar ones again. Some people accept their role, even it is was minor or more a case of not actively stopping it rather than having actively caused it. They look to see what could be done to ensure it doesn't happen again.

* Admitting your mistakes reduces the stress that you might get found out anyway. And when you admit your mistakes you have opportunity for improvement, and you will often find other people are willing to help you and will often also think more positively of you.

* Mistakes are not necessarily a bad thing. If we try new things we are likely to make mistakes. To some extent, if we don't make mistakes then we are not trying hard enough. We generally learn far more when we make mistakes than when we do things right. The key is to avoid situations where our mistakes could have disastrous consequences, and to ensure we learn from our mistakes.

* If you do things in secret and you make a mistake no-one will notice. As such you are less motivated to avoid making mistakes and there is less drive to do something about them once made. If you do things in the open where your mistakes will be openly visible then you are more likely to try harder to avoid making them and you will rapidly learn not to do them again. Be wary however of the other tactic when your mistakes are likely to be clearly visible, of not trying at all. You learn quickest when you do try as hard as you can, accept that this may lead to some mistakes, but get the rapid feedback to enable you to learn from them.

COMMON SENSE LIVING

Being Alive and Attitude of Mind

Live your Life in the Present

* The present moment is all we ever have. Now is the only time we have power to do anything. Now is the only time you can ever be happy or appreciate your life.

* Live your life in the present; in this hour that you are in now, in this moment you are in now. By all means occasionally spend some time thinking about the past, which often includes feelings of guilt, or the future, which includes feelings of fear, but spend most of your time in the present.

* This moment is all there ever is. All our regrets about the past and worries for the future are distracting us from our living right now and from the simple joy of life. Sadness and worry come from thoughts about the past or the future. Let go of the past and the future and appreciate the totality of the now.

* Most people are weighed down by worrying about what might happen in the future and feeling guilty about what they did or didn't do in the past. Any spare thinking time left over is used up in concern that maybe they should be doing something different to what they are doing in the present. There is no time left over for living our lives now to their full potential. Stop obsessing about the past or fearing for the future, and if you believe you should and could be doing something different in the present, do so, otherwise just focus on where you are and what you are doing now.

* Becoming skilled at living in the present has very significant physical and mental health benefits as well as making us feel much better and appreciative of life. Living in the present can significantly improve your immune system and enables you to cope better with sickness or other health issues.

* Most of our time will quickly fade into a never again to be remembered past. Particularly time we spend with our minds wandering about in the past or potential futures. If we are to have any hope of remembering our present we need to be focused on it, typically for a period of at least seven or eight seconds. If you want to be able to remember having been alive you need to be in your present as intensely as you are able.

* Live your moments as they pass, because they are your life. All too many people get towards the end of their lives and find that they have not been living, but have been waiting to be living. Why lose the best years of your life always working and worrying merely to retire to a life of ease and luxury when your best years are behind you. With a balanced approach to life you can work but also ensure that all your years are the best years of your life as they pass by.

* Use the knowledge that your life is finite to ensure you live your life fully. There is no mythical future where your real life will be. Your real life is the one you are living right now.

* You are going to die with your To Do list unfinished. Don't tell yourself you have to wait until it's done before you can enjoy life. You can enjoy your life now. This doesn't mean you need to go out and blow your life savings on a whim. You can be happy living the life you are in now, mostly doing the things you are doing now, by spending more of your time being in the present.

* Living your life in the present is not a call to attempt to try to maximize the pleasure in everything you do, seeking out some hedonistic paradise. For the most part, living your life in the present is

The Bumper Book of Common Sense

best served by knowing you are using your time in a meaningful way and putting your full focus into whatever it is you are doing without the distractions of other thoughts. Meaningful ways of using your time include learning and developing yourself, doing the work you are paid for, helping others, creating.

* Do not waste your time wishing you were in another moment, or in someone else's moment. Be in the moment you are in now. By wishing you were somewhere else, you are simply throwing away your time.

* If you don't like the moment you are in, look to change it if you can. But even as you act to change it you are still in the moment you are in, and you should be aware of it and make the most of it just as with any and all other moments.

* If you don't like the moment you are in, and you can't change it, then simply experience it. Like it or not, it is still the totality of your life; although if the moment is bringing you physical pain you may want to adopt techniques to try to manage it.

* You should never feel a need to 'kill time', or be impatient to get it over with, simply because you are waiting to be in some other moment. Whatever you are doing recognize it as the most important thing for you right now. Every moment can be given a purpose and appreciated if you are clear about what is important to you in life. Appreciate it as the totality of your life right now and fully engage in it. Future moments will be along soon enough and you will better experience them if you have learned to live in the moment.

* Even chores and what might be considered mundane activities can be made interesting and pleasurable by focusing on doing them, rather than focusing on why you'd rather not be doing them. Live fully in the moment of doing them. Maybe turn them into challenges, for example do them in a different way, or swap over the way you use your hands, or seek out how to do them better or quicker.

* The moment you have now is as real and as valid as any moment anyone has ever had and anyone ever will have. Do not regret not being some one else some place else some time else. The only place anyone can ever be is in the moment they are in.

* All moments are just as all others. The particulars change, but the essence of existence is the same. Each moment comes and it goes, as it always has and it always will. You live in your moments and others live in theirs. None are more or less important than any others, though some are more keenly experienced than others. Experience your moments, be aware of them, and your moments will be as real and as meaningful as anyone else's moments ever.

* Life is more exciting and with far more opportunities if you accept and react to what is happening rather than what you believe should be happening.

* Take time to appreciate life. Savor pleasurable moments: pay attention to them and be aware of being in the moment. Don't spoil moments to be savored by trying to judge them, or analyze them, or trying to improve them. Just experience them. Focus less on your thoughts and more on what is going on around you.

* Be mindful of being; observing what is both around you through all your senses and also what is within you in terms of thoughts and emotions. You can take great pleasure out of almost anything if you do it mindfully.

* Don't allow yourself to become so focused on the little things that you miss the wonder of life itself. Appreciate the splendor and the miracle of the world around you. Imagine how magical it would have appeared to people from 100 years ago.

* Any time and any place is where you are now. Experience it and make the best of it, because it can't be any other way. Life is all in the present moments. It can be lived or it can simply pass by. Beauty

and fascination exists all around us if we just open our minds to it. Appreciate the beauty of the rain, don't simply get wet.

* When walking, walk. When eating, eat. When with someone, be with them.

* The most important person is the person you are with. The most important thing to do when with someone is to be with them by giving them all your attention, rather than letting your own thoughts be running through your head.

* Most people, to paraphrase Leonardo da Vinci, look without seeing, hear without listening, touch without feeling, eat without tasting, move without being physically aware, inhale without smelling, and talk without thinking. Look at things around you with new eyes and there will be much to discover.

* Develop a heightened sense of perception. Become more aware of colors and shapes and smells and tastes. Be aware of the total reality of the moment you are in and your surroundings.

* Every time you are out walking try to notice something you hadn't noticed before.

* Savor your food and drink by paying detailed attention to it. Be aware of the taste and how it feels. Feel the texture. Does it have a smell. Is it warm or hot. All too often we barely notice what we are eating.

* Be aware of your body sensations. Name the feelings in different parts of your body: hot/cold; tight/loose; tender/sore; heavy; tense; moist; etc. etc. Then explore them. Awareness of body sensations can help us better control our physical bodies and help us mentally cope with problems.

* Many potentially pleasurable experiences are wasted through letting ourselves be distracted, for example by listening to music. We don't truly multitask so doing multiple things at once is detracting from the pleasure of doing them one at a time. Watching TV whilst eating detracts both from eating and from watching TV.

* Practice self-awareness; be aware of your experiences in the here and now. It will strengthen your ability to take control over yourself and make you better at hearing subtle thoughts within your brain. One tip to help habitually trigger self-awareness is to regularly tell yourself what you are doing, and to be aware of your body and what you can feel as you do so. Another tip is to adopt a half smile during the day – it has a curious tendency to help you be more aware of the moment.

* You can quickly bring yourself into the present by just focusing on your breathing: in, hold, out, hold, in, etc. Once you have done this a few times then focus on the sensations of where you are and what is around you, and become aware of yourself existing as a part of all existence.

* A technique to bring yourself into the here and now: "Become fully conscious of your body, be conscious of any feeling sensations, be conscious of your body existing. Expand out to be aware of things close by. What can you see and hear? Tune in to imagine anything close by as an extension of yourself. Then become conscious of anything else within range of your senses. See and feel and hear and smell, and feel any movement of air." Try to do this regularly through the day, and you will become more tuned in to being aware of your Now.

* Learning to be in the moment is a skill to be practiced. Don't give up because you fail to suddenly be an expert at it. Practice it, forgive yourself when you fail, and practice again. As with any skill, keep practicing and you will get better at it.

* Stop every now and again and just be aware of yourself being. Be focused on the sights and sounds and other impressions around you, and of yourself just existing in time and space. Treat it as a pause button on your busy hectic day. Find a way of regularly reminding yourself: some frequent sound or activity.

The Bumper Book of Common Sense

* Break your routines so that you can pay attention to doing something different. Do things in a different order or in a different way to the way you usually do them. Do different things to those you usually do. Do them at different times.

* If your mind is overrun with thoughts, you can use awareness of your breathing to calm it down. Focus your whole being onto your breaths, in and out. If your mind wanders, simply bring it back.

* There are no ordinary moments. They are all exceptional, and are all miraculous, because you are there to experience them, so long as you have the vision to do so. Learn to make every moment count because one day there will be no more, not for you at least.

* No matter how real the moment now is, it is one of a multitude of moments and it will rapidly pass and fade. Do not rely upon your memory to hold it firm. If you want to hold on to anything from the moment, including some thought that may have occurred to you, write it down.

Today is the Day

* Life is shorter than you think it is. Every day is precious. Live it. Make the most of it.

* Everyone has plans for doing the right things tomorrow. The trick is to do them today.

* Your future is dictated by what you do today. Your future is dictated by the decisions and choices you make today.

* Make each day the best it can be. You can achieve great things, live an extraordinary life, but only by doing the things you know you ought to be doing right now. Your life is now. Not in some vague future, which in any case will never be anything other than now. If you are not able to appreciate being alive now, and not able to give your all now, you are not going to be able to do it tomorrow.

* Do not be continually waiting for your life to begin, waiting for obstacles to be overcome, or things to be dealt with first. You are already living your life, every day, including today. Make progress today on what matters to you in life.

* For most people their life is daily wasting away. Time is not an infinite resource and will pass all too quickly. If you are not moving forward each day, you are moving backwards. If you are doing nothing worthwhile each passing day you are doing nothing worthwhile with your life.

* If you are not moving forward in your life, day by day, you are moving backwards. What can you do today that will take you closer to where you want to be?

* Don't count the days; make the days count. If you are looking forward to some day in the future, going on holiday for example, rather than be impatient for the day to arrive, try to do as much as you can before the day arrives. The time will pass by much more satisfyingly.

* Be effective today. Every day should be a day worth living, at the end of which you can say that was as good as I could reasonably have made it in terms of what matters to me, given the circumstances.

* Your life is finite. If there are things you want to do, get on with doing them. Things left to be done someday are unlikely to get done.

* Days with familiar patterns and routine pass very quickly. To slow time down do something new and different each day: take a different route; eat something you haven't tried before; read something you wouldn't normally read; talk to someone you don't know well; listen to a radio station you haven't listened to before.

* Too much time is wasted on the trivial or the empty. Time in which we achieve nothing more than the passing of time, or doing things which bring us only regret afterwards.

* Each day do at least one thing you fear or feel uncomfortable about, something to take you out of your comfort zone. And try to do at least one thing each day that you enjoy.

* Every day provides a myriad of opportunities to move just a little bit further forward, to learn a little something new, to get just a little bit better organized, to be just a little bit better.

* You will not be able to make each day perfect. But you can make each day better than it might otherwise have been had you not made the effort.

* Make the remainder of the day the best it can be. You may not have had a good day up to the present moment, but there is still the rest of the day. What can you get out of the rest of the day that would be more than if you didn't bother at all.

* Make the most of the days you are in good health, body and mind, since misfortune may affect either in the future at any time.

* We all have the same amount of time each day and each week. Some people sit around not able to get on with or do much of anything; the days, the weeks, and the years pass by in frustration and angst. Others get on with the things they need and want to do, and have enjoyable and satisfying lives.

* Your life is the time you make use of. People who waste their time, doing nothing in particular, to no useful end, have very brief lives no matter how long they live. There is plenty of time to have a fulfilling life if you make use of your time. For the most part, those who complain about not having enough time are those who make little use of the time they have. There are many people who get bored on a Sunday afternoon yet still wish they could live longer.

* Make your day as interesting and enjoyable as you can. Think happy thoughts on your way to work. Learn something, create something, write a poem, outline a story, progress your life's goals.

* Every morning start your day with enthusiastic expectation. Start each day with a new resolve. Be a new person each day.

* Start each day anew. Be finished with your previous day. Do not start a new day weighed down by thoughts of what you didn't do the day before. Do what you can with each day, and accept though learn from your mistakes and shortcomings. Try to be specific about something you could have done better; not to beat yourself up about it, but to resolve to do different in the future. Be specific about what you will do next time in similar or analogous circumstances.

* Be very explicit about what you are looking to achieve today. Try to be realistic. Write it down at the beginning of the day and take account of any known other demands on your time. At the end of the day write a short report on how well you have done. If you've come up short identify why and what it is you will do next time to get better at estimating and better at doing.

* Start each day with a smile. It will help make you feel good about yourself. Think of each day as a new start filled with potential opportunities. You have a fixed amount of days in your life and you should seek to make the most of each one. Be optimistic about the possibilities of each new day and smile about it.

* You can restart your day at any time. Just because the day so far has not gone well, there's nothing stopping you from starting again, with a smile and a resolve, to make the best of the rest of the day.

* A sense of urgency helps ensure a focused and directed energy towards achieving our life goals. We should want to get on and make progress in the things that are important to us at every opportunity. Don't imagine that you will always have plenty of time available to focus on what is

important to you. Things happen. Seek to make use of the time you do have to make as much progress as you can.

* Our days are usually far more fulfilling if we set out to make them so rather than expect our days to be boring. How our days go are often self-fulfilling prophesies.

* Most people go through life thinking that today is not one of their better days. On this basis they go through life with maybe only a handful of better days – if any. But you have it in your hands to make every day one of your better days simply by making the best of it that you can.

* If you have worries when you wake up in the morning, or even occurring to you during the course of the day, get them all written down. You'll feel better about it.

* What has passed has passed. You can't do anything about the past. But you can decide what you are going to do now and in the future.

* Make your work and home environments pleasant. Clear away clutter, keep it clean, put some good thought mementos about, and invest in a decent coffee mug or teacup. Be pleasant to people during the day. Dress in a way that makes you feel good and confident.

* Do not dwell on your approaching death, but appreciate your remaining life. It is not what you have failed to do with your life to date that is important; it is what you can do with the time you still have.

* Life is much briefer than you think; after all, where did the last 5, 10, 20 years go? Appreciate every day. Appreciate the rest of today. Use the rest of the day in a meaningful way.

Do the Right Thing Right Now

* We are what we repeatedly do.

* We have but to obey ourselves.

* We have a thousand or more opportunities every day to do the right thing or to continue doing the right thing. The more we make the effort to do so, the better we will get at doing it.

* Ask yourself, how are you spending your time right now. Are you doing what is important to you? Are you doing something that is contributing to your long-term goals? Could you be? Continually be reminding yourself of the big picture of what you want to do with your life, and be looking for opportunities to do things that fit in with the big picture.

* Daily living requires us to spend much of our time on things that are not directly contributing to our long-term goals. Nevertheless we can still ensure we do them in ways that are true to the sort of person we are or want to be. There is still a right way to approach them and to do them.

* Not everyone is as conscientious as you. This doesn't mean you should let your own standards slide. Be willing to do what you believe is the right thing even when others don't.

* The life you lead is dictated by the decisions you are continually making or are continually avoiding making.

* Before making a decision about what to do next, or if you find yourself on the verge of doing something you know you shouldn't, take a few deep breaths and verbalize internally. You are more likely to make what you know to be the right decision if you pause for a moment and be very clear about what the right thing to do is.

* If what you're doing right now isn't working, do something else.

* Do everything you do as well as you can. Don't worry about whether or not it is the right way, simply do it the best way you can.

* Grab any opportunity as it goes by, be wary of waiting for a better one. If you grab the opportunities that come by, more are likely to come by. If you let them pass whilst waiting for others, less are likely to come by.

Be Positive, Happy, Optimistic, and Appreciative of what you have

* You can feel in a good mood, feel happy, feel energetic, feel positive, feel alert, by just choosing to be so. Just snap yourself into such positive moods and then get on with your day in that positive frame of mind. Practice it. You'll find you can do it, and if you keep practicing it you'll get highly skilled at doing it.

* You can choose what state of mind to be in. Some states of mind are positive and beneficial to our general well-being, and some are negative and harmful. Optimism is good for your health. There are no benefits in being in a negative frame of mind, and in the longer term, dwelling on the negative will damage your health.

* You can choose how much you let a situation bother you, and how long you stay in a particular frame of mind.

* Don't live your life on autopilot. Choose to live the best life you are able. Live each day as fully as you can, and be enthusiastic and passionate about everything you do. Be excited about your life and your future.

* Do not judge your worth through comparing yourself with others. You'll be set for disappointment. There will always be others more successful or better off than you are in some way. Instead focus on your own life. Set your self-worth by comparing yourself with your past self. By continually looking to improve yourself you can rightly judge yourself as more worthy than you were before. And note that this isn't about your financial worth it is about the sort of person you are in terms of how you live your life and how you relate to others.

* Take yourself and life less seriously. Life isn't a competition. There are no winners or losers. We all end up dead.

* Celebrate your successes, particularly if you've worked hard for them. If you've done something great then take pride in it, and claim and accept the praise and glory that comes with it.

* Our brains and bodies are affected by what we pay attention to. We will be more positive if we pay attention to positive, uplifting, optimistic ideas and inputs, and will be more negative if we pay attention to negative and depressing inputs. We can all choose what we pay attention to.

* See your circumstances in a positive light and see the plus side and the benefits. Learn to consciously seek the positive in whatever you are dealing with.

* Not every day will be good, but there will be some good in every day. Notice it, and focus on that rather than the negative parts of the day.

* Take pleasure from what you have, and don't be envious of what others have or may have, or upset because you haven't got more.

* We will be far more successful in our endeavors with a positive self-image, since our subconscious minds will direct us according to our self-image. And our self-image is one we can and should

The Bumper Book of Common Sense

create for ourselves, one we should choose for ourselves, rather than one to let others impose on us.

* Be optimistic not negative about the future, and work out how you can increase the likelihood of things going well, and take action accordingly. If appropriate, understand the risks and consequences should things not go well, and plan accordingly. However once you've taken what action you can, look to the future with hope, not worry and stress. Once you've done what you can, there is no point in wearing yourself down with a negative attitude. Much better to feel good with a positive attitude. If things don't turn out well then deal with the issues as they arise.

* Being an optimist – glass half full rather than glass half empty – has significant health benefits, leads to much higher levels of well-being in general, and leads to higher levels of activity and persistence.

* Being an optimist doesn't mean ignoring or being unrealistic about risks. We should assess and take account of risks even whilst being optimistic.

* We usually get the outcomes we expect. We are consistently proving ourselves right. Be positive about how you expect things to turn out and they will go much better than if you don't.

* Don't get upset by minor inconveniencies or trivia. For example when in a queue and you perceive other queues as going faster than yours, or when the person in front of you on the motorway is going slower than you think they ought, or someone spills something on you. These things happen and they don't really matter, and they certainly don't justify you getting upset or angry about them. If it had happened a year ago is it really something that would still matter? Presumably not. So why should it matter when it happens?

* If bad things happen, shrug it off and get on with your life. Don't let it eat away at you or spoil the rest of your day. Let it go, albeit dealing with any issues that may been to be dealt with.

* To some extent self-justification, whereby we interpret the things we have done in a positive light, is a good thing and keeps us positive. However where we let self-justification kid ourselves that we are never wrong or make mistakes we fail to improve and continue to make avoidable errors.

* Appreciate the world as it is; and let go of any disappointments at it not being as you would wish it to be.

* Develop a general attitude of gratitude for the good things in your life and the good things people do for you. Appreciate what you have rather than be bitter about what you don't. For the vast majority of us life could be an awful lot worse, and has been for most people in the past and still is for many in third world countries. Be grateful for what you have and make the most of the opportunities you have the potential to create for yourself.

* Write down the things you have to be grateful for, and regularly remind yourself of them.

* You will not live forever. Be aware of death lurking close behind. It will help make you more appreciative of the time you have, and less obsessed with your own self-importance.

* Don't obsess about trying to do and experience everything. Focus on appreciating the experiences and things that are within reach.

* Don't forget to live and appreciate your life whilst striving for your goals. Don't wait until you've achieved them. The destination is only a very small part of the journey, and once you get there you'll probably be off again. Since the vast majority of your life is the journey, enjoy it as you go along.

* You are successful when you are moving towards the achievement of worthwhile goals whilst remaining true to your values. Success is not about any comparison with others.

* Living life to the full is not about being loud and brash and pushing people out of the way so that you can do what you want to do. Living life to the full is about striving to be better, about taking and seeking out opportunities, about taking calculated risks, about having respect for and liking other people, and being self-aware as you do so.

* Let go of expectations about people or circumstances that creates some idealized view of what to expect, which you then judge them against and generally find that they fall short. Rather, simply experience people or circumstances as they are, and appreciate them for what they are, without judging them.

* Enjoy your experiences. Even the ones many might label as bad. They are all a part of your life. Accept and experience your life rather than be forever judging your experiences as good or bad.

* Don't feel sorry for yourself when things don't go the way you would have liked. Self-pity wears you down, and achieves nothing positive. It makes you unhappy. By all means let certain feelings wash over you for a few minutes. There is nothing wrong with having feelings. But then put them aside and get on with your life.

* Accept yourself as you are – looks and shortcomings and weaknesses and all - and move on from there. You are what you are, but you can also upgrade yourself.

* Accept wealth or good fortune without arrogance, and be ready to let it go.

* There can be considered to be two types of happiness. Hedonistic happiness is the pleasure from the moment. It is short lived. Eudemonic happiness on the other hand is the more general contentment we get from knowing we have purpose in our lives and we feel we are fulfilling our potential. It is important to understand the difference. It is eudemonic happiness that we should be seeking.

* Hedonistic pleasures do not raise our general sense of (eudemonic) happiness. Buying things, winning things, physical pleasures, only give us a short-term boost to our happiness. Avoid getting addicted to continually trying to top up your hedonistic happiness in the belief it is the only way to be happy.

* Comfort and luxury don't make us happy. Something to be enthusiastic about makes us happy.

* Happiness doesn't depend on what you have, it depends on what you think. Being happy and contented is largely about attitude of mind and being appreciative of what we have. Beyond a basic minimum, having more material possessions rarely has a significant effect on our happiness.

* We think something in particular will make us happy, however once we have it we very quickly see our new circumstances as the norm and are generally no happier not long after we have obtained whatever it was. There are multiple factors which impact on how happy we are, and changing one of them in particular is unlikely to have a significant long term affect.

* Being rich or poor is not dependent upon how much you have, but on whether or not you are content with what you have. You can however be content with what you have whilst also striving to better yourself and your circumstances, and those of others you care about.

* The richest man is not he who has the most, but he who needs the least. A person who is satisfied with what they have is as rich as any person can be so long as they retain a sense of purpose in their life.

* How happy we are with our circumstances is dependent upon what we compare them with. We can see our circumstances in a positive light by comparing them with something worse, or in a negative light by comparing them with something better. The circumstances themselves are unchanged, only our attitude towards them has changed. Whether we are happy or miserable with our circumstances is thus dependent upon us, not them. Note that even if we are happy with our circumstances this doesn't prohibit us from trying to improve them.

The Bumper Book of Common Sense

* The only good predictor of how happy you are going to be tomorrow is how happy you are today. If you can't be happy today it is highly unlikely that circumstances will result in you being happy tomorrow.

* If you have worries that are preventing you from being happy, then plan out in explicit actionable terms how you are going to tackle them.

* Happiness is not something to strive for; happiness is something to be experienced through appreciation of the moment. Happiness is not a goal; happiness is how you choose to live your life. If you can't learn to be happy in your current circumstances, then you are unlikely to be happy in your future circumstances no matter how much material gains you make.

* Happy people are more aware of what is going on around them, are better able to solve problems, and come up with more new ideas for action to take in a given situation.

* Be happy whilst you are alive, because it won't be forever. Life is a one shot journey. Appreciate it and enjoy it as you pass through.

* You can be happy if you choose to be, irrespective of your circumstances. Happiness is a conscious choice, not an automatic response. The more you act and behave like you are happy, the happier you will feel.

* Happiness arises from focusing our attention to what we have control over - our thoughts, our actions, our reactions - rather than worrying about what we don't have control over.

* One of the keys to happiness is controlling the explosion of choices in our lives. Many people are happier working within constrained choices rather than continually having to seek out optimal choices in an uncertain environment, and being continually worried that they may have missed something.

* Smile. People feel happier when they smile. If you often have a smile on your face, people around you will be more pleasant, and you will be judged more sociable and intelligent.

* You are more likely to be happy if you keep yourself healthy, motivated, trusting of others, and if you care about others.

* Just because we choose to be happy in our lives it does not mean we can't or shouldn't strive for more. You can be happy and ambitious.

* Set realistic expectations and be happy when you meet or exceed them, rather than set unrealistic expectations and be unhappy at not meeting them. To stay in a positive state of mind find ways of coming out ahead of your expectations over and over again, even if only in small ways.

* The happiest people are often those who subject themselves to the strictest discipline, who work hardest, and who limit their pleasures.

* Enjoy simple pleasures. They are not hard to find or create if you want them. A walk in the woods, a good book, music, comedy, a fine glass of wine, a pleasant evening with family or friends, or even on your own.

* Music is a simple pleasure we can all enjoy, however you can significant enhance this pleasure by really listening to it. Try to separate out the separate instruments and listen to their individual contributions. Listen for underlying melodies and rhythm. Listen to the words.

* Make up photo albums of your favorite pictures that you can go through from time to time. Ask for copies of other's pictures to include, such as pictures from your parents of when you and they were young.

* Keep a copy of quotes or stories that you find inspiring, or jokes that always make you smile.

* Very little is required to lead a happy life. Enough food, shelter, spare time, access to knowledge, people to talk to. In modern western societies, and for many elsewhere, these are readily attained. The wanting of more than this is in our own minds, and any unhappiness that arises from not having lots more stuff is self-inflicted.

* If last thing at night you focus on the good things that have happened during the day you are more likely to wake up happy.

* Sitting up straight rather than slouching makes you feel happier, and it helps people get higher scores in tests, though for some females it may not work due to their being more self-conscious.

* People are generally happier after a good night sleep.

* Make yourself happier. Listen to upbeat music, dance, be grateful, be more loving, be more social, do acts of kindness, express gratitude, be optimistic, read or listen to more jokes or humor, watch comedies, take pleasure in little things like taking a relaxing walk. Spend money on experiences rather than things, they provide lasting memories.

* The news, TV, and media in general are sensationalist and depressing. They are not a true reflection of the world because they are biased towards shocking us. Watch and listen to much less of it and you will find yourself much more positive and optimistic.

* Music and exercise are both helpful in getting you out of a bad mood.

* We are happy when we make the most of our time; unhappy when we don't.

* Happiness isn't about what's going on outside of us, it's about what is going on inside of us. Happiness arises from the quality of our thoughts, and arises from feeling good about ourselves and others. Our own thoughts have the greatest impact on our happiness, and we can choose our own thoughts.

* In seeking happiness for others, you will find it for yourself. A happiness shared is a happiness more than doubled.

* It is hard to be unhappy if we love and are loved. What prevents us loving and being loved is usually our critical and judgmental nature and tendency to think only of ourselves. If you can change this you can create the environment for finding love.

Be Proactive

* Don't stand idly by as life happens to you. Don't just react to life. Have life react to you. Make your own plans. Effective sportsmen and women don't just focus on how to react to their opponents moves, they plan their own offensive moves and have others react to them. You can do the same in life.

* Give up complaining; get on with doing. Do what needs to be done, or be stressed and miserable. Your choice.

* Do not desire life to be easy. A life without challenge and struggle is unlikely to be particularly satisfying. You will be most happy in your life if you are actively working towards something meaningful, and overcoming obstacles that stand in your way.

* An imperfect idea acted on is better than a good idea not acted on. Small deeds done are better than great deeds that never get beyond the planning stage. What we think or what we believe, no

The Bumper Book of Common Sense

matter how brilliant or noble, is ultimately of little consequence except in so far as it leads to what we do. It is what we do that is of consequence.

* Life rewards actions, not thoughts. People who succeed do things that people who don't succeed don't.

* Good things don't come to those who wait; they come to those who work hard on what is important to them.

* Err on the side of action. Failure in action is better than the nothing that arises from inaction.

* The pessimist complains about the wind; the optimist expects and waits for the wind to change; the realist adjusts his sails.

* If you're not sure what the right thing to do is, choose the thing that seems the best. Better to get on and do something, and then possibly change direction, than to remain uncertain and do nothing. If you can't choose between a number of options then choose whichever is the least or the most effort depending upon whether you want to get it done quickly or you want to learn from it. If you still don't know which one to choose flip a coin and if you feel uncomfortable doing the one that wins, do the other one.

* We fail to achieve only because we are afraid we might fail to achieve, so we don't try. But if we truly made the effort to achieve, we would achieve. It might not be all that we set out to achieve, but be significant achievement none the less.

* You can live your life consciously or unconsciously. You can make things happen or you can have things happen to you.

* What you get out of your life is a function of what you put in. If you don't put very much into your life, don't expect to get very much out of it.

* The difference between being behind and being ahead is not very much. Maybe an extra 10%. Make that extra 10% effort and you could get well ahead of the game.

* You'll be surprised how much you can achieve by just setting out to do it. Many people think achievement is far harder than it is. They believe there are obstacles and blockers everywhere. But the truth is most of these melt away as you get close to them or prove to be easily overcome. Most people in this world drift along. If you have a clear vision and are willing to vigorously but intelligently pursue it you are already in a very small minority. Much of the world will step aside to let you pass, and some of it will even help you since decisiveness can be attractive.

* Differentiate vision that is a call to arms as a realistic goal that you will put in place plans to strive for, from a vision that is a vague hope that just drifts along in front of you as wishful thinking.

* Don't wait for someone to solve your problems for you, or wait for perfect circumstances in order to tackle them. Get started on solving your problems, and ask others to help you where necessary.

* If you want help from others don't wait for them to come and offer: ask for their help, but don't get upset if they say no.

* Don't go through life waiting for a favorable break. Go out and create your own favorable breaks by having and trying lots of ideas. You don't need them all to work. Just one working is probably enough. Don't see ideas that don't work as failures, see them as steps on the road to the ones that will work.

* Most people go through life expecting to hit a bull's eye with one shot. In the end most people either don't shoot because they fear they won't hit the bull's eye, or take one shot, miss and give

up. The ones that hit the bull's eye are the ones that no matter how poor their first shots, they keep shooting and adjusting until they hit it.

* There is a degree of uncertainty in everything, and we should base our actions on the best assumptions and reasoning to be had, not on some unrealistic expectation of certainty.

* Be willing to take risks, albeit calculated risks. It is foolish to take risks with life and limb except in extreme circumstances. But if you wish to develop and move on you should take risks in terms of moving beyond the boundaries you feel comfortable with. However be aware of consequences and be wary of risks that might also affect other people. If for example you have family dependent upon you, then you shouldn't be taking risks that would leave you penniless. If you are on your own then you might take risks that would simply be irresponsible if you had a wife and children dependent upon you.

* Attempting to avoid any risks is likely to be counterproductive. We often advance only by taking calculated risks. If our ancestors had never taken calculated risks it is unlikely we would have survived as a species.

* Don't get upset when risks don't pay off; it's the nature of risks. Take lots of risks, calculated risks, and some of them will pay off.

* Do not be afraid of making mistakes. Get on with life. If you are afraid of making mistakes you will be forever holding yourself back. You will make far more progress by getting on with something and then learning from the mistakes you make as you go along, than you will by holding back until you believe you are ready.

* Use your talents and skills. Apply your knowledge and experience. Release your creativity. Pass on your enthusiasm and positive attitude to others.

* Anything worthwhile is worth the effort. We need challenges if we are to develop and grow and get any sense of accomplishment. Don't be forever looking for an easy life. Seek out and embrace challenges and make your life worthwhile.

* Most people regret the things they didn't do far more than the things that they did do. Adopt a 'will do' attitude when not sure whether or not you should do something. If you get the opportunity to try something new, do it. If you want to make something, make it. If you want to change something, change it.

* Don't waste your life looking for a pot of gold at the end of the rainbow: mine the opportunities that are already all around you. Don't look for greener grass on the other side: plant your own greener grass.

* We should approach life as an adventure, in which we are willing to take calculated risks and to experience new things. Whether we like it or not, the world is always changing. In the long run, playing it safe and staying within our comfort zones is more likely to put us at risk than embracing change and adapting to it.

* Say yes to invitations, say yes to getting involved or helping. Don't take on things you can't or won't do, but take on things that get you active or get you interacting with other people.

* Once it is clear to you that something must be done, get on and start doing it as soon as you can.

* Your mind can be reprogrammed to be positive, to be proactive, to be always seeking to improve. It's your mind. You can take control of it if you wish. Use your time in the car, on buses, on trains, sitting around with nothing to do, to listen to audio books about motivation. They will help you reprogram your mind. Don't listen to them just once, listen to them many times, and listen to lots of different audio books. You can often rent them from libraries for a fraction of what it would cost to buy them.

The Bumper Book of Common Sense

* A particularly useful and powerful idea is to think of yourself as a company with your conscious self as the Chief Executive Officer (CEO). Ask yourself how your company is performing: is it growing and improving, or is it stagnating? What is the mission and the goals of your company? Do you have tangible and realistic plans for achieving your goals including clear medium and short term goals? How are the different 'departments' doing: health, relationships, finance, career? You want all your departments performing well, not just one or two of them. What is the culture and what are the values of your company? How well organized is the company? Is it making the most of its resources? What are the key processes – ie.. habits and routines - that enable you to be effective? Do you need to upgrade them, and learn from experience? Are you investing in new practices and learning new skills? How well is the company perceived in the outside world, and do you need to invest in a bit of PR? If your company is not the best it could be, what do you need to do to make it so? After all, you are the CEO, it is your responsibility and your opportunity.

* Take responsibility for what is going on around you. This includes not just for what you do, but also for what you don't do, but could. Note that taking responsibility is not the same as taking the blame, though you should be willing to own up to things that are your fault. However blame never solves problems; it is people who accept responsibility that solve problems.

* It is easy to dodge our responsibilities, but we can't dodge the consequences of our responsibilities.

* Look for the solution, not for who to blame.

* You don't have to wait for others to make the first move. You can make it.

* Get on and deal with small problems as they arise. If you don't they will grow into bigger problems later on. Better to deal with minor disruptions as you solve small problems than have major disruptions forced on you at a later date.

* Find work that you enjoy, and that you are suited to. Success is not the key to happiness; happiness is the key to success.

* Try to be passionate about the things you spend most of your time doing. Even if you feel unable to change your current job for one you believe would be more enjoyable, you can make your current job more enjoyable by setting personal standards and challenges.

* Do what you are best suited to in the circumstances. Play to your strengths. Note however that only you know what you are best suited to so take responsibility for getting involved in an appropriate manner. Don't wait for others to see your strengths and invite you – they won't; not any more than you are doing so for them.

Do what you Believe is Right

* Have the courage to do the right things, and to stand by your beliefs and reasoning. Listen to and act on your conscience.

* One man with courage makes a majority.

* If you have an idea you believe in, do not be afraid to be different, to disagree, to go against the tide, to stand alone. Creators are different, they disagree, they go against the tide, and they stand alone.

* You'll need to accept that many people will be upset about your doing things differently and any successes you might have. Don't let that put you off trying to do things differently.

* Don't assume that what the majority do is the best. It's simply the average. You can do way better than average, but not by simply doing what the majority do.

* Stick steadfast to doing what you believe is right, all the time you believe it is right.

* Be willing to question what you believe is right in the light of new evidence or new arguments. If the majority of people believe something different to you, it doesn't mean they are right. But it might. Look to understand why they believe what they do, and keep or change your mind accordingly.

* Always be willing to change your mind if you have reason. It takes great courage to do so, but it is the right thing to do.

* Do not trouble yourself with the behavior of others. Trouble yourself with your own behavior, and seek to influence others by your own example.

* Do not worry about what others think of you. Amongst the billions of people in the world those that know of your existence are few indeed, and even those that do know you spend very little of their time thinking about you, just as you spend little of your time thinking about them.

* Do not worry about what others think of you. They do not know you as well as you know yourself. What matters is what you think of yourself. If you don't think much of yourself then seek to do things that will make you think better of yourself. Finding ways to altruistically help others usually works.

* Live your life on your own terms, not by trying to live up to other people's expectations of you. You don't need the approval of others if you have the approval of yourself.

* By forever striving to be famous or successful you are slaving yourself to societies ideals not your own. We can be free by just living our lives on our own terms.

* It's better to be at the bottom of a ladder you want to climb than at the top of one you don't.

* If you've done things that make you feel bad about yourself, do not let yourself get drawn into the state of mind that then gives up on yourself. It is never too early or too late to start doing the things that make you feel better about yourself.

* We are what we do when no one is looking.

* We are as responsible for what we don't do as for what we do.

* Character is built in the little moments. You have many hundreds of opportunities to do the right thing every day. Keep trying to do the right thing.

* Most of the things you must, should, or have to do are not absolute demands, and thinking of them as such will create worry and anxiety. You should choose to do things because of how you want to live and interact in the world rather than because you feel duty bound to do so.

Face up to Your Fears

* The people who tend to experience the most success in the world are those who accept uncertainties and fear, try anyway, learn from their experiences, and keep trying new things. Not only do they then keep improving but they live a more satisfying, proactive and fulfilling life, and one that seems longer.

* Fear is one of the biggest reasons why we don't make the progress in our lives we know we are capable of, particularly fear of the unknown. We all experience fears and anxieties, even those who don't appear to. However we can overcome fear by taking action, by deciding that our future happiness and growth is more important than our fear of stepping into the unknown. Look to do

The Bumper Book of Common Sense

something every day that takes you a little out of your comfort zone and gets you used to taking steps into the unknown, albeit in a controlled manner.

* Face up to your fears if they are standing in the way of you achieving your potential. Do what you know to be necessary and you will be at peace with yourself.

* Don't let fear hold you back from doing the things you want to do. Be aware of the risks in any more extreme activities, but be aware that there is some degree of risk everywhere.

* Courage is not the absence of fear; courage is doing what is right despite the fear because there are things more important than fear.

* When we fail to face up to our fears when we have the opportunity to do so, we are strengthening the hold the fear has on us.

* Rather than trying to suppress what scares us, sometimes it is better to feel the intensity of it, and then choose to face up to it regardless.

* You should seek to do something that scares you a little every day; things that make your heart beat a little faster. Be prepared to take risks, albeit calculated risks. It helps you feel alive.

* Phobias are extreme fears of things or circumstances that don't really have much danger. If you have phobias that are preventing you from doing things you know you should or want to do then you should seek ways to overcome them. If the phobia is extreme and impacting on your life then get professional help. If the phobia is less extreme ways of overcoming it include:
    o Gradual exposure. Take very small steps where you start to come into contact with the phobia but from a safe distance that you can gradually reduce;
    o Imagine yourself in situations where the phobia is present again taking it a small step at a time;
    o Watch videos or look at pictures that put you in contact with the phobia but in a virtual rather than a real way;
    o See others behaving normally in the situation you have a phobia in;
    o Seek to determine if there are other factors at play that may be behind or contributing to your phobia and seek to tackle them;
    o Learning to be aware of and to be able to control your breathing whilst exposed, and to be able to calm and quieten your mind;
    o Keep a diary of your exposures and use a scale of 0 to 10 to record your level of anxiety each time you were exposed, 0 being no anxiety at all and 10 being total fear. Look to assess circumstances under which you were less anxious and look to build on them.

* Questions to ask yourself if you are afraid of failure or have a particular concern such as losing your job:
    o What is the worst that can happen?
    o What would you do if the worst happened? What actions would you take?
    o What opportunities would exist if the worst did happen? What strengths could you draw on? What alternatives might you have?

    Once you've recognized that you can cope even if the worst does happen, look to see what you can do now to lessen the probability of it happening.

* If there are things you are afraid to do, or don't believe you can do, but would like to, create visions in your mind of yourself doing them. Gradually increase the strength of the visions, making them as vivid and real as you can. Then just go ahead and do them in real life.

* If you are having trouble visualizing circumstances you are afraid of, put them into a humorous context.

* Do not fear change, embrace it. Change is the very essence of life. Without change there is only the boredom of being. With change there is the enthusiasm of becoming.

* Some ways of helping you develop a more courageous attitude include:
    o Practice little things like asking a shop assistant for help if you can't find something;
    o Regularly try something new, maybe try some food you haven't tried before, or talk to someone you don't know well, or try some game or skill you haven't done before.
    o For the things you know you have a fear of doing but wish you hadn't, seek out ways to gain gradual exposure, and see it as a challenge to overcome the fear;
    o Behave like you are someone who is courageous. If you know someone you would like to be more like, pretend you already are like them as you approach some given activity;
    o When faced with something you are reticent about, ask yourself what's the worst that can happen, and what is the best that can happen. You'll usually find the best outweighs the worst.

* Run towards your fear, particularly if it is standing in your way. If you recognize you are putting something off as a result of fear, then just getting on with it can be a very liberating and rewarding experience.

* Confronting and pushing yourself through your fear is ultimately less stressful than living with the fear gnawing away at you.

* Sometimes you will have strong feelings of fear and doubt, trying to hold you back. Particularly in the early hours of the morning. Experience them for a while, and then put them behind you. They are not real.

* Most of us occasionally experience the fear of being 'found out'. A fear that other people will one day realize we are not as perfect as we think they think we are. This should be seen as healthy self-doubt that keeps us focused and working hard. The alternative is when we believe we are perfect and deserving of all the good things we think people think of us. We are not perfect, any more than others are as perfect as they often appear to us. Thus accept the occasional self-doubts and then move on, doing the best you can.

* Whilst sometimes we may not be able to control events around us, particularly if caught up in extreme circumstances, we still have a choice in how we accept the inevitable.

* It is not actual events that are the cause of our suffering but our interpretation and response to them.

* Much of what we fear is the result of ignorance. The more we know and understand something, generally, the less we fear it, though of course the increased knowledge may make us realize just how dangerous something is. However being wary of something is not the same as being afraid of it. Much of what people fear, they wouldn't if they understood more about it.

* Don't be forever worrying about what might go wrong. There is some risk in everything we do, in everything we eat or drink. Don't let it hold you back from enjoying your life.

* Approach problems as though you have no fear, irrespective of whatever fear you may feel, and you are more likely to succeed in tackling them than you would otherwise do. Just as you will be readily able to walk along a plank that is low down to the ground whilst you may be unable to do so if it was high up.

The Bumper Book of Common Sense

Do the Best You Can in the Circumstances

* Sincerely and regularly ask yourself what is the best thing for you to do right now? And then do it, the best you can.

* We can never be fully secure in life. Life is transient. Circumstances change. Things happen. There is always a risk, and some risks we can't control. But some risks we can.

* Focus on what is within your control rather than worry about what is not or simply hoping for the best. Accept that chance events sometimes go against you. Don't get upset by that. Accept that it is the nature of the world and keep focused on what is within your control.

* You are not perfect, so don't live your life in fear that you may do something that shows you are not perfect. Don't try to live up to an image of being perfect. Getting things wrong from time to time is normal. Laugh at your mistakes. Learn from your mistakes. Move on.

* Always do the very best you can in everything you do. Don't worry about being the best, and don't measure yourself against some external standard, which is likely to be either too high or too low for you personally. Measure yourself against your own best achievable standard. Personal excellence is what you should be always seeking: no more, no less. It's more fun than just doing, and you learn and grow.

* Judge yourself on whether you have done the best you can in the circumstances, based upon what was within your control. If things happen which are genuinely outside of your control then don't worry about them or blame yourself for the resulting outcome. Just react to them as best you can.

* Do the best you can in the time available, or in the time that you are willing to spend, and accept the outcome. Engage fully in what you are doing. You should not judge yourself against how well you did, but on whether or not you did the best you could.

* Doing your best is about making best use of the time you believe it is reasonable to allocate to the task. Be wary of the pursuit of diminishing returns when the benefits in continuing are less than the benefits you would gain by doing something else.

* Do every task diligently and with a positive attitude and you will generally feel good about yourself.

* We can and should do ordinary things extraordinarily well.

* If you cannot make the effort to be effective in the small things, don't expect to be effective in the big things. Be continually looking for how to do things better. Seek every little improvement, no matter how small.

* Play to your strengths when you can. We all have different capabilities and abilities, and we should look to take advantage of where we are relatively strong, and avoid areas we are relatively weak, albeit in so far as circumstances allow.

* See everything you do as an opportunity to learn. If things don't work out as well as you would have liked, then so long as you reflect on what you could have done better you have increased the chances of them working out better next time. When first learning something you only need a few attempts and you will dramatically increase your abilities.

* Deal with the world as it is, not with it as you wish it was. By all means try to make the world a better place, but always recognize the reality of how it is.

* Given you find yourself in circumstances you'd rather not be in, you can only experience it, change it, make the best of it, or learn from it. Why worry about it?

- Freely acknowledge that life is full of difficulties. Recognize them as part of the natural order of things, and face up to and deal with them as best you can. Don't let them weigh you down. Turn them into challenges to yourself. Rather than running away from them, feel good about getting on and tackling them.

- Note what is termed the positive thinker's prayer:

    God grant me the courage to change the things that can be changed

    The grace to accept the things that cannot

    And the wisdom to be able to distinguish

- There is something worthy of note in almost all circumstances.

- The world is an uncertain place, accept it, and plan as best your can for the uncertainties. Don't get upset when the dice rolls against you. Adapt, act, and treat it as part of life's great adventure.

- Successful outcomes are dependent upon things that are within your control and things that are not. The wider environment and chance often have a significant impact on how things turn out. Thus your efforts are not necessarily a guarantee of success. However thoughtfully doing your best gives you the greatest chance of success, and don't let poor outcomes put you off continuing to do your best in the future.

- Sometimes it is best to accept a loss or make a sacrifice in order to avoid a greater loss.

Take Control of Your Own Mind and Thoughts

- Just as we train our body and get physically fitter so can we train our minds and become mentally stronger and more robust and resilient.

- Whether you succeed or fail depends on your own way of thinking. If you are happy to make excuses and give reasons for why failing to succeed is not your fault, then you will fail to succeed. If on the other hand you take responsibility for what is happening around you and seek to overcome any difficulties you encounter then you are on the road to success.

- If you fill your mind with self-doubt you will struggle and fail. If you believe you can you probably will. Those who succeed are those who believe they can and will succeed.

- If we have positive expectations we have a much greater chance of success than if we have negative expectations.

- Create strong mental images of how you wish to be, and your brain will help you be that way. Keep practicing being the way you want to be and you will get better at being that way.

- If you want something of yourself, put it in clear words, be specific, and explicitly ask yourself.

- If you want to know what you yourself want, then sit alone somewhere quiet and undisturbed and let your mind roam free. Too many of our thoughts during the day are simply responses to other people.

- You can be greater than you are. Know that you are capable of great things. Now set out to do great things.

- In extreme circumstances people can do extraordinary things. Why not seek to do extraordinary things under normal circumstances. Create a vision of yourself as being truly exceptional in the things that you do. Create it as a dominant thought in your head and then live it out. Get rid of the

The Bumper Book of Common Sense

limiting thoughts that hold you back and just live as the exceptional person you are capable of being.

* Replace 'I should' with 'I will', then do.

* To make a significant change in your life you need to bring yourself to a new state of being where you have changed. To do this you need to be very clear about what you want the new state to be. Think about it, imagine it, and let your sub-conscious embrace it. Then just start behaving like you have already changed.

* You don't need to wait till the New Year to make your life changing resolutions.

* Don't let yourself be defined by how others see and label you. Define yourself to be whatever it is you want to be.

* The drifting, wandering, incessant shifting of our attention makes us incompetent and miserable. The primary ability we have that makes us human is our ability to focus our attention through our self-awareness. When we let our attention shift about in an automated way outside of self-aware control we are being less than human. A skill we need to develop is to make our self-awareness continuous and controllable. When it isn't we are liable to give into temptations.

* Precision of thought sets you free.

* We mostly go through life half asleep, merely responding habitually to the circumstances in front of us. This sometimes leads us astray, as we go for the easy option and do things pleasurable in the short term but bad for us in the long term. We all however have the capacity for overcoming our base programming and take control.

* To be able to exhibit self-control we need to get in a state of self-aware attention that sits above our thoughts. We must be able to be aware of our thoughts without being emotionally influenced by them.

* A state of self-control is achieved when our self-awareness is able to control our thoughts, silencing them when we say so and moving us into specific action when we decide to.

* People with higher levels of self-consciousness tend to be harder working, are more consistent in their actions, their actions are more in line with their values, and they are more honest about themselves.

* You are responsible for yourself. You are responsible for the state of your home environment, for your weight, for your general health and well-being. Bad things happen. They happen to everyone. You are responsible for how you react to them and whether or not you let them get you down.

* You are in control of your life. You may or may not be able to change everything around you, but you can change some of it and you can change how you feel about it.

* You may not be responsible for what happens to you, but you are responsible for how you react and respond to what happens to you. Don't drain your energies by worrying about what has happened: use your energies to identify and implement a solution.

* Life is happening to you whether you like it or not. Do what you can to control it, but however things turn out, accept it and be happy. Why not? You are where you are in the circumstances you are in. All you have full control over is how you feel about it. Do you prefer to be happy or miserable?

* Don't let your mind keep wandering. Keep it focused on the achievement of your goals.

* Unless you are able to suppress your negative thoughts, they will suppress you.

* When something happens that upsets your plans or intent you will initially respond emotionally, instinctively feeling hard done by. However you can then allow yourself to continue like that, and stay in a negative frame of mind. Or you can accept things have happened that you didn't like, but look to make the best of them. By doing so you can quickly get back into a positive and healthy frame of mind.

* Don't get upset by the things that bother you. By all means try to do something about them, but pent up anger or resentment won't help you. Accept things first, and then tackle them with a clear mind.

* When your mind is troubled ask yourself whether or not there is anything you can do about it right now. If so, do it. If not, focus on what you can do now with your time.

* If something or someone has annoyed you, note that time will pass, and you can spend that time with the pain and stress of annoyance, or you can spend that time with a sense of calm, and with a resolve to deal with, if it needs dealing with, the issue that has annoyed you.

* Garbage In, Garbage Out. Take control of what knowledge and experiences are coming into you through what you read or watch or experience. It is affecting the way you think and the way you behave.

* Your happiness depends on what you choose to think about, what you do, and on your habits. You alone can control your thoughts and actions and habits.

* Your thoughts become words; your words become actions; your actions become habits; your habits become your character; your character becomes your destiny. You are the architect of your own destiny.

* Replace unhelpful beliefs by helpful beliefs. Our emotions draw upon our beliefs and beliefs will give rise to positive emotions and some to negative. Beliefs likely to lead to problem emotions include:
    o Everything should work out the way I want it.
    o I should be able to always do the right thing.
    o Other people should always be fair and nice.
    o Somebody is to blame if things go wrong.
    o Other people are always judging.

    More positive and useful beliefs include:
    o I can deal with any situation.
    o Life isn't fair.
    o It's how we deal with things, not what happens, that brings peace of mind.
    o Everyday is precious.
    o Things go better when we approach them positively.
    o There are far worse things that could happen

* Trying to suppress negative thoughts often results in their becoming more prominent in our minds, rather than less, due to the polar bear syndrome, whereby people who are asked not to think about a polar bear end up thinking about one far more frequently than they would have otherwise. Rather than trying to suppress negative thoughts let them come to mind, but try to focus on positive thoughts.

* You thoughts come and go. Just notice them, listen to them, without judging them. Become conscious of repetitive negative thoughts. Become aware of how frequent they are, and develop a habit that enables you to replace a particular negative thought with a particular positive one.

The Bumper Book of Common Sense

* Many of our negative thoughts arise from wanting the world to be different than it is. 'He shouldn't have said that', 'I should be thinner', 'People should respect one another', 'Children should be well-behaved', 'I shouldn't have done that', 'He should have asked me about ...', 'It's unfair that it should have happened to me'. Such thoughts are common and they stress us and wear us down. You need to replace such thoughts with acceptance that the world is as it is, and what has happened has happened. It serves no useful purpose to argue with or regret what has happened. Accept it fully and without question, and move on from it. You don't need to condone or be happy about what has happened, but you do need to focus solely on where you go from here.

* If you are feeling down, get all your negative thoughts down on paper. Expunge them from your mind. Then write down opposite feelings. Write down how you would like to be thinking or feeling, positive thoughts. Then repeat these positive thoughts to yourself and make them real in your mind, displacing your earlier negative thoughts.

* Do not compare yourself to others. If you do, you will be eternally stressed.

* We think we are thinking most of the time; but it's not true. Most of what we consider thought is just our mind mindlessly regretting the past or worrying about the future or just fantasizing. There is little useful end to the overwhelming majority of our thoughts.

* Try to calm your internal chattering to yourself. It is very wearing and it is to no useful end. It means you miss half of what goes on around you. Ever found yourself going from one place to another with something on your mind and forgetting almost everything in-between. That was the result of your internal dialogue. It rarely brings you more insights. Your insights come from when your mind is quiet, not when it is noisy. Overcome your mindless chatter by giving all your attention to the present moment and to your current task. If some other thought does come to you, write it down, then you can let it go in the certain knowledge you can come back to it later.

* Look for the opportunities that lurk in problems, and if you don't find them, think of problems as learning opportunities and a way of improving your solution searching skills.

* Setbacks and problems are not things that you should let prey on your mind and get you down. Rather they are opportunities to learn and grow. You don't need to seek out setbacks and problems, but you certainly shouldn't be afraid of them, and you shouldn't be afraid of taking risks that will on occasion lead to setbacks. Take them in your stride and move on.

* A fear of criticism leads to a lack of initiative and imagination, lowers self-confidence and self-reliance, and generally holds people back. It also leads to a failure to act on what would otherwise be useful feedback. Try not to react emotionally to criticism, instead look to see if there is anything you can take away from it. If not, forget it and move on.

* Change worries about 'What if X happens?' into, 'If X happens, what then?' There are usually plenty of options.

* Use your imagination to create, not to worry.

* If something is demanding your attention, ask 'what is the desired outcome?', and 'what is the next action?'. Thinking this way will put you in charge.

* The past has past. Accept it. You don't need to deny it. It was as it was. You can however choose to do and be different from now on.

* From this point forwards.

* Forgive yourself. Value yourself as a human being and recognize you have strengths and weaknesses. Don't continually beat yourself up or criticize yourself about your weaknesses, failures or mistakes. Forgiving yourself is not about suppressing negative thoughts or experiences, but rather about not letting yourself overreact to them.

* Don't let negative thoughts overwhelm you. Tell yourself that from now on you will do all that can reasonably be done. Neither you nor anyone else in the world can do more.

* For many people it is common to lie awake at night having their troubles playing over and over in their mind, in a way that is of no use and at a time when nothing can be done about them. If you find yourself in such circumstances tell yourself that there is nothing that can be done about them right now, and be clear about the next action you will take relevant to the given problem. You might find it helps to write this down.

* Do not worry about trifling things. Though the way you deal with trifling things is often the same way as you deal with important things.

* No point in worrying. If there's nothing you can do then live with it. If there are things you can do, do them. Worrying makes things worse, not better.

* Develop the habit of looking for solutions rather than dwelling on problems.

* It may have been a long and frustrating day. Things may have gone against you. People may not have behaved as you would have liked them to behave. There may be a pile of issues that need sorting. You can be justified in being stressed and feeling worn out and in having a drink and watching meaningless TV and being short with your wife or partner or kids. Or you can say that's done for today and I'll deal with tomorrow tomorrow. Tonight I am free and with the people I love and I'll appreciate the calm of being with them. How lucky I am.

* Try to be conscious of how your negative attitude towards someone or something is largely derived from prejudices, stereotypes, or atypical personal experiences.

* Rather than look at new information in terms of how it can be used to confirm your existing beliefs look at it in terms of how it can bring into question your existing beliefs. Your existing beliefs are not right, they are simply the ones you have. You should always be looking to improve them, and this is best done by finding flaws in them and then modifying or changing them. The more you look for where you might be wrong the closer you'll get to being right. It is by being wrong that new possibilities and opportunities open up.

* We need to live our lives based on the way the world is, or can reasonably be made to be, not on the basis of what we wish it were.

* Learn to accept the world as it is rather than resenting it for not being as you would like it to be, though don't let this stop you from wanting to change it.

* You can feel in a good mood or you can feel weighed down. It is all in your mind. With one your body will be getting healthier and you will get things done, with the other … Your choice.

* If people act stupidly or incompetently around you, rather than get angry with them, be grateful for your own Common Sense. And try to understand if there is some particular reason they are acting the way they are. Generally it is because they perceive circumstances differently to the way you do. It can be useful to understand why that is so.

* Short of doing things that are illegal or immoral, give yourself permission to do the things you want to do. Be in control of your own life, albeit accept full responsibility for the consequences of your actions.

* Any fool can criticize, condemn, complain, and make excuses, and most do. If you find yourself doing so, stop it. There are better uses of your time, such as figuring out what to do next.

* Let go of self-complaint such as 'Why did this happen to me?' ' Why am I always the one who …'

The Bumper Book of Common Sense

* Think of everything you do as meaningful and purposeful; even if your first thought is to think of it as a chore. You can give some meaning and purpose to most of the things you do, even the things you have to do. You can recognize that you are doing them for a good reason, if not why are you doing them. And you can look at how to do them as effectively as you can.

* Think of yourself as an essential cog in the universal consciousness, as important and as significant as any other cog. Our lives and everyone else's lives are governed mostly by chance, and it is chance that we happen to have been born in the environment we were and with the characteristics we were born with. It is thus not how successful you are that matters, since this is mostly the result of chance, it is how you make the best of whatever circumstances you find yourself in. You can be as significant as anyone else in the universe simply by making the most of the particular circumstances you find yourself in and by being aware of yourself and your environment as you do so.

Don't just React, Think

* Don't just do, think. Don't fall into the trap of being busy all the time, because it is likely that much of the busyness is either unnecessary or is an unproductive use of our time. If you stop and just think about things from time to time you will be more effective with the time you do spend doing.

* Your ability to think is your greatest asset, not your ability to do. Thinking then doing however will generally have the greatest payback.

* The human brain has a remarkable ability to absorb information and adapt to challenging unfamiliar environments. But if you don't use your mind, you will lose it.

* The vast majority of what we do and think is simple instinctive reaction to what is around us. Moreover many of these instincts are ones that evolved in a very different environment to the one we now live in. The only tool we have to go against our automated reactions is self-aware conscious thought, which we can use not only to go against instincts and automated reactions but to create new ones. It does however require effort.

* Habits are what allow us to do most things quickly and effectively. Without them we would not be able to do anything. However in some circumstances our habits are the wrong thing to do. We should be particularly wary of habits when something is important or something is different. Many people continue to apply habits when they are not appropriate.

* If we have made a sacrifice in order to do something, we will tend to keep doing it, even when it is no longer the right thing to do. Thus we often have an aversion to cutting our loses.

* Instead of event -> reaction -> outcome, whereby we immediately react to an event leading to what may be an undesirable outcome, look to pause in response to an event. Think about what outcome you wish for, and react accordingly, ie. event -> outcome -> reaction. Thus when you find yourself instinctively starting to react to an event, allow yourself to become conscious of that fact and ask yourself if your reaction is going to have a desirable outcome. This should give yourself sufficient self-control to change your reaction if necessary to one likely to have a more desirable outcome. We can all learn to do this if we practice doing so.

* Think about what you are doing, and do something about what you are thinking.

* We act on the basis of information. However don't take everything at face value. Some information you come across will be misleading or simply false. If you are about to make an important decision or take s action on the basis of some particular information, ask yourself about how confident you are in the credibility of the information.

* Don't pretend you understand things that you don't, and don't be afraid to ask clarifying questions; though there may be occasions when it is inappropriate to interrupt to seek explanations. If you

frequently find yourself not understanding the things you are engaged in then either you are in the wrong job or you need to do some rapid and intense learning.

* The things we do, and the things we don't do, have consequences. Sometimes they are unforeseen consequences. But often they would not have been unforeseeable consequences, if we had spent a little bit of time thinking, and I don't mean wishful thinking.

* Great things are achieved through a mix of idealism and pragmatism: the vision and enthusiasm of the idealist, tempered by realism and the attention to detail of the pragmatist. Some degree of idealism is necessary to give a sense of purpose and direction. A degree of pragmatism is necessary to ensure that feasible plans are made and are followed through.

* To achieve great things you must not only act, but also dream, you must not only plan, but also believe.

* Elements of effective thinking include being clear about your long term goals and how to go about achieving them, the effective and realistic assessment of circumstances and information, and the ability to prioritize and make decisions that are in the best interests of your long term goals.

* Ideas don't move mountains. Effort and action moves mountains. However ideas help ensure the right mountains are moved and that effort and action are applied to best effect.

* Think through future difficulties and what could be done now to influence them: fire prevention in order to reduce the amount of firefighting you will need to do.

* Perseverance alone is not enough. Beating your head against a brick wall will likely do more damage to your head than to the wall, no matter how much you persevere. There are other ways to bring down or go round a wall. Perseverance is most valuable when intelligently applied.

* If at first you don't succeed, try and try again, and then give up and try to do it in a different way. You need to be persistent in trying to achieve your goals, but don't persist in using techniques that are not getting you there.

* Have patience. Not everything has to be done immediately. Not everything is ready to be done immediately. If you want people to come round to a way of thinking, it sometimes takes a bit of time. There are many things which can't get done right away, but can get done eventually.

* If particular strategies work in our lives, largely derived from experience, try to understand why they work. We will then be better able to adapt our strategies when circumstances change, as they eventually do. If we do things solely because experience shows us that they work without understanding why, we will be slow to adapt to changing circumstances.

* Set aside an hour once a week when you can be on your own without distractions and just think about things. Have a paper and pen so you can write stuff down. Just think about what's bothering you and what you can do about it. Think about whether you are living the sort of life you want to live, and if not what you can do to get closer to doing so.

Work Hard and Overcome Adversities

* There is a storm that rages about us and we must battle to stay the course. Though others rarely see the storm that lashes about us, as we rarely see the storm that lashes about them.

* Life is a challenge. Very very few people get an easy life, even if it might seem to you that many do. The best way of tackling life's challenge is to work hard; to work very hard. Appreciate the occasional time you have for personal pleasure and relaxation, but don't begrudge or run away from the hard work. Just get on and do it.

The Bumper Book of Common Sense

* Working hard isn't just about doing lots of hours. It's about focus and attention whilst you are working. If you are continually allowing yourself to be interrupted either by yourself or others whilst working on a particular task then it is likely it will take far longer than if you were able to focus exclusively on it. Many people find themselves having to work lots of extra hours and getting stressed out by it when they could achieve far more with fewer hours by being far more focused.

* Life is a balance between work and play. Don't always be looking to increase play at the expense of work. Acknowledge that you should pay your way in the world, and not begrudge working hard; and rather than always be looking to do the least you can get away with, look to put a bit extra in.

* Don't brainlessly forever seek a life of ease and comfort. Adversity and challenges help and enable us to grow. Don't run away from them.

* Don't expect to get things for nothing. Life isn't easy and you must be prepared to make sacrifices if you want to achieve or obtain things.

* The more you sow, the more you grow, the more you reap. If you are lazy or avoid doing the things you know you ought to do, then you will have difficulties and stress.

* We feel bad about ourselves when we know we could have done better, when we have let ourselves down. Why not always do your best, then you will feel good about yourself.

* If you want to feel alive, do not seek out easy tasks, seek out difficult tasks, and endure.

* Life is more interesting and meaningful if you tackle the difficult things rather than the easy things.

* Do not see difficulties as a problem, rather see them as a marker which makes life worthwhile through providing the opportunity to apply our skills and to learn, and as something we will be able to remember in the general forgetful malaise of life.

* Think of anything you do which you find hard, or are reluctant to do but know is the right thing, as exercise which is making you stronger. It is.

* The pleasure of knowing you have worked hard to achieve and done your best is far more satisfying than the pleasure arising from self-indulgence.

* We treasure far more that which we have had to work for, than that which has simply fallen into our laps.

* What we may gain from realizing the opportunities that lie hidden in problems often far far outweigh the losses we might suffer from the consequences of the problem. Often the more difficult the problem the greater the opportunity.

* Things and circumstances are never as they ideally should be. Rather than bemoan this fact we should make the best we can of things as they are whilst also looking to influence things as best we can.

* Sometimes bad things happen. Rather than getting down about it, you need to simply accept it and do what you can. You cannot change the past, but you can change the future.

* Be prepared to make sacrifices, in advance, if you are to achieve. The more you put in the more you will get out. Too many people expect it all to fall into their laps by magic. Too many people believe they have rights without responsibilities. Life doesn't work like that.

* Great success usually requires a level of dedication that's incompatible with a normal social life.

* Do not expect life to be easy. Expect it to be a struggle and stand ready and firm to meet life's problems and challenges as they occur. It is difficulties that show us what we are and make us what we become.

* In accepting that life is difficult you become more proactive in dealing with the challenges rather than just bemoaning the fact.

* Most people give up at the thought of hard work, and wonder why life doesn't go their way. Be resilient. When most people are giving up, be someone who is just warming up.

* In most endeavors there will be ups and downs. Two steps forward and one step back. Don't be discouraged or disheartened by the step backwards. Accept it as the natural rhythm of things, and plan how to take your next step forwards. Accept the rough with the smooth and be ok with it.

* People who are successful have usually had failures on the way, but kept going. Indeed it is rare for those who have not had failures to be successful. Success means doing things others haven't, and that means trying to do things which are difficult. You will therefore fail from time to time. Success comes not from avoiding failure but from learning from failure. People who succeed without making much effort, often find their success relatively short lived since they lack the skills and endurance to hold on to it.

* Be tenacious. Never give up. If you have a goal or a dream, pursue it. Do your best to achieve the things that are important to you. Don't let obstacles or failures put you off. Overcome them and learn from them. Great things are achieved by those who keep going, and keep getting back up after any fall.

* Find a hero to call to mind when times get tough. Someone who has battled with the trials and tribulations and setbacks and tragedies of life, and overcome them.

* We don't always get what we want straight away. We have to keep chipping away until we win through.

* Have faith. Almost any challenge can be overcome if you have faith. Whilst it can be, it doesn't need to be, a religious faith. You can simply have faith in yourself, in others, or simply that things will turn out ok in the end.

* Positive thinking without positive action is nothing more than dreaming.

* If you have a purpose, no amount of difficulty should pain you. Difficulties are merely weeds growing on the path you travel.

* If you have a 'why' you can endure almost any 'how'. Think about what in life is really important to you, and remind yourself of it when times get tough.

* No matter how big the tree, if you keep swinging at it with a sharp ax it will eventually fall.

* We are generally more resilient than we believe we are, and whilst we often believe we will have difficulty coping under certain circumstances once we get stuck in we will usually find the difficulties fade away.

* Get into the habit of finishing what you start, and keeping any promises you have made to others or yourself. After the novelty of doing the interesting bit has worn off, get down to the hard graft of finishing it off.

* Use what skills and abilities you have, and do what you are doing with all your might.

* Many people work hard on the wrong things. Working on the right thing is more important than working hard, though working hard on the right thing is most important. Learning to work hard is

The Bumper Book of Common Sense

itself a skill that can be effectively applied even if you originally learnt that skill whilst working on the wrong things.

* Avoid the temptation to cheat or be dishonest. Whilst it can lead to short term gains, it will leave you always looking over your shoulder.

* Don't be concerned about whether or not others are better than you. Maximize your potential and the use of your own abilities. Hard work will often produce better results than talent.

* Working hard doesn't mean always rushing about. You can both work hard whilst also being relaxed about life and appreciating it as it passes by.

* Whilst you should work hard, you also need to rest. If you try to simply work hard all the time you will burn out and start to hate what you do. Ensure you take breaks and time off.

* If you succeed in something, be wary of complacency and believing future success will now come easily. You will need to work hard to continue to succeed. Also avoid the fear of needing to keep succeeding and thus a tendency to back away from continuing to try. You can only do your best. Welcome success but also accept that not every future activity will lead to future success. Just keep doing your best and accept the outcome. Finally you can feel at a bit of a loss after a success. Suddenly your focus has now gone. It is normal. Take a bit of time to celebrate your success then get on with the next activity or target.

Life isn't Always Fair; Accept It and Move On

* Life is not always fair: people we believe are less competent than we are, are sometimes more successful than we are; other people sometimes get credit for things we feel that we have done. We think that way about other people, and other people think that way about us.

* Sometimes there's not much you can do about life being unfair. But here are a few observations which may or may not help lessen the blow when it happens to you:
    o More competent people do tend to do better than less competent people in the longer term. It's not always true, but it does tend to be true;
    o People who are less competent, but are in challenging positions, will probably be highly stressed;
    o If you perceive certain people as being less competent, then it is likely others do as well;
    o If someone else takes credit for your work, then remember that you are more likely to be able to repeat it than they are. And of course you will avoid doing so in a way that allows them to take the credit again;
    o Maybe there is someone watching over us and there will be a final reckoning.

* We sometimes get unfairly criticized for things that were not within our control. Sometimes we criticize others for things that were not within their control.

* Some people are born into an easier life than others. There are others who had it better than we did. It's not fair. On the other hand there are many more others who were born into a much harder life than ours and who have had it much worse than we have. That's not fair either.

* Don't become upset when others get better breaks than you; when bad things undeservedly happen to you. Don't focus on feeling sorry for yourself; get on with dealing with your own life as it is, not as you believe it should be.

* People can be successful in almost any environment they find themselves in, if they accept responsibility for their own lives, work hard, and seek out and seize opportunities. There are many poor to rich stories, and most of them result from hard work and a positive attitude.

* Face up to the fact that life is full of difficulties and problems and uncertainty, and that you cannot always escape from pain and discomfort. Accept it as part of what makes you aware and alive, and get on with what matters most to you.

* You don't need to try to try to escape every discomfort. You can live with some discomfort. It is your expectation that you should try to escape it that is often most distracting, not the discomfort itself. However be sure that the discomfort isn't actually doing you harm. If it is, you should do something about it.

* Misfortune happens. Be proactive in trying to avoid it or in trying to get out of it; but don't get down when it occurs. It happens. Get through it. Move on.

* Misfortune is often the birth of fortune. There is often opportunity in misfortune so long as you are willing to look for it.

* You can't unscramble eggs. But you can make an omelet.

* When things don't go the way you want, deal with it or let it go. Don't dwell on it.

* Sometimes we have to do things we don't want to do. By all means try to get out of things you don't want to do, but assuming you get to the point where you have to do it, then don't begrudge it. Make the best of it that you can. If you accept it and engage in it you might even like it.

* Stop feeling sorry for yourself. Self-pity and playing the victim does you no good. Yes life is sometimes unfair and yes sometimes you are unfortunate. But feeling sorry for yourself doesn't make it any better and does make it worse. It saps your energy. It eats away at you and makes you powerless.

* Things happen as they do, and not as you would wish. There are limits to what you can do in the circumstances. Be content with what you can do rather than frustrated with what you cannot.

* If someone has hurt you, and it is not part of some deliberate campaign against you, then let it go. People, including you, hurt each other all the time without realizing it, and it is rarely deliberate. Harboring feelings of anger or resentment do you far more harm than it does the person you feel has thoughtlessly wronged you.

* Disappointment either makes you bitter or makes you resilient. Your choice.

* You are never truly a victim of circumstances. Bad things happen, but it's your choice to accept them and be weighed down by them rather than be invigorated by them and doing something about it.

* Not everything in the world is fair: fact of life. Nor is there any reason it should be. Don't get upset about it. Get on with living in the real world, changing what you can, accepting what you can't.

* Don't get upset when you are unfairly done by. Just deal with it in a way that is your own best long term interests. This will often mean just letting it go.

* We tell our children that they can't have everything they want and expect them to understand. Yet as adults we get upset when things don't go our own way. From time to time we should remind ourselves not to be so childish.

The Bumper Book of Common Sense

Accept and Embrace Change

* The future isn't always a continuation of the past

* There are continual pressures for doing things in a better way, in a more cost-effective way, and thus continual pressures for change. This may be at the level which relates to the way you do the things you do, or it may be at the level which relates to whether or not you should be doing the things that you do. These pressures are constant and relentless. For a while it may seem that things can go on the way they are for ever. But it's not true. Change is an inherent part of the world we live in and you either ride with it or you get left behind.

* If you are not yourself the instigator of change when there are better ways of doing things then you could well become the victim of change. By not taking advantage of changes that would make what you do more cost effective, you are increasing the likelihood of other changes that would lead to what you do becoming obsolete.

* Change is frequent. Believing something won't change in the future is a risky view. Just because we can't visualize the change doesn't mean it won't occur. Just because something hasn't happened in the past doesn't mean it won't happen in the future. Just because change has not occurred for some time does not mean it won't occur sometime soon.

* Change will happen whether you like it or not, whether you want it to or not. We must therefore be ever ready to change ourselves, to adapt. If we keep doing the same things, no matter how successful they might be at one time, then eventually they will be holding us back.

* People and circumstances come and go. Sometimes things seem stable for a while, but eventually they will change. Sometimes they will change rapidly and unexpectedly; for good or bad, though often they are just different. If circumstances are good, appreciate them. But if they change, go with it, and adapt to the new circumstances rather than hanker for the old.

* Do your best to change what you want and can change; and adapt yourself to what you can't change.

* Don't fight against change. Change is what makes life interesting. Don't fear it, embrace it, and appreciate life as much during the course of change as you do during more stable times.

* See changes as opportunities not threats. Change will happen. You can fight it and may even hold it back in the short term, but change will happen because circumstances are always changing. Better to either accept change and adapt to it or nudge it in a direction you believe to be more appropriate.

* There is a balance to be struck between never being willing to change one's views and changing them on a regular basis. A balance between holding onto views no matter what, and changing ones views regularly based on whatever the latest piece of evidence happens to be. A balance between being stupidly stubborn and being fickle.

* Frequent changes in direction can be highly disruptive and demotivating, even if they are theoretically the best thing to do. Sometimes it is better to keep up the momentum of doing things in a less than optimal manner than risk losing momentum in what may only theoretically be a better way of doing things. This however does not mean we should turn a blind eye to what the best way of doing things are. We should always look to be aware of these and take opportunity to improve and move in the right direction as opportunity arises, which it frequently does.

* We are making decisions about change all the time in that unless we are deciding to change then we are deciding not to change.

* Don't fight changes that are outside of your control. Change is the way of things. Best to be able to adapt quickly and go with the flow rather than grow weaker through trying to fight or avoid change.

* Change is not always good, or the right thing to do. Some change is inevitable and you should accept it. However not all change should be accepted. Challenge change if you believe you should, but in doing so seek to understand why it is someone is trying to make the changes. If you have this understanding you will be better able to confirm you are right in challenging the change, and better armed to develop tactics for going about your challenge.

Continual Self-Development and Improvement

* Be as good as you can be at everything you do.

* Understand where you want to be in a year or 5 years time. Do a gap analysis on where you are now vis-à-vis where you want to be, and then define the specific actions you need to take to close the gap.

* Every 6 months or so, ask yourself questions, write down the answers, compare them over time, and decide on a couple of areas to focus on making the effort to improve:
    o Is my diet contributing to or detrimental to my feeling alive during the day;
    o Is my diet contributing to or detrimental to my being healthy in old age;
    o Do I have lots of energy during the day, or am I tired or fatigued for much of the day;
    o Which of my habits are positive and improve the quality of my life and which detract? Am I consistently seeking more of the former and less of the latter;
    o Do I spend much of my day progressing my own agenda, or other people's;
    o What goals inspire me;
    o Am I regularly learning and improving or am I mostly unchanged month after month;
    o Do I spend most of my time focused on the task I want to get done, or am I constantly interrupting myself;
    o Do I have a single list of all my important commitments;
    o Do I mostly enjoy what I am doing;
    o Am I positive about my own abilities and my getting done what I have said I will get done;
    o Am I over time getting less cluttered or more cluttered;
    o Do I always have a notebook or equivalent with me to capture important or creative thoughts;
    o What environments are most conducive to my working effectively and productively?

* If you are to increase your self-effectiveness over time you need to undertake regular self-assessments. Otherwise the days, weeks, and months will drift into years and you won't notice your failure to move on. Questions to ask yourself regularly – once a month or every 2 or 3 months – and keep a written record of the answers, include:
    o Have I achieved or made significant progress towards my goals?
    o Is the quality and quantity of my work improving and increasing?
    o Have I been co-operating well with others?
    o Have been making good use of my time and avoiding procrastination?
    o Am I persistently following through on my responsibilities?
    o Have I been reaching minor decisions promptly?
    o Have I been over or under cautious?
    o Have I been reducing bad habits and increasing good habits? Which ones?
    o Is my overall health improving or deteriorating?

The Bumper Book of Common Sense

- - Have I paid attention to family issues and do my partner/children feel closer to me or further away?
  - Have I been respectful of others?
  - Are my finances in better or in worse position than they were?
  - Have I done some things to help others without expecting reward?
  - Have I been unfair to anyone, and if so how?
  - Do I feel better about myself or worse? If significantly either way, why?

* Every day be looking for small steps you can take in the direction you want to go. Every day ask yourself:
  - What is the one small step I can take today towards reaching my goals?
  - What is the one small step I can take towards improving my health?
  - What is the one small step I can take towards improving my competence at work?
  - What is the one small step I can take towards improving my relationships with my partner, my parents, my children, my friends?
  - What is the one small thing I have a special ability or aptitude for that I can make use of today?

  You only need very small steps, but look for and implement them anyway. If you are struggling with even small steps then you should try even smaller steps.

* Seek to do something every day to improve just a little. Every day try to be just a little bit better than you were the day before.

* Self-development is not just a theoretical learning experience. Put to practice what you learn and modify and adapt it. Get better at what you do and get more done.

* Life is an opportunity for continuous improvement. Be ever on the lookout for small things to improve. Always be seeking to draw out the possibilities that lie in each moment.

* When you feel you are being unfairly criticized, either ignore the criticism or try to understand whether or not there is anything behind it that you should be aware of and that you can learn from. Don't get defensive and argumentative.

* See criticisms from others as an opportunity to improve. You need to get beyond your natural emotional response to criticism to having a think about whether or not there is something positive you can take from the criticism. In the absence of criticism we can become very arrogant and blind to our own shortcomings with calamitous consequences.

* To get the full benefit from criticism we must accept we have failings and shortcomings and thus there is plenty of opportunity for improvement.

* People who have a tendency to blame others for their own mistakes or misfortunes will not learn from them. Those who err on the side of accepting personal responsibility will learn and be less prone to making such mistakes or having such misfortunes fall on them in the future.

* Be happy to embrace change or to face unfamiliar circumstances. They are tremendous opportunities for learning and self-development.

* Don't run away from the things you can't do, or can't do very well. Don't be embarrassed about what you don't know. They are opportunities to grow if you are willing to admit your limitations, at least to yourself, and then look to go beyond them.

* Forever be seeking out experiences from which you can learn. Whilst you need to do your best to succeed, rather than fear failure welcome it as a learning opportunity. The more failures you have the more you are trying and the further along you are to eventual success. Most people never succeed because they avoid any circumstances in which they might fail.

* Do the hard things life throws at you; don't run away from them. You get stronger if you do things that are hard; and opportunities are often hidden away in things that at first look daunting.

* If what you are doing is not getting you to where you want to go, you need to do things differently. Don't keep kidding yourself that 'if only you could work harder' everything will be ok.

* If you keep doing things the same way you will keep getting the same outcomes. You need to do things differently in the future if you want to get better results. Learning from experience isn't about wishing we'd done things different in the past but about us doing things differently now and in the future.

* Learning from experience doesn't occur just because you are immersed in particular relevant circumstances. Many people don't learn from experience. Learning from experience is about reflecting on what has happened and thinking about what could have been done differently and why this might have made a difference.

* Do more of what works, less of what doesn't, and try new things.

* Write a half page or one page brief on what it would take for others to see you as amazing. Identify two particular actions that would take you in that direction – then take them.

* You have shortcomings. You can either try to deny this to yourself. Looking for excuses for why it was circumstances or other people that were to blame for your behavior or actions. Or you can happily seek out an understanding of them so you can work on trying to reduce or eliminate them. If we understand our own shortcomings, not only can we work at overcoming them, but we can take mitigating actions to minimize the negative consequences arising from them.

* Keep trying to raise your standards and to eliminate your shortcomings.

* We can make ourselves feel good by improving ourselves relative to our past selves.

* Get the systems you regularly use, at home or at work, working effectively and efficiently, such that you don't notice them, and all your attention is on what you are doing without being distracted by how you are trying to do it.

* Stick to your mission, but listen to and adjust in the light of feedback, even if it is negative. Ignore any negative feedback which you can't make use of to improve.

* Identify the one thing you think will make the biggest positive difference in your life. Identify it and do it.

* You can improve your persistence simply by practicing difficult and demanding tasks.

* Life is like riding a bicycle. If you don't keep moving forward you'll fall off.

Life is What you Make Of It

* So far as the universe is concerned you are not special. The universe does not revolve around you and you are not unique. The universe has laid out no destiny for you. You are one of billions of self-aware creatures that are the product of natural occurring events. You just happened, through

completely random processes, to have been brought into existence. It's up to you what you do with your life. The universe doesn't care.

* There are opportunities all around you if you keep your eyes open, seek them out, think about them, and you are willing to work at them even when they are far from certain. Continually seek to improve your own skills and capabilities, and see life as something to be positively engaged with rather than something to fear or hold back from.

* When opportunity knocks most people can't be bothered to get up to open the door.

* Taking small opportunities when they present themselves can sometimes start the ball rolling to great opportunities. And it gets you into the habit of seizing opportunities as they pass by.

* Never pass up the opportunity for new experiences unless you judge them too dangerous. Many opportunities only pass by you once.

* People who are consistently lucky are probably generating their own luck by noticing and acting on opportunities, having positive expectations, and working hard to overcome adversities.

* We have free will: we can indulge our animal instincts and revert to the level of beasts, or we can develop and apply our reason and intellect and soar with the angels. We are free to choose to develop or not develop ourselves, and thus choose for ourselves what we will become.

* There is a huge difference between the enjoyment we get out of using our skills and ability to take on a challenge, as regards the dull pleasure we get out of watching TV. We remember our time of taking on a challenge; the many hours we spend watching TV just pass away into oblivion. Do more of the former, much less of the later.

* You can achieve almost anything you want to so long as you believe you can and you enjoy trying. You need to enjoy trying otherwise you will give up long before you get there. Becoming expert in almost anything, so long as you are physiologically capable of it, is largely down to how much effort you put into it.

* Life has no more or no less meaning than that you choose to give it.

* Those who gain their identity from many areas of life are more resilient to failures than those whose life worth is focused on only one area.

* Be wary of defining yourself solely through one aspect of your life. You should define yourself through your working life, your personal life, and your relationships. Having goals from different aspects of your life will help you deal with difficulties that may arise. Personal objectives outside work, and strong relationships, for example, will help you deal with loss of your job, retirement, or some other particularly stressful event.

* Find your personal spirituality through asking yourself:
    o What makes you feel calm and at peace?
    o What makes you feel connected to others?
    o What brings you comfort?
    o Where do you get your inner strength from?
    o What gives you a sense of purpose?
    o What do you think is important in life?

* Success in life is not about what you accomplish, but about how you tackle the circumstances you find yourself in.

* Our moral decisions are a lifelong process. Just because we have done something bad in the past this does not mean we have to define ourselves as a bad person. You can redefine yourself to be the person you want to be regardless of what you have been or done in the past.

Live your Life with Purpose

* You only live once. This is it.

* Ask yourself questions about how you want to live your life. You have huge control over your life, but only if you choose to take it, and only if you have a direction to go in. Most people simply drift through life, living their life on automatic as they simply respond to others around them; and they then wonder what happened. It doesn't have to be like that. Think about what you want and how you want to live your life and work towards it.

* Life is short. Appreciate and be purposefully aware of how you are spending your time. Be ever looking at improving how you live your life.

* Don't live your live being always busy but not achieving very much. Look to simplify much of your life so that you can focus you time and efforts on things that matter to you and help make you feel that life is worth living.

* Don't passively wait for life to happen to you, because most likely it won't. Go out and make life happen. Have a reason for living, and live.

* Seek to ensure you are spending much of your time working towards your goals and doing what is important to you. Even a small step is infinitely better than no step at all.

* To get to your goals, either find a way, or make one.

* You don't always need a Plan B. Be committed to Plan A: work at it and overcome obstacles to it along the way.

* Incredible things are within your grasp if you have a clear view of what you want, proceed methodically, with an open mind, and put in the legwork.

* If you don't have a plan for your life, don't be surprised to be outpaced by those who do.

* Have something you feel passionate about and indulge it, so long as it is not harming other people or yourself. Something that really matters to you and for which you will stand up for and for which you will make considerable effort to help and support. You should generally show dedication to anything you believe in, but you should have one or two things that stand out.

* To get great things done in the light of opposition, proceed with energy and invincible determination. There are few who would be able to stand in your way.

* Without a purpose, your life will be hollow. If you haven't found a purpose take time out each day to think about it until you have. Find a worthwhile goal and commit yourself to it.

* Meaning in this world is what we choose to create for ourselves, not something we discover.

* Have lots of interests, but not more than you have time for. If you have many different interests you have things to fall back on should you become frustrated in one of them.

* Just because we cannot prove our beliefs to others this does not prohibit our choosing to live by them, and probably being happier for it.

The Bumper Book of Common Sense

* A better future is created by those who dream of a better future and work hard to make it happen.

* Follow your dreams. You will have problems and difficulties in your life whatever you do. Better the problems are ones that help move you towards a worthwhile end when you solve them rather than just be problems to be solved.

* Have life goals. If you have difficulty identifying them, imagine how you would want to live your life if you won the lottery, and you've got all your celebrating out of the way. How would you want to live the rest of your life? You don't need to win the lottery to work towards what you really want.

* The journey towards your primary life goals is what gives your life meaning, and for many life goals the journey is the goal. Having goals that relate to making the world a better place and the lives of those around you a better place is not one that you strive for, achieve, and then move on to something else. It is something that you achieve and continue to achieve by continually working towards doing so.

* Many younger people, and some not so young, have dreams, and maybe even goals they work hard to strive for, relating to becoming stars, to achieving celebrity status. If you are one of them recognize the reality that only a very very few make it. This does not mean you should not dream, and certainly doesn't mean you shouldn't work hard. However a few observations:

  o Enjoy the journey. Irrespective of your eventual life achievements, you are living your life as you go along. Notice it and enjoy it. Ultimately it is not where you end up that matters, it is how you travelled.

  o Be very wary of arrogance and assuming small successes mean large successes are in the bag. If you get taken on by a professional football club, for example, you are not on your way to superstardom. Only a very small percentage of those that get taken on make it to the big time. You may be one in a thousand. One in ten thousand maybe. But there is a long way between that and being one in a million. If you achieve small successes it should be a prompt to work even harder, not an excuse to sit back.

  o Don't pass up more mundane but good opportunities that come along whilst continuing to dream or strive. If you do not have time for other opportunities because you are working very very hard, then continue to do so, there is every chance the opportunities will return. However if you pass up the opportunities because you are still dreaming, and just waiting for a better opportunity to come along, then you may find the opportunity passes by for ever. You can usually take advantage of available opportunities whilst still working towards your goal.

* Only a few can become truly great. However we can all become good in something, and in being good we will be much better than most.

* Living your life for purely hedonist pleasures is unlikely to leave you feeling you've lived your life with purpose. Purpose is found in helping others and in helping make the world a better place. There are many ways of doing this.

* To help you find meaning in your life, ask yourself the following:
  o How and for what would you like to be remembered?
  o Are you living your life in a way that you will be happy with when you are old?
  o For what would you like to be able to look back on your life and say, I did that?
  o What are the strengths that you could really build on to achieve something?

* Those who are completely happy with the world as it is are unlikely to put much effort into trying to change it. Seeking out things to be unhappy about, and seeking to do something about them, can give you some purpose.

* To achieve your primary goal in life: ensure your goal is realistic and moral, and you wish to achieve it for the right reasons; write down all your reasons for achieving your goal, the more the better; imagine how you would behave if you were highly motivated; be clear about the sub-goals down to a level where you know what to do on a weekly and monthly basis; consider the things that will stand in your way and distract you and work out how to overcome them; get on with it on a daily basis; every day re motivate yourself and resolve to do better. If you are not making progress, re-plan, with a focus on overcoming the things that stand in your way.

* To achieve greatness, have a clear vision of what you want to create, have a plan, be organized, work hard, and have patience. Notice what is working and what isn't, and adapt to do more of what is working and less of what isn't.

* The achievement of great things requires:
    o Desire – a clear vision of what you want to achieve;
    o Decision – a personal commitment and action to work towards your given goals;
    o Faith – the belief that you can and will achieve;
    o Persistence – continuing in the light of setbacks and difficulties;
    o Engagement – to get others inspired and involved;
    o Organization and Planning.

* If you have ambition, you are willing to work very hard, and you are willing to keep learning, you can rise to the top of any profession you have a modicum of talent for.

* If you want to be at your best you need to ensure there is a gap between where you are now and where you want to be; a gap that is not easy to cross. You need to spend some of your time striving to do what is difficult rather than simply trying to do everything that is easy.

* Our legacy in life is the things we create or the impression we leave on other people. Look to create something unique. Look to leave a positive impression.

* You are unique, and what you have to offer the world is unique. Do not try to be someone else; just be the best you that you can be. No one else can be you, and no one else can give to the world what you can. Don't waste the unique gift that only you can give to the world.

* Be an expert in something. You can't be an expert in everything, but you can be an expert in something. Being an expert in something gives you a competitive advantage in something. Moreover being an expert in something gives you a general credibility that goes far beyond whatever area it is you are an expert in.

* You have a duty to yourself, your family, and the world to do what you can to contribute.

* Don't judge yourself on the basis of your achievements, judge yourself on the basis of your intent and on how you live your life. If you have the intent to make the world a better place, and you live your life true to values compatible with making the world a better place, then you are living your life with as much purpose as those who more visibly achieve great things.

* Find significant meaning in loving those close to you. Don't allow yourself to drift apart from your family or once close friends. Relationships can sometimes be difficult and it is easy and very common for once close relationships to be either rent apart or be allowed to wither for relatively trivial reasons whereby both sides feel aggrieved about some issue and neither makes the move to bridge the opening gap. This is to the significant long term detriment of both parties. Be the one that bridges the gap. Be the one willing to make an apology, even if you don't think you ought.

Play to your Strengths

- Like it or not we live in a highly competitive world. Whilst we don't need to be eternally competing in terms of being the best when measured against other people, if we are to have a reasonably contented life we need to try to be the best we can be and that means making best use of our strengths and minimizing the consequences of our weaknesses.

- Playing to your strengths will help your general well-being. You do however need to understand what your strengths are: they are likely to be, but are not necessarily, what you are best at. Your strengths will generally be the things you feel energized by when applying them, the things you feel are 'the real you'. There are many online tests you can take to assess your general character strengths. Once you understand your strengths look for ways to frequently deploy and improve them.

- Find what you are passionate about and that is likely to be where your strengths lie, noting that your strengths are not just the skills and abilities you have now, but also the ones you are in a strong position to acquire. If you feel passionately about something then making the effort to improve your related strengths should come easy to you.

- Make a list of everything you are good at. We all have talents and skills we are good at. List them out. Even small things. And list out the things you consider yourself to be poor at. Then seek to build on your strengths, and to eliminate or go round the weaknesses that are preventing full application of your strengths.

- Look to be different, look to be unique, look for where you can make a difference. It is difficult to be better than everyone else in something lots of other people are trying to be the best in. However you can create your own niche that takes advantage of your unique set of strengths and passions and ways of resolving your weaknesses.

- Avoid situations that expose your weaknesses, except of course when you are deliberately seeking to learn to overcome them.

- We all have certain skills and abilities where we tend to be better than many others. This may come about because of inherited characteristics, or simply because we have made the effort to improve them. Look to continue to develop them and also look to find areas of life where you can exploit them.

- You can't learn everything so focus on learning and improving your skills in areas you have some ability in. Better to learn things you pick up relatively easily than struggle to learn things you are not well suited to and others will pick up much quicker than you will. Seek to exploit your areas of personal competitive advantage rather than simply become mediocre at things others will have a competitive advantage in.

- Understand and work around or compensate for your weaknesses. Don't let your weaknesses stand in your way. Stay away from endeavors where they are likely to hold you back. Note that you could work hard to overcome your weaknesses, and sometimes this might be worthwhile, but often your time is better spent further improving your strengths. A common way of compensating for weaknesses is to work with others who are strong where you are weak.

Sometimes Do Nothing

- Some problems will just work themselves out if you leave them alone. Whilst this should not be an excuse for not addressing issues that need to be addressed, sometimes it is best just to leave things for a while and see how they turn out. If they continue to get worse, then you can take action.

* Don't let your goals become a tyranny. You don't have to live your every moment focused on your goals. You need some time free from any specific focus in order to give your mind the opportunity to think creatively about things you might not have otherwise thought about.

* Don't get paranoid about optimizing every moment of your day. Sometimes you need to just sit around with nothing to do. Just appreciate being alive. Sit back and relax without it being some optimized relaxation event. Watch a bit of TV, read something. Don't feel as though your 'day off' has to be filled with leisure events.

* It is important to spend some time just 'being' as opposed to always 'doing'. Be capable of being at peace from time to time. Learn some simple meditation techniques for clearing your mind. Spend a little bit of time each day just sitting and clearing your mind, being at peace with yourself. Get up very early occasionally and listen to the early morning tranquility.

* Occasional indulgence in nostalgic thoughts is good for you. It helps you relax and keeps you connected with who you are.

* Sit peacefully and do nothing. For a while your mind is likely to chatter away to itself, but after a while you should feel an inner calm and more deeper thoughts should start to poke through which you would never hear amongst the noise of everyday life.

* To enter into a state of peace sit still, comfortably, eyes closed, listening. Imagine you are waiting for a particular sound. Imagine what the sound would be like, even though you are aware that you are not hearing it. Spend a few minutes in this state and you should find yourself feeling calmer and less stressed.

* Have a long relaxing bath. Try using oils or bubble bath, unless your skin is too sensitive. Have scented candles, a good read, and a fluffy towel. It works for men as well as women.

Daily Living

* Few of us come anywhere near close to exhausting our energies or our abilities. We can all achieve far more than we do.

* Develop routines for parts of your day, generally the early and late parts of the day. They will help ensure you get each day off to a good start and make good use of what is for many the most productive part of the day. They will help ensure you are aware of what is important for the day and help you focus on making progress on what is important rather than simply what imposes itself on you. Routine later in the day will help you take stock of the day and put it behind you whilst thinking about what is important for the next day. This can help you, and be part of helping you, relax before going to sleep.

* We all have our own niche within which we live and work. Be the best you can be within your niche.

* Read a lot. Read books, not just bits of newspaper articles and magazines. And read books on different topics and in different styles. It will give you lots of different perspectives on life.

* From time to time find a good book to enjoy. Reading a good book can be one of the best experiences you will ever have. Don't however be afraid to abandon a book you are not enjoying: don't feel compelled to read it until the end.

* Keep a diary/journal into which you write every day. Life goes by faster than you realize. Most people will struggle to remember much of their past lives. A diary will help you remember. Include both external and internal things. What is happening around you, what are you doing, but also what is dominating your thoughts.

The Bumper Book of Common Sense

* Write your own history. Write down what you can remember from your childhood. Time will pass and you will either forget much of your past life or bits will only occur to you from time to time. When you remember bits make a note of them and add them to your history.

* Get involved in sports or activities. Don't just watch on the TV. If a sport or activity piques your curiosity or interest go and get involved. Most sports and activities have places for beginners to get started. Being involved in sports or activities is enjoyable and relieves stress whereas watching TV doesn't.

* Get involved in community events or local clubs. You meet new people with some shared interests or goals. It helps you connect with what it is to be human, which is to engage in group activities. It provides you the opportunity to contribute openly and honestly without seeking reward.

* An appreciation of art in whatever form will add a significant extra dimension to your life and give your life more meaning.

* Learn to play a musical instrument. It involves lots of different parts of your brain.

* Be environmentally conscious. We have to share this world with billions of others, and everyone should do what they reasonably can in their own circumstances to help protect it, irrespective of what their neighbors are doing.

* For the most part you don't need lots of possessions. Possessions enslave us. And lots of possessions not only cost you money to buy but are a continual cost to maintain, insure, fix, and generally worry about when something happens to them. You've almost certainly got far more than you really need. Your lives are likely to be richer rather than poorer through having far fewer of them. Be happy with what you have and look to have a few quality possessions rather than lots of trash.

* The less you are wedded to luxuries the freer you are.

* Don't be obsessed by status and money. People who measure life's worth in terms of status or possessions or money are rarely happy.

* Be thoughtful, but not lazy; be humble, but not timid; be proud, but not arrogant; be kind, but not weak; be bold, but not a bully.

* Be good natured and kind most of the time. Pay people complements, let people in front of you in a queue if they appear in a rush, give up your seat on public transport if someone looks like they need it more than you, hold doors open for people, say thank you. There are a multitude of ways you can be kind to others. You and they will feel better for it.

* Do good deeds, anonymously if you can, or at least without any thought of return, whenever you can. Something simple like removing a brick from a cycle path could save someone's life. Why not do it?

* Be truthful and honest and caring, and you will be a more balanced and contented person.

* Do new things, try new foods, go to places you haven't been before. New experiences make your life feel fuller and help it seem longer. You will find lots of new things you enjoy and occasionally some you definitely don't, which you can put down to experience. However don't be continually seeking new thrills and intense excitements, which do little to widen your experiences. Don't be continually trying to seek out every more intensity in your experiences.

* Expect the unexpected. Prepare for future uncertainties by building in flexibility, such as having fall back options, taking precautions against certain possibilities which might have extreme consequences, and having some resources in reserve that can be readily brought to bear should they be needed.

* Use public transport from time to time, or all the time. It gives you a different perspective on life. You can read or write whilst on a bus or train. You may even get to talk to people.

* Life is not about your achievements; it's about your experiences. It's not the winning, it's the taking part. Enjoy life as you go along.

* There is little that is more worthwhile than shared experiences with those you love.

* Be curious and you'll never be bored.

* Be alive. Don't go through life as if in a drunken stupor. Be aware of yourself and notice the world around you. Most people notice very little. But with conscious effort you can become much more observant. Observe with all your senses, not just your sight. Listen and smell too. Practice explicitly describing the things you see and sense.

* Notice things. Look around you and test yourself on what you've seen. What color was …? What was … wearing? Are shoes shiny or scuffed? How did they wear their hair? What color eyes? What facial features? If you make the effort to notice things you feel more engaged with life.

* Do what you love doing. You can always find the time.

* Find a balance between doing and being. If you are forever doing and spend no time being then your life will just be eternally busy and largely meaningless. Find a balance between your outer world, where you interact with others, and your inner world where you reflect upon your own being and existence.

* Don't be forever trying to distract yourself from daily living and just being with yourself. You don't have to be forever seeking out new and more intense experiences and pleasures, and if you are you are at serious risk of moving on to harmful experiences and pleasures.

* Hobbies can be good for you. Something that you enjoy doing and you don't need to be continually worrying about how well you are doing. It helps reduce stress and can boost your creativity. You may well find yourself having lots of good ideas whilst engaged in a hobby. Keep any materials you need for your hobby neatly stored somewhere so you can get it out and start using it again quickly.

* Over indulgence in pleasure is as meaningless and as much a waste of your life as always working and never indulging in pleasure. We should take pleasure, but occasionally, when we can appreciate it and it creates good memories. Being drunk every night, or watching TV every night, brings us dull pleasure, but each day becomes much the same as any other, and to no good end.

* Look to limit treats to relatively rare occasions. Only then will you appreciate them and get real pleasure from them.

* Practice moderation in most things. It's ok to indulge yourself from time to time, but addictions and compulsions will usually cause serious problems.

* Don't worry about the little stuff, and get on and deal with the important stuff. Worrying about the little stuff saps the energy you need for dealing with the important stuff.

* Occasionally just go and do what you want to do, so long as it doesn't involve harming or potentially harming others and it keeps within the law. It is ok to be selfish from time to time, because you matter as well as other people. However there is no excuse for being selfish all the time or even particularly often. People who are generous are generally happier and more satisfied people.

* When you commit to living the life you want, luck and opportunity will be on your side. Welcome adversity as steps along the way and as an opportunity to grow and learn. Always be looking to

improve. Keep your sights firmly fixed on your goals albeit whilst retaining respect for others. Take charge of yourself. Dare to live.

Self-Talk

Why Self-Talk is Important?

* You live almost your entire life within the confines of your head. Life is what you think about most of the day.

* A person is what he thinks about all day long. New thoughts can remake you. You can alter your life by altering your attitude and by changing what you spend most of your time thinking about.

* You are what you allow your mind to let you be. You choose what thoughts you allow to dominate your mind. And you are defined by your dominating thoughts.

* You can change who you are. Just because you have done bad things in the past this does not make you a bad person who will continue to do bad things in the future. You can choose to be different principally through the way you choose to think of yourself. It is our ability to choose for ourselves, to be able to overcome our habits and 'natural tendencies', that make us human. You can become what you choose to be.

* If you feel a little bit ill, and you want to avoid doing something, you can convince yourself that the illness is real, and as a result you will feel, and quite probably be, much worse. On the other hand, if you feel a little bit ill, but there is something you really want to do, you'll convince yourself it is nothing, and for the most part it will be. Your mind cannot override all real illnesses, but it can override many minor ones.

* If you see yourself as having no control over your life, then you won't have. However if you see your life as being in your own hands then you will look for ways to achieve what you want to achieve, and rather than accept problems and constraints as limitations you will see them as problems to be overcome. Humans are brilliant problem solvers when they set their minds to it.

* Self-talk and autosuggestion are the means by which our conscious mind can influence our subconscious and thus our habits, instincts, and tendency towards action. Keep your goals at the forefront of your mind and your mind will subconsciously be looking for ways to help you move towards them.

What to Say to Yourself

* We have within us a voice which is often doubting us, holding us back, telling us we are too tired to do something, or that something is too difficult, or that it's ok to put something off for now because we can come back to it tomorrow. But we can talk back to that voice – tell it not to be ridiculous, or tell it you are going to do it anyway. You can take back control by talking to yourself about what you are going to do and arguing against your doubts.

* If you tell yourself you are very tired, you will feel tired. If you tell yourself you are happy and full of energy you are more likely to be. Our thoughts can seriously limit or enhance our energy for getting on and doing things, and for the most part under normal circumstances we can control our

thoughts. There are however limits and you will still need sleep for example, and sometimes it is best to take a break and a nap, but not for too long.

* Put a voice in your head that is confident and strong and positive and which replaces any nagging doubts.

* Learn to talk kindly to yourself rather than continually putting yourself down or thinking negatively about yourself. Be less judgmental towards yourself. How would you respond to a close friend who was putting himself or herself down. Be your own close friend. Rather than self-talk as a critic and disciplinarian in the light of self-control shortcomings, self-talk as a mentor and close friend.

* Regularly say to yourself: "I can do all things!" The "I" is a reminder that you take personal responsibility, the "can" is a positive assertion and mental attitude, the "do" is recognition that you are someone who takes action and gets things done, the "all" means you will tackle all that comes your way, and the "things" means it doesn't matter what it is. There are no problems or hurdles that you cannot tackle as best as they can be in the circumstances.

* Self-talk: "do it now", "do it now", "do it now", …

* Make up some affirmations that you regularly repeat to yourself: "I am highly capable and get on doing things when they need to be done." "I will do it now because it is the right thing to do right now"; "I am a good organizer and keep everything in its place." Affirmations are a way of speaking to your subconscious, which is susceptible to suggestion.

* You affect your sub-conscious through verbal repetition, and your subconscious affects how you behave.

* Autosuggestion isn't just about repeating mantras to yourself: you need to do so with emotion and self-belief. Your subconscious responds to emotions and feelings, not just words.

* It is useful to have certain regular reminders as part of your self-talk: 'smile', 'behave now', 'concentrate', and regularly say these to yourself and say them to yourself in response to certain external circumstances.

* When faced with something you know you ought to do, but are procrastinating over, tell yourself: 'I don't have to do this. I will choose to start now, or I will accept the consequences of delay.' You have the power of choice and thus responsibility for your own life.

* Replace self-talk about what you 'should do' or what you 'have to do' with talk about where you are trying to get to and the choices you are making in order to get there. When you talk to yourself about what you 'should do' or 'have to do' you are reinforcing the fact that you don't really want to do whatever it is, and you are creating a feeling of burden or guilt that you then rebel against. Much better to keep focused on your goals and the fact that you have the opportunity for moving towards them. Thus make your self-talk be about what you 'choose to do'.

* Instead of talking to yourself about what you should, must, or ought to do, talk to yourself about what the next specific thing you can get on with and the circumstances when you can do it. Instead of 'I must do …' say to yourself, 'Next time <circumstances> I will <specific action>.'

* An alternative to using 'I' in your self-talk is to use 'You', as in, for example: 'You can do this'. Try both and if one feels more motivating than the other use it.

The Importance of Positive Self-Talk

* We all talk to ourselves in our heads, but we aren't always conscious of what we're saying or how it's affecting us. Be aware of what you are saying to yourself.

The Bumper Book of Common Sense

* The average person talks to himself several thousand times a day, and 80% of it is negative. Ask yourself, 'Is this thought helping me or hurting me? Is it getting me closer to where I want to go, or further away? Is it motivating me, or blocking me with fear and self-doubt?'

* Most people's self-talk is negative: doubts and fears, imagining the worst, reliving mistakes and failures, being annoyed at other people, general worrying. When not thinking negatively, thoughts are often confused, or fantasies not relevant to real life. Frequently the same thoughts go through our head hundreds or thousands of times. In such ways people are wasting 90% or more of their waking lives. Work at replacing negative thoughts and emotions with positive ones. It may take time, but keep trying. Your relationships with others and your general level of happiness will improve.

* Continual negative thinking has a physiological effect on your brain that makes you less able to think effectively.

* Don't compare yourself negatively to other people. We all have different qualities and skills. When comparing ourselves negatively to others we are usually comparing ourselves with the best in other people, with some ideal composite of others, not with other people as individuals in the round.

* When unpleasant thoughts come into your mind remember you don't need to accept or dwell on them, though you may want to problem solve things that worry you.

* Banish any negativity from your self-talk, either negativity about yourself, or negativity about others close to you. Negativity is like a sore that you need not have. If you let it, it will trap you for years, possibly your whole life, and it is of your own making.

* Don't let negative thoughts remain in your mind. Drive them out with positive thoughts.

* Don't let your mind wear itself out worrying or on non-productive thoughts. Put it to use thinking about how to handle things, motivating you, generally putting you into productive creative moods. Or empty your mind to let productive thoughts pop into your head.

* We all live to a greater or lesser extent in a fantasy world. Choose a fantasy world that helps you move forward in your life.

* It is important to be positive in your thinking. Believe things will turn out well. However this doesn't mean ignoring that things might go wrong. We should think about what things might go wrong in order to plan for dealing with them, or for taking action to mitigate against them going wrong.

* Forgive yourself for not being perfect and for your past wrong doings. It is what you think and do now that matters now.

* If you believe you can't do something, ask yourself if the same would be true of someone who is highly effective. Think of some role models, people you admire, people who get on and do things. Tell yourself that if that person can do it, so can you. Get on and do it.

* If you want a positive and fulfilling life you need a positive mindset. In order to think positively, you must replace the negative thought processes that are running through your mind and replace them with positive ones. Moreover it is not difficult to do, it is just a habit to get into.

Personal Characteristics and Behavior

We are able to Modify our Characteristics and Behavior

* Our personal characteristics are not fixed. We can change them if we want to. It may not be easy, and it won't happen suddenly, but we can do it if we want to do it. We can change our personalities and our characteristics through changing our behavior. And we can change our behavior through becoming and being aware of the behavior we want to change from and being clear about the behavior we want to change to. Then be continually looking to suppress the behavior you are changing from and adopting the behavior you are changing to.

* The more we act in a certain way the more the behavior becomes ingrained and the more we continue to act that way. We can change an automated behavior by deliberately and consciously acting in a different way, for a month or so, until the new behavior becomes automatic.

* Being a pessimist or an optimist is a choice we make rather than an unchangeable personal characteristic. Whilst we may be instinctively pessimistic, we don't need to remain so.

Always be Looking to Improve

* Strive to fulfill your potential. Most people fail to do so. Be different to most people.

* Be alert to the opportunities that exist, wherever you are, to improve and to practice your thinking and other skills.

* As you go through life you can and should be always trying to be a better person by learning from others and by learning from your own and others mistakes. You should always be tinkering with your life.

* Take responsibility. Blaming others does not help you move forward. Nobody cares about your excuses and your complaints.

* Take responsibility for what you can do something about, albeit don't let others unfairly blame you. Take responsibility for your own life choices and actions.

* Don't wait for others to determine who you are, based on their impressions and opinions of you; decide for yourself. Other people don't really know what's inside of you, or what your potential really is. Whilst positive reinforcement from others is welcome, it shouldn't be what dictates what you become. You should dictate what you become.

* If you want to see the world in a different way, you need to change yourself. If you change your attitudes and behavior you will see the world as a different place.

* You are unlikely to improve your circumstances if you don't first improve yourself – in terms of skills and capabilities and in terms of attitudes and thoughts.

* On balance your own competitive advantage in the world is best served by capitalizing on and improving on your strengths than on improving on things you are not so good at, though there may be some weaknesses that you do need to overcome in order to avoid squandering gains from your strengths. Being very good at one thing is generally of more value than being mediocre at lots of things.

* It's ok, and even a good thing, not to be always trying to be the best in everything. But you should try to be best in something.

* Be continually looking to improve yourself. There are small and big ways you can improve: do both. Many small improvements, over time, add up to very significant big improvements, without necessarily a lot of noticeable effort. And you should be continually working on any shortcomings

The Bumper Book of Common Sense

– procrastination, poor organization, indecisiveness, laziness, negative self-talk, etc. - or at least those that you feel are holding you back from what you want to be or where you want to go. Over time however what you perceive to be these shortcomings should change as you make improvements and as you progress with your goals into more challenging areas.

* Be wary of theories that promise effortless success. Gurus are everywhere and there are captive audiences for those who preach simplistic solutions. However most supposedly new theories are just variances of old ones repackaged with fancy names and dressed in new clothes. Whilst the gurus can readily find examples of those who have succeed in applying their new ideas, there will be many who have tried and failed who don't get a mention.

* Don't be lazy in your thinking. Be curious and inquisitive. Look to ensure you understand arguments before you come to a conclusion. Ask questions of others to help improve your understanding.

* We get physically stronger by placing physical demands on our body. Similarly we can develop mental toughness by dealing with difficult or challenging circumstances.

* There is little point in getting stressed about what you cannot do anything about. However don't accept circumstances you are not happy about too readily. We are often able to do more than we think we can. Be aware of the fact that most progress comes about as a result of individuals not accepting things as they are and seeking to do something about it.

* Learn to be flexible. "You can't change the wind, but you can adjust your sails to reach your destination." Look to adapt yourself to circumstances. Look to learn or know about a large repertoire of approaches and techniques for making decisions, solving problems, making plans, communicating, etc.. Choose the approach or approaches that best fits the particular situation.

* Learn to be creative. There are many opportunities that derive from thinking about things differently to the way other people are thinking about them. Being creative is far more a learned skill than it is an inherent ability.

* Identify specific qualities that annoy you in others and then work to ensure you yourself don't have or exhibit those qualities. It is not uncommon that we do exhibit the very qualities we dislike in others.

* We will have been wrong in the past because we may not have had or understood all the relevant facts, or because our decision making or problem solving skills were not as good as they could have been. Refusing to admit we could have been wrong is refusing to admit information can be wrong or misunderstood or taken out of context and refusing to admit our decision making and problem solving skills could ever be improved: neither of which is true.

* Have the strength of mind to change your mind and admit you have been wrong in the past. You will have been wrong in the past, and it is a question of whether or not you are willing to admit it or not. If you are, then you have the opportunity to be less wrong in the future. If you are unwilling to admit it, then you will continue to be just as wrong in the future.

* Sometimes we know we did the wrong thing. Often this will be when we didn't do something when we know we should have: other people would probably not have noticed, but we noticed. Or we may have reacted to someone in an inappropriate manner, or we let frustration or some other negative emotion get the better of us. When you become aware of having done something you wish you'd done differently, reflect on it for a while. Don't be annoyed at yourself, after all what has happened has happened, rather thing through the specific circumstances and strongly imagine yourself deciding differently should similar circumstances arise in the future.

* If you fail in something, don't get down about it. Look to understand what you might have done to better succeed, and move on. It can feel quite devastating at the time, but if you learn from it and move on, you will look back on it as part of the normal process of learning.

* Once a week reflect on what in the past week didn't go as well as you would have liked. Maybe something you failed to do or a mistake that you made. What could you have done differently or better? Write down your thoughts and your commitment for doing things differently in the future. If you spend a bit of time on this each week you will be continually improving and bettering your chances of future success.

* Some important behaviors to cultivate and learn for those who work primarily with their minds:
    o Be able to remain relaxed in the light of lots of inputs;
    o Be able to sort through ambiguous instructions to determine what needs to be done.
    o Be able to spot and act on issues before they become a crisis;
    o Be able to adapt rapidly to changed circumstances or to the realization that things are not as expected;
    o Be able to adapt when things go wrong or there are significant obstacles;
    o Be able to work well with everyone and anyone;
    o Be able to renegotiate agreements;
    o Be able to effectively manage your energy through the day.

* Some important behaviors and ways of seeing the world to cultivate and learn for those who wish to be at peace with themselves and with the world:
    o Accept reality without judging it. The world is as it is, accept it or do something about it;
    o Accept people as they are rather than wishing they were different;
    o Don't get annoyed at your own shortcomings. Try to do something about them, but don't get annoyed about them;
    o Tackle and deal with problems, don't run away from them;
    o Be open and honest with the possible exception of when you know it might hurt someone for no good gain;
    o Be open to and occasionally seek out challenges. Don't back away from them;
    o Feel comfortable being on your own from time to time;
    o Accept that all humans are in a sense equal and have the right to be treated decently;
    o Appreciate the little things in life. Be aware of the world around you;
    o Have your own sense of right and wrong and use it to guide your life. It doesn't have to be the same as those around you;
    o Don't be afraid to go against the tide. You don't need to rebel against everything, but nor do you need to accept what the majority believe about everything.

Understand Yourself

* Be aware of your own strengths and weaknesses. Make a list of them. You will interact far more effectively with the world if you play to your strengths and avoid circumstances that bring out your weaknesses. Note however that what you might think of as a weakness may be more of a personal characteristic and in most circumstances may not be a problem, and certainly not something that should inhibit you during most everyday situations.

* Be aware of your habits and tendencies. If you are conscious of them you will from time to time be able to stop yourself automatically doing things that you know you will regret later.

* Accept that you have prejudices, biases, and a tendency to stereotype. It is a part of how our brains work. However in accepting it, you can also be aware that they can lead you astray, and thus make the conscious effort to compensate.

* Distinguish between what you can't do, because they are well beyond your physical or mental capabilities, and things you haven't done because you haven't learnt how to do them. Many people confuse the two and describe them both as things they can't do. However many things that one person would say they can't do, and thus won't make the effort to do, another person would simply get on and try to do, and will eventually succeed.

* Be realistic about the commitments you make, to yourself and to other people. Continually making commitments that you then fail to keep can be very wearing. Don't commit to things you are unwilling to go out of your way to get done.

* People are frequently overoptimistic about their future personal performance predictions, and take on more than they are capable of doing. Learn to be realistic about what you are able to do. By all means be challenging, but be realistic. A particularly common situation is that whilst people set a target that would be readily achievable if it was the only thing they had to do, is not achievable given the other demands on their time.

* Acknowledge you are not perfect, and be willing to show humility. You make mistakes. Your balancing of probability is sometimes inappropriate. Your mental models of how the world works could always be a bit better. You believe some things that are not true. There are many things you don't know. The average person knows less than 0.0001% of the available knowledge in the world. You may know a bit more than the average, but every other adult knows some things that you don't. If you find yourself believing that you are always right then take this as a warning sign that you are more closed minded than you ought to be. You should always be willing to adjust your beliefs and opinions based on new information or new arguments; and if you find you never do this, the problem is with you, not with the rest of the world.

* Reflect on yourself and your circumstances from time to time. Disassociate yourself from the immediacy of your actions or thoughts and just be aware of yourself as one person amongst billions. Feel a contentment at being, and determine whether you are where you want to be or could reasonably expect to be in life. If not determine what you can and will do about it.

Be Curious and Open Minded

* Be curious and inquisitive. The world is a fascinating place and you should have a sense of wonder about it. And the more we know the more interesting it becomes. Take an interest in a wide range of topics and you will never be bored.

* Engage when reading or listening or watching something. Take notes, do drawings, think about what you are seeing or hearing.

* When most people call themselves open-minded what they mean is that they respect the right of others to have ideas different to their own. However being open-minded also means having an attitude of distrust towards our own ideas, and actively taking an interest in anything that might help us improve or modify them, or better still enable us to discard them for something better.

* Develop a general insight into topics by being open minded about them and reading and listening to all sides of the arguments, for and against. There are usually multiple sides to an argument or story. Insight comes from having a multi-viewpoint understanding rather than simply a prejudiced one-sided view. Your insight may still lead you to a give viewpoint, but it should be based on recognizing there are other sides to the argument, and appreciating that others have a good reason for holding them.

* A characteristic of open-mindedness is a general willingness to more readily accept statistical evidence rather than rely on personal experience or anecdotal evidence.

* Be independent. Think for yourself about important issues. Don't believe everything you read. Don't conform to the priorities, values, and perspectives of others unless you are sure you agree with them.

* Be open about not knowing something. When we pretend we know something it creates a more stressful situation – we become afraid we might get found out. Generally it is better to be open and then we can learn something. However this needs to be kept within reason. It is not appropriate to be continually interrupting conversations you are involved in; people will soon be looking to avoid having conversations with you.

* Be willing to change your mind, where appropriate, in the light of new evidence, changed circumstances, or just the realization you got it wrong.

* Have a tolerance for ambiguity and for complexity. By all means try to resolve ambiguities and understand complexity, but not through oversimplification or prejudicial assumptions. We should see ambiguity and complexity as challenges and opportunities to better understand the world, not as threats to be responded to with intolerance and bigotry. If we can't resolve the ambiguity or understand the complexity, then we should simply accept it.

* Be open to other ideas. You are not a god who magically knows everything and is right in everything you think about. On the other hand don't wander around with eternal self-doubt. Have ideas around which you base your life but always be open to other ideas that might help you modify or change them.

* Being open-minded does not mean you need to be indecisive. You can act with purpose on the basis of what you believe to be the best information you have, without having to convince yourself it is absolutely right.

* It takes effort to remain open minded, particularly under difficult circumstances. You may pride yourself on being open minded, and it may be that you are, but that doesn't mean you always are or will always remain so. Beware of getting arrogant about your own open mindedness.

* Be wary of difficult circumstances and a sense of urgency. They make it very difficult to avoid jumping to conclusions.

Be Aware of your Surroundings and Circumstances

* Be aware of your surroundings and what is going on around you, and the fact that you might be impacted by what is going on. This includes your immediate surroundings but also the wider 'what is going on in the world' surroundings.

* Be aware of the wider context and potential implications of what you do, and try to take this into account. Ask yourself from time to time whether what you are doing will have an impact on or consequences for others beyond what is immediately obvious.

* Try to be well read and know what is going on around you and in the world in general. You should know a little about a lot and a lot about a little. Don't try to know a lot about a lot because you will fail and find your energies dissipated to little good value.

* Be aware that there are often different perspectives on something, and those with different perspectives may come to different conclusions. Often different perspectives are not either right or wrong, they are simply different. Rather than reject perspectives different to your own seek to understand them.

The Bumper Book of Common Sense

* The better you understand someone else's point of view the better you are able to interact with them to mutual benefit. It will also help you to predict how they will react in particular circumstances and thus help you to prepare your own responses.

* Appreciate that your decisions, actions and words have ramifications. You might not be able to fully appreciate or understand the ramifications all the time, but sometimes it is pretty obvious. If they are the ramifications you want, then well and good. If not, maybe you should think again. There are many different ways of getting to an end point. You don't need to run over everything in your path to get there, and if you do try to do so, don't be surprised if you meet resistance and obstacles.

* Be discerning. All things are not equal. Appreciate things that are good and be critical of things that are bad.

* Be ready to take advantage of opportunities that may arise. For example, in football, a striker who follows up on a strike on goal just in case there is a rebound, will be ready to take advantage when this does occur. Whilst it might be unlikely to occur on any given occasion it is likely to happen sufficiently often to significantly improve his scoring rate.

Be Positive and Confident and Appreciative of Being Alive

* Try to develop a true sense of joy at being in the world. Appreciate the wonder of being alive and feel it as an uplifting sense of being within yourself. Admire without desire.

* Adopt a positive hopeful attitude. You will get far more done if you are positive and hopeful about what you are doing or need to do, and look to make the best of whatever circumstances you find yourself in. Don't be unrealistic about what you can do, but you should certainly err on the side of believing that you can do things, because if you make the effort and are willing to tackle the adversities you probably can.

* Whilst being positive is an important part of success and getting things done, don't use it as a substitute for working hard and developing your skills and abilities. None of us would want to be under the knife of a surgeon with a positive attitude but without adequate training.

* Walk tall, walk straight, and look the world right in the eye, and you'll feel much more confident.

* Confidence arises from knowing you are prepared for the worst, and then focusing on doing your best.

* Be assertive when you need to be, though never aggressive. Being assertive is acknowledging that you have your rights and you have a right to state them. Not being aggressive means you acknowledge that other people have rights, and the right to state them.

* Be constructive rather than destructive. Being skeptical is for the most part being destructive, though sometimes it is appropriate: some ideas do not deserve to survive and can and should be taken apart through skepticism and asking why. However it is all too easy to be continually skeptical and negative. Some ideas are the best to be had and focus should be on improving them in a constructive manner rather than simply destroying them and leaving nothing in their place.

* Don't be a whiner; someone always finding fault and saying what's wrong, but never coming up with solutions that you are willing to run with yourself. If you see things that are wrong, think about solutions that you can engage in, not simply solutions for someone else to have to implement.

* Be grateful for what you have and your circumstances. Much of what you take for granted would be considered real treasures by many others. Your circumstance could almost certainly be a lot worse.

* Be grateful when others do something for you. Be sure to at least say a thank you to people who help you.

* Be happy in your life. Whilst it is a good thing to be continually trying to improve and making the best of things, don't be in a continual state of unhappiness about yourself and your circumstances.

* See negative thoughts as an opportunity. They arise from a problem. Problems are opportunities. They are challenges. Opportunities and challenges are what inspire or force us to develop and grow. Thus tackle problems head on with a positive attitude and the knowledge that you are going to get the best you can out of them.

* Take pride in the things you do well, and try to do everything you do well. Including the little things.

Relating to Others

* Be compassionate. Be quick to forgive others; though don't let yourself be taken advantage of.

* Have respect for others. They are living thinking feeling human beings just like what you are. And just because they think different to you, doesn't mean you should think of them as being wrong or mistaken. Having respect means respecting their right to think differently to you.

* Behave with integrity. Don't make promises that you can't keep, and keep the promises you make, if at all possible. If you can't, then tell people and explain to them why.

* Practice what you preach. Be honest in your dealings with other people, and do not deliberately mislead them. Except in so far as you genuinely have their interests at heart.

* Care about other people and behave in ways that benefit them. Our lives don't really make much sense without other people. We are happier when we know other people care about us; and they won't unless we care about them. People get more satisfaction out of having done something for someone else than having done something for themselves. However, of course, you can't please all the people all the time.

* Cooperate with others. We get far more done when working cooperatively with others. It isn't always easy working with others since other people often have their own views. However with most people we can develop healthy working relationships that suit both our and their ends. To do so however we need to be flexible and willing to give way on things that are not so important to us, but also assertive when we need to be about the things that are important to us. We then need to be creative about finding solutions that enable us to work with others to satisfy our ends in a mutually beneficial way.

* Treat others fairly. You should not be looking to take advantage of other people. You may feel as though you have a right to take advantage of gullible people so long as you stay within the law. You may even be able to rationalize it to yourself through thoughts such as if you don't do it, someone else will. However there are many vulnerable people and taking advantage of them is simply loathsome behavior.

* Be generous both in terms of helping others and in terms of your thoughts about others. You will get great satisfaction and feel better if you give to others who are in need, albeit in a way that doesn't hurt their pride. You should also give others the benefit of the doubt in terms of how you think about them.

The Bumper Book of Common Sense

* Be a volunteer. It is a great way of making new friends and generally helps you feel more positive about yourself.

* Be kind. If you get the opportunity to help others, do it.

* Think positively of others and give them the benefit of the doubt. You can't expect others to think better of you than you do of them.

* There is no need to be deliberately cruel to anyone or living creature. Sometimes it may be appropriate to get rid of an animal pest; but you can generally do it without necessary cruelty. Animals feel pain and can suffer. There is no excuse for deliberately killing anything, not even an ant, without good reason.

* Don't be envious of others. You do not know their circumstances. How they have worked to gain what they have. What misfortunes they may need to bear or have borne. Where their circumstances are leading them. Focus on your own situation and seek to avoid unhelpful and demoralizing comparison with others.

* Don't get arrogant, or think of yourself as better than others. And remember that the graveyard is full of indispensable men and women.

* Accept responsibility for helping certain others develop. This would certainly include your own children, but it may also include others that you might feel some sense of responsibility for, or who you know looks up to you.

* If you want to change others then you are more likely to do so by acting as a role model rather than by actively trying to push them to change.

* Develop and show empathy. Empathy is about recognizing and to some extent sharing other people's feelings, feeling as they do, without judging them. We all have a significant ability to be empathic, but most people do not recognize it because they let their own feelings and emotions dominate. If you learn to suppress the extremes of your own feelings you will become more tuned in to the feelings of others. Do however be careful you are not just 'assuming' other people's feelings: it is easy to misread others, and for example assume someone with a straight face is in a bad mood, whilst they may simply be in a reflective mood. A couple of words with them should enable you to quickly tell the difference.

* Have and show consideration for others. Being considerate means being aware that your words and actions might impact someone else, and modifying your words and actions in advance to reduce or eliminate the negative impacts on others, even when inconvenient to yourself.

* Be relatively open about what you want to do, what you are trying to do, and about how you feel. You know all these things, but others don't. Many of us behave as though we assume other people see the world from our perspective; because it is obvious to us we implicitly believe it should be obvious to them. But it isn't. Do not expect people to help you, or to be sympathetic to you, or to respond to you in a way you believe to be appropriate, if you haven't told them about what you are trying to do or the state you are in.

* Be wary of being too vociferous about your views. There is every possibility they may change in the future. If you are the sort of person who never changes their views then it is likely you are a closed minded bigot and others will almost certainly see you that way.

Self-Motivation (aka Willpower)

What is Self-Motivation?

* Self-Motivation, also termed willpower or self-control, is the self-discipline to do what you know you should when you should, despite having a desire to do otherwise.

* Self-motivation is being able to work now for reward later.

* A major part of self-discipline is an ability to delay self-gratification and to avoid impulses that are contrary to our long-term interests.

* Self-motivation is about doing the harder but more valuable thing, when you have the option of doing the lazy or easy thing.

* Self-motivation is what induces us to take action when we have the option not to.

* Self-motivation applies to control of our thoughts, control over our emotions, control of our impulses, and control over our actions.

* Our levels of willpower change during the course of the day. A state of low willpower is termed psychologically as ego depletion. Signs of ego depletion, and thus the likelihood of having poor self-control, include a stronger reaction to things, with stronger positive or negative feelings, and stronger desires. Thus you have periods where you have both less self-control but also stronger desires.

Why you should Look to Improve your Self-Motivation

* Few people in life get anywhere near realizing their full potential. For many, this is a regret in later life; and a continual pain as they pass through life. True, you can always blame circumstances, how you never had or have the breaks or the opportunities or the luck or the support. You can always consider yourself a victim of the vagaries of life. But the fact is we all have it within ourselves to achieve a tremendous amount and be happy doing so. Our success or failure in doing so is largely down to us, and not circumstances or other people. Our success or failure is down to our willpower, and significantly increasing our willpower is something we can all learn.

* The world is an amazing place, if you can rise to its challenges. With self-discipline you can.

* With a strong personal motivation you can achieve almost anything you want from life.

* People who are able to exert self-control are generally happier, healthier, able to deal with life's downs, get on better with other people, do better in their careers, and live longer than those less able to.

* Great ideas are nothing without the self-motivation and perseverance to follow them through to implementation.

* Knowledge of what we ought to do is rarely the problem. Good self-control enables us to do the things that we know ought to be done when they ought to be done. This leads to less stress and generally a happier more satisfying life.

* Increased willpower leads to increased stamina.

The Bumper Book of Common Sense

* The ability to delay instant gratification and focus more on long-term success is vital for achieving important aims and ambitions.

* Good self-control is the one personal characteristic most believe they lack, but would like to have.

* Most of our large problems arise from not facing up to and dealing with small problems when they arise.

* A lack of self-control, willpower, underlies many problems people have. We are surrounded by temptations, and it is often difficult to resist. People are continually struggling with desires that are tempting them to do the things they know they ought not.

* Those who lack self-discipline lack freedom. They are unable to control their lives by their own choices and thus they have their lives dictated by other people.

* People tend to overestimate their levels of self-control and underestimate their vulnerabilities. You need to work to improve your self-motivation and self-discipline simply to get to the level you believe you are already at.

Self-Motivation is Like a Muscle

* Willpower is not a personality trait which you either have or haven't got. We all have willpower, and how strong it is is dependent upon a range of factors such as how well we sleep, our diet, our general state of health, and the extent to which we have purposefully set out to strengthen it.

* We can develop and improve our self-control, our willpower. Willpower is like a muscle that we can strengthen through exercise and practice, and which grows weaker if we don't exercise or apply it. Resist temptations. Do things you don't want to do. If you always look to take the easy route you will never develop self-control. Some general self-control exercises:
    o If you are right handed, use your left hand for certain tasks;
    o Ensure you thoroughly brush and floss your teeth morning and evening;
    o Do some regular exercise routine;
    o Improve your posture in terms of sitting up straight;
    o Always be neat and tidy;
    o Keep a record of all your bad habits during the day, noting them down as or shortly after they occur;
    o Stop yourself from using certain swear or inappropriate words;
    o Always deal with chores, such as the washing up, straight away.

* Willpower will be strengthened through persistent effort to do so. Just as it takes time to build up a weak muscle, so will it takes time to build up your levels of self-control. You would not expect a weak muscle to suddenly be strong simply because you started to exercise it, so don't get disheartened when your willpower doesn't either. But if you keep at it, if you persist, if you focus on initial small victories that you can build on, you will eventually succeed.

* Self-control can become a habit.

* By improving your will power for a particular task you are improving it in general, and thus improving it for all sorts of different tasks.

* In order to practice small acts of willpower you need to get into the habit of noticing what you are about to do and doing the more difficult thing instead. Choosing something relatively trivial is a good way to start, something that won't overwhelm you.

* If you've been struggling with something, and successfully applying your willpower to it, it is normal to find yourself weakened later on. Thus people who have made extensive use of their willpower during the day find it difficult to continue to do so in the evening. They thus become more short tempered with their families and have a greater tendency just to flop down in front of the TV. Some tactics to mitigate against this include:
    o Manage your glucose to ensure you have some in your brain later in the day;
    o Walk away from any emerging arguments later in the day before they become severe;
    o Keep temptations at arm's length later in the day;
    o Develop automated responses for dealing with temptations;
    o Develop good habits for later in the day which take little effort to implement.

* If we have struggled and won a battle to overcome our desires through the application of willpower, we are often in a weakened state and less able to overcome the next desire or temptation that comes along. Thus we are often well disciplined with our eating habits during the day but find ourselves unable to resist temptation late in the day.

* We have the same stock of willpower for all different types of tasks. Once it's depleted it's depleted for any tasks requiring it. Signs of depleted willpower include:
    o Things bothering you more than they should;
    o Feeling things more strongly than usual;
    o Finding it more difficult to make your mind up about even simple things;
    o Finding it difficult to exert yourself.

* Making decisions depletes your willpower, and makes you more susceptible to temptations. Don't rely on willpower later in the day – structure your environment so you don't need to employ willpower.

* At times when we have to exhibit high levels of self-control, such as students during exam times, other aspects of our lives requiring self-control suffer – for example our diet, or exercise, or ability to keep things tidy.

* Your willpower will be lower when you are anxious, angry, depressed, or stressed. Reducing your stress levels will increase your willpower.

* Stress impairs willpower. It leads to short term focus, whereas willpower is about being able to focus on the long term. People who are stressed are more likely to indulge in unhealthy foods, have bad habits, use drugs, drink heavily, etc, etc. Managing your stress is very important if you want to improve your willpower.

* People who suffer continual pain will tend to find themselves with a regular shortage of willpower. This is a major contributor to the reason they are often bad tempered, as their minds are engaged in a continual struggle to ignore the pain.

Manage and Take Account of your Energy Levels

* It is important to manage your energy levels during the day. Certain things will drain you as you go through the day, but it is important to also be able to top yourself up so that you still have the energy to do useful things later in the day.

* You can better manage your energy through having a healthy breakfast. Examples of a healthy breakfast include:
    o High fiber cereals and skimmed milk;

The Bumper Book of Common Sense

- o   Porridge or muesli with skimmed milk;
- o   Low-fat or nonfat yogurt with fruit;
- o   Peanut butter on wholemeal bread;
- o   Fruit smoothies (with skimmed milk);
- o   Bran muffins;
- o   Oatmeal with raisins or berries or walnuts;
- o   Hard-boiled egg with wholemeal toast;
- o   Grapefruit.

* You can better maintain your physical and mental energy through having small and healthy snacks during the day as opposed to having a big meal in the middle of the day or by not eating at all. However watch you don't end up eating a large number of calories.

* Negative emotional thoughts will significantly decrease your energy. Tackle them and don't let them linger. If you find them coming into your head take some deep breaths and seek to replace them with positive thoughts. Do something active.

* Except where circumstances significantly change you should look to do things when you'd committed to do them. Anything not done at the time you'd committed to having it done saps your energy, even if it is relatively unimportant. If you are unable to do something when planned, re-plan it or decide it doesn't need doing at all, rather than just leave it as something undone.

* Lack of, or inadequate, sleep will seriously impair your mental energy, your willpower. Get plenty of sleep during the night, and during the day a short nap can restore focus and willpower. Not too long though, about 15-30 mins max.

* Do your most important work of a mental nature early in the day when you have the most mental energy and willpower.

* Our brain manages its energy levels, and seeks to conserve mental energy when our glucose levels are low or decreasing. At such times you are more likely to give in to temptation and immediate gratification. You are also more prone to taking risks when glucose levels are low.

* When your mental energy levels are low your decisions will tend to be based on short-term gains and delayed costs. You are also more likely to stick with the status quo and less inclined to compromise. If forced to make decisions under these circumstances look to compensate by giving increased weight to longer-term consequences and being clear about the reasoning behind your decisions.

* When your willpower starts to drop, focus your thoughts on the benefits of doing the right thing. Self-talk to tell yourself that the future will be better through doing doing the right thing now, that your life will be more worthwhile, and that you will feel much better.

* Continually trying to do what is difficult now helps make it a habit and strengthens your future willpower.

* You can top up your brain glucose levels through occasional high fiber snacks and fruit and vegetables, albeit keep an eye on your calories.

* Sweets and soft drinks and junk foods can give you a boost which for a short time makes your brain feel alert. However it is only for a short time and you will quickly find yourself feel drowsy not long after.

* Coffee with caffeine can help give you a boost, however only up to a point. Once you've had about 4 cups in a given day you will not be getting much more of a boost and it can start to have a

negative effect. Much more than this can also disrupt your sleep and you should avoid taking caffeine after about mid-afternoon.

* Fatigue, whether physical or mental, is, initially at least, simply our brain's automated attempt to conserve energy. We are actually capable of far more if we can motivate ourselves through the fatigue, as long distance runners regularly do. We are capable of going further and continuing for much longer than our initial feelings are suggesting. Of course if you keep going you will eventually reach true physical or mental limits. But these are often a long way the other side of the initial sense of fatigue.

* Trying to sustain challenging efforts over a long period of time will be difficult or even impossible without our managing our energy levels. We need to mix up periods of sustained effort, with periods of moderate effort, and periods of complete rest. For example, if you are working for months or years on challenging projects, then a weekly pattern of a couple of sustained effort days, a couple of moderate effort days, a light effort day, and a day of complete rest may be appropriate. You will need to find your own effective mix, but don't be tempted to just keep pushing for the sustained effort all of the time. You will burn out, such that in the long term you are less effective than you would have been with a more balanced approach.

* The ability of our brain to cope and effectively undertake different tasks undergoes cyclic rhythms. A daily cycle rhythm is called a circadian rhythm, but there also exist rhythms that repeat several times during the day or night, known as ultradian rhythms, and those that extend over several days or longer such as a month or a year, called infradian rhythms. As a result both of our daily rhythms, and ones that occur a number of times during the day, we will find ourselves better able to focus and concentrate at certain times rather than at other times. It is worthwhile, within reason, trying to take advantage of your natural rhythms and make use of the times you are able to focus and concentrate to do more intellectually challenging tasks, and taking rests or doing simplistic tasks when you are less able to do so, or feel tired. You will need to understand your own body rhythms for yourself, which are mostly genetic, and learn when in the day you are most alert, and try to take advantage of it. The following are tips generally applicable, though don't take them as gospel, and if something different works for you do what works for you:

    o Most people are most mentally alert in the mornings;
    o Most people are at their physical peak in the afternoon, though there is generally a dip mid-afternoon;
    o In the evening both the mind and the body are generally relaxed;
    o The mind and the body are generally at their lowest between about 2am and 5am;
    o Don't despair if after you've mentally worked for a while, about 50 mins or so, your concentration starts to lapse: it is normal, take a break, and return to the task a bit later, after say 10 minutes or so.

* Develop tactics you can fall back on when your willpower has been depleted. Don't fall into the negative cycle of continually allowing yourself to fall victim of temptations later in the day due to depleted willpower and then simply beating yourself up about it. Be realistic about your falling mental energies and ability to resist temptations later in the day, and adopt tactics accordingly. Tactics include some degree of toping up of your glucose levels, removing temptations, having specific plans about what you will do rather than leave it vague, choosing things which are relatively easy to do, and doing things with other people in a low temptation environment.

* Avoid leaving yourself having to make choices later in the day, since it is likely your willpower will be relatively low and you are much less likely to make good decisions. If you have good intent for what you want to do later in the day, be clear about what it is you are going to do and when. Avoid for example leaving yourself with a choice about which of two good things you should do. You are far more likely to do neither than you would be if you were clear about the one good thing you are going to do.

* Develop good habits and good fixed routines that are automatic and thus take very little effort or self-motivation. This becomes particularly important later in the day.

Have and use Inspiring Goals

* Motivation requires purpose, it requires goals. You cannot be determined without being determined about something in particular. The more particular your goals, the more vivid they are, the more motivated you can potentially become. In the absence of clearly defined goals, we become attached to daily acts of trivia.

* Don't have too many goals. A few goals or even just one goal that really matters to you are of far more value than a large number of goals. You can do anything, but not everything.

* If you have a goal or a purpose that really inspires, you need never be bored again. Purpose gives you energy, and with the right purpose you should be using any spare time towards its achievement, either through planning, or developing supporting skills, or seeking out useful information, or through doing work towards its achievement.

* Have a big goal, something that you feel really strongly about, something you would feel really proud about achieving. Imagine yourself as having achieved it and feeling that pride, and carry it around with you. And ensure you make some progress towards your goal today. Something small, but something on the way. You only need make small steps; so long as you keep taking lots of them.

* Strive to be the best you can be in your particular niche, and set a goal to be so.

* A good source of inspiring goals is to find something you are dissatisfied with: something you know could be and should be better; something you can do something about. Get your emotions to work for you, in that the more strongly you feel about something, the stronger should be your motivation for doing something about it.

* The amount of willpower you are able to bring to bear to get something done is directly related to how committed you are to doing it. If you are not truly committed then do not expect to be able to call up significant willpower.

* Many of our difficulties with getting on with things arise as a result of lack of desire rather than lack of self-discipline per se. When faced with a task that you do not feel like doing, do not immediately assume it is simply about self-discipline. Instead, identify your underlying reason for needing to do the task. Tap into the motivations, emotions, and feelings that underpin the root cause reason the task needs doing in the first place.

* If you do not feel motivated by your goals, if you do not get a sense of inspiration and energy through thinking about your goals, then you have the wrong goals.

* If you have no goals or purpose it is little wonder you get bored and lack self-motivation.

* Set your intentions and your life will follow a path towards achieving them.

* We should have a convincing goal that is so compelling that we can call upon it to get us going in the morning, and to guide us away from the bad habit desires that loom up in front of us. Be very specific about the goal and ensure you are able to visualize it and write it down. If visualizing your goal does not significantly strengthen your resolve to get on with doing the right things then you need to work on strengthening the desire to achieve it, or find another goal.

* Where you have a goal or something to achieve focus most of your day-to-day visualization on successfully doing the things that will get you to your goal rather than simply daydreaming about having achieved your goal.

* Keep your long-term goals at the forefront of your mind. They help build up your immunity to temptations during the day. They should also help you decide what to do next on a regular basis, and also keep you open to relevant moments of opportunity that might just happen to pass by.

* If you've got something planned and scheduled then you are far more likely to get on and do it than if you just have some vague idea that you ought to do it sometime. Ensure you have regular planned times for progressing your goals. If you are not regularly moving towards your long-term goals, then you are moving away from them.

* Seek out accomplishments you can feel proud of: large and small. Get in the habit of setting and accomplishing challenging tasks. Keep a record of your accomplishments.

* Spend a few minutes at the end of each day to reflect on whether or not you have done something that day to take you nearer your goals. Be clear about what you can and will do the next day to take you just a little bit nearer.

* If you have something you really believe in you can often inspire others to help. Most people are quite happy to be led by others, and if you have a clear vision and are willing to lead you will not have too much difficulty finding people to follow you.

Take Inspiration from Others

* Look to find an opportunity to be with people who are significantly better than you at what you do or with people who are high achievers. Set aside any feelings of inferiority you might feel and allow yourself to be inspired by them. See what tips you can pick up from them, and feel uncomfortable about yourself to the extent that you are determined to move your game to the next level.

* Take inspiration from others, whether living or dead, whether real or fictional. You are the hero of your own life and there's no reason you can't learn from other heroes by trying to emulate them.

* You can envisage yourself as a type of hero to help you deal with certain circumstances. Many heroes in mythology, fiction or fact, have had to deal with adverse circumstances and came through. Homer's epic "The Odyssey" for example depicts the wanderings of a Greek warrior trying to find his way home. Vengeful gods dog his path at every turn, but he stays true to his course and eventually succeeds in reaching his destination. You can visualize your own experiences as an odyssey, a series of challenges to be overcome as you journey on to your destination.

* Reading about someone else's endeavors increases our desire to engage in similar endeavors. Thus read about those you admire and would like to emulate.

* Read inspirational stories. Read about people who have overcome adversity. Read about people who have achieved great success having started out with nothing very much. If you read the autobiographies or biographies of people who have succeeded despite difficulties you'll realize that many of them were people not unlike yourself.

* Regularly read inspiring motivation books or listen to audio or even attend seminars. The more you expose yourself to motivational material the more it will seep into you, and the more ideas you will come across that you can try out and occasionally find of real benefit.

* Being part of a social group in which members encourage each other can be a great motivator. Hang out with people who are enthusiastic and energetic: it is contagious. But do absorb their enthusiasm rather than simply feel bad about yourself for being less energetic.

* The best way to adopt a given behavior is to mix with people who already display that behavior.

The Bumper Book of Common Sense

* Ask yourself whether you would be proud or ashamed of your behavior in front of others. Visualize yourself being on hidden camera with an audience watching you.

* We are social animals, and we care about what others people think and know about us. We can make this a motivational tool by making visible to others how we are getting on doing the things we are trying to do, or not doing the things we are trying not to do. We are more likely to excuse our own shortcomings if we keep them to ourselves then if they are openly visible to others.

* People are less likely to give in to undesirable temptations if they are being watched. Thus those with religious beliefs or belief in some higher power are less likely to give in to certain types of temptation.

* Tell other people about what you are going to do by when, or better still give them a written copy of your commitment. Knowing that other people, particularly people we respect, know what we are trying to do, can bring to bear the very strong motivation of not wanting them to think less of us.

Self-Motivation is your own Responsibility

* We are totally responsible for our own sense of purpose.

* What you seek lies within yourself, not within others.

* We are all able to change our behavior if we choose. Our past failures and our current circumstances are no excuse. It is our conscious ability to choose that defines us as human beings.

* If you turn your work or other tasks into a playful challenge you will instinctively put in more effort through having higher energy levels and motivation. Set personal bests, aim at clear targets, compete with yourself and others. When things don't go well, rather than get depressed, rise to the challenge as you would if you were playing a game.

* Keep the resolutions you have already made rather than continually making new ones. Get into the habit of succeeding to do what you have set out to do rather than continually moving onto something else before you do.

* Where there is a will there is a way. Where there is no will there is usually an excuse.

* Be tough with yourself, be decisive, and accept full responsibilty for your actions and your inactions.

Get into the Right Mindset

* Motivation requires hope and expectation. Have something to strive for and believe you will get there.

* Our mindset has a significant impact on our behavior. If we have a fixed mindset whereby we believe we were born a certain way and that won't change, then it won't. However if our mindset is one that believes we can change, then we can. People with a fixed mindset tend to be black and white thinkers, and think in terms of winning and losing. For them it is the end result that matters. If they fail they think in terms of not being good enough or of circumstances having conspired against them, and they give up trying. People with a flexible mindset more readily acknowledge shades of grey and that it is the journey that is most important. They look to keep improving and are less stressed by failure, seeing it as a challenge to keep improving till they succeed.

* The outcome you expect is the outcome you get. Believe you are going to have a great day, and you probably will. Believe you will have a horrid day, and you probably will. Believe you are the sort of person that tackles and deals with problems and you will be. Believe you are overwhelmed and unable to cope and you will be.

* To achieve great things often requires great sacrifice.

* Don't expect to achieve great things without substantial effort. The more effort you put in the greater your chances of success.

* There are always hurdles to overcome if you are doing anything challenging or difficult. It's simply the way things are. Nothing to get down about or upset about. Simply things to work out how to deal with, and then tackle, adapting as necessary.

* Adversity is not something to get you down; it is something to raise you up. Adversity gives you opportunities to grow and to see things from a different viewpoint. Indeed it is often only in adversity that we see particular opportunities.

* Don't kid yourself that there is some future best time to get on with the things you need to get on with. The best time to get on with whatever needs to be done is as soon as you can, irrespective of whether or not you feel like it. Don't wait until you feel motivated to get on with what is important to you.

* Do the things you are afraid to do, assuming they are not unacceptably dangerous. You learn more rapidly and you get more opportunities when you move out of your comfort zone.

* Don't let the fear of failure hold you back, unless of course it is a rationale choice based upon the real damage the failure might do. Whenever we attempt something new or something difficult there is a significant risk of failure early on. It is an essential part of the learning process. If you hold back because of that fear you are cutting yourself off from that learning process.

* Do and fail and you will be better able to do next time. Don't do, then you'll never do.

* A burning desire and a definite plan will get most things done.

* Get into the habit of seizing any opportunity that comes your way. Any opportunity to be active, any opportunity to take responsibility, any opportunity to learn, any opportunity to try something new.

* Don't sit and wait for opportunities to come your way, go out and create them.

* Don't see most of what you want to do as difficult. It's simple. Just do it. Don't spend hours agonizing over whether to do something you know you should do. Just do it. It's simple. Tell yourself it's easy and it will be.

* Start your day with a couple of easy quick wins. Ticking off a couple of your to do items will set you up in a 'get on with it' mood that can help you get started on some of the bigger tasks.

* Do things that need doing straight away. You are more likely to succeed by taking action as soon as you see it needs doing rather than waiting and battling with yourself. Try to get into the habit of just getting on with doing the right things. See yourself as the sort of person that does.

* Doing something imperfectly is sometimes better than not doing it at all. Although sometimes if something can only be done imperfectly it should not be done at all.

* When you have a goal or target to achieve, you should approach it with a sense of urgency, and passion to get it done. Tasks are much easier if you approach them with a determination to get them done rather than with a reluctance.

The Bumper Book of Common Sense

* Make tasks harder or more challenging. You are often more motivated and involved in a difficult task than you are in an easy one. One way of making a task harder is to reduce the time you give yourself to do it; seek to complete tasks in half the time of your estimate of how long it should take.

* You need a still mind in order to exercise a strong will. It is difficult to act with purpose if your mind is full of turbulence.

* If you are able to focus on one thing at a time, without distractions, then there is little distinction between work and play, there is simply the now in which you are being and doing. That is why we are often efficient in getting something done at the last minute. It has got to the top of both our priority list and is both the most important and most urgent thing for us to do. We can have the same efficiencies if we can get into the totally focused mindset.

* Do what you are doing to the best of your abilities, putting all your effort and concentration into it, and be satisfied with that because you couldn't have done more.

* If your objective in any given circumstance is to try to do your best, then you can be confident you will do so. If your objective is to reach some level of achievement then you are likely to be anxious about your ability to do so. Always make your objective to be to try to do your best, and do so. Then simply deal with any consequences that arise.

* Have a timer handy. Tell yourself you are going to work on a project or task, and only that project or task, for a set amount of time. Set the timer and plug away at the task. When the timer goes off, pack it up for now and move on to the next project or task.

* You can't do everything. Get doing everything out of your head. It will paralyze you such that you do nothing. Focus solely on a something you can do. There's always something you can do.

* Don't focus on how far you have to go. Focus on having steps along the way and making progress towards the next step.

* We give up more often because we feel overwhelmed by what needs to be done rather than because we feel as though we can't do something in particular. Forget about all that needs to be done. Focus down on to the something that you can do. If it still seems too much then you haven't focused down enough, focus down still further until what you can do seems readily doable: then do it.

* Don't let thoughts about what you can't do stop you from getting on with what you can do.

* A small step in the right direction is better than no step at all, assuming the effort could not be better spent elsewhere.

* It's never too late to get involved. Don't hold back from doing something just because you could have done more. Doing something is always better than doing nothing.

* The brain loves questions and pays more attention when there are questions involved. Rather than simply telling yourself you must do something, such as 'I must eat better', ask yourself, 'what can I do today to eat a little better?'; or rather than simply saying to yourself 'I must get more exercise,' ask yourself 'How can I get a few more minutes of exercise today?' Questions set the mind off looking for solutions. However avoid setting yourself big questions that will simply overwhelm you. Ask yourself small questions that will get you moving.

* Every day ask yourself, "What would I do today if I were a better person?"

The Use of Visualization

* Visualizing yourself practicing a skill or exercising actually has many of the benefits of actually doing it for real and can play an important part in helping you become more proficient. You need to make your visualizations as vivid as you can.

* You can think through possible scenarios in your head to visualize how they would work. If you have a potential aim, but are unsure of whether or not it is realistic, then play it through in your mind in as much detail as you can.

* To help you deal with particular future events, you can generate your own mind movie of how you would like events to run. Imagine the specific event, making it as real as you can in your mind. Think about how you would handle variations. When the event itself comes about you will have trained yourself for it. Be wary however of assuming the real world will behave in accordance with your visualization, it may not – be prepared to adapt.

* Some example uses of visualization to support general habits and everyday circumstances:
    o Imagine yourself not eating everything in front of you. Imagine yourself stopping before you've eaten everything and either getting up and leaving or telling others you have had enough;
    o Imagine yourself refusing an offer of some sweets or turning down the option of a dessert;
    o Imagine yourself avoiding the aisles in the supermarket that have sweets and biscuits and cakes;
    o If you are regularly self-critical, imagine someone you care for making the mistake you beat yourself up about. Imagine yourself comforting them. How would you try to make them feel better? What would you say?
    o If you find yourself regularly responding negatively to someone – possibly when they say something in particular or under certain circumstances – imagine yourself responding in a calm positive manner, as vividly as you can;
    o If you get agitated in certain situations – when driving, or travelling by train for example – imagine yourself staying calm and feeling kindness towards others around you.

* Make your visualizations as vivid as you can. Try to visualize small details, including sounds and smells and tastes if appropriate. Try to imagine yourself feeling as you would feel in the circumstances. The more vividly you can imagine the more your brain will respond as though you were experiencing the actual circumstances. You can use this to help overcome your fears and also to practice doing things. Some tips on doing such visualization:
    o Do it regularly even if only for a minute or so;
    o Find a quiet place where you can close your eyes and not be distracted;
    o Imagine yourself in the setting you are interested in, with as much detail about sounds and smells and taste and touch;
    o Imagine your body and mind actually performing the task. Imagine yourself talking if relevant, including the tone and loudness of your voice;
    o Imagine the scene unfolding in a positive way, including how other people respond;
    o Don't force yourself to go beyond what you are comfortable with. Scale back imagery if you are finding it difficult. A little but often is important.
    o Once you are comfortable with your visualizations you can extend them into circumstances a bit more extreme, but only taking each new step as you feel comfortable doing so;
    o Once you have made significant progress with your visualizations you can start to take steps in the real world. Again take it a little at a time.

- Fantasizing about your perfect world may make you feel better, but it has a negative impact on you achieving your goals. Better to use your visualizations to imagine yourself doing the things you should be doing.

- Just visualizing a better life will not make it happen. You need to follow up with actions to make a better life.

Learn to Take Control of your Now

- Dare to release the full potential of who you are capable of being, by bringing yourself fully into the present moment and then just doing.

- Fake it till you make it. Live your life as though you are already the person you would like to become. You will find yourself rapidly becoming that person. So act like someone who is confident, decisive, and effective. Act like someone who is good at giving presentations or speeches. Act like someone who is good at mixing with people at a social do. Act like someone who just gets on and does the right thing. Become the person you want to be by being that person right now.

- It is only at this very moment that you can do or change anything.

- Seize the moment, for it may not come again.

- Be resolved right now and you will get things done.

- Ask yourself: why not me? Why not now?

- We all have enormous reserves of willpower, and in extreme circumstances we would almost certainly be able to tap into them. They are there to be tapped into at any time; it is just making the decision to do so now that is usually missing.

- If you are not guided by a clear sense of purpose, you are likely to fritter away your time and energy on short-term interests to the detriment of long-term interests.

- Dream about the things you want to achieve. Dream about them and take action right now to do something towards achieving them.

- Don't wait until you are in the mood you would like to be in. Pretend you are already in that mood and do what you would typically do if you were in that mood. It will put you into that mood. Why wait for the mood to only come when you have little use for it. Create the mood for yourself.

- If you can get into the habit of getting on doing what should be done when it should be done you will significantly reduce the amount of negative stress in your life and be far more successful in your endeavors.

- For many things we do not need willpower per se, we just need to make a black and white decision and then keep to it. Whenever you are faced with a given situation, don't struggle with it, just do what you've decided to do. It will soon become a habit.

- If there's something you should be doing but are putting off, keep repeating to yourself 'Do it now. Do it Now. Do it Now. ....' until you give in and get on with it.

- If you are feeling lethargic, one way of motivating yourself is to get more oxygen. Do some light aerobic exercise such as going for a walk, or do some stretching or some deep breathing.

* Keep yourself hydrated, preferably with water. If you are dehydrated you will tend to be sluggish and tired. A glass of cold water can be refreshing and help you to get started on something.

* When we laugh or sing or dance or hug someone we release chemicals into our bodies that give us a lift.

* Just being able to see ourselves in a mirror increases our self-awareness and our self-control.

* You can get yourself in the mood for a particular task by putting yourself into the physical state in which you would normally do it. For example, if you are working from home, dress in your work clothes and adopt similar postures to those you adopt when at work.

* We get more tired when we aren't doing things than when we are.

* Your energy levels will go up and down during the day. Do the best you can with the energy levels you have rather than abandon doing anything because you don't have lots of energy. Even if your energy levels are relatively low you can still get on with some routine tasks. Note however that if you regularly have low energy levels you should look to do something about it through improved diet and health.

* We imagine our future selves as almost superhuman. We put off doing things now expecting our future selves to have no trouble dealing with whatever it is. However your future self is not a superhero able to do things your present self cannot. If you want to be able to get things done in the future you need to be able to get things done now.

* We view our future selves as a different person about whom we are less concerned than we are with the present us. We then load him or her up with the tasks we don't want to do. To improve our chances of doing the right things now we need to feel connected to our future selves, through strongly visualizing ourselves as being our future selves.

* People tend to think the future will be some idealized world without the constraints and distractions of today. They significantly over estimate their ability to exhibit self-control relative to their ability today, and overestimate the time available tomorrow. Best to accept that tomorrow you will make the same decisions as you will make today, and make today's decisions on that basis.

* When faced with a choice between doing the right thing and doing something that is easier or requires less effort, then visualize the outcome resulting from doing the right thing and the outcome arising from not doing it. Try to be as vivid as you can in your visualization, and don't kid yourself it is a one off. The decision you make now will most likely be the same decision you will make next time.

* Don't be mentally lazy. Overcome your automatic tendency to simply drift along. Be aware of yourself and look to make decision consciously rather than make them without any thought. You may find this difficult at first, but keep trying; you will get much better at it.

Making Changes

* Ensure the things you do have a purpose that you understand. Don't do things simply because you've always done them. Times change and things that may have been appropriate in past circumstances may no longer be so in current circumstances. Be ready to change with the times.

* Trying to make big changes in one step usually fails. It is usually best to make big changes through making a sequence of small changes. By all means try to make big changes, but if that doesn't work don't get discouraged. Many changes that you can't make all in one go, you can make if you do it a bit at a time.

The Bumper Book of Common Sense

* Making small changes enables us, our brains, to gradually adapt without being overwhelmed by the fears that arise when trying to make big changes. If you find yourself struggling just go back to smaller steps that you can do without too much effort.

* Changing long ingrained habits takes time. Most people fail because they expect instantaneous success, and when they don't get it stop trying until next time when they repeat the pattern. By taking small steps however almost any habit can be broken or changed.

* Changing a habit takes time and patience; typically it can take between 2 weeks and 6 months, and for some habits it can take years.

* Some examples of making small changes:
  o Eating a little less of unhealthy foods – throw a little bit of what you are eating away – just a crisp or two or a bit of chocolate;
  o There are many ways of getting just a little more exercise, taking some steps instead of the lift or escalator, walking a little further than usual, standing up instead of sitting down whilst doing something;
  o Cut down on your spending; look at ways to save just £1 a day;
  o Look to meet more people by going to places where people are. You don't need to talk to them. Practice your small talk at home;
  o Make more productive use of your time. Start by just making a list: note down one idea a day for a couple of weeks of what you could do to be more productive. Then choose one of the ideas and start to implement it in some small way. Build up from there, both by progressing with one idea and starting on other ideas. Don't be overly ambitious by trying to do too much too quickly. Just build up slowly. It is far better to succeed in taking small steps than to fail to take big steps.

* If you wish to make big changes in your life then you generally need to make big changes to your environment. We are, to a very great extent, creatures of habit, and react to our environment in instinctive ways. To change our instinctive behaviors requires us to move out of the environment in which they have become instinctive and into a new environment within which we can set up new behaviors.

* If you are having trouble trying to make changes in your life, then ask others to help. Tell them what you are trying to do, and work with them to identify ways in which they can help.

* If you want to make big changes in your life, do so one change at a time. Dissipating your energy across many changes just means you are likely to fail in all of them.

* Making changes, doing things that aren't already habits, can be uncomfortable. However the very fact that you feel discomfort is a sign that it is going against the grain. And if you keep it up you will get into a groove and the discomfort will lesson. Thus rather than seek to back away from the discomfort, embrace it.

* When looking to make changes ensure you create positive feedback for your new behavior and negative feedback for your previous behavior.

Overcoming Temptation and Bad Habits

* Most of our life is governed by our habits. It is hard work applying our conscious brain to overcome the natural instincts and habits of our unconscious brain. It can be done, but it is hard work and as the day progresses we are less able to do so. One of the best uses of our conscious brain is therefore to turn any bad habits we have into good habits.

* Your habits are not just physical habits such as smoking or eating or watching TV, but mental habits such as your tendency to procrastinate, how you respond to things that annoy you, how you manage your lists of things to do, etc.

* Ask yourself if your habits are supporting your goals or holding you back.

* If you don't conquer your bad habits, they will conquer you.

* When we surrender to our base desires we have momentary pleasure followed by a long period of guilt. When we gain mastery over our base desires we obtain a lifelong flow.

* We are often unaware of just how strong a grip certain bad habits have on us. If you have a bad habit you think you ought to change keep a record of when you find yourself giving in to it, a written record of some form. This will not only make you more aware of its occurrence but will also give you a measure to use once you start to try to tackle it. Be ruthless in recording every incident, no excuses. Depending upon the nature of the habit you might keep a small notebook or piece of paper with you to record particular incidents.

* You can create an additional motivational pressure on yourself to adopt a new habit by openly reporting your progress. This could be by putting up a chart where others can see it, or it might be by creating a blog or some other means to openly report progress on the internet. You do however need to be ruthlessly honest in your reporting, and feel the embarrassment when you fail to make progress or find yourself lapsing.

* Read up as much as possible about the habit you are trying to change, and pick up tips from others as to how to go about it.

* Seek to change one bad habit at a time. Changing bad habits is not easy. It can be done, but it will require a lot of effort. If you try to tackle more than one at a time there is a high chance you will fail with them all, whereas if you do one at a time you have a far higher chance of succeeding and then being able to move onto another. One reason New Year resolutions fail is you take on too much at a time. Better to list out your New Year resolutions and then sequence and space your intent to adopt them through the year, only moving onto another one once you have completed an earlier one. Be sure however before you move on from one bad habit to another that you have fully succeeded with the earlier one. Don't shift your focus too soon and then find yourself relapsing.

* If you are to change a bad habit you need to want to change it. You need to label a habit as a bad habit. If you don't, you won't change. If you do, you can bring to bear all the tools of habit change, and in time you will succeed.

* Any time you give in to temptation, ask yourself if you feel better as a result. Usually we feel worse. Try to remember this when faced with future temptations.

* You do things because you want to do them. Whilst you would like to change your bad habits, there is nevertheless some reason why you do them, some payback you are getting from doing them. Try to identify what it is about a given bad habit that leads to you doing it. Make it a challenge and a game to seek out an understanding of why you continually give in to the bad habit. Once you understand why, you can look for alternative ways, good habits, which can give rise to the same payback.

* One reason some people struggle to overcome certain bad habits is because the bad habit gives them an excuse not to risk trying and failing. If you can blame your bad habit for not succeeding you can retain a self-belief that you are really highly competent. It is worth seriously questioning yourself about this. If you think it might apply to you then you need to recognize just how destructive this way of thinking is. It will hold you back your whole life.

* Believe you can change your bad habits. Because you can. Have faith in yourself. We all have great strengths within us. It is through continually trying to tap into them that we learn how to tap into them.

The Bumper Book of Common Sense

* A significant barrier to overcoming temptations or negative behaviors is self-doubt. If you are telling yourself you will fail to change, then most likely you will; it is a self-fulfilling prophecy. However we are all capable of change, and if you recognize this and tell yourself this on a regular basis then you will be able to change. Ensure you self-talk is positive and encouraging rather than negative.

* Our brains like habits because they require little effort. It takes a lot of energy and effort to break a bad habit. But any bad habit can be broken if you persist and make the effort – usually in about 30 to 60 days, though some may take longer.

* Don't kid yourself that overcoming long established bad habits is easy. It isn't. If you believe it's easy then when you have set backs you are more likely to give up. If however you recognize that it's hard, then you are more likely to put in more effort, be persistent, and put setbacks behind you as you reaffirm your commitment and continue with the struggle.

* There will be obstacles and difficulties on your road to habit change. You will sometimes not be successful in adopting your new habit or giving up your old because of a given obstacle or difficulty. Work out how to overcome obstacles. If your tactic for doing so doesn't work then find another. And keep adapting your tactics until you succeed.

* Whilst trying to break a particular bad habit avoid putting yourself into the environment which typically triggered the bad habit, at least until your new habit or behavior has taken a strong hold.

* For certain bad habits it may be appropriate to seek help from others, whether friends and family who you can tell about your intent, or from local help groups, or from online support forums.

* Treat temptations as opportunities to develop self-control. When you feel you are about to give in to a temptation adopt a 10 minute rule, whereby you tell yourself you can now give in to the temptation but will wait 10 minutes before you do so. You may or may not still want to give in after 10 minutes but at least you've given your self-control some exercise.

* In the light of temptation, it is often more effective to delay the pleasure of giving in to the temptation rather than outright denying the pleasure. Thus a promise of a reward of a dessert at the weekend might help overcome a temptation during the week better than simply denying yourself. Or you might set rules relating to the times of day when you can indulge – such as no biscuits until after 6pm. Those that learn to postpone their pleasures also find the self-control to moderate their pleasures when they have given themselves license to indulge.

* When you are being drawn in a direction you don't want to go in, remind yourself of your long-term goals. Visualize the consequences of you always giving into this temptation and the negative impact it is going to have on your ability to achieve your goals.

* Create negative associations with your bad habits. Visualize the damage they are doing to you every time they are in front of you.

* Be more consciously aware of the impact your habits now are having on your future self. For certain long term habits that you want to change, write out a message to your future self about what you are doing now and how you intend to change. Then write down two messages from your future self, one from a future self that has failed to change, talking about the regret and the consequences of not having changed, and one from your future self having changed and the positive impact it has had on your life. Carry these messages around with you and refer to them when you find yourself about to give in to the habit.

* Write down the bad habit you want to change and elaborate on the reasons for doing so. Be very clear why you're doing it: the benefits of doing it and the downsides arising from not doing it. It may not be just about you and your longer term health and wealth but also about family and particularly children: you are probably the most important role model they will ever have in their lives, whether you want to be or not.

* You don't need to start on your habit change straight away, and indeed it might well be better to set yourself some future date on which you will start, some week or two in the future. It gives the intent more gravitas, and enables you to prepare. Set up your notebook. Write down your motivations. Pre-plan how you will handle certain temptations.

* We are more averse to losing something than we are pleased at getting something. We feel worse about the loss of £10 than good about the gain of £10. Thus when it comes to choices between instant gratification and delayed reward, focus your mind on the long term reward, the benefits of having the reward, and ask yourself if you are willing to give that up for the sake of the instant gratification, knowing that if you do give in you will also do so next time.

* Fixating on a temptation whilst trying to avoid it is draining of your willpower, and you are likely to eventually give in. Much better to distract yourself and get it out of your mind. One good way is to focus on lofty thoughts. Focus on your long-term goals and your values. People with religious beliefs can focus on the values derived from their religion, but anyone can draw inspiration from their own long-term goals.

* Rather than trying to give up bad habits focus on putting in place the good habits that will eventually replace them.

* Train your mind to recognize when you have a choice rather than always letting yourself run on autopilot.

* People who are distracted are more likely to give in to temptations. Thus when your mind is preoccupied you are more likely to act on impulse. Keep temptations out of sight and out of reach when doing something that is occupying your mind.

* We are not continually at risk from bad habits. They hit us at certain crucial moments and in certain circumstances, for a few minutes or even less at a time. We are thus faced with occasional moments of truth; and if we can get through them, the temptation loosens its grip as other thoughts take over. If we can recognize the circumstances and conditions under which temptations arise, we can develop strategies to avoid putting ourselves in the specific circumstances in the first place, or develop alternative responses when in those circumstances. For example drink some water whenever you are tempted by an unhealthy snack. Or take deep breaths, or go for a walk, or give someone a ring, or have some other little ritual which will distract you long enough for the urge to pass.

* You just need to ride out the wave, and the urge will go away. Some strategies for making it through the urge: deep breathing, self-massage, eat some frozen grapes, take a walk, exercise, drink a glass of water, call a support buddy, post on a support forum.

* Use self-awareness to override automated bad habits. When you feel the onset of some bad habit, be deliberately conscious of it being your brain following some pre-determined path. And be aware of your ability to consciously rewire your brain by wilfully doing something different to what you instinctively feel like doing. The more you wilfully do something different the stronger you are making a rewiring of your brain take hold.

* If you want to change your habits or behavior you don't have to, and shouldn't try to, do it all at once. All or nothing approaches are often all for a short while, and then a lapse changes them to nothing: and you give up. Small changes that you work at and put all your effort into, and come back to secure after lapses, are more enduring; and eventually the final change becomes just another small change to make.

* If a bad habit is proving particularly difficult to overcome, set your sights lower. A small step in the right direction is much better than continually failing to take a larger stride. Take as small a step as you can succeed at. It doesn't matter how small the steps: if you take them and you keep taking them you will cover the distance.

The Bumper Book of Common Sense

* Take it a day at a time. If you can't take it a day at a time, take it an hour at a time. The hours run into days that run into weeks that run into months. Focus on succeeding in the present and the future will look after itself.

* After a slip up, instead of focusing on how you have failed again, focus on the fact that with every attempt you are making progress. If you are struggling, don't target total success, target doing better. You will grow in self-confidence and get into a mindset that believes you will eventually succeed.

* Don't get upset if you slip up, but immediately reaffirm your commitment and get back to it.

* Be very wary of the 'what the hell effect' after you have had a minor failure when working on giving up a bad habit. Minor failures are common, and you can continue on the road to success by immediately returning to your good intentions. But if you adopt a 'what the hell' response, and allow yourself to binge on your bad habit, you will be significantly sliding back to failure.

* Giving in to temptations or urges can lead to feelings of guilt or shame, which leads to further lapses as a temporary comfort, leading to further feelings of guilt, etc. Often it's not the first weakness that is the problem, it's the 'what the hell' attitude that follows.

* Your environment is the largest determinant of your behavior. There are some environments when you would never give in to the bad habit, and others when you frequently do so. When trying to change your own habits and behavior look at the cues in your environment, and eliminate those that are hindering you and strengthen those that are helping you. Change your environment in ways that make the habits you want easier and the habits you don't want harder. And keep away from places or circumstances that are the triggers to your negative behaviors.

* Become aware of and analyze the triggers that lead up to your giving in to temptation. There is usually some chain of behaviors, possibly triggered by some particular cue in your environment, which leads up to the 'bad' behavior. By understanding the chain of behaviors you can identify places you can break the chain and redirect yourself in a direction less destructive or negative.

* When temptations are close at hand they override or block out our good intentions. The best way to stop yourself giving in to temptation is to not let the temptation pass in front of you. For example, it usually takes less willpower to avoid buying sweets than it does to not eat the sweets that are in front of you. But you may need to adopt tactics to ensure you avoid buying sweets, like staying away from the aisles that sell them.

* Much of self-control is about not putting ourselves in the way of temptations. Thus, ironically, people who are confident about their willpower are often more likely to relapse because they are over optimistic about their ability to overcome temptation and allow themselves to be put in the way of temptation.

* Watching the news or programs about troubles and crime leaves us susceptible to comfort temptations, such as food and drink. By all means take an interest in the news and crime programs, but in moderation.

* For habits of a repetitive nature, such as smoking, or regular snacking, then learn to substitute some surreptitious action when you feel the onset of the urge. For example you might lightly clench your fist, or become more conscious of your breathing. It should be something you can do for a couple of minutes or so, time enough for the worse of the urge to pass, and allow you to get on with something else.

* For any bad habits you want to break look for common patterns and set up countermeasure or substitute behaviors. Once you identify and recognize triggers to the onset of specific negative behaviors, you can develop automated responses to lead you in a positive direction, which you employ whenever you sense the onset of the negative behavior. If you are having difficulty initiating the substitute behavior keep playing it over in your head, imagining yourself being successful in your response to the triggers.

* Pre-plan how to avoid or deal with certain temptations you are prone to giving in to. If you are prone to buying things when you go out, for example, only go out with so much cash and no credit or bankcards. Make appointments in your calendar to deal with something you've been putting off. Make use of software applications to stop you accessing certain on-line sites during certain times of the day. Be clear about what you are prone to give in to, and be creative about keeping yourself away from the temptation.

* A technique for changing particularly tenacious bad habits. Keep a notebook with you and ask yourself, and write down responses to, various questions when you find yourself exhibiting the behavior you are trying to change:
    o When and where did it happen?
    o What were the specific environmental circumstances or triggers?
    o What was going through your mind as the feeling whelmed up that led to the behavior?
    o What specifically where you doing?

    If you can analyze answers to these questions and come up with patterns, you will be in a strong position to do something about tackling the habit, such as through changing your environment, avoiding certain circumstances, putting in place a counterstrategy or enter into specific self-talk as the behavior starts to take a grip.

* Take one bad habit at a time. Write it down in a private notebook and be clear that you definitely want to give it up. Identify and record a circumstance of giving in to the bad habit and write down the circumstance and triggers that gave rise to it. Identify at what point you might have been able to resist, and what you could have done, physically or in terms of self-talk, that would have either helped you resist or have taken you out of the circumstance that gave rise to the instance. Identify the specific warning signs for next time and what you are going to do next time. Then do the same with another circumstance under which you give in to it. Keep analyzing. Keep identifying tactics. Keep trying to apply the tactics. If the tactics fail it simply becomes another circumstance to be analyzed. At first it could be hard work. But persist at it and it will get easier. All bad habits can be broken if you decide you are going to do so, and just keep trying in a systematic manner.

* When thoughts about giving in to your temptations are playing on your mind, try calming techniques and reminding yourself that you are in control of your own behavior. Remember that the past has past, and that in future you don't have to let yourself give in to temptations. Remind yourself of your goals and commitments.

* Your willpower is weaker when you are tired, and you will find it more difficult to resist temptations later in the day. Prepare for this, and ensure you don't put yourself in the way of temptations when tired or later in the day.

* Take inspiration from others. Read about others who have overcome adversity in general or with respect to the particular habit you are trying to break. It can be done, and others have done it.

* Promising or making a commitment to your spouse or someone you respect that you will change a bad habit can be a strong motivator.

* Beware of the self-talk that says you can give in to temptation today because tomorrow is going to be different. Whilst you may genuinely believe this, it's not true. The decisions you make tomorrow are very likely to be the same decisions as you make today.

* Set strict rules for yourself. One way we give in to temptations is through the 'one won't matter' argument. A strict rule of 'not even one' is a counter tactic.

* When looking to give up bad habits, be careful how you reward yourself for some success. If you reward yourself through allowing yourself to indulge in the bad habit 'just this once' then you are most likely on a slippery slide.

The Bumper Book of Common Sense

* People who feel they have done well and exhibited high levels of self-control are often less on their guard and prone to then giving in to temptation as a kind of reward for their earlier good behavior. For example, having resisted temptation to buy sweets whilst out, we can be prone to eating something sweet when we get home. Being aware of this can help us be on our guard against it.

* Moral licensing is when we believe it is ok to do something 'bad' because of all the 'good' things we have been doing. In reality it is a weakness and an excuse, not a justification. It is only right that we should reward ourselves for doing good things, however there is no excuse for this reward to be 'bad' things. There is no moral justification for doing bad things just because we did a few things we consider to have been good.

* Be wary of rewarding a success with a bad habit, particularly one you have given up or are trying to give up.

* Beware of the halo effect where a virtuous choice makes our not so virtuous choices seem more acceptable. People who have a salad with a burger perceive their meal as having less calories than having a burger on its own! People who choose a healthy main course often indulge in unhealthy drinks, starters and desserts but still feel good about their choices. People get seduced by labels such as organic, low fat, bargain, buy 1 get 1 free, and end up eating and buying and doing more harm than good. Not that organic, etc. is bad, just that we get seduced into having more of it or other things alongside it.

* A technique when trying to overcome some specific temptation or bad habit. Whenever you give into temptation put some fixed amount of money into a jar, and once the jar reaches a set amount take the money out and send the equivalent amount as an anonymous donation to an organization that you actually despise. Ensure you do this, and ensure the organization is one that you genuinely do not like – maybe some extreme political organization.

* A tactic to try, in certain circumstances, in support of changing unwanted behavior is to dramatically increase it to a level that becomes unpleasant. You need to understand the norm for the behavior and then dramatically increase it. Be careful not to move into territory that is actually dangerous, but a short controlled 'shock' to your system can help jolt you out of a habit that is doing you significant long term harm.

* When looking for strategies for resisting a temptation or changing a bad habit we should look to apply multiple strategies all at once. Single strategies on their own, or one after another, are often not enough. Strategies to be employed, as many at the same time as possible, include:
    o Avoidance of being in the situation where the temptation or bad habit manifests itself;
    o Promise of a reward later if you avoid the temptation or bad habit;
    o Do something else to take your mind off it;
    o Remind yourself of the bad consequences if you proceed with the temptation or bad habit;
    o Remind yourself of the good things that will come about if you succeed now and in the future to avoid the temptation or bad habit;
    o Have alternative responses ready for when you feel the temptation starting to take hold.

* Don't be paranoid about overcoming every temptation. It is not good to always give up pleasure now for future benefits. Doing so will mean you will largely miss out on the pleasures of living. You know for yourself however whether giving into certain temptations are a part of a slippery slope or just an occasional and acceptable lapse.

Understanding and Tackling Addiction

* Addiction arises as a result of short-term solutions to a need that then comes to be relied upon. To counter addictions you usually need more than just 'willpower'. Serious addictions such as to drugs

or alcohol or gambling or eating or any type of activity that is doing you physical, mental, or financial harm needs treatment and professional advice. The following are some general ways of tackling less serious addictions:

- Follow self-help courses specific to the addiction. There will be plenty of such courses available as DVDs, books, or through internet sites;
- Join a self-help group specific to your addiction. You shouldn't have trouble finding one local to yourself through the internet. Alternatively seek help from others you know will be sympathetic. Having others to talk to who understand your addiction is usually a great help, and the mutual support strengthens our own commitment to change;
- Seek to understand what underlying need the addiction is satisfying and find viable less harmful alternatives;
- Develop a more positive thinking approach to your life. Being positive and having some inspiring goals should largely weaken or eliminate any holds addictions have on you;
- Keep a diary of when you give into your addiction and the circumstances leading up to it. Regularly review it and start to adopt tactics for avoiding the circumstances that lead up to the addiction;
- Adopt general habit breaking techniques.

* Dopamine is a chemical released into our brain that triggers us to pursue things that offer up the promise of pleasure. It is such a powerful motivator that we can get into a state of endlessly pursuing pleasure but never actually achieving it: which is the usual state of addiction. It is also a root cause of our over indulging in snack foods, shopping, television, e-mail checking, online poker, sex sites, etc. It is not the actual pleasure we experience that keeps us coming back for more, but the continuing promise of pleasure to come. By being more explicitly aware of this, and aware that we are not actually experiencing pleasure, we can gain better control.

* When tackling an addiction be wary of not simply creating another. Thus, for example, don't replace smoking with over eating.

* If you are battling against addiction keep away from places or environments where there are temptations.

* Once you've made some progress in tackling an addiction, don't see a relapse as a complete failure. If you relapse, immediately go back to battling. If you do so, it will get easier.

Implementing Good Habits

* Employing will power to do something drains your energy. Use your self-control to develop good habits, which then become automatic and don't then continually require will power.

* The more you do something the more likely you will do it again in the future. Like a path through the undergrowth, the more times you follow the path the clearer it becomes and the easier it is for you to go down the same path in the future. Persistence will lead to you succeeding in ingraining good habits.

* There is no short cut to forming habits. Repetition is the only way. At first it requires conscious effort, but keep at it and eventually it requires very little or no effort at all.

* If you are struggling to develop certain good habits, don't give up. It takes a lot of effort to turn something that isn't a habit into a habit. However if it is a good habit it is worth persisting with the effort. Good habits once ingrained enable you to do things efficiently and with little thought, enabling you to focus your efforts on other things.

The Bumper Book of Common Sense

* You are more likely to succeed in adopting good habits if you plan out how you are going to implement them. Adjust the plan in the light of the practice in attempting to apply it. In particular identify any blockers or common difficulties that get in your way, and how you will overcome them.

* If you find yourself never able to do something, make a plan. Decide when, then just get on and do it when the time comes. Don't be put off by occasional failures to do so. Keep trying and it will become a habit.

* Create, or frequently put yourself into, an environment that is conducive to your good habit. Depending upon what the habit is, you can surround yourself with reminders of it, and put into easy view lots of tips about how to just get on with it.

* Identify a new habit you would like to form and tell yourself you only need to commit to it for 30 days. It is easier to motivate yourself to keep up a new habit if you know it is only for a limited amount of time. At the end of the 30 days the new habit will often be so well engrained that it takes little effort to maintain it. If it is not, and you have made a genuine effort, then it should be easy for you to decide to continue trying.

* Improving a little each day adds up to big and lasting changes.

* Continually take action towards what you want and away from what you don't want. Even small actions in the right direction are worthwhile and help us get into the right habits.

* It you are looking to develop a number of good habits, focus on putting one in place at a time. Once you have established a given habit it requires little effort to maintain, and you can then turn your energies to establishing another habit. Trying to implement more than one good habit at a time often requires too much effort and you are likely to fail in all of them.

* Set high standards for yourself in everything you do. You will be more inspired, will grow more and faster, and will achieve more.

* One way of adopting a new habit is to tack it onto an existing habit such as doing something straight after breakfast or dinner, or straight after some other habitual action.

* Find yourself role models and copy them, albeit not too overtly if they are physically present in your environment. When faced with circumstances where you have difficulty doing the right thing, imagine what your role model would do, and imitate them in doing it.

* If you want to adopt a new habit, pretend you have already adopted it. Set your mind to tell itself that it is already what you do. A 'fake it till you make it' strategy.

* When trying to adopt a new habit, put visible reminders to yourself in your daily environment to keep the intent at the forefront of your mind.

* Find ways to increase the pleasure associated with good habits. For example: healthy food does not need to be bland; see studying as building up a picture of how the world works which is part of the fascination of life, see exercise as a building up of your body.

* Reward yourself for adopting good habits and behaviors, but ensure the rewards are not themselves bad habits. You can set particular targets linked to particular rewards, though it is usually best to reward behavior rather than results. Don't however reward yourself before you have achieved the target or demonstrated the desired behavior.

Keep Getting Back Up

* The will is strengthened through battling on through adversity.

* Resilience is our ability to keep going in the face of difficulties. To keep going despite failures and setbacks. To manage our negative emotions so they don't drag us down. Resilience is a skill we can all learn.

* Resilience requires being able to accept harsh realities, finding meaning when times are difficult, and being able to improvise with whatever is at hand. To build up your resilience: accept the reality of your situation; be prepared to accept a long hard struggle; and don't feel sorry for yourself.

* If you want to achieve something worthwhile, expect there to be difficulties along the way. If you accept that there will be struggles and difficulties to overcome then you are less likely to get downhearted and demotivated when they occur. When you make a commitment to achieve a goal then also make a commitment to tackle and overcome the difficulties.

* Don't take rejection personally. People are not rejecting you, they are rejecting what you have put in front of them. Improve it. Rejection means you have something to be rejected and it is easier to improve on something that has been rejected than it is to create something in the first place.

* There are many obstacles in life standing between you and your goals, and you will have failures and setbacks along the way. But keep bringing to mind your goal, and your intent to relentlessly pursue it, and you will soon be back on your feet.

* See every blow and defeat as experiences from which you can grow stronger. Like a video game where when you start out you will have failure after failure, but slowly you will learn and get better and eventually, if you persevere, you'll get pretty good at it.

* You will tend to have your own personal standard with regards how many times you try and fail at something before you decide enough is enough. If it is not many times then you should increase it considerably. Many people quit when had they tried a little longer they would have succeeded.

* Success is born of failure. Failure is a brilliant learning opportunity. The more you fail, so long as you are making the effort to succeed, the closer you are getting to success.

* See failures as a natural part of the learning and improving process. Indeed you generally learn far more through failures. Having failures, assuming they are the result of action rather than inaction, proves you are pushing at your limits, which you need to do if you want to improve.

* Don't beat yourself up when you fail. It has happened. Now get back to it.

* Getting things done requires patience and perseverance. If you believe it can be done, or that it might be possible, then persevere. Success in anything is usually 1% inspiration and 99% hard work.

* Most success stories involve people who persevered in circumstances when the majority of people would have given up.

* It is not talent that will get you to where you want to be, it is staying power.

* Repetition turns small steps into giant strides.

* When faced with a challenge don't give up at the first sign of failure. Adapt your plan. Learn what works to get you closer to where you want to get to, and what doesn't work. Keep trying and adjusting until you succeed. Adapt other people's ways of doing things to your own circumstances and learn by trial and error.

The Bumper Book of Common Sense

* It isn't whether or not you fall down that matters, it is whether or not you get back up. Learn to be persistent and keep getting back up and you will succeed where others fail.

* It doesn't matter how many times you've failed; so long as you don't give up you will eventually succeed.

* Life is not about how fast you run, or high you climb, but about how well you bounce.

* The steady tortoise will beat the spasmodic hare.

* When feeling unmotivated reaffirm your belief in yourself. Tell yourself that you are the sort of person that just gets on with things. Get on with something.

* It is not crisis or adversity that is the problem; it is the way you react to it which is the problem.

* Beating yourself up about your own lack of willpower, being overly self-critical, is counterproductive. It leads to less motivation, not more, and drives us towards depression. Being understanding with yourself, forgiving yourself, but still being determined, increases your motivation and chances of gaining the self-control you are looking for.

* From time to time we will resolve to make big changes, particularly when things appear to be getting on top of us. And making the resolution will make us feel better for a while. Once we start however it is not so easy, and we often fall. If we then beat ourselves up about it we will make little progress. If however we hold on to our determination to change, and see failure as experience which we use to adjust our behaviors as we try again, then we are likely to eventually succeed. If rather than abandoning our resolutions because of a setback we think through how to do things better the next time, then we are on the road to fulfilling our hoped for change.

* You will often set yourself overly ambitious targets and then fail to achieve them. Often however you will make some progress, albeit far short of what you intended. All too often people see this as failure, get discouraged, and drop back into habits that negate even this small progress. If however you see it as a sign that you can succeed and resolve to continue and build on this small success you will continue to succeed.

* It requires less skill to destroy than to create. It requires less work to knockdown than to build. It is easier to criticize than it is to create something that can be criticized. Thus don't despair because other people are criticizing. If there is something useful to be extracted from their criticism to help you improve, then make use of it. But the fact that they are criticizing says more about them than it does about what you are trying to do.

General Self-Motivation Tips

* It's hard to be motivated when you are confused. Simplify your life and you will have greater focus and be more motivated.

* Determination and persistence will overcome most obstacles.

* It is not necessarily discipline you need, just a disciplined approach.

* Sometimes be a visionary and sometimes be a doer. But don't try to be both at the same time.

* The will to win is not as important as the will to prepare to win.

* We have far greater stores of energy than we normally deploy. We work far within the limits of what we are capable of. Put more of your stored energy to use and move closer to your limits. You'll be surprised at what you can achieve.

* Clear your workspaces and keep work well filed. You are able to exhibit higher levels of self-control in a neat and tidy environment. Clutter and difficulty finding things is very demotivating and holds you back from getting on with things.

* You will generally feel more motivated in well-lit areas – preferably daylight and with fresh air.

* If you want to spend some time studying or practicing a skill then decide when you are going to do it and for how long, and put it into your calendar as an appointment with yourself. You are more likely to then do it than if you just keep it in your mind.

* Spend more time with people who give you a lift and less time with those who drag you down and drain your energy. Be someone who lifts other people up.

* Distance yourself from those who are a bad influence on you, though depending upon your personal circumstances and relationship with them you may try to talk to them first. You may find they don't realize the affect they are having on you and be more than willing to help.

* Too much listening to other people's woes stresses us and this impacts on our motivation. This includes listening to it on TV, particularly the News, but also other programs. This doesn't mean you shouldn't listen to the News or watch stressful programs, it is a part of life, just be wary of getting immersed in too much of it.

* A lot of TV and junk food makes you lazy and listless.

* High calorie refined sugar foods and drink give you a temporary boost and then bring you down for far longer than for which you benefited from the boost. Avoid them.

* Dehydration slows down your brain and body. Regularly drink some water during the day.

* Chewing some sugar free gum increases the flow of blood to your brain and helps you concentrate better.

* If is easier to hold on to your principles 100% of the time than it is to hold on to them 99% of the time. Once you give way on your principles 'just once' because of unique or particularly circumstances, you find unique or particular circumstances are everywhere.

* Learn about yourself: what motivates you and what demotivates you. What sort of music inspires you and lifts you up. Do certain smells make you feel more alive? Do some foods make you feel sluggish? Use your self-knowledge to help you get things done.

* Whilst you should seek positive inspiring goals, sometimes you can find inspiration from what you want to avoid. How will things turn out if you continue as you are, or fail to do the things you know you ought? Is that how you want things to turn out?

* There are many influences on our behavior, pulling us in different directions. The more we understand these influences the more we are able to resist or strengthen them.

* If you are regularly too tired to do anything in the evenings after work then you need to do something about it as you are wasting away a significant amount of your time, arguably your most valuable time, your discretionary time. However in order to tackle the tiredness you need to understand the contributing causes, and treat them as bad habits to be overcome. Potential causes could be one or more of:
    o Lack of goals and vision about what you want to do with your own time;
    o Poor organization at work such that you don't feel you are achieving anything during the day;
    o Poor eating, drinking, or exercising habits;
    o Poor traveling habits.

The Bumper Book of Common Sense

* A balance between too much and too little anxiety is best for getting on and doing things. Too little anxiety leaves us unmotivated to make the effort; too much anxiety prevents us focusing on the task itself.

* When trying to do something, such as eliminating bad habits and adopting good ones, think in terms of 'haven't succeeded yet' rather than 'keep failing'. Have lots of little rewards along the way for progress and big rewards for significant successes. One suggestion is to make up little reward cards for yourself where you can tick off 5 or more good habit activities and earn yourself some specified small treat.

* When using rewards to help motivate yourself ensure the rewards are ones that help you grow rather than ones that keep you distracted and addicted.

* In order to gain long-term commitment it is important that people accept inner responsibility for their actions. Having people respond to strong outside pressures such as large rewards or punishments does not engender personal responsibility. Ironically, small rewards are often more effective in engendering long-term commitment than large rewards.

* Telling others about your motivational goals can provide an additional impetus since you will want to avoid the embarrassment of failing to living up to your word. However ensure you are positive about your expectation of achieving your goal, don't build in ready-made excuses that will weaken your feeling of shame should you fall short.

* Meditation, whether religious or not, increases our ability to focus and concentrate and our overall self-control. It helps us become less prone to impulses and distractions.

* A technique for increasing your will-power in the present is to slow down your breathing. Slow down to about 4 or 5 breathes a minute. A few minutes of this will help you feel calmer and more in control. Do it when faced with a temptation you are about to give in to. Ensure you are slowing down your inhaling and exhaling; don't do it by holding your breath.

* Exercise does wonders for your self-control. It doesn't have to be strenuous. Going for a walk or jog will significantly reduce stress levels and increase self-control. Think of exercise as something that restores your energy rather than drains it.

* Everything seems a little more possible after a brisk 30 to 60 minute walk.

* We tend to be more motivated to move away from things we fear or dislike than we are motivated to move towards what we would like or desire. By weakening or eliminating our fears we free ourselves up to focus on achieving.

* If you are fully committed to your goal, maintain motivation by focusing on what is left to complete it. If you are not fully committed, focus on what you have already accomplished.

* Our brains generally respond better to external input than to internal input. For example, when exercising we will usually keep going longer if someone is telling us to do so rather than if we are just telling ourselves. You can increase the likelihood of responding to your internal thoughts by writing them down, talking aloud to yourself, or putting them on tape and playing them back. Different parts of your brain then light up to respond to this what has become external input.

* You can prime your brain to feel more motivated to do a given task by reading motivational words or quotes. Write them out on cards and put them out in front of you when you have the time to get on with something but are hesitant about just getting on with it. You should seek out your own words or phrases but the following are some just to get you going:
    o Do It Now;
    o The world belongs to those who do;
    o Achieve;

- o Execute;
- o Discipline;
- o With Purpose;
- o Awaken;
- o Empowered;
- o Energy;
- o Bold;
- o Whilst others sleep;
- o This next hour: use it or lose it;
- o I can and I will;
- o With each step;
- o We are what we do;
- o Drop by drop the glass is filled;
- o The time will pass anyway, put it to use;
- o Some succeed because they are destined. Some succeed because they are determined;
- o The difference between ordinary and extraordinary is that little bit extra;
- o Do not let what you cannot do interfere with what you can do.

* Don't pursue willpower perfection. You can not and should not try to control everything you think, feel and do.

Dealing with Stress and Worries

Dealing with Trauma or Despair

* If you have been experienced a particularly traumatic event then seek professional help, or accept it if it is offered.

* However bad your personal circumstances you will not be alone in experiencing them. There are many organizations and groups to help people with all sorts of issues. If you feel in a state of despair, use them.

* A way of dealing with a traumatic event is to write about it and how you feel. This is often more effective than talking about it to friends.

* Whilst you may not be able to completely eliminate bad memories about traumatic events, you can reduce the frequency of your thinking about them and you can stop them dominating your life.

* We have an instinct against stepping into the unknown, and some people stay in abusive but predictable relationships rather than try to escape into uncertainty. If we can consciously recognize our instinct, and recognize it as derived from our distant evolutionary past, we can consciously take action to better deal with modern day circumstances. If you are in an abusive relationship you need to acknowledge that you are near rock bottom and whilst escaping may be a step into the unknown it is also a step into a better world. However it is essential you find someone or some authority to go to for help: there are many organizations highly skilled in helping victims of abuse.

The Bumper Book of Common Sense

* In addition to what might be termed traumas are events such as loss of a partner or close family member, or a serious enforced change in lifestyle such as through severe injury, which give rise to strong feelings of grief. Such an event will result in all kinds of difficult emotions and it will feel like the pain you are experiencing will never let up. This is normal. Grief affects different people in different ways and there are no 'normal' stages people go through, though there are common strong emotions people feel such as disbelief and guilt and anger and fear and a profound sadness, as well as physical symptoms such as fatigue and nausea and aches and insomnia and those arising from a general lowering of immunity. In such circumstances it is vital to get support, from family members or friends, from counsellors or therapists, from a support group of which there will almost certainly be one not too far away, and from your faith if you have one. It is also important to try to look after yourself. Get into little routines that ensure you eat properly, get a little exercise, and keep clean. Face up to your feelings by writing about it in a private diary or journal, and if you have lost someone close maybe write to them, or put together a photo album celebrating their life, or get involved in something that was important to them. Certainly do not turn to alcohol or drugs to numb the pain. Accept the pain of grief, but then seek, step by step, to find a continuing life.

Recognizing and Managing Depression and Stress

* If you are very depressed, particular if you have thoughts about suicide, then seek help.

* If you find your life is lacking any meaning and your thoughts are turning to suicide, go spend six months working for the Missionaries of Charity. It will likely transform your life.

* If you are depressed go out and find ways to help other people who are in need. Join a volunteer help group. You will learn to appreciate life once again.

* When faced with high levels of stress our brains will sometimes go into a self-protection lock down mode. This can be a crippling liability. If you find yourself in such a state then try to take very small actions that at least get you moving. They may not seem much, but by keeping them up, and keeping them small enough so that you can actually do them, you will gradually start to get out of this state.

* Learned helplessness arises when we have frequently experienced failure or being controlled or being abused and we have become fatalistic about never being able to take control over our own lives, and we stop trying. Should you feel like this then you need to seek out small opportunities for taking control, small opportunities where you can make decisions and choices. If you can show yourself that you are capable of making small decisions, no matter how small, you will come to realize that you are also able to make bigger choices. And rather than slipping back into a negative fatalism should one not work out, think in terms of having made a choice, learnt from it, and moving on the next opportunity to make a choice.

* When you feel overwhelmed it is important to take action. You cannot deal with everything, but if you get on with something worthwhile you will calm your mind and be able to better focus on what is important. If you are not sure what is most important don't let yourself stay in a state of overwhelmed inaction. Do something, anything. You can always change it to doing something else if you consider something else to be more important.

* Continual worry and stress take a physical toll on our bodies and we will get sick more often and for longer. If you are under stress for a prolonged period you will age considerably.

* Be aware of signs of problems arising from stress and take action before they become serious. Most major health problems which occur when middle-aged, such as heart attacks, arise from an accumulation of stress and poor eating and exercise habits. You are continually 'getting away with it', and thus ignore the symptoms. But you are not really getting away with it, because one day it will become catastrophic. You need to deal with the issues when they don't seem so important, because if you don't, by the time they become important it is already too late. Signs of problems building up include:

- o Frequent exhaustion;
- o Inability to get a good night's sleep;
- o Significant changes in weight, up or down, without very obvious causes;
- o Frequent constipation or diarrhea;
- o Being prone to getting spots or skin blemishes without obvious causes;
- o High blood pressure and frequent palpitations or dizziness.

* If you get stressed when driving, do something about it. Instead of getting upset by other drivers go out of your way to be courteous to them. Play soft music rather than loud or jerky music, and don't listen to the news or other things that might rile or agitate you.

* No matter how bad things are, always remember that they could get worse.

* If you are the partner of someone who is depressed you are likely to readily become angry and blaming. Watch out for this, it won't help and it is likely to lead to a spiraling out of control. Try to develop tactics to stop yourself engaging in negative emotional interactions, which may include walking away for a while.

* If you are having some relationship problems, don't over think them. Beyond a little bit of thought, the more you try to analyze a relationship problem the worse you are likely to feel about it. You are likely to either become self-righteous or you try to construct some fantastical psychological explanation for what is often simply thoughtless behavior. Relationship problems need to be tackled, but by talking to the other person and telling them how you feel, not by trying to psychoanalyze their every action.

* Stress makes us less socially competent. We become obsessed with ourselves and pay less attention to others. If you are with someone who is stressed recognize that the stress will be impacting on their ability to interact with you. Be more patient with them and look to stay calm yourself.

* You need to be willing to give if you want good relationships. This doesn't mean allowing yourself to be a doormat, however neither should you be seeking to get your own way all the time. Don't get stressed when things don't go the way you would like, so long as sometimes they do.

* People who are seeking always to maximize will tend to be more successful, but will also be more stressed and unhappy, than those who are willing to accept when things are good enough. You can be successful, happy, and content without the stress of permanently looking to maximize every moment or every interaction.

* You may be unsure of whether or not you are suffering from stress. The following are some common signs to look out for:
  - o You feel resentment against people who seem to have a better life than you;
  - o Minor niggles dominate your thoughts;
  - o You say 'should', 'ought', or 'must' a lot;
  - o You find it hard to motivate yourself;
  - o You feel tired most of the time;
  - o You lack confidence and self-esteem;
  - o You have prolonged health problems;
  - o You feel life could be so much better if only …

* Dealing with stress is largely about dealing with how you think. Firstly you need to accept that the world is as it is, and not get upset that it is not as you would like it to be. Secondly you need to take control of the issues that are stressing you, which is largely about being clear about what they are

The Bumper Book of Common Sense

and determining how you are going to tackle them. And thirdly it is about following through on how you have decided to tackle the issues that are stressing you.

* List all the things that worry you and decide what your next step for each one is. Your stress levels will reduce significantly.

* We are unlikely to deal with stress effectively if our response is hostile and confrontational either towards others or towards ourselves. Nor are we likely to deal with significant stress through denial, hoping it will go away, or trying to escape through distractions. You may feel that smoking or TV or drinking is 'relaxing' you, but it is invariably storing up further problems. The best way of dealing with stress is to recognize it, and take responsibility for dealing with it, possibly with the help of others.

* When getting yourself out of a stressful situation all you can do is start from where you are and begin to take steps. If you focus on where you want to be, you will be despondent and demoralized about how far you have to go. If you move from where you are you can be successful in making progress.

* Be aware of your negative thoughts and consciously recognize them as weakening you. Think through whether they are telling you something useful. If so, what is it? If not, put the thoughts behind you.

* Take specific action to deal with circumstances that are stressing you. Identify what you can do then pull out all the stops to do it.

* Sometimes we can avoid a situation that is stressing us through putting off dealing with it, and doing something else instead. However this only provides us with a temporary relief, and the stress will generally be worse in the longer term. If something is bothering you, deal with it. Don't let it fester. Tackle it head on.

* Much of stress, and the cause of burnout, is taking on too much; when you are continually setting yourself too many goals or tasks, and are continually failing to reach or complete them. By all means take on challenges, but many people take on more than they have any chance of accomplishing without working 24 hours a day; and then they beat themselves up because they failed. This is very common, and you need to face it head on. Rather than continually taking on too much, you need to match what you are taking on with what you can reasonably do within the time available.

* Stress comes largely from unkept agreements with yourself. Keep your agreements, cancel them, or renegotiate them. Don't just let them pass by.

* Procrastination is the root cause of much of the stress in our lives. And it leads to a catch 22 since one of our responses to stress is further procrastination thus leading to more stress and worry. Learn techniques for overcoming procrastination.

* Many things that turn out difficult and stressful would have been much easier if tackled earlier.

* When you are stressed your body is craving a decision, any decision: fight or flight. It is the indecisiveness that is feeding your stress. Improving your decision making skills can significantly help you reduce stress, coupled with the recognition that if you can't choose between two options, either because you haven't got time or the pros and cons even out, then just go with one, either the one you feel instinctive about, or the one that seems easiest, or the one that seems most difficult if you want to learn from it.

* Often your stress results directly from habitual modes of behavior. You need to be more aware of this so you can change the habits that give rise to or contribute to eventual stress.

* It is often not the doing of stressful things that creates stress in us, it is not being able to switch off from it. It is having it follow you around when you are doing other things that are not in

themselves stressful, and having it disrupt your sleep. By learning to still and relax your mind you can deal easily with what might otherwise be exceedingly stressful circumstances.

* Stress relief strategies that don't work include: gambling, eating, surfing the internet, shopping, drinking alcohol, watching TV, or procrastination. Stress relief strategies that do work include: exercise and playing sports, doing a creative hobby, prayer – if you are religious, listening to calming music, reading, or taking action to address some particular issue that is stressing you.

* Being unemployed at home able to watch TV in the afternoon may sound relaxing, but it would for most people lead to a very stressful life. Better to spend your time doing what you can to get back into paid employment. This might even include doing some unpaid charity work just to keep your hand in at interacting with people, to get more contacts, and to be able to show prospective employers that you are willing to work.

* Failure to feel in control of our lives leads to both anxiety and stress. Thus people unemployed or in menial low paid jobs are often more stressed than those in high-pressure jobs. Make the effort to get more control by working hard and learning new skills to get yourself into paid or better paid employment, and to get yourself into positions where you are trusted to make your own decisions.

* Stress can be reduced by gaining control over the things you are responsible for. If you feel as though you are not in control look for ways to gain more control. If you are willing to be proactive and show initiative with respect to the tasks passed to you, those giving you the tasks are more likely to let you get on with them in your own way. However you must be willing to take responsibility, ensure you go out of your way to understand what is really wanted, and make the effort to get them done for when they need to be done by.

* Look to have at least an hour a day that is yours to do with as you will. It doesn't matter what you do within reason, so long as it is your own choice and it is not part of everything else that is going on during the day.

* Having a place you can call your own, with things around that relax you, can be a great way of reducing stress. If you don't have a space you can call your own, you can just have a box with a collection of things that make you feel calmer, which you can get out when you are on your own from time to time and lay out in front of you.

* You can reduce stress by listening to relaxing music, or taking some form of aerobic exercise, or finding something to laugh at, or owning and looking after a pet. Before buying a pet however be sure you are willing to take the time to look after it.

* Whenever you are feeling stressed take five minutes or so to concentrate on your breathing, and taking deep breaths. This will increase oxygen flow to your brain and will help you relax and soothe your nerves.

* You can significantly reduce your stress levels by spending more time being aware of the present; letting go of continual thoughts of the past and the future and the emotional clenching that results. You can still bring past and future to mind but in a matter of fact way in order to learn lessons or make plans rather than just having them living repetitively in your mind without resolution.

* The more you can live in the present, the less problems will weigh you down. We feel overwhelmed or stressed by problems because we are worrying about the future. If you focus on living in the present then problems no longer get you down. You can work in the present on solving your problems without getting stressed by them.

* A common cause of stress is a mismatch between what is happening and what you expected to be happening. If you accept what is happening and get on and deal with any issues that genuinely need dealing with, then you will be much less stressed.

The Bumper Book of Common Sense

* Not all stress is bad. Stress helps you focus; gives you energy and purpose. It is too much stress that is harmful. You know when you are too stressed because it is bothering you. If you are happily getting on with a busy life, even a very busy life, then you are highly unlikely to be over stressed.

* Stress is an opportunity. Something is not right and the fact that you feel stressed about it is telling you this. If you take it as a call to action rather than wallow in the self-pity of it you have the opportunity for improving things and growing stronger and more able in doing so.

* Too little stress can lead to boredom and a general feeling of ennui. You need to seek out some challenges that involve some stress. Our bodies need some stimulation and reason to perform.

Learn from Mistakes and Failures and Put Them Behind You

* Don't get too worked up about your mistakes or past decisions. Once they are made they are made. Feeling bad about them doesn't make them any better. If you can do something to rectify or partially rectify the situation, do so. If not, accept your mistake, learn from it, and get on with what you can.

* Forgive yourself. Nobody is immune to error. Learn from it, resolve to avoid similar mistakes in the future, and move on.

* Don't rationalize your failure or look for excuses. Though you can, and many do, find excuses, it doesn't help you move on. Whatever your excuse might be, it was simply a factor you should have taken into account but didn't adequately do so. Look for ways to succeed next time, not excuses for failing last time.

* Whilst it is appropriate to focus on the positive and put negative experiences behind you, ensure that you learn from them. The well-used saying that "those who cannot remember the past are condemned to repeat it", is as applicable to ourselves in our daily lives as it is to society more generally.

* It is your failures that give you the most intense learning experiences. Treat failures as the best feedback opportunities you are ever likely to get.

* Adversity and failure are intense learning experiences, and those who have failures and learn from them will generally learn quicker and more effectively than those who don't have failures.

* It is often better to have tried and failed than not to have tried at all. There are people who won't try something so that they can say to themselves, and others, that they could have succeeded if they had. Maybe they would, and maybe they wouldn't. They will however have learnt nothing. Whereas those who tried and failed will probably have learnt something, will be better able to succeed in the future, and are more in touch with reality than those who didn't try.

* Failure is the opportunity to begin again, wiser and better able. Failures along the way make you stronger and make the eventual success all the more likely.

* Somebody who can justly be called smart is not so because they don't make mistakes, but because they don't keep making the same mistakes.

* Become sensitive to the small mistakes you make during the day. Actively recognize any small mistakes you make and think about how you might try to avoid them in the future. Keep a note of them and how you can take action to avoid their re-occurrence – you are more likely to learn from your mistakes if you write them down.

* If you have big things that go wrong, think about whether there were any warning signs you could have picked up on, and ways in which you might have tackled the issue earlier if you had been more aware of it. How would you recognize it or a similar situation emerging again in the future?

* Don't get over anxious about a social faux pas. In the vast majority of cases they are far more obvious and significant to you than they are to others. Whilst you are at the center of your own world and such things are very obvious, you are not the center of other people's worlds. What might linger in your mind for days, months, even years, will have mostly gone from others within minutes. And even if it does linger in others for some particular memorable reason it will have far less significance to them than it does to you.

When Feeling a Bit Down

* Keep things in perspective. With the exception of extreme circumstances, whatever happens, life will go on.

* Things are often not as bad as they appear to be. Try to see things in a wider context. How will they seem in a year's time? How would they seem to someone in dire circumstances in the third world, or to someone who has only a few months to live, or to your ancestors living a hundred years ago in dire poverty? How would someone you respect as being high effective respond to the situation you are in, or what would they say to you? For the vast majority of us, no matter how bad our troubles they are as naught compared to the daily troubles of most during most of history, and the troubles of many others today.

* You are lucky to be alive. If you think about it, the odds of you existing with your particular mix of genes and early life experiences, are astronomically low: think about the chances of your parents meeting, or your parents parents; think about the chances of you being conceived just when you were. So appreciate being alive.

* If you worry a lot, 90% of what you worry about never happens. And what does happen is usually easier to deal with than you thought it would be.

* Much of our unhappiness arises from having high expectations about material possessions. If we lower our expectations we may well feel better. In truth many of us have far more than we need and can get by with much less.

* Many people judge their own worth by comparing themselves to others. They see others doing well and get down about how they themselves are doing. But there will always be others doing better than you in some way. And most of the same people you compare yourself to are comparing themselves to others and also feeling down. It is much better to focus on your own life, live your own life, and leave others to live theirs. If you are unhappy about aspects of your life then determine what you can do about it, and go about doing it.

* A common source of unhappiness is the realization we are failing to achieve our life goals, or the realization that we are living our lives without any meaning. In such circumstances your concept of success is probably focused on material gain or on seeking power over others. You can change such unhappiness by defining and striving for life goals which are more focused on your own self-improvement and on being more focused on making life better for others.

* Don't worry about questions you can't answer: 'How long have I got to live? Am I going to suffer serious problems as I get older? Will my children keep in touch when they leave home? Rather than worry about such things, put your energies into living healthy, saving money for the future, being good to your children, etc.

* Rather than let negative emotions and thoughts run around in your head, write them down. Negative thoughts are less wearing if you write them down than if you just leave them running

The Bumper Book of Common Sense

around in your head. Once you've written them down you can think objectively about what you might do to tackle any underlying issues.

* If you are feeling down write down 3 or 4 things you have to be grateful for. Remind yourself of how luck you are to be alive and of all the good things you have.

* Sometimes all you need is a bit of relaxation time. There are many ways of relaxing, including: deep breath relaxation, muscle and body relaxation, doing stretching exercises, yoga, meditation, focusing on the here and now, relaxing visualization, exercising, taking a walk, reading, having a bath. Some people would claim that watching TV helps them relax, and it may if you do a little of it. A lot of TV however will very likely increase levels of anxiety. Watching too much of the news, for example, which is far more often down beat rather than upbeat, will sap your energies.

* To change the way you are feeling, change what you are doing.

* If you are feeling down get active. Do something physical.

* If you are feeling down, ring a good friend, go for a walk or a jog, listen to some energizing music and preferably dance around to it, be kind to someone, do something active that you enjoy.

* If you are feeling down find a very quiet environment and just let things wander through your mind. Try and detach yourself from your thoughts and just let them pass through your head without judging them.

* If you make a mistake and feel highly embarrassed, note that it is often far less obvious to others than it is to yourself.

* You can go around thinking that everyone is out to get you, that when people are laughing they are laughing at you, that the words people say to you or about you have been carefully chosen. But it's unlikely to be the case. If you believe you have been verbally attacked you are far better to ignore it or treat it in jest rather than take it to heart.

* If you are feeling anxious your views will be much narrower than they would otherwise be. Do not try to solve problems if you are feeling anxious. You need to get yourself into a positive frame of mind. Do something you are good at for a while, or think about some of the good things in your life.

Take Responsibility for Dealing with your Unhappiness, Worries or Problems

* You must deal with long term stress. If you don't you will be prone to illnesses, depression and a host of physical and mental problems which will do you real harm.

* You need to deal with things that are worrying you. Make a plan and take action. Worry left to fester will damage your health.

* Talk to yourself as a best friend you've known all your life would do, giving yourself home truths about how to deal with the things that are stressing you.

* If you are generally unhappy in your life, it is time to move on. Don't see it as a distressing concern; see it as feedback on your current life, responding to which will improve your life.

* Not all problems in life have a solution as such, particularly problems about our relationships with others and about how we live our lives. Some problems need to be transcended, which leads to them going away because we see the world in a different way.

* If you are unhappy it may be because you are striving for the wrong things. If your happiness is based upon comparing yourself to others, or on your material possessions, then be aware that striving for material possessions and popularity rarely leads to any form of long-term happiness. Helping others, learning and developing, living relatively simply, are all more likely to lead to happiness in life.

* Much of what upsets us arises from a belief that things should be different to the way they are. People should treat us fairly; people should appreciate our efforts; people should know when we are upset; unlucky things shouldn't happen to us. But things unfold the way they do, not the way we would like them to. Accept that and deal with things as you find them.

* This is your life. The alternative is complete none existence, and that will come about soon enough. Most of what you feel upset about is the result of your own attitudes towards life. Circumstances are what they are. It is not circumstances that cause you to be upset it is your attitude towards circumstances, and in particular your expectations about circumstances. You expect the world to revolve around you and everything to fall in place the way you want it to. It doesn't. If you can accept that and deal with life as you find it, adapting to it as best you can, influencing it as best you can, then you can deal with almost anything.

* No matter how bad things are or seem to be, raise your sights and see the possibilities - for they are always there.

* Whenever you have a problem see yourself as the problem. By seeing yourself as the problem you can also see that the solution lies with yourself. If we see ourselves as victims of problems we lose the motivation, the creativity, and thus the means to go about resolving them.

* Accepting responsibility for all the problems you have, sets you free. It gives you the power to do something about them.

* People who are always blaming others for why things aren't going right are rarely happy.

* If you blame your failures and lack of success on others, you are unlikely to be any more successful in the future. If you accept them as being your own fault, but rather than beating yourself up look to change yourself, your behaviors, and your actions, then you are far more likely to be successful in the future.

* People who are driving never get car sick. If you are overwhelmed by problems then you need to get organized, be clear about what your next actions are, and work through them in priority order: get into the driver seat.

* Worry and anxiety should be seen as danger signals. And danger signals are a good thing not a bad thing, since they are a call to action. The response should be identifying solutions, planning them out, and taking action. If you find it difficult to get on with tackling a given worry adopt a 'do something small' approach. You don't need to solve it all in one go, and by doing something towards solving it you will build up some momentum in tackling it, which you might struggle to do if you try to tackle it all at once.

* Simply avoiding circumstances we feel anxious about but know we should engage in will generally mean the anxiety will be increased in future circumstances, and will mean we are missing out on aspects of life. Much better to adopt strategies that enable us to manage our anxiety. We usually find that once we engage in such activities they are rarely as bad as we feared.

* Procrastination leads to increased anxiety.

* Our anxieties tend to be driven by either a fear of not being worthy, or a fear of losing control. If you can pinpoint the cause of a particular anxiety you are more likely to find a way of addressing it.

* The freer we are in our heads the more creative and productive we can be. Get your worries out of your head, and deal with them, or put in place a plan to deal with them.

- If you have worries, particularly ones that are keeping you awake at night, then decide what needs to be done about them, and do it. You need to get your worries sorted if you are to release the creative energy to help you be proactive in what matters to you. If you don't address your worries they will be continually sapping your energy and dragging you down.

- Be wary of running away from your problems and fears. You can often distract yourself or find other things to do other than to deal with some problem or fear you have. But if it is one that keeps coming back, that possibly keeps you awake at night, then you need to face up to it head on and deal with it. Most problems and fears can be dealt with if you think about them and think about what options you have and make decisions and take action. Even those for which you can't find any desirable outcome, there is a best that can be done in the circumstances.

- If you are worrying about something, ask yourself what can you do about it now. You don't need to necessarily completely solve it, though you should if you can. But just working out what the next thing to do is, and doing it, significant reduces your feeling of stress about it. Worry makes problems grow; action makes them recede. Even 5 minutes of action can significantly reduce the amount of worry and stress you feel about something that is bothering you.

- Embrace your problems. Problems are good for us. They help us to grow, to develop, to learn; they give us a sense of satisfaction; they enable us to focus and apply the skills we have been developing for years and possibly decades. Do not run away from problems, go out and meet them head on with a joy in your heart. How dull and lifeless life would be without problems.

- Identify a particular problem that you have been avoiding, and which is stressing you, and brainstorm creative ways of dealing with it. You need to distance yourself from the thought of actually implementing the ideas as they occur otherwise you will be very limited in the ideas you come up with. Think of the ideas as advice you might give someone else who has the same problem. If you initially focus on just trying to generate novel ideas there is a good chance you will come up with ideas that hadn't previously occurred to you and which you are more likely to give a chance than those which had already occurred to you, and which you have been avoiding.

- Don't get stressed by challenging circumstances. Be willing and happy to take them on. They are part of what makes life worthwhile. Get into a mindset that sees them as something that help you to be the best you can be. Indeed without challenging circumstances you should ask yourself whether or not you are really taking on anything worthwhile.

- Don't ignore problems. Small problems can easily escalate. Many crises could have been avoided if they had been addressed before they had become serious.

- Get things finished. Starting lots of things but not finishing them gives rise to considerable stress. If you have trouble finishing things, start fewer things until you get better at finishing them.

- Worrying without actually doing something about it wastes time and drains energy. Once a week ensure all your worries and tasks are written down with clear identification of the next thing you are going to do. Every day keep your To Do Lists up to date.

- Not making decisions is a common cause of stress. Once there is no more information to be had, then you should get on and make the decision. If you can't decide on the best decision then toss a coin, or go with whichever one you feel instinctively best about. Make the decision and then deal with the consequences. Be aware that delaying the decision is making things worse.

- Change, or the possibility of change, can be very stressful. We have an expectation things should be the same, and get stressed when they aren't. However it is unrealistic to expect things to always be the same, and indeed society would be a far poorer place if it was. Accept that times change and adapt as best you can to the changes and be open to the fact that change gives rise to opportunities if you are on the lookout for them.

- We can reduce stress by taking control of what is happening around us and planning more.

* Sometimes, when faced with seeming insurmountable problems, you need help. It's natural. You don't need to fight against it or be embarrassed. Accept any help that is offered you, so long as it is genuinely offered in your interests, and appreciate it.

* If you're worrying about something happening ask yourself 'so what if it happens?' What will be the worst that can happen? In many cases it will not be so bad, and even if it is, if you can prepare for what you would do in those circumstances then it is less likely to prey on your mind.

* If you're worrying about something that might happen, tell yourself it will either happen or it won't. If you can do things to make it less likely to happen, or to mitigate the consequences should it happen, then do them. If you can't, tell yourself that worry won't help one iota. If it happens you'll deal with it. In the meantime get on with your life.

* If you feel guilty about something, either do something about it, or let it go. If you have difficulty letting it go think about what you would say to a close friend in such a situation. Would you beat them up about it, or tell them to get over it?

* Whatever problems you face, know that other people have faced similar and worst problems. Some of those people have been overwhelmed by them and some have overcome them. Whether you are overwhelmed or you overcome is dependent upon you, not the circumstances.

* When your head is full of worrying thoughts, focus on your breathing and let it slowly become deeper. Be aware of all your thoughts but keep focused on your breathing and the thoughts will gradually subside.

* If you are prone to panic attacks and fast breathing, learn breathing techniques to enable you to slow your breathing. It will calm you down.

* Regret does nothing for you. Rather than waste your energy on regret use it to pursue what is important to you. Things don't always go well, and sometimes you make mistakes. But regretting it does nothing for you. Move on.

* Don't seek excuses for how you are or what you do by blaming your childhood and your parents. Your parents were not perfect, but no parents are. Any more than you are perfect if you are a parent. Once you are grown up you need to take responsibility for your own life. If you consider your parents to blame, then you need to blame their parents, and so on.

* Do not let some incident from your past be an excuse for how you are now or for the actions you take now. You either believe you have free will or you don't. If you do, then take responsibility. If you don't, then accept that others have every right to constrain or punish you.

* Living with guilt, self-blame, or regret, will hold you back from living your life constructively and happily. Put them aside. By all means plan to correct things if you believe you can and ought, but don't let the negative feelings eat away at you.

* Don't dwell on negative questions such as 'how could I have been so stupid?' or 'why does everyone have an easier life than me?' Replace them with positive questions about what can you do going forward.

* If you have had some major trauma in your life that keeps gnawing away at you then you need to get professional help. If you don't believe it is significant enough to go get professional help then you need to put it behind you. You need to find ways to stop thinking about it, and find ways to reduce the stress you feel whenever you do think about it. Find some positive memories to bring to mind when the bad memory surfaces.

* You cannot bring about changes in the physical world through thought alone. If you think badly of someone and something bad happens to them, it is not your fault.

* If there is no remedy, why worry.

The Bumper Book of Common Sense

* Most of the stuff people worry about never happens.

* Don't let yourself get stressed by taking on other people's problems. Help them when you can if you have good reason to do so, but other people are responsible for their own problems.

Turning Problems and Worries Round

* To tackle long term stress problems, write them down on a piece of paper. If you try to deal with them solely in your head you will keep going round in circles. By writing them down you can list out causes and consequences and circumstances and write down actions you need to take to tackle them.

* If you believe your life is in a rut, that you not making any progress and you are not particularly happy about it, then the following are some tips for changing your mindset:
  o Have an honest look at your life and think about what is holding you back – is it about relationships, or the work you do, or some bad habits you've gotten into, or a combination. Maybe there's nothing you can put your finger on, but just a case of you having gotten too comfortable and complacent in your life;
  o Become more consciously aware of yourself and what you are doing during the day. Seek to be more focused on the now, totally focusing on the activity you are doing and seeking to be as aware of being in the moment as you can. Seek to see the things around you in a new light, try to see them as though they were things you hadn't seen before, and be curious about the detail;
  o Set yourself some goals or targets. Something challenging but not overwhelming or unrealistic. Be time bounded in regards the goals or significant progress towards the goals. What would you like to have done in the next month, what would you like to have achieved over the next 12 months;
  o Learn some new skill or take a course. Seek out new acquaintances. Putting ourselves into new situations and meeting new people gets us into a different mindset that mitigates against seeing life as a continual bore.

* You can handle most of what life throws at you if you believe you can. Moreover by adopting an attitude of facing up to difficulties and tackling them as best you can you will get better at tackling difficulties, much like doing physical exercise strengthens your muscles.

* Tough times are great opportunities to reassess what we're doing in our lives and change and improve our approach to what we are doing.

* In some ways the more difficulties we face the more opportunities we have to grow and the more we can take pride in the way we are living our lives.

* Look for the opportunities that exist in every situation. Circumstances may not be as you would have liked, but if you are always positive then some good will usually come out of them, or at least more good than might otherwise have come about. It is not uncommon for situations which are initially undesirable to turn out to have unexpected benefits; sometimes even greater benefit than might have been gained if the situation had not arisen in the first place. For example persons made redundant often end up finding or doing something better than they would have done had they stayed in their original job.

* We have the ability to reinterpret the way we think about past events in our lives. We can think of past events as failures and that we ourselves are a failure. Or we could think of ourselves as someone trying out different approaches and being a learning machine that is now much more likely to succeed in the future.

* We can control our interpretation of the meaning of a situation. We can use this to shift our mood or emotional state. For example, by acknowledging certain feelings as being perfectly normal – such as the stress of dealing with change or too much work – we then feel more in control rather than simply feel overwhelmed.

* If you are involved in something you would like to get out of, but feel unable to make a clean break, then you can take it slowly by gradually reducing your commitment, and preferably by starting or increasing your commitment towards something else. If you do this over a period of time then there will come a time when the break becomes much easier and not such a daunting prospect.

* Analyze your regrets to determine what you will do in the future in similar circumstances.

* Voluntarily giving some of your time and energy to a charity or organization or event you believe in, can be very rewarding and make you feel much better about yourself.

* You need a personal vision to put into perspective what might otherwise be a constant stream of worries and annoyances.

* Depression doesn't cause negative thinking; negative thinking is the root cause of depression. To beat depression you need to change how you think about the world and about yourself.

Memory

Memory Tends to be Meaning Focused

* We tend to remember meaning rather than the words. After someone's speech we will remember what we understand the speaker was trying to say rather than the specific words they used to say it.

* It's hard to remember information you don't understand and can't put into some context. We remember things better if we can relate them to things we already know.

* You don't need to try to remember everything. Much information, for example, is readily available on the internet. There is however a balance. We should try to remember sufficient basic facts about a topic such that we provide our minds with an architecture off which we can hang the details should we have a reason for looking them up. This enables us to put the details into some sort of context that is meaningful. Thus knowing and remembering some key dates from history, and their significance vis-à-vis different empires or countries or people, enables us to put in context other dates we don't know off by heart. Without this remembered historical architecture in our heads we would struggle to put other dates into any meaningful context.

Make Associations and Patterns

* Things are easier to remember if we can form patterns with them. Remembering the pattern then helps us to remember the original information. Disorganized and random information is very difficult to remember.

* We find it easier to remember information we can visualize. Try to turn abstract ideas into something you can visualize either directly or through use of analogies and metaphors. Use exaggeration and absurdities to make the visualizations stronger.

- You are more likely to remember something if you can make it personal, relating it to something that has personal meaning to you.

- Information is easier to remember if other associations are made, such as rhymes, smells, tastes, or visual layouts. Absurd connections between ideas are also usually much easier to remember.

- If there is something you want to remember, make up or use a rhyming saying, generally the sillier the better. Information embedded in rhyming poems or sayings is usually much easier to remember than the same information in a simple list or sentence format. Particularly if you also create a vivid mental image to accompany it.

- Memory tricks usually rely on creating links between the things you want to remember and something you already know. For example link a sequence of things you want to remember to a place you know well, linking specific items on your list to specific aspects of the place you know. Then later when you mentally walk or look around the place you know well you should find you can recall the items on your original list. Variations of this technique have been used to enable remarkable feats of memory.

- If you have a sequence of things to remember, creating a story that leads from one item to the next will significantly increase your ability to remember the items. Make the story vivid and absurd, increase the sizes of things in your mind and make them do silly things.

- To remember a sequence of letters you can make up a short saying or story using each letter as the first letter of a word. Using humor helps.

- We find it almost impossible to remember number sequences that have no meaning to us. The trick used for memorizing such things is to turn them into something that has meaning. For example you might be able to turn a number sequence into a date.

- Break long sequences of letters or numbers into 'chunks', whereby you can use a trick for each chunk, and you can find a way of remembering the sequence of chunks.

- Be wary of choosing unusual passwords or hiding places. It they don't have any meaning for you unless you write them down you are likely to forget them. Better to choose something with a link that will come to mind later. If you make quick decisions about passwords or hiding places you are more likely to follow the same logic when you want remember. If you try to be clever about choosing them, you will find it harder or impossible to follow the same logic later.

Write it Down

- To improve your chances of remembering something, write it down. The very act of writing it down, assuming you do it slowly and deliberately, improves your memory of it.

- Why try to rely on memory when you can write it down? Keep a list or notebook of things to remember and simply look at it now and again. You may never forget anything important again. This includes information about people, for example shoe and ring and dress and trouser sizes for people close to you, information about children or interests for acquaintances.

- Writing something down that you want to remember frees up your mind to do some thinking without the continual interruption of ensuring yourself that you still remember the thing or things you wanted to remember.

- If you are going out to buy certain things, then make and take a list of them with you.

* Use a calendar for any dates you need to remember, and, just as importantly, mark the days on which you need to do things: when to go out and buy presents or cards, when to send cards, when to undertake preparatory action in support of upcoming events, etc. etc.

* When you get someone's business card, jot down on the back when you met them, in what context, and any details that might help bring to mind their face.

* Don't try to remember thoughts, write them down, particularly creative thoughts or things you know you want to remember. Always have a way of recording such thoughts with you, a piece of paper and pen or a recorder. It is worth the expense of buying a decent audio recorder if you like such devices.

* Keep checklists for things you do which you might have to do again such as organizing events or making trips. You can improve such checklists based on your experience of using them.

* Our minds are not particularly good at remembering things. Our minds are good at reviewing options, identifying possible solutions, and making decisions. But it doesn't do these things very well if it has to keep trying to remember what the options are, or what factors to take into account. Write these things down and let your brain do what it is good at.

* We often find that things occur to us in the night that had slipped our mind during the day. Always have a pen and paper close by your bed so that if you do wake up with thoughts of something you can write it down. Don't assume you will remember your thoughts in the morning.

* The use of mindmaps, also called spider diagrams or radial patterns, can help memory. A key word or phrase is put in the middle of a blank piece of paper, often in landscape format, and lines drawn out with words on or at the end of the lines representing related or sub- ideas. Further lines can then be drawn radiating out from those lines representing further sub-sub- ideas. It is usually much easier to recall information in this format than it is in long lists. Some guidance which helps them to be better remembered includes making use of different colors, underlining or highlighting key ideas, making use of the spacing in some visually significant way, avoiding too many words, and adding symbols, sketches or pictures.

Pay Attention

* For long term memories to form you need to pay close attention. If you are multitasking, for example doing e-mails or writing whilst also listening to someone, you will find it difficult to remember what that person said.

* Our memories for details are lousy unless we've made the effort to pay particular attention. Our brains focus on memorizing meaning. For example, try to draw the details on a coin from memory – you've been handling them for years, decades, but the details are likely to be sketchy unless you have spent time studying them.

* We have far more difficulty remembering things we did on autopilot than things we were paying attention to at the time. If you want to remember doing something, such as checking things when you leave the house, think deliberately about doing them, maybe noticing some detail in the surroundings as you do so.

* We are much better at remembering faces and occupations and where people are from than we are at remembering people's names. Key elements of improving your ability to remember someone's name when you first meet them, which you will get better at with practice, are:
  o Notice detail about their features, albeit without being obvious or interrupting the flow of your meeting or interaction with them;
  o Ask them to repeat their name if you didn't get it clearly, or possibly to spell it. Jot it down if you can;

The Bumper Book of Common Sense

- o   Mention their name back to them a couple of times. It reinforces it in your mind. However don't go overboard;
- o   Envisage, possibly immediately afterwards, links between them and their name. Use your imagination. You are looking for a way that when you see them again, or recall their features or characteristics, then their name will also come to mind. A typical way of doing this is to take some feature, exaggerate it in your mind, and then find some play on words you can use to link their name to the feature. Alternatively you could make some play on words with their name and relate exaggerated images. However keep all this to yourself;
- o   If you forget their name, apologize and ask them, or ask someone else, or look them up. You may find, for example, that they are on an e-mail you were also copied in on; whilst you might not be able to recall their name, you might if their name is amongst a number of names you can see listed.

* You can improve your memory of the things you are trying to learn or remember by working at it: pick out salient points, make your own summary notes, and try to structure new information against your current understanding.

* Items that stand out, so long as you notice them, are likely to be remembered. Thus if you have a list of things amongst which is one or two you really want to remember, make them stand out in some way, eg. by highlighting them in a bright color. You are much more likely to then remember them.

* At the end of a meeting, or having read something, get into the habit of summarizing to yourself the 3 main points you would like to remember for the longer term.

Memories can be False or Mislead

* People reconstruct their memories in positive self-flattering ways. They see their past through rose-tinted glasses, and can even come to believe what are largely fantasy memories. Ask a husband and wife what percentage of the housework they themselves each do, and in the vast majority of cases and sum will be considerably greater than 100%.

* We tend to remember things that reinforce what we already agree with or believe, and are less likely to remember things that don't; which of course then further strengthens our existing beliefs.

* We tend to have a very strong hindsight bias where we believe we knew how things were going to turn out before they did. Before events we rarely come to a strong conclusion one way or the other about how they will turn out, but after the event we clearly remember thoughts that related to the way they did turn out and largely forget those that related to the alternatives, leaving us with a strong impression that we 'knew it all along'.

* Memory has a habit of exaggerating or minimizing pleasant or unpleasant sensations.

* Having extracted meaning from something, we may then have a false impression of the detail that gave rise to that meaning. Take the common case of people witnessing a traffic accident. They often report having seen very different things. This is because they will have put the bits of information they did see from their particular viewpoint into a coherent understanding of what they believe happened, and then believe that that is what they did see happening - which they didn't.

* The patterns we create to link things and thus remember them may be figments of our imagination.

* False memories can be created by implicit or explicit implications and suggestibility on the part of the person asking us about what we can remember. There have been frequent examples of injustices resulting from careless questioning of witnesses to, or victims of, crime. And there have been many proven cases of psychotherapists teasing out supposed repressed memories which in

fact never existed. The techniques used to supposedly 'reveal' repressed memories are the same techniques that are very effective in creating false memories. Note that truly traumatic events are not repressed, particularly repeated ones: the view that people repress such memories as some form of defense mechanism is a myth.

* To some extent our memories evolve each time we remember, and what we are remembering is the last time we remembered. Like Chinese whispers our memories are subtly changed each time we remember, influenced by the circumstances and our feelings at each remembering. This accounts in part for people being experts after the fact. Their memories of their earlier beliefs are strongly influenced by how they know things have turned out, and they overestimate the accuracy of their earlier beliefs.

* The following are some common memory biases:
    o We tend to remember the positive things resulting from the options we chose or decision we made more so than the negative things. Our memories support us in seeing ourselves as having made good decisions in the past;
    o We remember things in a self-flattering way, in a way that justifies our actions and makes us feel good about ourselves and what we did or didn't do.
    o We overestimate our involvement in things that turned out well, and underestimate our involvement in things that turned out badly;
    o We tend to remember the past in a more exaggerated manner than it actually was. We can thus come to believe our school exam grades were better than they were or that we were better at given sports or activities than we actually were, albeit assuming we believe ourselves to have been better than average. If we believe we were worse than average we tend to remember ourselves as having been worse than we actually were;
    o We incorrectly remember our past attitudes and behaviors as being consistent with our current attitudes and behaviors;
    o We can come to mistake what were in fact dreams for real events, and we can come to believe that real events were in fact remembered dreams;
    o We remember more details about people who are similar to us than about people who are different. We are also likely to distort our own memories based on stereotypes and prejudices;
    o We tend to remember humorous events better than non-humorous ones;
    o People are more likely to hold as true statements that they have previously heard vis-a-vis ones they haven't, even if they don't remember having heard them;
    o Uncompleted or interrupted tasks are remembered better than tasks we have completed;
    o We can misattribute the source of our memories, whereby we attribute a memory to an incorrect context or circumstance. We can sometimes for example mistakenly believe that we saw in person something that we actually saw on television;
    o We sometimes believe certain ideas were our own when in fact they were ones we have read or heard about;
    o We tend to remember concepts presented in a picture format better than concepts presented in a word format;
    o We remember things at the beginning and end of lists better than we remember things in the middle;
    o We recall personal events from our late teens and early twenties better than personal events from other periods in our lives;
    o We can often remember the idea behind what someone said whilst forgetting the verbatim wording of what they said. If we get the wrong idea we can thus readily misremember what they actually said;
    o We tend to displace recent events further back into time than they actually were, and bring remote events further forward in time;
    o Things that stick out are more likely to be remembered than other items.

The Bumper Book of Common Sense

* As a result of memory biases, when we meet people we once knew a long time ago we feel we have changed significantly whilst they have barely changed at all.

* Whilst our memories change as they are influenced by our beliefs and biases at the time we are remembering, our confidence in those memories also increases. We thus have the double whammy of both a changing memory and a stronger belief in the truth of what are becoming increasingly false memories.

Impact of Health and Way of Life on Memory

* Regular exercise boosts your memory, and this is increasingly important when you get older. Good exercise for your memory includes swimming, cycling, or reasonably brisk walks.

* Good sleep is important for effective long-term memory.

* Being overweight generally impairs memory.

* Food rich in antioxidants seems beneficial to memory, including berries, plums, oranges, grapes, spinach, and broccoli.

Some Everyday Memory Tips

* Place things where they will trigger useful memories. For example if you need to take something out of the house with you, put it next to the front door.

* If you are regularly misplacing certain things, such as keys, ensure you identify somewhere where you will keep them and ensure you put them there whenever you have finished using them.

* Reading aloud can improve your memory. If there are important things you want to remember, try reading them out aloud, though don't annoy other people whilst you are doing so.

* Simple repetition will help you remember. You should also try to express whatever you are trying to remember in different ways. Say it out loud, see it written as words, see it shown in a more visual form, possibly record it and play it back to yourself multiple times.

* A technique used by actors is to associate words or things to be remembered with actions. If you have the opportunity to associate what you want to remember with physical actions this can increase your likelihood of remembering if you are able to then perform the actions as part of your remembering.

* It is common to walk into a room and forget why you went in there, generally more common as you get older. If this has happened to you, try to mentally retrace your steps to think about what you were doing when you initially decided to go into the room. If you still don't remember, literally retrace your steps and go back to what you were doing. If you find yourself frequently forgetting what you wanted to do, get into the habit of visualizing yourself doing what you intend to do before you do it.

* If you have mislaid something and can't remember where you left it, the following are some tips to help find it: focus on where you were and what you were doing when you last saw or used it; think about whether it is something someone else might have borrowed or moved; be systematic in your searching, starting with the most likely place, but be sure you search everywhere in a given place checking any nooks and crannies – most people when they search for something end up spending much of their time searching again places they have already searched. When you search under and

inside settees and drawers, make sure you search them fully – using a torch can help ensure something doesn't lie unnoticed in a shadow.

* If you are having trouble remembering something that is on the tip of your tongue, or for which you keep coming up with what you know to be the wrong thing, best to stop thinking directly about it. Take a break or think about something completely unrelated for a while. Or approach the topic from a completely different direction.

* If you frequently find yourself forgetting whether or not you've switched the iron off, or the oven off, or locked the front door, it's because you are in automatic when you do these tasks. Get in the habit of explicitly paying attention to what top you are wearing every time you do one of these tasks. Then when you come to think about whether or not you did it you'll find yourself remembering what you were wearing and also remember actually doing the task itself.

* We are more likely to remember things when in the state we were when we originally experienced or learnt them, or when the environment, circumstances, or other conditions match those when the memory was first established.

* You are likely to remember information if you are in a similar state as when you first learned it. When studying for exams it is good advice to do your revising and test papers in a similar environment to that which will be relevant in the exams itself. Thus with relative quiet and sitting up at a table.

* Your memory of an event, or something you read or experience, will be better if you think beforehand about your expectations and what you are looking to get out of it. Reading a summary of something beforehand will help you remember what you read more so than if you just read it.

* You can significantly increase the likelihood of remembering something long term if you review it, and test yourself on it, at regular intervals. These should be progressively spaced out – for example after an hour, a day, a week, a month, and finally after about 4 or 5 months. Summarize for yourself the core principles of given topics and then set yourself a sequence of reminders following the above pattern to review them.

* If you are trying to remember things that are similar to each other, the memories can interfere with each other. You should look to either avoid learning similar information close together in time, unless of course they are part of the same 'learning', or ensure you focus on the differences.

* One set of facts can often overwrite a similar set of facts. When you are learning, give yourselves breaks to avoid simply having more recently learned facts overwriting facts learned early in the same session, particularly if they are similar. Also, don't be surprised to find that something once familiar becomes difficult to remember what it was originally like after it has changed. For example if can be difficult to remember the previous telephone numbers of people you know, or places you knew when younger which have since changed. If you see that something or someplace is going to change, and you might want remember it, then make sure you get some written or picture copy before the change.

* You can change a bad memory into a neutral or a positive memory by adding some new happy associations with it. Whenever you have a bad memory you'd rather not have think also of something positive – maybe a happy tune, or put some beautiful image around it.

Some Observations Relating to Memory

* Things we experience or learn in the presence of distinctive smells or sounds or sights or tastes or feelings are more readily remembered when again in the presence of the same. A way of trying to remember is to find a 'hook' relating the current circumstance back to the original circumstance.

The Bumper Book of Common Sense

* Just because we or someone else is positive about the accuracy of a memory does not mean the memory is accurate.

* In the presence of given smells we are more likely to recall events from when previously in the presence of those smells. It is not uncommon for childhood memories to suddenly resurface as a result of encountering some particular smell.

* Emotions influence our memories. Information learned whilst emotionally aroused is more likely to be remembered, but information learned just before a strong emotion is less likely to be remembered.

* We remember the unusual rather than the usual. You leave home every morning to go to work. You will only tend to remember those specific occasions when something different occurred. If there is something in particular you want to remember then you need to make something about it different to usual circumstances.

* We better remember things learned whilst in a positive frame of mind than those learned when in a negative frame of mind.

* Given information in a list we are more likely to remember items at the beginning or end of the list than items in the middle.

* How an experience ends has a more lasting impact on us than the length or even the intensity of the experience itself. Thus always look to end any experience on a high note.

* We have a tendency to perceive recent events as more remote than they were and remote events as more recent than they were. This is sometimes knows as the telescoping effect.

* Many common metaphors relating to memory are inaccurate and misleading. Memories are not buried in our brain, such that when we dig them up they are perfectly preserved. And we do not record in the deep recesses of our brain everything we ever see or hear. At best we remember odd moments from the past and reconstruct many memories by filling in what we presume must have been the case, and often it wasn't.

* Allowing yourself occasional nostalgic thoughts helps you feel more positive about life.

* Caffeine drinks help you feel more alert but they don't help your memory. In the long run you are better off getting more sleep whilst revising than spending more time studying on a caffeine high.

Memory Training Tips

* When studying to remember, frequent testing of yourself significantly increases what you remember, even though it generally doesn't feel like it. Thus far better to study and regularly test yourself, than just to keep studying.

* Take a relatively simple crossword puzzle and work out the answers but don't fill in the crossword itself. Then when you've finished try to fill in all the answers without referring back to the clues.

* Learning to visualize is a cornerstone of a powerful memory. Techniques to improve your visualization include:
  o Look at an object then close your eyes and try to see it in your mind's eye. Open your eyes to see it again, and again close your eyes. Keep trying this till you see at least an outline with your eyes closed;
  o Relax somewhere on your own, close your eyes, and try to describe out loud any images you perceive, no matter how vague. Practice should help to strengthen the images;

- o Try drawing. Your drawings don't need to be realistic. Just representative to you of what you are trying to bring to mind. Try looking at something, then look away and draw it from memory, looking again, then adding more detail. But avoid judging how good your drawings are. You are not trying to be someone who draws well. You need to see it as simply a skill like handwriting where you only need to write well enough to be able to read it back to yourself.

* Familiarize yourself with certain locations such as buildings, or shopping centers, or streets or gardens you know well. They provide excellent hooks on to which you can put lists of things you want to remember. Give the places in your location an order, such as would occur naturally as you walk through the location.

* Learn a simple rhyming scheme for numbers, such as 1 – sun, 2 – shoe, 3 – tree, etc. Use whatever comes into your head, but then learn it by heart such that it becomes instinctive and automatic. Then when you have a list of items you need to remember, associate each one in sequence with the items you have associated with the numbers. Make the associations vivid and preferably absurd or humorous. You should then find it easy to later on remember the list by stepping through the items you have linked to the numbers.

* By identifying letters with the numbers from 0 to 9, then any number sequence can be turned into a letter sequence which can then be used to create a simple rhyme or story, based for example on a word for each letter, which can be relatively easily remembered. The initial number sequence can then be recreated based upon a memory of the rhyme or story. Details of techniques such as this are readily available through memory books or the Internet.

* You can and should train yourself to improve your working memory, ie. your memory for 7 plus or minus 2 bits of information. Practice with a sequence of random(ish) numbers 7 digits long. Read it once then try to recall it backwards. Once you are comfortably doing it with 7 digits, practice with 8, then 9.

* Rote learning is not a very efficient memory technique. Giving some meaning to what you are trying to remember increases the efficiency of memory. Techniques for remembering particular lists of information including making up some story with the items in, or linking items to another sequence of items you have already learnt.

Communication

Face to Face Communication and Listening

* Verbal communication has three components: the words, the way the words are said, and body language. The words themselves are often not the most important. When talking about feelings and attitudes for example the words you use have little impact and far more important are your tone of voice and your body language.

* In asking people personal questions, the questions can come across as either considerate and caring, or come across as an interrogation. Tone of voice and body language are vitally important in how personal questions come across.

* Think about what you say. Is what you are saying or about to say likely to help the situation or hinder it?

* When interacting with others and discussing particular issues, try to deal with one issue at a time. Often many issues will get mixed up together making it largely impossible to see your way through

The Bumper Book of Common Sense

any of them. However if clearly understood and dealt with one at a time, the way forward on at least some of the issues will often become clear.

* Try to always have a pleasant manner about you, even if you don't feel in a good mood. Find a particular pleasing mental image, one that makes you feel good, which you can bring to mind anytime you feel a little down or you have an unpleasant thought. People are more comfortable talking to people who look friendly, and are more open to be positively influenced by them.

* Ensure that the environment in which face-to-face communication is to take place or is taking place is not inappropriate. It shouldn't be too noisy, or have too many distractions, or be such that you can be overhead when you'd rather not.

* If you have a particular message to get across ensure it is the right time. If the other person's mind is on something else, or for whatever reason they are not in a responsive mood, then don't press it. If you try to communicate at the wrong time they may be dismissive of an idea, which at some other time they may have been positively disposed towards. If appropriate ask the other person if it is convenient to discuss a given issue now, or agree some other time.

* Be sure that you talk clearly such that the other person can comfortably hear you, neither too loud nor too soft, nor too quickly. Be aware that as people get older their hearing tends to deteriorate, so, albeit without being too obvious, speak slightly louder when talking to older people, though be aware of any signs that indicate you might be talking too loudly.

* If you have a strong accent and are talking to people who don't have the same accent, talk slightly slower and clearer.

* Avoid using acronyms unless you are sure the other person or persons will understand them.

* When talking with other people and they say something you either didn't quite catch or didn't understand, seek clarification. Don't bluff it. They will assume you understand unless you say otherwise. Many a problem has arisen through misunderstandings that could have been avoided with a little bit of open honesty about not understanding.

* When somebody is talking to you, you not only need to understand what the other person is trying to say, but also show to that other person that you understand. One way of doing this is to summarize what they have been saying; in your own words rather than by simply repeating their own words back at them. If appropriate, replay key points back to check: for example 'So what you are saying is …', or 'So if I understand you right …'. Better to clear up any misunderstandings there and then than to take them away with you and have them cause problems later.

* When trying to get someone else to understand something, don't assume they do. Take responsibility for the other person's understanding, and if appropriate check. Get them to tell you what they understand in their own words, or find different ways of saying or getting across your message. If other people don't understand you, it is your fault rather than theirs. It is your responsibility to communicate in a way that they can understand.

* Much as you may like to believe otherwise, you don't know what the other person is thinking, any more than they know what you are thinking. If you want to know that the other person is thinking you need to ask them questions, and if you want them to know what you are thinking you need to tell them.

* The following are conditions under which people will often stop listening to what you have to say:
    o If they realize the topic is of no interest or relevance to them;
    o If they are struggling to hear what you say;
    o If you are using terms they don't understand;
    o If there is some off putting disturbance or distraction;
    o If they have something else on their mind;

- If you are pressurizing, threatening, or attacking them;
- If you are patronizing them, putting them down, or trivializing their views;
- If you are not giving them a chance to speak or you are ignoring what they have to say;
- If you are not paying attention to them; looking somewhere else or doing something else at the same time;
- If you are giving them advice that they clearly don't want.

* Communication isn't just about you transmitting. It's about you receiving. You will not transmit effectively unless you are also able to listen effectively such that you understand the extent to what you are saying is being received and understood. And if you suspect it isn't you need to be able to adjust your transmissions accordingly.

* If you want to be effective in your face-to-face communications then you need good listening skills. You need to understand what the other person is saying or trying to say. This requires:
  - Paying full attention to the other person and giving them your undivided attention. Don't carry on doing other unrelated things at the same time, don't prematurely interrupt them, and don't be thinking about what you want to say whilst they are still talking;
  - Don't let your mind go wandering off onto other topics whilst the other person is talking. If important topics pop into your head, stop the other person for a moment with an apology, write it down, and then return your full attention to them;
  - Don't interrupt. Let people finish their sentences;
  - When the other person stops and you are ready to reply, pause a couple of seconds to give them time to add anything else and to give you time to ensure your own response is appropriate;
  - Be non-judgmental about what they are saying. Focus on understanding what they are saying, not on whether or not you agree with it or how you feel about it. As soon as you start to listen emotionally you will stop effective listening;
  - Think of thoughtful questions which both prove you are listening, to clarify anything you don't understand, and also to help direct the conversation in the direction you believe to be appropriate. Good questions enable you to control the direction of a conversation with a minimum of talking yourself;
  - If what they are saying is complicated try to paraphrase it and play it back to them to give them a chance to determine whether or not you have really understood and potentially explain again or in a different manner;
  - Pay attention to their body language and pick up any additional information about what they are saying or how respond to what is being said. You might well pick up, for example, an understanding of whether they approve or disprove of statements they or you are making;
  - Adopt a listening body language posture. Look like you are paying attention through leaning forward, making a significant amount of eye contact, having an open posture, nodding your head and smiling and responding with short sounds, and generally try to look friendly and pleasant, albeit in a way appropriate to the subject matter of the conversation. Ensure your body is faced towards the person who is talking to you.

* Barriers to active listening to the person you are with, include:
  - Trying to analyze what the other person is really thinking;
  - Thinking about what you are going to say next or what your view is of what is being said;
  - Thinking about something else whilst the other person is talking, or remembering some experience of your own;
  - Focusing only on what you agree with;
  - Judging what the other person is saying;
  - Looking to 'win' any argument that may be part of the interaction, or simply focusing on coming out of the interaction 'looking good';

The Bumper Book of Common Sense

- o Changing the topic whilst the other person clearly still wishes to continue with the given topic;
- o Not taking the subject matter seriously, whilst the other person is being serious;
- o Automatically agreeing with everything the other person is saying without really thinking about it.

* Listening is not as easy as it might seem, and many people, most people, usually have other things on their mind whilst they are supposedly listening to someone else. Ensure your mind is solely on the person who is speaking, and if you find your mind wandering immediately bring it back onto the words being spoken.

* People get angry and frustrated if they feel they are not being heard.

* If you are an effective listener people will be much more positively disposed towards you and will like you much more than they might otherwise have done. You will also get far more out of the interaction through learning more and understanding the other person better.

* When engaging in conversation look the other person in the eye, albeit without staring, nod and lean towards them, and show that you are listening with the occasional 'uh-huh' or similar and through asking questions.

* If looking to check understanding don't simply play back the same words, which only indicated you heard the words, not that you understood them. Look to paraphrase the words or replaying it back in some different way.

* Be wary of interrupting at inappropriate points or finishing off sentences for the other person. You should interject to some extent to show that you are listening and interested, but you need to let the other person say what they are trying to say.

* Be responsive to how your questions are answered. It should be clear whether or not the topic is something the other person will feel comfortable about discussing in more depth.

* Remember that in most circumstances it is of more value to you to understand the other person's point of view than to give your own. Ask yourself of the circumstances, is it better that you learn something or that they learn something.

* Be inquisitive about what someone is saying, be curious. Take an interest and try to learn more through asking questions and generally engaging with them, rather than simply acting as a sponge. Try to find out what is really of interest to the person who is talking to you.

* Hold back and suppress any feelings the communication may be giving rise to in yourself.

* If you have any doubts that what you are about to say may be the wrong thing, hold back from saying it, particularly if your emotions are aroused. Once you have said something, you can't take it back. Even with apologies, it is said. Many an otherwise good relationship has been soured sometimes irretrievably as a result of something hastily said.

* Use 'I' statements when the interaction becomes emotional. Rather than talking about 'You always …', or 'You make me …', talk about 'I feel … when you …'.

* The real art of conversation is not only to say the right thing at the right time, but also to leave unsaid the wrong thing at the tempting moment.

* Make use of silence. People generally are nervous of silence and will try to fill it. You can ask a question, and even after you've had a response, by nodding and smiling, but not speaking, the other person will often continue with more detail simply to fill the silence.

* If you find yourself talking too much, then look to bring the other person or persons into the conversation by turning some of the subject matter into open questions directed at them. Then pause to give them time to answer and hopefully take over some of the talking.

* When brokering an agreement or an understanding between two parties, try to get them to understand each other's viewpoints through having each summarize the other's position. It is worth spending some time doing this, since once it is done each party will have a much greater understanding of where the other is coming from, and they are then likely to reach a mutually agreeable position much quicker.

* Try not to bluff in face-to-face conversation. Bluffing occurs when you pretend to know something that you don't. People often bluff so as not to appear ignorant or to avoid being seen to be not in the know. However bluffing leaves you at a disadvantage and you will often find it difficult to play an active part in the continuing conversation either because you are missing some important piece of information or because you will be on the back foot worried about being found out. In most cases it is best to be simply honest about not knowing something. You will then get some more information and also able to continue to play an active part in the conversation.

* People who are lying do not tend to show overt signs of nervousness. Rather they tend to show signs of thinking more, tend to be more impersonal in their tone, and are more evasive. Note that we are worse at judging when someone else is lying than we think we are.

Body Language

* The way we hold and move our bodies reflects what we are feeling and thinking. It happens automatically and for the most part without our realizing it. Moreover there is a consistency in how we do this from person to person. Some of it is universal and some of it is dependent upon our culture. The signals we give off in this way are what is known as body language, and the fact that other people consciously or sub-consciously pick up on these signals is why this is also termed non-verbal communication. And like any communication the signals we give off can be true and can sometimes be false, and other people can interpret them correctly or can interpret them incorrectly.

* Body language, non-verbal behavior, is about how we position and hold our bodies, it is about our facial expressions, and our eye movements, and it is about the gestures we make with our hands, arms, shoulders, body, legs, feet or a combination of these. Where our body language contradicts what we are saying verbally, it is usually body language that is being more truthful.

* People react to your body language, usually sub-consciously. You can change how people instinctively react to you through changing certain aspects of how you hold or move your body.

* Most of our non-verbal behavior is automatic. We don't think about it and usually don't notice it happening. However we can consciously overcome some of it, or a lot of it, with training and practice. Most people you come across won't have done so and thus will be 'honest' in their body language.

* You can significantly improve your reading of body language by both learning the principles and by observing people as they go about their normal lives. However be subtle when observing people's body language. People don't like being watched and can get upset or aggressive about it.

* Much of our body language derives from our instinctive response to danger, which is generally one of freeze, flight, or fight. Our responses occur very quickly, and we instinctively react in an honest non-verbal way. Even if we have learned to control certain aspects of our body language our first instinctive responses are usually outside of our conscious control.

* Freeze was often an effective response to danger in our prehistoric past since many dangerous animals tend to attack moving prey. Freeze is a common modern day body language response

The Bumper Book of Common Sense

when we feel threatened by someone or when we ourselves have done something or are planning on doing something we know to be wrong. We will tend to be stiller than normal, or maybe a little hunched up as though trying to hide.

* A body language flight response to a threat is a leaning or pointing of our body away from what or who we feel threatened by, or possibly seeking to put something between us and whoever we feel threatened by.

* A fight non-verbal response to a threat is typically exhibited through signs of aggression such as glaring or tightened muscles.

* A single act of non-verbal behavior can often be misleading and individual non-verbal signals are at best indicative. Thus people may exhibit particular non-verbal signals for specific reasons relating to the environment they are in, so be aware of context and the potential impact it may be having. For example, someone may have their arms crossed in front of them because they are being defensive, or it might be because they are cold. However whilst a specific non-verbal signal in isolation from others can be very misleading, taking a number of signals together, with them giving a consistent non-verbal message, is likely to be a very powerful indicator.

* Dilated pupils is a sign that someone is attracted or very interested in what they are looking at. Constricted pupils indicate dislike, though of course bright lights will also make our eyes constrict. As always context is very important.

* If someone feels threatened they will look to block their eyes, for example by squinting, lowering their eyebrows, or by subconsciously shielding their eyes. A furrowed forehead is a general sign that something is causing them some discomfort or anxiety, either something that has been said or something that has just occurred to them. Dropping eyebrows very low is a general sign of weakness or submission.

* If we hear something we particularly don't like we will tend to try to block our eyes for a short time, either with our hands or just closing them. Someone who suddenly remembers something they'd forgotten will often exhibit this behavior.

* Blink rate is much higher when we are not relaxed.

* A strong gaze can indicate either a strong like or a strong dislike. Other facial or context clues should make clear which it is.

* Use of your eyes is an important part of face-to-face communication. You need to regularly look at the person or persons you are talking to, but be careful not to stare. When you want to emphasis a point ensure you give eye contact.

* Not looking at the other person or facing away from them will send out very strong signals that you are not interested in them or what they have to say. However just because someone looks away from you whilst you are talking does not necessarily mean disinterest or displeasure. It may be they are just trying to be clear about their own thoughts or be otherwise thinking about something in particular.

* As an interviewee keep focused on the interviewer. If you keep looking around the room you will give a strong impression of either disinterest or superiority.

* Looking askance at someone is a sign of being suspicious about what they are saying.

* We all have genuine and fake smiles; with the ability to generate fake smiles being something we learn from early childhood. Genuine smiles involve much more of the whole face, with the corners of the mouth being pulled up towards the eyes. A false or polite smile has the mouth being pulled more out to the side.

* Positive emotions and agreement are expressed in terms of relaxed facial muscles, a head tilt, and wide eyes.

* When someone is upset or disagrees with you their facial muscles tend to tighten up. The jaw tightens, the eyes become fixed and with a slight squint, the lips and mouth area tighten, the neck is stiff, and there is no head tilt.

* When someone hides their lips or is pressing them together it is a sign that something is bothering them. It may, but doesn't necessarily, mean they are lying.

* Puckered or pursed lips is a sign of disagreement or thoughts about an alternative to something that has been said.

* If someone touches or licks their lips whilst pondering options this is often a sign of indecision and insecurity.

* If someone, possibly only briefly, sticks their tongue out through their teeth it is an indication that they have either been caught out or they feel they have just gotten away with something. If you observe this at the end of talking to someone you need to think about whether or not they might have just taken advantage of you. You might want to look for the opportunity to explore what it might have been and whether or not you can still do something about it.

* A raised chin is generally a sign of either confidence or defiance.

* Nose touching can be a sign of someone lying or avoiding the truth.

* Ear touching can be sign of indecisiveness.

* Indications that a person is confused are wide-open eyes, raised eyebrows, and mouth possibly slightly open.

* Nodding or shaking of the head simultaneous to and aligned with what is being said is generally a sign of honest expression. However if it is delayed or not aligned it could be a sign of deception or lack of belief in what is being said.

* Signs that someone is feeling uncomfortable and that something is bothering them include arms being crossed in front of them, touching of their neck or throat, rubbing their palms on their legs, rubbing their forehead, touching their cheek, touching their arm or shoulder, adjusting their clothes, and general fidgeting.

* A closed posture, for example arms folded in front of you, will make people instinctively think you don't want to communicate with them, or that you are probably disagreeing with what they are saying.

* When people shrug their shoulders to indicate lack of knowledge, a full two-shoulder shrug tends to be genuine. A half shrug, or one shoulder shrug, tends to indicate they are being evasive.

* Generally, though again it is very context dependent, people move their arms and hands about and raise them up more when they are happy and excited. Arms and hands kept still and low down is generally a sign of lack of engagement or concern. People will usually refrain from moving their arms around when with people they don't like, or when they are being less than open with the truth.

* When it comes to handshakes, someone offering their hand with the palm down suggests they are looking to dominate; with the palm up suggests they are being submissive. If they use both their hands they are seeking your trust.

The Bumper Book of Common Sense

* When people hold their arms behind their back they are generally telling others not to get close. People of higher status often do this.

* During business meetings, when a person leans back with hands interlaced behind their head and elbows out, it is a sign of dominance.

* When we are confident we spread out, claiming territory. When we are less confident we close up and claim less space.

* Hand steepling, fingers touching but with palms apart, is a sign of high confidence. It can be used deliberately to display self-confidence and emphasis of a particular point.

* Interlacing of fingers or wringing of hands is a sign of nervousness. People who feel significantly distressed will often rub their palms.

* Having your hands hidden from those you are talking to gives them an instinctive sense of unease. Keep your hands visible.

* Thumbs up, such as when holding lapels, or thumbs sticking out of pockets, tends to be a sign of people who are feeling confident. People whose thumbs are in their pockets and the rest of their hands hanging out tend to be feeling a lack of confidence.

* Don't point your finger at people. They don't like it, and in some cultures it is deeply offensive. If you want to point at someone better to do so with an open hand gesture, palm up.

* People's hands tend to shake when under stress or when they are feeling very positive. Which it is should be very obvious from the context. Note of course this is only meaningful if someone's normal hand state is still.

* Nail biting is a sign of insecurity or discomfort, though in a particular context they may just have a bit of loose nail they are taking off.

* People with a high status tend to sit in much more relaxed positions than those with a lower status. People tend to cross their legs when they feel confident. Those in a lower status will usually sit more formally and tend to be more on the edge of their seats.

* If someone who is sitting starts to kick with their feet, as opposed to just a little bit of jiggling, it is likely they have heard something that is causing them discomfort. Also if they are jiggling their feet a lot and then suddenly stop, it is a sign they are feeling stressed.

* People lean their bodies towards others when attracted by or agreeing with them, and lean away when repelled or disagreeing. We also open up the front of our bodies when agreeing and close up or put up barriers when disagreeing.

* A slight body bow when you meet someone is a sign of regards and respect. If you avoid exaggeration it will put someone in a more positive frame of mind towards you.

* Feet and legs tend to point towards a subject of interest.

* If you looking to join people who are already talking together it is generally obvious whether or not they are welcoming you into their conversation by whether or not their feet move out towards you. If their feet remain fixed pointing at each other then they are not wanting you to join in.

* If you are talking to someone and their feet or one foot is gradually shifting away from you, it is a sign they are keen to get away. Also if someone clasps their knees whilst sitting it is a sign then want to get up and go.

* If someone's body is facing you, but their feet are facing away, it is very likely they are keen to get away. This may not be because they dislike you or what you are saying. It may simply be that they genuinely need to be somewhere else.

* Someone stood with feet wide apart is likely to be in a confrontational mood.

* A person's personality and state of mind is to some degree reflected in their walking style. Whether someone walks fast or slow is to some extent a reflection of them, and if their style changes from what is usual it is almost certainly because of some state of mind change, assuming there is not some physical explanation.

* Be wary of assuming body language in people from a different culture. This can vary from the fact that some cultures have different norms with regards comfortable distances between people to the fact that in some cultures a nod of the head means no and a shake means yes.

* Cultural norms with respect to touching vary significantly. If you are in a different culture or meet people from a different culture, don't be rash in judging them on the basis of their non-verbal behavior.

* If you move to a culture different to the one you have hitherto lived in, learn the basic acceptable norms with regards greetings and how close people stand together. Otherwise people will feel you are either too familiar or too distant.

* Non-verbal signs that someone might be feeling uncomfortable or stressed for reasons such as the novelty of the situation or because of something else that is going on in their lives, can be similar or even identical to signs that they may be lying or trying to deceive. You thus need more clues, or to be more familiar with the person's normal behavior, to distinguish deception from innocent discomfort.

* If you are looking for signs of deception in someone you need to make them feel as comfortable as you can, so you remove non-verbal signals relating to discomfort or stress which can be similar or identical to signs of deception. It is also best to avoid having anything between you and them such that it is easier to spot non-verbal signs relating to the feet or hands lower down – the very fact of them seeking to hide these is itself a non-verbal clue. You are then looking for consistent and repeated non-verbal behavioral responses to particular questions or topics of discussion.

* People who are trying to hide something from us will often build a physical barrier between them and us. Deliberately moving to sit behind a desk, for example, or putting things on the table between them and us.

* People who are being honest and open will be consistent in the non-verbal messages they are sending out. If they are not, then something is not quite right. It might not be dishonesty, but it is something that is making them feel uncomfortable.

* When talking to someone, look to ensure your body language is attentive and open. This means facing people directly rather than being angled away from them, avoiding having your arms crossed in front of you, generally leaning towards them, maintaining good eye contact, and responding to what they are saying with nods or verbal intonations such as 'uh-huh', 'hmmm'.

* Clothing influences how we see others and influences how others see us, whether we like it or not. In any formal or semi-formal environment dress appropriately and neatly. Unless people know you well, they will respond to your image and the way you look. They shouldn't, but they will, because in the absence of knowing you better it is all they have to go on. Also wear clean clothes, stand straight, face people you are talking to, and look them in the eye. Don't cover your mouth when you are talking to them, and smile a lot.

* Pay attention to your appearance. Be clean and neat. Maybe have something to help you stand out from the crowd, but nothing too obvious or ostentatious.

The Bumper Book of Common Sense

* If you work you will generally need to conform to certain conventions, and in certain situations there is suitable and not suitable. If you do seek to shock, don't be surprised if people act in ways you'd rather they didn't.

* Pay attention to personal hygiene. Keep your body and hair clean, wash your teeth thoroughly and regularly, ensure you don't have unpleasant body odor or bad breath – and if you do, do something about it. You will be much more self-confident and relaxed if you are smart and clean.

Presentations and Public Speaking

* In a group environment, particularly though not exclusively in a work or business environment, presentations are an effective way of getting your point across. A combination of the fact that you have a captive audience, visual material, spoken material, and the clarification you can provide in response to questions. Make presentations a highly effective way of communicating. It is important however that you make the effort to give good presentations, and don't lose the interest of your audience.

* Be clear about the purpose or objective of the presentation or speech: the key points and what it is you want to happen as a result of it. Ensure you clearly articulate this to yourself and try to summarize the key message in 30 seconds or less. If you are unclear about what you are trying to achieve then so will your audience be. Ensure everything in your presentation material or speech is focused on and supporting your purpose or objective. People will not remember details from a presentation or speech. About 3 key ideas is as much as most people will take away. Ensure you are clear about what the key ideas are that you want them to take away.

* Ensure your message is one capable of being understood by your audience, that you present it in a way that they will understand, and that is relevant to them. Keep the structure of your presentation or speech simple and obvious. You don't want to lose your audience part way through which you will if it is complex. Ensure you keep your language simple, and if you are going to use abbreviations or specialist terms be sure they are ones everyone in the audience will immediately understand and know.

* Think about your audience. Why will they be there? What are they looking to get out of the presentation or speech? What is their level of understanding about the subject matter? Try to make your presentation or speech come over as something that helps solve a problem or answer questions that they may have. Clearly state the problem or question you are answering in your introduction such that they sit up and pay attention.

* Having a story that you can narrate which gets your point firmly across is a powerful technique. Putting a story in the form of a personal anecdote, even one you've made up, so long as it is credible, will generally get people listening carefully.

* If you have an idea for a story then follow these steps. Introduce the characters and set the scene, a bit of poetic license in providing some little details to add color and bring the scene and characters to life. Introduce the difficulty or challenge one or more of the characters face. Talk and walk through the sequence of events in resolving the difficulty or challenge, possibly with one or two false starts, no more, and keeping the scene alive through use of adjectives and adverbs. Draw out the conclusion you want to make and the lesson you want to stick in the minds of your audience. Keep the story relatively short but also ensure it keeps moving along.

* If the presentation or talk is important then put the effort into preparing it, and rehearse if you can. You need to focus not only upon the facts and material to be presented, but also the style, pace, and tone. If you have a practical demonstration to give, practice it several times, preferably in the place you will be doing it.

* If you get nervous before a presentation or speech then look to control your breathing. Also remember that a bit of nerves provide some adrenaline, which is not a bad thing.

* It is often appropriate to have handouts in support of presentations. You need to ensure that the distribution of handouts does not disrupt the presentation itself, or distract the listeners' attention. Whether you give out handouts before, during, or after the presentation depends on their purpose vis-à-vis the presentation itself. If you hand them out before or during ensure you take time to introduce the handout material itself, and if you want people to look up details be specific in leading them through the material.

* Ensure you get people's attention at the beginning of the presentation. If people are still milling about or talking ask them to settle down. If appropriate deal with administrative matters quickly and efficiently - fire exits, lunch arrangements, etc. - and then get onto the subject matter in hand.

* If you have a longish presentation or speech ensure you have some water you can sip once your mouth starts to dry.

* Face towards your audience when presenting so that you are maintaining eye contact. Look to maintain eye contact with individual members of the audience for a few seconds at least. If you have a large audience then looking towards a group further back will give the impression to the individuals in that group that you are looking at each of them individually.

* If you have presentation material don't stand there looking at it, except possibly occasionally as you wish to point out particular points. Talk to your audience not to the visual aids. Never turn your back on your audience. Ensure there is nothing on the floor where you are presenting that is likely to trip you up.

* Whilst ideally you should be so familiar with your material that you require only a quick glance to ensure it comes reliably to mind, this is not always the case. An option is to have a copy of the material in front of you where you can glance down at it whilst still facing the audience. However try to only do this occasionally, you don't want it to appear you are reading from a script. Or you may want to put key points on to cards, which you have in front of you. In this case ensure the slides are clearly numbered and the cards are clearly numbered with the slide number to which they apply. It is very easy to get lost amongst your cards. Again you need to be able to glance at the cards rather than have to read from them.

* Smile a lot during your speech or presentation. Ensure you look confident even if inside you are not. Keep erect, don't start slouching. Keep looking at or towards your audience.

* Speak slower than you would in normal conversation. Ensure your voice can be heard clearly by all the audience. Avoid a monotone voice. Include pauses for effect, and put emphasis on key points. If you have difficulties varying your voice then make use of rhetorical questions which gives rise to a natural variation.

* Be wary of using jokes. A bit of humor can be appropriate, but jokes will often offend someone, and you need to ensure you don't offend anyone.

* If you are feeling nervous during a presentation, remember that your nervousness will not be as obvious to your audience as you might think it is. We have a highly exaggerated sense of our own state which will not be coming over anywhere as near as strong to the audience as it will be to ourselves.

* Try to make the ending memorable. Get their attention. Avoid being too predictable. You need a change of pace. It is best to get to the ending unexpectedly, since this will often leave it lingering in the audience's mind.

* Don't let your presentation, and time for questions if appropriate, overrun the pre-arranged time period. People will have agreed to be present for a set period. Don't expect them to stay longer, and in any case some will leave and disrupt the remainder of your presentation.

* Some common shortcomings in presentations to be aware of and thus to avoid:

The Bumper Book of Common Sense

- o Forgetting that you need a clearly defined beginning, middle, and end;
- o Having a weak or no conclusion;
- o Using acronyms and other terminology that you might know well but some of your audience doesn't;
- o Not rigorously checking spelling and grammar;
- o Not getting your timing right so that you have to rush or even run out of time;
- o Failing to provide your audience with the opportunity to raise questions;
- o Putting too much on your slides, and simply reading off them;
- o Turning your back to the audience as you read off the slides, or spending a lot of time looking other than at your audience;
- o Crossing your arms in front of you as you speak.

* After you've done your presentation and you are feeling calm again, think about what you could have done better, and be clear about what you will do differently in the future. Even highly polished public speakers were, for the most part, initially not very good, but made the effort to learn to get better.

* Tips in terms of preparing slides for an effective presentation:
  - o Ensure all slides follow a master layout style with consistent use of headers, footers, logos, font, size of text except where deliberately changed for emphasis, etc.;
  - o Ensure your topic matter is organized into a smallish number of sections, no more than about 7, though 4 or 5 is probably better;
  - o Have key images or metaphors supporting each key point or topic you are covering. Use them to bring the topic to life for your audience;
  - o Use clip art sparingly and with a particular purpose. Remember your audience may have seen the same clip art used elsewhere and have different associations with it;
  - o Ensure each slide has a distinct purpose, and that it clearly satisfies that purpose;
  - o Generally you should limit yourself to one image per slide, and to 5 or 6 bullet points. Try to avoid a long sequence of bulleted slides;
  - o Do not clutter your slides or put too much on them;
  - o Avoid having a topic run over more than one slide. Each slide should be able to have its own unique title;
  - o Ensure your opening introductory slide makes clear to the audience why they are here and what they will get out of it. It should summarize the topics to be covered but not give the main points themselves;
  - o Ensure your full set of slides tell a story;
  - o Avoid use of clever slide build-ups except where important to your delivery. Advice sometimes given is that if you put a full slide of info the audience is distracted from your message of the moment. However unless the slide is particularly busy the audience is usually more distracted by wandering what is coming next. If the full slide is presented it only takes them seconds to glance at the full slide and then focus on you;
  - o Ensure that what is on your slides can be read by those at the back;
  - o Remember that people best remember beginnings and ends, so ensure your key points are covered in these, except of course where you deliberately want to build up suspense towards your conclusions;
  - o Take the time to make your slides look good and professional;
  - o Once you've drafted out your slides ask yourself whether or not they effectively get your message across. Ask someone else to review them before you use them.

Meetings – When you're Responsible for Them or Leading/Chairing Them

* If you have taken on responsibility for a meeting that you consider has little value, or for which the objectives can be achieved in a more effective manner, cancel it or make other arrangements. However you should probably seek the viewpoints of others involved before you do so since you may not have appreciated the value of the meeting to them.

* If you are responsible for a meeting you have a responsibility to prepare for it and to ensure that the meeting can achieve its' objectives in the shortest reasonable time. Time is a precious resource and whilst meetings are often a vital means of achieving objectives and communicating they are also a major drain on time since poor use of time multiplies up by the number of attendees.

* When preparing for a meeting for which you are responsible, give consideration to the following:
    o Be clear about the meeting purpose and any outcomes you are seeking. Ensure that having the meeting is the best way of achieving the underlying purpose;
    o Be clear about who needs to be at the meeting, and if certain people are critical to the achievement of the meeting's objectives that they are available and expect to attend at the time and place, and that that your meeting is in their calendars. You may need to choose the when and where to suit those critical to the meeting, and should seek to minimize the disruption for them;
    o If there are a number of objectives or topics to be covered be clear about priorities, and order the meeting such as to ensure these are covered as a minimum. Ensure however that you believe you have time to cover all the topics intended to be covered; being as realistic as you can about how long given topics might take, particularly if there are potentially conflicting viewpoints to be discussed;
    o If the meeting is one of a series of meetings on the given topic, ensure that early in the meeting any issues outstanding from the previous meeting are dealt with – including the status of any follow up actions that were agreed at the previous meeting or were continuing from the previous meeting;
    o Make allowance for domestics – ensure time for coffee and toilet breaks and for lunch if appropriate. Ensure the meeting room itself is available and booked and appropriate for the number of people, and that any facilities required such as projection equipment have also been sorted. Make sure any security arrangements such as advance notice of people arriving are addressed;
    o Identify any information that should be distributed prior to the meeting to optimize the likelihood of achieving the meeting objectives? As a minimum this should include the Agenda and possibly a statement of the meeting purpose;
    o Is there pre-work or pre-thinking that should be done by the attendees in advance of the meeting? If so, ensure they know in time to prepare. If other attendees will be bringing material to present ensure you have made appropriate arrangements for this. Ideally you should have the material sent to you in advance so you can make it available using the facilities you know will be available. Many a meeting has been significantly disrupted whilst attendees try, and sometimes fail, to get their material ready using the facilities available;
    o If particular attendees are expected to make specific contributions ensure they are aware of this. Note that one way of ensuring participant involvement and interest in meetings is to have different people lead different Agenda items; but ensure they know this and have agreed it beforehand.

* If appropriate prepare the meeting location for the meeting in advance of the start time, including ensuring any computer and projection equipment is set up and working and that any presentation material is ready for presenting.

* At the beginning of the meeting deal with any domestic issues such as fire regulations, intent for any breaks and lunch arrangements, any security or confidentiality reminders, and any rules that you want observed.

The Bumper Book of Common Sense

* An important aspect of running effective meetings is to ensure everyone respects the timings. Start the meeting on time, and don't disrupt the meeting for latecomers. (In an environment where the organization is such that many people have back to back meetings you might relax this to starting within 5 minutes or so.) Ensure the meeting finishes on time, since at least some of the attendees will have made other arrangements based on the timing. Have a clear view of how long you believe each topic on the Agenda should take and don't let any significantly overrun since the whole meeting will then be at risk of overrun or having certain topics not covered. Note that many people will just keep talking and discussing, and it is your responsibility as the person running the meeting to ensure the meeting keeps to its timings. On occasion, if something particularly important is being dealt with, you may need to break this rule. However there is a big difference between letting topics overrun because there is significant benefit in doing so, and just letting topics drift.

* During the course of the meeting:
  - If certain people are dominating the conversations, you may need to stop someone talking too much, or make a point of bringing in others;
  - Be an instinctive 'yes' person when it comes to ideas from other people at a meeting rather than a 'no' person. Most people have an instinct to quickly judge other people's ideas before they've been thought about, which demotivates the originator of the idea and puts them into a negative mode vis-à-vis other ideas that might be proposed;
  - Do not dismiss anyone's inputs. Even what you perceive to be bad or naïve ideas should be acknowledged and a reason given for why it is not appropriate to progress them further without making the person who made the suggestion feel stupid – and of course it may be you misunderstood the idea;
  - If people wander off topic, bring them quickly back on topic. If they have raised something important, then make arrangements for it to be discussed once the meeting is over or is followed up in some other way such as through raising and recording an Action. The people attending the meeting have come for the meeting's purpose and discussing other things is a lack of respect for their time;
  - At the end of each agenda item, briefly summarize what was said, and ask people to confirm that that it is a fair summary. Be explicit about any intended follow-up and ensure these are recorded in notes that will then be distributed after the meeting;
  - Note down items that require further discussion;
  - Do not let the meeting break up into separate groups of people talking amongst themselves. Only one person should be talking at a time, and should be talking to the meeting as a whole;
  - Be aware of expressions and body language that suggests different views to those being expressed. If you suspect someone appears to disagree with points being made, then explicitly bring them into the discussion;
  - If you disagree with someone give a reason for why you disagree;
  - List all actions that are generated at the meeting. Make a note of who is assigned to do what, and by when;
  - At the close of the meeting, quickly summarize next steps and inform everyone that you will be sending out a meeting summary.

* Ensure that if you are too busy to make notes yourself during a meeting that you have someone else do so. However choose someone who is capable of taking decent notes and understand what is going on. Make the notes from the meeting as good as you can: whilst, for most purposes, they don't need to be a blow by blow account of what was said at the meeting, they should capture any useful information that was revealed that attendees might be interested in, and they should be clear about any agreements that were made either as decisions or as actions on individuals for following up on. Note that it is the notes that will remain long after the meeting itself has faded from memory. It is very frequent that different people will walk away from a meeting with different memories of what was agreed. It is vital to use the meeting notes as a means for getting a consensus on what was agreed, either formally through agreement at the next meeting, or informally through the expectation that people will get in touch if they disagree with the notes. Ensure you make the notes from the meeting available to all the attendees within a few days of the meeting itself.

* At the end of a meeting consider what went well and what didn't go so well, so you can learn and improve. Ask others for their viewpoints. Many meetings are poorly run, and you may not be as good at running meetings as you think you are. Make the effort to improve how you run meetings through seeking some feedback.

Meetings - As an Attendee

* If you are being asked to attend a meeting ensure you are clear about what the meeting is about and that you consider it necessary for you to attend. If you are not clear, seek clarification. You don't want to waste your time attending a meeting that lacks a clear purpose or does not have the right attendees to achieve its purpose.

* Prepare in advance. Go to meetings with a clear idea of what you want from the meeting, not just to react to what other people want. Think about what particular points you want to bring up, and make sure you write them down and take them in with you: don't rely on your memory. Focus on the question you are looking for answers to rather than preparing answers to the questions you think you might be asked.

* A meeting is a period in your life when you have the opportunity to influence others. Don't waste the opportunity.

* Be punctual for meetings and appointments. Being late for meetings is being disrespectful to the others attending, irrespective of whether or not you are the most senior person attending. If you are late you are wasting other people's time. Don't keep people waiting if you can help it, and expect others to be on time as well. Note that if you have back-to-back meetings you may need to make some allowance for the time to get between meetings, and make apologies in advance that you may be a couple of minutes late or be looking to leave a couple of minutes early.

* If there is no chairperson for the meeting, then feel free to take a lead.

* If you believe the chairperson is being ineffective, you may want to help them along. However don't get into conflict with the chairperson or try to take over their position unless they are happy for you to do so.

* Make your contribution to the effective running of the meeting by not distracting the meeting away from its purpose. If a topic is of no interest to you, and you don't have particular expertise or knowledge to contribute, then you shouldn't feel the need to contribute, unless your viewpoint is explicitly sought, or you believe you have an insight others might have missed and which will usefully help the meeting along. Many people feel a need to talk at meetings in ways that don't help the meeting along.

* Ensure you understand any points being made which are potentially relevant to you. If you don't understand something relevant to you, say so. Seek further clarification. However if you don't understand something that is not relevant to you, then your seeking clarification is wasting the time of the others present. Of course you may need to seek the clarification before you know whether or not the matter is of relevance to you. Do so, but stop seeking any further clarification once you understand that it is not.

* Don't multitask during meetings. If you do, you will find you remember very little of what was being discussed.

* If a meeting looks like it is going to overrun you are within your right to leave at the time set for its completion, although it may be in your best interest to stay on.

* In the few minutes or so after a meeting go over in your head any key points that you would like to remember in the future, and write them down. Don't rely on the meeting notes, unless they are your own, since those producing the notes may not have the same interests as you.

The Bumper Book of Common Sense

* If you receive the notes of a meeting and you believe they are factually inaccurate or have missed important points, then reply to the person responsible for the meeting to say so. Even if they don't re-issue them you will have your own records you can refer to in the future should the need arise.

Meetings – Other General Points

* There are many bad meetings, and many people in organizations or clubs frequently complain about meetings they are involved in, but do little about helping to improve them. If you are responsible for a meeting take responsibility for making it as effective as you can. As an invitee to a meeting try not to attend meetings you believe will be ineffective. And if you are an attendee at an ineffective meeting do what you can to help it run a little more smoothly, albeit without showing up the chairperson.

* Meetings often have, or need, a cross over point which takes them from divergent thinking, which is about getting different ideas out into the open, to convergent thinking, which is moving towards conclusions and consensus of outcome. Cross over points can occur too early or too late. Too early means premature decisions without all options having been adequately explored. A given decision may be being forced on the group. Ways of opening up the options in such circumstances is asking questions such as: 'Before we settle on this, can we just see if anyone has any further reservations we haven't discussed so far?' 'Could I just ask a couple of questions?' 'Can we just review how we've come to this particular solution?' If the cross over point is arrived at too late then it is unlikely for the consensus or conclusion to get arrived at in the time allocated.

* In meetings it is important everyone is in the same state of mind at the same time. If some are still exploring options whilst others are drawing to a conclusion, there is likely to be a lot of confusion. If you can recognize that this is the case you can help the meeting to either return as a whole to identifying and exploring options, or to confirm the focus is now on drawing conclusions.

* At a meeting everyone present is giving up their time to be there. If they were not at the meeting it is likely they would be spending most of their time directly contributing to whatever activities they are responsible for or involved in. In a meeting they are only doing useful work for the periods the meeting is focused on the topics of direct interest to them. It is thus important that meetings seek to maximize the time the topic matter is relevant to each of the individual participants. This is best done by keeping on topic, and whilst on topic get through the subject matter as quickly and effectively as possible, taking advantage of the full range of viewpoints available at the meeting.

* Some of the characteristics of an effective meeting are:
    o All those who are at the meeting have a good reason for being there, and all those who need to be there to achieve the meeting's purpose are there;
    o The purpose and objectives of the meeting are understood by all in advance of the meeting;
    o If the meeting is a sequence of meetings, actions and progress since the previous meeting are adequately covered early during the meeting;
    o It is clear who is chairing the meeting, and they keep control of the meeting;
    o All discussions during the meeting are relevant to the meeting's purpose and objectives, and the meeting does not have different groups of people talking at the same time;
    o The meeting follows a prearranged agenda and works its way logically through the items, albeit there is flexibility in the light of emergent information or circumstances;
    o People stick to the Agenda topic under discussion and deal with each topic before moving on to the next topic;
    o Individuals are allowed to say their piece, assuming it is relevant;
    o The meeting has time to discuss all the topics on the Agenda, albeit it may set up follow up meetings for items that it becomes clear can't be covered in the time available;

- The meeting does not go on longer than it needs to to achieve its end, and doesn't go on longer than scheduled;
- The need for any follow ups are agreed with clarity of who is responsible for what by when;
- It is clear who is responsible for taking notes, and important decisions, agreements and actions are noted down and distributed to all after the meeting;
- There is a focus for ensuring actions agreed are followed through, either explicitly by whoever led the meeting or by other means such as a follow up meeting.

* Some of the characteristics of an ineffective meeting include:
  - There are many people at the meeting who have nothing useful to contribute;
  - The meeting is over-structured, and important issues are not discussed because of inflexibility;
  - Arguments keep getting repeated, and there is a lot of jumping around between the Agenda items;
  - Topics which have already been covered and moved on from, are returned to;
  - Individuals are frequently interrupting each other;
  - Individuals are focused on pushing their own agenda, and not focused on seeking common agreement;
  - Certain individuals dominate the meeting, whilst others say nothing;
  - It is not clear what the meeting is trying to achieve;
  - A lot of time is spent on points not relevant to the purpose of the meeting;
  - Too much time is spent on early Agenda items and later Agenda items that are just as or more important are not discussed at all;
  - People are expected to stay beyond the end of the scheduled finished time;
  - People come away from the meeting with very different understandings of what was agreed;
  - No or ineffective notes are taken, such that agreements or decisions are not followed up, and further meetings are required to go over agreements that had already been made.

* People seriously overestimate their memories. At meetings lots of agreements can get made, understandings arrived at, and actions agreed, but unless there are explicitly written down as an output from the meeting they get forgotten about or people come away with very different recollections. Anything you expect as a follow up from a meeting, get it written down or ask for it to be written down as part of the meetings notes. Do not rely on making a 'mental note' – the brain doesn't work that way - and do not rely on everyone having the same understanding of the agreements.

Written Communication Including E-mail for Business

* Effective writing is important. Misunderstandings that arise from poorly written communication can waste time and lead to the wrong things being done as a result, the consequences of which can vary from the mildly inconvenient to the catastrophic.

* Ensure you are clear about the purpose of your writing. Is it to clarify and explain ongoing developments, is it to initiate action, is it an audit trail record, is it a product in its own right such as a design description, is it instructions for someone to follow. In some cases it may be more than one of these, but do be wary of having information fulfilling multiple purposes. If you are not clear about the purpose or aim then you risk not achieving any purpose or aim. Don't start until you are clear about the purpose.

The Bumper Book of Common Sense

* Be clear about who the writing is aimed at. What is their existing level of knowledge and therefore what can be left out or referred to, what is the essential information that needs to be included, and how should the writing be structured to best convey the information and meet the aims with regards the particular reader or readers. If there are different groups of readers how can you structure the material to enable them all to effectively read and grasp it? Thus you might include details that would only be applicable to certain readers in an annex or separate sections such that they can be readily skipped by those who don't need to read them. However be wary of trying to satisfy too many disparate groups with a single piece of writing since you might end up satisfying no one.

* A common circumstance in business or technical writing is writing reports which have conclusions or recommendations, and a lot of supporting argument. Ensure that you provide a concise summary of the conclusions and recommendations at the beginning, but with a good structure of the supporting arguments so that the reader can dip into the bits of particular interest. Note that different bits may be of interest to different people.

* Structure your writing to make it easy to take in. If you have a lot of information then identify a logical sequencing of sections and sub-sections such that the reader gets 'chunks' of information which builds up their understanding and also enables them not to have to read the whole document or report in one sitting. The context of any part of the document should be immediately obvious from the section or sub-section heading under which it sits.

* When producing writing to argue a case then ensure you start with a clear statement of the problem or issue you are addressing, and then lead the reader logically through to your conclusion or argument in a way that is easy to follow. Ensure everything you include is relevant to the argument you are making and part of the logical sequence of points being made. Ensure your conclusion or concluding statements are clear and that it is crystal clear what you want the reader to do or think as a result.

* Keep your writing focused on the achievement of its purpose. When writing at school you were expected to 'display your knowledge' in your writing. Writing in a business context is not about you displaying your knowledge. It is about you communicating what needs to be communicated as economically and concisely as possible.

* The shorter your writing and documents the more likely they are to be read, assuming of course they have the information in that the reader needs to know. If the information is too short, and for example simply states the writer's opinion without supporting arguments, then it can be even more useless than being too long.

* Ensure the start of your writing is as strong as it can be. Many people start reading something but don't finish it, particularly if it is long. Thus, depending on the nature of your communication you need to ensure essential information is passed across very early on in your writing, and that the reader is encouraged to continue reading. Note that encouraged does not mean tricked or blackmailed by promising them information only if they continue: people do not respond well to this and will most likely stop reading there and then.

* Make extensive use of headings and sub-headings. Ensure they are informative, and provide the reader with the opportunity to readily dip into and find particular information that may be of interest to them.

* Every paragraph in a document should have a clear purpose and convey a single idea. If it doesn't, change it or get rid of it.

* Every paragraph should be part of a structured sequencing of ideas linked to the purpose of the sub-sections, sections, and thus the whole document. If paragraphs do not flow naturally one from another then the reader is unlikely to make ready sense of what you have written.

* Avoid long and complicated sentences. However ensure there is some variation in your writing. Lots of short sentences can also be distracting.

* Ensure that you are consistent in your ordering of topics. If you introduce a sequence of topics in a list, then keep to the same ordering when you come to describe them in more detail.

* Avoid use of phrases that can readily be replaced by single words. There are many such phrases, such as 'in view of the fact that …' can usually be replaced by 'because' or 'since'. A good check is to say it aloud and imagine you were saying it to another person.

* Don't use words, phrases, acronyms, or abbreviations the reader might not understand or might misinterpret. Or if you do, explain them when you first use them, and try to add other context to make it easy to remember or guess what the word means.

* Use diagrams or pictures where they help convey ideas. Whilst diagrams often take a lot longer to prepare than a paragraph of text, they can get the idea across much more powerfully, particularly if there is also text to ensure they are not misinterpreted. If you have diagrams or pictures ensure they are clearly labeled and ensure they are clearly put into context by, and referred to from, the main text.

* Make use of layout, white space, and some variation to make the reading easy on the eye and not appear as simply a lot of dense difficult to read text. A solid wall of text can put many people off.

* Keep your writing simple in terms of words used and in terms of formats and fonts. People will think the writing more intelligent.

* Spell correctly and pay attention to grammar. Poor spelling punctuation and grammar can put someone in a very negative mind vis-à-vis whatever you are trying to say, in addition to making your writing ambiguous or difficult to understand.

* Some common shortcomings in written communications:
    o Ideas not connected or flowing very well. A general jumping around in terms of ideas;
    o Difficulty in understanding what the point being communicated is;
    o Unbalanced coverage of material, with far too much on some topics and not enough on others;
    o Some of the subject matter being unrelated to the point being addressed;
    o Failure to cover or mention some obviously relevant issues;
    o Controversial statements being made without any supporting argument.

* For anything important that you write, ensure you proofread it or ask someone to do so for you. Pay attention to spelling, punctuation, and grammar. When proofreading ensure that your message comes across effectively and in an appropriate order, that everything included is relevant and important, that you avoid use of buzzwords and meaningless phrases, and that you've avoided ambiguity.

* We are usually very poor at reviewing our own work because we often see what we meant to say rather than what we have actually said. If you are reviewing your own work, if possible leave a gap of a few days or longer so that when you do review it it will be with fresh eyes; you are then far more likely to spot your sloppy sentences and waffling ideas.

* The need for good written communication, in terms of clarity of purpose and argument, structure of the writing, good spelling and grammar, applies as much to short reports or memos of a couple of pages or less as it does to long reports and documents. Just because a memo is only a couple of pages long, or less, does not give the excuse for poor structure or grammar. Someone who is busy may have dozens or hundreds of memos coming across their real or virtual desk every day. They are as likely to put aside a poorly structured short memo or report as they are a poorly structured long report.

The Bumper Book of Common Sense

* In a business environment e-mails should be grammatically correct and structured for easy reading. Many people neglect to think of the person who is expected to read the e-mail and simply dump down their thoughts, often even neglecting to ensure correct spelling. Unless the e-mail is personal between friends, then this is unprofessional and will distract people and put them off reading and responding. There is no excuse for poor structure and spelling and grammar with e-mails any more than there is with any other form of written communication.

* When sending e-mails to busy people, and many busy people could well be getting 100 or more e-mails a day, you need to get to the point more or less immediately and make it easy for them to respond to you. Tell them what you want in the subject line and keep the e-mail itself short and uncomplicated – a maximum of 4 or 5 sentences. Don't ask multiple questions. If you can get the whole message into the subject line, then do. You can complete the message with an EOM standing for End Of Message, so they immediately know they don't need to open the e-mail.

* If you wish to deal with different topics by e-mail, it is usually better to deal with them by separate e-mails that can be responded to separately than combining them into a single e-mail. It makes it easier for them to respond, and you avoid the risk of them not answering at all should there be one point that is more difficult to respond to than the others

* Never write long e-mails. People don't read them. If you have a lot to say put it in an attachment. If you believe they need more detailed information put it in an attachment or a link so they can print it or deal with it at their leisure. If you put detail in the e-mail itself they are unlikely to read it and will put it aside whilst they deal with easier to respond to e-mails.

* Make it as easy as you can for someone to respond to your e-mail. Be very clear about what you want from them, ensure you avoid ambiguity, and provide them with any information they might need to help them make a response. If you point them at where they need to go to find supporting information they are more likely to put the e-mail aside to be dealt with later than if you provide them with the information as an attachment.

* Be very wary about what you put in an e-mail. They often seem relatively informal, almost like speech, but they are nevertheless a permanent record which is very easily copied. And they have a habit of getting to people you didn't want them to. Never send an e-mail that you would be embarrassed by if it went on general distribution. You never know who might get hold of an e-mail and what they might do with it.

* Be very careful of any information you post on-line or send digitally. Information on networking sites or twitter or elsewhere can potentially be seen by anyone, and can be a permanent record. What, for example, might a future employer, possibly years in the future, think of you as a result of what you have written? Even information sent in confidence to friends or supposedly protected from open access is at risk. Friends don't always stay so for life, and many supposedly protected places can be hacked and the information openly released. Once it is out there you can't necessarily suppress it.

* Sometimes it is better just to pick up the phone and talk to someone rather than bounce e-mails between you. For example when looking for a mutually convenient time for a meeting.

* Written and spoken language are processed in different parts of the brain. If you are having difficulty trying to express something in a written form, try talking to yourself about it; it may get you out of your rut.

* If you are writing something out by hand for others to read, or even for yourself to read in the future, ensure your writing is readily legible. Scribbled notes that you or they can't reliably read back are not a lot of good, and can be harmful.

* As the recipient of some written communication, try to ensure you understand what is being said before you pass judgment on it. In particular try not to focus only on what you agree with, and dismiss what you don't agree with. If the writing is well structured and presented it should help

improve your understanding of the topic and you should be open to it potentially changing your mind or preconceptions.

* If you are the recipient of a relatively long piece of writing, make notes as you go through it. Pick out and note down key points. Drawing up your own mindmap of the information being presented can be useful. Decide whether or not you want to keep your notes long term, and if you do ensure they are put somewhere you can find them again.

* Try to get behind poorly structured arguments to understand what the writer intended. Whilst the responsibility for presenting a well-structured argument lies with them, it may also in your interests to seek to understand what they intended. It is for you to determine however whether or not it is worth making the effort: there is an opportunity cost in struggling with poorly written documents in that you could be using the time on other things. It may be better to give them a ring and ask them to explain in person or over the phone.

* If there are ambiguities or aspects of the writing you are not clear about, then get back to the author and seek clarification, assuming it is important enough to you.

* Ensure you understand what, if anything, the communication is asking of you, and any timescales involved. If you can respond straight away, do so. If you need to respond but cannot do so straight away you need to put a reminder to yourself either in your calendar or on some form of To Do List.

* Be careful when forwarding or replying to e-mails. Don't inadvertently send your e-mail to persons you didn't intend to, as frequently happens when people inadvertently 'reply to all'. And be aware that what you may be sending or forwarding might include a chain of e-mails which may contain information or comments that shouldn't be passed to certain others.

* If you have been given a document to formally review and comment on ensure you do so within the timescale requested, or decide you will be unable to do so and let the author or whoever is requesting the review know. Be as specific as you can about your comments, and don't get drawn into rewriting the document for the author – if it is far off the mark, say so, and suggest a better way of structuring the document and what topics should or shouldn't be included.

Use of Different Forms of Communication

* When you are communicating you are usually seeking some response from the recipient. Think about what that response is and ensure your form and content of communication has the best chance of eliciting that response. Make it as easy as you can for people to respond the way you would prefer for them to respond.

* Advantages of written communications include the fact that they can be edited and revised and shaped to meet the particular needs of the communication. They also provide a permanent record that can be reliably referred to in the future, and one that can be readily replicated. They give the recipient time to study them and consider an appropriate response. Written communication is usually best for complex messages.

* Disadvantages of written communication vis-à-vis verbal communication is the lack of immediate feedback on understanding of the impression created. Verbal communication can be adapted to the particular circumstances, and can respond to uncertainties or questions the recipient may have in order to provide greater information or understanding. Written messages can also take a long time to compose.

* Information presented pictorially often influences more than information presented textually. Pictorial items are more immediate and more easily grasped. However pictorial information can also be more ambiguous and there is a risk of people taking away a different message than the one

The Bumper Book of Common Sense

intended. A picture paints a thousand words, unfortunately they may be different words to different people.

* The personal touch is important when dealing with personal matters. Don't e-mail or text a message if your recipient would respond better to a personal phone call or a discussion over coffee. Face to face communication is particularly important if you want to reprimand or criticize someone.

* Storytelling and use of analogies and metaphors can be a powerful way to get your point across and to help people understand difficult to grasp concepts. They can be used in both written and aural communication. It is worth developing and remembering a range of stories and analogies and metaphors to illustrate key points relating to issues important to you.

* If you are trying to communicate a position to win over other people to your point of view then look to be able to state your position in a single sentence and then present your arguments in order, with the strongest first. Review all your arguments and ensure they are supporting your argument in a way that is relevant to the people you are presenting your argument to. If some of your arguments are complex or at risk of going over their heads then simplify them or don't use them. Ensure you end your statement of position in a concise and memorable way that summarizes your points.

* When giving people instructions to do something, be clear about the following:
    o What is the output or end point, and how will it be clear that it has been achieved. Is there any specific measure of completeness that must be satisfied?
    o Are there any particular instructions relating to how the task must be done, such as standards or procedures to be followed?
    o What are the time expectations? Must it be completed within a given amount of time, or will any time do? Not giving any time expectation risks it being left and not done at all as other priorities will almost certainly always come along;
    o Are there any intermediate targets or milestones that need to be completed within a given time? Do you want these to be reported, and if so how?
    o What level of progress reporting along the way do you want, if any?
    o Are there any other particular people you want them to involve or keep informed?
    o Ensure you pass to them any information you have that might be relevant or useful to them, or let them know where to go to find it;
    o Ask them to come back to you if they are having significant difficulties along the way, or they believe completing the task on time is at risk?
    o Be clear about circumstances when you would like them to come back to you irrespective of whether or not they think they are having problems.

General Effective Communication Tips

* Good communication should be complete, concise, clear, concrete, correct, considerate, and courteous. Communication should answer questions such as who, what, where, when, and why. It should say what it needs to say as briefly as possible. It should be focused on the receiver or audience; use specific facts and figures and active verbs; use a conversational tone; include examples and pictures when needed; be honest, tactful and good natured.

* Be clear about what you want to communicate and why. What is the primary idea or message you want the recipients to understand as a result of your communication? Ask yourself what you want most from the communication.

* If a communication is intended to be about something, keep it focused. Don't clutter it with detail that is not relevant or necessary to the achievement of the communication's purpose.

* If you can say something in only a few words then do so. Don't pad out your communication or use long words when short words are just as good. Being able to express something simply rather than in a complex manner, without losing any of the essence of what is being said, is a rare skill, but a vitally important one, and one you will get at better at simply through persisting in trying to do it.

* Other people can't read your mind, and it is unreasonable to expect them to pick up nuances in your body language. You must say what it is you want them to know or what you would like them to do. Don't assume they magically know, no matter how obvious it is to you.

* Interpreting coded messages requires information additional to that included as part of the message itself. Any piece of communication can be considered a coded message in that the words used are intended to represent something. A common understanding of the words and the context of the message are required for it to be correctly interpreted.

* Redundancy in a communication can help reduce errors, though this must be traded off against the fact that it makes the message longer, and if done where not necessary or appropriate may psychologically turn the listener off. You can achieve redundancy through simple repetition or through saying the same thing more than once but in different ways. Generally it is more acceptable and appropriate to use redundancy in spoken communication than in written communication.

* Be conscious of the potential need to give background information and to put things in context. It provides less likelihood of misunderstandings, and makes it more likely people will make effective use of the information. If however it is not needed it makes the communication longer and can hide the message you are trying to get across.

* Be precise in your communications and avoid vague terms. The more specific and precise your words the more likely they will be understood and the livelier and the more interesting your communication will be.

* If it sounds hollow, it is probably empty. Don't let yourself be 'impressed' by someone using terminology that doesn't seem to mean anything. If they are unable to re-express it in simpler terms, then unless it is clearly highly specialised terminology that should only be used for communication between experts, then there is a high likelihood it is nonsense.

* People who consider that their thoughts are 'too deep' to be put into words are kidding themselves, and trying to kid us. Thoughts that cannot be expressed in (word) language are of no practical use.

* If you either don't understand something, or recognize you might have misunderstood, then seek clarification, verbally if opportunity allows, or written if appropriate.

* Rather than make assumptions, ask questions. Don't assume you know what other people are thinking or feeling, or assume you know why they are behaving as they are. You will likely be wrong, irrespective of your own certainties. Ask questions.

* The quantity and quality of your questions is a measure of your level of interest, and good questions can go a long way towards enabling effective communication. They make the other person think in a different way, which just telling them things often doesn't. A short sequence of questions and answers can often get to the heart of a matter faster than any other method.

* Avoid questions that put the other person on the defensive. Questions which start with "Couldn't you …", "Shouldn't you …", "Wouldn't it be better if …" are all likely to appear as criticism, with the subtext that you have come up with better ideas than they have. Better to ask questions of a more 'brainstorming manner' such as "What might be ways of …", and then if appropriate

The Bumper Book of Common Sense

bringing in your own ideas as part of a joint activity. It is best however to lead them into coming up with the ideas themselves rather than you overtly stating them.

* Ask people open questions rather than closed questions, unless you are explicitly looking for a very specific answer. Closed questions are ones they can answer with a simple one-word or phrase answer and avoid giving any useful follow up information or wider understanding. Open questions are ones requiring a more elaborate answer, and generally are questions which start with what, when, which, why, where, how. Open questions seek to keep an interaction going and enable new topics to be opened up and explored.

* People understand and respond quicker to positive messages than they do to negative ones. Put your communication in as positive a way as you can. For example, focus on what you can do for someone rather than on what you can't, or talk of things being a challenge or opportunity rather than a problem.

* Clichés are powerful ways of getting an idea across; however look to vary them a little, maybe by adding on an additional surprise ending. A useful way of doing this is to take the cliché literally. Or look to take one that is the opposite of what you want, then swapping it around.

* Analogies provide us with a powerful way of communicating new or novel ideas to others. However they can also be misleading.

* With respect to any type of communication, the two periods of greatest attention are at the beginning and at the end. Information presented at the beginning or the end, or both, is more likely to be remembered, more likely to be read, and therefore more likely to influence others, than information presented or communicated in the middle. If you have key messages to get across ensure they are included in the beginning and or the end. Do not expect people to pick out key points that are hidden away in the middle details of a communication, whether written, spoken, or presented.

* If you have good and bad news to give, it is usually best to give the bad news early. You come over as being more open and honest. Also by leaving the good until towards the end you come over as more modest.

* Don't write to someone when you are feeling emotionally charged, or if you do, don't send it to them until you've had time to review it when you are feeling calm. If you've written something whilst emotionally charged you may want to get someone else to have a look at it before you send it.

* The following is a summary list of skills and attitudes which will support you in being a good communicator:
    o Be very clear about what the message is that you are trying to communicate;
    o Ensure that what you are looking to communicate is accurate;
    o Take responsibility for your messages and whether or not they have been effectively received. Be conscious of the possibility of misunderstandings;
    o Listen to the other person's or people's feedback and body language as a response to your message, being as empathic as you are able, and reflect upon it;
    o Try to see things from other people's point of view. What is likely to be their viewpoint when receiving a given message;
    o Respond calmly to emotional responses from others;
    o Repeat your message should you think it might not have been understood, albeit explaining it in a different way that should help with understanding;
    o Listen to the other person's viewpoint and seek to ensure you understand it;
    o Adopt a negotiating, win-win for all, attitude that acknowledges the other party has a view which may be different to your own;

- Encourage the other person to speak more;
- Take different opinions as an opportunity not a threat;
- Be open minded and acknowledge differences;
- Explain objectively, and try not to be judgmental;
- Pay attention to any direct feedback;
- Be assertive albeit without being opinionated or aggressive;
- Be willing to share your thoughts and emotions, albeit without being over the top;
- Address people by their name;
- Be as clear and precise as you are able, keeping to the point, and avoiding jargon and use of obscure terms;
- Try to provide concrete examples in support of abstract ideas;

Potential for Miscommunication

* Be aware that what you intended to communicate is not necessarily the message the recipient has understood, and similarly that what you pick out from someone else's communication is not necessarily what they intended.

* Communication is the effective transfer of an idea from one person, the sender, to another, the receiver. A communication can become distorted by:
    - lack of clarity by the 'sender' of what they are trying to communicate;
    - mistakes or slips of the tongue on the part of the sender;
    - the sender accidentally leaving information out;
    - distortions, interference, or noise in the communication medium used to convey the message such that what is transmitted by the sender is not precisely what is received by the receiver;
    - external distractions which mean part of the information is missed by the receiver;
    - internal distractions which mean the receiver has other thoughts in his or her head and does not pay attention to part of the message;
    - mishearing on the part of the receiver;
    - use of language on the part of the sender which the receiver does not understand;
    - misinterpretations on the part of the receiver, for example due to ambiguities;
    - intellectual biases on the part of the receiver leading to the message being interpreted in a different way to that intended. This could arise for example as a result of cultural differences, or just different backgrounds between sender and receiver.

* There are many different types of 'noise' that can interfere with a message, including:
    - Environmental Noise, which physically disrupts communication, such as loud background noise or poor quality copies;
    - Physiological-Impairment Noise, where physical impairment such as deafness might limit effective communication;
    - Semantic Noise, caused by different interpretations of the meanings of certain words;
    - Syntactical Noise, such as grammatical errors;
    - Structural Noise, where the message is poorly structured leads to ambiguity or incomplete information. For example, unclear and badly stated instructions or directions;
    - Cultural Noise caused by stereotypical assumptions that leads to misunderstandings;
    - Psychological Noise whereby our attitudes can make communication difficult.

- Other people may not have the same background as ourselves and may not be able to interpret a given piece of information, or worse may have a background which leads to them interpreting information differently to how we implicitly do so. Ensure enough common ground to put given information into context.

- Where there are ambiguities people will tend to interpret them in a way that suits themselves often without realizing there was an ambiguity in the first place. We often don't recognize the ambiguities in our own writing because we know what we mean. Always sit back after you have written something to check for clarity and ambiguities.

- Note that it is usually better that someone cannot interpret a message and that they seek clarification, than that they misinterpret it, and unknowingly proceed on a different assumption to that intended.

- If there is no feedback to give confidence that a message has been correctly received then miscommunication can go unnoticed leading to future problems.

Creativity

General Observations about Creativity

- Creativity is not something some people have and others don't. We all have the ability to be creative. Just get on and do things. Don't judge that it has to be 'good'. Creativity comes out of just letting yourself go.

- Anyone is capable of being creative, so long as they can find something to be passionate about.

- People are creative in some areas of their life and conformist in others.

- Many new innovate ideas come from persons outside the establishment, because they bring with them new ideas.

- Creativity is about having unconventional, but feasible, ideas. Simply having unconventional ideas is not being creative. There are a very large number of potentially unconventional ideas. The skill is being able to have unconventional ideas that can work.

- Good but new ideas tend to pass through three stages. First, they are ridiculed. Second, they are opposed. Third, they are accepted as being self-evident. Do not be put off if at first there is a lack of appreciation of your new idea. So long as you believe in it, that is enough whilst you continue to develop it.

- Most good ideas need an individual with courage and perseverance to see them through to acceptance.

- Great ideas don't succeed just because they are great ideas. They need to be developed and thought about, and need a lot of hard work and dedication.

- Good ideas don't sell themselves. To sell a good idea you usually need to sell yourself. People will often be more sold on your passion and dedication than on the inherent merits of the idea itself.

* People will often resist or reject even brilliant ideas. We need to be creative and innovative in how we sell or illustrate our ideas.

* Don't expect others to readily embrace your creatively ideas. Creative ideas often threaten others either because it would upset their way of doing things or because they feel as though they should have had the idea.

* There is a need for both conformity and innovation. Conformity is needed to provide a common means of communication and common values necessary to be able to work together. Innovation is needed to be able to see that things can be done differently and to deal with novel situations.

* Good and successful ideas are often ones that are simple but concrete, unexpected but credible.

* What comes to be seen as a work of genius usually starts out as a confused incoherent draft. Works of genius rarely if ever arrive fully formed. Don't be critical of your first and early drafts. Get as many ideas down as you can without judging them. Turning them into something coherent, well expressed, and well argued, comes later through hard work and perseverance.

* It is a myth to believe great creative ideas arrive largely complete. Most creative ideas develop and are improved by hard work and rework. Most works of genius are created by an unswerving commitment, hard work, and patience.

* We are not all the same. Some people get creative by following a highly structured approach, others just leap about. Most of us are somewhere in-between. If it works for you then do it your way. If you struggle being creative then maybe you should try shifting to being either more structured, or less so.

* Much seeming spontaneous creativity is the result of extensive and constant experimentation, most of which fails.

* New ideas don't come out of nowhere, no matter how novel they seem. They come from making connections.

* People are not their ideas. People you dislike or don't respect can, and often will, have good ideas. Similarly just because you like or respect someone does not mean their ideas are necessarily good or the best that could be had. Clearly you should give more weight to someone who has been seen in the past to have had good ideas. But never take ideas as gospel. Ensure there is a good rationale behind them.

* You need to work at being creative. Many people who go through a highly creative phase can often become very conservative and fixed in their ideas. It's nothing to do with them getting older, it's all to do with them no longer making the effort to be creative.

* It requires less skill and effort to knock something down than it does to create and build. It is easier to criticize than it is to create something that can be criticized. Thus don't be disheartened by criticism since what you are doing is worth far more than what the person criticizing is doing.

* You need to sleep well and get exercise if you are to be generally creative during the day. Whilst a lack of sleep may occasionally spark some off the wall thoughts, you are far more likely to be creative after having slept well.

Sources of Creative Ideas

* Most new ideas derive from existing ideas but applied in a different way.

The Bumper Book of Common Sense

* Many, possibly most, new ideas come from taking an idea that applies in one domain and then applying it in another. Thus underpinning many of the sources of creative ideas is exposure to ideas in many different domains.

* Analogies play a key role in creativity, because they suggest new directions or variations that may be useful. Most creative ideas are variations on a theme, but the variation is one that others have either not seen before in the particular context, or have not seen with sufficient clarity to be able to take advantage of or make practical use of. If you have a challenge you are looking to be creative about approaching, then use brainstorming type techniques to come up with direct analogies, lots of them, then use the different analogies, possibly in some mixed up way, to generate different ideas about how you might tackle the original challenge.

* Much creativity arises from making connections between things that hadn't previously been connected in order to satisfy some need. Being able to make conceptual comparisons and analogies between things that are seemingly unconnected is an important way of identifying new ways to do things.

* Try to identify particular attributes or characteristics of whatever it is you want to be creative about, and then look to vary specific attributes and characteristics, one at a time or in groups, and see what ideas it stimulates.

* A particular aspect of creativity is to make use of objects for things other than what they were created for. For example: take advantage of the shape of something, using it as a container or holder for example; use something as a tool, almost anything can be used as a hammer; break something down into its constituent parts and use the parts for something, the material on old clothes for example can be reused as coverings; turn objects into ornaments, possibly after some colorful and bright painting.

* A useful mnemonic to bring to mind when looking to create new ideas by varying the attributes of some thing or some things you already have in mind - SCAMPER: Substitute, Combine, Adapt, Modify, Put to other uses, Eliminate, Rearrange.

* Look at familiar things in a new way. Take them out of their usual environment and place them in one completely different, and then look to adapt them to that new environment.

* Look at circumstances you are seeking to be creative about from many different viewpoints. Imagine yourself very small. Imagine yourself a child. Imagine yourself being someone who is always decisive. Imagine yourself being someone you admire.

* Look at placing yourself in the situation you are looking to be creative about, as the primary actor or object. Imagine yourself as a type of cartoon character, and hypothesis as to how you might feel or what options you might have.

* Compressed conflict involves identifying 2 conflicting words that capture the essence of what you are looking for, then look to see what other situations or analogies are also faced with this seeming conflict, and how they have gone about resolving it.

* Your subconscious is far more creative than your conscious mind. To boost creativity, have clearly in your mind what it is you want to be creative about, then distract your conscious mind through doing a Sudoku, or counting backwards in 7s, or listening to multiple radio stations at the same time, or doing a short puzzle that requires concentration from your conscious mind. Then return to see what creative ideas pop into your head.

* Spend some time on your own. Creativity flourishes in solitude. But not if there are distractions such as TV or radio. You need to be able to hear your own thoughts. But you also sometimes need to interact with people to help develop ideas and get fresh perspectives.

* The best way to get a good idea is to have lots of ideas. In generating good ideas quantity often leads to quality. When you start to generate new ideas, keep going. It is only by continuing to try to generate new ideas that we often start to get into truly novel ideas.

* A number of small variations can quickly lead to something very different to the original.

* If you have a problem to mull over, go for a long walk alone.

* Creative thinking gives rise to opportunities. Good places to look for opportunities are in the things that inconvenience or annoy you – there are usually opportunities for making things better. If something bothers you, rather than get upset, think about what you can do about it.

* Opportunities often exist in the little things that go unnoticed by most people. Be curious about anything that strikes you as odd, no matter how small.

* Good ideas often arise from being dissatisfied about some existing product or service. Rather than bemoan things not being as you would like them, think about how they could be better.

* Good ideas often develop by building on and adapting ideas from others, and great creators frequently do so. Note that building on ideas from others is not cheating or dishonest. It is natural. Borrowing extensively from one source in particular, without explicitly acknowledging it, is cheating and dishonest.

* Other people are a great source of creative ideas, even if they don't realize it. They will see things from a different perspective than you do, and thus any discussion with them has the potential of opening up new ideas. It can be particularly useful talking things through with someone who knows little about the particular subject matter because they won't be constrained by existing ways of thinking about it.

* If you ever have weird ideas pop up into your head, write them down at the first chance you get. There is a good chance it is your subconscious coming up with a novel approach to something, though it may not be immediately obvious what it is that it relates to.

How to Boost your Creativity

* Learn to quieten your mind. If your mind is constantly filled with worries and regrets and thoughts about everyday life you will not get, or at least not hear, any creative thoughts that come to you.

* Always have a notebook and pen with you so you can immediately write down any creative thoughts or ideas that come to you. Do not rely on remembering them. Such thoughts often fleetingly pass through your mind, and even if they momentary have a great impact other thoughts will usually very quickly crowd them out, and often they won't come back again. Having noted down thoughts into a notebook, you should then regularly review them and move them to somewhere more permanent, such as an ideas folder, or an action list.

* Creativity thrives on wide ranging knowledge, curiosity about different topics, being willing to challenge the status quo, and letting go of judgments.

* The mindset for creativity includes openness to new idea, curiosity about anything and everything, willingness to think differently, perseverance in trying to understand or develop an idea, being willing to take risks, taking a structured approach, toying with ideas, taking personal responsibility for your thoughts and actions, and tolerance for ambiguity.

* Sometimes be willing to break long accepted rules, so long as it is not unethical or illegal or particularly dangerous. Creativity often arises from being willing to take a different path to others.

The Bumper Book of Common Sense

* Reading a lot, particularly on different topics, and having many different types of experiences, increases the potential for creativity since it opens the mind to more concepts with which to draw analogies.

* Reading or listening to jokes is a way of getting your mind used to making new connections since jokes generally involve some punchline which involves some lateral thinking shift.

* Do things you wouldn't normally do. Try new games or activities you wouldn't normally play or do. Go to events you wouldn't normally go to. You don't need to make a habit of them if you don't enjoy them, but you should at least try many different things.

* Things that you would normally do in a particular way, do them differently.

* Meet people from different backgrounds. They will give you different perspectives on life.

* Walk a lot. It is a mild form of exercise and gets oxygen into your brain. Moreover walking seems to facilitate getting your subconscious in touch with your conscious leading to many ideas occurring to you that would not have otherwise done so. Other forms of light exercise have a similar effect, cycling, swimming, gardening, jogging, tai chi, etc, but they are not all conducive to you jotting notes down, which you need to do if you are not to forget them.

* At least once a month do something you haven't done before, or go somewhere you haven't been before. Once a week make the effort to talk to someone you haven't talked to before or someone you don't know very well, to the extent that you find out something about them (from them) that you didn't know before.

* Discuss ideas with other people. A lot of ideas come about as variations on a theme, and if you are discussing ideas with others you may well find they open up new avenues, or new avenues suggest themselves to you as a result of their different perspective.

* Plants, flowers and trees facilitate creativity. Being surrounded by green colors will lead to more creative ideas than being surrounded by red colors.

* The brain can be 'primed' for certain types of thinking. Creativity can be facilitated by briefly looking at unusual modern art.

* If you find you are stuck when trying to come up with an idea, finding yourself continually coming back to the same ideas which you know won't work, then try looking up a word randomly in the dictionary and then looking at how to make it relevant. It might help get your mind out of a rut and onto a different path of thinking.

* You can stimulate your creativity by taking two random objects and think of some way they can be used together. Or look up two random words in a dictionary or encyclopedia and look for ways of linking them together. Or take two contradictory ideas and then look at how you can reconcile the contradiction.

* The right hand side of our brain is focused on creativity, energy, dreams. It is more intuitive and concerned with wholeness. The left hand side of our brain is logical, short term, and practical. It tends to break things down into parts and seeks to give them structure. We need to make use of both sides of our brains to achieve our potential. Ways of doing this include visualizing our goals, enjoying our work, and creative play. By working on challenges we enjoy, more of our brain gets involved.

* Different means of communicating use different parts of our brains. Use different means: write things by hand; type things into a computer; speak to others or into a tape or even just out loud to yourself. You will be more creative.

* Some ideas for stimulating your creativity in general:

- o   Buy plain pots and vases and decorate and paint them;
- o   Try new foods and drinks;
- o   Experiment with cooking;
- o   Read magazines on topics you wouldn't normally consider;
- o   Randomly look up words in a dictionary or articles in an encyclopedia;
- o   Take an everyday object and think of unusually uses for it;
- o   Visit museums, zoos, art galleries;
- o   Visit bric-a-brac shops;
- o   Take a trip to the theatre or opera;
- o   Listen to a range of different types of music that you don't normally listen to;
- o   Listen to different types of classical music;
- o   Do an evening class in some subject you know little about;
- o   Go listen to some lectures or attend some event;
- o   Do some DIY projects;
- o   Go out and fly a kite;
- o   Learn a new language, it usually puts ideas together in a different way.

* If you are looking for creative ideas for something in particular, after you've had a session thinking about it, stop for a while and do something relatively mundane, something not too demanding and completely unrelated to whatever the subject matter is. Go for a walk or a swim, do some light chores, do a puzzle, read a magazine. You should find new ideas pop into your head. Note that we often get creative ideas during what are our non-optimal parts of the day. If we are the sort of person that is alert and highly productive in the mornings, we will often find insightful creative ideas occurring later in the day.

* If you are looking for creative ideas for something in particular pick out an object at random and then try to force a connection with it. Or take a walk round an art gallery or a museum, where a wide variety of visual stimuli may well prompt some ideas. Make sure you have pen and paper with you to jot down any ideas that come to you or you may readily forget them.

* People who remember their dreams are generally more creative. Keep a notebook by you and jot down what you remember of your dreams when you wake up. Regularly doing so will lead to you improving your memories of your dreams.

* You can learn to better remember your dreams, and extract creative thoughts from them, by learning to recall them as you wake up and writing down what you remember. When you wake in the mornings, or awake in the night, rather than immediately open your eyes stay as you are and try to recall your dreams. Bring anything you can remember about them clearly to mind, then open your eyes and write down what you remember. Ensure you have pen and paper to hand and do this immediately. By getting into the habit of doing so you will find yourself getting much better at remembering your dreams. Once you do get effective at remembering your dreams you can move onto a state of being aware of yourself whilst still dreaming and learn to consciously guide your dreams.

* You can set your subconscious off being creative by asking yourself specific questions. By regularly asking yourself a given question you increase the likelihood of your subconscious mulling it over, and ideas can then simply occur to you when you are not particularly expecting them. You can strengthen this by writing the questions down, and regularly reading them, or recording them and listening to them, or simply saying them out loud to yourself.

* People who are happy or in a good mood are more creative and less prone to making errors.

* Creativity is stimulated by having a passion about what you do. By having a real interest in it. If there is something you find interesting then experiment with it, play with it, explore it.

* Look for the funny side in many of the things you come across. Note that humor is frequently based upon a lateral thinking twist to what is otherwise a normal situation.

* Develop a curiosity for and interest in new ideas. Don't try to judge them. Just take an interest in them, explore them, and seek out variations on them.

* Write a lot. Don't judge your writing. Don't try to write well. Just write. Anything that comes into your head. If you want to improve a piece of writing, you can do that by revising what you've written later. But when initially writing, quantity matters more than quality.

Brainstorming

* The best way to have a good idea is to have lots of ideas. When initially looking for ideas focus on generating many ideas, good, bad, or indifferent.

* Brainstorming with other people, where you feed ideas off each other in a non-judgmental and fun way, is likely to lead to more creative ideas than each individual involved might have come up with in isolation.

* When brainstorming, no ideas are too silly or crazy, and people should be encouraged to hitchhike on each other's ideas. Good ideas often emerge from combining or morphing ideas which on the face of it didn't initially appear particularly strong.

* Some general guidance notes in support of brainstorming sessions:
    o Think about who to invite. People who are likely to have something to contribute, and people from a wide range of backgrounds. Avoid having people in attendance who are likely to be critical or are likely to intimidate others.
    o Ensure the location is conducive to the session. Provide water and tea and coffees, and possibly snacks. Possibly props relevant to the subject matter.
    o Generally sessions of about an hour are most appropriate, though you may have more than one session with breaks in between. Less than this then some people may not have got started. Longer and many people will flag.
    o Ensure there is a facilitator who will make sure ideas get put up and judgment is suspended. The facilitator must also make sure ideas are focused on a clear problem, and that ideas keep coming, possibly by pointing to ideas which can be explored further.
    o Ensure someone is available to record up on flipcharts or elsewhere all ideas that are raised as they are raised.
    o Be very clear about the subject matter or the problem to be solved.
    o Be clear about the ground rules, which are that all participants are equal, and all ideas are captured, at least as part of the initial capture exercise. There is to be no criticism or judgment of initial ideas.
    o Encourage people to build on other people's ideas and identify variations on themes already expressed.
    o It can be useful to have various props which people can play around with and which could trigger further ideas. Don't have them overtly related to the subject matter – you are looking to avoid constraining people to obvious thoughts.
    o A techniques to help to continue to generate brainstorming ideas after they start to dry up is to take an object which has nothing to do with the topic being explored, identify its attributes, and then look to see what ideas may flow from looking at how those attributes or variations on them might be relevant to the issue you are looking at

- o Separate out identification of ideas from evaluation of ideas. Once you start to evaluate ideas you will dry up in terms of generating ideas. Thus keep looking to generate ideas for some time before you begin any evaluation to sort out the promising ideas. However involve a range of people in sorting the ideas otherwise you will simply end up with the prejudices of whoever is doing the assessing.
  - o Write up the ideas both pre and post assessment and give it wide distribution.

* In terms of generating an initial set of ideas brainstorming in groups is often less effective than getting people to initially come up with ideas on their own, since when in a group many people will not make much effort and will hide in the crowd. However to further develop ideas, and to push towards more creative ideas, working in a group will lead people to keep generating ideas after they would have stopped had they been on their own.

* When evaluating ideas from a brainstorming session be aware that there will typically be some ideas which are easy to implement but will only have limited benefits and some ideas which will be difficult to implement but if they come off will have significant benefit. It is often useful to evaluate ideas into these two categories since if you simply look to identify "the best" ideas you may find yourself either rejecting difficult to implement ideas in favor of easy to implement ideas or simply focusing on the greatest benefit ideas which may not come to fruition and missing a lot of easy wins. By splitting into the two categories you can get on and implement the easy ideas, whilst then setting up teams or projects to investigate further and follow up if appropriate the more difficult ideas.

* You can and should brainstorm with yourself. Put down a problem you want to solve, or a goal you want to achieve, and on a piece of paper with pre-numbered lines keep putting down ideas until you have a minimum of say 25 or 50. Initial ideas might not be feasible but if you keep looking additional ideas will emerge, and by combining ideas, or taking variations on themes, some good ideas could well arise. You can look to add further ideas the day or days after. Sort out or assess your ideas only after you have finished generating them. Sift through them, maybe with a multiple pass technique whereby at each pass you just tick off the better ones of those that are left. If further variations on a theme occur then just get them down. Or if you can link ideas together to get a better idea.

* Techniques to use in support of brainstorming with yourself:
  - o Try to see things from the viewpoint of a different time or place;
  - o Try to see things from the viewpoint of a different person;
  - o What would you do if you were omnipotent, and could do anything you wanted?
  - o Pick some words at random from a dictionary and try to relate them to whatever it is you are brainstorming;
  - o Think of
  - o Do a SWOT assessment: Strengths, Weaknesses, Opportunities, Threats;
  - o List down assumptions or barriers and then look at what needs to be done to overcome them;
  - o Look at the opposite of some of the ideas you have;
  - o Use exaggeration: make things bigger, smaller, fatter, thinner, multiplied;
  - o Write ideas that come to you very quickly one after the other without thinking.

* Reverse brainstorming is where we take a challenging statement and then look at how we might do the opposite. Then take the ideas generated and reverse them to see what they suggest for what it is we would like to do. Reverse brainstorming can help get people who are naturally negative on board and it can be fun.

* The concept of using Visually Identifying Relationships (VIR) is to take 4 pictures, one which is used to relax you, and the others to act as stimulants. Write down observations that arise from looking back from one picture to another, occasionally using the relaxing picture to step back from time to time. Initially just list out observations arising from looking at the pictures but then look to

The Bumper Book of Common Sense

see how these observations facilitate ideas with respect to the topic under consideration. You can build up a portfolio of pictures which you can then mix up the choice of to support your personal brainstorming or possibly group brainstorming sessions.

* A variation on the theme of Brainstorming is Brainwriting, where people write down ideas on pieces of paper and then swap it with others to see if they can build on the idea or have it prompt them with new ideas. The pieces of paper with sequences of ideas continue to get passed round. It should be done in silence.

* The Nominal Group Technique is where people work independently but get access to each other's ideas and the opportunity to build on them.

Ways of Encouraging or Discouraging Creative Thinking

* Arguably the greatest suppressor of good ideas is an environment in which people feel they are being judged. In a judgmental environment people hold back on ideas, whether strong or weak, and noting that even weak ideas could if explored have opened up routes to other much stronger ideas.

* High monetary rewards directly linked to producing creative output can be demotivating and interfere with creativity. It both puts a pressure on, which can disrupt the creative process, and it also makes the creative person themselves much more judgmental about their own work, in terms of asking themselves 'is it worth this large monetary value?'

* People who are competing for a prize will tend to do less imaginative work than those of similar abilities who are not competing. Moreover after winning or failing to win the prize they will work less hard.

* If people are told to generate good ideas, they will generate far fewer good ideas than if they are told to just generate lots of ideas and worry about whether or not they are good later.

* We often have a natural tendency to be negative about new ideas. To counter this, first focus on the potential benefits of a new idea before you consider the negative. Often there are useful aspects of ideas even when in the round they are flawed. If you simply launch into the negative you will miss any potential useful ideas that may be contained within them. Note that even when an idea is flawed in the round there are often aspects of it you can make use of.

* When a new idea comes up to be judged, start by focusing on the positive aspects of the idea, then on other interesting aspects of the idea and possible variations of it, and only when you've exhausted these move on to potential issues or negative aspects of the idea. It is vital to keep any negative thoughts until the end otherwise they will prematurely kill not only the idea itself but also possibly very promising variations of it before they can be explored. Lots of good ideas get killed prematurely because of a too early focusing on the negatives.

* When we simply state issues with an idea they are seen as obstacles and we get into a negative mindset. If we state issues as a question we can employ creative problem solving techniques to come up with answers.

* Instead of responding to ideas and suggestions with a 'Yes, but …' respond with a 'Yes, and …'. Using "But …" implies criticism whilst using "And …" implies good, and can be improved with suggestion about how to go about it. It also encourages the other person to be creative in thinking about to look to improve the idea rather than have them becoming defensive about it.

* Types of responses which kill or discourage new ideas:
    o 'It's been tried before.'
    o 'It's not my/your responsibility.'
    o 'It won't work.'

- - 'It will be too expensive.'
  - 'Now is not the right time.'
  - 'Put it in writing.'
  - 'You might be right, but …'
  - 'It will take too long.'
  - 'Others wouldn't approve/agree.'
  - 'What we have works. Don't fix or change it.'
  - 'It's a stupid idea.'
  - 'It wouldn't work here.'

* Ways of encouraging ideas:
  - 'What options are there?'
  - 'How could we make it work?'
  - 'It's a great idea, now what can we do to get it going?'
  - 'What other ideas can you come up with?'
  - 'Who else has any suggestions?'
  - 'What can I do to help?'

* Ways we lose our creative powers:
  - Letting the approval of others be more important than our own. Ie. let other people's opinions drive what we do and think.
  - Always putting other people first. The best way to help others is to help ourselves first.
  - Asking for permission when we should be deciding for ourselves.
  - Holding yourself back because you don't want to take risks.
  - Demanding guarantees, only progressing if you expect certainty.
  - Stretching ourselves too far.

* Principles that give us creative power:
  - Free yourself from the expectations of others. Live your own life, and find your own destiny. Pursue what you love.
  - Reclaim your creativity. Become curious and freethinking. Free your imagination to deal with life's challenges.
  - Think big. Have big dreams and goals.
  - Don't be apologetic about what you want. Have a dream and go for it.
  - Suspend disbelief. See opportunities and possibilities.
  - Create options. Create choices to give you greater flexibility.
  - Persist. Keep trying again and again and again. Keep learning from your mistakes.

* Most good ideas are defeated by irrelevant issues.

* Don't continually have noise around you. If you are plugged in listening to music all the time you are unlikely to get much in the way of creative ideas, except possibly if you are listening to calming background or classical music that leaves your brain free to have random thoughts.

* Don't fill all your time with TV and being busy. You'll never give your brain a chance to make itself heard. Sometimes do things with relative silence around you. You could be surprised at the useful

and creative thoughts going on inside your head that will stay hidden from you unless you give them a chance to be heard.

Getting and Being Organized

Being Organized Sets you Free

* . Being organized will leave you with more time on your hands since you won't be wasting time finding things, or even redoing things that you've lost. You will also be much less stressed if you can quickly find anything you might want to find, and you will be able to quickly get on with productive tasks

* Be well organized and you will be more motivated to do things.

* Being organized puts you in a much better position for doing extraordinary things than those who are less so. It enables you to focus on what you are looking to do rather than being continually distracted by trying to prepare for doing it.

* Being organized is not in conflict with creativity; in most circumstances it is a vital precursor to creativity and spontaneity. It frees your mind to focus on a particular subject, and to quickly take advantage of and act upon creative thoughts.

* Clutter contributes significantly to lethargy and procrastination; to a feeling of being weighed down and overwhelmed and stressed. This is also true of an e-mail Inbox that just keeps getting bigger and bigger. Clear clutter and be disciplined about it. You need a reason to keep something: you use it to make life easier; it has a strong personal value to you; it is particularly beautiful or pleasing. You will feel much better with less clutter.

* Being unorganized helps us maintain a pretense to ourselves, though not to others, that we are really highly capable at everything but can't fully demonstrate it right now because things are, temporarily of course, a bit of a mess. We have a fear that if we got highly organized we would find we are not as good as we like to pretend to ourselves we really are. Ironically of course we would be highly capable in some things if we got organized, though not in everything. Most people thus fail to be highly capable in something because they don't want to be seen not to be highly capable in everything.

* Keep your house clean and reasonably tidy, though not obsessively so: you will feel much calmer. Ensure others in the household do their bit. By getting into the moment you can actually enjoy tidying up and cleaning. Take pride in keeping tidy and clean and banish negative thoughts about 'having to do it'.

* When travelling on long journeys make preparations. Use checklists to check what items you may need to take with you, and check your transport and accommodation arrangements. If taking your car check oil, water, lights, etc. beforehand.

How to Get and Stay Organized

* Develop a clear vision of the sort of home environment you want to live in. It will largely be within your power to create that environment.

* Set up your organizing systems so that you are absolutely clear about what you will keep where. Make use of storage boxes, files, and compartment organizers, with appropriate labeling. Have a place for everything, and keep it there when not in use. This includes having places for commonly used items such as keys and phones, which is where you put them when you are not carrying them around with you. A lot of problems with clutter and not being able to find things is a result of not having firmly decided where things should be kept.

* Have a place for borrowed or rented items. Keep them there unless you are using them.

* If you feel overwhelmed with the amount of work to clear up, to de-clutter, to decide about where things should be kept, then write down a list of all the areas that need sorting, to a level of detail that any given area can be done in half an hour or so. And then start to work down the list. It is important however that the solutions to the clearing up are long term ones, not just moving stuff to somewhere else 'for now'. And once an area is cleared or sorted, make sure it stays cleared and used as intended. Note that it is better to have lots of small areas each of which you can get done in one session than a small number of big areas that you start on but don't really get done properly. Thus break up rooms or even areas within rooms into smaller areas like individual drawers or shelves. So long as you don't let areas slip after you've done them, and so long as you are making progress, you don't need to rush it.

* Once areas are well organized be absolutely ruthless in ensuring they stay organized.

* Whenever something is not put back in its place it will pile up to become clutter. It only takes a few moments to put something back in its place when you are done with it; if you don't you will waste time looking for it later, or waste time looking for other things amongst the clutter it has helped to create.

* Be ruthless with stuff you never use. Get rid of anything that wastes time, space, energy, or money, unless there is a blatantly good reason for keeping it. Will you ever use it again? If so, under what circumstances? Most people have a habit of holding on to huge amounts of stuff 'just in case', and it weighs them down, even if put away out of sight. And once you have decided to throw something out, do so; don't leave it lying around.

* Have fewer possessions. If you have fewer possessions you will have less clutter, more space; a life with few possession tends to be more liberating. Most people could readily cut their belongings by 50 – 90% and actually increase the quality of their lives. Much of your belongings generate a feeling of guilt: clothes that no longer fit; books you haven't read and in truth never will; games you never played. Get rid of them, and you get rid of the guilt. Useful or beautiful – if neither, bin it. Imagine you are about to move and want to make a fresh start. What would you keep? Imagine it would cost you by the box to move stuff. What is and what is not worth the expense? You don't need to wait till you move to get rid of the stuff that you have no good reason to keep.

* Don't hang on to things for old times sake, at least not more than one or two things. You can always take a photo as a reminder, which is likely to invoke just as strong emotions as the thing itself.

* Buy quality not quantity. Generally buy fewer things. You don't need most of what you buy. And when you do buy something new look to find something old you can throw out.

* Once a month go round the house finding things you haven't used for 12 months or more and throw them out, or give them to charity. A piece of clothing, a book, some gadget, something in the kitchen.

* When you tidy something up, think about how it got that way in the first place. Deal with the habits that create the mess. Decide what you need to do to prevent it happening, not in general, but specifically in response to each item you come across to tidy up.

The Bumper Book of Common Sense

* Organize your paperwork. Bits of paper with contact information should be put in a contact book or equivalent, and reminders should go onto some form of List. Throw out information you don't need and file away information you do or might.

* Deal with hard copy mail more or less as soon as you get it. Pay bills and invoices promptly, unless you deliberately want to delay for cash flow or other reasons – in which case identify when you will pay it and put it away until then, with some way of reminding yourself. File or throw the paperwork away as soon as you have finished with it.

* Some essentials in a digital world:
    o Organize your files and other information into an electronic filing system that is easy to use;
    o Ensure you ruthlessly keep files where they belong and where you will know where to find them some long time in the future;
    o Keep your passwords safe;
    o Regularly back up your work.

* Keep your organizing systems simple. If necessary add refinements once they are working. We often surround ourselves with systems more complex than they need to be. Set up something complicated and you are unlikely to follow it for long. Simplify whenever you can.

* Be organized without being bureaucratic. Getting organized is a means to an end, not an end in itself. You are getting organized in order to be effective and efficient in getting things done. You should get far more out of being organized than you have to put into getting and staying organized.

* Include time slots in your personal and family agenda for clearing up. Always be on the look out for anything that can help you or your family to be more organized.

* If you're not sure what to do, get on and clear something up. Clear out some e-mail, throw something away, clear a space, put something where it belongs.

Organize Your Workspace(s)

* Ensure your workspace is ergonomically sound. With a little bit of care you can avoid unnecessarily tiring yourself or doing yourself an injury whilst working. Pay attention to normal posture, reach, and lighting. Any aches or pains are not normal and you should make adjustments to avoid or stop them. Ensure the area you regularly work in is well lit.

* Keep a ready stock of supplies for anything you use regularly: paper, post it notes, envelopes, stamps. Have good quality staplers and hole punches and pens and pencils if you use them.

* Organize your paperwork. Ensure you have a structured filing system for any information you wish to keep, paper and electronic. Put and keep things in their files. Clear out from the files anything you no longer want or need to keep. Keep your desk and workspaces clear of all paperwork except that which is relevant to what you are working on. If you have a number of 'active' work projects then keep them in neat folders and in a place that is separate from your primary workspace.

* If when starting a new piece of work you have a clear desk to get started on, you will feel much more motivated than if the desk is littered with other half done projects.

* Get rid of loose papers. It they hold bits of information or reminders, copy them into notebooks or wherever you keep that type of information: if you don't have anywhere, create somewhere. If they are bills or other things that need to be actioned, action them or at least get them into an action folder. If it is something you might need in the future then get it into an organized set of files.

* Organize your kitchen so you immediately know where everything is, and you can access frequently used items in an easy and efficient manner. Make use of organizer material such as boxes and dividers to avoid having bits lying around, including in the refrigerator. Keep plenty of worktop or table space clear. Don't keep bits of food you are not really going to eat. Clear out your fridge once a week or fortnight and throw out expired food.

* Get the dishes done shortly after you've finished eating. Never leave them till the next day. This includes drying them and putting them away.

* Be neither a perfectionist nor a slob when it comes to keeping your home tidy. You have better things to do than to be continually tidying up and cleaning, and a messy home will get you down.

Make Extensive Use of Written Reminders

* Do your shopping with a list and avoid busy times. You will save a significant amount of time and money.

* Set up a number of standard meal recipes and a ready list of ingredients. Plan what meals you intend for most days of the week and do your shopping accordingly.

* Use a reminder scheme for up and coming events, such as birthdays and anniversaries. Set a time for when you should sort out presents, well in advance of the event itself, say a month before. Ensure you have wrapping paper and sellotape and labels.

* Keep a notebook for details relating to anyone you buy presents for – keep details of useful information that might help you choose what presents to buy: shoe and clothes sizes for example. Keep a note of presents bought. Put down ideas for presents whenever they occur to you – scribble down the ideas when they occur and transfer them to your notebook when you can. If you see good presents at any time during the year, buy them and put them away assuming there are no date restrictions.

* Maintain an X-Mass card list with all necessary information – such as addresses and names of other family members. If you don't have it create it in advance of next X-Mass and keep it up to date: keep it with or as part of your notebook for presents. Set a date well in advance to buy your cards, do the cards, and send the cards. You can buy the cards when they are cheap in the New Year and keep them for the following year.

Always have Pen and Paper with you

* Always carry something with you to take notes with. Capture any ideas and thoughts you would like to remember as they occur to you; if you don't you will forget them. Note down information gleaned about people, not lots of details, but key information that is worth knowing and remembering, and which might help you develop a closer relationship with them. Review the notes you take regularly and transfer them to where they belong: a to do list, a filing system, a list of ideas, a journal.

* Never rely on your memory. Always write down anything that occurs to you that you would like to remember.

Manage your Finances

* Manage your money. Keep a basic track of your incomings and your outgoings. Spend less than you earn. If you don't you will get into debt and your life will be very stressful. Don't buy things

The Bumper Book of Common Sense

you can't afford. This doesn't mean never use credit. But if you do use credit be sure you can afford to pay it back and don't get caught up in only being able to afford to pay back the interest. You don't need most of the luxuries of life if you can't afford them. You will be far less stressed and thus have a higher quality of life without luxuries than you will be with them if they also lead to money troubles.

* If you are in debt, deal with it. The most important step is to get your outgoings below your income, and keep them that way. Look to keep your interest payments as low as you can, and ensure you are regularly paying off some of the capital you owe. Whilst certain high cost purchases such as property or cars may be exceptions with regards seeking to avoid debt, you need to ensure you can comfortably pay off the interest and that you can cope with potential future changes in interest rates.

* Any scheme for making easy money is almost certainly either a scam or illegal. Be very wary of any scheme that asks you to put up money up front or requires you to provide personal details to people you don't know, except where you have very good reason to trust them. There are many people who are looking to take advantage of anyone who is vulnerable or is otherwise open to being exploited.

* No-one can predict specific outcomes of the financial markets consistently across time. Investors who believe they or others can predict market outcomes lose a lot of money. Even in the short and medium term, there's no way of telling which way the market will go, although in the long run they do exhibit consistent upward trends. Be very wary of believing that with a little bit of weekend analysis you can somehow outthink the markets. Remember that there are two types of investors: those who don't know where the market is going, and those who don't know that they don't know where the market is going.

* After fund and transaction fees have been included, actively managed funds don't perform consistently better than the market average. For a while some will do better than average, whilst others will do worse. But it is just statistical trends. Some, for a while, will seem to do better than average over a longer period of time. However that is just because there are a lot of funds and statistically one will do better than the others for a while. In the longer term it will however drop back as some other fund rises up the statistical league table. Be wary of being seduced by a fund that has performed well in the past, and certainly don't see it as a sure thing: it isn't.

* Don't try to pick individual stocks. Invest in as many as possible so you can match the market average. Don't be tempted to sell at the 'perfect' time. Adopt a buy and hold strategy. The more often you trade the lower the returns. Transaction costs of trading – commissions to brokers – really dent the returns.

* Never put your nest eggs all in one basket. In particular only put money you can afford to lose in highly speculative investments.

* A penny saved is a penny earned. There are lots of ways to cut back on monthly spends, and lots of sources of advice on the internet.

* When you go shopping, have a list, and largely keep to it. Try to keep to a single weekly shop for food and necessities. There may be occasional bargains but don't get seduced into buying more than you need, unless it will genuinely save you money: the best bargains are usually none food necessities. If you find you need to go out for something extra, buy it and only it. Don't browse: in, buy it, out.

* Don't go food shopping when hungry. Eat before you go. Similarly when going out for a meal with the family, particularly if you have children, ensure you and they have something to drink before you go.

* Buying cheap goods can be a false saving if they are of low quality and only last a fraction of the time higher quality goods will last. Before you buy cheap goods look to check that they at least have a reasonable reputation. Often low quality goods will break after a few uses, or even not work at all.

Some low quality goods however have stood the test of time and are commonly used because they are good enough for the use to which they are put.

* Save for a rainy day. Don't spend everything you earn. Most people can save if they try: buy less – you don't need lots of things; buy second hand – you can often buy good quality second-hand products from charity shorts or car boot sales for a fraction of the full cost; buy previous generation products – they often have all the utility you really need and are much cheaper than the latest generation; share rarely used tools with your neighbors or friends; do your own house repairs; only buy new clothes when your old ones wear out; don't take out gym or other memberships that you only occasionally use; beware of buying add-ons to expensive products; learn good petrol saving driving habits; be aware of gas and electricity use around the house – simple changes can significantly reduce your energy bills; insulate your home and buy energy efficient appliances and light bulbs; turn down your thermostat a bit and wear warmer clothing.

* If you can afford it at all, look to set aside at least 10% of what you earn as savings for the future. Put this money somewhere where it can earn interest that is higher than inflation. Be wary however of particularly high interest options since these will also tend to be higher risk options. And do have a look over your overall finances. There is no point in saving money that is earning a lower interest than that at which you are being charged for your debts. In such circumstances use money you might have otherwise saved to pay off any debts that have higher interest payments than you can get on savings.

* Generally insurance is not good value, in that by definition what insurance companies pay out will be less than the value of the goods covered, since the insurance companies will themselves be taking a cut to cover operating costs and profits. Thus for many goods it is best to forgo the insurance and pay for repairs or replacements when they become necessary. However for some products or outcomes insurance provides peace of mind and also covers against the worst that might happen. Thus house insurance, car insurance, certain valuables, and dependent upon circumstances life insurance, are often prudent to have.

* Keep a summary of your finances which will make sense to others should you die suddenly – this is very important if you have family and dependents. It's selfish not to do so.

Maintain your own Personal and Professional Portfolios

* Your Personal Portfolio is a master filing system for all aspects of home and family information, which you use:
  o To keep track of all information which you may need future access to;
  o To provide an organized approach to dealing with a range of home and family matters such as financial management;
  o As an easy to use reference system for information and guidelines that might be of interest, including checklists that you can improve through use;
  o As a tool to support your personal learning and self-development and those of members of your family. Thus record various assessments of yourself, identify areas of strength and weakness, list out your long and medium term goals, record information relating to sources of self-development, and keep track of your self-development activities;
  o As a place to keep your personal or family diary, and also memories of particular events or incidents;
  o As a place to keep items to inspire and lift you: inspiring quotes, lists of music that lifts you, copies of jokes that always make you smile, copies of particular photos or pictures that make you feel good.

* Your Personal Portfolio is something you use throughout your family and home life, and it is never too late to start. It is also a discipline, and a set of information, you can pass onto your children.

- Benefits of producing and maintaining your Personal Portfolio include:
  - To remove many unnecessary frustrations from home and family life arising from not remembering information you've known at one time;
  - To help ensure you do the things that need to be done;
  - As something to look back on in the future and to pass on to others.

- Your Professional Portfolio is a master filing system for career and self-management, which you use:
  - To record the detailed history of your career and capabilities, including a record of your successes and outputs and the things you feel proud of;
  - To help you manage your career development, including the undertaking of a SWOT analysis (Strengths: what are you good at relative to other people; Weaknesses: what are you weak at; Opportunities: what opportunities open up as a result of your strengths, how can you exploit your strengths; Threats: what might be holding you back.) The SWOT analysis can be used to help you identify what to spend more of your time on within your existing area of employment, to identify what additional training you should seek out, and possibly to plan out a career change;
  - To support your self-management, both time and information management;
  - As a self-development management tool;
  - To provide an easy to use reference system for information and guidelines relevant to your work;
  - To keep a record of your work.

- Reasons for developing and maintaining your Professional Portfolio include:
  - In order to manage your professional development and your career;
  - In order to improve your productivity;
  - In support of your being able to demonstrate to potential employers that you are suitably skilled for the tasks to be undertaken;
  - To help ensure that you have a range of skills relevant to your profession, or to the potential opportunities that may come in the future.
  - As something to look back on in the future;

- Maintaining your Personal and Professional Portfolios is a lifelong affair. It is something you will continually add to over time, and continually be looking to rearrange or improve.

- You can keep your Portfolios in hard copy or electronic format or a mixture of both. If you have your Portfolio in an electronic format, ensure you keep it regularly backed up.

Learning and Teaching

Learning is Good for You

- If you are learning and growing intellectually you will be happy and your life will be enriched.

- You become smarter by continually using your brain. And by continuing to use your brain as you get older you will lessen the chances of premature aging and getting Alzheimer's.

* The more you sweat in peacetime the less you bleed in war. By continually learning life skills you will become better able to deal with life.

* By continually learning the skills and knowledge that is relevant to your area of paid work you will increase your chances of staying in paid work and increase your prospects for earning more.

* The more you learn about people and the way people are, the better you will be able to interact effectively with them.

Never Stop Learning

* In an ever-changing world, being learned is not enough. You need also to be a learner. Being a learner is more important than being learned.

* The world is forever changing around you, whether you recognize it or not, whether you accept it or not. If you are not learning and progressing and changing yourself and your behaviors then you are falling behind. Your past successes and adaptations to your environment will not be enough to ensure future success and adaptation.

* You are never so expert in something that you can't benefit from continuing to try to improve.

* Anyone who stops studying or continuing to develop themselves simply because they have finished school or college, or because their workplace is not sending them on courses, is doomed to mediocrity in their work and in their life.

* Many people stop learning relatively early. Whilst still in their 20s they become fixed in their ways and make no effort to keep developing and looking for new experiences and updating their mental models. They become risk and failure adverse and settle into routine life and thought. It doesn't have to be that way, nor should it be that way.

* Cease to learn and you cease to grow. You are never too old to learn or to upgrade yourself.

* Only a fool knows everything. There are always new useful things or things of interest that you can learn.

* It is practice not talent that ultimately matters. Unless you have some physiological disadvantage, then extensive practice will bring extensive skill. It is the quality and quantity of practice, together with a self-belief, that enables people today to be more capable than most of those of yesteryear, not a dramatic improvement in their genes.

* You can never run out of things to learn, and the more you learn the more you realize that. Much of what you think you know is only an approximation or is only one point of view. You can always learn more.

* You should be open to learning at all times. Almost any opportunity, particularly when interacting with others, is a potential opportunity for learning.

* We can and should be continually developing ourselves physically, mentally, and emotionally. There are many hundreds of opportunities each day when we can make decisions to be improving ourselves physically, mentally and emotionally; most in small ways, but they accumulate. Small decisions about what we do or don't eat. Opportunities for a bit of exercise. Opportunities about how we do or don't let our mind wander and about our self-talk. Opportunities about what we choose to do next, and about whether or not we choose to continue or stop what we are doing. Opportunities to control our instinctive and emotional responses to what is happening around us. Every day hundreds and hundreds of opportunities, some big, most small, to get better and better.

The Bumper Book of Common Sense

* Any and all problems are learning opportunities.

* Experiment. Try new things. Find out what works best for you by trying alternatives. Don't assume that what you are doing now is in any way optimal. And even if it was optimal at one time, changes in circumstances or environment may mean it is no longer so. Test to find when and in what circumstances you are most productive. When do you get your best ideas. What stresses you. Look for patterns then use that knowledge to improve.

* Having learnt a skill or some knowledge, even if you don't want to continue to improve, you should keep what you have learnt topped up. Regularly practice the skill, or review the knowledge. If you don't, it will weaken and become forgotten.

* Put aside some money each month as your Personal Research and Development Budget. Use this money to improve your skills, buy books, attend learning events, try and buy new productivity tools. Upgrading yourself enriches your life and provides new and better job opportunities.

Learning is your Own Responsibility

* Take responsibility for your own learning. It is not someone else's responsibility to ensure you learn and develop. It is your own responsibility. If someone with as much vested interest in you as yourself is not willing to take responsibility for developing you, then why would anyone else?

* Don't be put off by the fact that learning is sometimes difficult. At first, everything is difficult. It is by progressing in the light of difficulties that you learn. How far would a sportsperson get if they stopped because they were getting a little tired or had a bit of an ache. Work your way through the difficulties and what was once difficult becomes easy; you've learnt, and you can move onto the next set of difficulties. If you give up because it is difficult, you have only yourself to blame for not learning anything very much.

* Your employability depends upon your current skills. It is up to you whether or not you keep developing them, keep them up to date and learn new ones. If you don't make the effort to keep your skills up to date, then your employer can always find someone else who has more up to date skills and someone who makes more effort to keep their skills up to date.

* Lack of a higher education should not hold you back: if you are willing to work hard, and be an avid reader, you can learn more thoroughly through being self-taught than most people learn from college or university. And once you've been in employment for a while, and had time to develop a 'track record', whether or not you have had a degree or similar becomes less important: what becomes important is whether or not you continue to develop.

* Formal education is valuable. Self-education is invaluable.

* Your skills and abilities are malleable. If you try something and you are no good at it you can either adopt the attitude that it's because you lack an innate ability, and give up, or adopt the attitude that you haven't learnt it yet and get on and learn it. With the latter attitude you can get better and even good at almost anything, though it is worth targeting your learning at things that seem to come easier to you, at things you enjoy, or at things that other people avoid.

* Those using self-imposed deadlines in academic settings perform better than those not imposing such deadlines, though externally imposed deadlines were even better. If you are not working to a set of deadlines set by someone else, set your own, and work hard to achieve them.

Most People can Learn Most Things

* You can improve at almost any skill if you make the effort. Learning skills is far more about making the effort than it is about any inborn ability. And this is also true of thinking skills such as being creative.

* Those that became great at what they do did so because they worked very very hard at it.

* Your body and your brain are both highly malleable. If you learn and practice and put the effort in you can shape them both in almost any way you choose. Training and practice can take you to near the top in almost anything, and is far far more important than natural ability alone, though if you want to become the very very best at what you do choose things you appear to have a natural inclination for, or things that others shy away from.

* In our information age you can learn almost anything you wish to learn. The internet and ready access to books, either to buy or borrow from libraries, means you have far more information and practical advice at your fingertips than anyone in the world had even 30 years ago.

* Every expert was once a novice. If you want to become an expert in something, learn about it and put in the focused dedicated hours.

* To become a true expert generally requires about 10 years of intense practice with a practice rate of about 1,000 hours a year: about 20 hours a week. Most people can become a leading expert if they put in this amount of practice.

* When getting better at something, a skill or physical activity, we will hit limits. When we start to learn something we generally make rapid progress - albeit often through lots of small spurts interspaced with periods of seeming lack of progress - but gradually the amount of progress we make for the amount of effort we put in significantly diminishes. In order to become highly skilled or an expert we need to keep putting in efforts to improve even though the returns seem to be getting smaller. It is these continuing smaller improvements that then set us above the majority.

Learning Styles

* Learning style preferences are different for different people: whether you learn better when information is presented to you aurally or visually, with text or diagrams; whether on your own or in a group; or whether from detailed ideas and examples up to high level concepts and theories, or from high level concepts down into detailed examples. You will learn more readily and be more motivated to learn if information is presented to you, or you present information to yourself, in a way that matches your preferred learning style. It is worth understanding your own learning style preferences because it will enable you to learn more effectively. Most people do if they think about the circumstances under which they most enjoy learning. However there are tests you can readily find online if you are uncertain or you just want to confirm.

* If you are making extensive use of the learning styles you are weak in, you will be learning less and be motivated less than you would otherwise be. Seek to understand your own learning styles and play to your strengths in terms of how you learn and review and revise what you learn.

* Though you will have certain learning style preferences you shouldn't try to rely on them exclusively, because you will not always have information presented to you in that way. And if you try to rely only on information presented in your preferred learning style, you will miss out on much of the insights and understandings that arise when information is presented in alternative styles. Thus don't avoid other learning styles, though you may need to complement them with your preferred style.

The Bumper Book of Common Sense

- If you find large amounts of information is being presented to you in a style that is other than your preferred, and you can't do much about it, then ensure you take or prepare your own notes in a style that is better suited to you, for when you come to revise the material. Thus you might turn lots of written material into a more visual structure using mind maps or pictures, or you might look to voice record some of the material such that you can listen to it. You might also go seeking out alternative sources of the material, such as video presentations on the Internet, or find someone you can discuss the material with.

- When learning and taking notes, use note taking which works best for you in terms of later review and revision: long-hand detailed notes, key phrases, drawings, mind maps or variations therein of. You may want to voice record your notes for subsequent playback.

- Some people learn primarily visually, others aurally. Visual learners like to see pictures and diagrams. If you have a preference for visual learning, or you are teaching someone with a preference for visual learning, then use diagrams and pictures and charts and flowcharts and make use of symbols to represent words or phrases. You should also make use of the space and layout on the page and use color coding and highlighting of key words or phrases. If you prefer aural learning, then you prefer lectures and tutorials and group discussions. When reading text you might want to read some of it out loud, and you should look for opportunities to talk through what you are learning with others. If you are interacting with others who are aural learning focused then look to get them engaged in discussion.

- Some people learn primarily through reading and writing, some through doing. If you learn primarily through reading and writing then you should be looking to take notes as you learn things and look to summarize and précis information and make up lists and mindmaps. If you learn best by doing then get involved in practical experiments whenever you get the chance, but also try to think through what ideas mean practically and visualize doing them in your head even if you can't do them for real. Try to be as vivid as you can in your visualization. If you are teaching people remember there are a lot of people who learn best this way and often don't get the chance to engage in practical experiments. Help them visualize by giving them real life examples to think about.

- People who are extravert tend to learn by doing things and by talking to and with other people. They learn through engaging in physical activities and group discussions and have difficulty working on their own. They work best when working and revising with others or a friend, albeit they need to keep focused on their studies. A good technique for extroverts when learning, is to review material as though preparing to explain it to someone else. Introverts prefer to be given time to reflect on information and often prefer to learn and revise on their own. They prefer to be given time to think about things before talking about them. In group discussions they prefer to listen and think it over for themselves, and contribute when they are ready rather than being actively brought in.

- Some people learn best through learning a step at a time, through having concrete information that they learn in a logical sequential manner, relating the information to what they already know. If abstract ideas are presented to them it is important they are given examples they can visualize. Others prefer high-level concepts and to understand the essence of something before they try to look at the detail. They are comfortable jumping around between ideas as they look to uncover the links and a wider context that relates the ideas. Generally people who prefer learning a step at a time prefer to be given clear guidance and instructions about what to learn and how to revise, with clear deadlines. Those who prefer dealing in high-level concepts are happy just to get on with things themselves though can have a tendency to get distracted. Those who prefer detail should be encouraged to see the wider context within which the detail exists, and those that prefer high-level concepts should be encouraged to write down or draw up a coherent and complete picture of those concepts and then explore them with example details.

- Some people need to personalize information, need to feel an emotional attachment to it either through seeing how it relates to them, or through feeling a personal connection to the people they are learning with or being taught by. Others are quite happy with abstract ideas and an impartial engagement with others about it.

- An aspect of the different learning styles people have relates to the circumstances or environment in which they best learn and focus. For example:
  - Time of day: different people are at their best at different times of the day.
  - Physical settings: some people work best with neat and ordered surroundings, others are more comfortable and creative in an unstructured setting.
  - Sound: some people need quiet, whilst others find certain background noises soothing or even motivating.
  - Light: the intensity of light affects different people in different ways.

- Try to be aware of other people's learning styles, particularly people you frequently communicate with. If you can present to others what you are trying to get across in a way that is aligned to their preferred learning style, you are more likely to succeed in doing so.

- When presenting to a large audience, where it is likely there will be many different learning styles, adopting many different styles at once will increase the likelihood of your message getting across to a larger number of people: thus visual aids, talking, allowing some interaction, practical demonstrations if possible. Also try to provide both general concepts in a big picture type of way, whilst also providing a structure into which more detail can be provided, and against which you can give some concrete examples. You are looking to touch all the bases with regards people's learning styles, though you may want to focus on certain key elements of your audience if you are aware of their likely learning styles.

What to Learn

- Think about your long-term goals. In addition to your specific short-term actions, it is likely that improving your skills and abilities will be an important part of helping you get to your goals. Be specific about what skills and abilities you can usefully learn or improve, and then set about learning and improving them through structured learning courses.

- Imagine and write down a eulogy for yourself at your funeral. What do you believe it would say? And what would you like it to say? Cover your personality, achievements, personal strengths, family life, professional success, and behavior towards others. What is the gap? Then develop a personal learning program targeted at giving you the knowledge and skills to close the gap.

- We all have some natural strengths and weaknesses. In broad terms we should seek to improve what we are already good at such that we become exceptional in something rather than simply improve what we are not so good at but likely to still remain one of many. Alternatively seek out topics that others steer away from so you can develop some form of competitive advantage over others. With careful thought about your own abilities and potential you can seek out a topic in which you can become uniquely expert.

- Notwithstanding that it is generally of more long term benefit to get better at what we are good at than to get better at what we are not good at, sometimes certain weaknesses hold us back. In such circumstances we might decide to learn to be better at what is holding us back, though we might simply find ways to get round our weakness.

- Identify a topic that you are interested in. Identify some particular aspect of the topic that you are interested in. Then learn everything about it so that you can become a world expert.

- We should consider learning to be a lifelong activity. However it is better to learn a few things deeply than try to learn everything superficially. There is far too much for us to learn very much about everything, and we will thus fail. The days of the person who could be an expert in many different fields is past.

The Bumper Book of Common Sense

* With regards your given area of paid work, or what you would like to be your given area of paid work, identify areas for structured learning that will help you become the best you can be. Seek to take advantage of whatever learning opportunities are provided by your employer, but even if they are not provided you should seek to learn and improve for yourself. It is in your own interests to become the best you can be at what you are paid to do.

* Write your CV. If you were to find yourself out of your current employment would your CV be one that would make you employable? What skills are in demand, and do you have them. Ensure you take the opportunity to keep yourself employable, and take advantage of what your current employer offers. Don't wait for your employer to upgrade you, use your employer to help you upgrade yourself.

* Success in life is sometimes more about accepting and adapting to change than it is about getting better at what is becoming a redundant skill. Better to have some ability in something that is useful than a lot of ability in something that isn't.

* Learn not just to learn, but learn how to get better at learning. And always be willing to question yourself about whether or not you are learning the most appropriate things.

* Thinking analytically is a skill that can be taught and learnt, and improved with practice. It is a skill where failures can be valuable learning experiences, so long as you reflect upon them rather than just beat yourself up about them. Unfortunately too many people seem to think of thinking and analytical skills as something you either have or don't have, with most people of course believing that they themselves do have them. Most people however are poor thinkers, just as they are poor at any skills they have not learnt or trained for.

* If you don't already know about the following, learn about it: nutrition – know what foods are good for you and which are bad; the environment – know what is good for the environment and what is bad; managing your budgets - so you understand when and by how much you are spending more than you are earning; your body's limitations - so you can avoid unnecessary injuries such as a bad back; basic repair of items; basic safety and how to avoid creating hazardous circumstances; and the basics of Common Sense in general as given in this book.

* Learn how basic things work and learn how to repair everyday items. You don't need to try to become an expert in everything around you and forever fixing things. It is time consuming and unlikely to be good use of your time. However don't be afraid to try simple repairs. There is basic maintenance on your car you can and should learn how to do, and you can have a first look at fixing many household items: though ensure you take appropriate safety precautions, like switching off electricity first if appropriate. Learn a little bit of sewing. There is ready how to guidance on anything you are likely to come across available on the internet.

* Learning isn't, or shouldn't be, predominantly about putting lots of facts into your head. We can only ever learn a tiny percentage of the facts that exist. Learning should be predominantly about: knowing how to find facts we need; having sufficient structure or understanding of topics to be able to put facts into context; and knowing how to make some practical use of the facts we learn or find. Dependent upon your interests and areas of work you should however seek to have learnt facts relating to your own specialist niche.

* There are a huge amount of things you could potentially learn. You can't hope to learn more than a tiny fraction of what can be learnt. Don't try. Learn what is of practical use and learn about one or a few things in depth, rather than lots of things superficially.

* Many people, most people, take their verbal skills for granted. Yet our thinking is constrained by our verbal skills. Keep improving your verbal skills and you will be enriching your thinking skills and your life in general. Always be looking to improve your vocabulary. Ensure you look up any unfamiliar words you come across. Don't just look up the definition of the word itself, but look up the origin of the word, since many words are interrelated and in learning one word you may gain an understanding of a whole family of words. And when you come across anything you consider well written, reread it. Examine it and look at what makes it so good, so you can look to emulate it.

When writing and you feel a word you are using is not quite right, use a thesaurus to seek out the correct word.

* When you learn how to fix a problem, try also to think about how the problem came about and how you might avoid it doing so again.

* Learn from your failures and difficulties. How could you have done things differently? How would you do things differently in similar circumstances in the future?

* Learn not to fear failure. If you fear failure it is likely you won't take risks or try to do very much. Thus don't be embarrassed by failure or mistakes. Take them as a sign you are pushing at your limits and thus likely to be learning and improving.

* Listen to, and actively seek out, feedback. Feedback can be hurtful, but you need to avoid getting emotional about it and simply treat it as an opportunity to potentially learn something. Use it in a positive manner to seek out areas of improvement you might otherwise be blind to.

Attitude of Mind Towards Learning

* The mind is not a vessel to be filled, but a fire to be kindled.

* The best students are those who question what they are learning rather than simply worshiping it.

* When we learn we should not simply be looking at how to make what we do more efficient, but also questioning whether or not we are doing the right things.

* Be willing to admit you don't know something. In admitting you don't know something you are likely to learn something. If you hide the fact you don't know something, you learn nothing.

* If you are in a group learning environment and you don't understand something, don't be afraid to ask. Just because others haven't asked doesn't mean they all understand: and chances are that if you haven't understood then many others won't have either. Of course you don't want to be regularly disrupting the group by continually asking questions. If you understand very little of what is being said then either you shouldn't be there, or you need to wait for a follow up opportunity to understand better – you do not have the right to spoil the session for everyone else.

* The more we think we know the less we are likely to learn. Only by accepting we know little can we learn much.

* You won't get smarter by hiding from yourself how well you understand things. Get into the habit of testing how well you understand things and seeking to improve your understanding. Rather than be embarrassed by how little you understand something see it as an opportunity to learn more and to better understand, which you wouldn't have done had you continued to kid yourself you really understood.

* When you take up a new skill or subject of interest, you can progress from novice to amateur reasonably quickly. However going from amateur to expert will take a long period of sustained training or learning and practice. Amateurs have a habit of considering themselves more expert than they are, and are often less aware of their own shortcomings than are the true experts.

* It is not those who are smartest or who have the best physiological advantages that become the more expert or skilled, it is those who work hardest at it so long as you are learning in a way that you get regular feedback and the opportunity to keep improving.

The Bumper Book of Common Sense

* Test your understanding of ideas or of how things work by explaining them to yourself. Seek out where your understanding breaks down rather than simply kid yourself you have a full understanding.

* People overestimate their knowledge and understanding of things because they largely think about them in the abstract rather than specifically. If we want to be sure we understand something we need to be very specific about it. Think about how you would explain something to someone who keeps asking why or how.

* Overcome any reluctance you might have to making mistakes, at least as regards what you are trying to learn. Making mistakes is an inherent and absolutely essential part of learning. It is part of the feedback process without which skills cannot be learnt and information cannot be turned into know-how: know-how being the ability to use information to do something effectively and with minimal expenditure of effort.

* It is by trying to do things that you can't do that you learn to do them.

* See yourself as someone who is continually learning and improving.

* One key difference between adults and children when learning physical skills, and one reason children learn much quicker, is that children don't care about making fools of themselves.

* Test new ideas. Be curious about things. Never stop looking for opportunities to learn and experiment. If new ideas work, adopt them. If they don't, try other ideas. And remember your environment is frequently changing and different things will work in different environments. If you aren't continually experimenting with change and always evolving to be fittest in your environment, then eventually you will go the way of the dodo, where you find you are no longer suited to nor able to survive in your environment.

* Each day we should be looking for opportunities to learn. Most of us meet other people every day and thus every day have opportunities for learning from them or improving how we interact with them. Think about how you have interacted with someone and think about how you might do better next time either with that person or with others in similar circumstances.

* Whilst you should be open to new ideas and frequently willing to try new things, don't be obsessive, and note that routine tasks are good for you some of the time and help you avoid being overwhelmed and stressed.

* You can learn from anyone, from anything you read, from anything you watch. Just suspend judgment and prejudice, observe what is going on, and try to understand why.

* The more we understand why things work the more adaptable we become. We learn why things work by asking why and seeking an answer.

How to Learn Tips

* Have a strategy or plan to achieve any particular learning or skill development aim that you have. Understand where you are trying to get to, and what steps will get you there. Plan these out, understand what resources you need, and set out a timetable. Look for ways you can measure your progress. It is likely you will be too ambitious with your initial plan and timetable. Don't get disheartened, adapt it.

* Spend a bit of time ensuring you have got the best resources or learning material you can reasonably get hold of. Good learning material can significantly speed up your learning process. Potential resources include what is available on-line, books, access to people, specific courses, and clubs or other places people who are interested in a given subject get together.

* There is usually a large amount of material available about anything you want to learn. Seek it out. You will learn far better by looking for and using good material than you will by plowing through poor material or trying to learn by trial and error.

* Set targets for what you are trying to learn and look to track your progress towards achieving them. Note however that you need to measure whether the learning is effective, not only that you've spent time on it.

* Keep a 'skills file' or 'learning record' to help you structure your learning and keep you on track to achieving your learning objectives. Within such a file or record you should keep: examples of your work; any feedback you get on your work including results of tests; a basic diary of what you've done when; and your own reflections on your development.

* If you want to succeed in something seek to learn from those who are already experts. Stand on the shoulders of giants.

* Be glad when you meet someone better or more capable than you are at something. See it as an opportunity to listen to and observe them. Try to learn something from them.

* Copy and emulate people you admire or wish to be more like. If they have written things in a style you wish you could adopt, then copy out a big chunk of something they have written word for word, several times, and you will feel yourself absorbing a bit of how they think. Plagiarism in terms of taking someone else's work as your own is clearly wrong, but trying to adopt and adapt someone else's general style is not, and is simply a part of how we all learn - unless of course you then take one person's style as the only basis for your own, which is then likely to become plagiarism again.

* Learn from other people's mistakes, not only from your own. You haven't got time to learn only from your own.

* Ask questions. You learn by asking questions and then getting or seeking answers. Everyone is more expert than you at something. You can learn something from anyone if you can find out what they are knowledgeable about and ask them questions. Never be ashamed to ask questions about anything of which you are ignorant. Never stop asking questions and you will keep finding better answers.

* Go out of the way to occasionally read stuff you wouldn't normally read. You are more likely to stumble upon new ideas. Generally you learn more from people who disagree with you, or hold contrary views to you, than you do from those whose views are the same as your own.

* If you want to improve your understanding of something talk to people who disagree with what you believe, rather than to those who agree. The different perspective is likely to prompt useful variations in your current views leading to a deeper understanding.

* Much of what we learn is through feedback. We do more of what we believe works and less of what doesn't. Which is what is meant by learning from experience. We should seek feedback in any action or behavior we want to improve. The quicker and more frequent the feedback, the quicker we learn. To be continually learning we need to be continually seeking feedback.

* Don't set up your means of feedback in a way that avoids bad news or a negative response. Better to get an honest bad opinion then a misleading good opinion.

* To become an expert:
    o Find a coach or a mentor who can provide you feedback on technique and set challenging but achievable goals along the way;
    o Copy techniques of existing experts;
    o Practice in a way that will get you feedback about how you are doing;

The Bumper Book of Common Sense

- o Persevere. Improvements come in spurts, interspaced with long periods when you seem to be making no progress. But you need to keep training and practicing through the fallow periods to get to the spurts of rapid improvement.

* You need to step outside your comfort zone as part of your learning. You learn by trying to move beyond what you already know and are comfortable with.

* To learn a new skill you generally need to be pushing at your limits. This means you will be continually 'failing'. This is a vital part of learning and improving. If you are not frequently failing then it is likely you are not trying hard enough and you will not be learning nearly as effectively as you could be.

* The learning of physical skills benefits significantly from repetition. However don't mix, in close proximity of time, the learning of different but similar skills. They will interfere with each other, making the learning far less effective.

* Mentally practicing a skill, rehearsing it in your mind, contributes to your getting better at it.

* If you are trying to learn a skill, then read up on or get taught the best way to do it, then practice, practice, practice, with focused practice sessions and pushing the envelope as you do so. Get a mentor or someone who can help ensure you are not practicing bad habits. It is important to get frequent feedback which you use to continually improve your performance.

* When developing skills look at how masters do it. Then try to copy them. Compare your outputs with theirs and look at how to improve.

* When being trained or doing classroom learning, go beyond what you are being taught or you are being asked to do. Do this over the same period you are being taught about it, in the evenings or weekends. You may tell yourself you'll come back to it later, after the course has finished, but you probably won't, you'll have other things to do. So put extra effort into any structured or formal training: read more about it, look up more on the internet, ask questions of your teachers.

* Have patience when learning a new skill. Keep practicing and you will learn it. If you expect to magically learn it with little effort you will be disappointed. If however you put in the effort, and keep putting in the effort, and keep going despite obstacles and sometimes slow progress, you will succeed in getting very good.

* Improvement is often not a linear response to our learning or practice efforts. Often we are seemingly making no improvement at all, then we make some quick and significant improvements, get to a new level, and then seemingly level off again. Do not get disheartened during the periods of seeming lack of improvement. Without you continuing to learn or practice during these periods you would not make the dramatic improvements later on.

* Plan a regular time to study or train, and choose a place appropriate to the study or training, where you will not be distracted.

* When you undertake a given study or training period have a particular goal in mind for that period. Possibly have some minimum that will give you a sense of having achieved something, and also some more challenging target. Don't be too ambitious with study periods however since you may end up trading quality of study for quantity, and thus seemingly get through a significant amount of work but not have covered it as well as you should.

* You can get into an alert concentrated state of mind by pretending you already are – and adopting body and facial expressions as though you are.

* Your brain learns what it pays attention to. When you are paying attention to something your brain is rewiring itself. The more attention you give something, the stronger the rewiring, and the better your learning. One way of ensuring focus is to limit the time you spend on different aspects of your learning. You might spend 30 minutes reading, then spend 10 minutes reviewing what you've

learned and then 10 minutes seeing what you remember. By limiting the time on each aspect you help increase your focus.

* When learning try to use as many of your senses as you can, most obviously visual and sound but others if you can. When you use different senses you activate different parts of your brain which improves your ability to recall information at a later date.

* Don't back away from using old fashioned repetition to learn basic facts and lists. It is an effective way of learning basic factual information such as dates, or lists of people, or tables of information.

* Don't kid yourself that you can learn or study just as well whilst listening to music with words. Music without words is likely to be less distracting though not as effective as studying in silence. However if there are lots of other distractions around you, listening to some classical or instrumental music can help you concentrate.

* When you feel sleepy, take a short break; you will not learn much if you are not alert. If you take a nap during the day limit it to no more than about half an hour. Much longer than this and you are likely to feel worse afterwards rather than better.

* There are limits to what we can do. You need breaks to give your brain time, subconsciously, to absorb and organize the information and to replenish its energy.

* If you are reading a book for information or knowledge then taking notes as you go along will help you focus on what you are looking for and help you remember. Either note down key points, or represent key ideas in some visual way. When making notes be sure they are readable and make sense. There is little point in taking notes that you are unable to read or understand later.

* For almost any subject there are a few critically important concepts which once you have grasped provide the scaffolding off which most of the rest of the subject matter hangs. These are your mental models for the particular subject matter. Be continually looking for how best to summarize key ideas and how best to relate them both to each other and to other ideas you already know. Look to represent key concepts in a diagrammatic, visual, or mindmaping format.

* Start with basic ideas before trying to tackle more complex ones. If you don't master the basic concepts first you will rely on memorizing more advanced concepts rather than understanding them. You will then end up misunderstanding and misapplying the concepts.

* Look to integrate theory and practice where you can and it is appropriate. Learning some theory and then getting the opportunity to practice what you've learnt is particularly effective.

* Be an active learner by asking yourself questions that you can seek out the answers to as you continue your learning. Don't be concerned about the fact that you don't understand something but see it as an opportunity to better understand. There is a lot of satisfaction in finding ourselves understanding something we previously hadn't.

* When looking to memorize or learn through testing yourself, ensure you know the subject matter reasonably well before you begin to test yourself. Otherwise you might find that the wrong answers you give whilst doing the tests themselves stick in your memory and interfere with the right information.

* If you are trying to remember information you are learning then you need to regularly review it and remind yourself of it. Typically you should space out your reviewing of the material with initially closely spaced reviews, and then more spaced out ones. Example spacing might be 1 day after, then 3 or 4 days after, then a couple of weeks, and then a couple of months later. If in reviewing it you find you have largely forgotten it, then you might need to reinstate more regular reviews.

* The wider your vocabulary and understanding of words the greater your ability to grasp and generate concepts. Whenever you come across a word you don't know, look it up, or make a note of it and look it up later.

The Bumper Book of Common Sense

* A very good way of learning something is to try to teach it. Even if you are not intending to actually teach it, prepare material as though you were, and ask yourselves questions that you imagine a student might ask.

Effective Reading

* Learn to be an effective reader. It will save you a lot of time and will significantly increase your ability to learn effectively.

* Adapt your reading approach to what you are reading and to the purpose of your reading.

* If you are reading a novel or fiction for pleasure, then you can take your time, or skip past bits, dependent upon whether you are enjoying a part of the story, or you are bored by it. If you are bored by it, but still wish to continue reading, then you can adopt speed reading habits. If you wish, you can just go to the end of the book to see how things turn out, though you may find yourself missing some of the rationale and subtleties, which may not be all neatly packaged at the end. Don't feel guilty about skipping through books you are reading for pleasure. It is your time, use it as you see fit. There are no benefits in forcing yourself to read long sections of a book you are finding boring.

* When reading for pleasure try to immerse yourself in the story by removing distractions, particularly if you are finding the book a little hard going but wish to persist. Don't multitask with also listening to music or the radio or TV, unless it is relatively innocuous instrumental music, which helps cover up other possibly distracting sounds rather than being itself distracting.

* Speed Reading for extracting information from a book or article can be very effective. With a little bit of learned technique you can readily double your reading speed without any loss of comprehension. And if you are reading a book to simply extract some particular information from it, you can readily learn to do this 10 or more times quicker than you might have otherwise done.

* The following are some general tips on speed reading which anyone can adopt without necessarily training yourself in speed reading, though it is worth the effort of practicing and following some structured guidance:
    o Don't read as though you are saying the words out loud. You can recognize words far quicker than you can say them. A way to practice this is to hum softly to yourself whilst reading.
    o You don't need to read word by word. You can understand groups of words and move your eyes across text taking in two, three, or more words at a time. And note that the notion of what you are reading is largely contained in certain key words. So long as you see these as you move across the text you are likely to readily understand what is being said without having to focus on every word.
    o Hold the text slightly further away from you to make it easier to take in groups of words at a time.
    o Use your finger or a pointer to run along below the words you are reading. This will both keep your eyes from wandering around which slows you down, but also gives you the opportunity to slowly speed up your reading by speeding up your pointer.
    o Remove distractions. If you also have the TV or radio or music on it will significantly slow up your reading and you will not be able to concentrate as much. We don't really multitask, we just keep swapping between tasks, and continually shifting our attention to the TV or radio or music will be highly disruptive.
    o If you have things on your mind then, as with external distractions, your reading will slow up significantly and you will take less of it in. Better to deal with the distraction first, possibly by writing down your thoughts on it.
    o Set yourself a time limit for what you are reading, a reasonably challenging one, and then set out to extract what you can from the text within that limit. With a bit of practice you will find

you can get the vast majority out of a piece of a text in a fraction of the time it would take you to read it through word by word.

* Even if you are skilled in speed reading sometimes take you time. If you are reading good quality fiction for pleasure you are likely to appreciate it more if you take it slowly. And technical information usually needs to be taken slowly.

* When you are reading a book or a long report in order to get information out of it and to learn you need to be an active reader. Otherwise you will spend many hours reading and get little or nothing for it. Elements of being an active reader include:
    o Know why you are reading it and what you want out of it;
    o Get an overview by skimming the contents pages, looking at pictures, glancing at bullet points, reading the preface or introduction. Look at summaries and reviews of the book, for example as available on Amazon;
    o Think about and write down questions you are looking for answers to;
    o Mark up parts of the book as you go along to highlight key points, assuming the book is yours to do this on. Note that you don't want to mark up large chunks, which defeats the purpose, but key points you can grasp within a few seconds when you look back over it. You can put down the key points in the front of the book so that when you look for them again you don't need to go hunting.
    o If the book isn't yours, you can either make notes on your own paper as you go along, or you can use post it notes to mark key points and come back to them later.
    o Use mind mapping or sketches to list out the key points in a structure that helps you understand how they relate to each other;
    o Focus on the beginnings and ends of Chapters and Sections and create your own Chapter or Section summaries;
    o Don't feel obliged to read word for word – given your goal you might be able to quickly extract sufficient information for your purpose, or may even conclude that the information you want is not actually in the book or report.

* You can extract most of the useful information out of a non-fiction book that is not overly technical or factual in about 30 minutes by first being clear about why you are reading it and what you are looking for. Using the contents list and skimming the early and later parts of chapters will enable you to very quickly pick out key concepts and home in on the information of most use to you. The rest of the book is simply supporting details and examples or anecdotes.

* Don't sit reading for hours on end. Take a break of 5 minutes or so at least every hour.

* Improving your vocabulary will improve your reading. You will grasp ideas quicker and easier and your reading won't be disrupted by either having to spend time looking up a word, or continuing your reading with a misleading or lack of understanding. When you come across new words ensure you understand them, and keep them in a little book that you review from time to time. If you remind yourself of newly learned words a few times and think how to use them, you will soon learn them. If you just look them up without making a note of them you will probably not remember the next time you come across the word.

* Note that buying a book does not impart its knowledge to you. You need to make the effort to read it and to think about it.

Obstacles to Effective Learning

* Some people never learn anything because they understand everything too soon.

The Bumper Book of Common Sense

* The biggest obstacle to learning is the belief that we already know it. A beginner is generally more open to new ideas than an expert.

* You won't make much progress with your learning unless you plan for and have dedicated learning sessions.

* Getting upset at feedback and seeking to defend yourself from what you might see as criticism will merely cut you off from the opportunity of learning from the feedback. Not all feedback will be useful, but some of it will be, and if you merely get upset at it you will miss out on that which could be useful.

* If you avoid testing yourself as you progress with your learning you will get an unrealistic impression of what you have learned, and fail to review and revise certain essential elements of what you are learning. Ironically many people avoid testing themselves for fear that they might not have learned as much as they would have liked and as a result miss the opportunity to adapt their learning to ensure they are being effective in their learning.

* Lack of sleep will significantly hamper your learning. Being highly stressed, and having a poor diet and little exercise will also seriously hamper your ability to learn since they sap your motivation and energy.

Tips for Exams

* Much learning includes the taking of exams as a way of supposedly proving you have learnt the relevant material. Effective preparing for exams can make a very big difference to how well you do in them.

* Treat learning for exams as a marathon not a sprint. Do it over a long period of time, not all crammed into a couple of weeks before the exams themselves. Learning over a long period of time also makes your memory less dependent upon the particular circumstances whilst learning.

* Start revising for exams early, through ensuring you understand the material. Create summaries and mind maps as you are learning. They help you understand the material and are also something you can use to support your revising.

* Plan your revision, scheduling which topics you will revise when. Include repeated review of material already learned. Early in your revision timetable check out which topics you don't understand very well and get some help in understanding them. Then deal with the topics you find it hardest to remember.

* Don't try to study late at night or when you are tired. Whilst you can use coffee or other stimulants to keep you awake you will not be learning very well and will have difficulty recalling what you learnt under these conditions when faced with exam conditions.

* Your brain effectively rehearses and tries to make sense of what you have been learning whilst you are asleep, and puts it into long-term memory. It is far better to do some revising and then sleep on it, than to keep revising and lose sleep as a result.

* Get practice doing test questions under similar conditions to those that will exist in the exam itself.

* Review your results from doing test questions to identify your weaknesses, not just through learning the answer to the specific question but determining whether there is a part of the relevant topic you haven't understood very well.

* Ensure you learn and memorize key facts, equations, quotes, dates, etc.

* If the exam involves writing essays develop your style for writing essays within the time constraints that will exist in the exam, such as whether you jot down the key ideas and ordering before you start using a particular format such as mind mapping. Ensure you have easily readable handwriting, and practice writing essays by hand. It is very different to typing them up on a computer, both in terms of the 'wear' on your hands, and also writing on a computer allows you to readily go back and edit in a way that is difficult and looks messy if you do it by hand. You can be a very good essay writer on a computer but struggle badly in an exam if you haven't practices writing essays by hand. Note that essays written with good handwriting tend to receive higher marks than equivalent essays written with poor handwriting.

* Prepare yourself before your exams in terms of blood sugar levels, and avoid stimulants that might create a peak but then a significant drop in performance. Also use of stimulants can inhibit normal memory functions.

* Find ways that work for you with regards relaxing before the exam: deep breathing for example, or listening to some music.

* Take some water in with you to an exam if you are allowed to. Best to take the label off so that it is obvious you are not trying to cheat. But only sip at it during the exam. You don't want to drink so much that you then want to go to the toilet.

* At the start of the exam spend a few minutes looking through the whole paper before you begin in earnest. Be sure you pace yourself and ensure you answer questions with the highest marks. Note that you will generally get more marks by answering all questions even if some not very well, than answering fewer questions but more perfectly. It is usually much easier to get 3 or 4 marks on a question with a total of 10 marks than it is increasing a score of 6 or 7 to a full score of 10. If you are doing questions involving maths or analysis activities ensure you show your working out since you can get marks for that even if you get the final answer wrong.

* If you are having trouble remembering during an exam, try to keep relaxed. Take some deep breaths. Try to recall the circumstances under which you learnt or revised the material. Jot down what you can remember, and remember that even poorly answered questions can still pick up some marks.

Teaching

* In teaching we are often also learning. Qui docet, discit: He who teaches, learns.

* Good teaching is aimed at skills and knowledge just beyond what the pupil already knows. It extends their knowledge and understanding but is not so far as to be beyond their comprehension. Often such learning involves giving them basic structures to add to ones they already have, and off which they can hang further information.

* Look to précis any long or complex ideas you want to get across to others. If you want someone to understand something long or complex you need to give them a simplified framework they can readily understand, on which you and they can hang the details and subtleties.

* Ensure those you are teaching understand the basic concepts before moving on to more complex concepts. If you don't they will focus on memorizing rather than understanding ideas, and slowly get more and more lost. Test understanding by getting those you are teaching to explain concepts in their own words and to elaborate upon them.

* If you are teaching something new to the student you need to present it in a way that tries to make it seem familiar. This is both to help remember, and to help overcome a natural aversion to things that are novel and new. Generally you need to go from concrete examples they will readily understand to abstract ideas and then show how the abstract ideas lead back to further concrete examples.

- Encourage people you are teaching to ask questions. It gets them thinking, and also helps you understand where the limits of their current understanding are. Never tell someone that their questions are stupid. It will switch them off thinking about what you are trying to teach them.

- If preparing material for teaching or revising, keep it in reasonably small chunks with a clear hook for each chunk and clear identification of key concepts.

- People learn best in an environment where there is much praise for steps in the right direction, and where rather than criticism you point out possible alternatives and improvements.

- In certain circumstances telling people they are smart as an attempt to motivate them can be counterproductive since they may come to believe they have to be that way all the time and will thus avoid challenging tasks in case they don't live up to expectations.

- If you are using learning styles the student is weak in they will be learning less and be less motivated. Some students are predominantly either visual or aural, and some students need concrete demonstration or examples to learn effectively. If you are teaching an individual it is useful to understand which style is predominant and look to exploit that. If you are teaching a class where there is a mix of students with different learning styles you need to adopt multiple styles.

- If you are teaching, it is vitally important you get feedback from those you are teaching. Without feedback you do not know if they are learning, and you do not know if your teaching methods are being effective. If you get feedback you can adjust your teaching methods to make them more effective. After all teaching isn't about what you are outputting, it is about what the students are inputting.

- To help children get into good study habits:
    - Set up a study area that is where they will get into the habit of studying. Somewhere they will not be continually distracted and somewhere they will have materials and files to hand;
    - Show them how to organize files and study notes and material for different subjects;
    - Set up a homework study routine. Set times of the week when they are mentally alert and won't have other activities that interfere or lead to frequent conflicts;
    - Teach them to plan when they will do their homework, soon after they have received it. Have them use a visible calendar to record their plans on.

Fitness, Diet, Health, and some Notes about How your Brain Works

General Health

- For good heath: eat lightly, exercise regularly but not too vigorously, breathe deeply, live moderately, and maintain a positive interest in life.

- Look after your body: it is where you live.

- Your health is your greatest asset and good health far outweighs almost all other considerations. Health allows you to engage in productive activities, at work and at play. It allows you to enjoy the company of your friends and family. And it allows you to live with vigor. Eat healthily. Exercise regularly. And if you drink or have other vices be moderate in their application.

* Keeping reasonably fit and eating healthily is important not only to help keep us from wasting huge amounts of time through being tired for much of the day and being regularly sick, but also to keep us alive and capable for longer. Whilst there are no guarantees, and bad luck can happen to anyone, in general people can have an extra ten or twenty years of meaningful and productive life through moderate exercise, having a good diet, and avoiding particular habits such as smoking, lots of alcohol, and frequent dangerous drug use. It is blatantly Common Sense to look after yourself.

* Your body is your body. It's you. You don't need to look like someone else. Don't get it artificially altered just because you'd like to look like someone else. And if you do want to go ahead with alterations, at least be aware that sometimes things go wrong, and often whatever you get done causes significant problems later in life. If you want to look young then being happy and smiling will be far more effective that artificial alterations of your face or body.

* A major issue with people in middle age is being overweight, drinking too much, and being inactive. It leads to a general listlessness and mild or severe depression. Losing weight and getting some exercise will significantly improve both long term health prospects and help you feel much more alive and interested in life.

* Being healthy as you grow older is a major, possibly the major, contributor to the quality of your life. The best way of being healthy as you get older is to follow good healthcare advice. Don't pretend you don't know what it is, you do. And don't use the excuse some of it is contradictory. Some of the precise details may be contradictory, but the basics aren't. Ignore it at the expense of your own health and the quality of your life.

* If you don't look after yourself, you can't look after anyone else, at least not in the long term.

* Be aware of the limitations of your body both when exercising and in normal everyday life. In particular be careful about carrying and lifting things. Back problems are common, and are largely self-created.

* Deal with constipation problems. Constipation is a serious drain on physical and mental energy. If you have constipation problems see your doctor. Better dietary habits, usually involving more fiber intake, will probably be a necessity. Whilst you can take medicines to help in the short term, you should not have to rely upon them in the longer term.

* Look after your teeth and gums. It doesn't take long to ensure you properly clean your teeth in the morning after breakfast, and at night after you've finished eating and drinking for the day. Problems due to bad teeth and gums can be very disabling later in life, and significantly reduce the joy of life.

* If you smoke, give up cigarettes. They don't relax you, they are simply a habit that is slowly killing you, lowering your quality of life now and in the future, and they are also a waste of money that you could do a lot of other things with.

* Regular alcoholic drinking not only loses you the time drinking, but also seriously impairs the rest of the day or much of the day after, and leads to long-term health problems. You are unlikely to achieve very much if you are a regular heavy drinker. You can have a good time drinking without getting drunk or having hangovers. Add sparkling water to your wine, keep toping up your gin and tonic with extra tonics, and top up your beers with lemonade.

* Don't listen to lots of loud music or otherwise have your ears exposed to loud noises, whether you are young or old. It will damage your ears to your regret later in life.

* Pent up anger, frustration, or resentment over long periods of time can significantly increase the onset of cancers or other serious diseases.

The Bumper Book of Common Sense

* Too much stress going on over a significant period of time can seriously damage your health and your quality of life. Be aware of it, and deal with it. See advice given elsewhere in this book and readily available on the internet and through your doctor.

* If you are having recurring health problems, don't ignore them. Look to find out what the cause is, getting a proper medical opinion, and do something about it. Most problems can be dealt with relatively easily if dealt with early. You can also experiment with your own diet and exercise regimes. There is a lot of advice readily available on the internet. Look at what appears relevant and experiment with it in moderation.

* If you have concerns about your own, or your children's health, seek medical opinion. People have died through not having things checked early enough even though they were worried about them.

* Visit your doctor from time to time for recommended checkups and go to your dentist every 6 months or as recommended. Catching problems early makes a huge difference to the quality of your life and can literally save your life.

* Medicine is not an exact science and mistakes happen, despite good intentions. Human errors occur, and medical errors are a significant cause of death. Additional visits to doctors and testing often lead to unnecessary procedures and hospitalizations, which carry equally unnecessary risks, and empirical evidence reveals no difference in life expectancy between those who undergo annual check-ups and those who don't. You can't be a victim of medical error if you are not in the system.

* Test results are not 100% reliable, and are subject to 2 types of error, false negative and false positive: false negative meaning the test does not show a result when it should, and false positive meaning it does show a result when it shouldn't. The base rate bias in particular means that tests for rare conditions can frequently show false positive results, with possibly 99 in 100 or more of the positive results actually being false. Yet both doctors and patients tend to treat test results as though they are unquestionable correct. If you have an unexpected test result, take the test again. It is unlikely to be wrong twice in a row.

* Find out the dangers, as well as the benefits, of undergoing testing, a course of drugs, or a medical procedure. Look up all the relevant data, particularly that relating to false positives.

* Vacuuming, dusting, and cleaning hard floors at least once a week can make a big difference to the quality of the air in your home. Also keep outdoor pollutants outside your home by not letting shoes be worn into the house.

* Laughter has physical, emotional, and cognitive benefits, reduces stress, boosts our immune system, and strengthens our heart. Listen to humor and read jokes and funny stories. However avoid humor that is aimed at belittling others.

* Massage can have a very relaxing effect on our bodies and clear stresses that may be the root cause of some common aches and pains.

* Get some sun, but not too much. Too much exposure to the sun increases your risk of cancer and leads to premature aging of the skin.

* Spend some time outdoors in natural habitats, woods, the seaside, around lakes and rivers, in the countryside. It's particularly important that children get to be out in these environments from time to time, and important for them not to be plugged in to music or other distractions whilst there.

* How healthy we feel and indeed are is strongly influenced by our state of mind. If we are negative or stressed our bodies will feel and be less healthy than if we are positive or relaxed. When we dwell on the negative aspects of an illness we are likely to be making the illness worse.

* Whether or not people feel ill is often psychosomatic. Many illnesses are of course real, but many illnesses occur only because people tell themselves they are ill. When flu bugs are about some

people will succumb at the first sniffle whilst others will ignore minor symptoms and not succumb at all.

* Positive affirmations strengthen our immune system.

* Our minds significantly affect how we feel about many of the foods we eat. We can all happily eat foods if we believe they are one thing but would feel physically sick if we discovered they were something else much less palatable.

* Our attitudes and expectations significantly affect how well we respond to medicines and drugs. If we believe they will work they are far more likely to do so. We will often respond to placebos in the same way as real medicines so long as we believe they will work. The human mind can produce effects as strong as the most powerful drugs.

* Just as we can often make ourselves feel and actually be physically healthier through positive thinking, negative thinking can be physically doing us damage and contributing to the onset of more serious illnesses.

* Faith, hope, and determination, if they are strong enough, can cure us of many illnesses and diseases, though not all.

* Our brain is capable of producing physiological changes in our bodies, just as the state of our body affects our brain.

* Your body will react to how your mind perceives it. If you think of yourself as getting old and on an inevitable decline, your body will feel that way. You can't stop your body aging, but you can slow it down considerably by having a positive mindset.

Diet and Eating

* Good nutrition is essential if you are to maintain an optimum state of mind, body, and spirit. What you choose to eat will make a huge difference to your well-being and the length of your life. There is plenty of advice about good eating habits: find it and use it.

* Learn how certain foods and drinks affect your energy levels, and use this information to optimize your energy levels in support of complex tasks.

* There are subtleties and complexities about food and drink and their effect on maintaining your health and brain in a good condition. Whilst there are some black and white areas in terms of good and bad, there are many grey areas since different foods can affect different people in different ways. The way food is prepared and cooked and how different foods are eaten together or after each other, can also affect their impact. You need to learn about your own body and how it reacts to different foods and drinks.

* Foods which take a long time for our intestines to digest and break down are generally better for us because they provide a steady supply of energy to our brain and body rather than peaks and troughs. The speed with which different types of food can be broken down to create the sugars used by our body and brain is known as the Glycemic Index (GI), with a low GI being good. Foods with a high GI lead to our bodies having to create a lot of insulin in order to regulate the sugars created and this is bad for us, and over a long period of time can lead to diabetes.

* Proteins provide our brains with amino acids, from which neurotransmitters are created. These carry signals between our brain cells and allow parts of the brain to communicate effectively with each another. Lack of protein will make our thinking literally more sluggish.

The Bumper Book of Common Sense

* Vitamin C has a lot of health benefits. It helps protect the body from infections and helps the body repair itself. It helps reduce certain types of body stresses that contribute to various cancers, and also helps prevent heart disease. It helps reduce lead toxicity levels which can cause health problems in urban areas and also helps keep the eyes healthy. Our bodies are unable to produce vitamin C for themselves and thus we obtain it through various fruits and vegetables such as blackcurrants, oranges, watermelon, cabbage, lettuce, and peas. Taking lots of vitamin C will not of course protect you in any absolute sense from health problems, but the likelihood of getting health problems is a probabilistic matter and taking vitamin C moves the probabilities further in your favor. However taking more than recommended dosages will not provide additional benefits, though note that smokers are recommended to take more vitamin C than non-smokers.

* Your brain gets its energy from glucose. A steady but moderate supply of glucose will help keep your brain alert and able to think through complex problems. A poor supply or wildly fluctuating levels will lead to you feeling tired and unable to think things through. Good foods for maintaining a steady supply of glucose include peanuts and cashew nuts, fruits such as apples, blueberries and pears, as well as cheese, fish, meats, olive oil, and vegetables. Note that it is best to eat fruits in their natural form rather than simply as juices, since the fiber helps moderate the speed of absorption. And avoid drowning these foods out with sugar either by sprinkling sugar on or taking them with other high sugar foods. Other sources of a steady supply of glucose include bread, rice, pasta, potatoes, yogurt, and milk, albeit all in moderation. Whilst many foods such as sweets, desserts, and soft drinks also contain sugar and thus glucose they do so in high doses, which give an initial 'sugar rush' and hyperactivity, but then results in the body reacting by increasing insulin which soaks up the sugar and leading to less glucose going through to the brain.

* Your brain cells need a good supply of oxygen, and a lack of iron in your diet will reduce your blood's ability to carry oxygen, leading to poor concentration, a lack of energy and general tiredness. Sources of iron include lean red meat, egg yolks, red kidney beans, lentils, dried apricots, fortified breakfast cereals, broccoli, wholegrain cereals and wholemeal bread.

* A small snack if you haven't eaten for about 3 or 4 hours helps keep your blood sugar level stable: some nuts or a piece of fruit. However you need to manage your overall daily calorie intake.

* Coffee or tea is good for boosting your brain performance, in small doses. 2-4 cups a day is fine, but don't add sugar or cream. Too much coffee or tea leads to a degradation in your performance. Go for the high quality coffees with minimal treatment of the coffee beans. If you want more than 2-4 cups a day then drink decaffeinated coffee or herbal teas for the rest. However neither do you want too many cups of decaffeinated coffee: in the first place unless explicitly labelled as caffeine free they probably still contain some caffeine, and it is also highly acidic so if you take it a lot can contribute to heartburn, ulcers, inflammatory bowel conditions, and other disorders.

* The key to a healthy balanced diet is not to ban or omit any foods or food groups but to balance what you eat by consuming a variety of foods from each food group in the right proportions for good health. The five food groups being: fruit and vegetables; bread, rice, potatoes and pasta; milk and dairy foods; meat, fish, eggs and beans; and foods and drinks high in fat and/or sugar; though the later should only be eaten sparingly.

* Tips for eating well: base meals on starchy foods; eat lots of varied fruit and vegetables; regularly eat some oil rich fish containing Omega 3; eat foods containing whole grains rather than refined; cut down on saturated fat and sugar; try to eat less salt - no more than 6g a day – other herbs can often be used in its place; foods rich in vitamin B such as chicken, potatoes and bananas can help improve your memory and keep your brain healthy; drink plenty of water - equivalent of about 2 litres during the day; don't skip a healthy breakfast; and eat regularly during the day, with small healthy snacks in between not very large meals.

* Eat some fish regularly: salmon, herring, mackerel, anchovies, sardines, tuna. Have it baked, boiled, grilled, or poached. Not fried.

* Organic foods are better for your health and for the environment.

* Many herbs and spices have health benefits and you should add them to your food if you get the opportunity. Examples of those believed to have benefits include: Rosemary, Thyme, Sage, Mint, Basel, Oregano, Cinnamon, Parsley, Garlic, and Chili Peppers.

* Drink enough water each day to maintain a healthy level of hydration – generally a couple of litres though the bigger you are the more you should drink. Note that most drinks contribute to this though you should ensure most of it is water itself. Drink more if you get a lot of exercise or live in a dry climate, or if you are pregnant or breast feeding. Spread your drinking out during the day.

* Drinking lots of water will help you eat and drink less of what is not good for you.

* Some foods or ingredients which sap your energy or are harmful to the brain include: Alcohol, Artificial food colorings, Artificial sweeteners, Corn syrup, Frostings, High-sugar "drinks", Hydrogenated fats, Junk sugars, Nicotine, and White bread. A little occasionally won't do you any harm, and indeed you can't avoid some of them in moderation, but they will be bad for you long term if they are a significant part of your diet. Keep an eye out for related advice.

* Alcohol kills brain cells. Nicotine causes narrowing of the capillaries that restricts the delivery of oxygen and glucose to the brain via blood flow.

* Bad for your brain and bad for your general feeling of well-being is overeating. People who regularly eat too much sugar over a long period of time often become diabetic. They are significantly more at risk of becoming regularly depressed, having problems with their memory and ability to process information, and getting dementia or Alzheimer's disease.

* As you get older, particularly past 40, your metabolism slows. This means that if you continue to eat as much as you did when you were younger you will put on weight.

* Avoid fast foods, fried foods, and cakes, biscuits, donuts etc, or at least keep them to very occasionally. They are bad for your health.

* Recognize that takeaways and restaurant and café foods generally contain far more fat, salt, and calories than food prepared at home. Be wary of eating a lot of it, and look for options that at least reduce the amount of the fat, salt, and calories you are eating – such as smaller portions, and fewer starters or deserts.

* Foods cooked in restaurants are often deliberately made to taste good through the use of unhealthy additives. They also rarely use high quality ingredients. Restaurants are a business trying to make a good profit.

* Eating out leads to you eating more and drinking more than you would at home. Eating out is usually a pleasant experience but don't over indulge either in how often you go out or in what you choose when you are out.

* Be wary of snacking. There are often a lot of calories in snacks, it can add many hundreds of calories to your daily intake without you noticing. You don't need to cut it out altogether, but try to cut down on it, try to have less when you do snack, and go for healthier snacks.

* Most people underestimate how many calories they consume.

* If you have a large plate you tend to eat more, and less with a small plate.

* Generally eat less. Stop short of feeling full, irrespective of how much you still have on your plate. A full belly will generally dull your brain in the short term, and there is lots of evidence that thinner people live a lot longer than fatter people.

* Eat less processed foods.

The Bumper Book of Common Sense

* Reduce the amount of refined sugars you take. Avoid or at least reduce your sugar intake in drinks and in sweets, cakes, biscuits, etc.

* Rather than focusing on what you shouldn't eat, focus on what you should. Eat healthy foods whenever you're hungry and there will be less desire to eat unhealthy foods.

* If eating is a response to feeling stressed, seek alternative ways of dealing with stress, such as reading, listening to music, writing a diary, or various breathing techniques, possibly linked to yoga or tai chi.

* Heavy meals at lunchtime will make you tired and sluggish in the afternoon. Keep lunches light.

* Avoid eating late at night. You should leave at least 3 hours between eating a meal in the evening and your normal bedtime. If not you are likely to find your sleep disrupted.

* If you find yourself regularly feeling angry or sad or lethargic it could well be as a result of poor diet.

* Lack of vitamins and minerals are significant contributors to general apathy, having difficulty concentrating, and general negative moods. You need a variety of foods such as fruit, vegetables, fish, dairy products, cereals, meat, albeit much of it in moderation and with alternatives if you are vegetarian or you otherwise can't or won't take particular foods. If you don't get a varied and balanced diet, take a multivitamin: once a day.

* Sometimes we eat even though we are not hungry. When we are bored or stressed for example, or when we feel tired or sometimes when we are thirsty. Instead of eating take a drink of water, take a walk, talk to someone, or chew some sugar free gum.

* The reason most people fail with their own control of their weight is they are continually looking for ways around the simple commitment of eating fewer calories and getting more exercise, ie. consume fewer calories than you burn. The diet industry implies there are ways around this simple commitment, which there isn't.

* Dieting is usual counterproductive in the long term. It is easy to lose weight, and almost any scheme you try will enable you to lose weight. But your body adapts by learning to better store fat, which then leads to increased weight when you stop dieting. Rather than diet, it is far more important to adjust your life style through good eating and exercising habits. New habits leading to you losing a pound a week or every couple of weeks will be far more successful than crash diet to lose 20 or more pounds in a couple of months and then a promise of changed habits.

* There is little difference in effectiveness between different types of diets. They result in reductions in calories and thus whilst you stick with the diet you will lose weight. Rather than agonize about which diet to adopt in terms of which would be most effective, instead adopt whichever diet you believe will be the easiest for you to stick to.

* A particular danger for dieters is if on a given day they exceed their self-imposed allowance, they consider the day a failure and are likely to lose their self-restraint for the rest of the day. They will then binge eat far more than they would normally putting themselves back not just a day but potentially a week or more.

* Diet drinks can be counterproductive since they trick the body and brain into expecting but not getting a glucose spike which can lead to you having less energy and less self-control.

* Tactics for successful long term weight loss and control:
    o Don't have sugar rich foods to hand;
    o Wash your teeth earlier in the evening, to discourage late night snacking;
    o Lose weight slowly through changing habits rather than special diets or fasting;

- Develop automated habits for specific circumstances;
- Eat off smaller plates and drink caloried drinks from smaller glasses;
- Eat more low calorie high volume foods – fruit and veg;
- Chew your food for longer and leave some of it on your plate uneaten;
- Put a picture of a fat person on the fridge.

* If you are looking to lose weight, then whenever you are faced with either a temptation you know you shouldn't give in to, or you don't feel like doing some exercises for when you had planned to do so, bring to mind your motivations for losing weight: unattractive body shape, concern about diabetes and ill health, or lack of energy. Tap into the emotions that are the root cause reasons for wanting to lose weight, and bring them to mind in support of avoiding temptations or getting on with what you know you ought. If convenient look in the mirror.

* If you are struggling to lose weight, keep a food and drink journal, where you keep a note of everything you eat or drink. Best to record it before you eat, and write down the calories. If you don't eat after noting it down simply cross it out. People who do so generally lose weight twice as quickly as those who don't.

* Control over what you eat starts with control over what you buy. Don't go food shopping when you are hungry, and don't get seduced into buying more than you intended through special multi-buy offers.

* Use a cookbook and keep a file of meals that work well, particularly if you have children who often have varied and incompatible tastes.

* Occasional fasting, once a week or so, is good for you and helps you live longer, so long as you don't then look to compensate by overeating on other days.

* Occasional eating of foods recognized as being bad for you, so long as they are not dangerous, won't do you any harm; but keep it to occasional, and don't binge when you do.

* Advice on healthy and less healthy foods changes over time, and you need to keep an eye out for such advice. However be wary of simply hooking on to a particular piece of advice that just happens to suit your prejudices, and using it as an excuse to continue to indulge certain habits that in truth you probably know you should be moderating. The best simple advice is to eat in moderation and to eat a variety of foods. If whatever advice you choose to follow takes you too far away from this then you have only yourself to blame for the consequences.

* Don't kid yourself that a little bit of exercise will compensate for poor eating habits. To burn off the calories of a fast food meal you would need to vigorously exercise for most of the day. Exercise has many benefits but for most of us controlling our calories is far more important for weight control than lots of exercise.

Exercise and Breathing

* Physical exercise is good for you: it helps you avoid high blood pressure, helps with weight control, helps with sleep, helps keep your mind active, helps you feel good about yourself, helps with positive thinking, and also helps alleviate stress. Try different types of exercise – walking, jogging, swimming, cycling, aerobics, dancing. Gardening or housework can also be a form of exercise so long as you make it so and let it get you a little breathless.

* Our brains need oxygen. If you increase your lung capacity through exercise or breathing exercises you can increase the amount of oxygen that gets to your brain, and your brain will work better. You will find yourself having good ideas.

The Bumper Book of Common Sense

* Exercise helps to maintain your body weight by balancing your energy intake (food eaten) with energy output (exercise). Take small steps if you're new to exercise - use the stairs instead of the lift at work, get off the bus one stop early and walk the rest of the way. But note that trying to be super fit is not a particularly good thing unless you are a professional sportsperson; and it can and often does lead to problems such as injuries and long-term damage to your body.

* Don't rush to get fit. If you try to do lots of exercise when you are not used to it you will almost certainly injure yourself and thus be unable to continue. See getting fit as a medium-term goal, and build up gradually. It is far more important to do a little frequently than to do occasional heavy sessions. If you do a little frequently you will find yourself slowly increasing what you do.

* Excellent forms of exercise almost anyone can do at any age are Yoga and Tai Chi. Some of the benefits of yoga and tai chi are: flexibility, strength, agility, muscle tone, mental calmness, improved balance and body awareness, better mental concentration, improved circulation and detoxification, and a general reduction in stress. But don't rush into it. Start slowly and gradually build up.

* As you grow older your muscles will grow weaker. Most people as they get older will benefit from a little strength training a couple of times a week. This is not about building up big muscles, but about retaining the muscles you have. There are many forms of strength training ranging from structured gym sessions to simple home exercises using little or no equipment, with the latter being most appropriate for most people. It is important to leave 48 hrs or so between strength exercises to give your muscles time to rebuild. It is this rebuilding which is the source of the increased strength.

* You should look to do some aerobic type exercise where you get slightly out of breathe for a minimum of about 2 hours a week, though preferably spread throughout the week in 15 to 30 minute sessions. Most sports provide aerobic exercise, as does brisk walking, jogging, swimming, bike riding, dancing, running around with the children, or even use of certain games consoles that encourage physical interactions. It can also include some of the more physical household or gardening chores. It is often more motivating to do aerobic type exercise with a partner or in a group or class.

* An exercise option for those who are continually busy is short 'power workouts' where you exercise intensely but only for a period of 5 minutes or less. Should this appeal to you however you should take some professional advice. You could easily do yourself some significant damage if you simply leapt into doing it.

* Try to do balancing and stretching exercises at least 2 or 3 times a week, for periods of about 10 or 15 minutes. Look to schedule this for a regular time during the week. Be careful however not to push yourself and end up injuring yourself. Stretching helps keep you flexible, helps reduce stress, and generally improves circulation and energy levels.

* Try to set yourself a goal with regards your exercising. It may relate to weight loss or improvement in overall body shape or some measurable improvement in endurance or strength or agility. You will feel more motivated if you are aiming towards some goal and over a period of time you can see yourself making progress. And of course once you achieve a goal you can reward yourself in some way and set another. Any goals you set however should be medium term, 6 months or a year, with moderate short term goals. Don't rush to achieve significant goals.

* Some variation in your exercise routines can help avoid them becoming boring and have you lose the motivation to keep them up, as well as ensuring a more balanced strengthening of your body. You should try different types of exercises from time to time, maybe a bit of swimming now and again, or some jogging, or some one on one or team sports. Different types of exercise will exercise different muscles and different parts of your body rather than have you only strengthen or flexing a relatively small part of your body.

* Be mindful of potential injuries. If you are about to do an exercise session do some light warm up exercises first. If you have pains be mindful of them. Sure you can have the willpower to continue through the pain, but if the pain is telling you about an injury then you are likely to aggravate it by

continuing through it. And remember your longer term exercising will be significantly hampered if you have injuries.

* It is important to be able to differentiate injury pain, which is your body telling you something is not right, from discomfort which arises from pushing yourself and which you can keep going through. The former tends to come on quickly as a sharp pain. The latter tends to slowly build up from an initial aching, though again if it becomes a sharp pain you should stop, unless you are a professional with expert advice.

* Don't sit around too much during the day. If your job or daily life style is one that involves you sitting down all day, look for opportunities to get up and walk around, or spend some time standing up. Your brain will respond well to increases in oxygen arising from just moving around a bit rather than continually sitting. You are more likely to get creative ideas and thoughts whilst walking around. You should look to get up and walk around for about 5 minutes or so each hour.

* Look for any excuse or opportunity to be a bit more active. Stand up when on the phone; walk up stairs rather than use escalators or lifts – at least for a couple of flights at first; walk relatively short distances rather than use the car; do your housework with some vigor rather than as a chore; don't stock up on desserts at home, but go down to the local shop to buy them as and when you want them.

* Regularly going for a walk is good for you. Not only is it a bit of mild exercise, but walking can be excellent for clearing your head. You will find good ideas often occur to you whilst walking, so long as you don't drown them out through continually listening to music.

* From time to time spend 5 minutes just mindfully breathing. Find somewhere quiet where you won't be disturbed, set an alarm for 5 minutes of so, sit comfortably, and just breath in and out whilst being aware of yourself. Let thoughts come and go but keep bringing yourself back to being aware of your breathing. Look to count 1 – inhale, 2 – exhale, 3 – inhale - up to 10, and repeat. Keep practicing and it will become a very useful technique for bringing calm during what may be hectic days.

* Do deep breathing exercises a couple of times a day. Sit or lie comfortably; put one hand on your stomach and one on your chest. Inhale slowly through your nose, but ensure your belly puffs out before your chest. Fill your lungs. Then slowly exhale through your mouth. Try to release almost all the air out of your lungs. Repeat 4 or 5 times.

* A breathing exercise to help you relax. Close your lips and breathe in through your nose for about 4 seconds. Then hold your breath for about 8 seconds, and the slowly exhale through your mouth for about 8 seconds. Repeat 4 or 5 times. Then continue just breathing normally but remain aware of your breathing for a while.

Sleep

* Sleep is vital to overall well-being, and many problems arise when you do not get enough or good enough sleep, such as: increased susceptibility to colds and other infections and slower recovery times; general fatigue and lack of motivation and self-control; difficulty concentrating and poor memory; poor problem solving skills; general moodiness and irritability; general feeling of being overwhelmed with small problems; increased likelihood of accidents; tendency to put on weight; and increased risks of general health problems..

* People vary in the amount of sleep they need but most adults need between about 6 and 9 hours a night, and children into their mid to late teens need more. If you feel tired during the day, or find yourself stressed not long after waking up, then it may be that you are not getting enough sleep, though there may also be other factors such as poor diet.

The Bumper Book of Common Sense

* Generally, getting up at around 6am, or sunrise if it is earlier, seems to be an optimal time for having high levels of energy during the day, though if you are sure a different time works for you, so be it. This means the time you go to bed should be such that you get a good nights sleep, generally no later than about 11pm, preferably earlier, though again learn and do what works for you.

* Seek medical help if you cannot solve your sleeping problems; though note that many of the problems with sleeping arise from poor application of good sleeping habits, from being overweight, and from stress. Long term stress related sleeping problems usually arise when people take on more work than they can cope with, or they are doing things they are not suited to; though sometimes there may be a particular short term stressful situation.

* Do not do work or chores at the expense of sleep time, unless there is a particular rare and urgent need. For the most part lack of sleep will cause many more problems than delaying a particular task.

* To help you sleep well:
    o Eliminate bright lights and any significant sound. This includes the light and sounds from clocks or electronic devices in your room. You are likely to sleep better in total darkness. Use comfortable earplugs to eliminate noises if necessary;
    o Have good quality bed linen and nightclothes if you wear any;
    o Ensure comfortable temperature and avoid humid extremes. Note that it is better to have your room cool rather than warm, so long as you are warm under your bedding;
    o Develop regular schedules allowing for in general about 7 or 8 hours of sleep, though individuals do vary in needs. Try to go to bed at a regular time, not too late, and get up at a regular time, preferably fairly early;
    o Try not to stimulate your brain in the 30mins or hour or so before you intend to go to sleep: reading something not too thought provoking is better than watching TV or browsing the internet;
    o Limit what you eat and drink in the 2 or 3 hours before you go to bed, and certainly avoid anything with sugar or stimulants for at least 4 or 5 hours before;
    o Avoid exercising in the 3 or 4 hours before you go to bed, though do ensure you are getting some exercise during the day;
    o If you have difficulties, try to develop a bedtime ritual. This could include a relaxing bath (not too hot or cold), listening to relaxing music, slowly dimming lights, a jotting down of things on your mind including reminders for the next day;
    o If you have difficulty quietening your mind when you are trying to sleep then learn some meditation techniques. Whilst you don't want to be meditating when trying to sleep, the techniques will help you relax your mind;
    o If appropriate make arrangements with your partner to ensure they don't disturb your routine.

* If you regularly get only about 4 or 5 hours sleep a night, and feel it isn't enough, then adopt an approach known as 'sleep restriction'. You estimate how long you are likely to sleep then you plan on getting up after this amount of time, setting your alarm accordingly. You don't let yourself stay in bed, even if you want to. You get up and get on with your day (or early morning). And the same the night after. You do this for a week or so, and then if you find yourself regularly sleeping through to your alarm, increase the time you allow yourself to sleep by 15 minutes. Eventually you should find yourself sleeping more regularly, and should gradually find yourself settling into a more sustainable sleeping pattern.

* If you spend a couple of hours unable to get back to sleep in the early morning start to get up earlier. Let your sleep patterns adjust to finding a new earlier get up time.

* Tips for getting back to sleep if you wake in the night include:

- - Keep pen and paper close by and write down things that are on your mind and what you are going to do about them;
  - Read something not very exciting or thought provoking;
  - Have a warm milk based drink.

* A particular suggestion if you find it difficult to get to sleep or get back to sleep having woken in the night is to get comfortable and into a sleeping position and environment and then replay the day just passed in your head in as much detail as you can. Try to remember the details and live it again in your mind.

* A common cause of not being able to sleep, or get back to sleep, is having your worries and problems playing over in your mind in a repetitive manner. In such circumstances you need to tell yourself firmly that there is nothing you can do about your problems right now, if appropriate right down the actions you can take in the morning or when you can, and also recognize that many problems that loom large in the night are often dealt with relatively easily in the morning.

* During the night our emotional minds dominate. When we wake up in the night we often have worrying thoughts which during the night we find difficult to control. Our more rationale mind is only able to put them into perspective during the day. Don't get overly concerned about your night time terrors.

* Whilst you may feel that alcohol can help you get to sleep, it leads to less restful sleep.

* If you are having trouble sleeping, maybe you are not trying hard enough during the day.

* Getting too much sleep can be as bad for you as too little. Unless you have trouble getting enough sleep look to see if you can get by on a little less sleep. In particular getting up early in the morning can give you some time to get on with your own important tasks for an hour or so before the pressures of the day lead you off doing things which are largely driven by other people's priorities rather than your own.

* There are different views even amongst the experts on whether a nap at lunch time or in the afternoon is good for you. If it works for you, don't feel guilty about it, but generally it will be best between 12 and 3pm. Note however that the experts do agree on keeping it to a shortish period of between about 20 and 30 minutes. Longer than this and you will feel more sluggish for much of the rest of the afternoon rather than refreshed. Drinking a strong coffee before you take a nap should help in that it takes about 30mins to have an effect.

Meditation and Relaxation Techniques

* It is important to be able to calm your mind from time to time. Meditation is a technique to enable you to do this. Meditation can significantly reduce feelings of stress and significantly slow aging and deterioration of the brain. Regular short periods of meditation, say 5 or 10 minutes a day, can also significantly improve your general ability to focus.

* The following is a simple general meditation technique. Sit in a chair, still, away from distractions or noises. Have your feet flat on the ground, sit up straight, and have your hands on your lap. Don't fidget. Close your eyes. Become aware of your breathing. Say to yourself 'inhale' and 'exhale' as you do. If your mind wanders bring it back to 'inhale' and 'exhale'. Once you are focused without your mind wandering you can stop saying to yourself and simply focus on your breathing. Whenever your mind wanders return to 'inhale' and 'exhale'. Try this for 5 minutes a day at first, building up to about 15 minutes a day. Don't get downhearted if you fail to keep focused. Just keep practicing. You will start to see benefits so long as you keep trying.

* Another simple relaxation technique. Lie on your back, legs uncrossed, arms relaxed at your sides, eyes open or closed. Breathe deeply for a couple of minutes to help you feel comfortable. Then

The Bumper Book of Common Sense

focus on the toes of your right foot. Feel any sensations. Keep focused for a minute of so. Then slowly move your focus to the bottom of your foot, again feeling any sensations, and keeping your breathing even. Slowly move your focus to your ankle, and slowly move it up your right leg being aware of each part of your body as you pass through. Once up at your hip repeat with your left foot and leg. Then slowly move your focus up your body up to your shoulders. Move your focus to the end of your fingers on your right hand and slowly move it up your right arm. Then your left hand and arm. Then up through your neck and throat, up your face to the top of your head. Finally imagine yourself just above your head. Continue to breathe deeply for a while and then slowly just be aware of yourself as a whole again. You should be feeling very relaxed.

* A further relaxation technique relates to progressively stressing and relaxing the various muscles in your body. Lie down in a comfortable position. Do a bit of deep breathing to help you relax. And then slowly, starting with your right foot, tense up a group of muscles tightly, for about 5 or 10 seconds, and then relax them. Slowly work through the muscles in your body. Do the tensing and relaxing several times for each group of muscles. As well as generally relaxing you may find you have muscle groups which spend a lot of their time being tensed up without you realizing it, and this technique will help you be more aware of them and more able to relax them. If you find in doing this that you have a lot of pain when tensing up certain muscles, your may have something wrong which would benefit from a visit to your doctor.

* Seek from time to time to simply bring your mind into the present and look to just focus on the present moment. Find somewhere quiet, where you won't get disturbed and look to find a comfortable seating position. Then simply focus on one thing, either some imaginary thing in your mind, some particular simple phrase, or some particular object in front of you. Possibly a candle through any object will do. And simply focus all your attention on it. Don't worry about other thoughts that come into your head. Just keep bringing your attention back of the object of focus. At first you might find it difficult to hold your attention for very long, but if you keep practicing you will get better at it. And once you do get better at it, you should find it quite relaxing, and you may well find new and creative thoughts occurring to you.

* Practice visualization. Find somewhere quiet where you can be comfortable and not disturbed. Close your eyes and imagine yourself being somewhere you know reasonably well and that you find peaceful. Maybe somewhere in the woods or by a lake or the sea. Then imagine being there, with all your senses. Feel yourself being there; try to imagine the details and the colors. Imagine the sounds and the smells. Try to feel a breeze or the warmth. You could use natural nature sounds from CDs if appropriate to your visualization – they are easily obtainable. If you keep practicing visualization you will get better at it.

* Yoga and Tai Chi both provide effective ways of relaxing, though you need to spend the time learning them. Doing classes will help you get the technique right and get the most from them.

* Look to make relaxation techniques a part of your way of life. Set aside some time each day or each week for application of your preferred technique or techniques. Don't worry if you can't instantly get into great technique, just keep practicing and you will get better at it. Avoid applying relaxation techniques when you are sleepy: you are likely to simply fall asleep.

Body Posture

* Having a good body posture has many benefits, including:
    o It helps ensure you breathe properly, which has the knock on effect of increasing your concentration and thinking ability as a result of getting more oxygen to the brain;
    o You feel more alert and comfortable in everyday life;
    o It improves your image, noting that people with good posture appear to be smarter and more attractive. People with a good body posture exude an aura of confidence and capability;
    o People with good body posture tend to feel more self-confident;

- Good body posture helps avoid health complications that arise due to bad body posture. Many back problems or circulation problems arise from bad body posture.

* A good body posture for sitting in a normal four-legged chair is one that is between a slouched position and a forced sitting up straight position. This is sometimes described as a 'poised' sitting position, and is one in which the weight of the head is being passed by the spine into the chair, and the ribs can move freely. In a good position you do not need to force yourself to breathe properly because it will come naturally from the posture. Some common habits which prohibit sitting properly include: tightening your lower back in order to sit straight; dropping your head forward; throwing your shoulders back; tucking your legs under the chair. If you are sitting for a long time however you will find yourself needing to shift your posture from time to time, and you should get up and have a walk around every now and again.

* Good body posture is about maintaining the nature curves of your back. It is not about keeping your spine totally straight, which can be as bad for you as always slouching. A good posture is one you feel comfortable with and can maintain with little effort. When standing it means your weight being distributed evenly across the balls of your feet. Look up on the internet pictures and descriptions of what good posture looks like in different circumstances, and make the effort to ensure you have it by practicing in front of a mirror.

* Some common causes of poor body posture, often leading eventually to poor health include: repetitive motions without frequent breaks; being immobile for long periods of time during the day such as staying sat down for hours at a time; slouching over using a computer or other electronic devices for long periods of time; frequent walking with heavy backpacks; lifting heavy objects without ensuring you keep your back straight whilst doing so.

* Some tips for developing and maintaining a good body posture:
  - Be conscious of your body posture and when you are aware it is not good, put it into a good posture;
  - Eliminate bad habits which lead to poor posture such as lying down whilst reading or watching TV, or working in bad light which invariably leads to you slouching;
  - Try not to sleep on your stomach;
  - Try to use good quality chairs that have a firm, but not hard, back support, and preferably a high back that allows you to have your shoulders supported;
  - Place your backside into the innermost edge of the chair, not the middle or edge which will lead to you leaning or slouching badly;
  - Sit with both feet flat on the floor. Sitting with legs crossed will result in your back not being straight;
  - Try to have a good bed and pillow. A bed that is firm, though not hard, and a pillow that supports your head;
  - Avoid regularly carrying heavy items that put a strain on your shoulders and back and lead to you frequently adopting hunched shoulders and back. If you do need to regularly carry heavy bags consider using a bag with wheels or rollers;
  - Do exercises to strengthen your back such as simple stretching or yoga. Though take it easy at first, ensure you are using the right techniques, and only push yourself as you feel comfortable doing so;
  - If you find it difficult to change your posture consider getting a shoulder and back massage. This should loosen your joints and make it easier to adopt a good posture;
  - If you have frequent back problems then see a chiropractor or physical therapist and get a proper assessment of the causes, likely to include poor posture, and what you can do about it.

* Body posture affects how your brain operates. Having your arms folded, for example, can prohibit creative problem solving. You will be better at solving anagrams lying down rather than standing up. You are also more likely to be creative if you are gently pulling on something rather than if you are pushing against something.

The Bumper Book of Common Sense

Your Voice

* When talking or speaking ensure you are doing so loud enough for others to be able to hear you comfortably, albeit without shouting or being particularly loud.

* Be wary of ensuring you don't speak in a monotone. Let your voice follow its natural speech pattern, which should include variation in pitch.

* If you are telling a story or relating an event, live it in your mind as you tell it. This will reflect in your voice and give the story more life.

* Use your face and your body to imitate and emphasis what you are saying. This will reflect back in your voice itself.

* Slow down when delivering important points. It will give them more impact. And also pause before and after them. Though not for too long.

* Be aware of how your voice sounds by taking recordings and playing it back. If there are aspects of your voice you don't like, practice adjusting them, and get regular feedback through further recordings and play back.

* You can improve your voice through singing out loud, on your own, in the car for example whilst listening to music, or when alone at home. Also pay attention to news readers and practice imitating them.

* Having good breathing habits will improve your voice. Look these up on the internet and practice them.

* To keep your voice in good shape during the day ensure you keep yourself hydrated, preferably with water.

* If your voice is important to you or your job, take some singing or acting lessons.

Dealing with Pain

* If you are getting recurrent pains for reasons you don't understand, then go and see your doctor.

* We all sometimes have to deal with pain, and for some people pain is a part of their daily lives. Prolonged exposure to pain can leave us bad tempered and hamper our getting on with our lives. Use painkillers when you reasonably can, though sometimes prolonged use of painkillers can itself be harmful. Meditation techniques can help enormously, but it is best to get professional advice rather than try and probably fail to learn it from a book.

* If you are in pain, rather than trying to ignore it, feel it and accept it. You are likely to feel less pain as a result.

* Swearing can often help you tolerate pain better.

How your Brain Works

* When we do things we build up neural pathways in our brain. The stronger the neural pathways in our brain the easier and more natural we find doing the things they are associated with. Thus the

more we practice something, the stronger we make the associated neural pathways, and the easier we are able to do it in the future.

* Our brains are far more flexible and malleable than most people think. Our brain reconstructs itself, rewires itself, as a result of our learning experiences. Our brains change in response to what we practice doing. As you learn or practice a skill your brain rewires and makes more room for it. Even mental practice contributes to this rewiring of your brain, though not as strongly as with physical practice.

* The key to rewiring our brains is self-awareness. Because of the existing neural pathways in our brain we have an automated tendency to do the things we have done in the past and which has led to the existing neural path landscaping of our brain. We thus have a natural and 'instinctive' tendency to behave in certain ways in response to the circumstances we find ourselves in. But through self-awareness we can consciously do things that go against these automated responses. Because there is a part of our brain, the frontal lobe, where our sense of self-awareness sits, which has the ability to override our natural tendencies and automated responses. And when we exercise this ability, through focused conscious effort, we are rewiring the other parts of our brain that dictate our automated behaviors and responses. If we do this often enough, and persist with our conscious efforts, we eventually create new automated behaviors and responses. Thus when we wish to change existing habits, at first it requires significant amounts of conscious effort to do so. But the more we succeed in doing so the easier it gets until after a while our new habits become themselves automated requiring little effort to implement. This wiring, or re-wiring, of our brain with regards a given habit can take between a couple of weeks and 6 months, though often about a month is enough.

* The application of self-awareness uses a lot of energy, which your brain gets from glucose. A steady but moderate supply of glucose will help keep your brain alert and able to apply the self-control necessary to override your automated responses to circumstances. A poor supply of glucose or wildly fluctuating levels will lead to you feeling tired and unable to think things through or apply self-control. Note that it is the glucose that occurs naturally in foods such as fruit and vegetables and fish and meat that helps generate a moderate supply, whilst the glucose in sweets and cakes leads to spikes that then bring you crashing back down. How well your brain is able to convert glucose into energy is dependent upon how tired you are, and it is much harder to maintain self-control later in the day. It is best to develop habitual behaviors for later in the day rather than rely on willpower to do the right things.

* Our brains have an ability to mimic other people, through what are termed 'mirror neurons', which help us understand what other people are feeling. This is why people who spend a lot of time together often start to mirror each other's postures. Usually this mimicking is subconscious, though in some professions people are trained to do this as an influencing technique. This also explains why seeing someone else doing something we are tempted by, such as smoking or eating sweets, triggers a desire in ourselves to do likewise. It also leads to us experiencing other people's emotions, good or bad, which enables us to empathize with them, but can also lead to a triggering of such emotions in ourselves.

* Your subconscious is primed by your environment, by whatever you are sensing at a given moment in time. Though you are rarely aware of it every physical object you are encountering is triggering associations in your mind. This is continually going on at a subconscious level and your feelings and thoughts are influenced by these subconscious associations. Thus you can find yourself getting in to certain mental states directly as a result of your environment. For example you will find it more difficult to get into a productive focused state of mind if you are surrounded by clutter and reminders of other things you should be doing.

* Men's and women's brains are wired differently, with women's brains being more balanced between left and right hemispheres leading to them generally being more intuitive and more tuned in to emotions than men. Men have a tendency towards greater visual and spatial skills and women towards greater language skills. This however is not absolute, and there is huge variation in individuals and these variations overlap.

The Bumper Book of Common Sense

* Our brains get into different states and we can, with practice, learn to change the state we are in. The different states are labeled as brain-wave states, namely:
    o Gamma wave state: generated during situations of extreme stress, leading to our being able to transcend typical activities, such as when people perform incredible feats;
    o Beta wave state: generated during active conscious thinking and concentrated problem solving;
    o Alpha wave state: generated during a relaxed alert state;
    o Theta wave state: generated during drowsiness, when daydreaming, or during light sleep. Note that unusual ideas can often pop into the head during a theta wave state;
    o Delta wave state: generated during deep sleep. Our physical healing is accelerated when in this state.

* Different parts of our brain light up when we're thinking of ourselves as opposed to when we're thinking of other people. However when we think of our future selves it is often the part of our brain that relates to thinking of other people that lights up. This in part explains why it is often difficult to make sacrifices in the short term for the benefit of our long term. In order to be better able to make short term sacrifices for long term gains we need to feel a stronger connection with our future selves. Explicitly envisage your future self in a similar manner to how you see yourself in the present.

Common Sense Working for a Living

Take Responsibility for Enjoying and Finding Meaning in your Work

* Look at how to make your work life more meaningful. After all it takes up a large part of your life. You need to take personal responsibility for this: it is not for others to inspire you, it is for you to find inspiration. See your job in terms of its context and contribution to the wider organization, and the wider organization's context in terms of its contribution to the world. Your job is so much more than just something to be done.

* You can see your work as a daily drudgery, solely as a way of earning money, or as a purposeful contribution to society. It's up to you how you see it. But how you see it will fundamentally affect the quality of your life.

* Be clear about what you enjoy doing, and what you are good at, and set about seeing how you can do these things as part of your working life. Having a job you enjoy and you are good at will be a major step towards having a fulfilling life.

* Find work you enjoy doing and you are suited to. If you are working solely for the money, but hate the job, you are throwing away a large part of your life. If you are not enjoying your job, you don't necessarily need to quit it and look elsewhere, which might be difficult in terms of earning money. However look to understand what you like and don't like about your job, and look to do more of what you like and less of what you don't. You may have some flexibility about how you go about doing your job, or might be able to agree with your boss some changes, or take a different job within the organization you are in. Generally people are happier doing what they are good at, and if you can exploit this then you will also be of more value to the organization you work for.

* If you don't particularly enjoy the work you are doing, and have ideas about your ideal job, you can move towards it without abandoning your current work:
    o Be clear about what you would like to do and why;

- Get good at what you do now by developing your underlying skills of time management, decision management, critical thinking, communication, and interpersonal communication; and also develop your behaviors – being open minded, positive, etc. These skills and behaviors apply to any job;
- Develop other more specific skills or understanding relating to your ideal job. Take any training or other opportunities that may be relevant or opportunistic in your existing job, or do it in your own time;
- Look for any opportunities to move in the direction you want to go in;
- Mix with people who already work in the area you would like to work in.

* Be wary of allowing yourself to be promoted into positions you are not competent for and which you will not enjoy. By all means be ambitious and seek to move on. But remember work is a major part of your life and if you are unhappy in your work you are likely to be unhappy in your life. A little extra money won't compensate for this.

* People who are excellent in a supporting role often fail when promoted to a leadership role because that is not where their strengths lie. Be aware of your own strengths and weaknesses and don't push yourself into roles you are unsuited for, and likely not to be competent in. Note that this is not an excuse not to keep trying to progress. Maybe you don't know if you are suited to a leadership or more senior role without trying. However people do allow themselves to be promoted beyond what they clearly know to be their own level of competence, and whilst they may earn more they are significantly more stressed as a result and the quality of their life can be low.

* Look to recognize the parts of the job you are less than competent to carry out and compensate through getting others to help you out or to do them on your behalf.

* It is not as difficult to run your own business as you might think. What skills have you that someone might pay for? What can you make and sell? What can you buy and sell for more than you bought it? There are millions of ways of making money. Find one that plays to your skills and capabilities. However ensure you have a viable business plan, and it is usually best to test out some of your ideas before giving up an existing well-paid job, particularly if you have family dependents. And be prepared to have to work very hard at it.

Take Control over your Work and Responsibility for Getting the Right Things Done

* Many people avoid hard work and claim they are working smarter, whereas in reality of course they are working no smarter than anyone else. Working smarter means being very well organized and having very good time management skills, including an ability to keep track of and focus on what is important whilst not allowing less important tasks to become a crisis. Very few people do this.

* In order to do things of value rather than just be busy all day long you need to know how your job fits into the wider company processes and business, know what are the unique responsibilities and accountabilities of your job, and know what is expected of you. Just because your boss hasn't explicitly told you to do something doesn't mean you don't have a responsibility to do it. On the other hand nor are you free to just do what you feel like.

* People usually have more freedom and discretion in their jobs than they think they do, particularly those in management positions.

* Understand how your work interacts with and affects others. You may be doing what you consider to be a good job, but it is how your work combines with others to give rise to outputs for the organization as a whole that matters.

* When faced with a problem look to identify options for dealing with it and discuss them up the management chain, don't just pass on the problems themselves.

The Bumper Book of Common Sense

* Be willing to bend the rules to get things done. It is easier to ask forgiveness than permission. An exception is where safety is concerned. Safety rules are there for a reason and need to be followed unless there is a good reason why not, such as it being safer in the particular circumstances not to follow them. Another exception is where ethics is concerned, both with regards your organization's ethical codes and also with regards your personal ethics.

* If you don't take control of your work, by doing the things that need doing when they need doing, then your work will take control of you, and force you to do things when you don't want to do them.

* Unless you schedule time in your daily calendar to do important but none urgent things, and treat that time like a meeting, it is unlikely you will get round to them. It is usually best to do important things early in the day when your energy levels are higher. It will also give you a sense of accomplishment for that day that you can build on.

* In the morning, when you get into work, assuming you have some discretion in what you do, spend the first hour on something of long-term importance. Don't look at your e-mail except to glance to ensure there is nothing urgent that you need to take action on.

* Learn to manage your energy levels during the day. Take immediate brief breaks every hour or so and ensure you get up and walk about a bit. Express appreciation of others. Spend more time on the activities you do best and enjoy. Focus on one thing at a time.

* Reduce interruptions. Don't be continually responding to the phone, unless of course that is your job, and review and respond to e-mails only at set times during the day.

* If your work involves frequent interactions with others, then adopt good note taking habits with regards key ideas you may want to remember in the future, and whatever agreements you may have come to. Don't rely on your memory. Remember however that your note taking is a means to an end, not an end in itself. You don't need to write down everything. And of course your notes are your own, so feel free to be creative in making them work for you. Add color or highlights or observations in the margin. Having good notes can significantly improve your work effectiveness.

* Last thing, when packing up from work for the day, list 3 or 4 priority things for you to do the next day.

* Rather than complain about being too busy, be grateful you have plenty of work to do, and learn how to handle it, through being well organized and being an effective manager of your time.

* Get into a mindset of seeing your work as a challenge to be enjoyed rather than endured. Get efficient and organized and develop a strategy for dealing with too much work. Set yourself an intent for a given number of hours each week, more than you are paid for but limited to a maximum none the less.

Boosting your Employability

* Do more than you are paid for and eventually you will be paid more for what you do.

* You get responsibility for big jobs by proving you have outgrown responsibility for small jobs.

* We prepare for being successful in doing big things by doing the very best we can in the small things. Excellence is not an act, but a habit. Always be the best you can be, and do the best you can in the circumstances.

* Don't kid yourself that you don't need to work harder because you are working smarter. You need to both work harder and work smarter than those around you.

* Look to bring value to others. Be worth something to them.

* If you work for an organization, unless you own it, it does not owe you a living. You should seek to be of value to the company, not just to increase your own employment prospects but also to help the company or organization itself to stay in business. If it goes out of business, so do you, and you will also be potentially stigmatized as having been part of a failed company.

* Find out what you are good at, then do more of it. Leverage your own competitive advantage. Don't wait for others to tell you how best to use your strengths for the betterment of the organization you work for; get on doing so for yourself.

* Take advantage of your time working to upgrade yourself, to expand your competencies and skills. Learn as much as you can about your given work area. Take whatever training opportunities are available. Learn from others with more experience or knowledge by frequently asking questions. Be sensitive to feedback from others, don't get upset about it, accept it and use it to improve yourself. Regularly ask yourself what you've done in the past few months to improve your competency and skills.

* It's not what you know that makes you a valuable asset; it's what you are able to do with what you know. Don't just seek out knowledge; seek out the skills to turn knowledge into useful action and output.

* To make or keep yourself employable and maximize your opportunities for advancement develop a Personal Development Plan. Proactively look to take advantage of any development opportunities your organization may have to offer, including access to mentors. In developing your Personal Development Plan have and record a clear vision of what you want to achieve and where you want to get to. Make a realistic assessment of what knowledge and skills you currently have, identify what knowledge and skills and experience you need to get to where you want to be, and find ways of closing the gap. Maintain a diary of progress and take any corrective actions you deem necessary to overcome blockers or emergent issues.

* Do not wait for your organization to develop you. It is not they who are responsible for your self-development, it is you. Don't wait to be put on a course or offered development opportunities, seek them out for yourself. If you are proactive you can get a lot from your organization that will be of benefit to your development.

* If you are a professional, look to write articles or papers. It will be a great boost to your career and will give you a lot of credibility.

* Show people you know what you are talking about. Show off your experiences, albeit without being arrogant about it. Make people feel comfortable about believing in you.

* If you are keen to progress fast within your organization then get involved in the current crisis or high visibility projects within the organization, and put in a lot of effort.

* Spend about 10% of your time as an employee looking for ways to do your job better: training, reading, brainstorming, thinking about whether you should be doing what you are doing and identifying more productive things to be doing or ways of doing what you do. If others are doing similar things to you, understand how they are doing them. You will usually find some good tips, or even completely different ways, for going about doing what you do.

* If and when you write your CV pay attention to layout, spelling, and grammar. Don't be afraid to make it long, though not too long. Give people a reason for wanting to talk to you.

The Bumper Book of Common Sense

Be Professional in How you Behave

* Be professional and show respect in all your work dealings. If your organization has specific values then exhibit them. Look to foster good relationships in the office, including and especially cross department, and seek out win-win resolutions to any issues.

* Be honest and reliable in all of your business dealings, just as you should be for your personal dealings.

* Don't complain about the people you work with. They are as they are. You should recognize how they are and take responsibility for your own interactions with them, or in extreme cases limit your interactions with them.

* If you work in the service industry then be courteous and seek to serve. Even if you don't work in the service industry this is generally good advice.

* People do judge others by appearances, even when they don't mean to. Dress appropriate to your work environment.

* Have values and live by them. Don't be late for meetings. Don't make commitments you can't keep and make every effort to keep the commitments you've made.

Work Life Balance

* Don't take your work stresses home to your family; nor your family stresses into your work.

* You need to balance your home and your work life. If one dominates to the detriment of the other you are likely to have significant short, medium, and long term problems.

* Seek to limit the amount of time you spend in work, and learn to get your work done in that time. Don't forever be doing extra or worse still not doing extra but continually feeling stressed because you haven't.

* Work hard when at work, even stay a little longer, but when you have finished your work for the day, put it behind you. Don't bring your work into your personal life. If towards the end of the day there are things you haven't done then you need to make a clear decision to either stay and finish them or put them off till the next day. Don't go home thinking maybe you should have stayed. Of course you might deliberately decide to 'take work home with you'. So be it. But ensure you set yourself a clear period of time whilst at home to do it, and switch off from it the rest of the time you are at home.

* You will be far more effective in your work if you can put it out of your mind during the periods you are not working. Focus on your other interests when not at work, and learn to put your work out of your mind.

* Beware of investing all your energies in your career and leaving little left over for your family. If you are not also putting a lot of energy into your family relationships, it is very likely they will be deteriorating. It is not worth sacrificing a good loving relationship with your family for a little extra success at work.

* Remember that your career is not who you are, it is what you do, for now.

* Don't wait till you retire before you enjoy life. Live your life as you pass through. Switch off from your work in the evenings, at the weekends, and during your holidays. Work when you are at work. When you're not at work put it out of your mind by focusing on other things.

Common Sense Living on your Own

* It's ok to be on your own, but you should look to have friends and acquaintances and keep in touch with your family.

* Living on your own is better than living in a relationship that is not working and which is not going to work.

* Be content with your life. Be happy with what you have and the opportunities that living on your own give you, rather than feel sorry or self-pity for yourself.

* You need to feel comfortable living on your own, even if, and especially if, you would rather not. Don't be desperate to avoid being on your own. If you are, you will most likely end up with someone you are not particularly suited to and any such relationship is likely to be unsatisfactory and to fall apart, sooner rather than later. If you are comfortable on your own you can take your time finding the right person to be with.

* If you want to find a partner to share your life with, then be clear about what sort of person you are looking for, and remember physical characteristics will change; better to think in terms of general qualities which are more likely to last. Someone who will care for you and about you and not just about themselves. Then find out where you are likely to meet such people. Possibly not where you currently hang out. Spend time there. But take it slow. If you try to push it, it is very likely you will attract people with different characteristics to the ones you are looking for.

* Don't spend all your time down the pub. There is nothing wrong with spending some time in the pub, but don't let it become your only escape from loneliness, at least not if it also means significant drinking.

* Invite other people who are on their own round to watch a movie or play a board game, and include some snacks and drinks, though avoid alcoholic drinks if they are driving. People with families are unlikely to be responsive to such ideas though people with partners may be so long as you invite the partner along as well.

* Don't spend all your time outside of work or college or wherever being on your own. Go out to places where there are people with similar interests to your own. If you struggle to find somewhere you feel comfortable then look to take some classes in topics that interest you. Not only will it provide you with some time when you can be with other people but you could well make new friends who you can spend some time with outside of the classes themselves.

* Living on your own is a great opportunity for doing your own projects and being creative. Learn to cook well. Learn new skills. Eliminate bad habits. Get into a positive mindset, and learn to eliminate negative thought patterns.

* Get out of the house. Take walks. Join a gym. Go to museums, libraries, art galleries. Get or keep reasonably fit.

* Regularly do something new. Don't let yourself get into a rut. Every week do something or go somewhere you haven't been before.

* Learn and regularly practice small talk. You will often find yourself in queues or places where you are close to others. Practice basic small talk; you'll quickly get better at it. You are not looking to make friends with everyone you meet, just looking to be comfortable talking to them. If you can do this with strangers you'll get good at it with people as you get to know them better.

* Consider having a pet. A dog can be a great companion and can get you regularly out of the house as you take it for walks. Do however look after it, and ensure you spend the time and effort to house train it if necessary. A dog can do a lot of damage if left in the house on its own and if it is not well trained. Other pets such as cats or rabbits or fish can also be company.

* Keep a diary or journal.

* Keep your house clean and tidy. Don't be a slob. Wash up after you. Throw rubbish away rather than leaving it lying around. Put things away after you've used them.

* Ensure you have a comfortable bed and somewhere comfortable to sit. Have somewhere comfortable for visitors to sit.

* Decorate as you like, but not so as you would be embarrassed to have people call round. Pictures or posters on the walls can quickly create a cheerful effect, but not too many.

* If you are living on your own it is not uncommon to feel uncomfortable or even worried at the idea that someone could break in. Some ways of alleviating this include getting an alarm fitted, ensure you have good locks on all your doors, ensure you keep your windows locked or such that they cannot be opened more than a small amount, keep a heavy bat or club of some sort by your bed, and ensure you have a speed dial on your mobile to someone you can call for help if you are sure someone has or is about to break in.

Common Sense Relating to Getting Older

* Don't regret getting older. It is the way life works. Just ride with it. You can appreciate and make the most of life whatever age you are.

* As you get older don't expect a lot of respect from younger generations, at least not in certain societies. Don't get bitter about this; it's the way it is. How much respect did you give to older generations when you were younger?

* Age is not an impediment unless you believe it is. Many people have taken up new challenges in their 50s, 60s, and 70s and been highly successful.

* People need something to live for, something to look forward to. This is true at any stage of life, including old age. Once you have retired, having goals is more important than ever. Also get some structure to your days. Know in advance what you are going to do for most of the day before you get up in the morning.

* Maintaining social relationships plays a significant role in maintaining both mental and physical health as you get older. Having friends and soul mates helps you live longer and helps you look and feel younger. Looking after pets and plants has also been shown to help maintain or improve mental and physical health relative to those in similar situations with nothing to look after. There is little doubt that having electronic 'companions' will also play a significant role in this regard in the future.

* Once you retire and leave your work environment you need to develop new social interactions. During our working lives we readily have plenty of social interactions; which even if they don't extend out of work still satisfy a need to feel part of a group or groups. For many people these very suddenly stop when they retire. Many people very quickly find themselves isolated and alone or just with their partner. It is important to join groups and stay at least moderately socially active.

* It is often a good idea to get some part-time paid work after you retire, or do some volunteer work, but it must be work you enjoy and can add value to.

* Light exercise can preserve health into old age. This includes walking, gardening, moderate cycling and swimming, and some of the softer martial arts such as Tai Chi. Vigorous exercise in later years is likely to be as bad for you as no exercise.

* Older persons who regularly walk, even just for half an hour or so a day at a relatively sedentary pace, show, on average, significantly less mental deterioration than those who don't.

* As you get older, particularly past retirement, keep your mind active. Nothing ages a person quicker than an idle mind. You should continue to have mental goals even in old age, and whilst there may be some deterioration in brain ability, it is not severe except when the brain is not used or because of disease. Crosswords and other puzzles will help keep the mind active, but you should be trying to do much more in terms of both continuous learning and also looking for ways of passing on your thoughts and wisdom. Some tips for keeping your mind active:
    o Reading a good mystery novel and trying to work it out as you go along, helps to build up your brain's problem solving capabilities;
    o Whilst walking round supermarkets or shops think about why they are arranged the way they are;
    o When buying just a few items do the arithmetic of adding up prices in your head;
    o Rather than passively watch TV engage with whatever you are watching. Try to predict what is likely to happen next, or try to read body language;
    o Talk to people whenever you can;
    o Write. Write as much as you can. Write your autobiography and write you own book on lessons you have learnt from life. Put in as much detail from your life as you can;
    o Take up, or renew, a hobby;
    o Learn something new, such as a foreign language or a musical instrument. There are likely to be local classes on all sorts of subjects where you can not only learn something new but meet other people as well;
    o Learn new games, not just how to play them, but the strategies for playing them well.

* As people get older they tend to become more sure of their views and opinions, less open to other views and opinions, and less curious; thought patterns become narrower, more limited, and repetitive; we become more obsessive about small things. Our brains atrophy unless we actively do something about it. We can help counter this by opening ourselves to a much greater direct awareness, without thought or judgment, of our surroundings – including sight, sounds, taste, smell and anything else we sense.

* There is some impact on our abilities as we get older, though it is not as pronounced as many people think it is. Whilst some aspects of our quick thinking, attention span, and ready recall may decline with age, we are, assuming we keep using our brains and thinking, able to call upon a far greater store of knowledge and experience which means that our overall abilities can continue to increase until well into our 60s or 70s.

* As we age our brain is less able to cope quickly with the large amounts of information we are continually bombarded with, which is in part why it gets more difficult to remember things as we get older. One way we can compensate for this is to focus our attention on one thing at a time. For example, if you are doing something that requires concentration, have fewer distractions: turn off any background TV or the radio or music.

* Our ability to switch quickly between tasks, which give the illusion of multitasking, declines with age. Don't see it as declining mental ability and simply adapt by removing distractions when concentrating or studying.

The Bumper Book of Common Sense

* Once we get into middle age our working memory, whereby we hold information in a sort of temporary store, weakens. Thus we have a greater tendency to forget something that was in our minds just a few moments ago. Compensate by writing things down.

* As you get older look to get more organized. You will be more likely to forget things as you get older, and also less able to readily cope with having lots of things on the go at the same time. If you don't adapt to this you will find yourself getting more confused and actually feel as though you are less able to deal with the normal demands of daily life. However if you compensate by getting more organized such that you make use of structured lists and keep things in a set place and you plan your time you may well find your overall effectiveness at getting things done actually increases rather than decreases.

* As you get older you can improve your memory by thinking more about the underlying meanings of what you are trying to remember.

* Much of what is seen to be memory decline in old age is a self-fulfilling prophesy, in that people who expect their memories to decline will find it does to a far greater extent than those who believe that keeping their brain active will also keep most of their memories in good shape.

* Overeating seems to lead to people ageing prematurely, whilst eating too little weakens the body and makes you more prone to illnesses. However you should generally err on the side of eating less than more, and rarely if ever eat until you are feeling bloated. Try to get in the habit of stopping to eat even if you are feeling only slightly full.

* Smoking and drugs in general are likely to lead to premature aging and early death. Not only will you die earlier but your later years will be poor quality. Many people look and indeed are old at the same age that others are in good middle age health. Even if you have been smoking for most of your life, cutting back and stopping can still have significant benefit for the rest of your life when compared to not doing so.

* Death is inevitable. Accept that fact and make the most of the time you have. The times you spend worrying about death or getting old are wasted times, which you could enjoy doing other things. Moreover by living your life rather than worrying your life you are more likely to live longer.

* Be prepared for your own death. And this is not just something for when you are old; you should be prepared at any time in your life after early adulthood. If you can accept that life is limited and could be taken from you at any time, you should feel more appreciative of life and ensure you do not build up regrets in terms of what you spend your time doing and in terms of your interactions with other people.

Common Sense Survival Tips

* Pay attention when engaged in potentially dangerous activities. Danger is potentially all around us, but we are generally safe so long as we behave appropriately. If we don't behave appropriately then we are liable to be killed or injured, or get someone else killed or injured. Most fatal accidents and injuries could have been avoided if someone had paid more attention to what they were doing.

* Develop good safety habits with everyday things and it will be a habit you can fall back on under unusual circumstances.

* Even very complex tasks can be learnt such that we can do them without paying much attention – take driving for instance. However as soon as something out of the ordinary happens you need to be able to give it your full attention more or less instantly. Don't get complacent about complex or

dangerous tasks, and ensure you don't do anything to compromise being able to react very quickly should something out of the ordinary happen.

* Driving is very dangerous; don't take it for granted. There are far more deaths and injuries arising from driving than most people realize and statistically it is far more dangerous than flying or taking trains. After 9/11 in America more people died because they switched to driving rather than taking planes than actually died as a direct result of 9/11 itself.

* Driving is familiar and we readily get into a false sense of security and invulnerability. However the consequences of a momentary lapse of attention or from making a small mistake can be very severe. Under normal circumstances you will get away with using your phone or allowing other distractions whilst driving; however if something out of the ordinary occurs at the same time it can be and sometimes is lethal, if not to you then to someone else.

* If you drive a car, use your indicators to tell other drivers and pedestrians what you want to do. If you don't you are far more likely to have or to cause an accident. Other people do not magically know what you are planning to do with the potentially deadly weapon you are supposedly in control of.

* Driving a car with a bad cold, or doing anything for that matter with a bad cold, is as dangerous as doing it after a couple of alcoholic drinks. Avoid doing it if possible, and if you can't then be more careful than usual.

* Don't drive through flooded waters or in other dangerous conditions, unless of course it is more dangerous not to. You are not as invulnerable in a car as you think you are.

* House fires happen, usually at night. Have a plan so that everyone in the family knows what to do in the event of a fire in the night. Ensure children in particular know how to try to get out of the house. Children have a habit of trying to hide when they panic, such as in a closet or under the bed. Make sure they know what to do and if they are young practice it with them. If a route out involves a window that does not open easily, leave something close by it that you could use to break it – make sure your children know what to do and to be careful of broken glass.

* Know your evacuation routes when you stay away overnight.

* Have a fire extinguisher in your home and know how to use it and what sort of fires it can be used on. PASS: Pull the safety pin out; Aim the nozzle; Squeeze the handle; Sweep side to side close to the base of the fire. Have a fire blanket in the house that you can get to quickly – probably best in the kitchen since that is where you are most likely to need to use it.

* If you are caught in a fire with smoke keep close to the floor. Smoke and heat rise. Beware of closed doors, and check how hot they are before opening them. Check high up: being careful not to burn the palms of your hands if the doors are hot; use the back of you hand if you are unsure. If they don't appear hot open them carefully and close them if there is fire the other side. If they are hot, don't open them unless you have no option.

* If you are trying to escape from, or have escaped from, a burning house do not go back in to rescue possessions.

* Protect your home from burglary. Make sure windows are shut and locked, particularly at night or when the house is unoccupied, or might appear unoccupied. Ensure locks are secure on windows and doors. If your neighborhood is prone to break-ins then take extra precautions such as alarms and additional locks.

* If you live in an area prone to certain types of catastrophe – earthquakes, floods, bush fires, tornados – read up on advice about what to do and any preparations you can do. A couple of hours preparation could save you or your children's lives.

The Bumper Book of Common Sense

- Large numbers of accidents happen in the home. The following are some Common Sense tips for avoiding accidents in the home:
    - Do not leave clothes or anything else that can catch fire anywhere near where they can catch fire, including above ovens or gas hobs;
    - Be careful with candles or any other naked flames. Don't let anything near them or above them that can burn, and ensure the flames and any ambers are out when you leave the house or will be leaving them unattended;
    - If you smoke don't smoke in bed, and when you put your cigarette out ensure it is fully out;
    - Don't leave pans being heated in the kitchen unattended, and be wary of overheating anything with oil in it;
    - Be careful with boiling water. Don't leave it where someone could accidentally knock it over and be careful when carrying it around or putting it down;
    - Don't overload electric sockets;
    - Do not have mains connected electrical appliances in the bathroom;
    - Ensure any electrical appliances that can get hot are turned off after use and if you leave them for a few minutes ensure no-one is likely to go near them;
    - If you spill or have water anywhere near electrical appliances ensure they are switched off – unless of course they are intended to be used with water;
    - Do not leave damaged wires unrepaired;
    - If you have a gas oven, pay attention to ensuring the gas is never on when not lit;
    - If you use heaters be aware of the potential dangers they pose, dependent upon the type of heater;
    - When changing light bulbs in ceiling lights make sure you are on something sturdy as you do so;
    - Be wary whenever you climb up on something, including ladders. Ensure they are sturdy and you have a good grip. Preferably look to ensure someone else is also about;
    - Be wary of highly polished floors, and of mats that can slip;
    - Gardens can be very dangerous places. Tools can be dangerous: always use them with care and check they are in good working order before you use them;
    - Barbeques should never be brought indoors or have anything close by them which can catch fire;
    - If you live in a high-rise building, do not have windows that can be fully opened. Have restrictors put on them. If you have young children you may also want to do this with any upstairs windows they could potentially access;
    - Do not leave objects on stairs or at the top of stairs where someone can inadvertently trip over them or slip on them;
    - If bending down ensure there are no open cupboards or anything you could bang your head against as you get up again.
- When handling dangerous products read the warning labels or instructions. Most people claim they do, but in fact less than a third of people typically do. And poor handling of dangerous products is a ready cause of avoidable accidents.
- Ensure you and everyone else in your family including children know how to protect personal information over the internet. Use but don't fully rely on anti-virus and related programs. Don't go following links in unsolicited e-mails, even ones you believe have been forwarded to you by friends: your friends may not know about the links in their e-mails, and e-mails from friends may not have come from them. Ensure you and other members of your family, again including children, know how to manage and protect passwords. Be wary of any links from websites that are other than ones you know for certain to be safe.

- Recognize that young children can do almost anything with anything that is within their reach or which they could bring within their reach:
    - Do not leave things they can light a fire with within reach;
    - Do not leave things perched on edges where they can be knocked off;
    - Do not have anything hot where they could touch it, such as boiling pans on stoves;
    - Do not allow them to get through doors to go outside where there are roads;
    - Do not leave them with glass objects they could break and cut themselves on;
    - Do not leave medicines or household chemicals where they could get hold of them and could eat or drink them;
    - Do not leave them alone in the presence of dogs, no matter how tame you believe the dog to be;
    - Do not leave them unsupervised in or near a full bath, and check the temperature of water before you put children in it;
    - Use electric socket guards on any sockets young children could access;
    - Do not have open stairs where young children could fall down – put stair guards in;
    - Check there are no hazards in gardens such as ponds or pools which children could fall in or places they could climb up and fall from, or ways of them getting out of the garden unnoticed.

  Generally make the assumption your young child will get away from you unnoticed and thus you need to ensure there are no hazards nearby.

- Ensure you know how to switch off the water coming into your home – most homes have a shut off valve, and electricity – at a circuit breaker box, and gas – main gas shut off valve. Find out where these valves and boxes are so that in an emergency you know how to quickly switch them off. Gas shut off valves are usually close to the meter.

- If you have smoke or carbon monoxide detectors, ensure they work. If you don't have any, consider getting some.

- Keep torches handy in case of blackouts, and know how to find them in the dark.

- Recognize the possibility of occasional catastrophic happenings, including fires and burglaries, and keep essential documents safe and keep a duplicate somewhere away from where they could suffer the same fate as the originals. Important documents include insurance papers and information on valuables. Back up computer data regularly, and keep it somewhere separate from the original data.

- If you are traveling through likely wilderness or deserted areas, be prepared for the worst – such as your car breaking down. It can happen. Ensure you have some survival kit with you including survival blankets, torches, water, first aid box, knife, lighter/matches, map, and compass: preferably in a rucksack so that you can carry them should you need to – though it would usually be best to stay with a vehicle. Mobile phones often won't work so you may need to survive for a while. If you go off the beaten track always know which direction to go in if your transport should break down. Also make sure someone knows where you have gone.

- If you are caught out in the open in a lightning storm, ensure you stay out of water, away from tall trees, try not to be the tallest thing around, and don't lie down on the ground. It is usually best to crouch down on the balls of your feet. And note that most people struck by lightning will survive.

- Don't walk through flooded streets. There may be holes you can't see, and if the water is flowing you could get swept off your feet and possibly killed.

- If you find yourself in a car sinking in water, get seatbelts undone and open windows. You will not be able to open a car door underwater due to the water pressure.

The Bumper Book of Common Sense

* When out in the wilderness remember that many berries and plants are poisonous. If you don't know what it is, don't try to eat it. Even some plants and berries that animals eat can be toxic to humans. Note that liquids, preferably water, are far more important than food for survival.

* Protect yourself from theft whilst outside. Keep valuables out of sight, and don't have them somewhere they can be easily lifted or pick pocketed. Don't leave anything remotely valuable visible in your car: even a couple of pounds might be attractive to a criminal opportunist.

* Don't put yourself in danger of being mugged. Don't walk down deserted alleys or across deserted tracks, particularly not at night but also be wary during the day. Don't go flashing your money around if in local shops or down the pub. Generally don't go through areas which have a bad reputation, and certainly not on your own or when drunk. You should consider doing some basic self-defense classes.

* Most people in the street have a purpose. They are going somewhere or looking for something in certain types of shops. People out looking for victims, such as pickpockets, tend to be wandering about seemingly aimlessly. Beware of such people. If they then suddenly head towards you they may well have decided you are a suitable victim. Look to head away or surreptitiously protect yourself.

* If you are in a public place such as a train or café and you need to leave your things unattended for a while, asking someone to watch your things will make them far more likely to try to stop anyone who did try to take your things than they would if you hadn't explicitly asked them.

* Heed public notices when you are out. Warnings of dangers or possible criminal activity are there for a reason.

* Be careful if you are near dangerous places. Never try to beat a railway crossing. Don't lean over high balconies and be careful when near low railings with a significant drop on the other side.

* Don't jump into water that may be deeper than you to rescue an animal, unless you are a very good swimmer. You are far more important than an animal, and there are many cases of people jumping in to rescue animals only for them to be killed and for the animal to survive. And be wary of jumping any distance into water you don't know very well, even if you are a good swimmer.

* Don't get into arguments with aggressive people, irrespective of the fact that you believe you are in the right. You can't win an argument against someone with a violent or aggressive nature. They'll end up hitting you, or worse. It is not worth it and it can be very dangerous.

* As a pedestrian or cyclist in the presence of cars or other motor vehicles, don't assume the driver can see you. Keep out of their way. Be particularly careful in poor light conditions. Always ensure you look both ways when crossing roads, and even when crossing at traffic lights don't unthinkingly presume all the cars will stop. Be wary if you are crossing when there is more than one lane as a car in the lane immediately in front of you may stop but a car in the far lane may not.

* Freezing in the face of danger is a natural response. For many types of danger being motionless is an appropriate instant response, and it also enables you to evaluate the danger and prepare a fight or flight response. However staying motionless for too long could be putting you in severe danger.

* People caught up in disasters and severe catastrophic circumstances have a tendency to initially underestimate the severity of the situation, and have a tendency to follow the crowd. If circumstances are unfolding in a way that seems significantly out of the ordinary, then do try to figure out what is going on rather than simply seeking safety in the crowd.

* If you do night work, you are more likely to suffer from fatigue, lack of concentration, memory loss and mood swings. Be aware of this and make allowances. Don't expect yourself to work at peak physical or mental performance.

* If you are tired, you are more likely to make mistakes. Make allowances, particularly where safety is concerned.

* Be very wary of get rich quick or get rich easy schemes. They are either a scam or illegal. Some common characteristics of scams include them prompting for immediate action, them seeking personal information, or them looking for you to send off money before they provide you with anything. Note that most scams are trying to target large amounts of people and you can usually find out through internet search engines whether or not it is a scam.

* Be wary of any scheme or enterprise where you are being let in on a secret. They are almost certainly a scam. If they weren't they wouldn't have stayed a secret up until now, and there is no particular reason why you would be one of the first to be let in on the secret, despite what whoever is trying to let you in on the secret might tell you.

* Don't pay people up front for services or goods, unless they are a well-known reputable company. People you don't know very well who offer unbelievably good deals, and need some up-front money, are likely to be con artists. And even if they are not, if they don't do a very good job, or the product is not as you expected, it is unlikely you will get your money back.

* Advertisements can be very powerful and readily lead you into buying things you don't want. If you find yourself getting drawn into accepting an advertisement's arguments then before you commit:
  o How would you describe the product in your own words, without all the more extreme emotive words used in the advert itself;
  o Visualize the product in the setting you would use it, rather than the glamorous one portrayed;
  o Look at the advert without the voiceovers or music;
  o Ask yourself whether the product is a luxury or a necessity;
  o Ask yourself what difference the product is going to make to your life;
  o Ask yourself whether the price and general likely quality of the product are justified.

* You can try to get a better deal on a lot of things you buy, and generally you lose nothing by trying. You can always pay the asking price, or buy it somewhere else.

* Put comfort before fashion. If your clothes feel uncomfortable it's your body telling you to wear something else. Also uncomfortable clothes make you grumpy, self-conscious, and could lead to you having an accident.

* Listen to your hunches and instincts. If you sense something is not quite right about someone or something then this is your subconscious telling you something that you shouldn't ignore. The stronger the hunch or instinct the more seriously you should take it, and if there is any danger in the situation back away to somewhere safe.

* If you are getting recurrent pains or aches for reasons you don't understand, go and see your doctor. If you are regularly bleeding from your anal passage, go see your doctor. If you develop lumps on your body, go and see your doctor.

* Pain and worry tells there is a problem. It's not a bad thing, it's a good thing: it's an alarm. Now get on and deal with whatever it is warning you about.

* If you are visiting or living in a foreign country or culture, learn the basic rules of etiquette – it will save a lot of hassle and bad feeling and possibly worse, and it will also help you be more persuasive.

* Do not give up your current position until you have high confidence in moving to a different position: 'A bird in the hand is worth two in the bush'.

The Bumper Book of Common Sense

Daily Living Adages and Aphorisms

* Adages and aphorisms are useful ways of reminding ourselves from time to time of certain ideas in certain circumstances, and are also useful ways of planting certain thoughts in other people's heads. Having a good store of adages and sayings can help you get to the essence of understanding many circumstances, though always be wary they may be overly simplistic or even just plain inappropriate.

* Adages and aphorisms don't express basic universal truths. They frequently contradict each other and are only valid in the context of particular circumstances. Thus whilst absence may make the heart grow fonder, out of sight can also be out of mind. Although he who hesitates may be lost, haste can also make waste. Nothing ventured might mean nothing is gained, but it is often better to be safe than sorry. Many hands may make light work, but too many cooks can spoil the broth.

* Learn what is true; to do what is right.

* If the mind sows no corn, it grows thistles.

* The wise seek wisdom, the fool has found it.

* The wisdom of others only truly becomes the wisdom of ourselves through personal experience.

* A man who cannot sit alone and reflect will not find wisdom.

* Better to light a candle than to curse the darkness.

* If you don't know where you are going, it doesn't matter which route you take.

* Always be happy, but never be satisfied.

* The quality of your life is dictated by the degree of your commitment to be the best you can be.

* We are what we choose to do.

* One becomes what one does.

* What you do in the dark will be revealed in the light.

* Goals are dreams with deadlines and a plan.

* Take the road less traveled. The air is cleaner.

* It is only by swimming against the tide that you'll find the unspoiled beaches.

* Beauty is only skin deep.

* A pebble and a diamond are alike to those who cannot see.

* The sky is no less blue because the blind cannot see it.

* Find a job you are good at and that you enjoy and you will no longer need to work for a living.

* Live like no one else, so later you can live like no one else!

- You are unique. There never has been and there never will be another you.

- The reasonable man adapts himself to the world; the unreasonable man persists in trying to adapt the world to himself. Therefore all progress depends on the unreasonable man.

- If you are facing in the right direction, all you have to do is to keep on walking.

- If you are facing in the wrong direction, it doesn't matter how fast you run.

- Measure twice, cut once.

- Think about what you are doing and do something about what you are thinking.

- Dare to dream and have the courage to act. Think and Do.

- If not now, when? If not you, who?

- If it's to be, it's up to me.

- It's never too late to start being what you want to be.

- You can have what you want, so long as you go after it with all your heart.

- Your future depends on what you do now.

- You don't need to try to do everything; just do something.

- Deeds before words.

- We live in deeds not years.

- Give it a go.

- You miss 100% of the shots you never take.

- If you want to fly you must be willing to step away from the ground.

- A ship is safe in harbor: but that's not what ships are built for.

- It's no use waiting for your ship to come in unless you have sent one out.

- The early bird gets the worm, though sometimes it might be best to hang back just a little to check it isn't poisoned.

- Idle people have least leisure.

- Opportunity is missed by most people because it is dressed in overalls and looks like work.

- Plough deep whilst others sleep.

- There are no secrets to success. It is the result of preparation, hard work, and learning from failure.

- Success is not a destination, it is a journey.

- If you've got it, use it. If you haven't got it, get it.

The Bumper Book of Common Sense

- Every path has some puddles.
- Bad things happen: deal with it.
- When the going gets tough, dig deep.
- When the going gets tough – the tough get going.
- Be the mountain beneath the storm. All around you may be in a flap, but you can stand firm.
- It's hard to beat a person who never gives up.
- If you can do more, do more.
- Only those who work hard know the real pleasures of leisure.
- Solve each problem as you meet it.
- You can't fix a clock simply by setting the hands to the right time.
- You are your own knight in shining armor.
- Success is achieved by those who try, and keep trying.
- If you're going through hell, keep going.
- Be optimistic; what's the point in being anything else.
- Patience achieves more than force. Patience opens most doors.
- Give time time.
- A man may fail many times, but he isn't a failure until he begins to blame somebody else.
- Failure sucks, but instructs.
- If you have a 'why' you can put up with the 'how'.
- Life is not always fair.
- Nothing endures.
- The secret of life is not to do what you like, but to like what you do.
- Life isn't about waiting for the storm to pass; it's about learning to dance in the rain.
- You can't change the direction of the wind, but if you adjust your sails you can reach any destination.
- It is not the strongest that survive, or the most intelligent, but those that are most responsive to change.
- If you do not change direction, you'll end up where you are heading.
- If you want something you've never had you must be willing to do things you've never done.

* Things turn out best for those who make the best of the way things turn out.

* Trouble is opportunity in work clothes.

* Don't be afraid of the unknown. The unknown is not afraid of you.

* Lack of curiosity breeds mediocrity.

* If my mind can conceive it, and my heart can believe it, then I can achieve it.

* Be happy. Irrespective of what life throws at you.

* Don't strive for happiness. Be happy and strive to create and to do.

* Above the clouds is the bright sunshine.

* A deed well done pleases the heart.

* Success is not about what you have materially; it is about how content you are with your life.

* Relax. Don't take everything seriously.

* Come in out of the rain, unless there is pleasure or benefit in staying out.

* If you live with the lame you will develop a limp.

* Hate and envy wears you down, and do not hurt your enemy. It is like taking poison and wishing your enemy would die.

* Trust everyone, but cut the cards.

* Better to risk being cheated than never to trust.

* It is better to give a dollar than lend a cent.

* The wise say nothing in dangerous times.

* A wise man gets more from his enemies than a fool does from his friends.

* Never ascribe to conspiracy that which can be explained by incompetence.

* A guilty conscience never feels safe.

* Nothing is impossible for the man who doesn't have to do it himself.

* Don't spend £100 of time on a decision only worth £10.

* Profit and oxygen. They are not the point of life, but without them there is no life.

* Don't spend more than you earn, unless it is 'borrowing' for investments that are expected to give greater yields.

* If you find yourself in a hole, stop digging.

* You cannot eat your cake, and still have it.

The Bumper Book of Common Sense

* Enough is enough.

* Everything has a breaking point.

* A small leak can sink a great ship.

* We reap what we sow.

* Don't corner something meaner than you.

* After enlightenment, the laundry. (Zen saying)

* Our existence is but a brief crack of light between two eternities of darkness.

* In the long run ... we die. But between now and then is the rest of our lives.

General

Some Well-known Principles, Laws, and Razors

* Occam's Principle, also called Occam's Razor. All other things being equal, choose the simplest. This applies when looking for an explanation to something, deciding what to do, or looking for a solution to a problem. It may not always be correct, but it provides a useful and practical approach. Clearly as soon as the 'simplest' solution you have chosen is found wanting, move on to the next simplest which fits the facts.

* Murphy's Law states that if anything can go wrong, it will. Thus, expect the unexpected, and be aware of the possibility of things going wrong.

* In many areas of life a majority of the effects or consequences arise from a minority of the causes: the Pareto Principle or 80-20 rule. There are many ways this rule is used or variations of it. For example 80% of our effective output arises from 20% of what we do. 80% of an organization's outputs are produced by 20% of its employees. 80% of an organization's profit comes from 20% of its customers. Note that the 80/20 split is not expected to be exact in any sense, but it represents the idea that a relatively small percentage of the input gives rise to a relative large percentage of the output.

* Hanlon's Razor: Never attribute to malice that which can be adequately explained by stupidity. Or alternatively: do not invoke conspiracy as explanation when ignorance and incompetence will suffice.

* The Peter Principle states that in a hierarchy, every employee tends to rise to his or her level of incompetence. In the natural course of events there is a sort of inevitability about this as people who prove competent at a given level within an organization earn and eventually get promotion, which only stops once they reach a level they are no longer competent at. And organizations are generally very poor at subsequently moving people back down the hierarchy. The book on this topic also includes corollaries such as work is accomplished by those employees who have not yet reached their level of incompetence. The Peter Principle is amusing and frighteningly true in many organizations.

* Parkinson's Law: Work expands so as to fill the time available for its completion. The time for completion of an activity often becomes a self-fulfilling prophesy, since with the end point being some way off less attention is paid to it, and priority is often given to other tasks or to aspects of the task which are interesting but not essential. Only as the time for completion draws nearer is the work more focused on the essentials to get it finished. A corollary is that if no time is set for the completion of a task then there is a high likelihood it won't get completed.

Relating to Experience

* Experience is a double-edged sword. It gives us an intuition and examples relating to whether certain things will work or not and may allow us to solve problems quicker because we've seen similar problems in the past. However our experience may not be relevant to problems set in a different context or environment. Or past outcomes may have been due more to chance or factors other than our own endeavors. And thus experience could lead us off in the wrong direction.

* The positive aspects of experience include:
    o We know how to approach what needs to be done;
    o We know some of the pitfalls of adopting alternative approaches;
    o We need only limited time to plan, and have reasonable confidence in our estimates.

* The negative aspects of experience include:
    o We become constrained in our thinking and fail to see, accept, or even be willing to look for, better alternatives;
    o We often misapply or over generalize our experience, believing a given situation is analogous to a situation we have experience of, whereas in reality there are key differences;
    o People's experiences differ. Where experience is taken as the major driving factor behind a decision or plan, then the experience of the most senior person involved usually takes precedence. There is rarely any particular reason why this should be superior to someone else's, and if the area involves specialist understanding it will frequently be inferior.

* Just because some past decision of which we have experience led to a positive or negative outcome, this does not mean it was a good or bad decision. The positive outcome may have been far worse than would have been achieved had an alternative decision been taken, or the negative outcome may have been the best that could have been achieved.

* In practice, situations are rarely as similar to the past as they might at first sight appear. External factors may be different. There may be different people involved.

* Jumping to conclusions based on past experience is acceptable in most circumstances with which we are familiar and the consequences are not too severe. Now and again however jumping to conclusions will lead us astray, and thus if consequences are severe we need to be more conscious of our thinking.

* Be wary of simply preparing for the last battle. Be wary of looking to fix a problem that by the time you've come up with the solution will not be a problem anyway because circumstances will have changed.

Taking Advice

* Be open to seeking out and listening to advice from others. You are seeking out ideas you hadn't previously thought of.

The Bumper Book of Common Sense

* Don't feel hurt if advice is not what you want to hear. Whilst advice that conforms to what you want to hear is useful from a psychological and motivational viewpoint, it doesn't help you make better decisions. Better to get advice that derives from what you hadn't thought of and opens up other possibilities. As such it is important to understand why alternative advice is as it is. The simple "If I were you I would …", without any rationale for why, is not a lot of use. But the "If I were you I would do this because of …" gives you the chance to think through whether or not the reasoning is valid given your particular circumstances.

* Ultimately you need to make up your own mind and take responsibility for whether or not you take someone else's advice. Others don't necessarily know the particular circumstances as well as you do, and others don't necessarily have the same stake in the outcome as you do.

* The following are some general notes with respect to taking the word of experts:
  o Experts are not infallible;
  o Experts themselves may hold contradictory views;
  o We should ensure that the experts' view is consistent with other views and information;
  o People who are in the public eye, such as celebrities, are often treated as though they are experts when in practice they have no special knowledge or expertise in whatever it is they are being asked about;
  o An expert is an expert in something, and just because they are an expert in one thing does not mean they will be expert in something or indeed anything else. Of course, they might be, but it is unlikely;
  o Experts tend to frown upon new ideas;
  o The expert will be basing his advice on his experiences, which may or may not be similar to or relevant to your particular circumstances.

* We would significantly benefit from expert advice on many occasions. Usually, assuming they are genuinely an expert, they will know more about something than we do, and will have had more experience. And for most cases the experts' advice will be useful and will help us avoid problems and mistakes we would otherwise have had. However:
  o We should ensure that the costs of employing or involving the expert are not likely to outweigh any benefits we might gain through following their advice vis-à-vis what we would have done without their advice;
  o We should ensure the expert gives the reasoning behind the advice rather than simply the advice itself. A good expert will always be willing to do this;
  o We should ensure that expert provides us with something useful, rather than just continually telling us about other factors that need to be taken into account and investigated. Although it is reasonable for them to point out additional factors this should be alongside also giving useful and practical advice;
  o So long as we are open minded in listening to expert advice, if having heard it we disagree with it we should go along with our own convictions;
  o The expert may not have the time to understand the specific circumstances and whilst giving general advice applicable to general circumstances would if they had the time acknowledge that the advice is not applicable in the specific circumstances.

* Be wary of 'one size fits all' advice. Most advice can and should be tailored to the specific circumstances. There is no one right way to bring up children for example: there are different ways that work to a differing extent with different children. Someone who claims a specific fix will work without making the effort to understand the circumstances is unlikely to be giving good advice, though of the course the advice might work by chance in the specific circumstances.

* Don't get upset by people giving you advice you don't agree with. Listen to it, and if it is useful make use of it. If it is not, then set it aside. The people giving you advice don't understand the circumstances as well as you do, so don't be surprised or troubled that the advice is not perfect. It is simply a different viewpoint that may or may not be useful and for which you should grateful.

Note that even if you disagree with advice, it may prompt you in coming up with some other thoughts that you might not have otherwise done.

How to Improve your Common Sense

* Common Sense is more malleable than traditional IQ intelligence, and can be readily learnt and improved through actively trying to do so.

* In order to improve your Common Sense you need to first of all recognize that you can, and then to take responsibility for improving it.

* Read up on the principles of Common Sense, and related topics such as critical thinking, problem solving, and decision making, and indeed all the topics covered in this book. Don't just read one book. Read lots of books. Read different books on the same topic since they will give you different viewpoints and also reinforce key points.

* Read lots of self-help books, and preferably buy them. People who have spent money on a self-help book or course will usually be more confident that it will help them than they might have been before making the commitment.

* Take personality tests in order to better understand your own strengths and weaknesses. Improve your strengths and either overcome your weaknesses or find ways to avoid them manifesting themselves.

* Read a variety of good fact and fiction books. If is both a highly pleasurable experience and a very good way of developing your inner self and general wisdom.

* Gain experience in as wide a range of things as you can without putting yourself in physical danger. The wider the range of experience you gain, the more general will be the practical lessons you will learn.

* Volunteer. Get involved. Contribute. Particularly for things you've not done before.

* Find role models. They may be people you know, or they may be others you can read or otherwise find out about. You can learn a lot from role models. Not only can you get information and knowledge from them, but they can inspire modes of behavior. You can adopt an 'if they can do it so can I' attitude, and whilst the detailed way you behave will be unique to you, you can take a significant step towards adopting what you consider good behavioral practices just by trying to emulate someone who already has that behavior.

* Talk to people. People have different perspectives and you should try to understand what they are. You don't need to agree with them, but you should be aware of them. If you have difficultly talking to people or knowing what to say, then make a lot of effort to improve your small talk.

* Ask others about their experiences and their lessons learned and general guidance on life. You don't need to follow them, but much of them will be as hard won as are your own lessons learned and at least worthy of consideration.

* Slow down. Many errors you make could be a result of impulsive, hasty decisions. You should, for a time at least, seek to sacrifice decision speed for decision quality. When in doubt about a decision, sleep on it.

The Bumper Book of Common Sense

Common Sense on a Global Scale

* It is better to think the worse about what is coming, and take action to avoid it, than to think the best, and take no action.

* There are those who believe in climate change and those who don't. Whether or not the world climate is being significantly affected by human activities is not a matter for Common Sense, but one for effective analysis of the evidence. And it is blatantly obvious from the evidence that the world is being dramatically and significantly affected by human activity. Just because scientists occasionally get some of the details wrong, just because we don't understand some of the detailed mechanisms, just because dramatic climate change has occasionally happened in the past before we were around, just because a scientist sometimes goes against the vast majority, none of these negate the fact that it is blatantly obvious we are the root cause of significant climate change.

* Whilst there are significant risks in the adoption of new technologies there are also huge risks in not adopting them. New technologies offer the potential to make life better or sustainable for large numbers of people, however they need to be applied based upon research and a thorough and balanced understanding of their potential consequences.

* There is a need for ongoing and significant research into the effects of modern day technologies on humans and on the world. We just don't know many of the impacts. We need knowledge that can then inform balanced judgments, and be the basis on which decisions are made. For example, what are the impacts of genetic engineering? There are many who are vocal on both sides without the aid of adequate factual knowledge.

* Solutions to many problems often have side effects that can lead to new and sometimes worst problems. We need to be very aware of this as we tackle some of the world's more significant problems, and apply a systems thinking approach to seeking out appropriate solutions.

* There are many problems facing humanity that require people to work together. They will not be solved by different nations, different groups of people, all looking after their own interests. The world needs some common goals to get everyone working together, and to enable peoples to put aside past quarrels. Getting out into space would provide such a goal, as would a truly global effort to convert to sustainable energy and food production.

* We are all far more defined by being human than we are defined by some particular tribal characteristic. Many people are extremely nationalistic. Yet there is no real defining characteristic that makes people of one nation different in any fundamental way than people of another nation. The genetics of all people is mixed whether they realize it or not, whether they accept it or not. As with all tribal affiliations, whether they be national, religious, or whatever, the more extreme they are the more they show up the persons holding them as insecure individuals looking for someone to bully.

* For the world to prosper in the long-term people need to give up personal greed and laziness. Man's ingenuity is such that the world's problems are almost certainly capable of being solved, including hunger, shelter, pollution, climate change, and many others. However it requires a sense of humanity in which people are not out to look simply after their own personal interests at the expense of everyone else's.

* The problem is not that there are too many people in the world. The problem is that there are too many people in the world who are out solely for themselves.

* It is important that people's attitudes are changed from 'what I do is irrelevant, it is up to everyone else' to 'what everyone else does is irrelevant, I can at least do my bit'. Those who can but don't do their bit should be recognized as the selfish uncaring b****** that they are and stigmatized as such.

* If we want the world to be a better place we have a responsibility to do our bit to help make it a better place, rather than just blaming or waiting for everyone else. There are a multitude of ways we

can do our bit from showing kindness towards others, being positive towards others, being aware of the environment and avoiding pollution and waste where we can, being charitable, actively helping others in need, etc. etc. etc.

* Give a little bit towards making the world a better place. You don't need to make huge sacrifices. Just give a little bit. I little bit of your money, and a little bit of your time.

* Just because there is no consensus on what is the best thing to do, this does not mean you should do nothing. Do what you genuinely believe will contribute towards making the world a better place.

* What sort of world would you like to live in. One of co-operation, tolerance, compassion, achievement, education, kindness, peace, and freedom from poverty, war and injustice. Do what you can to nudge the world in this direction. Behave the way you think everyone in the world should behave, albeit without letting yourself be deliberately taken advantage of. Support those who you believe will help nudge the world in this direction.

* It is our capacity for reason and our ability to deny our desires and transcend our short-term self-interests that enables us to live in modern day societies rather than be subject to the aimless cruelty of the strongest. It is important to teach people thinking skills and teach them to improve their self-control.

* Do not begrudge government and the constraints imposed by modern society. Such constraints are an essential part of the complex highly innovative societies most of us live in. Anarchistic societies would largely be ones based on bullying. Note however that you don't need to agree with everything your government does and lawful challenges are a normal part of civilized societies.

* Don't begrudge paying taxes. Governments need to be financed. And those who earn more should pay more. The alternative to government is a world which would be far far worse for the vast majority of us. If we can afford it, we should make our contributions. The more we can afford, the more we are benefiting from government, and the more we should contribute. Those who adopt or encourage tax avoidance schemes are simply transferring the burden of paying onto those who can afford it less them they can. They are examples of the selfish uncaring b******* who make the world a less pleasant place than it could so readily be.

* Effective thinking and doing skills should be part of every school child's syllabus, and should be widely available as adult learning.

FURTHER READING

The books and websites below are ones that I believe the reader interested in the subject matter of this book would also have an interest in. They will provide more detail and different slants on particular aspects of what I consider to be Common Sense and thus I ask the reader to at least explore them.

Bad Thoughts: A Guide to Clear Thinking by Jamie Whyte. Lots of good, common, and well-explained examples of poor thinking.

Boost Your Memory – by Darren Bridger. Lots of good information about how memory works and ideas on how to boost it and make it work better for you.

Clear Thinking by R W Jepson. Originally published back in 1936, and describes many of the core principles of clear thinking, which have been understood for a very long time.

Develop your Leadership Skill - by John Adair. Relatively short book with exercises and checklists from a recognized world expert on leadership.

The Dilbert Principle by Scott Adams. Illustrates the many failings to apply Common Sense in a workplace context.

High Performance Thinking Skills by S P Reid. Describes a large number of thinking skills and how to go about adopting or improving your use of them.

Influence: The Psychology of Persuasion – by Robert B Cialdini. The key principles of how people are persuaded to comply with requests, based on social psychological research.

Irrationality: The Enemy Within – by Stuart Sutherland. Largely based on psychological research, and identifies many of the ways people make irrational decisions and act in irrational ways.

Lateral Thinking: A Textbook of Creativity by Edward de Bono. Edward de Bono;s early work which outlined his ideas on lateral thinking which have since become widely known and elaborated in many further books by himself and others.

The Little Blue Reasoning Book: 50 Powerful Principles for Clear and Effective Thinking – by Brandon Royal. Includes easy to read summaries of the principles themselves and also other useful thinking lists including common fallacies.

Make the Most of Your Memory – Guardian Shorts. Tips on making maximum use of your memory, and discussion of some common myths about memory.

Maximum Willpower: How to Master the New Science of Self-Control – by Kelly McGonigal. A practical book with exercises you can readily follow to significantly increase your willpower.

Mistakes were made, but not by me – by Carol Tavris and Elliot Aronson

The Now Habit – by Niel A Fiore. How you can overcome procrastination by learning to live in the present.

The Philosopher's Toolkit: A Compendium of Philosophical Concepts and Methods – by Julian Baggini and Peter S Fosl. Covers a large number of critical thinking topics and how they can be applied in a practical manner.

Positive Psychology: A Practical Guide – by Bridget Grenville-Cleave. A practical and accessible guide to adopting a positive outlook on life, based on researched psychology.

Practical Intelligence: The Art and Science of Common Sense by Karl Albrecht. Describes the importance of different ways of thinking about problems and issues and gives guidelines on developing them.

Ready for Anything: 52 Productivity Principles for Work and Life – by David Allen, a recognized world leader in personal and organizational productivity.

Rewire Your Brain: Think Your Way to a Better Life – by John B Arden, using latest understandings from neuroscience to identify practical ways you can improve the way you think and literally rewire your brain to adopt more useful ways of interacting with the world.

The Skinny on Willpower: How to Develop Self Discipline – by Jim Randel. The key principles of self-discipline presented in a humorous and easy to read fashion, with stick men and women.

Smart Thinking: How to Think Big, Innovate, and Outperform Your Rivals - by Art Markman. Specific suggestions on how to create new more productive thinking habits.

Straight and Crooked Thinking by Robert H Thouless. Originally published in 1930, albeit revised in later years, identifies most of the fallacious ways of thinking and arguing.

Stress Proof Your Life – by Elizabeth Wilson. A short description of 52 ideas to help reduce the stress in your life.

The Success Formula for Personal Growth – by Jerry Bruckner. 2000 easy to understand pieces of advice or observations from successful or influential people to help you lead a happier and more fulfilling life.

The Thoughts of Marcus Aurelius. Marcus Aurelius was Roman Emperor for about 20 years in the 2nd century. He had a philosophical outlook on life based on living a Stoic simple life, where we take responsibility for our own thoughts and actions. He left behind his writings which are available in various translations and also under the headings of Meditations, or just Thoughts of Marcus Aurelius.

What Every Body is Saying – by Joe Navarro with Marvin Karlins. Whilst much of body language is well documented this provides a good easy read through of the essentials.

Why we Make Mistakes by Joseph T Hallinan. Describes the root causes of many common mistakes and what we can do to avoid them.

Willpower: Rediscovering our Greatest Strength – by Roy F Baumeister and John Tierney. Practical guidance on how to improve our will power and self-control based firmly upon targeted psychological research.

Winning Arguments: From Aristotle to Obama – Everything You Need to Know About the Art of Persuasion – by Jay Heinrichs. About how to get your points across in a way that people listen.

Words of Wisdom: Philosophy's most important quotations and their meaning – by Gareth Southwell. A good collection of views and statements by the world's greatest recognized philosophers.

You are not so Smart by David McRaney. An easy to read description of the many ways in which we mislead ourselves

18 Minutes: Find your Focus, Master Distraction, and Get the Right Things Done - by Peter Bregman. Easy to read book with the core message that you need to focus on what is most important to you and avoid simply being busy all the time.

52 Small Changes – by Brett Blumenthal. 52 small changes you can make in your life, one a week, to you to a healthier and happier lifestyle.

76 Fallacies – by Michael La Bossiere. A description of the most common fallacies with lots of examples.

99 Ways to Get More Out of Each Day - by Gene Griessman. Lots of good tips for daily living presented in an easily digestible form.

100 Ways to Motivate Yourself – by Steve Chandler. Lots of useful ideas to help you to motivate yourself.

Various online articles relating to body language and effective communication by Stephen D. Boyd, Ph.D., CSP, Professor of Speech Communication in the College of Informatics at Northern Kentucky University, USA.

There are many websites which contain good Common Sense advice, albeit often mixed in with not such good advice or clear personal preferences and ideas of the authors. The following sites all provide a large amount of good material free of charge. They may charge you for extra stuff, but you can access a large amount of free and useful stuff without paying or having to register. However, as always, websites come and go so my apologies if these sites are no longer available when you come to try to access them.

www.helpguide.org: Provides general Common Sense summary guides on a wide range of issues relating to Family, Health, Lifestyle and Aging.

www.personalexcellence.co: A site dedicated to Personal Excellence, including a large number of articles on self-improvement. Impressive.

www.stevepavlina.com: A site to help you with personal development.

www.fallacyfiles.org: a comprehensive collation of a wide range of fallacies, easy to understand and with examples.

www.mindtools.com: a site largely focused on self-improvement and tips to help in the workplace and in the advancement of your career. A lot of good free stuff, and even more when you subscribe. Much of the information also available as an e-book by James Manktelow.

www.pickthebrain.com: a site dedicated to self-improvement, with lots of easy to read short articles on a wide range of self-improvement topics including motivation and productivity.

www.thegreatcourses.com: The Great Courses are a large selection of lecture courses you can purchase as either DVDs, Audio, or Streaming. They cover a wide range of subjects. If you get used to the lecture style they can be very informative and interesting. Some subject matter examples include: Creativity, The Art of Conflict Management, Decision Making. Well worth a look, and often have special offer deals.

www.wikipedia.org: doesn't need an introduction. Note however there are other related sites providing other openly available and collaboratively generated material such as www.wikibooks.org and www.wikiversity.org. These are all part of the wider vision of the wikimedia foundation - www.wikimediafoundation.org/wiki/Home - which has the vision of a world in which every single human being can freely share in the sum of all knowledge.

www.wikihow.com: not as well known as wikepedia, and independent of the Wikimedia foundation, has a vision of a world in which anyone can easily learn to do anything. The site provides open access to an ever growing number of How To guides.

Printed in Great Britain
by Amazon